Understanding
The American Public
High School

SAMUEL M. HOLTON
Professor of Education, University of North Carolina

Allyn and Bacon, Inc., Boston

Preface

EDUCATION LIKE POLITICS AND RELIGION, IS IN THE PUBLIC DOMAIN. EVERYONE has some experience of its processes, and its more controversial issues are debated daily in the communications media. Yet it is difficult to obtain an overall picture of the American educational system and the way in which the public high school fits into the general pattern.

This book is designed to help the reader obtain a coherent view of the nature and role of the American public high school. In particular it aims to provide the student of teaching with the right framework for a consideration of schools as institutions.

During teacher training, the pressures for developing technical competence in classroom management severely restrict the time available for treating the theoretical base for public education, and for studying its history, philosophy, sociology, and economics. For this reason a text giving a concise survey of these fields seemed required. This book attempts to provide such a survey, one which can form the basis for a systematic consideration of the role of the public high school in American society. The survey is divided into four sections dealing with the following aspects: (1) the school's relationship to the rest of society, (2) the school's program, (3) its operation, and (4) questions concerning staffing, housing, and the changing power structure. Since most teacher education programs include separate courses in educational psychology and adolescent development, this material is not treated here. Other matters, such as teaching methods, discussed briefly here, are considered in much more detail in other courses and texts.

One of the most important characteristics of the modern high school is that it is in a state of transition. A good teacher or administrator must be both alert to the need for change and capable of working effectively within the existing institution. A too optimistic view of present practice would hinder desirable progress. A too pessimistic view tends to obscure opportunities for progress within the existing structure. A text such as this should aid the student to develop a perspective from which to examine both the institution and possible ways to modify it.

In each section, I have made a general survey of the field, trying to state facts and avoid giving opinions. This survey is followed by a chapter of readings which have been selected to show some of the areas most under discussion at the present time. These are the areas where the changing nature of society and technological innovations are affecting the basic structure and philosophy of public education, or they are ones over which professional opinion is currently divided. Obviously, any selection of this kind could be far larger, but here the intention is only to indicate where the main centers of interest and controversy lie.

Samuel M. Holton

Contents

Section I

Secondary Education
in America

AMERICAN SECONDARY EDUCATION IS PECULIARLY PUBLIC. WHETHER THE high school is studied historically, philosophically, sociologically, or politically, the significant consideration is that it has now been assigned the task of providing for nearly all of the population within the appropriate age group. Evaluation of the school system, therefore, must be based on the extent to which it succeeds in carrying out this assignment.

Before such evaluation is undertaken, it seems desirable to consider (1) the historical background for the development of a *public* secondary school, (2) how conceptions concerning the functions of secondary education have been refined, (3) the arguments for using the school as an instrument of social reconstruction and the nature of that process, (4) the relationships between the school and other important social institutions, and (5) the immediate tensions of public education in urban America.

Each of the five chapters in the following section will discuss one of these topics, starting with the present American pattern of secondary education and how it has evolved in response to the development of new ideas and to changes in the structure of society. The readings in Chapter 5, and in Chapter 10, Section II, indicate just how wide-ranging some of the schools' responsibilities have become, and show a number of ways in which its role may change in the future.

1

The American Pattern of
Secondary Education

THE MODERN AMERICAN PUBLIC HIGH SCHOOL IS DIFFERENT FROM ITS
European counterparts and from its nineteenth century predecessor. Because these differences are not always understood by the American public,
this chapter is concerned with them and some of the subordinate questions which arise in considering them. What were the important stages
in the development of the school? What were the forces which modified
the European secondary school in America? To what extent are the traditions of the earlier school a hindrance? To what extent is the private or
independent secondary school like the public high school? Which developments in the American high school have parallels in other national
systems of secondary education?

The Tradition of Education for the Leisure Classes

Until the late nineteenth century, secondary education, anywhere in the
world, could have been defined as education intended for the leisure
classes. In many countries, it is still distinct from the education intended
for the lower classes and referred to as "common," "basic," or elementary
education. To understand the secondary schools of previous centuries, it
is necessary to search for the social or economic background of a leisure
class. Different types of leisure class education, for example, were found
among the Greeks, among the Romans, within the medieval church, in
the feudal society of the middle ages, and in Colonial America. Each of
these systems of education seems to have left its mark on succeeding (and
present) systems.

3

Among the Greeks two different economic and political systems existed side by side. In the city-state of Sparta, a militaristic ruling class was dependent on the continuing slavery of a conquered people. If the ruling class were to stay in power, it was felt that its members must be rigidly disciplined in mind and healthy in body. Young Spartans were therefore subjected to an intense training in the barracks, and from this system the philosophy of the state as superior to the individual developed to a high point. In Athens, by contrast, the base of support for the ruling class came primarily from commercial activity. The pursuit of knowledge was freer and the individual citizen was prized for his own worth rather than simply as a tool of the state. The issue of whether it is the function of the school to protect the society or to liberate the individual was apparent to the Greeks themselves and is still under debate.

Among the Romans during the imperial era, the basis for wealth and leisure was first a vast commercial empire that spread over the entire mediterranean world and secondly the military and governmental control of the equally expansive political empire of the Caesars. The wealthy young Roman of this period of the *Pax Romana* was trained for a career in government and politics.[1] The dependence of secondary education for many centuries on the study of the Latin writings of Caesar, Cicero, and Vergil suggests at least a continued view that what was appropriate for the leisure class of Rome was right for the leisure classes of other eras.

In the medieval period three systems of education existed, each oriented to a different group. The church developed an educational system designed to fit its own special needs. Besides teaching religious matters, this concentrated on administrative training, since the economic basis for leisure was the property of the church itself. Among the lay ruling classes, emphasis was placed on the system known as chivalry. This was needed to assist the perpetuation of feudalism. With the growth of small towns came a demand for artisans and a third form of education for youth, the apprenticeship, developed. Current efforts to provide within the public high school for various types of work study programs represent an effort to solve the problem, first recognized in the Late Middle Ages, of making formal provision for the education of artisans.

The renewal of commerce in the early stages of the Renaissance created a new leisure class in Italy and later in Northern Europe. With the new leisure came a new interest in materials from classical sources. The classical sources had a more optimistic view of the nature of man than that provided by the church literature of the time. Though at first knowledge of Latin and Greek was a legitimate key to the learning of the ancients, in time it became little more than a badge of membership in the

---

[1] For original material on the education of the ancients see Paul Monroe, *Sourcebook of the History of Education for the Greek and Roman Period* (New York: The Macmillan Company, 1913).

new leisure classes. The schools which taught Latin and Greek became the new secondary schools. These schools (called Latin Grammar Schools in England) which taught in Latin and studied Latin grammar and Latin authors remained the pattern for European secondary education for several hundred years and were the type of secondary school brought to America by the European colonists.[2]

Secondary Education in America

Colonial America was not much different in its social outlook from the mother countries. The same social forms and customs tended to prevail. The same common law governed in England and in the English colonies. Property inheritance laws facilitated the development of a landed aristocracy similar to that in the mother country. Nevertheless, there were forces at work which encouraged the more rapid development of democracy. Schools, traditionally the conservative force of society, felt the pressure.[3]

The first Latin grammar schools in America had been close copies of those in Europe. Doubtless the "humanistic" flavor of the European school had been modified by the Calvinistic theology of the Puritans. The "good life" was to be found not in the classics but in the Scriptures. In early New England, the argument for mastering Latin and Greek was that these languages were basic to the study of the Scriptures. (The tendency to retain an old form instead of developing a new one more appropriate to the need of the times still seems to be a problem for American education.)

In America, more than in Europe, the college preparatory function of the Latin Grammar School was stressed from the first. The important justification given for setting up higher education in Massachusetts was the preparation of ministers. While there were Latin grammar schools in other colonies, the pattern of life in New England was the most hospitable to them.

The first serious break with the Latin grammar school tradition came in the eighteenth century, about the same time as American nationalism began to develop and under the leadership of the same people. Special schools were set up to offer "practical" subjects. One of the most complete proposals for such a school was made by Benjamin Franklin. He suggested that instruction be carried on in English (customarily instruction in the grammar schools was in Latin) and that suitable instruction be offered in foreign languages, English grammar, rhetoric, literature, history,

[2] Ernest E. Bayles and Bruce L. Hood, *The Growth of American Educational Thought and Practice* (New York: Harper and Row, 1966), pp. 17–18.

[3] *See* Vernon L. Parrington, *Main Currents in American Thought* (New York: Harcourt, Brace and Company, Inc., 1927), Vol. I.

the sciences and other practical subjects. His academy, a compromise between his proposal and traditional practice, opened in 1751 and included two schools, one referred to as the Latin and the other as the English.

Franklin's proposal is a classic statement of the curriculum problem both then and today:

> As to their studies, it would be well if they could be taught *every thing* that is useful, and *every thing* that is ornamental: But art is long, and their time is short. It is therefore proposed that they learn those things that are likely to be *most useful* and *most ornamental*. Regard being had to the several professions for which they are intended.[4]

The influence of political and economic forces on leisure-class education, noticeable as early as in the civilization of Greece, continues to be evident after the creation of the academy. One of the primary forces in the school's development was the need for a larger middle class adequately trained to assume positions requiring some specialized and technical skill and to exercise more political responsibility. The view expressed by Franklin that the curriculum should serve a practical purpose has haunted American education ever since, but has not had much sustained effect on actual practice. Along with this idea, there developed a concomitant one that the more "ornamental" or aristocratic type of secondary education is also appropriate for non-aristocratic classes. These two ideas have been important influences in most of the efforts toward altering the American secondary school program.[5]

The academy, modified by its clash with the demands of the traditional, came to replace the Latin grammar school. In many cases the change consisted of adding the program of the academy to that offered in existing schools. In others it came from the development of new schools in new communities. By 1800, the academy seemed established as the basic pattern of secondary education in America.[6]

In the twentieth century attempts have been made to use education as an instrument for socially integrating the less well educated with the better educated. In the late eighteenth century Jefferson was similarly interested in the social importance of education. He believed that only the educated should be trusted to rule. To him the appropriate distinction between the old English and the new American aristocracy was that ability

---

[4] Benjamin Franklin, *Proposals Relating to the Education of Youth in Pennsylvania* (A Facsimile Reprint, Philadelphia: University of Pennsylvania Press, 1931), p. 11. Italics appear in the original. *See also* Thomas Woody, *Educational Views of Benjamin Franklin* (New York: McGraw-Hill Book Company, 1931) and R. Freeman Butts and Lawrence A. Cremin, *A History of Education in American Culture* (New York: Henry Holt and Company, 1953).

[5] Merle Curti, *The Social Ideas of American Educators* (New York: Charles Scribner's Sons, 1935).

[6] John S. Brubacher, *A History of the Problems of Education*, 2nd ed. (New York: McGraw-Hill Book Company, 1966), pp. 406–407.

rather than birth was to be the determining factor. He would have established a pyramid in which primary education was made available to the whole population and then the more capable were selected to go to district secondary schools. From these the students who would attend college were finally chosen. In the introduction to his bill for the education of the youth of Virginia he stated that:

> And whereas it is generally true that people will be happiest whose laws are best, and are best administered, and that laws will be wisely formed, and honestly administered, in proportion as those who form and administer them are wise and honest; whence it becomes expedient for promoting the publick happiness that those persons, whom nature hath endowed with genius and virtue, should be rendered by liberal education worthy to receive, and able to guard the sacred deposit of the rights and liberties of their fellow citizens, and that they should be called to that charge without regard to wealth, birth or other accidental condition or circumstance; but the indigence of the greater number disabling them from so educating, at their own expense, those of their children whom nature hath fitly formed and disposed to become useful instruments for the public, it is better that such be sought for and educated at the common expense of all, than that the happiness of all should be confined to the weak or wicked:[7]

In practice the academy failed to achieve the aspirations of Franklin for a practical curriculum and of Jefferson for a free education for the able children of the poor. It was a tuition school, operated by private trustees, attended by middle and upper class students who had received their elementary education in private schools or through other arrangements such as tutoring. The idea, advanced by Jefferson, of a single system or ladder of education in which students moved from the first grade through the university was not put into practice suddenly. Instead it developed more naturally in the situation in which there was no strong dual system such as existed in Europe where the common people attended one school (a primary school) and the aristocratic another (a secondary school).[8] Inherent in American thought in the first half of the nineteenth century was the idea that it was appropriate to provide secondary education for women. Some academies were established to provide specifically for the education of women; many were coeducational.[9]

As American political thought shifted from Jeffersonian to Jacksonian democracy, the aristocratic academy gradually gave way to the high school. The first public high school, the English Classical School, was founded

---

[7] Thomas Jefferson, "A Bill for the More General Diffusion of Knowledge" (June 18, 1799), quoted by Roy J. Honneywell: *The Educational Works of Thomas Jefferson* (Cambridge: Harvard University Press, 1931), pp. 199–200.

[8] Lawrence A. Cremin, *The American Common School* (New York: Bureau of Publication, Teachers College, Columbia University, 1951), pp. 49–82.

[9] John S. Brubacher, *A History of the Problems of Education,* 2nd ed. (New York: McGraw-Hill Book Company, 1966), pp. 406–407.

in Boston in 1821. It is not easy to draw an accurate line between the early high school and the academy; the two existed concurrently and their roles could differ from place to place. The academy sometimes served in a particular community as the public secondary school for that community, providing secondary education to the students of secondary age who wished to attend, regardless of their ability to pay a fee. The early high schools were predominantly free and operated as an agency of the government with a public school board, but some of them charged tuition fees. Academies were likely to have boarding students. High school students were likely to be day students.[10]

The question of who should pay for secondary education is still an important one in America. How much any family may have to expend in fees or indirect costs is still recognized as a significant issue in the democratization of education.

The high school was from the first an extension upward of the elementary school. Its patrons came from classes of people who were not "too proud" to attend a "public" school. Recognition that the term "common school" might legitimately include the high school program came in part as a result of an 1874 court decision in Michigan. In that state the Kalamazoo School District, operating under constitutional provisions similar to those in most of the states, had begun the operation of a public high school. In holding this to be a legal operation for common school trustees the court in effect recognized that secondary education was legally common education.[11] There had of course been no particular doubt that states could provide out of public funds for secondary schools just as they provided for colleges and universities. The question was whether a high school should be defined as a common school and operated within the existing authority for common schools.

Recognition that the secondary school program should be a part of common education was an important step in the development of a democratic system of education. The evolution was still not complete. What had been achieved was an education designed for the middle class and free of prohibitive cost under the supervision of a public board, not an education appropriately designed for all of the population of secondary school age completely free of expense.

The Victory of the Public High School

Whatever the pretension of American education in 1874 to democratic status, there were only approximately 110,000 students in public high

[10] Butts and Cremin, *op. cit.*, pp. 275–80.
[11] *Ibid.*, pp. 418–19.

schools in 1880. By 1890 there were approximately 200,000, by 1900 500,-000, by 1910 900,000, and by 1920 2,200,000.[12] The period between 1880 and 1920 saw the student population multiply 20 times and go from approximately 3 per cent of the high school age group to approximately 25 per cent.[13] By 1920, nearly 90 per cent of the students in the secondary schools were enrolled in public schools.[14]

It was during the period between 1880 and 1920 that secondary education became significantly public. The nature of the shift is apparent in the contrast between the reports of two committees of the National Education Association, made in 1893 and in 1918. The first, known as the Committee of Ten, reported concerning the secondary schools of the day:

> Their main function is to prepare for the duties of life that small proportion of all of the children in the country—a proportion small in number, but very important to the welfare of the nation—who show themselves able to profit by an education prolonged to the eighteenth year, and whose parents are able to support them while they remain so long at school.[15]

The second, known as the Commission on the Reorganization of Secondary Education, reported in 1918:

> Education in a democracy . . . should develop in each individual the knowledge, interests, ideals, habits, and powers whereby he will find his place and use that place to shape both himself and society toward ever nobler ends.[16]

In 25 years an institution designed for the leisure classes and aristocratic in most of its traditions was recognized as having responsibility for educating *each individual* in the society. (It was much easier to restate the philosophy than to make appropriate changes in the nature of the program. Indeed most of them still remain to be accomplished).

The twenty-fold increase in the secondary school population made it imperative to define standards. Also the expansion of college enrollments increased the problem of determining the relationship between the secondary school and the college. College people dominating the National Education Association demanded a definition of the secondary school's

---

[12] "Statistical Summary of Public Elementary and Secondary Schools, 1870–1946," Chapter II, p. 27 in *Biennial Survey of Education in the United States, 1944–1946* (Washington, D.C.: U.S. Government Printing Office, 1949).

[13] *Ibid.*

[14] *Statistical Circular*, Vol. 241 (Washington, D.C.: U.S. Office of Education, 1948), p. 1.

[15] Committee on Secondary School Studies, *Report of the Committee on Secondary School Studies Appointed at the Meeting of the National Education Association, July 9, 1892* (Washington, D.C.: U.S. Government Printing Office, 1893), p. 51.

[16] Commission on the Reorganization of Secondary Education, *Cardinal Principles of Secondary Education* (Washington, D.C.: U.S. Office of Education Bulletin, 1918, No. 35), p. 9.

role. In 1892, this pressure led to the appointment of the Committee of Ten and subsequently to several other committees (including the Committee on College Entrance Requirements, the Committee on Economy of Time in Education, the Committee on Six-year Courses, and the Committee on the Articulation of High School and College), prior to the creation in 1913 of the Commission on the Reorganization of Secondary Education.[17]

As a result of the work of these committees, the offerings of the public high school were standardized around 15 or 16 "units" of work from six basic fields—English, classical languages, modern languages, history, mathematics, and science. The "unit" was defined. The principle of "constants and electives" was enunciated. The high school was recognized as a four-year school, although the possibility of a six-year organization was also recognized. The principle of transferring from the secondary school to the college on the basis of graduation rather than examination became generally accepted.[18]

The appointment of the Commission on the Reorganization of Secondary Education represented the development of a new relationship between the high school program and the colleges. After this time it became evident to the critical observer that the colleges were as dependent on the public high school as the public high school on the college. The high school, however, had a broader responsibility than the mere preparation of students for college. Even as early as 1890 only a small portion of the secondary population continued into college. As the school became a service of the government, it became important that the education offered be appropriate for all.

The transition of secondary education from the status of a private school system, offering classical subject matter to the socially elite, to the status of a public school, attempting to design instructional material for all students within a particular age-span, came at the same time as a shift in the concept of government. In the eighteenth and nineteenth centuries government had been viewed largely as a device to protect people and their property. In the twentieth century it was coming to be viewed as a creative force in the improvement of the lot of the people.[19]

Trying to establish a program suited to the recognized needs of larger segments of the population led to experiments in two directions.

---

[17] William M. French, *America's Educational Tradition* (Boston: D. C. Heath & Company, 1964), pp. 155–61.

[18] Two survey views of this era and its developments are Edgar W. Knight, *Fifty Years of American Education* (New York: The Ronald Press Company, 1952); Isaac L. Kandel, ed., *Twenty-Five Years of American Education* (New York: The Macmillan Company, 1924). *See also* French, *op. cit.*, pp. 152–61.

[19] H. G. Good, *A History of American Education*, (New York: The Macmillan Company, 1962), p. 593.

One was with different types of specialized schools, the other involved including a variety of distinct curricula within a single school's program. Among efforts at creating more specialized schools was the development of the junior high school. Also tried were separate schools for boys and girls and for different racial groups, specialized commercial and vocational schools (with designation of the older type school as classical or college preparatory), and in a few places special schools for certain ability groupings.[20]

A more popular approach was the development of specialized curricula within a single school. The initial pressure was to provide vocational training of some sort for students for whom the traditional college preparatory program was the most unsuited. Some kind of commercial curriculum became a common offering. Generally, the student took the regular units of work in English and social studies, but would substitute business mathematics for algebra and such courses as bookkeeping, shorthand, typing, and office practice for the more traditional courses in classical and modern foreign languages. The popularity of proprietary schools offering secretarial training seems to have suggested the appropriateness of the same type of material in the public schools.[21]

Similarly, the need for skilled workers, which became most evident about the time of the First World War, gave an impetus to other types of vocational training.[22] The development of group testing and the idea of vocational guidance also had its impact. During these years some schools with as few as 1,000 students had as many as ten distinct curricula.

One of the reasons why separate schools and separate curricula were developed was that their presence allowed the pressures for revising the more traditional phases of the school program to be diverted. Rigid standards could be made to apply to the program designated college preparatory without hampering the adaptation of newer programs to the needs of other groups.

Perhaps proponents of this compromise between tradition and the various newer curricula failed to realize the strength of the pressure for a more practical and democratic curriculum. It soon became apparent that the principal distinctions being made in the specialized schools and curricula were social. Parents wanted for their children the programs which carried prestige. Teachers of vocational and commercial courses pointed out that inability to learn classical subjects gave no assurance of ability to learn vocational or commercial subjects. Pupils were generally not ready at the beginning of their high school careers to choose their vocations. The general responsibilities of the high school were widely

20 *Ibid.*, pp. 441–55.
21 Butts and Cremin, *op. cit.*, p. 581.
22 Good, *op. cit.*, p. 452.

recognized as of more importance than the specialized ones. One of the major influences on educational thought in this connection was *The Eight Year Study*, the report of which was published in 1942.[23] In this study it was shown, at least to the satisfaction of some, that success in college was not dependent on completing a prescribed pattern of courses at the high school level. Similar evidence was to be found after the Second World War in the success of veterans who had been allowed to enroll in college although they had never completed high school.

The current stage in public secondary education is sometimes referred to as that of the "comprehensive high school." It is this program which will be described in subsequent chapters. While specialized and comprehensive schools exist side by side, comprehensiveness is one of the dominant characteristics of the high schools in most communities. Several factors have contributed to the emphasis on comprehensiveness. Among them has been the decision that larger schools are more economical than small ones. Also important are shifts in our understanding of the learning process and in the nature of society itself.

Education is more complicated today than in the preceding periods of American history. It has to be, to cope with the problems of an urban economy with a mobile population. The difference is important both in the cities and in rural areas. In the rural economy which dominated the American scene of the last century, change was slow. George Washington and Abraham Lincoln would each have been at home in the time of the other, or even in the times of the Greeks and Romans. Neither would be at home on the modern farm or in the modern city.

The need for vocational education for the average citizen living on the farm in 1860 was comparatively slight. The need for civic education for the same citizen could be met with some degree of success by the home. Since comparatively little was known about health and sanitation, little had to be taught on these subjects in the public schools. Commercial recreation was practically unknown, and the school was not a place for play. While child labor was a problem prior to 1880, in the rural economy it was more clearly a problem of the family than of society.

It is doubtful whether the modern high school could have developed so comprehensive a program if it had remained in its nineteenth century rural setting. Nor would its character as an agency assuming the residual responsibilities for education be the same. Society delegates responsibility to various agencies in different periods. At one period the delegation will be to the home, at another to the church, and at another to the school as an organ of the state. The shift from a rural to an urban base has strongly influenced the relationship of these three social agencies.

[23] Wilford M. Aikin, *The Story of the Eight Year Study* (New York: Harper and Brothers, 1942).

Independent Systems of Education

Some understanding of the significance of the American public comprehensive high school in the mid-twentieth century may arise from a brief consideration of the nature of independent systems of secondary education in this country, and of public systems in Europe.

As will be seen from the map on page 14, the largest portion of students attending independent schools is to be found in the East and in the Midwestern States. The smallest proportions are to be found in the South and Far West. The most frequent explanation for the discrepancy has been that private schools are strongest where they developed in the early eighteenth century before the development of public secondary schools. In addition, the Catholic parochial schools are located in those sections where the Catholic population is more numerous.

Two main classes of secondary schools in America operate independently of the public school. Together they enroll approximately 8½ per cent of the secondary school students in the country. One of these is the private school operating either under the control of a single individual or under a private board of trustees, usually charging tuition, and independent of the control of any church group. The other is the parochial school, operated by some religious group for the purpose of including religious instruction in the education of its young members. The right of these groups to operate independently for so long as they maintain adequate standards has been well established. The sanctity of a private educational institution's charter was established by the Dartmouth College Case in the early period of the American Constitution's development. The parent's freedom to send his child to a private school was decided by the United States Supreme Court in 1925.[24]

There is considerable diversity in the types of private, non-parochial schools. Some are military. Some are maintained for one sex only. Most of them are boarding schools, but there is also a significant number of day schools. The quality as measured by tangible means varies. Many are conservative in teaching techniques, but some are strictly experimental and progressive. Some were established to take care of particular problems such as provision for mental or physical handicaps. Other schools provide for the education of a socially select or perhaps a talented group.[25]

The private, non-parochial schools now enroll approximately 1 per cent of the total secondary school population. (Some observers expect this number to increase in the next few years as a result of some criticisms

[24] Pierce vs. Society of Sisters, 268 U.S. 510, 535.
[25] Digest of Educational Statistics, 1964 (Washington, D.C.: U.S. Department of Health, Education and Welfare, 1964), pp. 26–27.

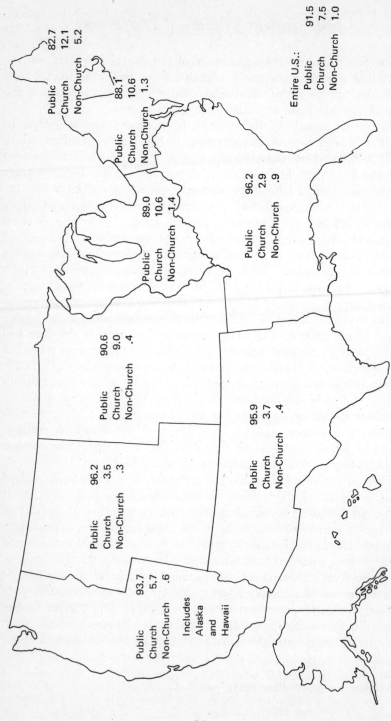

Percentage Enrollment in Public, Church Related, and Non-Church Related Secondary Schools in 1960–1961*

Public 82.7
Church 12.1
Non-Church 5.2

Public 88.1
Church 10.6
Non-Church 1.3

Public 89.0
Church 10.6
Non-Church 1.4

Public 96.2
Church 2.9
Non-Church .9

Public 90.6
Church 9.0
Non-Church .4

Public 96.2
Church 3.5
Non-Church .3

Public 95.9
Church 3.7
Non-Church .4

Public 93.7
Church 5.7
Non-Church .6

Includes
Alaska
and
Hawaii

Entire U.S.:
Public 91.5
Church 7.5
Non-Church 1.0

*Adapted from Digest of Educational Statistics, 1966 Edition (Washington, D.C.: U.S. Department of Health, Education, and Welfare, 1966), pp. 24, 31.

of public secondary education, the increasing affluence of the middle classes, and the tensions caused by racial integration.) When it is considered that, prior to 1880, these were the basic secondary schools, it may be seen how their relationship to the society has changed.

One of the questions which concerns the student of the American public high school is the effect which these schools may have on the problems of public education. One possible result of the existence of some types of private school is the population's division along lines of social class. This is seen as a stronger tendency in New England and along the Eastern seaboard than in other sections of the country. There is argument that where the children of influential and wealthy parents are sent away to school local public schools receive less interest and support.

Studies of the comparative achievement of the graduates of public and private schools with regard to such things as college entrance tests and subsequent success in college have tended to show that public school students do as well as or better than private school ones.[26] In most of these studies differences between different public or private schools were greater than those between the two groups treated as wholes.

For a long time one of the important differences between the public and private schools was in the area of teacher education. The private schools seemed to pride themselves on the fact that their teachers had little formal training in education and psychology. The present trend is in the direction of similar requirements for the teachers of both public and private schools. In some states, private school teachers must meet state certification requirements.

Among the other issues raised by the program of some private schools is whether coeducation is better than sex-segregated education. Also at question is the desirability of the military discipline of the military school, and the effects of sending children away from their parents during the formative period of adolescence. In some situations it seems important for the children to get away from home as soon as possible, in others it may be undesirable. A crucial issue for the student of democracy is whether it is better for every child to have the common experience of a public education or whether it is better for parents who wish a different training to have private schools available.

Parochial secondary schools in this country are operated primarily by five separate church groups: Roman Catholics, Episcopalians, Seventh Day Adventists, Lutherans, and Christian Reformed. Over 90 per cent of the students enrolled in parochial schools are in Roman Catholic ones. The table on the following page indicates the size of each group and the strength by regions. Most of these schools are day schools and in that

---

[26] Representative of these studies is Irving T. Lathrop and Thomas J. Kieffer, "College Achievement of Public versus Private High School Graduates," *The Clearing House* 33: 299–302 (Jan. 1959).

ENROLLMENT IN NON-PUBLIC SECONDARY SCHOOLS BY CHURCH
RELATIONSHIP AND BY REGION, 1960—1961 [1]

	U.S.	New England	Mid East	Great Lakes	Plains	South East	South West	Rocky Mtns.	Far West
All Non-Public Sec. Schools	1,109,443	119,970	350,486	273,278	99,016	112,216	36,244	15,459	102,774
Non-church	133,126	36,124	38,843	10,547	4,223	26,792	3,691	1,252	11,654
Church Rel.	976,317	83,846	311,643	262,731	94,793	85,424	32,553	14,207	91,120
Roman Catholic	887,481	79,077	291,639	241,225	86,814	71,001	27,957	11,660	78,108
Protestant Episcopal	16,180	2,653	3,495	1,235	854	4,280	880	190	2,593
Seventh Day Adventist	15,800	429	1,430	2,180	992	2,413	954	734	6,668
Lutheran	14,680	54	1,073	8,740	2,822	256	389	423	923
Christian Reformed	9,795		649	5,966	1,146	527	412	352	743
Jewish	6,522	196	5,531	553		80			162
Friends	5,041	598	4,009	106	160	45		99	24
Baptist	4,713	200	358	1,058		2,226	328		543
Methodist	2,923	430	829	33	130	918	476		107
Presbyterian	2,740		396	483	189	787	578	169	138
Other churches	10,442	209	2,234	1,152	1,686	2,891	579	580	1,111

[1] Digest of Educational Statistics, 1966 Edition (Washington, D.C.: U.S. Department of Health, Education, and Welfare, 1966), p. 31.

respect are more like the public schools than like the private boarding ones. Their principal reason for existence is to be found in the belief of their patrons that an education in which religion is not central is not a good education.

The educational methodology of most of the parochial schools would be considered by public school people to be conservative, but there has been a tendency on the part of those operating the parochial institutions to imitate the changes in technique which have come into public schools within the past 50 years.

Some officials of the Catholic church have been pressing strongly for public support of the parochial school program. Recently, for example, an attempt was made in New York to amend the state constitution to permit local school districts to make direct appropriations to parochial schools. In some states such provision has been made with regard to textbooks, health services, and school bus transportation on the grounds that these were services being provided to individuals rather than to the schools. Recent Federal legislation has recognized this principle in provision for support for elementary and secondary schools. Usually the states have maintained some nominal supervision over the church schools' standards, the certification of teaching personnel, and the enforcement of attendance regulations.

Many public school personnel feel that the use of public funds to support parochial education would be contrary to the principle of separation of church and state. It is also feared that support for Catholic church schools would encourage the development of an economically inefficient system of schools for other denominational groups and a weakening of the support for public schools generally. Pressure for expansion of the Catholic parochial school is, of course, strong in sections of the country where the Catholic population is large. The problem of social division along religious lines is less important in the more heterogeneous Middle West and the more homogeneously Protestant South.[27]

European Educational Systems

Since American and European secondary schools started from the same parent institutions and since it seems evident that American secondary education has been modified by the development of American democracy, it is interesting to look at the present status of secondary education in Europe.

In most of Europe the program of the Latin grammar school, as it

[27] For a survey of these problems see John S. Brubacher, *The Public Schools and Spiritual Values*, Seventh Yearbook of the John Dewey Society (New York: Harper and Brothers, 1944).

is called in England, can be recognized in the classical curriculum of the schools for the upper classes. Similarly there are distinct schools providing a technical curriculum reminiscent of the old academy program. Many of these are descendants of schools organized in the late eighteenth and early nineteenth centuries. While they do not have the social prestige of the classical schools, they are widely respected. The bulk of the youth of secondary school age attend school, however, either in continuation programs in the elementary schools, work in part-time programs of an evening or night school nature, or are in recently organized schools of lower prestige referred to in England and France as "modern" schools.

In Western Europe there is still much variation between such countries as Sweden, where the proportion of youth in secondary schools is high, and Spain and Portugal, where only a small part of the secondary age group are in school.

While public pressure for school reform is strong and much progress has been made in England and France toward providing for universal secondary education in a single track system, the tradition of the multiple track system in which the classes or different ability streams are educated separately is still quite powerful.

As a result of the Education Act of 1944, the British are taking large steps toward providing universal public secondary education.[28] The Secondary Modern School is apparently becoming popular in some sections of the country and approaches, at least in theory, the American comprehensive high school.[29] The French are making more cautious steps toward a similar modification of their schools.[30] In both France and England there is a serious shortage of college and university facilities for competent secondary school graduates. This tends to delay acceptance on the part of the public and colleges of the validity of more widespread college preparation.

The curriculum of most European secondary schools would seem to an American to be heavy in its emphasis on languages and classical literature, and light on social studies. The emphasis on languages is natural in an area in which people speaking different languages live close to one another. The tradition of using the secondary schools to prepare the whole population for citizenship is, however, an American development. At the same time that some Americans suggest a return to the old European pattern of secondary education, the recent modifications of

[28] H. C. Dent, *Secondary Education for All* (London: Routledge and Kegan Paul Ltd., 1949), pp. 111–29.

[29] For an American comment on the current situation see Jack B. Montague, Jr., "Another Look at English Secondary Schools," *The Clearing House* 37:430–34 (1963).

[30] S. R. Fraser, "Reform in France," *Comparative Education Review* 11:300–310 (Oct., 1967).

English, French, German, and Russian education have been in the direction of imitating American secondary education.[31]

Also apparent to the American observer is the dependence of the Europeans, particularly the French, on the school-leaving examination. This practice is more acceptable in a society in which the individual is to be tailored to the needs of the state than in one in which the school is to help the individual develop to the limits of his own potential. One result of frequent testing is that instruction is geared to preparation for examinations. More emphasis is placed on recall learning than on the development of understanding. Since passing a standard examination is necessary to proceed to the next level of instruction, the emotional pressure can be strong. This pressure is observed to be very serious in the French system, but it is also a problem in the English and Russian schools.[32]

Still another aspect of European education is the absence of lay school boards.[33] Only in England is the local education authority important in the schools' operation and even there it exercises less control over the curriculum, the selection of teachers, and the general supervision of the program than is true of the American school board.[34] In some European countries, notably France and Russia, the central control of schools results in a standardization that would seem objectionable to the American educator.

In the European school systems, except in Russia, coeducation is the exception rather than the rule. Men are the usual secondary school teachers in the boys' schools. Until recently all teacher training for secondary schools was given at the university level, and in special junior-college type institutions for the elementary level. Recent educational reforms, aimed at the development of more universal secondary education, have made necessary the development of more teacher training facilities.

[31] John Francis Cramer and George Stephenson Browne, *Contemporary Education* (New York: Harcourt, Brace and Company, 1956), pp. 65–69, 92–93, 443–47.

[32] James B. Conant, "An American Looks at European Education" in Francis S. Chase and Harold A. Anderson, *The High School in a New Era* (Chicago: The University of Chicago Press, 1958), p. 26.

[33] I. L. Kandel, *The New Era in Education: A Comparative Study* (Boston: Houghton Mifflin Company, 1955), pp. 131–36.

[34] *Ibid.*

2

The Aims of Public Secondary Education

THE SHIFT OF EMPHASIS IN AMERICAN SECONDARY EDUCATION FROM PRO-viding for a small leisure class to catering for an entire age group has necessitated significant changes in the statement of aims for the school. The following chapter discusses what changes have been made in the stated purpose and some of the questions raised by these transformations. Who, for example, has had the responsibility for speaking for the professional school personnel? How important is concern for the individual student's welfare in these statements of aim? How much attention is given to the welfare of the society? How much direction do the statements give for modifying traditions which were more appropriate for a more exclusive type of school? Are consistent trends discernible in the various statements put forward during the past half century?

Statements of Aim in the Twentieth Century

The Cardinal Principles of Secondary Education. Representative groups in the teaching profession have been considering the aims of education since about 1890. Perhaps the first full statement of aims emphasizing the public character of American secondary education appeared in the 1918 report of the Commission on the Reorganization of Secondary Education.[1] Entitled "The Cardinal Principles of Secondary Education," this was important for four reasons: (1) it broke with the older tradition that the secondary schools' function was to teach the classical disciplines to a very limited and elite segment of the total secondary age population; (2) it was an authoritative statement by a commission of the National Educa-

---

[1] *Cardinal Principles of Secondary Education* (Washington, D.C.: U.S. Office of Education Bulletin, 1918, No. 35).

tion Association; (3) it was couched in simple language, easily remembered; and (4) it has been widely used both by lay and professional groups as a starting point for the evaluation of existing practices and programs.

The seven "cardinal principles of education" have several shortcomings as aims for American public secondary education in the twentieth century. In spite of the fact that they were apparently based on an earlier statement by Herbert Spencer of the nature of a complete education, they lacked the logical completeness of Spencer's version. The areas listed included health, command of fundamental processes, worthy home membership, vocation, civic education, worthy use of leisure, and ethical character.[2] The relationship of each area to the other and to the total was not clear.

The second area was open to a variety of kinds of interpretation. Were the fundamental processes referred to "fundamental" to the other aims listed? If so, the heading was superfluous. Did this heading refer to traditional teaching content which would not be included under any of the other headings? If so, what other functions of education had been omitted?

The use of "worthy" in the third and sixth objectives and the inclusion of "ethical character" as somehow coordinate with the other five areas of concern revealed a preoccupation with moral values. Such a preoccupation was somewhat characteristic of the philosophy of Idealism in the late nineteenth and early twentieth centuries, but was destined to be replaced by a more objective approach. It was soon recognized that almost any practice or body of subject matter could be justified as a contribution to one or another of the objectives listed.

Recognition of the need for a more helpful set of objectives led to other attempts at formulation. Among others, both Bobbitt and Charters attempted to arrive objectively at a statement of aims.[3] In the 1920's, enthusiasm for scientific method led to an attempt to get a consensus from those considered competent to judge what the aims of education should be, and to make an item-analysis of the skills needed for effective living. During the same period, an attempt to formulate the aims by identifying all of the biological drives of the individual proved a failure.

The Social-Economic Goals of America. Each successive attempt toward reformulation bore the marks of the particular concerns of that immediate period of time. This seems particularly apparent in one list, entitled the "Ten Desirable Social-Economic Goals of America," circulated widely during the depression era. It was said to have been derived

---

[2] Commission on the Reorganization of Secondary Education, *op. cit.*, pp. 10–11.

[3] *See* Franklin Bobbitt, *The Curriculum* (Boston: Houghton Mifflin Company, 1918) and W. W. Charters, *Curriculum Construction* (New York: The Macmillan Company, 1923).

from an analysis of the ideals of America as they were found in the federal constitution. The list included: (1) hereditary strength, (2) physical security, (3) participation in an evolving culture, (4) an active, flexible personality, (5) suitable occupation, (6) economic security, (7) mental security, (8) equality of opportunity, (9) freedom, and (10) fair play.[4] While it may be difficult to see how such a list is to be derived from studying the federal constitution, the items are suggestive of important social problems recognized in the period immediately before and during the Depression. The title indicates that the intent was to list the goals of the society rather than the specific responsibilities of the school. Nevertheless it was promulgated by professional people as a guide to the school program, although its use was much more limited than that of the well-stated cardinal principles of education.

The Educational Policies Commission Report of 1938. One of the more authoritative listings of aims was the work of the Educational Policies Commission of the National Education Association, published in 1938.[5] Like some other statements, this one was considered descriptive of the functions of public education generally, as well as of secondary education specifically. The four major headings were: The objectives of (1) self-realization, (2) human relationship, (3) economic efficiency, and (4) civic responsibility.[6]

While it seems difficult to justify making economic efficiency and civic responsibility of coordinate importance with such areas as self-realization and human relationship, the listing appeared logical enough in its organization. Because the list was in outline form, its headings could be used for brevity and the sub-heads could be studied when more specific treatment was desired. Under each heading approximately a dozen objectives were set out as sub-heads. It was more difficult than in the case of the seven cardinal principles to misuse these objectives to justify traditional programs. The basic approach, reminiscent of Spencer's, was logical. It described the objectives of the educational process in terms of the individual as he relates to himself, others, the economy, and the state. The amount of emphasis on economic and civic efficiency reflected the recent distress of the depression era and the impending involvement in the Second World War.

The Imperative Educational Needs of Youth. Another approach was made later by the same Educational Policies Commission. It was not a revision of the 1938 objectives, but was an attempt to phrase them in terms of the needs of individual students rather than of the social rela-

---

[4] The High School Curriculum, Sixth Yearbook, Department of Superintendence (Washington, D.C.: National Education Association, 1928), p. 51; "What are Desirable Social Economic Goals for America?" The NEA Journal 23:6–12 (Jan., 1934).

[5] The Purposes of Education in American Democracy (Washington, D.C.: NEA, 1938).

[6] Ibid., p. 41.

tionships in which students were placed. First published in 1944, it was headed the "Imperative Educational Needs of Youth."[7] They were listed as follows:

1. All youth need to develop saleable skills and those understandings and attitudes that make the worker an intelligent and productive participant in economic life. To this end, most youth need supervised work experience as well as education in the skills and knowledge of their occupations.
2. All youth need to develop and maintain good health and physical fitness.
3. All youth need to understand the rights and duties of the citizen of a democratic society, and to be diligent and competent in the performance of their obligations as members of the community and citizens of the state and nation.
4. All youth need to understand the significance of the family for the individual and society and the conditions conducive to successful family life.
5. All youth need to know how to purchase and use goods and services intelligently, understanding both the values received by the consumer and the economic consequences of their acts.
6. All youth need to understand the methods of science, the influence of science on human life, and the main scientific facts concerning the nature of the world and of man.
7. All youth need opportunities to develop their capacities to appreciate beauty in literature, art, music, and nature.
8. All youth need to be able to use their leisure time well and to budget it wisely, balancing activities that yield satisfactions to the individual with those that are socially useful.
9. All youth need to develop respect for other persons, to grow in their insight into ethical values and principles, and to be able to live and work cooperatively with others.
10. All youth need to grow in their ability to think rationally, to express their thoughts clearly, and to read and listen with understanding.

An analysis of the areas of need listed will reveal six which were also mentioned in the seven cardinal principles: health (2), vocation (1), home membership (4), civic education (3), ethical character (9), and leisure (8). The inversion of the order is perhaps significant. Particular prominence is given to the vocational objective, and health and civic education are listed ahead of family-life education. Perhaps numbers (6) science and (10) rational thinking are an expansion or clarification of ideas that were included under "command of fundamental processes" in the seven cardinal principles. Related to the idea of vocational competence is stress on consumer economics (5) and related to the emphasis on "worthy use of leisure time" is the idea of developing aesthetic appreciation of art, music, literature, and nature (7).

[7] *Education for All American Youth* (Washington, D.C.: NEA, 1944), pp. 225–26.

It is difficult to be certain whether the expansion of the list between 1918 and 1944 was an *ex-post-facto* recognition of the addition of new course materials in the public high school program (particularly science, economics, and vocational programs) or really descriptive of some more logical analysis of the needs of youth. The listing did seem to have an advantage over the earlier statements in suggesting, with some degree of clarity, the important content for the school program. The emphasis on supervised work experience in the first item and the specific reference to the obligations of citizenship seem to represent an attempt to respond to the peculiar pressures of the war period for more effective vocational education and for military service. While both of these are, perhaps, legitimate concerns of public education, the emphasis is stronger than would have been thought necessary at some other period. The entire statement was probably intended as a counterbalance to the traditional concept of the high school as a college preparatory institution.

Indicative of the shifts in emphasis which may occur even in short periods of time are the revisions made to "Ten Imperative Needs of Youth" seven years later in a 1951 publication of the National Association of Secondary School Principals.[8] The words "and mental health" were added to the second statement; "and to have an understanding of the nations and peoples of the world" was added to the third; while "and to grow in the moral and spiritual values of life" was added to the ninth.

The unwieldiness of long statements, the ambiguity of short listings, the tendency to ignore both in the actual operation of the school program (except for justifying existing procedures) tended to worry the leading writers in the field of curriculum. Some of the educational philosophers had warned of the dangers inherent in the statement of aims. The problem of setting aims for groups of children (and even for whole nations) was that children's needs varied both in kind and in relative importance from one community to the next and from one child to another. On the other hand, changes were constantly taking place in the nature of society which tended to make the important emphasis of one period seem much less important in another. In the period between 1918 and 1950, for instance, the relative importance of vocational education, physical education, education for world citizenship, and family life education was seen to shift in the various statements.

The Behavioral Goals of the Modern Secondary School. A revised statement of the goals of the modern secondary school appeared in 1957. It was the result of a study sponsored by the Educational Testing Service, the Russell Sage Foundation, and the National Association of Secondary School Principals. Using panels or committees of consultants, interested laymen, and school personnel, a central editorial committee under the

[8] *Planning for American Youth* (Washington, D.C.: National Association of Secondary School Principals, 1951), p. 9.

leadership of Professor Will French carefully classified the *desirable changes in behavior* which should result from the educational process.[9] The final statement is clearly that of the professional student of secondary education influenced by informed lay opinion. While it is likely to stress the particular concerns of the mid-twentieth century, it builds more on the philosophical analysis of the school's role than on inherited curricula. It thus may become a guide for improvement, rather than a justification for continuing outworn practice.

Using a decimal system this listing proceeds from broad areas of concern—(1) Growing Toward Self-Realization, (2) Growing in Ability to Maintain Desirable Small Group Relationships, and (3) Growing in Ability to Maintain the Relationships Imposed by Membership in Large Organizations—to more specific sub-heads (*e.g.* 1.1 Developing Behaviors Indicative of Intellectual Self-Realization) and finally to quite practical immediate objectives (*e.g.* 1.11 Improving His Study Habits, Study Skills, and Other Work Habits). Certain aspects of the organization of these areas might be questioned at several points. For example, the separation of economic or vocational aspects of life from those labeled "cultural" seems somewhat artificial. It is awkward to insist on including under the heading "growth toward self-realization" the topics "cultural orientation" and "economic literacy" which could probably be covered under the headings dealing with the maintenance of group relationships.

The title, *Behavioral Goals of General Education in High Schools*, seems to indicate a stress on "general education." When it is noted, however, that vocational objectives are included, it becomes clear that the term "general" is not meant to be restrictive. No public secondary education is to be considered adequate or complete which does not provide for all of the areas listed. Perhaps in reaction to the general emphasis of this listing on behavioral goals, there have been others oriented more toward a "traditional" view of the school.[10] In response to such a reaction, the Educational Policies Commission issued a new statement in 1961.

The Central Purpose of American Education. American secondary education at that time was being blamed for everything from theorists' concern with "life adjustment" to the success of the Russian Sputnik. In this adverse climate, the Educational Policies Commission retreated from the logic of its earlier statements. It hauled down the flag in a

[9] Will French and Associates, *Behavioral Goals of General Education in High Schools* (New York: Russell Sage Foundation, 1957). Readers should refer to the complete report.

[10] For several statements of this more traditional view see Francis S. Chase and Harold A. Anderson, eds., *The High School in a New Era* (Chicago: The University of Chicago Press, 1958); see also Paul Woodring and John J. Scanlon, *American Education Today* (New York: McGraw-Hill Book Company, 1963), and Hyman G. Rickover, *American Education: A National Failure* (New York: E. P. Dutton & Co., Inc., 1963).

statement entitled *The Central Purpose of American Education*.[11] While reaffirming the Commission's commitment to the 1918 and 1938 statements of the cardinal principles and objectives of American education, it went on to state that "the development of every student's rational powers must be recognized as centrally important."[12] It also stated that the central purpose of American education was not its only purpose.

Whether interpreted as a politically inspired move to reassure the people of the traditionally sound stance of public education or as a compromise in which both the progressive and conservative views of education could be embraced, the statement added little. It progressed hardly any further than the 1938 statement in trying to define the school's role in terms that would give real direction to the public school teacher. Its language was quite similar to that of the Committee of Ten in 1893 and—despite its protestation of support for citizenship, vocational skills, and morality—its focus was much more restrictive than most of the previous twentieth century statements of purpose.

The Taxonomy of Educational Objectives. A more hopeful approach to the development of specific and manageable statements of objectives was undertaken by a group of psychologists working under the editorship of Benjamin S. Bloom of the University of Chicago. This group aimed to assemble, from existing materials, a statement of educational objectives sufficiently explicit to provide a reasonable basis for the development of objective tests. It was not apparently their intent to specify the appropriate educational goals of public education or of any other level or type of school, but rather to arrive at a classification system for possible goals.[13]

These objectives were classified under three main headings: (1) The Cognitive, (2) the Affective, and (3) the Psychomotor. These were defined in part as follows:

1. *Cognitive*: Objectives which emphasize remembering or reproducing something which has presumably been learned, as well as objectives which involve the solving of some intellective task for which the individual has to determine the essential problem and then reorder given material or combine it with ideas, methods, or procedures previously learned. Cognitive objectives vary from simple recall of material learned to highly original and creative ways of combining and synthesizing new ideas and materials. We found that the largest proportion of educational objectives fell into this domain.
2. *Affective*: Objectives which emphasize a feeling, tone, an emotion, or a degree of acceptance or rejection. Affective objectives vary from simple attention to selected phenomena to complete but internally

[11] *The Central Purpose of American Education* (Washington, D.C.: NEA, 1961).
[12] *Ibid.*, p. 12.
[13] David R. Krathwohl, Benjamin S. Bloom and Bertram B. Masia, *Taxonomy of Educational Objectives: The Classification of Educational Goals*, Handbook II: Affective Domain (New York: David McKay Co., Inc., 1964), pp. 3–6.

consistent qualities of character and conscience. We found a large number of such objectives in the literature expressed as interests, attitudes, appreciations, values, and emotional sets or biases.

3. *Psychomotor*: Objectives which emphasize some muscular or motor skill, some manipulation of material and objects, or some act which requires a neuromuscular co-ordination. We found few such objectives in the literature. When found, they were most frequently related to handwriting and speech and to physical education, trade and technical courses.[14]

One of the significant observations of the committee working on classifying objectives in the affective domain was the tendency of college teachers of survey-level courses to start off with statements of objectives which were in the affective domain and then, as the courses became stabilized, to regress toward those in the cognitive domain. The difficulties of *measuring* objectives dealing with interests, attitudes, and appreciations seemed to lead teachers away from efforts to *teach* toward them.[15] The same problem has been observed by innovators at the secondary level.

The Individual and the Society

During the twentieth century, much of the discussion of educational objectives has related to the resolution of conflicts between the needs and interests of the individual and those of the group or society. Sometimes concern was expressed over whether the school was to be "student centered" or more strongly society oriented.

Recognizing that democracy is the basic social philosophy might provide a solution to the problem. Democracy as a social philosophy may be described as that view of the relationship of the individual to the society in which it is assumed that the welfare of the individual is the most important concern of the group. It follows that in a democratic society, it is important that each individual be able to make contributions to the welfare of others, and further that what is not in the interest of individuals is probably not good for the group as a whole. Any statement of educational objectives for a democratic society which fails to recognize either the peculiar needs of individuals or the probable demands of social living is incomplete. The problem is not whether the school will be "student-centered" or "socially oriented" but whether the school recognizes that in dealing with the student it is dealing with the important social unit.

The more traditional view of the role of the secondary school seems to start from an assumption of values which inhere in the society apart

[14] *Ibid.*, pp. 6–7.
[15] *Ibid.*, pp. 16–18.

from its existence as a collection of individuals. In this view, the transmission of the cultural heritage and not the development of individual potential is considered the primary goal of any form of schooling whether public or private. Traditionalists are concerned with the development of individual potential, but they do not recognize this as the *primary* goal.[16]

Until 1961, the trend of the various statements of educational aims was toward an increasingly "democratic" approach. In each one the focal point seems to have been the individual student, while concern was expressed regarding all his contacts with other individuals in the social setting.[17] To the extent that any official statement can be made of the "professional" position of American teachers, these statements were official. They were statements made by major committees or commissions of the National Education Association or by its affiliated groups.

For example, the problem of conflict between individuality and socialization is dealt with in the 1957 listing of "Behavioral Goals of General Education in High Schools" not only in the three main headings (self-realization, small group membership, and large group membership), but also in the topical listings for the major sub-heads dealing with intellectual development, cultural orientation, mental and physical health, and economic efficiency.[18] This scheme suggests the interrelatedness of the social and individual phases of the educational process.

The next steps in the formulation of aims and objectives are difficult to anticipate. The statement of behavioral goals is complete enough to give some direction to teachers and curriculum makers. The approach of the 1964 *Taxonomy of Educational Objectives,* and similar emphasis by other educational philosophers influenced by developments in linguistic analysis, will lead to more and more careful statements of points of view. Attempts of traditionalist critics to limit school responsibilities to the academic or cognitive type of objective seem likely to be balanced by the public concern for integrating lower levels of society into the basic social fabric. Such integration may well require the school to pay much more attention to "life adjustment," and will reverse any trend toward retreating in the direction of selective education and limited educational objectives.

[16] Christian O. Weber, *Basic Philosophies of Education* (New York: Rinehart and Company, Inc., 1960), p. 49.
[17] For a listing which places more emphasis on the "cultural heritage" consult Francis S. Chase, "Making the High School a Place for Study and Learning" in Francis S. Chase and Harold A. Anderson, *The High School in a New Era* (Chicago: The University of Chicago Press, 1958), p. 189.
[18] French, *op. cit.,* pp. 92–213.

3

The Public High School and Problems of Society

THE DEMOCRATIZATION OF SECONDARY EDUCATION IN THIS CENTURY RAISES the question as to what extent the school should be used to solve the problems of society. The statements of objective described in the previous chapter indicate a focus on the needs of individual students. Nevertheless, the school program has a relationship with a number of social problems. Perhaps the two most significant are (1) the social stratification of the society into classes and castes, and (2) juvenile delinquency.

Social Stratification

Americans have been acutely aware for a least 20 years of the threat to democratic ideals posed by social barriers against Negroes and other minority groups. Less attention has to be paid by interested laymen to the problems resulting from other types of social stratification.[1] Studies are now available documenting how, even in public education, class stratification hampers the ideal of providing for the needs of each individual.[2]

Studies of Social Class in American Communities. Sociologists have found several different categories useful in describing social stratification within American communities. Among these have been income; occupation; years of formal education; social or political influence; family connections; moral or ethical behavior; type, location, and condition of

[1] Robert J. Havighurst and Bernice L. Neugarten, *Society and Education*, 2nd ed. (Boston: Allyn and Bacon, Inc., 1966), pp. 265, 362.

[2] *Cf.* W. Lloyd Warner and others, *Yankee City* (New Haven: Yale University Press, 1965), pp. 245–46.

housing; and prestige.[3] In classifying any particular individual or family, one of these is selected or several may be used together in some combining formula. The class status of an individual is to be viewed as changing to the extent that his relationship to others on the same scale changes.[4]

One of the commonly accepted American social classification systems makes use of upper, middle, and lower classes with the possibility of two subgroups in each class. Distinctions between these groups, in a setting in which four levels were identified, were described as follows.[5]

The Upper Class. The upper class is described as economically secure with the assurance of leisure time for the elderly and the women. The family relationship, frequently concerned with hereditary status, includes relatives over an extended area and intermarriage is within the same class. The home or place of residence may reflect the inherited status of the family with emphasis on such symbols of permanency as antique furnishings. The religious affiliation is likely to be nominal but will in many communities be with one of the older protestant groups in the community. The community interest is likely to be regional rather than local and there is little interest in local politics. With regard to education, this group usually attends college but seems to develop intellectual interests only when following some professional field. With regard to morality, the values accepted were described as "liberal protestant". There was evidence of clandestine drinking and infidelity. The women were described as likely to be protected and there was a tendency of the younger set to feel that they were above the law. Upper middle class families were able to move into the upper class through marriage, economic gain, and by such other conscious activity as buying antiques or moving into a more exclusive neighborhood.

The Upper-Middle Class. The upper-middle class is described as less secure than the upper class. The men are employed as professional people or as owners or managers of large businesses. The women may work part time. The immediate family is more important than the extended family. The family relationships are likely to be democratic. The homes reveal less emphasis on the historic tradition of the family. The religion is likely to be more important than with the upper class, with the denominational affiliation about the same as for the upper class, but including more denominational church groups. There is much more participation in local politics than in the upper group. The upper-middle class group has usually attended college. The pattern of morality is more seriously accepted and enforced within the class.

The Lower-Middle Class. The lower-middle class is economically less secure than the upper-middle class. Women are more likely to work full time. The men are less likely to own their own businesses. The homes are less likely to reflect the "traditional". There is more emphasis on quality in the upper-middle class group and on quantity in the lower-

[3] Thomas E. Lasswell, *Class and Stratum: An Introduction to Concepts and Research* (Boston: Houghton Mifflin Company, 1965), p. 11.

[4] *Ibid.*, p. 110.

[5] Morton Rubin, *Plantation County* (Chapel Hill: University of North Carolina Press, 1951), pp. 110–11.

middle group. The lower-middle class group is less interested in formal education and the children are less likely to graduate from high school.

The Lower Class. The lower class is characterized by little identification with the community. Its members are economically insecure, work for daily or hourly wages, draw some prestige and cohesiveness from their job classification. The families are clannish but individual family relationships are likely to be unstable. The residences are likely to be poor. When there is any participation in religious activity it is likely to be in cult or emotional type groups. Community activity is of a negative sort, and clashes with the law may be frequent. The children of the group are likely to quit school early and may have no apparent regard for the morals of the society.

The Relationship between Social Class and School Continuation. There have been many studies of school dropouts, some of large scope and carefully done, others of lesser significance. Many of these studies show a clear relationship between both success and continuation in school and the social status of the parents, as indicated by economic status, professional or occupational classification, the family's traditions of education, the availability of adequate medical care, and the presence of a stimulating environment at home.[6]

Many lower-class children quit school before reaching the leaving age specified by law.[7] This may indicate their parents' lack of concern for education. It may indicate a weakness in the school curriculum in providing for this group of children. It probably reflects the school officials' difficulty in keeping up with a highly mobile segment of the population. Students who come infrequently are likely to be distinct problems when they do come to school, but are not yet likely to be in a category in which legal action may be taken to place them in correctional institutions. Whatever the cause for their truancy, these children in general are doomed as adults to unemployment or to work at inadequate wages. They tend to marry early, have large families, and to produce more than their share of delinquency and crime. They and their children may in time become a caste of unemployables.

That there is a connection between the number of students continuing through high school and certain geographic factors related to income and way of life may be seen from the map on page 33. In four states less than 60 per cent of the 1961 ninth graders graduated from high school in 1965. These states were all relatively rural. Three had a per capita income of less than $2,100. Two of them had a large population of

[6] Harold C. Hand, *Principal Findings of the 1947–1948 Basic Studies*, Illinois Secondary School Curriculum Program, Bulletin No. 2 (Springfield: State Department of Public Instruction, 1949), pp. 12–15. *See also* Lawrence A. Van Dyke and K. B. Hoyt, *Drop Out Problems in Iowa High Schools* (Ames: State University of Iowa, 1958).

[7] W. Lloyd Warner *et al.*, *Democracy in Jonesville* (New York: Harper and Brothers, 1949), p. 205.

rural Negroes. Most of the 12 states with more than 80 per cent graduating were highly urbanized, and ten of them had a per capita income of more than $2,400.

Another dimension of the relationship of social class to school continuation is to be found in the expected life income for different educational levels of the population. This may be seen from the chart given below. It will be noted that between 1949 and 1961 the income for males in the lowest levels had increased by 64 per cent while that for the highest level increased by 52 per cent. Nevertheless, the total for the college graduate was three times that for individuals who did not finish elementary school. It is anticipated that employment opportunities for those with little education will become fewer and fewer as industrial automation increases.

ESTIMATED LIFETIME INCOME FOR MALES BY YEARS OF SCHOOL COMPLETED[1]

	1949	1956	1961
Less Than Eight Years	$ 98,222	$131,432	$151,348
Eight Years in Elementary School	132,683	178,825	204,530
One to Three Years in High School	152,068	201,784	234,960
High School Graduation	185,279	244,102	272,629
One to Three Years in College	209,282	278,130	333,581
College Graduation	296,377	372,693	452,518

[1] Digest of Educational Statistics, 1964 Edition (Washington, D.C.: U.S. Department of Health, Education, and Welfare, 1964), p. 127.

Social Class and the Costs of Secondary Education. The cost of school attendance aggravates the problem of social class reinforcement. The cost of participating in the full program of the public school either segregates those children of the poor who remain in school or serves to encourage them to drop out. Doubtless, the long battle to provide a free public high school seems to most middle and upper-class Americans to have been won. Tuition charges have been abolished. Transportation has been made available for most, and schools have been conveniently located for attendance. Nevertheless cost remains a barrier to free access by all of the children to the public schools.[8]

[8] Harold H. Punke, "Cost to High School Seniors," NASSP Bulletin 41; 202–211 (Feb., 1957).

PUBLIC HIGH-SCHOOL GRADUATES IN 1964–65 AS PERCENT OF NINTH GRADERS IN 1961–62*

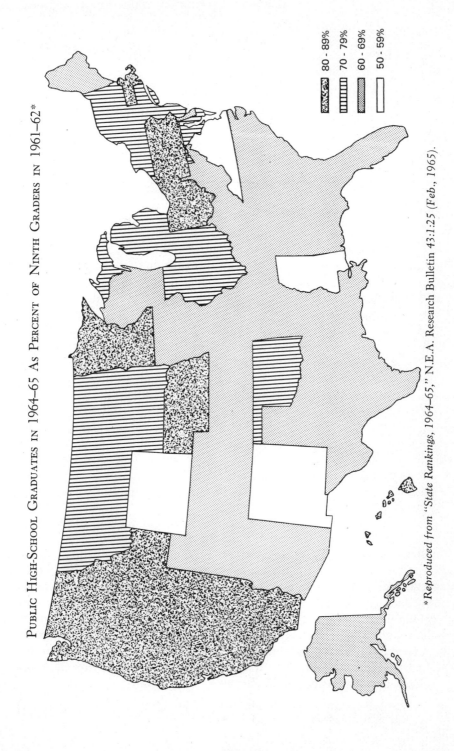

80 - 89%
70 - 79%
60 - 69%
50 - 59%

*Reproduced from "State Rankings, 1964–65," N.E.A. Research Bulletin 43:1:25 (Feb., 1965).

The costs of secondary education fall into three categories: (a) costs imposed for required materials such as textbooks, library books, gym suits, laboratory fees, paper, and writing materials; (b) those imposed for theoretically voluntary activities such as typing, athletics, subscriptions to the school newspaper or annual, graduation, band instruments, assessments such as for the junior-senior social, charity drives, club or class dues, and tickets to school functions; and (c) costs of maintenance while in school, such as for physical examinations, glasses or hearing aids, lunches, transportation, and clothes.

Studies have shown that items in the first two categories—which are associated with necessary or important school activities—might range from as little as $25 a year per student to as much as $200.[9] When it is remembered that the annual family income of many students of secondary school age is under $4,000, it is seen that even $25 per child is too much for some to bear. Put differently, it is estimated that for perhaps half of the population, the family income is insufficient to provide a decent level of housing, food, clothing and essential medical services. Although cost may not represent the principal reason for non-attendance, it must represent a serious barrier. The fact that the poorest classes have the most children to educate complicates the problem.

The American people have not yet stated to what extent they are willing to pay the maintenance costs of all children from tax funds. It can be assumed that the child who needs a school lunch but goes hungry will get less from his schooling than the child who is adequately fed. At as low a cost as 35¢ a meal, lunches for one child for a school year will amount to $63. The working class family with six children in school might then be faced with a total bill of $378. For many of them this would approximate a tenth of the family income to be spent for one meal during only half of the days in the year. The difficulty is complicated by people's aversion to what is recognized as pauper treatment. The pauper school gave way to the free public school partly because it was recognized that to give an elementary education to all regardless of economic status was better than to brand part of the society as paupers.

Since public education itself is an investment, a case can be made for spending some additional money to see that it is not wasted. Certain medical services (providing hearing aids, glasses, orthopedic help for the deformed, and dental assistance, for example) can be justified on these grounds. Some of the volunteer welfare agencies are attacking these problems, but the evidence is strong that much more must be done if all of the children who should be in school are to remain there and to profit to the limit of their potential. One of the major contributions of federal

[9] J. Minor Gwynn, *Curriculum Principles and Social Trends*, 3rd ed. (New York: The Macmillan Company, 1960), pp. 363–64.

programs under the Elementary and Secondary Education Acts has been provision for children in families with very low incomes.

The relationship between expenditures for education and the holding power of the school can also be important. Part of the nature of the relationship between tax expenditures and dropping out can be inferred from a study of the accompanying chart. Seven of the ten states with the

PER PUPIL EXPENDITURE FOR PUBLIC SCHOOLS COMPARED WITH
RANKING OF STATES IN PROPORTION OF FIFTH
GRADE GRADUATING (1964–1965)[1]

Rank[2]	State	Amt.[3]	Rank(%)[4]	Rank[2]	State	Amt.[3]	Rank(%)[4]
1.	New York	$790.00	13(79%)	28.	Vermont	$438.00	15(78%)
2.	Alaska[5]	643.00	40(64%)	29.	Missouri	437.00	31(66%)
3.	New Jersey	607.00	21(76%)	30.	Hawaii	422.00	6(84%)
4.	Connecticut	593.00	4(77%)	31.	North Dakota	422.00	14(79%)
5.	California	570.00	1(89%)	32.	Louisiana	418.00	29(67%)
6.	Oregon	569.00	7(83%)	33.	South Dakota	416.00	22(74%)
7.	Wyoming	554.00	46(59%)	34.	Nebraska	407.00	11(82%)
8.	Illinois	551.00	24(71%)	35.	Utah	407.00	36(65%)
9.	Delaware	536.00	30(66%)	36.	Florida	403.00	28(67%)
10.	Washington	534.00	8(82%)	37.	Texas	396.00	25(69%)
11.	Wisconsin	532.00	34(66%)	38.	Virginia	380.00	47(59%)
12.	Minnesota	528.00	12(86%)	39.	Maine	371.00	45(60%)
13.	Montana	516.00	17(77%)	40.	Oklahoma	366.00	23(73%)
14.	Rhode Island	514.00	14(85%)	41.	Idaho	332.00	10(82%)
15.	Michigan	510.00	16(77%)	42.	Georgia	330.00	42(62%)
16.	Nevada	505.00	5(85%)	43.	Kentucky	323.00	43(62%)
17.	Maryland	503.00	18(77%)	44.	North Carolina	322.00	33(66%)
18.	Massachusetts	502.00	9(82%)	45.	Arkansas	317.00	41(63%)
19.	Indiana	490.00	20(77%)	46.	West Virginia	315.00	44(60%)
20.	Pennsylvania	479.00	12(81%)	47.	Tennessee	300.00	32(66%)
21.	Colorado	470.00	27(67%)	48.	South Carolina	289.00	35(65%)
22.	New Mexico	470.00	49(57%)	49.	Alabama	288.00	38(64%)
23.	Ohio	469.00	2(86%)	50.	Mississippi	273.00	45(58%)
24.	Idaho	465.00	39(64%)				
25.	Kansas	462.00	26(68%)				
26.	Arizona	451.00	37(65%)				
27.	New Hampshire	448.00	———				

[1] *Adapted from "State Rankings 1964–65," NEA Research Bulletin 43;1:26 (Feb., 1965).*

[2] *Rank by Expenditure.*

[3] *Amount per pupil.*

[4] *Rank and percentage of fifth graders graduating.*

[5] *Alaska purchasing power is approximately ¼ less.*

highest proportion of students graduating from high school had a current expenditure for pupils in average daily attendance in excess of $500. Seven of the ten states with the smallest proportion of students graduating from high school spent less than $400. It should be noted, however, that other factors such as density of population are also important. Alaska and Wyoming are both in the top ten in the proportion of money spent and in the bottom ten in the proportion graduating.

Social Class in Relation to the Curriculum. There is evidence that the high school is seriously handicapped in providing for children of the lower classes. For instance, the school's teaching may be in direct conflict with the education the student is receiving at home. The student may learn at home to be aggressive, to fight with others his own age, to strike the first blow, to expect no quarter from any one. When he comes to school he is expected to be passive, to sublimate any aggressive tendency, to "turn the other cheek," to expect "to be treated right." Similarly, while the middle class pupil may be learning to trust authority, to expect protection from the law, to expect reward for good behavior and punishment for disobedience, the pupil from the poorer background may be taught to fear authority, to mistrust the law, to take what he can get.[10]

Several different programs and projects have recently been inaugurated in attempts to provide more adequately for differences in social background. Federally financed projects such as Operation Headstart, Operation Three P.M., and Operation Upward Bound have provided special experiences and tutoring for disadvantaged youth with the deliberate intention of compensating for inadequacies in cultural background. Doubtless techniques developed in such programs will serve to improve the more regular and systematic programs of the public school. (The principal weakness of such programs has been the tendency to bypass, in the initial stages, the professional advice available from professional personnel.)

School personnel often find it difficult to understand students of the lower class because most school board members and teachers themselves come from middle-class groups.[11] The teacher may not realize that when a pupil does not conform to middle class values, he may be conforming to the values of the social group from which he comes. For instance, the language which the school is trying to teach may not be acceptable in the home community of some students. A view and pattern of sexual behavior may be taught at home which the schools will not accept.[12]

[10] *Cf.* George Henderson "Role Models for Lower Class Negro Boys." *Personnel and Guidance Journal* 46:6–10 (Sept., 1967).

[11] Elizabeth G. Cohen, "Status of Teachers," *Review of Educational Research* 37:286 (June, 1967).

[12] Jack A. Duncan and George M. Gayda, "Significant Content of Group Counseling Sessions with Culturally Deprived Ninth Grade Students," *Personnel and Guidance Journal* 46:11–16 (Sept., 1967).

Sex standards are, and should be, important at the school. They present a real problem area in dealing with the pupils from lower-class homes. Similarly, throughout the whole pattern of attitudes and behavior problems, the teachings of the school and lower-class family may clash.

Those things which the school does for students from middle-class homes seem to be reinforced by the environment from which they come. When it teaches them to read, they receive the praise of their parents and move toward the goal of more mature living both in their own class group and in the society at large. When it teaches them to be thrifty, they become more acceptable members of their families. If the school rebukes them for discourtesy, the home will also rebuke them. If they get good grades, their parents are pleased and most of their peers will not be unduly critical—they, too, must please their parents.

Those things which the school teaches the children of the lower-class parent seem, at times, to be against the forces of the rest of their environment. If it teaches them to read, they may have little opportunity to practice their skill at home. If it teaches them to be thrifty, they may run into attitudes developed by the home based on cycles of comparative plenty and complete poverty. Courtesy in their home may be practically unknown. In some of these homes gratification of one's impulses seems to be the only basis for satisfaction in life.[13]

For these reasons it might seem that the American high school curriculum has little hope of being related to the problems of the lowest classes. It would certainly not seem sufficient to help them do better those things which they were going to do anyway. On the other hand it seems foolish to insist on teaching only such traditional material as Latin and algebra to students to whom such material seems so irrelevant. It would seem in their interest to spend more time helping them to understand those ethical values of that middle-class philosophy called democracy in order that they may be able to participate in the fruits of democratic living.

That geographical factors do influence the distribution of education can be seen from the map on page 39 showing the percentage of the total and of the non-white population with less than five years of schooling. For both segments of the population some southern states have three or four times as much illiteracy as some states in other regions. (A larger proportion of white adults in Arkansas, Georgia, Kentucky, Louisiana, New Mexico, North Carolina, South Carolina, Tennessee, Texas, and West Virginia were functionally illiterate than of the non-whites in Colorado, Maine, Massachusetts, Minnesota, Nebraska, New Hampshire, South Dakota, and Wyoming.)[14]

---

[13] *Ibid.*
[14] Data from the *Digest of Educational Statistics,* 1964 (Washington, D.C.: U.S. Department of Health, Education, and Welfare, 1964), p. 124.

The Classroom as a Social Grouping. The student in school is in a sense in a miniature society. As such, school and classroom are likely to reflect the characteristics of the social setting in which they exist. As early as the fifth grade the social lines between students have been found to have hardened.[15] The teachers who recognize the situation realize that sometimes they are unable to do anything much about it. When the differences in the groups within a particular classroom are large, it seems impossible to provide for all of them. Nor does it seem any more democratic to separate different groups into different classrooms. One of the major problems is that modes of controlling groups have to vary according to the group's attitudes. Where one group of students can be controlled easily, another requires more effort and a different approach.

The instructional material required also varies from one group to another. As early as the second or third grade, it becomes apparent that there are vast differences in backgrounds. Vocabularies differ and hence make provision for differences in the development of reading and spelling skills important.[16] Some children assume leadership roles easily and enjoy instructional techniques requiring creative participation by the group. Children from other class groups often seem to feel they cannot expect to exercise leadership and hence may not profit from techniques requiring initiative on their part.[17]

There are teachers who, by understanding the background of their students, have been able to use the classroom situation as an opportunity for breaking down—at least temporarily—the barriers among different social groups. Some schools seem to have been able to hold very low any feeling that the school program favored students of the upper-middle class.[18]

For those who wish the school to serve as the means by which class distinctions are obliterated and middle class values become dominant, the classroom is perhaps the crucial link in the whole educational system. The self-contained classroom of the elementary school may have a better opportunity than the departmentalized high school in this regard, because of the intimacy of the group.

The tendency of students to regard one another as individuals and not merely as members of an elite caste or class increases with the

[15] Celia B. Stendler, *Children of Brasstown* (Urbana, Ill.: Bureau of Educational Research and Service, University of Illinois, 1949), pp. 90–95.

[16] Robert L. Green, Louis J. Hoffman, and Robert F. Morgan, "Some Effects of Deprivation on Intelligence, Achievement, and Cognitive Growth," *Journal of Negro Education* 36:5–14 (Winter, 1967).

[17] George Henderson, "Beyond Poverty of Income," *Journal of Negro Education* 36:42–50 (Winter, 1967).

[18] Robert Marcus, Edward Bispo, and Irving Katuna, "Social Change and Curriculum Innovation," *Journal of Negro Education* 36:121–28 (Spring, 1967).

PERCENTAGE OF TOTAL AND NON-WHITE POPULATION 25 YEARS AND OLDER WITH LESS THAN 5 YEARS OF SCHOOLING: 1960*

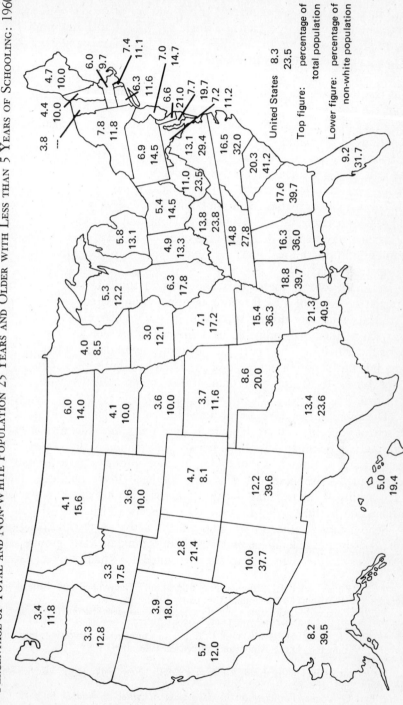

United States 8.3   23.5

Top figure: percentage of total population

Lower figure: percentage of non-white population

*Data from Digest of Educational Statistics, 1966 Ed. (Washington, D.C.: U.S. Department of Health, Education, and Welfare, 1966), p. 11.

opportunity for prolonged contact.[19] If the number of people with whom a student must come in contact in a single day is kept at a minimum, the opportunity for coming to understand and appreciate at least a few others who are different is increased.

One of the major problems in schools which attempt ability grouping is the tendency for these groupings to reflect the social stratification within the community.[20] Similarly the tendency in some high schools to offer different diplomas for different courses seems to increase class distinctions in the school.

Social stratification is not only evident within the classrooms of American public schools; it is also evident within the so-called extra-curricular or extra-class activity.[21] This problem is perhaps harder to deal with because the activities are voluntary. The children who have developed self-confidence and self-assurance at home and who know what will be expected of them in a middle-class-oriented program have a distinct advantage. Furthermore, they are more likely to be motivated to participate or excel.

It is well known to teachers and even to students that the extra-curricular activities of a high school are usually dominated by the groups of students who are already successful in the regular classes.[22] In the larger school there will probably be a sizeable group not participating in any of the activities. The matter of cost is an important consideration for some, but this is not the only problem. The cliquishness of certain social groups serves to freeze out some of the other students who might participate.[23]

The more academic types of activities, such as joining the staff of the school paper or annual, tend to require the same skills as the classroom and are dominated by the students who dominate the classes. The lower class is so severely handicapped in most instances as to be out of the running. Since these activities are considered to be public evidence of the quality of the teaching, faculty sponsors are not likely to encourage participation by those who do not already possess a high level of skill.[24]

School dances, other socials, and athletic activities also present problems. Socials are generally popular with upper-middle class groups who already possess the skills and interests required for satisfactory participa-

[19] Cf. William Van Til "Intercultural Education," *Encyclopedia of Educational Research* (New York: The Macmillan Company, 1960), p. 723.

[20] Cf. William M. Alexander and J. G. Saylor, *Modern Secondary Education* (New York: Rinehart and Company, Inc., 1959), p. 377.

[21] Hilda Taba, E. H. Brady, and J. Robinson, *Intergroup Education in Public Schools* (Washington, D.C.: American Council on Education, 1952), pp. 124–27.

[22] *Ibid.*

[23] Cf. August R. Hollingshead, *Elmtown's Youth* (New York: John Wiley & Sons, Inc., 1949), pp. 168–72.

[24] Earl G. Pogue, *Participation in Extra-class Activities as Related to Socio-Economic Classification.* Doctor's thesis, University of Illinois, 1949.

tion; but, unless they are carefully supervised, these activities can become too expensive or embarrassing for lower-class groups.[25] Even in competitive athletics, differences in outside training experiences,[26] costs, and social divisions in the locker room,[27] can make participation difficult or impossible for some groups. The problems seem to increase with the size of the school, since in smaller schools students tend to know each other better and, when talent is in short supply, each participant is and feels needed.

Some schools have been successful in minimizing social divisions in extra-class activities. By instructing students in school in dancing and other skills, insisting on keeping down the costs, avoiding fraternity- or sorority-type functions, and educating student leadership, school personnel can help to reduce cliquishness and class distinctions.[28]

One aspect of extracurricular life which deserves consideration as a possible vehicle for socialization is student government. This phase of student life at present reflects the same stratification patterns as the other activities discussed above. In some cases specific requirements for membership on the student council or for office in the student government have been drawn up "to see that the right students" are elected.[29] Sometimes these are academic requirements. At other schools the faculty itself nominates the candidates to be voted on by the students. Even when there are no such restrictions, students who seem to consider politics important come from those social classes in which the parents are also politically active. There is prestige involved and the students who feel comfortable in prestige positions seem to come from middle and upper class groups.[30] Furthermore the student government is usually identified with authority. Its members are expected to set an example of propriety. Students already in the graces of school officials are more comfortable in this role.

Juvenile Delinquency

Probably of much less significance than social stratification is the problem of juvenile delinquency. Nevertheless, some institutional provision has to be made by the society for dealing with this delinquency. The people involved are of secondary school age. The increased inclusiveness of the

[25] Hollingshead, op. cit., p. 172.
[26] Cf. Lynn M. McGraw and J. W. Tolbert, "Sociomatic Status and Athletic Ability of Junior High School Boys," Research Quarterly 24:72–80 (1953).
[27] Taba, op. cit., pp. 126–27.
[28] Alexander and Saylor, op. cit., pp. 607–610.
[29] Taba, op. cit., pp. 126–27.
[30] John J. Patrick, "Political Socialization of American Youth," Research Bulletin No. 3 (Washington, D.C.: National Council for the Social Studies, 1967), pp. 51–52.

school has increased the number of potential delinquents either under its direction or still within its legal clientele. Even if the delinquent is transferred to a correctional institution, such an institution must itself become a school. In other societies and times, schools usually dismissed the delinquent as beyond their responsibility. Using modern psychological tools, it is becoming possible to identify the potentially delinquent and to provide assistance before it is too late.[31]

Juvenile delinquency is not a peculiarly American problem, and many of its roots are to be found in the general conditions of modern living.[32] There is a clear relationship between the higher rate of delinquency and the prolonged nature of adolescence in modern society, as compared to the shorter and more clearly institutionalized period of adolescence in more primitive societies.[33] The relationship between length of adolescence and delinquency has been explained in several different ways. It has been pointed out that where there are stable social patterns with institutionalized roles for both parents and adolescents, there is less room for conflict between children and adult authority—particularly parental authority.[34] The child or adolescent has less need to rebel against adult authority because it is not personal but institutionalized.[35] It operates in clearly defined spheres and leaves freedom in other clearly defined spheres. Furthermore, in more stable social patterns the adult is better able to understand the mores of the younger generation; they have not altered since he was an adolescent. In periods of rapid social change, mores change and the adolescent feels trapped between his peers and his parents.[36]

The young recognize that the old are conservative. The old have accepted as inevitable, or at least as realistic, inequities in social custom which the young perceive as contrary to the ideal. The young cannot understand why the elders tolerate inequity. The elders cannot understand why the young will not learn to tolerate. Furthermore, antagonism may develop between the young and the old when a premium is put on youthfulness and vigor in a dynamic society. The old become jealous of youth while the young are becoming impatient of the slowness of change. The old feel the continuing need for the vicarious satisfaction of their ambitions in the young, while the young are impatient to be free of the solicitude of their elders.[37]

[31] Cf. Arthur K. Rice, "Commission Blames Schools for High Juvenile Crime Rate," Nation's Schools 80: No. 6:6–8 (1967).

[32] President's Commission on Law Enforcement and the Administration of Justice, Juvenile Delinquency and Youth Crime (Washington, D.C.: U.S. Government Printing Office, 1967), pp. 41–56.

[33] Ibid., p. 46.

[34] Ibid., p. 45.

[35] Ibid., p. 47.

[36] Ibid., pp. 147–48.

[37] Ibid., pp. 45–46.

While it is possible to overemphasize the importance of the sex drive of the adolescent, it is necessary to understand it as a possible factor in the conflicts between adolescent and adult standards. To the adult it is desirable that the adolescent sublimate his sex drive to socially accepted ends, but to the adolescent the process of sublimation is often difficult.[38] The situation is further complicated when sex becomes the symbol of the conflict between adult and juvenile tensions. Recent studies show that this factor is present in most of the cases of adolescent pregnancy and early marriage.[39]

Much delinquent behavior starts when a lack of academic success at school is intensified by adult pressure to be more successful.[40] A defense mechanism is then developed: the student denies the importance of school and starts playing truant. Since truancy is classified as a serious offense, it is likely to get the student into court, particularly if he comes from the lower social classes to start with.[41] The middle- or upper-class truant is likely to be treated differently.[42] The school which makes no provision for successful participation by a student who is required to attend may be laying the groundwork for truancy and hence of delinquency. When the potential truant is able to rationalize that the school's program is not intended for him, the situation becomes even more dangerous.[43]

The highest rates of delinquency occur among lower-class families.[44] Lack of respect on the part of lower-class parents for the law contributes to the nature of the delinquency. Similarly, the lack of suitable recreational facilities encourages the development of gang-type activity. The bulk of juvenile crime is committed by groups rather than by single individuals. Pressure for group acceptance and recognition is an important contributing factor. When the school can help in the process of integrating lower-class students into its activities program and thus provide acceptable outlets for their normal drive, it is helping to prevent juvenile crime.

The tendency of some upper-class groups to think of themselves as "above the law" encourages such things as juvenile drinking, excessive speeding, and vandalism. This kind of delinquency is a problem to school officials both because of their concern for the students and because school activities are frequently the focal point for the congregation of the groups involved. Nevertheless, the ultimate damage both to the students and to

[38] Cf. Ibid., pp. 199–200.
[39] Ibid., p. 149.
[40] Ibid., p. 223.
[41] Lloyd Allen Cook and Elaine Forsyth Cook, A Sociological Approach to Education (New York: McGraw-Hill Book Company, 1960), p. 239.
[42] Ibid.
[43] Cook and Cook, op. cit., pp. 239–41.
[44] William C. Kvaraceus and Walter B. Miller, Delinquent Behavior: Culture and the Individual (Washington, D.C.: NEA, 1959), p. 55.

society may be less than in the case of lower-class children's delinquency, since upper-class parents are more likely to be able to minimize it.

Recent years have seen a rise of discontent among the college-age population which has taken many different forms, including experimentation with drugs, campus revolts, draft card burning, and flagrant disregard for traditional sexual morality. Some of this activity seems motivated by a very laudable desire for social involvement. Some of it is perhaps indicative of deep seated problems of adjustment in the family. Since it is primarily a college phenomenon it is probably more of an upper-middle-class one. It becomes a concern for the public secondary school to the extent that such drive may be channeled constructively if better attention is paid to social problems in the social studies curriculum. It also concerns school officials when the activities of undergraduates become examples for the high school student. This is particularly possible in college communities.

The School as an Agent of Socialization

The question has already been raised as to whether the schools' objectives should be limited to the mastery of the traditionally oriented content or whether the public educational system has a larger responsibility as an agent of society. Can the school provide an opportunity for lower-class children to break out of the poverty-cycle of their parents? Can education be used as a social escalator on which whole groups may perhaps move upward in the scale of living? Can the force of education be used to lessen juvenile delinquency or will increased knowledge and confidence tend to create a generation of draft card burners and "hippies"?

Logically it would seem that—to the extent that the school is the agent of the whole society, dealing with the total population of secondary school age—it must have a concern both for the improvement of the society and, in a democracy, for the welfare of those whom it is teaching. The problems involved in the relationship of the school to other educative agencies will be enumerated in the next chapter.

4

The Public High School and
Other Social Institutions

EXPANSION OF THE PROGRAMS AND CONCERNS OF THE PUBLIC HIGH SCHOOL during this century raises very important questions as to what is its appropriate relationship to other and older agencies of society. Among the relationships which need to be considered are those with the various levels of government, the home, the church, other educational institutions, and the informal agencies of social life. A closely related consideration is the nature of the school as a bureaucracy.

The School and the Government

Responsibility for the operation of schools remains, as a result of the constitutional fathers' inaction, in the hands of the states. It has been a matter of conjecture as to why the subject of education was not mentioned in the federal constitution. Possibly, in the initial philosophy of federalism, education was considered the prerogative of the sovereign states. On the other hand it should also be noted that, except in the minds of people like Jefferson and Franklin, public responsibility for education was considered insignificant. Even in England education was a matter for private philanthropy. It was not until after 1830 that the states assumed much responsibility for schools and then the steps were in the direction of permitting local communities to take action rather than of permitting or providing the use of state funds for operation and maintenance. It was after the middle of the nineteenth century that education became clearly established as a joint local and state responsibility.[1]

[1] John S. Brubacher, A *History of the Problems of Education*, 2nd ed. (New York: McGraw-Hill Book Company, 1966), pp. 64–66, 575.

An understanding of the relationship of state and local governments in the matter of education is dependent on a broader understanding of their basic relationship to each other. In our American system it is the state which serves as the center of most sovereign authority. The local unit, such as the city, the county, or the school district receives its power and authority either through the application of the state constitution or through legislative delegation. The city, county, and the district school board are corporations of the state, chartered by the legislature to carry out governmental functions.[2]

Provision for public schools is now made in state constitutions. The arrangement is no longer permissive. Education is a function of government for which separate provision is likely to be made. In many states the school boards operate with a great deal of independence from the local government. In some areas, school boards levy and even collect their own taxes. School board members are frequently chosen in elections separate from those in which other local officials are selected. School district boundaries do not necessarily coincide with the boundaries of other governmental units and services. In some areas provision is made for the appointment of the school board by city or county officials and for the regulation of the school budget by these same officials. In other areas, however, the political and fiscal autonomy of the school units from the other local governmental units is complete.[3]

Extensive support from state funds serves to increase the centralization of responsibility in the hands of the state. Statewide regulations applying to attendance, the certification of teachers, courses of study, the adoption of textbooks, and the supervision of instruction tend to insure that at least basic minimum standards acceptable to the state as a whole shall prevail. Despite the control which the state legislature has over the public school system, it is important to recognize the areas of responsibility of the local school board and the voting citizens of the school district. From those properly certified by the state, the local officials must select the teaching and administrative staffs of their schools. The determination of policy within the limits set by state regulation is made by these officials with advice from the professional staff they select. The voting of funds for the support of the program beyond that provided by the state is the responsibility of some locally elected board or of the voters themselves.[4]

    [2] Edgar Fuller, "State School Systems" in *Encyclopedia of Educational Research*, 3rd ed. (New York: The Macmillan Company, 1960), p. 1386.
    [3] NEA Research Division, "Fiscal Independence of School Systems," *Research Bulletin* 43:117–23 (Dec., 1965).
    [4] Standard works in this area are Arvid J. Burke, *Financing Public Schools in the United States* (New York: Harper and Brothers, 1951), and R. L. Johns and E. L. Morphet, eds., *Problems and Issues in Public School Finance* (New York: Bureau of Publications, Teachers College, Columbia University, 1950).

It has become increasingly evident that in some states it will not be possible to raise all of the funds necessary for the support of education from state and local sources. What was until recently token support, designated for specific purposes, from the federal government has been increased in the last few years until it represents a major source. In addition, the federal government, through the United States Office of Education, provides much valuable assistance to state and local schools through such activities as gathering information about school practice over the nation.

School, Home, and Church

Among the problems facing the leaders of the American public high school is that of deciding the basis of its relationship to other established institutions and agencies. When one attempts to demarcate the responsibility of the home or school or church, he is faced by the fact that an individual's personality is a single whole and cannot be divided. If a student learns to appreciate literature at school, he will go home to read. If he does not have an opportunity to read at home, he will have difficulty at school. Similarly, if he does not get enough to eat at home, he comes to school hungry; and if he is not fed, he will have difficulty in learning the things which the school should teach. Or he may learn at church the importance of honesty, but unless he is also encouraged to be honest at home and at school, the church will find it hard to make its teaching effective.

Many of the students who come to school have an inadequate home background. Not more than half are in regular contact with any church group. Since the school is an agent of society as a whole, it seems logical that it should help the student get any essential teaching he has missed at home or elsewhere. In some cases it becomes necessary for the state to take a child out of his home to place him in a foster home or an institution which becomes for him both school and home. If so, the orphanage or correctional institution becomes an extension of the school.

In most cases there is not a serious conflict between home, school, and church. Each should desire for the student his development as an effective person and member of society. Each should respect his personality as an individual while helping him become a contributing member of society. Each can help him in a different way. The parent may lack the technical skill to teach some kinds of subject matter. He may lack the objectivity to help his child to think for himself. The school may be able to teach the student skills and help him to learn to think for himself, but cannot provide the personal security to be found in identification with home and parents. The important consideration is that each institution should respect the personality of the student.

Sometimes conflict between the agencies of the society arises in the area of technique. If one of the three agencies mentioned depends on indoctrination as its basic instructional technique rather than striving to provide for the rational maturity of the student, then it may find its effort opposed to that of some other agency. If the home has taught the student dogmatically that he should not respect members of minority races, the school will be hindered in trying to teach such respect. If the church teaches dogmatically that it is wrong to believe in evolution, the school is confronted with a problem. If each of the agencies can recognize the importance of allowing the student to weigh the evidence for himself, then none need fear the serious encroachment of the other. The inability of every agency to accept this democratic principle makes the issue more complicated than it would otherwise be.

The place of religious instruction in the public school curriculum is an important issue. Anyone who believes that a particular credo should be given preference over others may object to the school's insisting on toleration of many points of view. Thus the atheist complains when a Christian majority agrees to teach religion at school. Similarly, the Jewish parent may complain, or the Catholic, or the Protestant. When, however, the suggestion is made that religious discussion be limited in the school, some religious groups insist that this amounts to the teaching of atheism. The problem is not easily resolved, although various solutions have been tried.

Recent court decisions have dealt specifically with the issue of the place of religion in the public schools. For several centuries religion was one of the principal subjects in the school curriculum. Ever since the development, about the middle of the nineteenth century, of a public school system, the issue has been discussed. Horace Mann, himself, was concerned that there must be "a wall of separation" between church and state. The courts have now indicated that it is not appropriate to require a child to pray at school. Even though the teaching of religion is contrary to our form of constitutional democracy, most authorities suggest, however, that it is appropriate to teach *about* religion, but that any technique designed to require acceptance of a particular point of view is to be labeled as undemocratic. Perhaps it could be said that any matter which cannot be discussed objectively in the school setting should be avoided,[5] while at the same time it is evident that the teaching of civic

---

[5] *Cf.* Lewis G. Jones, "Religious Instruction in a State School," *Educational Review* 4:121–25 (Sept., 1892). Quoted by John S. Brubacher in *Eclectic Philosophy of Education* (Englewood Cliffs, N.J.: Prentice-Hall, Inc., 1962), pp. 530–32.

and moral values is consistent with the responsibility of the school as an agent of the society.[6]

Any definition of the role of the secondary school in modern America should make allowance for the fact that the society is also maintaining other agencies for education, some public and some private. Among these are the YMCA, the YWCA, the Boy Scouts, the Girl Scouts, community recreation departments, the Red Cross, and similar groups. Some of these have limited goals; others assume much responsibility for the education of young people. To the extent that these agencies contribute to the development of students and are consistent with the goals of a democratic society they may be encouraged by the school.

Articulation with Elementary Schools and Colleges

The development of the public high school has led to questions regarding its relationship to the school units above and below it. America was the first nation to attempt to make of these three different institutions a single educational ladder. The stages in the transition from secondary education as provision for the elite to secondary education as a part of a system of common education have been pointed out.

One of the most significant differences between the elementary and secondary schools lies in their outlooks concerning subject departmentalization. Typically elementary school organization is based on grade groupings with a single teacher working throughout the school day with the same group of students. In the secondary school there is some specialization. Each child will have several teachers during the school year and each teacher will have many different students. Because the organizational pattern of the elementary school is simple, it is possible to be very flexible: time allotments for different subjects can be varied from one day to the next and so can teaching techniques. On the other hand, the rigid schedule followed in the high school restricts the possibilities. It is also easier for the elementary teacher to know his students when he has 30 than for the high school teacher when his contact is with 150.

Traditionally, there has been an important difference between the attitudes of the elementary school and the secondary school toward the provision of common education. The elementary school was supposed to provide a worthwhile program for all of the children of all of the people. In the secondary school the tradition of selectivity is still quite strong.

[6] G. R. Snider, "Bible Reading and Public School Prayers," *Phi Delta Kappan* 48:516–17 (June, 1967).

Compulsory attendance laws in most of the states compel children to come to school until they are 16 years of age. Excessive retardation in the elementary school creates serious disciplinary problems.[7] Therefore, the elementary school has already accepted the idea that standards of grade placement must be flexible. At the secondary school level, students who are having excessive difficulty or ones who are serious discipline problems seem to have been encouraged to leave. The gradual development of guidance services may change the situation, but the influence of hardened tradition is important in delaying the development of democratic practice. Current public concern over school dropouts will also encourage a look at the situation.[8]

A third difference concerns preparation for the next level of education. While there is some feeling on the part of elementary school teachers, particularly in the seventh and eighth grades, that their function is to prepare students to do the work of the high school, the matter of preparation for further schooling is not a major issue in the policies of the elementary school. On the other hand, there has been a strong feeling on the part of some high school teachers and many lay citizens that a major responsibility of the high school is the preparation of students for college.[9] Teachers tend to want to identify with college colleagues. The fact that high school teachers are trained by particular college disciplines such as the department of history or of chemistry may have some influence in this matter. It is difficult to say whether in the years ahead the increase in the proportion of the total population going to college will solidify, or the new orientation of the colleges toward their responsibilities will help change the attitude of the high school teachers on this matter. Perhaps most important will be the pressure to provide a program appropriate for the total high school population.

Originally, the junior high school was proposed to provide for improved articulation between the elementary and secondary schools. Doubtless it has been somewhat successful in this undertaking. Nevertheless it, too, is frequently the victim of a clash between the traditional, selective philosophy of some of the personnel operating the high school and the more student-centered philosophy that seems basic to good elementary school organization. True articulation of the segments of the educational ladder seems to await modification of certain aspects of the secondary school program.

[7] Helen K. Mackintosh, Lillian Gore, and Gertrude Lewis, *Educating Disadvantaged Children in the Middle Grades* (Washington, D.C.: U.S. Department of Health, Education, and Welfare, 1965), p. 1.

[8] Jack Culbertson, "Attendance," *Encyclopedia of Educational Research*, 3rd ed. (New York: The Macmillan Co., 1960), pp. 99–100.

[9] *Cf.* William G. Brink, "Secondary Education-Programs," *Encyclopedia of Educational Research*, 3rd ed. (New York: The Macmillan Co., 1960), p. 1260.

Recently what may be a vocal minority of college personnel has criticized vigorously trends in the democratization of the secondary school program.[10] Whether this criticism represents awareness of the threat which democratization might pose to the traditional aspects of the college program is largely a matter of conjecture. It is a commentary on the nature of the communication within the colleges and universities that the changes recognized as desirable in the departments charged with studying public education should be fought with so much heat by some of those who are experts in other areas.

The School as a Bureaucracy

Closely related to questions about the American public high school's articulation with other agencies is consideration of the nature of its internal functioning. The control of American public education is distinctly bureaucratic. A popularly elected, or at least a selected, lay board has nominal control over the school program. There is a superintendent of schools responsible both to this lay board, and to a state superintendent of schools or department of education. The state officials are responsible to some elected official or officials. They are also responsible to the state legislature. The local superintendent of schools exercises supervision over a secondary school principal who is occasionally also responsible to a lay school committee or board and to supervisory personnel in the superintendent's office. The principal then has at least nominal supervision over certain staff personnel at the level of assistant principals, counselors, department heads, and eventually over classroom teachers.

One of the recurring problems in bureaucratic organizations is the delineation of responsibility. The situation is complicated in public schools because general policy decisions are supposed to be referred to lay groups and professional matters to be controlled by professional personnel. Arguments inevitably arise about which decisions are to be made by which group. In addition there is sometimes uncertainty regarding the role of parents. In general, the parent is considered one of the citizens supposed to operate through the lay board of education. This may not be so simple if what the articulate parents seem to want is different from what the professional school personnel believe to be in the best interest of the children. The relationships are also complicated by recognition that cooperation between the school and the home is important.

---

[10] For a summary of some of this discussion the student is referred to: Henry Ehlers and Gordon C. Lee, *Crucial Issues in Education*, revised ed. (New York: Henry Holt and Company, 1959), pp. 259–97.

The determination of what is taught is primarily in the hands of the teacher. The curriculum must be adapted to the needs of the individual students. Nevertheless, there are other influences operative as a result of the number of bureaucratic controls. There may be legislation passed by the legislature, a course of study promulgated by a state department of public instruction, regulations by the state board of education, textbooks adopted by a state textbook commission, board policy established by the local board of education, informal and formal controls exercised by principals and supervisors, and the reactions of parents—all in the background of the teacher's decision as to what will be taught or how.

Perhaps the most potent controls exercised by state school officials are those exercised through the processes of certifying teachers and accrediting schools. The certification of teachers generally serves to set minimum standards of preparation both in terms of professional course work in the field of education and in the areas of subject specialization. The accreditation of schools also tends to encourage maintenance of certain minimum standards in terms of such matters as course offerings, pupil loads, efficient size of administrative staff, library facilities, record keeping procedures, etc.

One of the dangers of bureaucratic control is that it may be difficult to modify the system to provide for the needs of students. Indeed, such control may prevent necessary changes to benefit whole classes of students. For example, a special emphasis on science which is of pertinence for 20 per cent of the students may take precedence over important provisions for the needs of 50 per cent. If the 20 per cent are the children of the most articulate and politically important, the possibility of their being favored becomes a probability and democracy is the loser.

In a large school rules and regulations become a problem. Fifty or sixty teachers working with 1,500 students sometimes lose the independence of action which seems essential for efficient teaching. In such situations, teaching units must be organized around specific amounts of time. There is little chance for providing for longer, more meaningful kinds of approach. Each teacher will be required to work with perhaps 150 students a day. Emphasis will probably be placed on formalized methods of instruction because the shortness of the period and the teacher's lack of familiarity with the student makes nothing else possible. There are likely to be rigid regulations for controlling the movement of students from class to class and during recess periods because there are many to move and relationships remain impersonal. There is little opportunity for supervising study or for careful assignment of work to be done at home. There are too many different teachers competing for the student's attention. It becomes necessary to decide which teachers may give tests on which days. Field trips and out-of-school activities must likewise be so routinized as to lose much of their effectiveness.

In a bureaucracy one of the solutions for such problems as impersonalization is to add additional personnel to take care of the area which seems neglected. The school has added among other programs a system of counselors and guidance workers whose major responsibility is to restore some of the concern for individual personality that the school lost when it became so highly organized.

It is also important to recognize that, in spite of the problems of bureaucratic control, most teachers do have much freedom of action in the classroom. Teachers recognized as competent are encouraged in many schools to consider courses of study as only suggestive. Use of a wide variety of teaching materials to supplement or even replace the textbook is encouraged. Principals and other supervisory personnel are likely to encourage much freedom of action and in most cases are not able to supervise so closely as to control. Each teacher is recognized as facing with each class a different set of instructional problems requiring different materials and techniques.

Summary

As a result of nearly 200 years of evolution, the relationship of the public schools to the government is one in which tax support comes from all three levels—local, state, and federal. Control is vested at the local level with varying degrees of supervision from the state, and there is remarkable similarity in actual practice over the entire nation.

Logically at least, the relationship of the school to other primary and secondary agencies of society is one in which the school is recognized as an arm of the government which acts for society as a whole, while other agencies exercise important responsibility and control as influential forces in the life of the individual student. There is no necessary conflict as long as each is respectful of the individual and of his right in a democratic society to be presented with the alternatives and permitted to choose between them.

Internally, the school system may appropriately be viewed as a bureaucracy in which there are well-defined responsibilities divided between the lay boards of control, the office of the superintendent of schools, the principal, and the teachers. This machinery tends to operate in such a way as to provide considerable freedom within limits to the individual classroom teacher.

5

Schools and the Social Crisis: Selected Readings

THE PUBLIC HIGH SCHOOL AS THE INSTRUMENT OF THE LARGER SOCIETY IS being expected to respond to the changes which seem to be taking place in the American way of life. Large segments of the population have moved and are moving into the cities and many of those who used to live in the cities have moved into the suburbs. Technology is changing the nature of employment opportunities. Legal barriers to racial integration have been removed and there is new attention to the problem of poverty in a land of plenty. Traditional views of sexual morality are being questioned. Juvenile delinquency and crime seem to be increasing. Military service in unpopular wars is a haunting specter for young males and their families.

Education in the Metropolitan Area

The large city school system is faced with most of the problems in the larger society, sometimes in more acute form. The influx of the poor into the city and of the middle and upper classes into the suburbs has resulted in a concentration of problems. The poor are more dependent on the school for basic education than are the children of the middle class. The relative decline in taxable property in proportion to the number of children to be educated has resulted in a decrease in the money available to pay for education and related services. The departure of the middle class to the suburb has removed both the sources of lay leadership and pressure for quality education available in smaller or more mixed communities. At the same time, the sheer size of the metropolitan school system tends to increase the amount of bureaucracy and its inflexibility of response.

54

One of the relatively recent indications of the seriousness of the social problems in our large cities has been the threat of open violence. Riots have already led to people being killed and widespread destruction of property. Many of the participants in these riots have been high school age youth and others in age groups recently out of school. In this first selection Daniel Levine, Associate Director of the Center for the Study of Metropolitan Problems in Education at the University of Missouri in Kansas City, indicates what seems to be the nature of the problem as it relates to the role of the school.

Defaulting in the Schools
and Rioting in the Streets[*]

Daniel U. Levine

The escalation in destructiveness of the civil disorders which began with rioting in New York four years ago and culminated in rebellious explosions in Newark and Detroit during the past summer has forced widespread realization that the nation's ideals and traditions may be destroyed unless rapid progress is made in solving the multiple social and economic problems of the inner core sections of our central cities.

Many perceptive observers have attempted to give the public informed guidance in considering why two great American cities faced what was virtually civil insurrection in the summer of 1967, and why officials in uncounted other cities were no longer able to maintain the fiction that, "It can't happen here." It has become frighteningly obvious that, "It *can* happen here," that "here" is nearly everywhere, and that the urban crisis which has developed in the United States can no longer be evaded or ignored.

Several of these observers, such as social scientist Daniel Moynihan, have pointed out that the rebellions in Newark and Detroit represented the economic protest of thousands who for various reasons are unemployed or underemployed and who, whether referred to as an "underclass" or a "lower class," realize that as conditions now exist they have no hope of fully participating in a modern economy. Others have observed that overt

[*] *The Clearing House* 42:274–77 (Jan., 1968). Reprinted by permission of publisher and author.

violence generally can be traced to youngsters and young adults swept up in the excitement provided by the chance to recklessly discharge accumulated anger and hostility which have been building over a long period of time.

These two observations are not mutually exclusive, nor do they exclude other factors which have been cited as igniting the spark that turns a smoldering fire into a raging eruption. There is evidence, for example, that organized effort by so-called black nationalist groups and by politically-radical elements played some part in fomenting the riots and in keeping them boiling after they started, and it is also widely recognized that small incidents involving the police can set off fireworks by bringing to the surface many years of intemperate and hostile relationships between law enforcement officials and the inhabitants of low-income ghettoes.

None of these explanations are fully satisfactory, however, because they miss the underlying cause which, unless adequately understood and dealt with, may eventuate in immeasurably more horrible confrontations in the future: the fact that in most large urban centers in the United States anywhere from one-fifth to two-fifths of the population consists of low-income people compressed into overcrowded and deteriorating communities where they feel—with good reason—that the mainstream of American life has passed them by.

As the United States has grown and as people have poured into the cities from rural areas, these neighborhoods have become so large that the social institutions which once reached into them with some effectiveness can no longer do so. Parents, as a result, are losing control of their children, who have become the victims of all the negative and soul-destroying influences that exist in the big city. That adults in the low-income core parts of the cities are losing an often desperate struggle to socialize their children in the middle-class goals of hard work and moderation is not very surprising, since the slums, as Joseph Lyford points out in an important book[1] about New York's West Side, exist precisely in order that the larger community may have a place to exile antisocial individuals unable to "make it" in polite society. Most people who live in slums, however, bitterly resent the fact that their community is a malignant "dumping ground" for the rest of the nation.

Add to this the fact that many of the poor are non-whites whose residence in low-income ghettoes is an ever-present and inescapable reminder that forces beyond their control will seemingly forever limit their social as well as geographical mobility no matter how hard they might strive or how much they might achieve, and it is clear that one has sufficient incendiary materials to set off the most spectacular of explosions. Behind all the specific causes which turn incipient brush fires into

---

[1] Joseph Lyford, *The Airtight Cage* (New York: Harper and Row, 1965).

raging conflagrations, then, is the general bitterness and alienation created when large numbers of people live in circumstances which encourage them to see themselves as being deprived of and cut off from opportunities and rewards available to millions of persons in more fortunate communities.

The possibility that disastrous domestic conflict will recur is likely to exist as long as masses of the poor, particularly the non-white poor, live separated from their fellow man in socially stratified slums and racially segregated ghettoes. Recognizing also that very few teachers are able to conduct effective instructional programs in the face of the alienation and the multiple social pathologies which permeate the inner-city classroom, it follows that the abolition of segregated educational patterns which help keep youngsters boxed in entirely low-income surroundings must be considered a priority goal for all educators. Granted that unemployment and intolerable housing conditions are more directly implicated as causes of violent social upheaval, it is also true that school experiences not only teach vocational skills needed to compete in an industrial society but also communicate attitudes and values which determine whether a student feels sufficiently a part of the larger society to function well in it or is alienated from it and unable to accept the demands it makes on him. The school may not be able to reach the present "lost generation" of hostile and embittered young adults and adolescents who are products of the segregated residential and educational patterns of the recent past, but it can provide desegregated educational experiences that combat the pervasive feeling of exclusion and isolation which is already beginning to cripple subsequent generations of younger students now growing to maturity in the inner core slums.

How well are we doing as a profession in helping to break down the barriers which separate Americans of differing social class and racial groups from each other? Judging by the fact that the overwhelming majority of low-income students are in predominantly low-income schools and the overwhelming majority of non-white students are in predominantly non-white schools, we have not been very successful in working to counteract the forces which lead to stratification and segregation in school district attendance patterns. Given the strength of these forces, it is patently unfair to expect the schools to fully overcome stratification and segregation created by other economic, political, and social institutions. Yet, the schools could do much more to destratify and desegregate attendance patterns than is now being done. Instead, we have allowed ourselves to be all but immobilized by what can be aptly characterized as the "Yes, but" Syndrome.

There are many manifestations of this syndrome at work with regard to the goals of placing youngsters in comprehensive-type schools which are not limited to a single social class or social group. One such example arises whenever educators pay verbal homage to this goal but show in their behavior that it is a low priority goal for them, a goal insufficiently important to warrant actually doing something to achieve: "Yes, it is desirable to have integrated education, and I am glad when Negro students enroll in previously all-white schools, *but* we are helpless to achieve more integration because to do so would require assigning some children to schools outside their immediate neighborhood." Thus it is assumed that traditional patterns of school district organization are somehow sacrosanct, and can brook neither reconsideration nor modification.

Similarly, the certainty that the schools cannot in the foreseeable future provide integrated educational experiences for every student—cannot, in other words, accomplish everything with respect to desegregation—becomes somehow transposed into the very different and illogical assertion that the schools cannot accomplish anything in the direction of desegregation, as when educators have argued: "Yes, segregation in education is undesirable and should not exist, *but* thousands of Negro students are piled up in the inner city far away from areas where whites are willing to attend school, and this prevents us from taking steps to reduce segregation."

When it comes to recent proposals for school district cooperation in allowing a limited number of non-white pupils from the city to attend suburban schools or to establish and maintain contacts among students and teachers of differing racial groups within the city districts or between city and suburban districts, once again verbal agreement about the importance of desegregation is all but universal, while willingness to act on this conviction has been evident in only a bare handful of suburban districts in the United States: "Yes, I sympathize with the problems the city schools are facing and feel that our predominantly-white student bodies would benefit greatly from contacts with non-white peers, *but* many of the parents in my district would oppose such programs and might even challenge them in the courts, so our hands are tied and there is nothing we can do to help our administrative colleagues in the cities."

Similarly, many suburban educators are aware of the existence of new curriculum materials, such as the basal readers published by the Ginn and Scott Foresman Companies, which show non-whites interacting in everyday surroundings with whites and which are every bit as good as previous versions that portrayed American society as if it consisted only of whites. Yet, so few suburban school districts are taking advantage of the opportunity to replace materials which perpetuate racism by ignoring the fact that non-whites constitute a significant group in American society that one can almost hear educators in positions of authority attempting to excuse this inexcusable failure by pleading, "Yes, it is desirable to use multi-ethnic readers which make students aware that the United States is a pluralistic nation with diverse groups of people in it, *but* many of our clients are so imbued with racism that they would be alarmed and would register complaints at something so small as the appearance of non-whites in the school textbooks of their children."

It is impossible to deny that the educator in the grip of the "*Yes, but*" syndrome makes points which are valid if considered only in and of themselves. The inadequacy of this response, however, is clear the moment it is recognized that our nation as we now know it today may be doomed unless the schools, like every other key institution in our society, place paramount emphasis on the elimination of social and racial divisions which are moving us rapidly toward a state of continuous civil war. How responsible, in this context, is the superficially-defensible response of the educator whose position is epitomized by a line of reasoning which argues, "*Yes*, I realize that unless we turn out citizens who will practice brotherhood in their daily lives our country will be destroyed by hatred and violence, *but* our job in the schools is to concentrate on academic achievement and not try to solve social problems which we had no part in creating"?

How pick the most suitable terms to describe the crisis toward which we are drifting? Conflagration? Race and class warfare? Mass slaughter? Insurrection?

How pick the most suitable terms to describe the reaction-to-date of the educational profession in the face of this threat? Inaction? Apathy? Irresponsibility? Passivity?

It little matters which terms are chosen, since any of those in the second set can be paired with any from the first set to portray the general failure of nerve in a profession in which many once took great pride and showed great courage concerning their efforts to establish the foundations for a genuinely pluralist society. How sad that as a profession we have succumbed to the shortsighted "*Yes, but*" syndrome which is almost diametrically opposed to the school's historic mission as the crucible for pluralism in the United States.

The Dropout

Universal secondary education is now a publicly-accepted American goal. While in the old rural economy the dropout was a problem to the educational idealist, in today's urban society he has become a danger to the public peace. In the rural setting of the late nineteenth and early twentieth centuries, the dropout could go to work on the farm. In the industrialized urban setting, there is often nothing for him to do but loaf. He becomes a prime candidate for trouble.

In the following article the Assistant Superintendent for Education of the Disadvantaged in New York City, and a former director of the NEA Project: School Dropout, describes some of the dimensions of the dropout problem.

Seven Hundred Thousand Dropouts*

Daniel Schreiber

In America today, the school dropout looms as one of the Nation's major problems. Presidents of the United States, Congress, Governors, special commissions, labor and business officials, educators, social workers, juvenile court judges—all have expressed their concern publicly and frequently. Recent reports and events, although seemingly disparate, highlight almost daily our Nation's anxiety over the impact that the school dropout is having on our economy and stability. Yet, the school dropout problem has been with us a long time, and the concern of educators to resolve the problem is not new. Almost 100 years ago, in 1872, a paper titled "The Early Withdrawal of Pupils from School: Its Causes and Its Remedies" was presented to the annual convention of the National Education Association.

The dropout problem has become more pressing now because of a multiplicity of factors which are largely extrinsic to the school and peculiar to our time. Some of them are:

☐ the high rate of youth unemployment, which is sometimes four times greater than the national average unemployment rate.

☐ the continuous rise in delinquency and crime among youths although large sums of money are being spent to counteract this development.

☐ large-scale migration from rural and farm areas to urban centers.

☐ the population explosion—approximately 3.8 million youths are reaching age 18 each year. This is a million more than reached age 18 in 1964 and previous years.

☐ the increase in the number of welfare families, especially in large cities, further heightened by a marked increase in the total cost of public

* *American Education* 4:6:5–7 (June, 1968), U.S. Office of Education. Reprinted by permission of the publisher and author.

assistance. (The projected welfare budget for New York City for the 1969 fiscal year is $1 billion!)

☐ the elimination of unskilled jobs through automation and the increased use of technology in farming, resulting in unemployment.

☐ the racial riots in the cities, in which the participants are overwhelmingly the unemployed, out-of-school youths of the area.

The urgency of the need to alleviate some of the problems created by the dropouts is demonstrated by the fact that two Presidents of the United States found it necessary to call Congress' attention to the situation. President Kennedy referred to it in his State of the Union Message in 1963. In his message to Congress on education in 1965, President Johnson said: "In our 15 largest cities, 60 percent of 10th-grade students from poverty neighborhoods drop out before finishing high school. The cost of this neglect runs high both for youth and the Nation." The President could have added that another 10 percent never reached the 10th grade.

Congress responded affirmatively, money was appropriated, projects were undertaken, and programs were introduced; but unfortunately they were neither drastic nor sufficiently effective, as recent reports evidence. On March 1, 1968, the President's National Advisory Commission on Civil Disorders stated: "The most dramatic evidence of the relationship between educational practices and civil disorders lies in the high incidence of riot participation by ghetto youth who have not completed high school." One day later, the Department of Labor, through its Bureau of Labor Statistics, reported that in the Nation's 20 largest metropolitan areas "32.7 percent of nonwhite youth aged 16 to 19 were without work compared with an 11 percent jobless rate of white teenagers."

Paradoxically, all of this comes at a time when the holding power of the Nation's schools is at its highest and the number of students going to college increases annually. In 1967, 721 students graduated from high school for every 1,000 students who were in fifth grade eight years previously. This compares most favorably with 302 graduates per 1,000 fifth-grade students in 1932, 467 graduates in 1942, 522 graduates in 1952, and 642 graduates in 1962. The anomaly lies in the fact that the 28 percent—the 279 former fifth-graders—who did not graduate from high school last year represents more than three-fourths of a million youths, many of them alienated and unwanted.

WHO DROPS OUT, AND WHY?

Numerous research studies dealing with dropouts have been made, and a review of the literature will uncover more than 1,000 references. Essentially they are undertaken on the belief that if we were to know why youths leave school before graduating from high school, we could help the next generation graduate. In the 1965 book, *Dropout Studies: Design and Conduct*, prepared by the National Education Association in cooperation with the U.S. Office of Education, Schreiber, Kaplan, and Strom indicate that the most valuable way to view a dropout study is in terms of its purpose. Usually a study will attempt to answer a specific question such as, How many pupils drop out of school? What are the reasons for dropping out? Who are the dropouts and what are they like? What happens to dropouts? Which pupils will drop out? What ways and means can be developed to reduce dropout rates?

Although each dropout is an individual whose reasons for dropping out are peculiar to himself, these studies have developed a portrait of an average dropout. He is just past his 16th birthday, has average or slightly below average intelligence, and is more likely to be a boy than a girl. He is functioning below his potential; he is below grade level in reading; and academically he is in the lowest quartile. He is slightly over age for his grade, having been held back once in the elementary or junior high school grades. He has not been in trouble with the law, although he does take up an inordinate amount of the school administrator's time because of truancy and discipline. He seldom participates in extracurricular activities; he feels rejected by the school and, in turn, rejects the school. His parents were school dropouts, as were his older brother and sister. He says that he is leaving school because of lack of interest but that he will get a high school diploma, in some way or other, because without it he cannot get a good job. He knows the reception that awaits him in the outside world, yet believes that it cannot be worse than remaining in school.

A study published by the New Jersey Department of Education in 1967, titled "Who Failed?" reports an interview with a highly perceptive youth. I am going to quote from it fairly extensively to demonstrate that the potential dropout knows that he is going to drop out of school but doesn't know how to prevent it. And neither does the school. Here it is:

"At first you don't realize you are going to fail. You sit in class while the teacher is explaining things and you just don't understand what she is talking about. You ask a question or two and the teacher gives you the answer, but you still don't understand. So you think you will find out from some of your friends what it's all about, *because you feel kind of ashamed to keep on asking questions.* It makes you feel like you're kind of dumb. I remember the first time I asked the kid next to me a question about the work, the teacher became angry and said that I should stop fooling around and pay attention. . . . You know there ought to be some time in school when you could get together with the other kids in your class and talk about the things you would be afraid or ashamed to ask a teacher."

He then goes on to describe his reactions to the first big test in that class: how he wrote answers to questions he made up because he was ashamed to hand in an empty paper and how he slouched in his seat so that he would be as inconspicuous as possible. Finally the papers were returned and charitably his was placed face down. Without looking at it, he folded it and placed it in his pocket. Let him tell what he did next. "I felt so upset I couldn't go to my next class right away. I went to the boy's room. I went into the john and took the paper out of my pocket to look at it. It didn't have a mark." Failure bred more failure, followed by classcutting and truancy, and finally the realization that there was no hope. "By April my parents had accepted the idea that I was going to fail and they couldn't do anything about it; the teacher knew I was going to fail, and she couldn't do anything about it; I knew I was going to fail and couldn't do anything about it. Somehow I found myself going around more with the other kids in the class who were also failing."

Could this boy have been helped to become successful in a different school with a different program? His failure became apparent in senior high school, but what of those pupils whose failure is obvious in the first and second grade? In one recent study based on information from the cumulative record cards of graduates and dropouts in an industrial community in Pennsylvania, the investigator uncovered two predictors of school failure and dropout proneness which should shock all educators. If a child, when he entered school at age six, came from a home where the father was not working and where there was no phone, the chances were eight out of 10 that he would drop out before graduating. Also, if he were not achieving academically after the end of the first grade and he had to repeat the first or second grade, his chances of not graduating were eight out of 10. He was condemned to failure at the age of six.

There are a good many stirrings now that should help improve the dropout situation as this Nation's cumulative efforts make themselves felt. Schools are starting preventive programs earlier; New York State, for example, has authorized public preschool education for three- and four-year-olds. Schools are paying more attention to remediation within the regular program and are taking more responsibility for working outside the formal setting. Closer community involvement is being built into many school activities because of the positive influence of the home and neighborhood upon youngsters' inclination to stay in schools.

The Federal Government has become increasingly interested in public education and in recent years Congress has responded by allocating substantial sums of money to help in developing and maintaining programs directly or indirectly related to the school dropout. It initiated and supported the Vocational Education Act of 1963, the Elementary and Secondary Education Act of 1965, Head Start and Follow Through programs, the Neighborhood Youth Corps, the Job Corps under the Economic Opportunity Act, and Manpower Development Training centers. The National Defense Education Act has funded programs, now under the Education Professions Development Act, to upgrade the quality of teachers and counselors. At the present time a task force at the U.S. Office of Education is preparing a study related to the dropout program authorized by a 1967 amendment to the ESEA.

DEALING WITH THE CAUSES

"Project Re-entry," a program supported by the bureau of guidance of the New York State education department, grew out of the 1963 summer return-to-school program which had been coordinated by the U.S. Office of Education. The program, designed to support the summer efforts of guidance counselors in local school districts, uses intensive guidance and counseling of both parents and pupils to encourage potential and actual dropouts to return to school in the fall. It also seeks to encourage participating schools to reappraise current programs for these pupils.

In 1963, Francis Keppel, then U.S. Commissioner of Education, stated, "The fundamental goal is not merely to keep children in school but to educate them. The test of success, therefore, is not merely the reduction of the dropout rate but the improvemnt of the educational product."

All of the new programs to combat the dropout rate have some good in them. At the very least, they demonstrate the Nation's concern and effort to resolve serious economic and social problems, but essentially they are rear-guard actions. They are not getting at the roots of the problem which is to educate all children for a meaningful, participating, successful life in a democratic society. For the overriding fact is simply that there is increasingly little place in our society for the dropout.

Our schools must recognize these facts and try to alleviate the early conditions associated with the development of attitudes and behavior which lead to dropping out. Motivation and the opportunity necessary to provide greater success in school must be offered. Otherwise, staying in school becomes an end in itself rather than a means to an end.

The United States, no matter how productive and affluent it is, cannot afford to have almost one million youths drop out of school each year to become unwanted and unemployed. The accumulation of the millions of excluded and alienated youths and young adults cannot and will not remain quiescent. We must reconstruct our educational system to provide relevant, successful experiences for all children so that they will become and remain an integral part of our society. We must, in the words of the National Advisory Commission on Civil Disorders, "make good the promises of American democracy to all citizens—urban and rural, white and black, Spanish surname, American Indian, and every minority group." To do less is to challenge the very fabric of our society and the possibilities for growth and stability in America.

The second article on school dropouts, written by an assistant principal, questions the frequent emphasis on the development of vocational skills as the appropriate approach to dealing with the dropout-prone adolescent. Claude Lammers, Assistant Principal, West High School, Minneapolis, maintains that, rather than specific skills, the need is for more emphasis on character and maturity. He would emphasize general education and the development of prevocational skills.

Automation, Dropouts, and Educational Dogma*

Claude C. Lammers

Certain concepts of secondary education in the United States are unrealistic and in need of change. This is particularly true of the time-honored "salvation through skills" dogma that has been greatly oversold.

In *Education for All American Youth: A Further Look*, published in 1952, the Educational Policies Commission of the National Education Association made this bold assertion: "The major adjustments with respect to the scope and purposes of secondary education have now been made." According to members of that commission, secondary education was to become a reality for *all*, regardless of interests or levels of ability.

The Educational Policies Commission anticipated that school attendance would become compulsory in all states until graduation from high

* *NASSP Bulletin* 51:31–39 (Dec., 1967). Reprinted by permission of the author and of the National Association of Secondary School Principals. Copyright: 1967 by the National Association of Secondary School Principals.

school or until age 18. Strong emphasis was to be placed upon *vocational* objectives. It would be the function of schools, according to that EPC report, "to develop saleable skills, and those understandings and attitudes that make the worker an intelligent and productive participant in economic life."

In spite of the phenomenal advance of technology and in spite of the rural-urban-suburban population interchange which is drastically reshaping the character of many city schools, the orthodoxy of 1952 is fundamentally the orthodoxy of today. There has been continued devotion to a program of job-oriented, universal secondary education.

Leaders in industry, labor, and government have vied with educators in pointing out the perils that lie ahead for the 7,500,000 young people who will drop out of school during this decade. Newspaper editors and columnists have joined the chorus. Said news columnist Sylvia Porter four years ago in a widely quoted article: "The teen-ager who drops out of school now and stays out dooms himself for life."

THE MYTH OF EARNING POWER

The doom awaiting the dropouts is, of course, calculated in dollars and cents, in terms of the amount of future income that these young people are sacrificing if they do not stay in school. The U.S. Chamber of Commerce has stated that each extra year in high school will add $17,500 to a student's lifetime earnings, and that four years of high school is worth $70,000. Census Bureau figures in 1961 indicated that the median income for males 25 years of age and over exceeded $5,500 for those who concluded their education with the twelfth grade as compared with less than $4,000 for those who left school at the end of the eighth grade.

To date, statistics such as these have been a chief stock in trade in awesome anti-dropout campaigns conducted by schoolmen, politicians, and the public-spirited generally. The trouble is that the figures are dangerously misleading because they are presented as if the comparisons were between segments of the school population that differ *only* in the amount of time spent in the classroom.

In reality, students who drop out tend also to compare *unfavorably* with graduates in native ability, verbal and numerical skills, personality adjustment, and attitudes toward education and work—all characteristics that have other roots than the mere circumstances or duration of formal schooling.[1] Differences in earning power between the dropout and the graduate must be attributed to these factors as well as to differences in education per se.

One can only conjecture as to the monetary value of additional education in the lives of individuals. Those who employ such an argument

[1] R. A. and L. M. Tesseneer. "Review of Literature on School Dropouts." NASSP BULLETIN. May 1958; pp. 141–153.

to counsel, lecture, and cajole youngsters to stay in school are indulging in a pretty superficial attack upon the dropout problem, and in the process are seriously deceiving both their clients and themselves.

But the words of doom do not end with predictions of limited earning power. "Unless you *at least* finish high school," the warning goes, "you may never get a job at all in the automated world we are entering." Here the counselor has obviously subscribed to the myth of automation as a giant scythe cutting away employment for the least skilled with each swing, thus making job security a matter of acquiring more advanced skills.

Again, the story is not as simple as the foregoing would suggest. While in certain areas mechanization has drastically reduced the need for unskilled and semiskilled workers, it is equally true that automation, with its use of computers and sensory and feedback devices, is also eliminating many jobs for skilled workers in both factories and offices and is even having a significant impact upon employment opportunities in the middle-management echelon.

THE MYTH OF JOB SKILLS

Despite the warning of the U.S. Department of Labor that only five percent of present jobs can be classified as unskilled, there is ample evidence that the increasing complexity of machines does not, as a rule, make the newly created jobs more complex or difficult. In discussing current trends, Edwin L. Dale goes so far as to claim that there is no indication that jobs with minimal skills are disappearing faster than those demanding higher skills.[2] He cites the example of an automated bank in which half of the jobs were scarcely up to a semiskilled level and included assignments such as feeding checks through a quick-photography machine.

Surprising as it may seem, both General Motors and the Ford Motor Company found it possible to train workers for newly automated plants in *less* time than had been required for their conventional assembly lines.[3] Highly significant is the conclusion of the NEA Project on the Educational Implications of Automation that "the complexities of the new technology do not necessarily call for an increase in manipulative skills."[4] Clearly, then, the notion that schools must justify their existence in terms of providing new and more sophisticated skills needs critical reexamination.

In spite of pleas for more training, the ironic fact is that our current levels of education have made possible a technological revolution of such proportions that American youth are faced with a backlash of leisure.

[2] Edwin L. Dale, Jr. "The Great Unemployment Fallacy." *New Republic*. September 5, 1964; pp. 10–12.

[3] James R. Bright. *Automation and Management*. Boston: Harvard Business School, Division of Research, 1958; Chapter 12. Also, Paul Goodman. *Compulsory Mis-Education*. New York: Horizon Press, 1964; p. 67.

[4] Virgil M. Rogers. "Automation: New Tasks for Schools." *New York State Education*. April, 1964; p. 19.

Gains in productivity per worker have come so rapidly that there has tended to be an excess of manpower in spite of enormous gains in the gross national product. The result has been a reduction in the workweek, earlier retirement ages, and a curtailment of employment for the teen-ager. As Jane Warters, a specialist in counseling, has said: "Except in time of war, the employment of youth is generally not needed or wanted."[5]

We continue to be told, however, that dropouts are unwanted because they are untrained and that they are turned away by employers because they do not have the specific skills taught in secondary schools. Yet, when employers use the high school diploma as a screening device, it is very likely that they are giving lip-service to the need for skills while they are actually more concerned about character traits and levels of maturity. They are looking for young people who show signs of having heeded admonitions to "grow up and settle down."

In discussing jobs for dropouts in the *Teachers College Record*, Robert A. Dentler points out that in a matter of a few years after leaving school most of the graduates *and* dropouts are employed. He cites a study in which employment rates were 94 percent for the graduates and 88 percent for the dropouts.[6]

THE MYTH OF SCHOOL ATTENDANCE

Although programs of persuasion and compulsion have kept the percentage of dropouts on the decline, the ineffectiveness of this additional instruction has been painfully apparent. In the opinion of Robert J. Havighurst, as many as 25 to 30 percent of the young people in slum areas fail to grow up successfully in the milieu of present-day schools.[7] Evidence of this failure is to be found in excessive absenteeism, apathetic and hostile attitudes, and meager academic achievement.

Urban youth from slum areas, with outlooks shaped by a legacy of poverty, despair, and discrimination, do not readily "buy" the idea of school attendance as preparation for employment—it is, instead, merely an alternative to idleness. According to James S. Coleman, this alternative imposes upon a youth "the indignity of going to a school he did not choose, to a teacher he does not like, to do things he considers childish."[8]

[5] Jane Warters, *High School Personnel Work Today*. New York: McGraw-Hill Book Co., 1956; p. 8.

[6] Besides age and training, the factor of color figures strongly in the rates of employment. It is more of a handicap to be nonwhite than to be a dropout, according to Dentler's "Dropouts, Automation, and the Cities" (pp. 475–483 of the *Teachers College Record*, March, 1964).

[7] Robert J. Havighurst, "Metropolitan Development and the Educational System," *School Review*, Autumn 1961, pp. 251–67.

[8] James S. Coleman, "A Future Without Jobs," *The Nation*, May 25, 1963, pp. 439–44.

There has been a lack of candor in our approach to today's youth, especially to those who are at odds with the requirements of formal education. At the same time, there has been a lack of foresight in the present curriculum when measured against the demands of the automated age. To meet these needs, I will sketch out a three-point program—a program which blends courses of action already accepted with other, more drastic changes. Altogether, my emphasis is upon breaking the constraints of educational dogma.

1. In Every Way Possible a Greater Sense of Worth and Purpose Must Be Aroused in Disadvantaged Youth.

Unless these young people can be made to believe in themselves and in their future, no proliferation of special educational programs will have a significant impact.

While some of the uneasiness and unhappiness of the disadvantaged in the school setting may be alleviated by accepting fewer years of education than the magic 12, the better answer is to *prevent* secondary school maladjustment as much as possible. To quote again from Robert A. Dentler's article in *Teachers College Record*: "For the current generation, our job is largely remediation and retraining. . . . In the long run, the best point of departure is a search for excellence in the early instruction in the central city schools."

This search for excellence has featured plans to improve staff selection and training, to reduce the teaching load, to develop new curricula, and to provide better facilities. It has been argued that neighborhood schools in communities having a high degree of social deprivation must have *compensatory* education; i.e., the programs of these schools must compensate for the lack of advantages which are normally available to middle-class children.

The compensatory concept gained impetus when aid to education and the war on poverty were wedded in the Elementary and Secondary Education Act of 1965. Although recent experimentation has probably done more to clarify problems than to solve them, the new legislation may yet prove to be a landmark in the development of urban education.

TEACHERS' ATTITUDES CRUCIAL

The attitudes of teachers and the techniques they employ are of critical importance—and unless these are given prior consideration, revisions of content are likely to serve little purpose. Youth who already lack self-esteem can be easily harmed if these low evaluations are reinforced by unflattering expectations encountered in the classroom.

Only teachers who can correctly assess the true potentialities of the disadvantaged—and who can communicate with them in a manner that avoids condescension—can arouse the needed interest, hope, and ambition. Adequate training, suitable temperament, and intense dedication are all essential qualities for inner-city teachers, and the job of finding and keeping these people needs constant attention.

The perfunctory manner in which so many of the educationally disadvantaged have been shunted into "basic," "remedial," and "slow-moving" classes has undoubtedly blighted the lives of large numbers of these young people whose true potential was never sensed by their teachers. Their school lives have become saturated with workbook exercises, with filling in the answers on page after page, day after day, *ad nauseum.* The watering-down of content, falsely predicated upon a general lack of ability, is humiliating for such students; it is not the content of courses, but the individual's self-respect and self-confidence that need to be brought "within reach."

Compensatory education is essentially a program of combating inner-city deterioration by strengthening the neighborhood schools. The limitations of this approach were highlighted last year in James Coleman's survey for the U.S. Office of Education entitled *Equality of Educational Opportunity.* Coleman concludes that the *quality of schoolmates* does more to determine the success of instructional programs than any other single factor. The leavening influence of students with relatively high aspirations has also been noted by Alan B. Wilson in his study of sixth-grade students in Berkeley, California.[9]

Those findings indicate that the most suitable classroom environment is one which reflects the levels of aspiration to be found in the *expanded* community. Such an environment waits on the formation of new school populations through some combination of these alternatives: (1) busing students away from inner-city schools, (2) building new school complexes (education parks) to serve the needs of large cross-sections of population, and (3) eliminating present barriers in housing opportunities for minority groups.

2. *Work-study Programs Must Be Developed as a Major Part of the Answer for Frustrated Students Who Are Failing in the More Traditional School Setting.*

As students mature, the gulf widens between those at the extremes of academic aptitude, and serious problems arise in fitting such individuals

[9] Alan B. Wilson. "Social Stratification and Academic Achievement." *Education in Depressed Areas.* (Edited by A. Harry Passow.) New York: Bureau of Publications, Teachers College, Columbia University, 1963.

into the mold of the comprehensive high school. Notwithstanding this, the tendency has been to look with disfavor upon those wishing to go to work (or to college!) before the prescribed amount of time has been spent in secondary school rituals. While an underachieving gifted student remains hidden from public view, it is not so with the dropout.

Many observers persist in looking upon the dropout as someone who has committed a quasi-delinquent and irrational act. On the contrary, given the nature of many educational offerings, he may have acted quite sensibly. Unfortunately, however, the dropout has been left to his own devices after leaving school, with few efforts to provide community or school-related programs to give him further direction. The dropout thus gains the further distinction of being a "left-out."

Those who think that the nation's welfare depends upon keeping all youth in full-time school until 18 might consider the following comment by Evelyn Murray, an official in the U.S. Bureau of Employment Security: "Most of the lower half of the class can do most of the world's work. Forty percent of the workers in 1970 will still be in the semiskilled, unskilled, and service occupations." In regard to the effect of work experiences, she states that "the retarded tend to disappear" since lack of intelligence shows up more in school than in most work situations.[10]

The spread of work-study programs in the present decade is a partial and belated recognition of the significance that must be attached to the problem of school-to-employment adjustment. In addition, programs such as the Job Corps, Neighborhood Youth Corps, and numerous local projects initiated through federal grants have also addressed the same problem. Besides certain immediate gains from the work programs, there is the possibility that attitudes will be developed favoring a return for further training in future years. At least the likelihood would seem to be greater under these circumstances than when students are retained in conventional programs in spite of growing bitterness.

3. The Emphasis upon Vocational Training Must Be Redressed in Favor of an Expanded Program of General Education.

As pointed out earlier, educational dogma has assigned to the teaching of skills a place of eminence that is inconsistent with actual student needs today. The automated age will place *more*, not less, importance upon general education.

Among those who have tried to describe our future under automation and cybernetics there are widely divergent views. Some persons of scholarly

---

[10] Evelyn Murray. "Work: A Neglected Resource for Students." *Personnel and Guidance Journal.* 41:229–233; November, 1962.

repute have forecast changes so fundamental that they are viewed by the general public with the same kind of skepticism that was accorded earlier predictions of space travel. Consider, for example, the estimate that two percent of our population could produce all the goods we need with the aid of machines that can now be envisioned!

Consider also the gloomy predictions as to the ability of those people currently in routine jobs to adjust to a bizarre (for them) new world of full-time leisure.[11] At the opposite extreme are those who see no revolution in the work-leisure pattern. In their opinion, the great reservoirs of human wants can only be met by combining our full manpower resources with our increasingly sophisticated machinery.

Between the more extreme points of view there is some semblance of a consensus. There tends to be some agreement, for example, that the workweek will be shortened. Jobs in production will decline in the face of further automation, but employment in service fields and in the public sector may offset these losses. In general, industry will favor those who leave our schools with *flexible* rather than specific skills. The rate of change in industry may be so rapid that workers will have as many as three distinct types of work during a lifetime.

Although local conditions may warrant some exceptions, the only logical course of action for a majority of schools is to concentrate upon general education and *pre*vocational training. The present vocational subjects need not be abandoned but could be offered for exploratory purposes, for nonvocational interests, and for the presentation of fundamentals upon which the student might build specific skills in on-the-job or post-high school training.

REDEFINING THE PROBLEM

The problem of the dropout must be defined in terms of the obligations of the total society. It is not enough to point the finger of shame upon those who have failed to fulfill the role assigned to them under the orthodox views of the past. Thus far, the term "dropout" has been a symbol for much of what is wrong with errant American youth; we are in need of a new term and concept which will more adequately and more honestly portray the current situation.

The basic problem is that there is an "idleness gap" resulting from the failure of the upward thrust of education to meet the downward reach of employment. The upward thrust of education must (and will)

[11] Robert Theobald. "The Cybernated Era." *Vital Speeches*, 30: 636; August 1, 1964.

be maintained, but this alone will not suffice. Business and labor, in the interest of national welfare, need to be concerned with the downward reach of employment.

> *More restricted than the broad concerns of the previous articles, but nevertheless significant is that expressed by L. Carroll King, Professor of Chemistry, Northwestern University. He questions whether many of the "successful" high school students, the ones who go on to college, are receiving the kind of education that will enable them to progress later on. The college dropout can also become a problem for society.*

Student Casualties*

L. Carroll King

The most important problem facing American education today is: There are too many student casualties.

The problem of student casualties is with us at all educational levels, but it is particularly acute at the high school-college interface. For at least 10 to 15 years, we have improved our teachers, we have improved our courses, we have improved our equipment, and then we have looked at the student as a statistic. If he survives our operation, fine; if not— there are always more students next year. Our procedure in the handling and treatment of students in the secondary schools and early college years is a violation of the student's right to individual attention and consideration.

Consider a typical situation at a typical large university with a highly select group of entering students. The faculty, each year, approaches the beginning course assuming that all the students will produce as indicated by advance examination records. What happens? Very few of them produce as expected. In a class of 500 at my university, one might make the following observations: Four percent of those entering the freshman course are exceptional and may be described as highly successful. Approximately

* *Education Digest* 32:29–31 (April, 1967). An address given before the Middle Atlantic Regional Meeting of the American Chemical Society, February, 1967. Reprinted by permission of publisher and author.

10 percent of the total do well enough that we are very happy about it. At least 50 percent of them, of course, do respectable work, but we are a little disappointed. The rest appear to have attained a plateau, and apparently do not intend to learn anything that they have not already encountered in their high-school activities. For the most part, they do passable work, but just barely. About 5 percent of them fail.

There are at least three possible positions one might take when attempting to understand this situation:

1. The high schools did not do a very good job. This is an explanation popular among college teachers. They suggest, first, that the student has only a superficial knowledge of the subject supposedly learned so well in high school. Second, they will observe that the student is clumsy and lacking common sense, and has very little ability to correlate experimental or factual information with theoretical concepts. Furthermore, the student lacks independence and self-reliance. The student wants to be told what to do and when to do it, and he wants to be told what he did and what it meant. The college teachers will say it's almost as if someone had been managing the student's life in detail from day to day, and he had never learned to make a decision by himself. All this is blamed on the secondary school.
2. The college course itself is dull, repetitious, and poorly taught. Most college teachers have heard this charge, particularly from students who do not do well, and occasionally from a secondary-school teacher who has been confronted with explanation 1.
3. For some reason, as yet unspecified, these students are not working at anywhere near the rated capacity we have been led to expect from their high-school activities and by the examination system which placed them in college in the first place. It is my opinion that this position may provide the best basis for trying to locate and understand the casualty problem.

Let us examine the problem in terms of the student and what is happening to him. The student is the casualty, the one branded by failure. It is time to ask: To what extent is our system responsible for these student casualties?

First of all, let us eliminate that 2 to 4 percent of our student population who are so good that they could get along without us. These, of course, are the ones we are most willing to take credit for. Let us also eliminate the petty charges whereby high-school and college teachers seek to pass the buck. Instead, let us consider that 10 to 15 percent of the very good high-school students who come to college and far too frequently fail outright, or do much less than expected.

TYPICAL DAY

Now let us examine a typical day in the life of one of these good students attending a suburban high school.

Our good student gets out of bed at 7 AM, he grabs something to eat, and at 7:30 is on his way to school. Classes begin at 8. During the next seven and one-half hours he attends at least four hours of subject-matter classwork plus a gym class and one other extraneous class, such as driver education. He eats lunch. If he is lucky, he has one study period.

He returns home at 4:30 PM, or later if he stopped to talk or get a haircut. If he is involved in any extracurricular activity, he gets home much later. By 6 PM he has just about enough energy left to make it to the dinner table. At 7 it's time for homework. For the good student, this means three or four hours, if all goes well. By 11 or 12 o'clock he can go to bed, his 17-hour day complete.

In four years on this schedule, Mr. Good Student accomplishes a lot. He should! No one else in the population works that many hours day after day after day. But after four years of this, Mr. Good Student is no longer Mr. Good Student. He is a tired old man. By the time he completes secondary school, we have asked him to do *too much, too fast, too soon*, and we have asked him to keep at it *too long*. At one time, this kind of demand was placed on the student when he was a little older and at the university. Now it starts when he is a child.

Mr. Good Student has had his heavy load, too much, too soon, too long, and has finally broken his back. He may go to college; but he cannot continue. At the college or university he comes to the realization that he is faced with four more years of 17-hour days. It is too much; he just quits. The tired, beaten, defeated Mr. Good Student asks for academic death.

In the past 15 years we have committed a crime against a generation. It is time we faced up to the fact that the human organism cannot work at a maximum rate day after day and year after year. There must be a time for rest. There must be provision for education at a more reasonable rate.

What can we do about this problem? Secondary-school teachers recognize the cause of student casualties, but they are trapped by the demands of parents, especially parents of first children demanding more homework. They are trapped by the demands of colleges and their ever-increasing standards for admission. They are trapped by a national college board examination system. The teacher is forced into the role of the overseer driving with a whip. He, in turn, is in the grip of a rigorous schedule imposed by a standard curriculum and standard examinations. The system created to serve the student and the teacher is rapidly making a slave of the student.

What can be done? First, we must revive the concept that the function of our educational system is to train students. This is the only legitimate function of the educational establishment and the sole reason for its existence.

Second, we must revive the concept that the student is an individual entitled to individual attention and consideration, and a right to proceed at his own rate.

Third, we must abandon the notion that the scholarly activity of teachers is responsible for the troubles of students. Direct and indirect benefits accrue to students associated with a teacher who is active in the development of new knowledge.

Finally, we must realize that the classroom teacher is the backbone of our educational system. We must rely on his judgment about students. In his consideration of students, we must free the secondary-school teacher from the tyranny of regimented curriculums, standardized examinations, college entrance requirements, and homework demands of parents. The teacher must have more freedom to develop his offerings according to the individual needs and talents of his particular students.

Juvenile Delinquency

It is both cheaper and socially more desirable to avoid delinquency and crime than it is to care for or rehabilitate the criminal. Previous articles have referred to the problems of the poor and minority groups. In the next selection Gerald Pine, Associate Professor of Education at the University of New Hampshire, discusses delinquency in the upper and middle classes.

The Affluent Delinquent*

Gerald J. Pine

At one time or another nearly everyone has assumed the role of delinquency expert. Public and professional comment on juvenile delinquency seems never to die nor fade away. Like sex, religion, sports, politics, and the weather, delinquency can always provide a subject for discussion. One dimension of the delinquency problem which has been a good conversa-

* *Phi Delta Kappan* 48:138–43 (Dec., 1966). Reprinted by permission of publisher and author.

tion piece of late is the occurrence of delinquent behavior in the middle and upper classes. Statistics released by the Federal Bureau of Investigation and other governmental agencies, the growing number of newspaper accounts describing the anti-social and aberrant behavior of privileged youth, and the frequency with which delinquency in suburbia is discussed during cocktail *tête-à-têtes* attest to an apparent rising incidence of affluent delinquency.

This paper examines the relationship between delinquent behavior and social class status. Its pivotal concerns are reflected in the following questions:

1. What is the extent of delinquent behavior in the middle and upper classes?
2. How is delinquent behavior treated in the middle and upper classes?
3. Are there any forms of delinquency which are more peculiar to one class than another?
4. What is the relationship between social class mobility and delinquency?
5. What are the factors which generate the affluent delinquent?

In attempting to answer these questions, I have expressed my notions in a series of propositions anchored so far as possible in research findings, in theory, and in my personal experience as a school counselor in an affluent suburban community.

Proposition 1. There is a significant relationship between an increase in a country's economic growth and a rise in delinquent behavior. There is evidence that a significant increase in the gross national product of a nation is accompanied or followed by a significant increase in delinquent behavior.

Teen-age crime, once little known in France, is up 400 percent over a decade ago. Prosperous West Germany is becoming concerned about crime by children, especially in the 14 to 18 age groups. Sweden, Denmark, Norway, Holland, and Switzerland all report increased teen-age criminality. Japan, which is enjoying the fastest rate of economic growth in the world, is also experiencing one of the most rapid escalations of delinquency.[1] Such trends offer a sharp contrast to the comparatively low rates of delinquency which appeared in the United States during the depression years.[2]

An increase in economic growth triggers a great deal of social and spatial mobility. The by-products of mobility and their role in delinquent behavior will be discussed in the propositions to follow.

Proposition 2. There has always been a considerable amount of delinquency in the middle- and upper-class segments of our society. Several investigations have attempted to ascertain the frequency and nature of

---

[1] *Boston Sunday Globe* (UPI), August 22, 1965, p. 53.
[2] Negley K. Teeters and David Matza, "The Extent of Delinquency in the United States," *Journal of Negro Education*, Summer, 1959, pp. 200–213.

delinquency behavior in the middle and upper classes by using samples vaguely defined as middle- and upper-class in terms such as: "upper-income group," "children of the professional class," "college students," and "group from relatively more favored neighborhoods." In contrast to the evidence based on official records, these studies, notwithstanding the general definition of class, indicate delinquent behavior is more equally dispersed among the various social classes than the average American citizen realizes.

In 1946 Austin L. Porterfield[3] compared the offenses of 2,409 cases of alleged delinquents in the Fort Worth, Texas, area with the admitted conduct of several hundred students at three colleges of Northern Texas. He found that many college students had committed one or more of the "delinquency offenses" but seldom had been so charged as in the case of their less fortunate counterparts.

Wallerstein and Wyle[4] distributed to an upper-income group a questionnaire listing 49 offenses under the penal code of the state of New York. All of the offenses were sufficiently serious to draw maximum sentences of not less than a year. Replies were received from 1,698 individuals. Ninety-nine percent of those questioned answered affirmatively to one or more of the offenses.

In response to a questionnaire which Bloch gave to 340 college juniors and seniors during the period from 1943–1948, approximately 91 percent admitted that they had knowingly committed offenses against the law, both misdemeanors and felonies. The groups sampled came from considerably better-than-average middle-class homes. Women students were as glaringly delinquent in this respect as men, although the volume of major offenses which they admitted to was somewhat smaller than that for men.[5]

In another study Clinard discovered that of 49 criminology students at a Midwestern university, 86 percent had committed thefts and about 50 percent had committed acts of vandalism.[6]

Exploring the implications of "white-collar criminality" in regard to delinquent behavior, Wattenberg and Balistrieri compared 230 white boys charged with automobile theft with 2,544 others in trouble with the Detroit police in 1948. They found the automobile theft group came from relatively more favored neighborhoods and had good peer relations.[7]

---

[3] Austin L. Porterfield, *Youth in Trouble*. Texas: Leo Potishman Foundation, 1946.

[4] James S. Wallerstein and G. J. Wyle, "Our Law-abiding Lawbreakers," in *Probation*, 1946, pp. 107–112.

[5] Herbert A. Bloch and Frank T. Flynn, *Delinquency: The Juvenile Offender in America Today*. New York: Random House, 1956, p. 11.

[6] Marshall B. Clinard, *Sociology of Deviant Behavior*. New York: Holt, Rinehart & Winston, 1957, p. 165.

[7] W. W. Wattenberg and J. Balistrieri, "Automobile Theft: A Favored Group Delinquency," *The American Journal of Sociology*, May, 1952, pp. 575–79.

An investigation was conducted by Birkness and Johnson in which a group of delinquents was compared with a group of non-delinquents. Each group included 25 subjects. It was found that five times as many of the parents of delinquent children (in contrast with the non-delinquent children) were of the professional class. Almost twice as many parents of the non-delinquents were classified in the manual labor status in comparison with the parents of delinquents.[8]

A study carried out by Nye in the state of Washington revealed that there was no significant relationship between one's position in the social class structure and the frequency and severity of delinquent behavior, i.e., the middle- and upper-class adolescent was involved in as much norm violating behavior as the lower-class adolescent.[9]

In summary, during the past 20 years there has been an accumulation of evidence to demonstrate that delinquency is not the exclusive property of the lower class; it appears to exist to a significant degree in all strata of our society. But if this is the case, why have we only now become so deeply concerned about the affluent delinquent? Certainly if we have been concerned we have not been "publicly" concerned to the degree that we are today. Perhaps the answer lies in the fact that within our social structure there is a protective shield which hides the affluent delinquent and which up to now has served as a curtain of silence making privileged delinquency socially invisible. Nearly 30 years ago Warner and Lunt, in their classic work *The Social Life of a Modern Community*, observed that the disparity in number of lower- and upper-class arrests is not to be accounted for by the fact that criminal behavior is proportionately higher among lower-class juveniles or that there are more ethnic groups whose children have been imperfectly adapted to city life. It must be understood as a product of the amount of protection from outside interference that parents can give members of their families.

Proposition 3. Official delinquency data has been and is biased in favor of upper- and middle-class youth. Delinquency is usually considered primarily as a lower-class problem. However, the research reporting significant relationships between delinquent behavior and lower socioeconomic status has been characterized by a built-in bias, i.e., the use of official delinquency statistics that do not reflect a considerable amount of upper- and middle-class delinquent behavior. Middle- and upper-class children are less likely to become official delinquency statistics, because their behavior is more frequently handled outside the sphere of formal legal institutions. The middle and upper classes control various means of preventing detection, influencing official authority, and generally "taking

---

[8] V. Birkness and H. C. Johnson, "Comparative Study of Delinquent and Nondelinquent Adolescents," *Journal of Educational Research*, April, 1949, pp. 561–72.

[9] F. Ivan Nye, *Family Relationships and Delinquent Behavior*. New York: John Wiley & Sons, 1959.

care of their own" through psychiatrists, clinics, and private institutions, thus avoiding the police and the courts—the official agencies.

In the following telling and graphic descriptions, Harrison Salisbury[10] describes the classic middle-class way of dealing with anti-social behavior:

> If sixteen-year old George and three of his friends "borrow" a nice-looking Pontiac convertible from the country club parking lot and set off on a joyride and are caught speeding by the county police they are taken to the station house all right, but nothing goes on the blotter. The parents come down, there is much talk, the fathers bawl the day-lights out of the kids, the boys promise to be good, the owners wouldn't think of making a charge, and by two o'clock in the morning everyone is back home, peacefully sleeping. There's no case, no records, no statistics, "no delinquency."
>
> When 17-year-old Joan gets pregnant after letting 18-year-old Dennis "fool around" at a beach party one summer night, she isn't sent to the Youth House. Nor is Dennis confronted with the dilemma of marrying the girl or facing a charge of statutory rape. There is an angry dispute between the two families. Joan's family blames Dennis. Dennis's family blames Joan. In the end Joan's father finds a doctor who takes care of Joan for $750. Joan is a month late starting school in the fall because, as her mother explains to the principal, she had a severe reaction from the antibiotics they gave her at the camp up in New Hampshire where she went in August.

In addition to the built-in bias of official delinquency data, studies reporting on the relationship between social class status and delinquent behavior are characterized by another critical shortcoming: a paucity of empirical material on a significant dynamic of social class—social mobility.

Proposition 4. A significant factor related to delinquent behavior in the upper and middle classes is the dynamic of social mobility. What bearing does movement from one social class to another class have on delinquent behavior? What are the implications of vertical movement between classes in regard to norm violations? The question of social mobility has an important place in the study of social class and its impact on delinquent behavior for two reasons:

1) Social mobility introduces a dynamic feature of possible change into a class system, and 2) it can alter the structure and patterns of class relationships as the consequences of mobility introduce changes into those close relationships.

Here I would like to share with you the results of a study designed to determine the significance of the relationships between social class status, social mobility status, and delinquent behavior.[11] The study was

---

[10] Harrison E. Salisbury, *The Shook-up Generation.* New York: Harper & Bros., 1958, pp. 107–109.

[11] Gerald J. Pine, "Social Class, Social Mobility, and Delinquent Behavior," *Personnel and Guidance Journal,* April, 1965, pp. 770–74. See also: Pine's "Occupational and Educational Aspirations and Delinquent Behavior," *The Vocational Guidance Quarterly,* Winter Issue, 1964–65.

conducted to determine the significance of the relationships between social class, social mobility, and delinquent behavior. Data were collected from a population of 683 pupils (grades 9–12) attending an urban high school. Information regarding delinquency was gathered by using a 120-item anonymous "delinquency inventory." The chi-square technique was employed to analyze the data, which showed that, in general, there is no significant relationship between social class status and delinquent behavior. A very strong relationship exists between social mobility status and delinquent behavior. Adolescents moving downward in the social structure are more heavily involved in delinquency; adolescents moving upward are least involved.

The primary conclusion made in this study is that delinquent behavior is less a function of the class an individual is in at the moment and much more a function of the class to which he aspires or toward which he is moving. In examining the relationship between social class and delinquent behavior, it is not only important to know what class an individual is in but perhaps more important to know if he is securely located in the class, if he has just managed a toehold in the class, or if he has just moved down from a class.

The findings indicate delinquent behavior is not a lower-class phenomenon. However, one aspect of the question of class differential in delinquent behavior which invites further investigation is the relationship between value system and delinquency. Social-class status may be more accurately measured in terms of value systems than in terms of economic factors such as occupation, housing, residence, and income. The lower-class boy moving upward into the middle class may be guided in his behavior by a middle-class value system and, therefore, might be more accurately described as a member of the middle class.

The behavior of the middle-class boy moving downward in the social structure may be influenced primarily by lower-class concerns, hence he might be more accurately described as lower class. It is quite possible for a child to live in a lower-class neighborhood and in the midst of a lower-class culture and still be considered middle class.

An explanation of the strong relationship between downward mobility and delinquent behavior may be found in Reissman's hypothesis[12] regarding the psychological consequences of "downward mobility." He suggests that these consequences can be channeled away from the individual to avoid injury to self-conceptions and self-respect. The individual imputes to others the blame for his or his family's descent in the social structure. His frustration and his failure are poured into an explanation that implicates society or society's institutions as the cause of it all. Hostile and negative attitudes toward others and toward authority develop.

[12] Leonard Reissman, *Class in American Society*. Glencoe, Ill.: The Free Press, 1959, p. 369.

If the intensity of the psychological consequences of "mobility failure" is in proportion to the degree of failure, then it is not difficult to understand the strength of the relationship between downward mobility and delinquent behavior. Certainly, downward mobility represents the greatest failure in the mobility process. For, in a culture which highly esteems the success value, what constitutes a greater failure than the failure to at least maintain one's status quo in the social structure?

Proposition 5. *Successful social mobility is a breeding ground for the development of delinquent behavior.* The research evidence presented in Proposition 4 indicates there is a statistically significant relationship between downward mobility of adolescents and delinquent behavior. Paradoxically, the downward movement of the adolescent may be the consequence of the successful mobility of his parents. Psychological tension and conflict often accompany successful movement in the social structure and may be expressed in delinquent behavior.

Successful mobility necessarily involves a major adjustment by the individual. He must reject the way of life of the group he has just left and assume the new way of life of the group he has just entered. It is a process of class "acculturation." Depending upon the change required, the reorientation of the individual can be enormous; depending upon the recency of the change, the reorientation can involve a great deal of insecurity.

"Successful mobility places the individual, for some period of time, in a marginal social position. The individual's former friends and associates may find him threatening; his success is a mark of their failure. His newly created friends and associates produced by his successful move may find him too 'different,' too 'raw,' and too recent to be accepted as a bona fide member. The individual thus finds himself suspended in a 'success limbo.' The insecurity he feels may produce reactions the same as those exhibited by failure."[13]

Not only does the individual experience the results of success or failure but his family does also. Whyte[14] found that the individual's family must become implicated in his success just as they do in his failures.

On a larger scale, our society must experience the consequences for its emphasis upon social mobility, upon seeking and achieving success. Tumin[15] sets forth the following as by-products of the stress placed on social mobility in American society:

   1. A "diffusion of insecurity" as more and more people become involved with trying to get ahead rather than developing any lasting

   [13] *Ibid.*, pp. 371–72.
   [14] W. H. Whyte, "The Wives of Management," *Fortune*, October, 1951; and "The Corporation and the Wife," *Fortune*, November, 1951.
   [15] Melvin C. Tumin, "Some Unapplauded Consequences of Social Mobility in a Mass Society," *Social Forces*, October, 1957, pp. 32–37.

and sure sense of the group and its needs. Traditional beliefs and values of society become threatened as behavior is more and more oriented toward "status acceptance and prestige ranking."

2. A "severe imbalance" of social institutions as a result of rapid mobility of the population as religion, education, and the family become tied to the struggle for economic success.

3. "Fragmentation of the social order" as more and more individuals become rivalrous with each other. Competition does not always lead to the greatest good for the greatest number.

4. "Denial of work" as the emphasis shifts from the importance of work and striving to the urgency of appearing to be successful. Preference is given to the open portrayal of *being* successful, as measured by the power and property which one openly consumes.

5. "Rapid social mobility" generates in the older portions of the population a cranky and bitter conservatism and worship of the past; and in the new mobile segments a vituperative contempt of traditions.

It is the accumulation and the complex interaction of these social by-products which fertilize the soil for the growth of affluent delinquency.

Proposition 6. The female-based household is a by-product of successful mobility and an important variable in the development of delinquent behavior. Success and the striving for success in the middle and upper classes is frequently the incubator of the female-based household. A number of studies have identified the female-based household as a characteristic of lower-class society and as an influencing factor in the development of delinquent behavior. And yet anyone who has worked with middle- and upper-class youth is keenly aware of the large number of female-dominated families in suburbia. In order to insure and maintain his success, father often becomes a "weekend briefcase-toting visitor" who is either absent from the home, only sporadically present, or when present only minimally or inconsistently involved in the raising of the children. Mother becomes "chief cook and bottle washer," assuming both the maternal and paternal roles.

It is not too difficult to understand how female-centered families in the middle and upper class can produce delinquents, particularly in the male adolescent population.

Because of the inconsistent presence or involvement of an adequate masculine model in the home with whom the suburban boy can identify, many teen-age males develop uncertainties about their masculine identity at a time in their lives when identity is a crucial matter. For the adolescent male who feels insecure about his sex identification, delinquency represents a demonstrative vehicle for asserting his masculinity.

Proposition 7. The emphasis on success in our culture has led to the elongation of adolescence, a contributing factor in the development of delinquent behavior. Another consequence of success in the middle and upper classes is the extension of adolescence as a period of growth and development. The emphasis on success in suburbia is epitomized in the pressures exerted on youth to get into college. For the vast numbers of young boys and girls who do go to college one fact is very clear: Adolescence doesn't end at 18 or 19; it probably ends at 21 or 22; and perhaps even later. Thus for a large number of our privileged youth at least four years have been tacked on to the process of growing up and four years can be a long time to wait to prove yourself—to demonstrate that you are a man or woman. Four more years of that social limbo we call adolescence are very conducive to intensifying the already existing feelings of anxiety, tension, restlessness, and rebellion so common to high school youth. Adolescence is becoming an "existential vacuum," a social process lacking purpose and meaning. To the degree we elongate the process of adolescence without providing purpose for its existence, to that degree should we anticipate more frequent socially aberrant and rebellious behavior.

Proposition 8. A middle- and upper-class "sheepskin psychosis" nourishes norm-violating behavior. In the middle and upper classes there is tremendous pressure placed upon youth to succeed. These pressures emanate from the dominating concern of parents for achieving and "getting ahead," and the feeling in youth of an ensuing sense of discrepancy between aspiration and achievement. "This strong focus in the middle-class milieu may induce the whole perfectionist-compulsive syndrome, in which children have impossible ideas of what they should accomplish; the result for some individuals is a combination of neuroses built around the individual's inability to achieve internalized goals of various types, e.g., learning to read, being on the honor roll, or getting into the college of first choice. . . . The stresses imposed through the conflict over aspiration and achievement wake a wide variety of symptoms. One of these symptoms may take the form of norm-violating behavior."[16]

Proposition 9. Middle-class values which once served as behavior controls are weakening. One of the identifying characteristics of the middle class is the tradition of deferring immediate gratifications for long-range goals. For years this tradition helped to instill in middle-class youngsters a capacity for self-denial and impulse control. However, there is mounting indication today that the strength of this tradition of focus on achievement, of directed work effort, and deferment of immediate pleasures is diminishing in a number of middle-class sectors. Impulse buying and installment plan financing are very representative of the "have-it-now" pattern of the lower-class culture. Concomitantly, compulsory education and a continuous promotion policy act to keep all youngsters in school regardless of effort, achievement, or future goal. These trends have tended

---

[16] William C. Kvaraceus and Walter Miller, *Delinquent Behavior: Culture and the Individual.* Washington, D.C.: National Education Association, 1959, pp. 99–100.

to lessen the view of middle-class youth that success is achieved through deferred gratification, frustration tolerance, directed effort, and self-control. If delinquency is on the rise in the middle class, it may be attributable in part to a diminution in the classical middle-class tradition of "hard work today and rewards tomorrow."

Proposition 10. Middle-class youth behavior reflects lower-class values. Currently, lower-class concerns and values are being sold to and bought by the middle-class consumer. Mass media and the advertising world have dipped deeply into the lower-class culture. Lower-class focal concerns such as force, duplicity, chance, excitement, trouble, autonomy, and "present pleasure" have been mined over and over again for use on the screen, the air waves, the picture tube, and the printed page. The effect of this cultural saturation has been the borrowing of lower-class concerns by middle-class youth. Adolescent fads, jargon, music, and behavior seem to mirror a number of lower-class behavior patterns. It would seem that the interaction of these recently assumed lower-class concerns with the other social and psychological by-products of social mobility constitute a powerful generative force in developing affluent delinquency.

Provision for the Disadvantaged

One of the most important tasks in providing an adequate education for all of the children of all of the people is to decide how to deal with the problems relating to the more disadvantaged segments of the population. There are in fact several disadvantaged groups currently recognized as representing particularly acute problems for democratic education. There are problems of race, problems of poverty, and in some sections of the country problems for Spanish speaking minorities.

In the first of the selections dealing with the disadvantaged the authors analyze three alternative policies for trying to equalize educational opportunities for different races. After describing these alternatives as essentially facets of a single solution, they indicate their awareness of the complexity of the issues and express the belief that school integration is in fact possible. Mr. Schwarz, a former high school principal, is a doctoral candidate at Harvard University. Mr. Smith and Mr. Pettigrew are members of the Harvard staff.

Collapse of Consensus:
Desegregation: Assessing the Alternatives*

Robert Schwarz, Thomas Pettigrew, Marshall Smith

There has been a collapse of consensus among liberal whites and militant Negroes about how to desegregate the nation's schools.

Some don't believe in integrated education any more. Some now claim it can't work.

Many young Negroes have given up hope of ever achieving racial integration and demand community control over all-Negro schools in the ghetto. White liberals find themselves split on the issue—much as they have been over the Vietnam War. There is virtual unanimity among liberals for moral as well as educational reasons that racially integrated schooling is desirable and must remain an ultimate objective. But there is sharp and often acrimonious debate over short-term policy decisions— with the educator typically caught in the crossfire.

One outspoken portion of the white liberal community is combining forces with white extremists who never accepted the goal of integration. Joining this fold are the most strident separatists among Black Power advocates, and together this strange coalition is trying to breathe new life into the "separate-but-equal" doctrine that the Supreme Court thought it had effectively laid to rest in 1954. While continuing to profess school integration as the ideal solution, these liberals are now repeating many of the contentions of such symbols of segregation as George Wallace and Louise Day Hicks, whom they were roundly castigating only a few short years ago: White Americans simply will not accept interracial schools; integration is demographically impossible to achieve anyway; integration is the pipedream of unrealistic "do-gooders" and intellectuals, and Negroes are happier and can get a fine education in truly first-rate ghetto schools. Old programs no longer identify the players in today's racial drama.

Long-range educational decisions, however, cannot be made on the basis of ideological contentions.

The future directions of our nation's schools are too crucial to be determined by the domestic aberrations of war and short-run expediencies. Educators must responsibly fashion a design for the rest of this century

* *Nation's Schools* 81:3:61–66+ (March, 1968). Reprinted with permission from *Nation's Schools* and the authors. Copyright 1968, McGraw-Hill, Inc., Chicago. All rights reserved.

out of the best information we have available and all of the alternatives as we can perceive them. Today's educational thinking raises three broad policies as future alternatives: 1) compensatory education, 2) decentralization and community control, and 3) desegregation and integration.

ALTERNATIVE I: COMPENSATORY EDUCATION

In 1906 Bernard Shaw wrote in the preface to *The Doctor's Dilemma*:

> Or, to take another common instance, comparisons which are really comparisons between two social classes with different standards of nutrition and education are palmed off as comparisons between the results of a certain medical treatment and its neglect. Thus, it is easy to prove that the wearing of tall hats and the carrying of umbrellas enlarges the chest, prolongs life, and confers comparative immunity from disease; for the statistics show that the classes which use these articles are bigger, healthier, and live longer than the class which never dreams of possessing such things.

For many years Americans had a stock answer to explain the differences in achievement level between advantaged and disadvantaged groups. It was clear that the advantaged had access to better facilities, curriculum and teachers. And that this access "caused" the differences in achievement levels also seemed "obvious." It is frightening to realize that in the face of mounting evidence contradicting this "answer", the reaction of many educators, policy makers, and journalists has not been to reject their beliefs but to advocate them more than ever, to call for "taller hats" and "larger umbrellas" for the ghetto.

Such a reaction has promoted increased ESEA Title I support for compensatory education leading to new materials, more adults in the classroom, and team teaching in the context of the "neighborhood ghetto school." There is little question but that the funding of massive compensatory programs for the ghetto dweller would be a simpler political solution than integration *if* compensatory programs really worked, *if* these schools did overcome the educational achievement deficits that the "disadvantaged" child brings to school with him.

The sad fact is, however, that segregated compensatory programs have not succeeded. If there exists such a program in a ghetto school that has enabled students to approach and *sustain* grade level achievements, it has not been rigorously evaluated and publicly reported. This unhappy truth is extensively documented in Chapter Four of the U. S. Civil Rights Commission's Report, "Racial Isolation in the Public Schools", in which results of major compensatory efforts from a number of cities are reported in detail. More recently the evaluation of the heralded More Effective Schools program in New York City by the Center for Urban Education produced familiar results.

Such results are not easily swallowed by those who have long assessed the quality of education in terms of dollar inputs. The discovery that pupil achievement levels are apparently insensitive to changes in traditional inputs (teachers excluded) hasn't been and shouldn't be blindly accepted. Those who disagree with this conclusion generally argue that either the compensatory programs have not been in effect long enough for improvement to be seen or that the programs have not been adequately funded. And in criticism of the evidence offered by the U.S. Office of Education's Equality of Educational Opportunity report (the Coleman Report) supporting the conclusion of little or no independent effect of traditional inputs, these same persons contend that even if the report's measures were adequate, the existing differences in school resources between schools is so small that it is impossible to estimate the relationship between school resources and achievement. Because the pupil-teacher ratio is so similar across the country, for example, we have no way of estimating the effect of reducing it from 25/1 to 6/1 at the elementary level.

It is impossible to offer absolutely conclusive evidence refuting any of these points. Critics will always claim that we must wait even longer to see the results, spend even more money, and provide more teachers per classroom. The burden of proof, however, is on these "true believers."

Actually, the most difficult fact for true believers to accept is that there is little positive effect in simply increasing the teacher-pupil ratio. Although the tutorial goal of Mark Hopkins at one end of a log and a single student at the other end is recognized as impractical, it, or conditions approximating it, is considered to guarantee success. But consider the economic and practical implications of supplying one qualified teacher for every six disadvantaged students as defined by ESEA Title I eligibility. David K. Cohen[1] estimates the initial costs in teacher training, salaries and classroom construction to be approximately $20 billion. He further estimates that the annual salary expenditures on teachers of poor children would increase from about $1.7 billion to about $8.6 billion, or from 8 percent to 43 per cent of the total instructional expenditures for *all* children. This line of reasoning assumes, of course, that enough qualified candidates could be found and trained, and that they can be persuaded to work in ghetto rather than suburban schools. It also assumes that the political will can be mastered to reallocate national priorities to the point where current ESEA expenditures are dramatically increased. And even if such a program were realized, there is little indication that it would be successful in truly equalizing public educational opportunity.

Reliance upon the mechanical solution of increasing the teacher-pupil ratio has been criticized on theoretical as well as empirical grounds.

[1] David K. Cohen, "Policy for the Public Schools: Compensation or Integration?" *Harvard Educational Review*, Winter, 1968.

Perhaps the most familiar criticism of this approach is that smaller classes are of no help if the teachers are too inflexible to adjust in teaching styles and instructional strategies. This notion gained indirect support from the findings of the Coleman Report and from the recently published British survey, *Children and Their Primary Schools*, commonly called the Plowden Report. In both reports, rough measures of the quality of the teachers in a school are strongly associated with the achievement of the students. The association is independent of the social class of the individual student and the student body and of the level of other school attributes. The relationship is much stronger for minority group students than for majority (white) students, and it appears to be accumulative in that it increases over the years from first to twelfth grade. Apparently, competent teachers are successful no matter what the class size.

The problem with such findings is that they lead to few direct policy implications. And though long-term policy directed toward recruitment of "smarter" teachers (more pay, better working conditions, and so forth) might eventually produce a solution for the ghetto, what about the next 10 years? Certainly increased attention to approaches for improving the quality of teaching seems to be called for and at the expense, if necessary, of standard hardware improvements.

ALTERNATIVE II: DECENTRALIZATION

A second alternative now being proposed for the ills of urban education is decentralization and community control. Since decentralization is in some danger of becoming another fashionable educational catchword, we should point out that the term means at least two distinctly different things to different groups of people. For educators, decentralization seems largely to be an organizational concept: It is a device for dealing with the administrative rigidity and bureaucratic inertia that inevitably characterize most large formal organizations. The movement to decentralize the New York City school system, for example, certainly predates the Black Power movement. New York reorganized its local school boards in 1961 in an attempt to let some air into the system, and, in 1965, 31 district superintendents were appointed to have jurisdiction over these local units. Although both moves were in part motivated by the desire to bring the schools closer to the people, there was no substantial transfer of power from the board's central headquarters at 110 Livingston Street to the districts.

In the past year or two, administrative decentralization has been talked about, and in some cases implemented, in more and more of our major cities. The Chicago school system, for example, has been divided into three large districts each of which is under the semiautonomous jurisdiction of an associate superintendent. In Washington a panel of outside consultants led by Prof. A. Harry Passow of Teachers College has recommended the reorganization of the school system into eight decentralized units; and in Philadelphia, Los Angeles, and Boston various decentralization plans have been put forward. But there is an increasing gap between the decentralized schemes recommended by schoolmen and the demands of militant black leaders. This gap is best illustrated by the reception accorded the report of the Mayor's Advisory Panel on Decentralization of the New York City Schools.

Although this is not the place to go into the details of the Bundy Plan,[2] it is worth noting that in the act leading to the creation of the advisory panel, the state legislature requested the creation of "educational policy units" that would:

> . . . afford members of the community an opportunity to take a more active and meaningful role in the development of educational policy related to the diverse needs and aspirations of the community.

The premise underlying this request is that:

> Increased community awareness and participation in the educational process is essential to the furtherance of educational innovation and excellence in the public school system within the city of New York.

It seems likely that the state legislature was led to think of decentralization in terms of increased community participation in educational policymaking because of the demands stemming from certain ghetto communities. One obvious source of these demands was the experience of parents and community leaders at East Harlem's Intermediate School 201 in the summer and fall of 1966. A less obvious, but probably more significant source, was the participation of many ghetto residents in various antipoverty programs. We are thinking here especially of the ill-fated community action program, which in its initial phase promised the "maximum feasible participation of the poor." But whatever the sources of the legislature's insistence on increased community participation in policymaking, the point worth noting is that the advisory panel's recommendation of "a community school system"[3] has achieved the improbable success of provoking the board of education, the supervisors' association, and the teachers' union to close ranks in opposition to it.

The relationship between decentralization and community control, on the one hand, and Negro American achievement, on the other hand, is undoubtedly more complex than advocates appear to assume. If the decentralization plan carves out ghetto districts and separates them from

---

[2] So named after the Chairman of the Mayor's Advisory Panel, McGeorge Bundy.

[3] The Bundy Panel recommended 30–60 autonomous districts, each with its own eleven member governing board (the majority of whom would be elected), which would have authority over all elementary and secondary schools within its district. Mayor Lindsay has since modified the plan to leave high schools under the jurisdiction of a central board.

"white" districts, racial segregation of schools may be institutionalized for generations to come. The result of such further educational ghettoization cannot be definitively predicted, of course, but present data would point in the direction of lower achievement and aspirations of future Negro students. But this need not be the case. New York City, or any other American city, *can* be decentralized in such a way as to further desegregation—though by itself, of course, decentralization cannot complete the task.

Black Power proponents brush aside such considerations. They are convinced that black community control alone can improve ghetto schools, instill racial pride, and elevate achievement. All of these contentions, however, are ideological assumptions, not demonstrated truths. Unlike the hard data which supports the efficacy of racially integrated schools, these critical assumptions are held to be true by fiat. To be sure, community and parental involvement as well as racial pride are values to be sought as ends in themselves. But their positive causal connections with achievement and later attainments are not as yet demonstrated. Like ardent supporters of ghetto compensation, Black Power advocates have the burden of proof for their sweeping assumptions.

ALTERNATIVE III: RACIAL DESEGREGATION

Critics of racial integration, white and black, often claim that it is a bankrupt strategy that failed; actually, it is largely a strategy that has never been tried. To the extent it has been attained in schools, it has typically succeeded in three key realms: the academic achievement of Negro children, the racial attitudes and preferences of white children, and the racial attitudes and preferences of Negro children. Each of these consequences merits attention.

The Coleman data, as analyzed and reported in chapter three of the Civil Rights Commission's *Racial Isolation of Public Schools* monograph, support with a large sample what limited research in individual school districts from White Plains to Berkeley has indicated repeatedly: Negro American children as a group evince and sustain substantially greater academic achievement if they are members of predominantly white classrooms. This effect is especially strong if the child begins his interracial education in the first three grades. And the achievement of white children in such classrooms is not lowered when contrasted with that of comparable white children in all-white classrooms.

Not all desegregation, of course, leads to superior Negro achievement. Interracial schools, like universal ones, can be good, bad or indifferent, since the mere racial mix of students is no magic guarantee of learning as some integrationist ideologists imply. But desegregation is the prerequisite of the ideal condition—the true cross-racial acceptance of integration. In other words, a *desegregated* school is merely an institution with an interracial student body, usually mostly white; it implies nothing about the quality of the interracial interaction. By contrast, an integrated school is a desegregated one with numerous cross-racial friendships and little or no racial tension. The Commission on Civil Rights, in closer examination of the Coleman data, discovered that the chief academic benefits of interracial education occurred primarily in the genuinely integrated schools.

Some researchers regard the improved learning of integrated Negro youngsters as a total result of social class and not race. That is, most Negro schools are comprised primarily of lower class children, while most white schools are comprised primarily of middle class children. Considerable research, including the Coleman Report, shows the vast importance for achievement of attending a school with a middle class milieu. Thus, these researchers conclude that it is actually the typically higher social class backgrounds, and not the race, of his new classmates that raises the integrated Negro child's test scores. There is no doubt that this social class effect is central to the process, but our interpretation of the relevant data to date is that there is also a racial benefit for achievement. In any event, this debate between researchers is strictly academic for the educational policy maker. With the most generous definition, only about one-fourth of Negro America is middle class. Consequently, the only way the vast majority of Negro students can attend schools with a dominant middle class milieu is through racial desegregation.

While important, high achievement test scores are surely not the only goal of education. Indeed, many integrationists argue for biracial schools solely in terms of the nonacademic benefits of diverse contacts. Preparation for the interracial world of the future, they insist, demands interracial schools today for both white and Negro youth.

Both the Coleman and Commission Reports speak to this issue, too.

The Coleman Report shows that white students who attend public schools with Negroes are the least likely to prefer all-white classrooms and all white "close friends"; and this effect, too, is strongest among those who begin their interracial schooling in the early grades. Consistent with these results are data from Louisville, Kentucky, on Negro pupils. In an open choice situation, Negro children are likely to select mostly-white high schools only if they are currently attending mostly white junior high schools. In short, integration leads to a preference among both white and Negro children for integration, while segregation promotes further segregation.

A Civil Rights Commission survey of urban adults in the North and West discussed in its report suggests that these trends continue into adulthood. Negro adults who themselves attended desegregated schools as children tend to be more eager to have their children attend such schools and do in fact more often send their children to such schools than comparable Negro adults who attended only segregated schools as children. They are typically making more money and more frequently in white-collar occupations than previously segregated Negroes of comparable origins. Similarly, white adults who experienced as children integrated schooling differ from comparable whites in their greater willingness to reside in an interracial neighborhood, to have their children attend interracial schools, and to have Negro friends. The cumulative nature of integration, then, is not limited to just the school career, but also tends to span generations for both whites and Negroes.

Those who consider only test scores in urging bigger and better ghetto schools might well think deeply about these racial attitude and preference data. Even if it were somehow possible to generate first-rate academic performance in ghetto schools, would not such institutions and their all-white counterparts be still producing yet another generation of racially bigoted Americans who regard racial separation as desirable and right? Children educated in racially separate schools naturally come to see the world through "race-colored" glasses.

Integrated schooling is not something paternalistically provided "for Negroes." Nor, for that matter, is it something "for whites." It is in a real sense an educational alternative necessary to the ultimate solution of the nation's most serious domestic problem. Integrated schools, then, are "for America."

ARE THESE ALTERNATIVES MUTUALLY EXCLUSIVE?

We have discussed the major ideas in education today[4] related to race relations as if they were alternatives, as if you had to choose one to the exclusion of the others. We did this because we feel it accurately reflects the typical context in which they are discussed. In particular, compensatory education, decentralization and community control are often presented as substitutes for racial desegregation. We reject such thinking. Our reading of the evidence to date leads to the belief that to the degree these ideas have merit they have still more merit in interracial schools. Thus, compensatory programs in integrated schools have frequently attained lasting success, in contrast to the typical failure of similar compensatory programs in virtually all-Negro settings.

We believe that there is a case to be made for decentralization and more community participation in the running of the schools, just as there is a strong argument for compensatory education, but only as these policies *accompany* the drive for integration rather than substitute for it. There is no question that school systems in large cities are overly bureaucratic and inflexible, and that they should become more responsive to local needs. We support the notion of strengthening the authority of

[4] The final sections of this article draw heavily upon our *The New Republic* article of January 6, 1968.

school principals and their faculties, and we share the hope that increased participation by parents in the life of the school will have a salutary effect on the motivation of the children.

But if these ideas make sense for segregated schools, they should make even more sense for integrated ones. Similarly, if teaching technics are developed in compensatory programs to capitalize on reduced pupil ratios, these technics should prove effective in an integrated setting. Integration *by itself* is not going to be enough to close the achievement gap. If experiments in decentralization prove to have a positive impact on achievement, these findings should influence our planning for *all* schools.

IS RACIAL INTEGRATION POSSIBLE?

But why make the case for integrated schools, ask members of the new segregationist coalition, if it is impossible to achieve? Even if it is demonstrably by far the most effective approach around which others revolve, is it not foolish and naive to pursue an unattainable goal?

Those who wish to abandon school desegregation "prove" its impossibility by pointing to the racial demography of our cities: Four of five Negro Americans who live in metropolitan areas reside in central cities, while half of metropolitan white Americans now reside in suburbs. Emphasizing New York City and Washington, D.C. as urban prototypes, they conclude that school integration is simply never going to be achieved. So why not "educate children where they are" and replicate in our schools the racial and social class homogeneity of housing patterns?

We are aware of these facts of racial demography; and we do agree with the unstated premise in this reasoning that housing patterns of racial separation will not erode rapidly enough to be of any real significance to the schools. But after careful study of this issue, we firmly believe the conclusion to be correct only if, once again, one is willing to make a number of critical assumptions about the future. The pattern of black central cities and white suburban rings makes future school integration impossible only if one: ignores the majority of American cities that are not likely ever to resemble either New York or Washington; assumes that Negro ghettos will not extend into suburbs (as Chicago's westside ghetto will soon expand into Oak Park); assumes that the single site model of so-called "neighborhood" schools will dominate future school plans despite its uneconomic features; assumes that the overwhelmingly white parochial system in key central cities will not cooperate more and more with public systems; assumes that virtually all school district and municipal boundaries will stay frozen.

In evaluating these crucial assumptions, the reader should keep in mind another demographic reality never mentioned by the apostles of separatism: Virtually the same percentages of Negro and white Americans reside in the nation's 212 metropolitan areas—roughly two-thirds of each group. In other words, Negroes comprise the same one-ninth proportion of metropolitan America as they do for the nation at large. As soon as we grasp this important fact, the question of racial numbers acquires a different dimension. Even metropolitan Washington D.C. has many more white than Negro school children, and this racial ratio has not radically changed in recent years.

But is metropolitan *cooperation* (consolidation is not required) truly possible? Were it necessary solely as a device to integrate schools, we would admit that it is, perhaps, utopian. Yet the forces pushing metropolitanism are far deeper. Duplication of services throughout the multiple municipalities of our typical metropolis are grossly expensive and wasteful, and the intensifying pressures on local budgets are generating cross-boundary cooperation in many realms. Two large southern cities— Miami, Dade County, and Nashville, Davidson County—have gone the full route and consolidated their metropolitan areas.

When metropolitan cooperation for racial integration occurs *without* financial incentives, we regard it as an important precedent. Thus, we deem the modest Rochester, Hartford, and Boston experiments as significant forerunners, even though the transporting of small numbers of Negro children to already-existing, overwhelmingly white suburban schools is not an ultimate solution.

Once the Vietnam War draws to a close and federal funds are again available for new domestic initiatives, major support for school construction will almost certainly become a reality. But how will it be spent? It could be spent largely by central cities to build fine new facilities deep in the ghetto—and thereby institutionalize school segregation into the next century. Or it could be used for metropolitan complexes drawing from large and heterogeneous attendance areas. Such school construction funds could be restricted to voluntary, suburban-central city consortia and thus become a powerful incentive for metropolitan cooperation in education. Unlikely? Well, similar federal programs for metropolitan cooperation in other realms have been operating successfully for some years.

Well planned metropolitan complexes spanning all grade levels and convenient to mass transit arteries would provide ideal settings for compensatory efforts, decentralization, and community involvement. Economies of scale would allow truly massive programs of compensation to take place under conditions of social class as well as racial integration. Pie-slice attendance areas would effectively set up decentralized districts without sealing in homogeneous districts by race and class. And though the size of these multiple-school complexes is often cited as antithetical to local participation, numerous educational innovations have been suggested to counter this: parental school boards for the complex with everything but taxing power; smaller individual schools than are now economically possible for "neighborhood" schools; centralized athletic, theatrical, library, medical and other facilities so superb that adults would wish to employ the complex as a community center. Quality takes on a new dimension in these terms.

School integration, then, *is* possible, but we must plan and strive for it if it is to be achieved. Platitudes about school integration being an ideal and ultimate goal are worthless, however, if by our actions we delay or obstruct the process indefinitely. No one claims that attaining school integration will be easy. Yet if the effort is judged impossible before it is made, the prejudgment becomes a self-fulfilling prophecy.

Recognition that large numbers of school age youth are out of school and also out of work has raised questions both as to the adequacy of the existing school programs and as to what can be done to remedy the situation. One solution tried both during the depression of the 1930's and again more recently has been to take these youth out of their home environment and place them in work camps. The specific operation of these camps has been contracted to industrial concerns. This has raised serious questions among school personnel as to whether such operation implied a failure on the part of the public school personnel. Others have suggested that the problem is rather the orientation of those in a position to advise. Franklin Parker, Professor of Education at West Virginia University, describes the scope of the Job Corps program and its antecedents.

Salvaging School Failures:
the Job Corps Acts*

Franklin Parker

Twice in our recent national life we have experimented with federally conceived, administered, and financed schools: in the Civilian Conservation Corps (CCC) during the depression of the Thirties and now in the

* *Phi Delta Kappan* 49:362–68 (March, 1968). Reprinted by permission of publisher and author.

Job Corps during the affluent Sixties. Both educational ventures arose during times of trouble, both were federally established to supplement the public schools, and both were designed to aid those youths whom state-supported education had failed to reach.

SIMILARITIES AND DIFFERENCES

In the 1930's we were in an unprecedented economic depression with over 12 million—one out of every four in the labor force—unable to find jobs. In the 1960's we are in unprecedented prosperity with skilled manpower in short supply while some three million are unemployed. Both the CCC and the Job Corps were concerned with out-of-school and jobless youths from low-income families. Both wanted to salvage dropouts from the public schools, unskilled and unsuccessful youths, many of them frequently in trouble with society. One motive in the CCC program was to provide financial help to the impoverished families of the Corpsmen; of the $30 per month earned by a CCC youth, $25 automatically went to his family. While Job Corpsmen and women voluntarily may (and most do) send allotments home, the prime motive is to teach salable skills with all this entails in job training, social behavior, and psychological confidence. A major intended by-product of the CCC was natural conservation, reforestation, road-building, and state and national park improvement. While some Job Corpsmen do work in conservation centers, the major goal is to impart those productive skills which are required in an urban society rather than to save trees and conserve soil.

The CCC was part of a cluster of New Deal agencies (National Youth Administration, Works Progress Administration, and others) designed, in Keynesian terms, to prime the pump of economic opportunity by government spending. The Job Corps is part of the War on Poverty agencies (Head Start, Upward Bound, VISTA, and others), perhaps Keynesian in theory but mainly designed to enable the hardcore poor to break out of the poverty cycle. The CCC and other New Deal programs were relief-giving and only World War II boom conditions brought full employment. The Job Corps and other War on Poverty programs are essentially remedial and intended to eliminate poverty; it is yet to be seen whether post-Vietnam America achieves its aim of becoming the Great Society.

Class instruction in fundamental learning skills was an afterthought in the CCC. Such instruction has been a carefully planned integral part of the Job Corps from the beginning. The education establishment as represented by the National Education Association was critical of the CCC as a rival, at least for money, to state systems of public education. The education establishment today generally favors the Job Corps and the other War on Poverty programs, although it wants to retain and increase federal aid to public education.

One fundamental factor common to the CCC and the Job Corps in conception and operation is that these agencies were deliberately established to supplement state systems of public education. To accomplish its purposes, the federal government could merely have pumped money into established agencies such as the public schools and welfare agencies. Instead, the Roosevelt Administration chose to create new agencies, to serve new wine in new bottles, with new labels like the New Deal. To a certain extent, as the War on Poverty indicates, the Johnson Administration is doing the same thing. It is understandable that politicians seek to dramatize their programs. It is also understandable that those who conceived the CCC and Job Corps were, insofar as salvaging failures was concerned, seeking alternatives to the established professional welfare agencies, the public schools, state vocational training programs, and state employment agencies—all of which have coexisted with poverty too comfortably for too long.

WHERE PUBLIC SCHOOLS FAILED

The public schools have served middle- and upper-class youths exceedingly well. They have not served deprived youths quite so well. They offer much to youths from good homes who are motivated, ready, and anxious to take advantage of learning opportunities. They do considerably less well in meeting the needs of sons and daughters of low-income families; those youths who happen to be slow learners, live in slum areas, come from broken homes, frequently move from place to place, are members of minority groups, and are often on relief or welfare. Each year during the past decade about a million such youths have failed to receive the education they need for "the good life" in our automated, urbanized society. By one account, this year 750,000 youths between ages 16 and 21 will be on the streets—out of school and out of work.

The public schools are almost invariably better in the suburbs than they are in the inner cities—better in the quality of teachers, in finances, staff, equipment, and student motivation. American public schools do not function well under modern slum conditions, either urban or rural, because all too frequently they are forced to use beginning or inept teachers. The best teachers usually want to teach the best students in the best schools in the best neighborhoods. Our public schools tend to reject seemingly hopeless cases and have not found ways of reaching them. The result is a growing number of young people whom the public schools have failed—the unreached, the children of failures, those with dark images of themselves, the frustrated, the alienated, the bitter, and the violent ones.

HOW POVERTY WAR BEGAN

Several factors shattered the complacency of affluent Americans, opened their eyes to poverty in the midst of plenty, prompted liberal intellectuals and politicians to bring into being a new War on Poverty, and encouraged innovators to turn from old agencies toward ones newly created to make dramatic breakthroughs. The Cold War, the drive for scientific achievement, the establishment of the National Science Foundation, the criticism of progressive education and life adjustment education, the impact of Sputnik I and the space race—all contributed to a quest for quality programs in American education. The Negro protest movement, as it gathered momentum after the landmark 1954 Supreme Court decision on school desegregation, also played its part in focusing attention on the poor, among whom are so many Negroes.

Harvard economist John Kenneth Galbraith's *The Affluent Society,* 1958, took passing note of the hardcore poor whom the majority of Americans seldom see, and is said to have influenced Catholic journalist Michael Harrington, whose *The Other America: Poverty in the United States,* 1962, dramatically described in human terms the stark dimensions of America's hidden poverty. President John F. Kennedy was said to have been impressed by Harrington's book and reportedly it was a factor in his setting up task forces to study manpower, training, and education. These task force reports probed the unduly high rate of rejections on Army induction tests for mental and physical deficiencies. Studies forecast that 26 million youths would enter the labor market between 1960 and 1970 and that, of these, 5.2 million would not have completed high school and 2.3 million would have a grade school education or less. By 1970 it was estimated that only five percent of available jobs would be open to unskilled persons. Such reports caused growing concern about poverty. Suddenly the topic became fashionable. President Kennedy's New Frontier administration set the tone and his task forces drew up the blueprint for national reappraisal. His tragic death touched the American conscience and made it easier for a sympathetic Congress to pass in rapid order a flurry of social welfare and education programs which his determined successor introduced. The Kennedy Administration planned, the Johnson Administration packaged, and the 88th Congress passed the historic legislation which began the Great Society effort.

THE GREAT SOCIETY

Lyndon Baines Johnson was briefly a teacher in a deprived area school. He served during the depression as state director of the National Youth Administration in Texas. Years later in revealing informal remarks to graduates of the Capitol Page School, he referred to one of his early heroes, Rexford Guy Tugwell, one of President Roosevelt's advisors, whose bold views were responsible for some of the New Deal's social welfare programs. Johnson told the pages that when he first arrived in Washington, D.C., 35 years earlier, he had a dream of remaking America, and now he had been given the opportunity to carry out that dream.

Johnson was a President in search of a program in 1964. With a major political victory in sight to make him President in his own right, he sought a program and a plan. It came wrapped in a phrase he had used in a few speeches and one which he raised to capital letters in an address at the University of Michigan on May 22, 1964: THE GREAT SOCIETY. Its aura and mystique enshrined what the education-minded President envisioned as the program which would place his administration alongside Wilson's New Freedom, Roosevelt's New Deal, Truman's Fair Deal, and Kennedy's New Frontier. He said: "We are going to assemble the best thought and broadest groups to prepare a series of conferences and meetings—on the cities, on natural beauty, on the quality of education, and on other emerging challenges. From these studies we will begin to set our course toward the Great Society."

THE WAR ON POVERTY

In his State of the Union message to Congress on January 8, 1964, President Johnson called for an "unconditional war on poverty—not only to relieve the symptoms of poverty, but to cure it and, above all, to prevent it." On introducing the Anti-Poverty Bill which created the Office of Economic Opportunity (OEO), he wrote to Congress on March 16, 1964, "I have called for a national war on poverty." Congressional hearings were held and the legislation was passed in August. Not until the election campaign was over was money appropriated for the OEO under the direction of Sargent Shriver, who then also directed the Peace Corps.

GETTING STARTED

The Job Corps came into existence on October 8, 1964. In the language of Title I of the multifaceted Economic Opportunity Bill, the Job Corps was described as an agency

> to prepare for the responsibilities of citizenship and to increase the employability of young men and women aged sixteen through twenty-one by providing them in rural and urban residential centers with education, vocational training, useful work experience, including work directed toward the conservation of natural resources, and other appropriate activities.

The Job Corps was an idea with a director and appropriate money but little else. In 10 weeks Shriver assembled an outstanding staff including as Job Corps director Otis Singletary, on leave as chancellor of the

University of North Carolina at Raleigh, and as head of program development Wade Robinson, Harvard professor and himself once a high school dropout. Two other educators were enlisted: Lewis Eigen from Temple University and David Gottlieb from Michigan State University, the last also a former high school dropout and now an acknowledged expert on educating the disadvantaged. Harold Brewer, director of employee relations for the International Telephone and Telegraph Corporation, planned the recruitment, screening, selection, and assignment of applicants. Christopher Weeks, a public finance and government efficiency expert, became deputy director. Wray Smith, previous head of Peace Corps training programs, was in charge of operations. Bennetta B. Washington, former principal of Cardozo High School in Washington, D.C., planned and administered the women's centers. David Paynter, professional baseball pitcher turned school superintendent, coordinated the conservation centers.

The Job Corps turned to the conservation agencies for staff to run conservation centers; to the Defense Department and Veterans Administration for old Army bases for training centers; to the General Services Administration for equipment and supplies (often surplus). To get out the word to potential applicants in urban tenements, country backwoods, and on Indian reservations, the Job Corps turned to the departments of Labor; Agriculture; and Health, Education, and Welfare; and also enlisted thousands of volunteers through 35 national organizations. The word went out through personal contact aided by filmstrips, posters, pamphlets, news releases, and always the "Opportunity Card," a postcard application form addressed directly to Washington, D.C. Within six months a nationwide screening network had been established: for male applicants, over 1,900 U.S. Employment Service offices, state employment services, and Community Action Program offices; for female applicants a newly named organization came into being, the Women in Community Service (WICS), a national confederation of women volunteers from Catholic, Protestant, Jewish, and Negro organizations.

On January 15, 1965—a cold, gray, snowy day—30 young men from the streets of Baltimore and the mountains of western Virginia and Kentucky arrived at Camp Catoctin, situated in a national park in the Appalachian foothills of western Maryland. The first center had opened. The Job Corps was in business.

PROFILE OF A CORPS ENROLLEE

The Job Corps has been under constant study; thus a great many statistics, profiles, and follow-up studies are available. As of May 1, 1967, 75,410 youth had gone through the Corps programs. In early 1968, 40,467 youths (30,585 males and 9,882 females) were enrolled in 124 conservation centers, 10 urban centers for men, 18 centers for women, and three special centers. From the total number who have stayed any length of time, the following profile has been compiled: The average male has had 8.8 years of schooling; the average female, 9.8 years. While 40 percent of the males in conservation centers read below the third-grade level, the average male in all centers had a 4.6 grade reading level; female, 6.2 grade reading level. Male competence in mathematics was at the 4.8 grade level; female, 5.5 grade level.

Males from rural areas comprised 19 percent; females, 5 percent. Small towns accounted for 40 percent of the males and 35 percent of the females. Cities of 100,000 or more have provided the remaining 41 percent of the males and 60 percent of the females. Of the males, 63 percent had no criminal record; females, 82 percent. Minor antisocial behavior was reported for 27 percent of the males and 16 percent of the females. Ten percent of the males and two percent of the females had one serious criminal conviction. Of the males, 65 percent had a full or part-time job before entering the Job Corps; females, 50 percent. Of the working males and females, 60 percent had earned less than $1.25 an hour, with a year's reported earnings averaging $639. Of the males eligible for the armed forces, 47 percent failed the induction test, 17 percent for physical reasons and 30 percent for educational reasons. Eighty percent of the males and females had not seen a doctor or dentist in the last 10 years and they averaged seven pounds underweight. Of both sexes, 60 percent came from broken homes, 63 percent from homes where the head of the household was unemployed, 39 percent from families on relief, 60 percent had lived in substandard housing, 64 percent had asked to leave school, and 49 percent had parents with less than an eighth-grade education.

FOLLOW-UP OF CORPS LEAVERS

A continuous series of sample surveys of the 109,610 youths who have gone through some phase of Job Corps programs as of Oct. 1, 1967, indicates that 76,301 or 70 percent got jobs, entered military service, or returned to school. Of these 76,301 youths, 59,515 or 78 percent got jobs; 9,156 or 12 percent went back to school; and 7,630 or 10 percent went into military service. Of those getting jobs, the average youth earned $1.71 per hour as against $1.19 before training, and 39 percent of those in jobs received wage increases. Of the 33,309 youths who were not in jobs, schools, or military service—most had not completed their Job Corps programs—one in seven wanted to re-enter the Job Corps; 56 percent were under 18 years of age; 19 percent had police records; and the remainder had other serious difficulties.

RECRUITING AND SCREENING

The Job Corps makes a special effort to reach eligible youths in high poverty areas and especially rural youths living far from employment offices. To do this it had, as of May 1, 1967, 873 paid screeners plus thousands of volunteers. Referrals of potential applicants to the screening centers are made by the Urban League, the Police Athletic League, the Young Women's Christian Association, and in 23 cities by state technical assistance panels of the Department of Agriculture. Recruiting and screening offices have a quarterly target number of applicants to contact. A typical example of target numbers and those actually recruited and screened by the WICS for fiscal year 1967 were 2,725 first quarter (3,064 actual), 3,717 second quarter (3,266 actual), 8,440 third quarter (3,872 actual) and 4,670 fourth quarter (actual figures not available). Of those recruited and screened, 70 percent show up at assigned centers.

Recruiters and screeners first ascertain whether or not other programs can meet the applicant's needs. They measure the applicant against Job Corps entrance criteria, screen in those most eligible, screen out those for whom the program is not suitable, and finally make assignments to appropriate centers, if possible near the applicant's home. Applicants with low reading skills or a special interest in outdoor work skills are assigned to conservation centers from which most are later transferred to urban centers. The urban centers get applicants with the highest reading skills and special vocational interests. Coordination and referrals are frequent among screeners for the Job Corps, the Neighborhood Youth Corps, and the Manpower Development and Training programs.

PROGRAM COMPONENTS

Conservation centers, managed by the U.S. Forest Service, the National Park Service, and other conservation agencies, accommodate 100 to 200 men. The conservation work consists of picnic and campground construction, involving such skills as masonry, carpentry, and landscaping; road construction and maintenance, involving surveying, heavy equipment operation, and truck driving; trail construction, involving power saw operation and maintenance, and surveying; fence construction; and building construction, involving carpentry, plumbing, masonry, electrical wiring, and blueprint reading. The Men's Urban Centers, accommodating 1,000 to 3,000 men each, offer vocational instruction in mechanical drawing, hospital work, art and photography, clerical and sales work, food services, laundry and dry cleaning, building trades and construction, plant farming, metal machinery, motor vehicle repair, machine operation, printing and duplicating, electrical repair and assembling, and metal fabrication and welding. The Women's Urban Centers, where 250 to 450 girls live, offer occupational training in clerical fields, health and medical services, assembly operations, and beauty shop operation. Remedial instruction includes reading, writing, speaking, basic arithmetic; and for women, home and family life, nutrition, child care, and art. There are recreation periods and physical fitness programs, counseling and guidance, and health services. About half the day is spent in classroom work or supervised job training, and half the day is spent in recreation and center maintenance. Instruction is highly individualized; the ratio is one staff member per 2.5 trainees; and the length of stay, depending on the type of training, may be from a few months to two years.

WHAT THE CORPS ACHIEVES

By June, 1966, statistics revealed that after nine months the average Corpsman had raised his reading level 2.3 grades, achieved two more years of schooling, and gained 10 pounds; 35 percent had been fitted with eyeglasses; and there had been 1.3 dental extractions and six fillings per Corpsman. More difficult to measure are social gains and behavior patterns related to jobkeeping, such as punctuality, cooperation, neatness, manners; and reactions to supervision, criticism, and difficult problems.

Of those completing an advanced training program, 85 percent start working or enter the armed forces or return to school. Salaries increase in proportion to the time spent in training, although those under age 18 have difficulty finding work. The Job Corps has induced the federal Civil Service to reduce its minimum age from 18 to 16.

Through conservation centers, the Job Corps estimates that as of Oct. 1, 1967, it had contributed $28,000,000 to the country in roads, fishing streams, timber stands, watersheds, picnic areas, firebreaks, and landscaping—besides the experience, work habits, health, and sense of accomplishment gained by the trainees.

The Job Corps is a growing education laboratory covering a wide range of vocational and academic abilities while specializing in rapid compensatory learning. Experiments are going on; manuals are being prepared, tested, and revised; sequential lesson plans are being fitted together to try to salvage those whom the public schools frequently have branded as failures. Educational materials developed in the Job Corps are being used in Canada's Project New Start, in the U.S. Air Force Air Training Command, in the District of Columbia Summer School Program, in 25 school systems selected by the NEA and the National Association of Secondary School Principals, and in over 2,000 public schools.

WHAT THE JOB CORPS COST

A year after establishing the Job Corps, Congress set the maximum cost per trainee for 12 months, excluding capital costs, at $7,500. Direct operating costs per trainee have gone down from $8,470 in 1966 to $6,950 in 1967 to $6,700 in 1968. At Congressional hearings on March 10, 1966, critics seized upon the cost and charged that training a Corpsman costs more than sending a student to Harvard University ($2,890 for tuition, room and board per nine months, according to a recent Harvard catalogue). Sargent Shriver replied that the Harvard student had thousands of dollars spent on his previous education while little had been spent on the Corpsman. He added that sums for the Corpsman not figured in the Harvard student's costs included an allowance, home allotment, clothing, medical and dental care, travel, and other sums. If comparable amounts were calculated for the Harvard student, his cost would approach or surpass the amount spent on a Corpsman. Also, a student pays to Harvard about one-third of the true cost, Harvard's endowment making up the rest.

One might also point out that 39 percent of enrollees come from families on relief and that if this 39 percent represented 15,000 families on relief for 20 years at $2,500 per family (such in fact has been the pattern of the poverty cycle), such welfare costs could total over $750,000,000. Further, it has been estimated that a Corpsman earning no more than $3,400 per year for 40 years would more than repay in taxes the government's investment. The chairman of Litton Industries, which manages one Job Corps center, has estimated that the investment per trainee will be recovered by the taxpayer in 5.1 years.

In the March 10, 1966, hearings, Representative Edith Green (D., Ore.) compared her estimate of the Job Corps cost per trainee, $9,120, with the national average public school expenditure per pupil, $484. The annual *instructional* cost per Job Corpsman, $957, falls into clearer perspective when compared with the annual pupil cost in New York City, $1,064, and in Washington, D.C., $765. The Job Corps dropout rate is 21 percent, compared with 31 percent who fail to complete high school in Washington, D.C. Also relevant is a comparison of the Job Corps annual instructional cost of $957 per enrollee with the per pupil cost of $1,072 in 21 inner-city schools in New York City, 80 percent of which are in culturally deprived areas.

INDUSTRY AND THE CORPS

Large corporations which have contracted to run Job Corps centers include the Packard-Bell Corporation at Charleston, W. Va.; Burroughs Corporation, Omaha, Nebr.; General Corporation, Clinton, Ia.; Philco-Ford, Guthrie, Okla.; United States Industries, Battle Creek, Mich.; Radio Corporation of America Service Corporation, Sparta, Wisc.; Thiokol Chemical Corporation, Clearfield, Utah; Federal Electric Corporation, Edison, N.J.; Litton Industries, Pleasanton, Calif.; International Business

Machines, New Bedford, Mass.; Graflex, Inc., Morganfield, Ky.; and Westinghouse Corporation, Edinburg, Ind.

Why does industry do it? Profit is an obvious motive, but under OEO's cost-plus-fixed-fee contract, Litton Industries, for example, makes 4.7 percent profit on its Job Corps center as compared with industry's average 6 percent profit on defense contracts. Industry sees the public service sector, particularly education, as a progressively larger market. With the rapid spread of automation and technology, industry more and more will have to train its own changing specialists. Much talked about now is the possibility that industry may run entire educational enterprises, both private and public.

Industry is often quick to change to whatever brings better results. It does not have to wait until ideas are dragged through faculty committees. Generally, it can hire, fire, reward, expand, contract, and move about rapidly.

Education-run centers may have better thought-out and more well-rounded academic and vocational programs, but the trainees like the real equipment, practical instructors, and job placement results which industry-run centers offer. Industry has a clear edge in organizing Job Corps centers, and the Job Corps chiefs in Washington know this.

TROUBLE IN THE CORPS

At first Job Corps officials in Washington were in a hurry to get started. In their understandable haste to site, staff, and fill centers they made mistakes. Some recruiters and screeners initially oversold the Job Corps idea, and youths arrived expecting to drive big bulldozers right away, have plenty of time for play, and be able to take over the local girls. Center staffs were as new as the raw recruits and in some centers did not have facilities in good receiving and operating order. The initial dropout rate was high. Some unpleasant and sometimes serious incidents broke out. They were immediately picked up by the press and presented in the worst light: knife fights, alleged abuses of townspeople, sodomy, rape, riots in centers too strict or too lax, and charges that women's centers were little better than brothels. Bad news made better reading than good news, and the unfortunate incidents were reported out of proportion to similar occurrences among non-Job Corps youth in communities across the country.

Congressional and other critics have seized upon the inflated reports of these incidents and made much of them. At basic issue is the fear in some Job Corps communities that wild youths, including Negroes from other parts of the country, will "raise havoc." Also, the Job Corps, unlike other OEO agencies which are locally managed, is administered from

Washington, and there is often antagonism to any federally administered operation. Although conditions have improved in recruitment, screening, and counseling procedures; in developing more wholesome relations with community groups; in center staffs who are more numerous, professional, and competent; and in more realistic academic and vocational programs —still, the Job Corps image needs to be improved.

CONCLUSION

Like other adolescents and young men between 16 and 22, the Job Corpsman is going through an ordeal of change. Deprived financially, socially, physically, culturally, and medically, he is more at home with ugliness, anger, and hate than with beauty, moderation, and tolerance. Like many in his environment, he may have grown up fighting, stealing, carrying weapons, and sexually aberrant. Effort and time are required to shake off this inheritance. He must find himself by proving himself. He needs better models than can be found in slums, higher values than can be gained in many broken homes, more attention in studies than the public schools have time to give him. He needs training to get that better job and confidence to hold it. The Negro needs assurance that blacks can win. He needs to step up the ladder. And that is one reason the symbol of the Job Corps is a ladder with an arrow in the middle pointing up.

The Job Corps is, hopefully, a way to make a taxpayer out of a public charge. Surely the cost is less than welfare dependency, juvenile courts, correctional institutions, prisons, and mental hospitals. Surely the cost is less than ghetto riots, pillaging, and guerrilla warfare in our cities. The more the Job Corps can succeed, the quicker it can go out of business, and the better this country will be. The Job Corps, like the CCC before it, is a practical program and a bargain for America.

Providing for the Adolescent Unwed Mother

School policy toward the pregnant high school age student has been a matter of considerable comment for several years. There has been some discussion in school law journals and articles as to whether and under what conditions such students could be expelled from school. The more enlightened position seems to have been that such students were more in need of the services of the school and of society than were other pupils.

*The next article, by Mattie Wright, Co-Director of the Com-
munity Services Project for Unwed Pregnant Adolescents, Chicago
Board of Health, describes a project which attempts to marshall the
services of all of the social welfare agencies in the community—
including the school, the welfare department, and the health department—to aid these students. Such a project might not be the
best solution in the smaller community, although even in relatively
rural areas such boarding facilities would certainly be feasible if
the problems were treated on a large-area basis. Another question
might be raised as to why, with coordination among public agencies,
it might not be possible to do a better job in many other facets of
education, including the general area of sex and family life teaching.
[Since the article was written, the pilot project has developed into
a program, administered by the Florence Crittenton Association of
America, called the Crittenton Comprehensive Care Center.]*

Comprehensive Services for
Adolescent Unwed Mothers*

Mattie K. Wright

The unwed pregnant adolescent girl presents both a dilemma and a
challenge to the helping professions. In part, the dilemma stems from
the lack of understanding of the mixture of medical, emotional, and
social problems involved when the phenomena of adolescence and out-of-
wedlock pregnancy occur concurrently.

Until recently, those services that do exist for unmarried pregnant
girls have tended to focus their attention on girls from middle or higher
socioeconomic groups, while girls in the lower socioeconomic brackets
have received little service. But even for those girls who do receive services,
planning has tended to be fragmented to meet a particular need and
has included little of the coordination of services essential to insure a
comprehensive approach to the problem. However, in recent years there
has been increasing recognition among both professional and lay groups
that services to the disadvantaged teenage unwed mother are especially
important, and that these services must be community-oriented and designed to meet her physical, educational, and mental health needs.

* *Children* 13:5:171–76 (Sept.–Oct., 1966). Reprinted with permission from the
author and of *Children*, Children's Bureau, Welfare Administration, U.S. Department
of Health, Education, and Welfare.

Pregnant girls and their families in the lower socioeconomic brackets have many characteristics in common with girls from middle and upper class backgrounds who are faced with the problem of an out-of-wedlock pregnancy, and I believe we indulge in pure fantasy when we assume otherwise. However, they also carry additional burdens and special problems often unknown to and not experienced by persons of other classes. Many of them are part of families in which communication with one or both parents is largely nonverbal; in which men are rarely seen as part of the sustaining continuity of family life; in which the "good father"— if there is one—is seen primarily as an economic provider; in which the mother feels she has little control over her own fate and even less over the fate of her children; in which serious and chronic medical problems are common. In addition to these disadvantages, these girls are stereotyped by the community as persons who feel no shame for having babies out of wedlock and who are poorly motivated, untreatable, and impervious to acceptable social standards.

Isolated from community resources, such girls are rarely known to any social agency except a public assistance service. Many of them do not make sustained use of what medical resources are available to them until they arrive at a hospital at the point of delivery—confused, frightened, and unprepared. Few resume schooling after their babies come.

In Chicago, in 1963, we made a modest beginning toward meeting the needs of such girls. It was only a beginning, for we were faced with an extensive problem: the rise in the number of cases. In 1964, for example, Chicago Board of Health reports indicated that 2,833 girls of 17 and under had given birth out of wedlock. In 1965, this number rose to 3,144—an increase of 11 percent. Over 75 percent of these girls resided in areas of the city characterized by the lowest per capita incomes, the highest rates of illegitimacy, and the lowest levels of educational attainment; 83 percent in 1964 and 85 percent in 1965 were Negroes. (These figures, of course, do not give the total picture because of under-reporting and "hidden pregnancies" in middle class groups.)

Concern over the lack of coordinated services for these girls prompted the Mental Health Division of the Chicago Board of Health, in February 1963, to set up the Community Services Project. This pilot demonstration was designed to meet on a small scale the comprehensive needs of a selected number of unwed pregnant adolescent girls. Initially supported by a 3-year grant of $169,000 from the National Institute of Mental Health, the project received a 4th year of support to try to build the program into the fabric of basic community services. This is now being done, as I will describe further on.

The project, carried out through the collaboration of the Board of Health, the Board of Education, the YWCA, the Community Referral Service, and a number of voluntary hospitals, offered an array of medical, educational, and mental health services without charge to pregnant girls who were living at home in unfavorable environments. At first, it served only 15 girls at a time, all of them under 16. In 1964, it served 30. All were Negro girls from areas characterized by poor housing, crowded schools, minimal job opportunities, and family disorganization. Many of them were from families in which the only adult was a mother or a grandmother.

An office was secured for the project in a public housing unit, situated in a culturally and economically deprived area of the city, inhabited predominantly by Negroes. In the beginning the staff consisted of a full-time director (a social worker), an additional social worker, a psychologist, a consultant psychiatrist, a teacher, a project coordinator (also a social worker), an administrative assistant, and a secretary. A second staff social worker was added in 1964. In addition, in November 1964, nurses studying for a master's degree in psychiatric nursing at the St. Xavier's College of Nursing were assigned to the project for their field work. Previously, nurses from the Chicago Board of Health instructed the girls in prenatal and postnatal care.

The following criteria were established for admission to the project: The girl must have been in elementary school; in her first pregnancy; not beyond the 7th month; without serious medical problems; and interested in attending school. Girls who were formerly students in classes for the mentally retarded were generally excluded from the project, although some exceptions were made.

EDUCATIONAL PROGRAM

While the initial planners of the project were convinced that medical and mental health services for these girls should be given major attention, they decided that offering the girls an opportunity to participate in an accredited school program was basic to insuring their involvement in the total project.

The educational phase of the program, offering both academic and home arts curriculums, was carried out in a large classroom in a YWCA center located in a housing project which also contained a mental health clinic, a Board of Health prenatal station, a district office of the Cook County Department of Public Aid, and a district office of the Youth Commission. The proximity of these facilities was of great advantage in coordinating services and maintaining a close working relationship between the staffs of the different agencies.

The Board of Education provided the teaching staff, work materials, carfare, and lunch. The school routine and curriculum approximated, as much as possible, those of a regular school classroom.

Early in the project it became apparent that one teacher could not be expected to have proficiency in both academic and home arts subjects, nor could she be expected to provide the remedial and individualized instruction that most of the girls needed. Therefore, in June 1964, the Board of Education replaced the one teacher in the project with two experienced elementary schoolteachers—one trained in academic subjects, and the other in home arts. It was then that the enrollment was expanded to 30 girls.

The teachers placed special emphasis on increasing the girls' incentive and self-direction. They also encouraged the girls to assume responsibility for completing work assignments, caring for materials and equipment, and showing consideration for their fellow students, teachers, and visitors.

A hot lunch, brought in from a nearby high school, was served daily. This not only insured that the girls got at least one well-balanced meal a day, but it also provided opportunity for instruction in table setting, serving methods, table manners, and cleaning up. Each girl was encouraged to learn to work efficiently and quietly while performing the homemaking tasks, to be polite, to converse in a pleasant voice, and to eat a variety of foods.

The skill, sensitivity, and warmth of the teachers enabled them not only to create an atmosphere for learning in which the girls felt secure and accepted, but also to stimulate the girls to raise their level of achievement. Many of the girls responded with greater self-discipline and purpose, not only in their academic performance but also in their behavior and attitudes. They showed marked regularity in school attendance, in contrast to their generally erratic attendance when they were in regular school.

The prescribed curriculum was enriched by a weekly arts and crafts class in knitting, crocheting, embroidery, rug-hooking, and toy-making, conducted by a volunteer. For three summers, a college student, recruited by the Careers in Social Work program, offered individual tutoring in reading to girls especially needing it. In addition, the YWCA offered the girls classes in typing and personal improvement after the regular school day ended.

From February 1963 through February 1966, we had 390 girls referred to the service. Of this number, 108 girls were accepted into the program. The remaining 282 girls were not accepted for the following reasons: advanced stage of pregnancy; chronic physical illness; severe emotional problems; mental retardation; inability to involve the girl's family; limits of project capacity. The excluded girls, however, were accepted for medical care by the cooperating health services.

Of the 108 girls who participated in the project over 60 percent were referred by the Board of Education or the Board of Health's infant welfare stations. Their ages ranged from 11 to 16 years, with a median age of 14. Fifty-nine percent were living in one-parent homes (mother or grandmother only).

Almost one-third of the participating girls had themselves been conceived out of wedlock. The median number of months the girls had been pregnant when admitted to the project was 5; the lowest number, 2; the highest, 8. Eighth grade was the median school level, but a few girls were in the sixth and seventh grades. Seven months was the median duration of enrollment in the project's school—1 month, the shortest period, 14 months, the longest.

The ages of the babies' fathers or putative fathers ranged from 14 to 34 years, with a median age of 17 years. Many were unemployed school dropouts.

MEDICAL SERVICES

Comprehensive medical care, including prenatal, delivery, and postnatal care, was provided for the girls by the Board of Health's Maternity and Infant Care Project, with support from the Children's Bureau.[1] Facilities used were the Board's maternity clinics, its infant welfare stations and special pediatric clinics for high-risk babies, and 12 participating voluntary hospitals. Costs which could not be borne by the girls or their families were borne by the Maternity and Infant Care Project, or, for girls who were receiving public assistance, by the Cook County Department of Public Aid.

In addition, the student in psychiatric nursing arranged special hospital visits for girls close to delivery, visited each girl in her home before delivery and immediately upon her return home, and conducted weekly maternal health discussions with the girls at the school. These meetings were divided into two sections—one for pregnant girls and the other for girls who had already had their babies. They were geared to providing essential health information and at the same time to helping the girls handle constructively the feelings and attitudes associated with their condition.

Excerpts from a report of the health discussion groups by one of these nurses, Judith Meehan, reveal something of the needs of these girls:

> . . . Although I found gross lacks in the girls' knowledge of the basic facts of life, I did not find this surprising or out of the ordinary for this age group. However, without the opportunity for weekly group discussions, I would not have known or been able to ascertain in what areas the deficit was the greatest, and, therefore, needed specific and special attention to fill.

[1] Close, Kathryn: Giving babies a healthy start in life. *Children*, September–October, 1965.

However, what the girls did not lack were gross misconceptions and misperceptions about their bodies—about the function of their bodies and about the care of their bodies. There was a definite need, therefore, to unlearn these misconceptions, misperceptions, and superstitions upon which they have been operating; and then, there was a definite need for factual information from me for the girls to use as a substitute—a realistic substitute. Some common questions and ideas expressed by the girls were: "How come the baby does not drown if it's in a bag of water?" "How do people have babies out of their side?" "Why do some people have stitches and some don't?" "What are the baby's soft spots for?" "If I lift my hands above my head, will the baby strangle?" . . .

It was with their profound curiosity about life—anything and everything—that I often found myself working. Eventually, I became conscious of my stimulating, nurturing, and fostering their curiosity as a very profitable and satisfying means of learning—as a gratifying substitute for their present learning via physical experience only. . . .

. . . Fear of pain during delivery was the most often expressed feeling. Guilt about being pregnant also came up often, but in a sense, it often felt to me like guilt about anything and everything—as if an apology for being alive.

Possibly the greatest demand on me and by me was to convey to each girl that she was important to me—that her ideas, questions, feelings, and thoughts about whatever she wished were important to me. . . .

MENTAL HEALTH

The third focus of the project—the promotion of mental health—involved individual and group counseling, psychological testing, and psychiatric consultation. In addition to scheduling periodic individual interviews with each participating girl, the social workers offered regular interviews to their mothers. However, shortly after the project went into effect, the social workers found that both the girls and their mothers felt threatened by individual interviews and broke many appointments.

Constant reaching out over a sustained period was often required to get both the girls and their mothers involved. Because of the common life experiences of the girls and their mothers, problems in communicating, and social isolation, the staff decided to complement the individual casework interviews with group discussions. We found that the group approach not only furthered our diagnostic understanding of the conflicts, strength, and needs of the girls and their mothers, but also improved both the girls' and their mothers' ability to work on their problems.

The girls met in groups of 12 to 15 each, once a week, for an "educational process and problem-solving discussion" led by the caseworker but carried on chiefly through a free and spontaneous exchange. The emphasis was on problems of living, self-directed learning, stimulation of varied interests, and expansion of horizons. Because these girls tended to be "action-oriented," to respond to the here-and-now, to be "doers" rather than "reflectors," and to fail to see relationship between cause and effect, attempts were made to build on what they had—to help them learn from their experiences and the experiences of others and translate, abstract, and generalize from these experiences rather than to view them in isolation or as something that "just happened to me."

The group offered the girls a broad opportunity for the development of positive relationships with authority figures and with their peers. The leader saw her role as keeping the discussion focused on the girls' immediate problems, controlling impulses, acting as mediator, and creating a growth-inducing atmosphere. In order to help them sustain the gains they had made and recognize that they would need help over a long period of time, not just during their active participation in the project, an after-school, biweekly discussion group was started during the girls' first week in regular school. The 18 girls in this group set up their own goals for these discussions—"to stay in school," "to avoid a second pregnancy," "to develop their personalities."

The leader's role changed with the mothers' group which also met biweekly. At their meetings she was much more directive than with the adolescents, although she did encourage free discussions. The emphasis was on strengthening the woman's mothering role by fostering better self-understanding, building feelings of adequacy, and improving their communications with their daughters. She also helped them plan special activities such as parties and outings with their daughters. Many of these socially isolated mothers developed firm friendships in the group.

CHARACTERISTICS OF THE GIRLS

Most of the girls we served had already repeated one or more grades of school and were functioning academically on a level 2 to 4 years below normal expectations. Many described themselves as having few friends and lacking physical attractiveness, talent, and skill. In general, they were poorly socialized, immature, and impulse-ridden, and had developed few inner controls. They often used aggressive behavior as a defense against feelings of emotional deprivation, dependency, inadequacy, low self-esteem, and isolation from others.

The initial response of the girl's mother to her pregnancy usually reflected high anxiety, stress, and hyperactivity. Feelings of guilt were projected onto the girl or to factors outside of the family. The pregnancy was viewed as an assault upon the family and, for a temporary period at least, it seemed to mobilize the family to better organization. However, the apparent ability of the family to cope with the problems it presented was usually only superficial. Putting up a facade is the mechanism such families have historically used to maintain themselves in the face of continuous and multiple onslaughts on every aspect of their daily lives.

We saw in mothers a deep sense of disappointment—the daughters for whom they had wanted a better life were now caught in the same bind as themselves.

The majority of the girls exhibited a noticeable regression to more infantile and dependent behavior. They said their sexual experience was no different from that of other girls their age and saw themselves as "victims of circumstances" or were generally puzzled that the pregnancy could have occurred. But their feelings of guilt were manifested through somatic complaints and through projecting responsibility for their condition on others. Many had real difficulty in accepting their pregnancy as fact and tried to carry on activities incompatible with their condition. After they had given birth they were usually able to talk about themselves more realistically and to express feelings of guilt, frustration, and unreadiness to assume motherhood.

Most of the girls expressed a desire to keep their babies. But they were rarely able to participate in discussions geared to planning realistically for the child. Many of them seemed to see the baby's identity as being inseparable from their own. They tended to turn to their mothers for direction.

Hence, the mother's own feelings and attitudes, reflecting many complex pressures, bore strongly on the plans for the child. Among these pressures were a strong cultural sense of obligation to care for one's own; the mother's sense of guilt about her own sexual behavior which had produced a child out of wedlock; and her identification with her daughter's situation. Frequently, a girl's mother regarded keeping the baby as a maturing experience for her daughter, or as a means of controlling her future activities, particularly with respect to any future sexual behavior. Some mothers also indulged in the fantasy that the new baby was providing them with a second chance to perform the motherhood role effectively, a role in which they felt they had failed with their own children.

The girl's relationship to the baby's father varied with the girl—ranging from a casual encounter to an intense relationship of long duration. The intensity of the relationship seemed to be associated with the degree of conflict and emotional deprivation experienced by the girl, particularly in her relationship to her mother. Girls often described feelingly how "nice" a boy had been to them and how affectionate, even when they knew he had been involved with other girls at the same time.

We interviewed some of the fathers of the expected babies. Few expressed any responsible interest in the girl's state of well-being, in participating in any planning in her behalf, or in continuing the relationship. Although the girls were unhappy and angry over such abandonment, they continued to engage in fantasies about the positive role the father would assume in their own and their child's life. Most of them had such a strong need for love and affection that they either attempted to continue a relationship with their baby's father or began seeing a new boy.

HOW THEY SAW THEMSELVES

The following excerpts from a record of a group meeting conducted by one of the project's staff social workers, Dolores Exum, reveal something of the girls' self-image.

. . . Ann started the meeting by asking me a direct question about whether I had had sexual relations as a teenager. Joan, Sylvia, and Mamie joined in a chorus, demanding that I answer. Susie and Carrie said that they wanted to be "counted out"—meaning that they were not pushing to have me answer.

I said I wondered why they asked this question. Joan said I was their "idol"—they did not act like it, but I had a lot of influence on them. Ann spoke of her South Shore friends (middle-class neighborhood). They live in houses and go to college; all the girls "put on airs." They take pride in being "virgins." She suspected that I was like the "South Shore kids." Some might be true virgins, but she suspected some knew a lot about birth control.

Since Ann brought up the question, I asked her if she had anything else in mind. She said she wondered whether it were possible to grow into adulthood without having sexual relations. The group thought it was possible, and they talked about what the teachers had said about their teen years. Susie mentioned that Mrs. A said she had grown up in a neighborhood like the ones in which they lived and "she had not given in." Frances and Marie thought it was "luck" that enabled a girl to avoid being seduced. Marie said she would never go steady again. . . .

I talked about my feeling that each girl had within her certain capabilities and strengths which she could use to make for herself the kind of life she wanted. . . . I said I was certain the girls in South Shore had to control their sexual urges, too. Perhaps some know more about birth control because they think it is a good idea to postpone motherhood until they are older and married. I used several examples of thoughts the girls themselves had expressed about how to avoid intimacy in dating relationships.

Mamie suggested writing down things you are unhappy about as a way of "getting things off your chest." Donna said it was "too bad that girls could not talk to their mothers." The only time she was able to feel close to her mother was when she was "high on the roof." Carrie explained that this meant "feeling good from alcohol." Her mother was like that too.

There was an exchange between Mamie, Donna, Carrie, and Ann about being "dragged down" by depreciatory remarks and how their relationships had become more strained with their mothers since their pregnancies.

I suggested that what they had been saying had something to do with why a girl seeks closeness with a boy, and that sometimes a baby was a by-product, which only intensifies a girl's difficulties.

The meeting had been extended past our regular hour. I suggested that we think about what we would like to discuss in our next meeting.

. . . As there were no comments, I suggested birth control. There was considerable enthusiasm.

PLANS AHEAD

As a result of its 3 years of experience in this pilot project, the Board of Education, in February 1966, established the first of several schools planned for unwed pregnant girls in Chicago. Known as the Family Living Center, the school is located in a modern, well-equipped, educational building of a church and is well suited for an academic and vocational training program. The school can accommodate 255 girls at one time, and it is expected that 450 girls will be served in it during a calendar year. As of June 30, 1966, 151 girls (91 in high school and 60 in elementary school) were attending the new school. Thirty of the elementary school-girls in this group were transferred from the original project school. They, along with the others, are receiving health services, as well as some of the additional services described in the demonstration program.

On the basis of the project's demonstration that comprehensive services for the adolescent unwed mother can be provided and effectively used through creative cooperative programing, expansion of the medical, social welfare, and mental health services of the Community Services Project is about to be launched, under a contractual arrangement between the Chicago Board of Health, the Illinois State Department of Public Health, and the Florence Crittenton Association of America.

The new services will be coordinated with the expanding educational services offered by the Board of Education. Together the two programs should go far toward meeting the needs of pregnant school-age girls in Chicago. They will be focused on girls remaining in their own homes during pregnancy who are isolated from the mainstream of urban living and who come from culturally and economically disadvantaged groups, including Appalachian white people, Negroes, Indians, and Puerto Ricans.

The staff of the Community Services Project will be enlarged to include additional social workers (male and female), psychiatrists, an obstetrician, a full-time nurse, and a nutritionist. In addition to complete prenatal and postnatal care for the girls and comprehensive health care for their babies, a network of other services will be offered the girls, their parents, and the putative fathers. These services will be given not only during the girls' pregnancy, but also on a continuing basis thereafter, as needed.

We will also continue recently introduced weekly discussion meetings with the teaching staff, led by a staff psychiatrist. These meetings have not only helped teachers to increase their understanding of the emotional and other factors operating in the girls' situation, but have also increased their ability to make the best use of themselves in their role as teachers. Similar discussions will also be carried out for members of other disciplines on the staff. Regular meetings of the entire staff will also be continued.

Our experience has taught us that comprehensive services necessary for this type of program require the use of many disciplines. It is, therefore, fundamental that staff members function as a team and share their individual training and skills for the improvement of the girls' complete well-being.

There is also a need for all professional disciplines to take a long hard look at the way in which they approach persons who come from other than middle and upper class socioeconomic groups. The time is long past when we can afford to see these people as "untreatable," "poorly motivated," and "impervious" to standards of socially acceptable behavior. Rather, we must assume an aggressive reaching-out role with them. The problem is not one of having to adapt the clients to the techniques and expectations of the various helping professions, but rather, of gearing our approaches to the clients' or patients' special needs and problems.

The Social Role of the School

The topic of the previous article raises what may be the fundamental issue in considering the school's role in a rapidly changing society. Should the school limit its efforts to doing those things which it has always done, or should it be constantly changing its curriculum to meet the needs of its students?

The issues involved are discussed at a very basic level in the next article. Sterling M. McMurrin is a former U.S. Commissioner of Education and since 1966 has been Dean of the Graduate School of the University of Utah.

What Tasks for the Schools?*

Sterling M. McMurrin

Among the large problems that are always with us, none is more persistent, more pervasive, or more basic than the problem of means and ends—of insuring that our methods, techniques, and instruments are adequate to

* *Saturday Review*, Jan. 14, 1967, pp. 40–44. Copyright Saturday Review, Inc., 1966. Reprinted by permission of publisher and author.

the ends we seek, that the ends are relevant to our abilities and, above all, not dominated and determined by our means. In a society that feeds on a rapidly advancing and sophisticated technology, the failure to have clear and forceful purposes and viable ends could be disastrous. We could become the creators of a technological order in which our ends would be defined and established by the instruments that were fashioned to serve us rather than by considerations of human value, an order in which the things that matter most would be at the mercy of the things that matter least.

Nowhere is the problem of means and ends more crucial than in education. Confronted by quite remarkable technical possibilities, we are failing to come to grips with the problem of aims and purposes and to define adequately the proper function of the schools—their specialized role in relation to the educative processes of the whole society and their immediate task in the education of the child. Certainly without clear purposes—large and small, direct and indirect—the schools cannot successfully plot their course amid the present revolution of numbers, dollars, and computers. Most revolutions are lost because their aims are ambiguous and ill-conceived. We cannot afford to lose the revolution in education by being overwhelmed by the new technology because we cannot match it with intelligent and resolute purpose.

Because education is a function of the society and its culture, its purposes are determined by them, by the character of the social institutions and by the values of the culture. In the United States or in any other democratic society, the purposes of education are multiple and complex. The schools, traditionally overconservative in their ways, must cultivate the capacity to change when the conditions of society call for something different or when educational research and technology demand the use of new methods.

The elementary function of education is the perpetuation of the culture. Education is an almost instinctive conservative force that secures whatever is of worth in the social structure and in the substance of the culture. The schools are subtle, sensitive, and highly effective instruments of indoctrination by which every generation gathers up the achievements of the past, employs them in the pursuit of its own ends, and communicates them to future generations.

Our society is marked by scientific intelligence, social conscience, and an acute historical consciousness; it possesses a remarkable capacity for invention and change. Since for us change is inevitable, unless we move forward with resolution our society is in danger of retrogression and our culture in danger of decline. We cannot live simply by the conservation and perpetuation of the past; we must be critical and creative.

The proper function of schools, therefore, is to be the chief agents of progress, whether it is the advancement of knowledge, improvement in the arts, technology, or the social conscience, in institutional organization and administration, or in the attainment of those large visions of the future which are the prime movers of history. For the schools, colleges, and universities provide the most effective means for the achievement of the intellectual skill, knowledge, understanding, and appreciation necessary to the analysis, judgment, and decision without which there can be no genuine progress. We depend upon them to stimulate that freshness of ways, attitudes, and ideas which alone can bring vitality and high achievement to a culture. Achieving an effective relationship between the conservative and creative functions of education is a difficult and unceasing task. Out of the dialectic of conservation and creation issue most of the basic tensions that develop between the schools and their communities.

"Education" refers to society as the totality of socio-economic-political arrangements. It refers, as well, to both the fabric and substance of the culture, its value structure, and its creative process. But in a democratic society the purposes and energies of education must be centered primarily upon the individual, upon the cultivation of his talents and abilities, both for his vocational preparation and the melioration and adornment of his life. And education for the individual means the securing of those conditions which are essential to an authentic individualism.

Deeply imbedded in the political faith of the American people is the belief that whatever contributes importantly to the life of the individual—whatever disciplines his mind, nourishes his values, refines his sensitivities, and prepares him for a productive vocation—contributes also to the solidarity of the society; and that it also brings strength and vitality to the culture and adds to it that authenticity and integrity of spirit without which no civilization can hope to endure. So the purposes of education must be sought across the total spectrum of human interest, experience, and value. The task of education seen in this context is nothing less than the achievement and preservation of a genuinely free society in which men are authentic persons who are masters of the forces which shape their world.

In the past, educators have invested excessively in the development of educational *methods*. There has been too little concern for the *substance* of education and a minimum of interest in its purposes. With the new curriculum reforms the question of substance is gradually gaining the attention which it deserves; but the purposes are still neglected and confused. The all-too-common domination of educational thought by the interest in methodology has meant that method has often been the major determinant of substance and purpose. Our schools would have been much stronger today and would now more effectively perform their function if we had brought the problems of method and substance and purpose into a more honest and effective relationship.

This does not mean that the methods of instruction can be treated indifferently. The discussion of the purpose of the schools, for instance, cannot ignore the developments in educational technology which must now become major factors in our educational planning. This would be an untenable and disastrous separation of means and ends and could lead to gross distortions in the whole structure of education—and, eventually, the destruction of the humane values that we seek through the schools. But the proper ends of education can be realized only if they are placed within the grasp of the schools, where the educational program is designed to conform to the immediate and proximate ends that our methods and expertness are capable of achieving. In view of the great promise of educational technology that it may make new things possible, we should refine our goals and be prepared to move in new directions of learning.

The central tasks of the school are the dissemination of knowledge, the cultivation of the intellect, and induction into the uses of reason. We expect the schools to do many things: to discipline the moral life by sharpening the powers of discernment, making the moral conscience more sensitive and increasing the sense of civic responsibility; to nurture the esthetic life by cultivating artistic appreciation and creativity; to strengthen the spiritual life by refining the sense of worth and value and investing life with meaning and purpose. But unless a school concentrates its purposes first upon knowledge and reason, it will not contribute importantly to these things; rather, it will confuse its purpose, dissipate its energies, and utterly fail in its responsibility.

This does not mean that the educational process should be subordinated to the simple communication of information. The quest for knowledge means far more than this. It entails the full development of the intellectual capacities of the individual, a development that is quite impossible in any other context. It is here that the mind achieves its powers of sensory perception and discrimination; here the individual learns to distinguish the meaningful from the meaningless and gains respect for evidence and for logical discourse. Here he cultivates his powers of intellectual sight, analysis, and generalization, his capacity to discern the universal in the particular, and his comprehension of cause and effect, of order and structure, and his understanding of the nature of theory and the relation of theory to practice. And most important, it is here in the actual pursuit of knowledge that even a child finds the joys of knowing and the virtue of intellectual honesty and develops the passion for truth.

There are, in effect, three primary functions of instruction, which are defined by the immediate task of the schools: the cognitive, the affective, and the conative functions.

► The cognitive function of instruction is directed to the achievement and communication of knowledge, both the factual knowledge of the sciences and the formal relationships of logic and mathematics—knowledge as both specific data and generalized structure. It is discipline in the ways of knowing, involving perception, the inductive, deductive, and intuitive processes, and the techniques of analysis and generalization.

It involves both the immediate grasp of sensory objects and the abstractive processes by which the intellect constructs its ideas and fashions its ideals.

► The affective function of instruction pertains to the practical life—to the emotions, the passions, the disposition, the motives, the moral and esthetic sensibilities, the capacity for feeling, concern, attachment or detachment, sympathy, empathy, and appreciation.

► The conative function involves overt behavior—struggling, striving, impulse, commitment, desire, decision, action, and the power of will.

I am not proposing a return to the theory of mental faculties that was long ago abandoned as a gross distortion of the complex character of the human mind and its behavior. But to see these basic categories in the description of the mental functions is to see the intricate and difficult structure of education and to sense the enormity of its task. Most of our work and most of our success has been with the cognitive function of instruction, which is admittedly primary. We know more about cognition and our tools and techniques are best adapted to its task. We are only beginning to move effectively in research into the regions of the affective and conative functions, and we have a long way to go before we will be on firm ground. Here especially there is need for openness, creativeness, and innovation in the substance and methods of education and in the preparation of teachers. The affective and conative facets of education, though less primary, are not less important. But they are more difficult to understand, assess, and negotiate. When we face the challenge of the new technology—how to employ for proper educational ends such instruments as television, teaching machines, or computer systems—our decisions must be made in the light of the total impact of instruction upon the individual, centering upon knowledge and the rational intellect but not violating the claims of the emotions and volition.

We should recognize here another useful distinction in the total structure of the educational process, what may be called simply verbal-conceptual education as compared with nonverbal-nonconceptual education. In occidental culture especially, our preoccupation with knowledge, reason, and abstraction has produced assumptions, methods, and habits of education that are directed primarily to the construction and communication of ideas and complex conceptualized structures that are highly dependent upon language and language skills. The educated person is one who can deal successfully in a kind of conceptual coinage, whose achievements are especially in the ability to use words and mathematical or logical symbols effectively and to reason discursively in the formation, examination, and exchange of ideas.

I would not depreciate the worth of this dominant element of our education. It is the chief foundation stone of our culture. Upon it depend our philosophic thought, our science and technology, and much more that is precious and basic to the whole structure of our civilization. But we must ask whether in immersing ourselves so exclusively in this cognitive function of education—in education for verbal-conceptual abilities—we have not severely neglected other important and sometimes simpler facets of personality and life—the esthetic pleasures, for instance, that accrue from sharpening the instruments of sensory perception, or the intrinsic values in the appreciation of poetry and art which are available to those whose education has cultivated their intuitive powers and refined their capacities for sympathy and feeling. Or consider the whole area of what we commonly and somewhat loosely call the inner life. This is crucially important territory about which we know little and do less. We cannot assume that because we have been so eminently successful in building a high civilization on the foundations of philosophy and theoretical science we are justified in our failure to explore fully the large possibilities that are open to us to augment and strengthen our cultural achievement.

It is a simple matter to theorize on what is appropriate or inappropriate to social institutions, but it is quite another thing to shape those institutions in practice to conform to the ideal concepts which we construct of them. The schools in fact are subject to countless divergent and conflicting pressures. Their problems are set for them by the real forces of society, and any serious educational planning must respect those forces. Certainly one of the central issues confronting us today is the question of whether the schools should serve other social functions than education as traditionally conceived—the question, for instance, of the limits of their custodial responsibilities, of their obligations to become recreation or community centers, or, far more important, of whether they should be employed as instruments of social policy, as in the enforcement of civil rights laws.

It would be more accurate, of course, to ask not whether these should be school functions, since in various ways they already are well established, but rather to what degree these should be school functions. For among the important causes of the schools' failure to achieve their educational goals is the habit of society of imposing obligations upon them which are foreign to their character, for which they may not be well equipped, and which have little or no relevance to the central purpose of education. More and more the schools are expected to share the tasks of the home in rearing the child, to assume a larger responsibility for the social life of youth, to take on social work which properly belongs to other public agencies, to accept responsibility for delinquency, to bear the blame for every moral deficiency of the individual or the society. The large failures of society in matters of civil rights and race relations, for instance, as expressed especially in the employment, income, and housing patterns of the great cities, have placed an enormous burden upon education. The schools are expected to effectively pursue the proper ends of education and at the same time solve problems of segregation and racial discrimination for which they may be in no way responsible and for which there are no solutions short of a complete and total effort by all agencies and segments of community life.

This is not to suggest that the schools can or should avoid the social tasks that are clearly a part of the educational enterprise and for which they can mobilize effective resources. They have obvious organizational advantages and professional competencies for mounting difficult social problems. But when society fails to recognize the limits that are proper in such matters, it seriously endangers the quality of future intellectual attainment.

The determination of the purposes and ends proper to education is the chief task of the philosophy of education, a discipline which in recent decades has fallen into serious confusion from which it is only now beginning to recover. For some time the philosophy of education has often been reduced to a more or less standard format in which educational policies and procedures are allegedly, by virtue of appropriate intellectual contortions and logical distortions, deduced from premises established in metaphysics, the theory of knowledge, or theory of value. This kind of argument has produced much confusion and not a little dogmatism. Certainly the basic considerations of education have relevance to the nature of reality, the nature of knowledge, and especially to value theory and specific value concepts. But such central issues in the philosophy of education as the purposes of education must be decided not so much by deduction from abstract speculative theses as by such practical considerations as the threat of cultural decline, the establishment of social justice, the national security, the need for strengthening the economy and for satisfying its manpower demands, the aspiration of individuals toward artistic expression, their vocational and professional interests, their anxieties and frustrations, and their demand for autonomy and freedom.

The nation faces a future that is fraught with difficulties and uncertainties. Threatened from without by enemies of overwhelming strength and affected within by the subtle yet powerful forces that issue from the clash of economic interest, the processes of urbanization and industrialization, racial tensions, and political struggle, and endangered by irrationalism, bigotry, and growing personal and social anxieties, it needs as never before the full development of its intellectual capabilities. This means nothing less than achieving the maximum possible education for every individual—education in the requisite knowledge and skills for vocation and profession, and education in that humane knowledge and wisdom that frees the mind from the bondage of ignorance and the spirit from hopelessness and fear. Only a full commitment of our intellectual, moral, and spiritual resources will bring to the culture the vital energy essential to greatness in the years ahead. And only an educational effort that far exceeds our past accomplishments will preserve the distinctive personal quality of life that must always be the mark of a free people.

Section II

The Program of the American Secondary School

THE PROGRAM OF THE AMERICAN PUBLIC HIGH SCHOOL HAS DEVELOPED IN three different channels: the formal curriculum, the extra-class activities, and the program of counseling and guidance. These three aspects are not separate responsibilities. Rather they are three different ways of providing for the needs of high school students.

In the following section, two chapters have been devoted to the curriculum. One deals with what seem to be the more traditional aspects of curricular organization and the other deals with their later modifications. The development of American education has been more frequently the result of redesigning old patterns than of creating new ones.

Difficulties which arose in attempts to reconstruct the curriculum forced the development of the program of informal or extra-class activities. The modern emphasis on the school as a laboratory sets the tone for improvement but the true potential of the informal program as an educative force is still seldom realized, perhaps because of the slowness of the public and even of the teachers to realize its importance and worthiness.

The development of counseling and guidance as a district feature of school organizations followed logically from the school's assumption of responsibility for providing for all of the children of all of the people in a program originally designed for the children of the few. These activities would be important, however, even if only the select few went to high school. School personnel have come to recognize that large schools in particular are likely to be impersonal. Most of the guidance services of the school serve to personalize its program.

Current pressures in American society are causing both professional school personnel and laymen to take stock of desirable additions to the school curriculum. Possible modifications range from total restructuring of existing courses through reorganizing the grouping of grades to new emphases on family life and vocational education.

6

Older Aspects of Curricular Organization

By the time the structure of the American public high school had become crystallized around 1900, it had developed several distinctive characteristics. Among these were the scheme of departmentalization, the Carnegie unit system,[1] a four-year pattern, the concept of graduation, the concept of passing and failing, and the concept of the high school as a college preparatory institution. These are so familiar at the present time as to seem hardly worth mentioning, and yet, none of them is essential to the role of the high school. Much of the suggested modification of the school during the past half century has related to these aspects. Some of the changes to be anticipated in the future will also affect them.

Departmentalization

Basic to the organizational pattern of the high school, as it had developed during the nineteenth century, was the concept of specialization in subject matter. This had been less true of the Latin grammar school because in that school the general subject matter was Latin, there was likely to be a single master, the student body was usually small, and there was essential continuity from one year to the next. The academy broke away from this pattern. Variety of subject matter was the theme of Franklin's suggestions. Later the Latin grammar school, in order to compete, found it had to add such courses as English and mathematics to its own curriculum in imitation of the academy's.

As the high school replaced the academy and began to grow larger and to employ more than one teacher, departmentalization became fixed.

[1] This system is explained later in the chapter.

127

Specialization seemed the logical approach to the staffing of a curriculum as broad as the one adopted. Furthermore, the pattern of the college had become established and specialization was becoming a part of the structure of that institution. The system of preparing teachers increased the trend.

Despite the advantages which stimulated its development, the system of specialization at the high school level also has serious drawbacks. The most obvious is that a teacher has to work with such a large number (usually 150 or more) of students in the course of one school day. The system also limits the selection of content for the curriculum. When the important formal instruction offered to a particular group of 16-year-olds is limited to subjects labeled World History, Algebra I, Latin II, Biology, and English Grammar and Literature, many of the problem areas of life in modern times will be neglected. Even those topics which are covered will probably be dealt with out of the context of their significance in modern living. The student is more likely to be judged on his mastery of the subject matter than to be encouraged to develop those particular skills and concepts which help him to become a more effective person.[2]

Recognition of the limitations imposed by the current type of daily schedule has brought the recommendation by Conant for a longer day with shorter class periods.[3] While this would help to increase the number of different courses a particular student might take, it would still not solve the other problems created by departmentalization. It would instead increase the tension and the problem of unity in the program for the student. It would also increase the number of hours the student must remain at school.

If the high school is to provide for specialized as well as general education, some departmentalization in the areas of specialization may be necessary. Not every student in high school need study shorthand. Similarly, high school physics may appropriately be a part of the learning experience of some high school students without necessarily being appropriate for all of them. It is in areas such as these, where instruction is to be provided for only part of the high school age population, that departmentalization is likely to seem most useful.

Specialization at the high school level is often justified on the grounds that it is traditional. Until other logical ways of organizing subject matter have been found, it may seem more convenient to depend on old approaches, as illogical as they may be to the new purposes of American secondary education. There is also pressure from colleges for students to present to them units of credit based on departmentalized instruction. It is, however, possible to report the results of high school instruction in

[2] Cf. Louise E. Hoch and Thomas J. Hill, The General Education Class in the Secondary School (New York: Holt, Rinehart & Winston, Inc., 1960), pp. 5–8.

[3] James B. Conant, The American High School Today (New York: McGraw-Hill Book Company, 1959), p. 62.

traditional ways without having to carry on using the same methods of teaching.[4]

What seems to be needed in the high school is some method of providing for specialized and high-level instruction, and yet avoiding the situation in which students see each teacher only briefly and can never feel more than some cog in the educational machine. For each student to be taught by fewer, not more, teachers seems the better approach to individualizing instruction, whether for the bright or the dull.

That it is possible to deal with a variety of types of subject matter without an extreme emphasis on specialization may be seen from a glance at the curriculum of the elementary school. A single teacher working with a group of not more than 30 or 40 students teaches a diverse range of subjects including reading, language arts, social studies, the sciences, health education, and even physical education. In many schools the elementary teachers are also responsible, under the supervision of specialists, for music and art. It is true that many of the concepts developed in the elementary school are of a simpler nature than those of the secondary school and may require less specialized background on the part of teachers. On the other hand, there is in the elementary program quite a diversity of teaching skills required to cover so wide a range of subject matter. There is probably very little difference in the complexity of the ideas being developed at the upper elementary grade levels and those of the high school level.[5]

It is interesting to note that, partly as a result of the climate of criticism in the early 1960's of all aspects of public education, there are strong pressures toward departmentalizing the elementary school curriculum. Some of these pressures have resulted in specific experiments in this direction. As yet there is no adequate proof of the success of such projects even in the achievement of limited goals such as mastering skills or subject matter. The vast weight of professional opinion of specialists in elementary education is opposed to this development.

The Carnegie Unit

The movement at the end of the nineteenth and beginning of the twentieth centuries to standardize both the high school curriculum and college entrance requirements led to the adoption of what has since been called the Carnegie unit. In defining this unit, both class work and homework were considered. All work which was followed for a specified number of

---

[4] Cf. R. L. Amsdon and J. S. Tertwilliger, "A Survey of Secondary School Marking Practices and Policies," NASSP Bulletin 50:1–37 (March, 1966).

[5] Cf. Hazel C. Hart, "Classroom Structures Rapidly Changing," Education 86: 195–201 (Dec., 1965).

class periods and which required a specified amount of out-of-class preparation was defined as of equal value. The length of the standard year of work in any subject was set at 120 clock hours. Work which did not require out-of-class preparation would count for half of the credit carried by work which did. The standard length of time to be expected for homework was to be twice the amount of time spent for class work.

While modifications in minor aspects of the measurement of high school credit have occurred, the basic pattern remains the same as that recommended in 1906.[6] The value of work is still determined by reference to the Carnegie unit. There are relatively few courses of irregular length in the high school schedule even though it might seem reasonable to assume that some subjects would logically require more time and others less. Some students can master standard units of work in much less than the usual periods of time and others require much more. Where, as in the case of Economics and Sociology, short courses are offered, they are likely to be scheduled for a semester and paired with another half unit course.[7]

While the length of the class period has been increased in many schools, the 45 minute period for a term of 180 days acts as a standard. Some schools, when they added time to the period, indicated to the students and teachers that the additional time was for supervised study, thus perpetuating an archaic distinction between teaching time and study time. The requirement of two hours' homework for every hour of classroom recitation has been largely abandoned for reasons to be discussed later. Such areas as music, art, and industrial arts are appraised at only half of the value of other more traditionally academic subjects such as mathematics and history. While the distinction is perhaps harmless, it contributes prestige to some subjects not justified by their content.

One danger of describing the high school program in terms of Carnegie units is that it makes the process of modifying the schedule unnecessarily difficult. If it were not so easy to count units, it might be easier to arrive at a more flexible scheme of organization. Admittedly, it is convenient to be able to transfer units of credit from one school to another. There is the presumption that these units describe similar learning experiences. The fact that, even if two students have the same recorded credit from the same school, they still have two different kinds of education is overlooked. The counting of credits is easy; the evaluation of learning is difficult.

[6] Ellsworth Tompkins and Walter Gaumintz, "The History of the Carnegie Unit," *NASSP Bulletin* 48:5–25 (Jan., 1964).
[7] See Grace S. Wright, *High School Graduation Requirements Established by State Department of Education* (Washington, D.C.: U.S. Office of Education, 1958), Circular No. 455.

The Four Year Program and Graduation

One of the distinctive aspects of the American high school program as it had evolved by the end of the nineteenth century was its length. European secondary schools were typically six- but frequently seven- or eight-year institutions. The way the American college evolved was responsible for the discrepancy between European and American secondary school systems. The freshman and sophomore years of the American college would in the European system have been a part of the secondary school's instruction rather than the university's.[8]

So chaotic was the college's status at the end of the nineteenth century that it was not easy to tell which of the institutions (many of which had evolved from former academies) were truly colleges and which were strictly secondary schools. College accrediting associations were then created in an attempt to straighten the matter out. They found that the easiest way to distinguish the college from the secondary school was to require students entering the college to have some standard quantity of secondary school training. Out of this confusion came the Carnegie unit, the four-year college, and the four-year high school. Even before the dust had settled, there was pressure to revise the secondary school program to make it include more than four years of work, but the four-year program had jelled sufficiently to resist such pressure.

The Carnegie unit discussed in the preceding section acquires its importance from the fact that typically 16 such units are required for graduation. Here the curious dependence of the high school program on subject departmentalization becomes most evident. Traditionally, the student who finds some way to complete the 16 required units in less than the traditional four years is entitled to graduate. The student who is unable to complete 16 units, including certain required ones, does not graduate no matter how long he may remain in school. The accumulation of units, not the passage of time, determines the completion of the secondary school program. Students may repeat courses several years in succession before successfully completing them. The number of years of attendance is not considered particularly significant. Nor is the education acquired outside of the formal 16 units considered in the process of measuring achievement.

School principals who think students might profitably take more than the standard four units of work each year are faced with the problem of persuading them that they should still remain in high school for the four full years. The principals feel the student's maturity is of as much im-

[8] John Francis Cramer and George Stephenson Browne, *Contemporary Education* (New York: Harcourt, Brace and World, Inc., 1956), pp. 217–18.

portance as the rate of exposure to particular subject matter. But, because the program has been described for so long to parents, students, and the colleges as a 16-unit program, it is difficult to make people see there may be merit in staying on after the regular requirements have been completed.

Aside from the question of counting credits, there is a more subtle problem involved in the use of a quantitative measure of educational accomplishment. Because individuals are different and yet everyone needs teaching, it is difficult to describe what constitutes appropriate minimum content to be mastered by all of them within the space of four years. It would, also, be difficult to be sure that four years is the best quantity of time for everyone to remain. It is for convenience that American secondary education is described as a four-year program instead of as a three-year, five-year, six-year, or eight-year one. It was likewise a matter of convenience which made it seem desirable that a student acquire 16 instead of 18 or 25 units of credit. The biggest problems arise when the rigid administrative convenience of the system becomes a barrier to intelligent adaptation of the program to the needs and conditions of the students who are attending.[9]

Development of the high school diploma as a symbol of completing the program also presents some very interesting problems. The necessity of establishing uniform standards for comparing types of achievement which by their nature are not comparable, is questionable. The more important the diploma becomes, the more serious becomes the question. When only a small portion of the population graduated from high school, and when it was obvious that many of those who did not were as competent as those who did, failure to graduate was not so important. When, however, the bulk of the secondary age population has begun to qualify for the diploma and when job opportunities and hence station in life become dependent on graduation, the matter becomes more serious.[10] (The fact that the curriculum bears little relationship to the job which the student may do after he leaves the school raises a further question: is it wise to place so much weight on graduation as a basis for employment?)

One of the by-products of having the diploma as a symbol of completing the high school program, and accepting it as a measure of quality, is a tendency to criticize the school for any weakness or failure of the graduate in his job or further education. The school's role, however, is to contribute as much as possible to the development of the student in many facets of his living; it should be only incidentally concerned with *certifying*

---

[9] *Cf.* Harold B. Alberty and Elsie J. Alberty, *Reorganizing the High School Curriculum*, 3rd ed. (New York: The Macmillan Company, 1962), pp. 28–30.

[10] Robert W. Young, "The Irrational Curriculum," *NASSP Bulletin* 51:46–52 (Sept., 1967).

his vocational or educational competence. The fact that the student himself may have been of low native ability, from a weak social background, or simply not yet mature enough to perform the tasks to which he has been assigned is likely to be overlooked.

The development of the diploma as a symbol has been accompanied by a tendency of the school, and the public at large, to ignore responsibility for students who do not graduate. Most school faculties will point with pride to the success of the graduates. The size of the group of students who fail even to finish school is frequently forgotten.[11] Emphasis on the students likely to receive diplomas results in encouraging some students to drop out. What cannot be completely ignored is that most graduates come from the upper social levels. When the symbol of success is reserved for achievement which is not necessarily otherwise significant and is affected by distinctions based on social class which are not desirable, there are serious grounds for criticism.

While the proportion of students remaining in high school until graduation is steadily increasing, the percentage for 1964–65 for the country as a whole was only 73.9 of the ninth graders. This ranged from a low of 57 per cent in New Mexico to a high of 89 per cent in California.[12] First time enrollment in bachelors degree programs in the fall of 1963 was only 53 per cent of the size of the spring graduating class and only approximately 41 per cent of the ninth graders four years earlier.[13]

Significant numbers of students who might continue profitably into college drop out after graduation from high school. They have been encouraged to feel that they are through learning and are ready to seek gainful employment. While this feeling may not be entirely the fault of the secondary school, it still seems unfortunate that there should be any indication that a student can safely stop his education short of the best development of his potential for which schooling is available. Careful studies still seem to show that there are approximately as many capable students who do not continue their formal education as there are who do.[14]

One of the techniques by which the diploma is maintained as a symbol is the graduation ceremony. Doubtless this ceremony serves useful purposes both as a public relations effort of the school among its patrons and as an incentive to students. Nevertheless there are hazards in the emphasis on diplomas which make it worthwhile to consider the possibility of a less dramatic ritual.

[11] J. S. Umstattd and Robert D. Thornton, "Secondary Education-Student Population," *Encyclopedia of Educational Research*, 3rd ed. (New York: The Macmillan Company, 1960), p. 1278.

[12] "State Ranking, 1964–1965," *NEA Research Bulletin* 43:1:24–27 (Feb., 1965).

[13] *Digest of Educational Statistics* (Washington, D.C.: U.S. Department of Health Education, and Welfare, 1964), pp. 6, 73.

[14] Robert J. Havighurst and Bernice L. Neugarten, *Society and Education* (Boston: Allyn and Bacon, Inc., 1951), p. 227.

Related to the pomp and ceremony is the practice of determining a valedictorian and of publicizing the academic ranking of members of the senior class. This custom seems to go back to the earliest days of American education. In the colonial colleges it was the practice to establish the social rank of students and to seat them in their rank order. With the development of more democratic ideas this was stopped, but the idea of recognizing the best students at the time of graduation from high school was allowed to evolve.

The development of the elective course principle has led to some abuse of the system on the part of ambitious students and their parents. Class standing has become of such social importance that hard subject matter or teachers may be avoided for fear that standing might be jeopardized. Pressure is felt by teachers to give some children better grades than they deserve. Since the decisions as to which students should get honors are frequently quite close, hard feelings are likely to arise between school officials and parents of children who are not selected.

As serious as any of these problems is the unreliability of the process by which the decisions as to rank are made. Numerical grades are averaged and quotients carried to the third, fourth, or fifth decimal place. Since the numbers themselves are not reliable to the whole unit value, the final result is almost meaningless. Out of a total of 16 grades, a difference of one grade based on a variation in a single teacher's estimate of the merit of a student's work could affect considerably his relative standing.

For those who accept the idea that the school should be less concerned with the approximate relative standing of a student than with his attainment of his own potential, the system of ranking seems out of place. For such people, each student not only starts with a difference in native potential but develops in a different environment. The school has accepted equal responsibility for the welfare of each student. The systematic rewarding of those who, because of superior potential or superior environment, have achieved the most obvious success is questionable. It is desirable to depend more on the idea that virtue is its own reward, that the merit of accomplishment is to be found in the intrinsic value of the thing accomplished and not so largely in the extrinsic recognition accorded by such devices as announcing class rank.

The Concept of Passing and Failing

In the minds of many teachers and students the last resort in motivation is the promise of a passing grade or the threat of failure. This practice fits rather closely into the system of counting course credits for graduation. Because it fits into the established order of things, it is one of the obstacles to modifying the traditional system. For instance, teachers sometimes defend unreasonable assignments by reiterating that unless the student undertakes them he cannot expect to pass the course. Better teaching procedures are by-passed because they complicate the matter of assigning passing or failing grades.[15]

The classification of students as ninth, tenth, eleventh, or twelfth graders who have failed one or more subjects is somewhat arbitrary. In most schools such classification is based on their possible ability to complete a program with a particular age group. In the social hierarchy of the school, social status is in part dependent on grade placement. Unfortunately, the student who is recognized as retarded is likely to be considered by both teachers and classmates as inferior even to the group with whom he is classified.

The problem in defining the basis for promotion is to decide what is to be the minimum level of acceptable work. For many years there was a great deal of faith in the existence of such a minimum. Secondary curricula of the eighteenth and nineteenth centuries describe the course work for a particular year as containing so many books of Caesar or Euclid. In later years, the English program tended to be described as consisting of the study of certain specific classics. Gradually the assumption was made that passing consisted of mastering a certain percentage of the material covered in the prescribed course of study.

When it was recognized that the total amount taught could not be measured, the difficulty of using the concept "passing = mastery of a percentage of the total taught" began to be realized also. For one thing, each student was likely to learn something different from a particular kind of instruction. For another, it was sometimes important to require complete mastery of some material before a student moved on to the next level. The mastery of 70 per cent of it did not seem to assure sufficient understanding to justify moving ahead.

The criterion for passing is often the development of sufficient competence to be ready to proceed to the next level. Students who are enrolled in Algebra I are expected to have mastered sufficient material to be ready to begin Algebra II. Students in Spanish I must be ready to continue with the work of Spanish II. The presumption is that the content of Algebra II or Spanish II is sufficiently well-defined for teachers to know what is a necessary prerequisite. The problem of determining what is essentially prerequisite is almost the same as that of determining a percentage of mastery. The necessary prerequisite would vary somewhat from student to student and the content itself must also be varied from student to student.

---

[15] *Cf.* Dan F. Cagle, "How May We Make the Evaluation and Reporting of Student Achievement More Meaningful?" *NASSP Bulletin* 39:24–27 (April, 1955).

A third concept of passing is based even more arbitrarily on the use of scores on particular tests or series of tests. In the attempt to avoid the subjectivity of the decision as to what constitutes satisfactory accomplishment for a particular grade level, teachers hide behind the notion of accepting the score obtained on objective tests. They fail to recognize that the selection of the score which is to serve as their "cut-off" point is itself quite arbitrary. Furthermore there is no recognition of the fact that causes for low achievement on the tests needed to be considered.

Systems of promotion from one grade level to the next are usually expected to provide motivation for students to work harder and to ensure some minimum level of proficiency at advanced levels. This expectation is based on an assumed constancy of the subject matter appropriate for different students at any grade level. If the curriculum is really tailored to individual needs, then there is no common basis for all students on which the percentage of mastery can be logically computed.[16]

Not only is it hard to define the appropriate passing level, it is hard to measure the learning which has taken place within any individual. Some students come to a course knowing much of the material which is to be taught. Others come with distinctly different orientation to the content of the courses. Particular instruction may have the effect of helping some students to fill in gaps in factual information, while it helps others to change their attitudes toward certain social problems. Each kind of learning is important, but it is not often possible to compare them. Nor is it possible to decide which skills, attitudes, and information are essential and which are merely desirable. Even when the students involved are well known, it is difficult to say what is desirable in terms of their development.

If the teacher is correct in his decision as to which are the essential skills, attitudes, and information, he is still faced with the problem of measurement. The easiest of the outcomes to measure is rote mastery of information. Even in this case, he is faced with serious problems as to whether the information is meaningful to the student—that is, whether he is capable of using it or whether it may have been memorized for the purpose of passing a test and will soon be forgotten.[17] The measurement of some skills is possible, but it is difficult to be sure whether the student will be able to maintain the skill until the time when he will need to use it. The measurement of attitudes is even trickier. There is the risk of interfering with the right of a student to maintain his own independence of action and opinion. It is not desirable to require students in a demo-

---

[16] A. Harry Passow and others, "Adapting the Curriculum to the Needs, Capabilities, and Talents of Individual Students," *Review of Educational Research* 27: 277–86 (1957).

[17] Robert L. Ebel and Dora E. Damrin, "Tests and Examinations," *Encyclopedia of Educational Research*, 3rd ed. (New York: The Macmillan Company, 1960), p. 1508.

cratic society to pretend to accept attitudes which they have not yet accepted. It is, however, important to inform them of prevailing attitudes in its culture.

The decision as to the appropriate mark is complicated further by the problem of whether to reward achievement in relation to an absolute standard or to the progress which the student has made. It seems unfortunate to say that a student who has made considerable progress has failed. It seems equally unfortunate to say that a student who may be at a relatively high level and for whom the work of the course was relatively inappropriate should fail because he seems to have made little progress.

The differences between students seem to make a farce of any aspect of the program of the school which attempts to establish standard subject matter or standard application of selective devices to the students. The most acceptable approach seems to be to expect each teacher to provide for each student the best experience he can, consistently with the fact that there are other students for whom he must also provide at the same time. The assignment of such marks as "passing" or "failing" must take into consideration the question of whether the individual student is more likely to profit from being allowed to continue to the next stage in the sequence or should be encouraged to repeat the present stage.[18] The decision is simplified somewhat if it is recognized that the next stage can be modified, must indeed be modified, to provide for a wide range of student abilities.

One of the problems resulting from the "failure" of students is the decision as to what the student who has failed is to do about his failure. In some cases the suggestion may be made that he should try some other course. This is sometimes, but not very frequently, an acceptable solution. If the course he failed is a part of the required program, there is the serious problem that eventually he must receive a satisfactory grade in order to graduate.

If there were a well-defined core of work which constituted the subject matter of a particular level, it would seem logical to have students repeat the course until they had mastered that core or a satisfactory part of it. When the difficulty of defining such a core is recognized, the prescription for repetition becomes less acceptable. Furthermore, if a student has mastered part of the work of a course, it seems wasteful to ask him to repeat the whole experience. There is also the problem as to how we may expect all of the students who have difficulty with a particular approach the first time to be successful on the second or third try.

The practice of having students who have done poorly continue work for an additional period of time in summer school has some

[18] Ernest O. Melby, "It's Time for Schools to Abolish the Marking System," *Nation's Schools* 77:104 (May, 1966).

advantages, but this does not necessarily provide for individual differences nor avoid the futility of blind repetition. Some analysis of the nature of each student's learning problems must be made if they are to benefit from the extra time spent. Provision for individual differences is one of the principal characteristics of good teaching.

It has been shown that repeating courses represented such a morale problem in some schools that many students dropped out altogether.[19] If the purpose of the school is to provide as much instruction as the child is capable of benefiting from, then any practice which encourages students to drop out of school prematurely is unfortunate. It may be possible that some of the students who drop out because they have been unsuccessful have made a wise decision; the burden of proof, however, seems to rest with a school which makes no particular effort to provide in a different way for students who find learning difficult.

That a student is asked to remain for a second year at the same level of instruction need not mean that he must be asked to repeat the same work in the same way. The size of the classes which any teacher is likely to have, the shortness of the class periods with which he has to work, and the difficulty of getting to know which students are repeaters and their problems are important factors which have to be considered. If conditions make it probable that the student will not benefit from repeating a grade, it may be less harmful to promote him.

The social stigma attached to being branded as intellectually inferior is a problem for most retarded students and for their schools.[20] A student asked to repeat a subject will be likely to find himself an outcast. He is older; his interests are probably different; and he has the stigma of being intellectually less capable. While these factors are not invariably present, nor in all instances as important as the other problems of providing adequate instruction, the fact remains that they may decrease very materially the effectiveness of the instruction offered.

An important consideration is that generally passing is considered a reward and failing a punishment. The situation has deteriorated in some schools to the extent that teachers openly threaten students that failure to do some assignment will result in failure in the course. The development of the idea that failure is punishment, or passing a reward, is unfortunate when it is desirable to recognize that different students have different capabilities.

Some schools have essentially said that any student assigned to a particular class must have some reasonable opportunity to receive a satis-

[19] New York State Education Department, Drop Outs: The Cause and Cure, (Albany, New York: New York State Education Department, 1954).
[20] Henry J. Otto and Dwain M. Estes, "Accelerated and Retarded Progress," Encyclopedia of Educational Research, 3rd ed. (New York: The Macmillan Company, 1960), p. 9.

factory grade on the coursework.[21] In the last analysis the only solution is to abandon or seriously modify the emphasis on promotion and on passing and failing, and to substitute a stronger emphasis on providing for each individual a program which seems appropriate to his status at a particular time. Study should be encouraged as the key to the solution of some problem and not because it will be rewarded by a grade or a unit of credit. Assignments must be made on the basis that they will help a student learn; the intrinsic value of learning must be stressed rather than any mark.

The High School as a College Preparatory Institution

The traditional program of the high school reflected the idea that it was primarily a college preparatory institution. One fact was overlooked: at no time have all of the graduates actually continued into college. If preparation for college is the same as preparation for living, obviously one need not be concerned that the high school is still frequently viewed as primarily a college preparatory institution. The justification, however, of coursework or teaching procedures which seem to serve no other purpose than as preparation for meeting college *entrance requirements* raises a serious question.

The early American secondary school was concerned with teaching Latin grammar to the prospective students of the colonial colleges. With the advent of the academy it was recognized that some secondary students were to prepare for something else. As the academy movement was absorbed by the better established Latin grammar school, the college preparatory emphasis again became dominant. Similarly the early public high schools were not considered primarily college preparatory institutions; but as they became more and more respected, they were absorbed by a college preparatory philosophy.[22] At the turn of the nineteenth century, the emphasis of the disciplinary psychology then in vogue made the distinction between what was preparation for college and what was preparation for life rather hazy. Thus the period of rapid expansion of high school enrollments found a basic curriculum which was justified on the one hand as a part of the liberal education and at the same time as preparatory for college.

Where there is a distinct, established curriculum which is said to be appropriate as preparatory for college, it is difficult to be sure which

[21] John I. Goodlad, "Some Effects of Promotion and Non-Promotion upon the Social and Personal Adjustment of Children," *Journal of Experimental Education* 22: 301–328 (1954).

[22] E. D. Grizzell, *Origin and Development of the High School in New England before 1865* (New York: The Macmillan Company, 1923), p. 42.

students should really be encouraged to take it. Many of the more capable students have no intention of going to college and yet they may eventually do so. Conversely there are some less capable students who know they will go and may be helped to learn how to do the tricks which will be expected of them in college. There may be a third group who are aware that the college preparatory program carries more prestige and who therefore elect it although they are not interested in going to college.

The traditional effect of emphasizing preparation for college has been to rob the high school of its initiative in planning for students the best program which could be devised for them. The smaller the school, the less likely is a student to have the chance to take part in coursework of any other type. Indeed schools seem sometimes to be as guilty as individuals of selecting their programs in terms of glamour or tradition, rather than practical value.

Part of the problem is quite simply that of prestige. Since the college is considered to have more prestige than the public school, it is perhaps logical that that phase of the high school program most closely identified with the college should also have more prestige than the other phases.[23] The matter is complicated still further because the students enrolled in college preparatory programs are themselves likely to come from the upper social classes.

Even within the curricula which prepare students for college there is a tendency for courses oriented toward the liberal arts college to have more prestige than those which prepare students for the technical or scientific colleges. Thus courses in classical and modern foreign languages tend to have more prestige in some high school programs than courses in mathematics and sciences. Courses which are required of all students tend to have somewhat less prestige, and the courses which are likely to be elected by students not in the college preparatory program tend to have the least of all. Specialized vocational curricula are likely (because they have some standards of selectivity for their student group) to have more prestige than the so-called general curriculum which is open to any student who remains in school.

The tendency of colleges to keep high schools informed of the achievements of recent graduates sometimes encourages teachers to think of college success as the chief measure of the effectiveness of the high school program. The fact is that approximately half of the high school graduates do not go on to college (see accompanying table). It might be argued that the student who will go on to college is actually of less importance as a measure of the high school's success than the student who will not. The student who will not be going to college is in need of as

<hr>

[23] For a satirical treatment of this problem see Harold Benjamin, *The Saber-Tooth Curriculum* (New York: McGraw-Hill Book Company, 1939).

effective a program of training as the high school is capable of giving because he will not have further formal education.

The school which is most concerned about the success of its students in college may actually try to duplicate the program which its graduates will take in their freshman year. A few teachers fail students at high school on the grounds that they are not prepared for college work in the same area! It would seem more defensible to assign passing or failing marks in terms of the objectives of the high school and then to make a separate notation in the student's record that college work may or may not seem indicated. Certainly college level standards or subject content should not be applied to students who have no reason for or intention of continuing into college on the slight possibility that they may later decide to do so.

FIRST ENROLLMENT FALL, 1965, AS A PERCENTAGE OF HIGH SCHOOL AND PRIVATE SCHOOL GRADUATES, SPRING, 1965*

Section	Graduates, 1965	Entering Freshmen	Percentage
North Atlantic States	704,086	305,765	43%
Great Lakes and Plains	779,975	428,986	55%
Southeastern States	535,493	272,365	51%
West and Southwest	615,546	431,048	70%
Outlying Areas	24,799	11,104	45%
(Service Schools)		3,658	
	2,659,899	1,452,926	54%

* Data from Digest of Educational Statistics, 1966 (Washington, D.C.: U.S. Department of Health, Education, and Welfare, 1966), pp. 49, 60.

While much that the colleges do seems to indicate an intention on their part to restrict the public high school in its own exercise of responsibility, there is also much evidence that the colleges are willing to leave the program of the high school up to the school itself.[24] College admission is more and more based on tests and estimates of aptitude for college work than on the accumulation of credit units. College entrance requirements, where they are still stated explicitly, tend to require only commonly presented work in English, language, mathematics, and social

[24] Alvin C. Eurich and John J. Scanlon, "Articulation of Educational Units," Encyclopedia of Educational Research, 3rd ed. (New York: The Macmillan Company, 1960).

studies. Provision is made for students to make up credits which are considered essential in such areas as language and mathematics after arrival at college. There is also a strong tendency toward giving credit for advanced standing which may be established through an examination process.[25]

ENROLLMENTS IN HIGHER EDUCATION 1889–1967
PER 100 OF POPULATION 18–21*

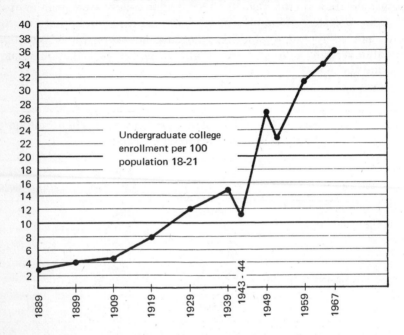

* Data from Digest of Educational Statistics, 1968 Edition (Washington, D.C.: U.S. Department of Health, Education, and Welfare, 1968), p. 70: "Ratio Undergraduate Resident Degree-Credit Students to 100 of Population 18–21." [Figures for 1967 estimated.]

If it can be shown that the public high school can provide appropriate instructional programs for all of the children of all of the people, it seems possible that the colleges will be asked to make similar provision. The pressure for admission to college has increased very markedly since the end of the Second World War, and college enrollments are expected to continue to rise.[26] Enrollment has risen from three percent of the age

[25] G. Lester Anderson, "Colleges and Universities—Organization and Administration," Encyclopedia of Educational Research, 3rd ed. (New York: The Macmillan Company, 1960).
[26] Ronald B. Thompson, Estimating College Age Population Trends, 1940–1970 (American Association of Collegiate Registrars and Admissions Offices, 1953).

group to approximately a third. The temptation, particularly in the private colleges and the universities, is to become more and more selective. It is to be hoped that the public pressure will be strong enough to break the traditional position of the college as a school for the few and to channel the energies of the college staffs into developing programs for all who have a need for further education.

While the more prestigious colleges may have the opportunity to prescribe what an individual secondary school may do by way of college preparation, they are at the same time still largely dependent on the secondary schools in their region for their student bodies. The public school officials within a given area can protect themselves from interference by colleges by planning together sound programs consistent with their responsibility to students who may not be going to college. The shifting of emphases from transcripts and units of credit to scholastic aptitude testing as the basis for college admission will relieve some of the pressure provided that the public school personnel are able to interpret such use of test scores to the patrons of their school.

Summary

It remains to be seen whether an institution as popular as the American public high school can be successfully reoriented. The practical or utilitarian values which seem to flow from departmentalization, clearly defined units of credit, an apparently just and easily justified scheme of grading, the ritual of graduation, and neat articulation with the college, make it seem foolish to discard them. The size of the whole system, the need for easy transfer of credit for an increasingly mobile population, the dependence of the schools on popular approval also makes modification difficult.

Nevertheless there is mounting evidence that real improvement of school practice may require just such modification. The need seems to be to bring teachers into closer contact with their students, to provide more flexibility in student progress within the school, to adapt the content within the course to the needs of particular students rather than to a total age group, to assume that the school will work with the student for as many or as long a number of years as seems appropriate to his situation.

7

Newer Aspects of Curricular Organization

WHILE THE SECONDARY SCHOOL OF TODAY IS NOT MUCH DIFFERENT IN ITS organizational skeleton from that of 1900, there have been many efforts during the intervening years at modification and these have left their mark. The close observer would be likely to conclude that the old school would never be the same again. Even well-informed laymen would recognize the nature of the change, although sometimes mistaking the purpose of it. The trends have been, at least in part, away from strict departmentalization, toward reorganization of the four-year program, toward an emphasis on individual programming, and toward the development of a comprehensive public high school. These, accompanied by the tremendous increase in the proportion of youth attending, have added up to a marked shift in the nature of American secondary education.

Away from Departmentalization

Among the most logical suggestions for modification in the last 50 years have been those for less strict departmentalization of subject matter. These suggestions have taken three forms: modifying the content of subjects (or at least of the organization of that content), modifying the time allotted, and modifying the teaching techniques. In theory, at least, these three elements have gone along together and have been dependent on each other.

Correlation. The first and simplest suggested modification is usually referred to as correlation. Correlation is the attempt to relate what is taught in one course to what is taught in the others which a student is taking at the same time. A first step in arranging for correlation has been to provide for shifting the sequence of course materials in such a way as to get related material into the same year. Thus, American literature and American history are both assigned to the eleventh grade. A second step in this process has been to provide that the historical sequence followed in the study of American literature corresponds closely to the sequence (and time allotment) being followed in the history class. Perhaps the English teacher will collaborate with the history teacher in the assignment of reports. If so, the history teacher will be concerned with the research carried out and the English teacher with the quality of the grammar and composition.

If the planning is carefully done, it is possible that aspects of the students' educational needs which might be neglected by both teachers working separately as not specifically in their province will be accepted as joint responsibilities. The development, for example, of research skills in the debating of such topics as public ownership of electric power plants gives an opportunity for understanding the nature of evidence as well as for the encouragement of speaking skills and the appreciation of issues in recent American history. The development of study skills may receive the concerted attention of both teachers. The tension created by the divergence of demands on the students in the typical departmentalized situation is reduced. To the extent that correlation is effective, education at the high school level becomes more nearly a unitary process rather than five or six distinctly unrelated ones. Presumably efficiency is increased.

Although much can be said for correlation, there are disadvantages which arise primarily out of the tendency to make the selection of subject matter central rather than the meeting of individual student needs. In the first place, correlation for the sake of correlation is artificial. While it does seem desirable to bring the study of American literature into a closer relationship with the study of American history, it may not be possible or desirable to set up a precise time schedule by which each may be developed as parallel to the other. While common assignments may be helpful and appropriate, it is not always desirable from the standpoint of the development of composition skills to rely simply on the correction of the projects done in connection with the history class.

Where the thinking of the staff has gone no further than correlation, it is not likely that the important areas of student need which are related to his study of history and to his study of English literature or grammar will be identified. As a step toward the identification of student needs and the modification of the program to provide for them, correlation gives some opportunity for recognizing the possibility for change. As a method of meeting the real needs of the secondary age student, however, it does not fill the bill. One of the first steps in many schools toward the scheduling of time for efficient learning has been assigning one teacher to handle both English and social studies. This provides the teacher with an opportunity to correlate the activities of the two classes and to use both class assignments and class time more efficiently. It has proved one of the most practical approaches to correlation.

The Broad-Fields Approach. A second technique suggested for reducing specialization has been referred to as "the broad-fields approach." This has involved a pulling together of related areas such as history, political science, economics, sociology, and geography into single units called social studies. Similarly, courses have been organized under the titles general science, general mathematics, and general business. This approach can represent a form of emphasis on specialization, but the nature of that specialization is usually more appropriate to the public high school's responsibility than was the former division of courses into ancient history, first year algebra, or physics, etc.

This step has been made easier because high school staffs are generally formed of teachers trained in such broad areas as English, social studies, mathematics, or science rather than in the more narrow specialties which would be found at the college level. It was therefore logical to reorganize their teaching and to aim to promote learning which could later be applied to a wide range of subjects. The coursework itself was to be drawn from the areas of specialization of the teacher involved, but it was to be organized on less narrowly defined lines than work at the college level.

As in the case of correlation, the use of a mechanical process—such as listing the ninth grade government course as Social Studies I—does not insure any real change. It is, however, a step in that direction. Alas, it is possible in many, if not most, cases to recognize that almost identical courses are simply being taught under a new name. In some cases, state courses of study or local curriculum materials even declare that Social Studies I is to be Civics; Social Studies II is World History; Social Studies III—U. S. History; and Social Studies IV—Economics and Sociology.

Probably the most helpful aspect of the shift from the specialized course content toward the broad-fields approach has been the development of text material for the new orientation. In this way a suggested outline for the new material is provided as well as suitable material for use by the students. Teachers whose general teaching technique is heavily dependent on text material are thus assisted to make the transition. Furthermore, parents and others who might feel that important areas of subject matter were being omitted, may be reassured by seeing that there is a body of content for the newer scheme of organization.

Some of the courses, such as general mathematics, have suffered in prestige from the fact that students oriented toward the college preparatory curriculum have continued to be assigned to, say, Algebra I.[1] This

---

[1] *Cf.* Milton W. Beckmann, "Is General Mathematics or Algebra Providing Greater Opportunity to Attain the Recommended Mathematical Competences?" *Journal of Educational Research* 47:505–511 (1954).

tended to give the general course a reputation for being a refuge for the less able students. The matter was frequently complicated still further by the failure of some school administrators to give teachers assigned the newer courses any clear indication of the purposes of the new scheme. It is also essential for the new courses' scope in relation to other courses already in the program to be delineated clearly.[2] Thus there has been a careless overlapping of the ninth grade general science course with the tenth grade biology course, or with general science courses offered earlier in the sequence. Obviously, these are weaknesses not in the idea itself but rather in its application.

As in the case of correlation there is no particular assurance that the major evils of over-specialization will be avoided by the use of the broad-fields approach. It still represents a distinct compromise between the idea of organizing subject matter around the needs of students and a system of organization based almost entirely on the logic of the subject material itself.

The Core Curriculum. Perhaps the most advanced practice is illustrated in the concept of the core curriculum. (The number of senior high schools using the core approach is expanding slowly; popularity at the junior high level is somewhat greater.)[3] The term "core curriculum" has been used to describe everything from the simple collection of courses which are required of all students in the school to the process of assigning students to a teacher who then plans with the students the units of work to be undertaken. For purposes of comment here the term is used to refer to a planned program for organizing the common areas of instruction for all students in the school around their needs and interests. In such a program there is an attempt to make systematic provision for a scope and sequence of common experience throughout the four years of the high school, for the development of important social skills and attitudes, and for the mastery of whatever subject matter seems to be essential in those processes. The primary emphasis is on the needs of the students. The mastery of a specific body of subject matter is made subordinate.

In schools offering a core program there is usually also provision for the separate study of specific skills and subject matter which seem essential for other purposes.[4] Thus vocational subjects such as typing, short-

---

[2] *Cf.* Rudyard K. Bent and Henry H. Kronenberg, *Principles of Secondary Education,* 4th ed. (New York: McGraw-Hill Book Company, 1961), p. 296.

[3] See Nelson L. Bossing, "What is the Trend Toward Core Curriculum in the Senior High School?" *NASSP Bulletin* 40:360–63 (1956). Also U.S. Office of Education, *Core Program: One Hundred Selected References, 1956–1960* (Washington, D.C.: U.S. Office of Education, 1961); also R. A. Gibboney, "Block of Time Programs in the Senior High School," *High School Journal* 44:248–50 (April, 1961); also Gordon F. Vars, "The Core Curriculum: Lively Corpse," *The Clearing House* 42:515–19 (May, 1968).

[4] Harold B. Alberty and Elsie J. Alberty, *Reorganizing the High School Curriculum,* 3rd ed. (New York: The Macmillan Company, 1962), p. 217.

hand, agriculture, or home economics would still be provided in the somewhat traditional way. Similarly, students preparing for college might take additional courses in foreign language or science. Physical education would be provided for in a separate block of time. While specific areas will be taught separately from those provided in the core, it is to be hoped that the same general principles of treatment would be applied to their teaching. In other words, the unit approach utilizing problem-solving techniques appropriate for the core—and which will be described in a later chapter—is also appropriate for many other parts of the high school curriculum.

The most radical core approach involves almost complete disregard for traditional schemes of subject organization. Instead, teaching is planned around the solution of problems which seem vital to the students themselves. Provision is made at the same time to concentrate on the development of such skills as composition, study and organization of information, and for the development of important social skills. The emphasis is on individual and group guidance as well as on the more traditional teaching functions of the school. Basic to the idea of the core curriculum is a new set of teaching procedures. The mere fusion of two courses such as social studies and English, while it may serve many of the same purposes served by correlation, is not sufficient.

Most of the difficulties which have arisen in schools trying out the core curriculum approach have resulted from too hasty an attempt to get into the program. Either teachers were not adequately prepared, or students and parents were not warned as to what to expect. On the other hand schools which have made more careful preparation for participating in the core program have found that it was likely to be considered the most effective part of the curriculum. One advantage of the core program is that the teacher can deal with fewer students. Instead of the customary 150 to 200 students, the teacher with two half-day core sections will have only 60 or 70. Because of the use of blocks of time longer than a single period there is also more opportunity for flexibility.

In the typical Junior high school using the core approach, two-thirds or more of the school day at the seventh grade level, half of the day at the eighth grade level, and a third of the day for the remaining four years may be assigned for the core curriculum. The rest of the time will be devoted to the various other types of specialization mentioned above. At some senior high school levels specialized courses may include work in English and social studies as well as in the more strictly vocational or prevocational areas.

Departure from Classical Content. Basic to all of the modifications in the traditional curriculum during the past 50 years has been a trend away from classical organization of content. First Greek and then Latin were dropped or seriously reduced in importance.[5] Next the classical organization of the history curriculum (which originally called for a year of ancient and medieval history, a year of modern European history, and a year of American history) was drastically changed.[6] Concurrently, the classical sequence of literary masterpieces in the English curriculum was modified.[7] Finally, the classically oriented sequence including plane geometry, two units of algebra and a half unit each of trigonometry and solid geometry is now under attack.[8]

Slowly the impact of the revolution in educational psychology is being felt. With the decline in favor of the idea of mental discipline, the concept of organizing curriculum material around the needs and interests of students is gaining influence. There is no longer any universally-accepted best approach to the study of history, English literature, mathematics, or science. Nor does the traditional content of these areas have so vested a position in competition with newer and more logically sound schemes of organization being developed. This is not to say that the hand of tradition does not weigh heavily on the shoulders of the school principal and staff who wish to provide a better program. It is much easier to continue to travel along traditional paths than to blaze new ones.

One of the important hindrances to developing new approaches is to be found in the tremendous size of the public high school program. Teachers are recruited from all over the nation, and frequently a staff of as many as 40 or 50 teachers may be representative of as many as 20 or 25 different training institutions. Inevitably, perhaps, older teachers feel threatened by the suggestion of a younger teacher that the traditional way of doing things may be improved on. Conversely, assimilating new teachers into a school which has made important modification of the curriculum can prove difficult.

As has already been suggested, the break with the classical tradition has been complicated by the association of the classical program with social prominence. If a knowledge of Latin was the badge of education, the parent who recognized the importance of such a badge wanted his child to have it. Indeed the school principal who wished to provide the best possible program for his student group was likely to be hesitant in suggesting that they be denied the same badge that was being provided in other schools for other students. The temptation was to try to provide for both the classical tradition and the newer approach. In this effort

[5] Norman J. Dewitt, "Classical Languages," Encyclopedia of Educational Research, 3rd ed. (New York: The Macmillan Company, 1960), pp. 215–20.
[6] Richard E. Gross and William D. Badger, "Social Studies," ibid., pp. 1297–98.
[7] Robert C. Pooley, "Literature," ibid., p. 471.
[8] E. Glenadine Gibb, John R. Mayor, and Edith Treuenfels, "Mathematics," ibid., pp. 800–801.

the larger school was in a better position than the smaller, for the larger had more teachers.[9]

It is reasonable to assume that as the revolution in the curriculum away from the classical content continues, it will gain momentum. The newer elements in the program, when they need to be replaced, will not have gained the foothold held by the older. The social prestige gained from having studied a particular subject will grow less important as more and more students have the opportunity for such study. Social prestige of this sort requires an economy of scarcity, and the universal nature of modern secondary education has rendered even the classical approach less scarce. More important still is the fact that school personnel have themselves become more and more proficient in recognizing the needs of their students and in developing better techniques to meet them.

The Reorganization of Secondary Education

Almost before the American public high school had become crystallized as a four-year institution there was some demand for its program to be reorganized so that it would articulate better with the elementary school's on one side and the college's on the other. President Eliot of Harvard and others were disturbed as early as 1895 by the rising age of students entering college, and the idea of starting the program of secondary education earlier was discussed. The work of G. Stanley Hall and others in the field of adolescent psychology around the turn of the century suggested the need for a school which would concentrate on providing something different and special for students between the ages of 12 and 15. The tendency of large numbers of students to drop out of school at the end of the elementary period was recognized and began to cause concern during the period before 1920.[10]

Emphasis on the Importance of Articulation. The establishment of an educational ladder based on putting together three distinct schools— the common, the secondary, and the collegiate—made it necessary to consider the problem of articulation. There were three points at which the three schools did not match. They had different objectives, they had different organizational procedures, and they had traditionally different social status. The problem of articulating the parts of the American educational ladder has had its impact on the development of the public high

[9] Cf. Norman J. Dewitt, "Classical Languages," Encyclopedia of Educational Research, 3rd ed. (New York: The Macmillan Company, 1960), pp. 211–20.

[10] William Van Til, Gordon F. Vars, and John H. Lounsbury, Modern Education for the Junior High School Years, 2nd ed. (New York: The Bobbs-Merrill Co., Inc., 1967), pp. 5–21.

school and will continue to lead people to suggest modifications of its program.

Gradual acceptance by the secondary school of the objective of providing for the education of all of the children of all of the people has brought it into closer harmony with the objectives of the elementary school. The administration of the secondary schools by the same school officials and lay boards of education has probably hastened the articulation of the two units. For so long as the secondary schools were private schools and the elementary schools were public schools, it was inevitable that they would have somewhat different orientations. A third factor that has served to reduce the distinctions between elementary and secondary education has been the trend toward a single salary scale for teachers in the two separate units and a parallel trend toward the same type of training program for both groups.

It should not be implied that the problem of articulating elementary and secondary schools has been solved.[11] There are still differences in the two programs which serve to retard their integration into a single pattern. There is still a tendency to regard the program of the high school as justifiably selective. There is still a tendency to regard the high school teacher's job as primarily that of transmitting subject matter and of protecting the standards of mastery rather than of meeting the needs of individuals. That steady progress is being made preventing students dropping out at the end of the elementary school program may be seen from the chart on page 152 showing the proportion of students continuing from the ninth to the tenth grades between 1930 and 1960. In spite of this and the rising age of compulsory attendance, the heaviest failure and dropout rate is to be found at this level.[12]

The articulation of the high school with the college is complicated by the fact that in most cases the high school is controlled by a local board of education while the college is likely to be controlled either by a private or a state board of trustees. It is also increasingly evident that there are students who could profit from an education extended beyond the high school period who cannot necessarily profit from the kind of courses available in the typical college. This difficulty may indicate a need to modify both the college and the high school. The rapid development of community colleges and other types of schools for vocational and adult education shows the direction in which further developments may be made.[13]

[11] Marian W. Hodge, "Articulation of Secondary and Elementary Schools," *California Journal of Secondary Education* 31:322–25 (1956).

[12] *Digest of Educational Statistics*, 1966 (Washington, D.C.: U.S. Department of Health, Education, and Welfare, 1966), p. 7.

[13] *Cf.* Irving E. Carlyle, Chairman, *The Report of the Governor's Commission on Education Beyond the High School* (Raleigh: The Governor's Commission, 1962).

Whatever differences may seem to exist between the training and philosophy of the elementary and secondary school teachers exist to a much larger degree between that of public school and college teachers. Perhaps the most fortunate aspect of the whole problem from the standpoint of articulating American education is that in this country public school teachers are trained in colleges and universities. This is less true in the school systems of Europe. The existence of departments and schools of education in the universities and colleges here means that most public school teachers do their training within the same social setting as other professional people in the community. It also provides for the development and utilization of research done by colleges and university personnel in the areas of education and psychology.

PROPORTION OF NINTH GRADE STUDENTS CONTINUING TO
TENTH GRADE 1930–1960*

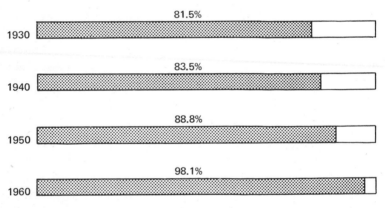

*Data from Digest of Educational Statistics, 1964 Edition (Washington, D.C.:
U.S. Department of Health, Education, and Welfare, 1964), p. 120.

The Junior High School Movement. Out of the pressures of the early part of the twentieth century for better articulation and provision for adolescents came the development of the junior high school. Publication of G. Stanley Hall's work on *Adolescence* was a contributing factor. This movement was given particular impetus by the rapid expansion of school enrollments in the urban areas. By building a new school unit the pressures from both the elementary and secondary school for additional space could be met.[14]

Some educational reformers recognized that a new school unit would be free of many of the problems which had plagued attempts to modify

[14] Columbus, Ohio, and Berkeley, California, seem to have been the first two school systems to establish Junior High Schools, in 1908 and 1910 respectively.

the programs of the older elementary and secondary schools. Subject departmentalization could be modified in the new program without interference from the colleges. At the other extreme more specialization could be provided in such areas as physical education, art, and music. The transition from the single teacher of the elementary school to the complicated schedule of the high school could be eased a bit. The holding power of the schools could be improved in two ways: (1) through the development of better guidance facilities, and (2) through easing students into the traditional program of the high school at the ninth grade level.[15]

Perhaps the chief contribution of the modern junior high school is the development of a program in which the students from 12 to 15 receive special attention. In the traditional elementary-high school organization, the seventh and eighth graders are placed physically in a school situation which they have generally outgrown. Furthermore, in most cases teachers have been more interested in, and better trained to work with, younger students. Similarly the ninth graders are likely to be neglected at the high school level. For instance, most of the extra-class activities such as the publications, socials, varsity athletics, and student government have been set up primarily for the eleventh and twelfth graders. The teachers are often more enthusiastic about teaching senior English or twelfth grade science. By placing the seventh, eighth, and ninth graders in one school under the supervision of teachers and principals who are entirely concerned with those grades, much more attention can be given to their development.

While the onetime argument for a school that was distinctly different for the early adolescent has been somewhat modified, the idea of concentrating students of approximately the same age level in the same plant still seems good. In practice a three-year span seems to provide for sufficient continuity within the program itself. There is still a recognized need for counseling and guidance services and for student activities which are easier to provide in a separate junior high school than in the seventh and eighth grades of an elementary school and the ninth grade of a high school. The junior high school also has the opportunity to provide for a core program appropriate to that age level and at the same time for specialized work both in arts and crafts and in some of the academic fields.

In some situations it has proved desirable to set up a six-year secondary school. This is known as a "junior-senior high school." If the full advantages of the junior high school program are to be capitalized, it seems better that the upper and lower divisions of such a school each be three years in length and be housed in separate wings of the building with their own administrative officers (perhaps as assistant principals). Such an

[15] Thomas H. Briggs, *The Junior High School* (Boston: Houghton Mifflin Company, 1920), pp. 162–74.

organization is more often found in sparsely populated areas where transportation is a problem. Frequently central facilities such as the auditorium, gymnasium, and cafeteria may be shared. Care must be taken, however, that in such sharing the program of the junior high school is not overshadowed.

The accompanying chart shows the relative decrease in the number of traditional four-year high schools, and the increase in the separate junior and senior high schools, and the combined junior-senior high

PERCENT OF PUBLIC SECONDARY SCHOOLS BY TYPE OF SCHOOL:
UNITED STATES 1919–20 TO 1965–66*

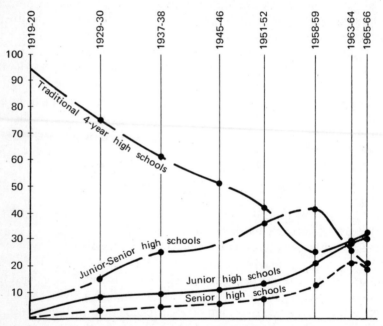

* Data from Digest of Educational Statistics, 1968 Edition (Washington, D.C.: U.S. Department of Health, Education, and Welfare, 1968), p. 46.

schools until approximately 1962. The proportion of reorganized schools grew steadily and at the present time there are more than three times as many of them as there are of the standard four-year pattern. They still contain by far the largest number of students. The very recent rapid drop in six-year high school seems to reflect a speed-up in school consolidation to provide more adequate programs.

Since about 1960 there has also been a trend, particularly in some of the metropolitan school districts, to experiment with a new four-year pattern in which grades five, six, seven, and eight were identified as a "middle school." Some of its proponents suggest it takes advantage of the greater sophistication and presumed earlier maturation of children in urban areas, provides for such things as subject departmentalization and specialization at the fifth and sixth grade levels, allows more specialized guidance services at the upper levels of the elementary school, and in New York City (where the proposal seems to have gotten its real start) provides for a smoother transition from *de facto* segregation of the races. It is difficult to be sure whether the new 4-4 pattern will become the dominant one.

Opponents of the middle school approach have pointed out that, even if evidence of greater sophistication in fifth and sixth grade children does exist, it is not clearly a sufficient reason for a new scheme of school organization. There are still more significant differences between fifth and eighth grades than between seventh and ninth graders or fifth and first. Most of the students of elementary education see earlier departmentalization, or subject specialization, as of dubious value. Those concepts to be taught to a fifth or sixth grader are certainly not so sophisticated as to be beyond the well-prepared elementary teacher at that level. Guidance services may well be needed for the 12 to 15-year-old group but they can also be used to advantage throughout the entire elementary school program. The peculiar problems of *de facto* segregation in New York City are hardly justification for such an approach in other areas with different problems and other possible solutions to the same problem.

The Community College. The expansion of secondary education as a public function following the Kalamazoo Case in 1874 and more particularly since 1900 may be regarded as indicating the American people's acceptance of the idea that education is an important public responsibility. Traditional distinctions between elementary and secondary education were not to be allowed to get in the way of providing education for any who might profit from it. By the same token it was logical that popular pressure should be generated for the development of publicly controlled education beyond the twelfth grade.[16]

Publicly supported state universities were, of course, already in existence; some of them dated from the early days of the republic. They were, however, controlled at the state rather than at the local level and were firmly entrenched in the traditions of the college. What seemed to be needed was a local school, controlled by the same, or similar, local boards of education, providing a program that was continuous with that of the high school, and which was little if any more selective in its admission requirements. Some communities began to meet this need between 1900 and 1920.[17] It was during the same period that the private junior college movement was getting started. The two movements have much in com-

---

[16] William M. Alexander and J. G. Saylor, *Modern Secondary Education* (New York: Rinehart and Company, Inc., 1959), p. 142.

[17] The first public junior college was established at Joliet, Illinois, in 1902.

mon—in many instances the only major difference is in the nature of the control and the diversity of the public programs.

The number of private junior colleges seems to be remaining relatively constant at approximately 250 since before the Second World War, and the number of public colleges is steadily increasing—in 1965 there were 381. Nearly 500,000 students enrolled in public institutions in 1961 and approximately 60,000 in private ones the same year.[18]

The community and junior colleges provide for three or four distinct types of students. There is likely to be a program of general education which may or may not be terminal in nature and which tends to be partly a duplication of the programs of the first two years of the four-year college. There is likely to be a terminal program of semi-professional or technical training which prepares students for job opportunities within the community. The third program is strictly college preparatory in its nature and represents an opportunity to complete all or most of the first two years of work, so that the student can go into the junior year when transferring to a standard four-year college. A fourth program provides continuation education for many students from a variety of walks of life.

While in many cases the community college charges a tuition fee, the fact of not having to pay for lodging and other student services makes the cost to the student a great deal less than for the four-year college. The tradition of the community college is to provide an appropriate program for as many students as possible.

The growth both in the number of community colleges and in the number of students enrolled has been quite steady. The pressure of students wishing to enroll in colleges has increased to the point that private and state colleges and universities may soon reach saturation. The community college offers an opportunity to relieve this pressure and perhaps even to make it possible for some universities to abandon the freshman and sophomore level of work to the community schools and to commit the use of their limited dormitory, laboratory, and library facilities to their upper level and graduate students.

The Compromises and Experiments. The process of reorganizing secondary education has involved interesting compromises with tradition. One which is quite evident is the maintenance of the four-year high school program even within the 6-3-3- organization. In the systems which have maintained separate junior high schools, the ninth grade is often regarded as the first year of high school, even though it is also recognized as the third year of the junior high school. In part, this is merely a matter of keeping the records for the reorganized secondary schools in the same form as those for the more traditional four-year programs. Records are kept primarily on the basis of the so-called academic phase of the program

[18] *Digest of Educational Statistics,* 1964 (Washington, D.C.: U.S. Department of Health, Education, and Welfare, 1964), pp. 84, 91.

rather than on the total program of the school. Like most such compromises, it is a basis for misunderstanding.

The preparation of junior high school and middle school teachers poses similar problems. Typically, the pre-service training of public school teachers has been for either the elementary or the secondary level. The elementary teacher has been prepared for teaching the primary or middle grades. The tendency in the preparation of high school teachers has been to stress the kind of subject specialization most appropriate to the eleventh or twelfth grades. Very little attention has been given to the preparation of teachers specifically for the junior high school. As a result it has been a common practice to use teachers prepared either at the elementary or the secondary level for grades seven and eight. It has generally been left to the principal or supervisory staff to develop the teachers' understanding of the responsibilities of the junior high school.

Local situations have sometimes made it appear desirable to set up junior high schools consisting of one or two grades rather than of the traditional three. There has been fairly uniform agreement among the students of secondary education that the three-year program provides for better continuity than the two-year one. A few schools have experimented with a seven grade elementary school and a five-year high school. This plan is less likely to provide a satisfactory program for the seventh, eighth, and ninth graders. One advantage in following a standard plan of reorganization is that national studies of such situations are likely to be available to teachers and staff. Discussions in national conferences, the development of appropriate text materials, and the training of new staff are all facilitated by some degree of standardization.

At the other end of secondary education, the decision as to whether the thirteenth and fourteenth years should be considered secondary or collegiate depends in part on the future plans of the student in the program. For so long as the objectives of the secondary school and the college are sufficiently different to make the distinction important, the staff of the community college must face a dilemma. Identification with the college tends to carry more prestige in the eyes of the community. On the other hand, identification with the public school will probably provide more genuine freedom to develop a program appropriate to the needs of both the students and the community. The community college is faced with the same dilemma with regard to the training appropriate for its staff. To the extent that the Ph.D. is primarily a research degree, it may seem inappropriate for the kind of program needed at the level of the thirteenth and fourteenth grades. On the other hand the status of the school seems sometimes dependent on the staff having more advanced degrees.[19]

[19] James W. Reynolds, "Junior Colleges," *Encyclopedia of Educational Research*, 3rd ed. (New York: The Macmillan Company, 1960), p. 742.

The Emphasis on Individual Programming

In the early days of American secondary education all students followed essentially the same curriculum. The expansion of the public high school's enrollment to include larger and larger sections of the population has been accompanied by the development of the idea of more individual choice in selecting a program. This led to the provision of electives, modification of graduation requirements, development of the concept of guidance, and—more recently—concern with remedial work. In more recent years there has been experimentation with programs of acceleration and enrichment, programmed instruction and language laboratories, use of television, and independent study.

The Emphasis on Electives. The first modern emphasis on electives began in imitation of a practice developed at Harvard under President Eliot. A variety of course offerings had been available in the program of American secondary education since the introduction of Franklin's academy. Part of the impetus for the work of the Committee of Ten in 1892–1893 was the confusion, recognized by college officials of the time, in the number and names of courses offered in the secondary schools. The effect of the work of that committee and of others which followed it had been to place the curriculum of the secondary school in an inflexible pattern. Modification of this pattern followed three distinct ideas: (1) the addition of the sciences and the modern foreign languages to the traditional pattern of academic courses, (2) the development of courses of a vocational nature, and (3) the development of subjects of a more general nature in such areas as art, music, crafts, social studies, and physical education.[20]

The substitution of modern foreign languages for Greek and Latin did not occur all at one time. It was a gradual process. In many cases students were encouraged to pursue both Latin and a modern foreign language. When the concept of mental discipline broke down and reverence for a tradition of classical instruction was discontinued, it became obvious that the reasons for studying a language would apply about as well to a modern language as to a classical one. In addition, the proponents of modern languages could build a case for the use of language as a means of understanding the culture of other peoples. Whether language instruction can stand up as a necessary part of an educational program designed to provide for the needs of most of the students of secondary school age remains to be seen. There has been renewed stress in the 1960's on language instruction resulting in part from the pressures of

---

[20] John S. Brubacher, *A History of the Problems of Education* (New York: McGraw-Hill Book Company, 1947), pp. 313, 447–51.

the cold war and the availability of federal funds to support special programs.[21]

The increase in science subjects in the curriculum has occurred primarily within this century. While the question as to whether they are to follow strictly the organizational pattern of the college courses or are to be organized in a broad-fields approach is not yet settled, it is fairly obvious that they are a very important part of the school curriculum. It is interesting to note that, partly because of commitment to the limit of 16 to 20 units as a standard high school program, the sciences are tending to hasten the loss of status by the classical languages. For instance, the student who is permitted to take only five units a year must choose between Latin and physics if he is also going to have English, social studies, mathematics, and a modern foreign language. The pressures of the 1960's have resulted in several far-reaching studies at the national level of the appropriate content for high school biology, chemistry and physics. These have led to the preparation of new materials including some differentiated for different ability levels. Also the availability of federal and foundation funds for the preparation of science teachers has tended to increase emphasis on specialization in the science fields.

Vocational emphasis in the high school program spread during the period between 1910 and 1920, receiving considerable impetus from the Smith-Hughes Act which made federal funds available. The development of vocational curricula will receive some attention in the next section. A part of this movement had to do not only with the development of whole curricula but also with the addition of such courses as home economics, typing, agriculture, and general business to the program of students in other curricula. While some of the college preparatory courses still seem to have more "intellectual appeal," it seems a matter of time before practical courses will become as acceptably a part of the school program for all students as the classics and modern foreign languages.

The trend toward larger school units has facilitated the development of a variety of courses in the areas of the fine and industrial arts. The satisfaction to be had in the appreciation and practice of art, music, and the shop crafts is sufficiently evident to require little additional justification either to students or to their parents. Few even of the most traditional of the critics of curriculum change are likely to be opposed to the opportunity for developing more proficiency in these areas. The spread of radio and television has tended to hasten the development of a higher level of cultural appreciation among the entire population. As in the case of all elective areas in the school program, additional time must be made available for the new studies or older and more static phases of the program must give way.

[21] Cf. Emma M. Birkmaier, "Modern Languages," Encyclopedia of Educational Research, 3rd ed. (New York: The Macmillan Company, 1960), pp. 861–83.

Electives in social studies have been created in accordance with the general feeling that schools should help students' development as members of society. In particular, there has been strong pressure for more attention to citizenship, economic education, and for broadening the history courses to include Africa, Asia and Latin America.[22]

Part of the problem concerning the development of a physical education program has been trying to decide what skills are really desirable and appropriate for teaching in school. There has been general agreement that the school must contribute what it can to the physical health of students and to their recreation, but no exact agreement has been reached as to how the mastery of certain specific skills in the sports area contributes to health.

Modification of Graduation Requirements. Just as the course titles recommended by the committees of the National Education Association between 1892 and 1911 tended to place the program in a strait jacket during the period following, so also the suggested college entrance requirements tended to place similar restriction on graduation requirements.[23] Gradually it became evident that, if the high schools were to provide for the new population coming into the school, some changes would have to be made. The first approach was the development of what were called parallel curricula. Thus the student in the college preparatory curriculum was likely to follow the same program recommended earlier, but other programs were provided for other groups.

A second approach has been to break away from the restriction of 16 units as a basis. Some schools have increased this minimum to 18 or even 20.[24] Another approach has been to continue to give only partial credit for some of the new elective phases of the program. Thus students might qualify for only 16 or 18 units of credit while taking five or more courses a year. In some cases different types of schedule have been arranged in which some units are referred to as "interest units" and are carried for only two or three periods a week. As will be noted in the next chapter, some of the new elective features (particularly in music) have been scheduled in the activities period.

The third and more basic approach in recent years has been to reduce the constant requirements for graduation to four units of English, two of social studies (usually including U.S. History), one in science (usually Biology), and one in mathematics. Whether this has really amounted to a liberalization has usually depended on the nature of the course offerings. Very small schools have frequently been able to offer only the college

[22] Richard E. Gross and William V. Badger, "Social Studies," *Encyclopedia of Educational Research*, 3rd ed. (New York: The Macmillan Company, 1960), pp. 1296–1313.

[23] John S. Brubacher, *A History of the Problems of Education*, 2nd ed. (New York: McGraw-Hill Book Company, 1966), pp. 413–17.

[24] "High School Graduation Requirements," *NEA Research Bulletin* 37:121–27 (Dec., 1959).

preparatory course requirements and hence all of the students would end up with this program. On the other hand some larger schools have had a more varied offering.[25]

The shift from simple emphasis on academic work to provision for some student needs through extra-curricular activities made the influence of graduation requirements less restrictive. Although graduation still looms large in the minds of the student and the staff, it is no longer the only concern. Many of the important aspects of the school's influence on its student body are not reflected in the academic program at all. The requirements for graduation have become so general as to be fairly readily applicable to the needs of almost anyone in the school population. The tendency of the colleges to move away from strict dependence on credit units has helped in this shift.

Perhaps more meaningful than a listing of graduation requirements and course offerings, is an analysis of the proportion of students at a given grade level enrolled in a particular course at a particular time. The table on page 162 gives an indication of the extent to which particular course offerings are actually selected. It indicates, for instance, that approximately 15 per cent of high school seniors have been allowed to make substitutions for the usual course in senior English. Surprisingly, with the exception of U.S. History, there is no common core of course work in the area of the social studies. For the majority of the tenth, eleventh and twelfth graders mathematics is not a part of the school program. Science courses beyond general or first year biology are selected by about a third of the high school population during any one academic year. Approximately half the student population take their science courses in the four-year period.

Emphasis on Secondary Education as General Education. It is hard to distinguish between the notion that we must provide within the secondary school for all of the children of all of the people and the idea that the secondary school's function is not preparing students for college or the vocations but rather for their education as citizens of the community. Almost automatically preparatory education is specialized education, and social development calls more specifically for general education.

One of the recent movements in secondary education has been referred to as "life adjustment" education. While the publicity given to this development attracted the suspicion of the conservatives, the impetus behind the movement was the recognition that the former emphasis on preparation for college or vocations had been appropriate for less than half the total population of the high school. The leaders felt the school's main responsibility was to provide an education appropriate for the total population.[26] Renewed concern about dropouts during the 1960's has tended to counter the criticisms of the late 1950's.

[25] *Ibid.*
[26] Rudyard K. Bent and Henry H. Kronenberg, *Principles of Secondary Education,* 4th ed. (New York: McGraw-Hill Book Company, 1961), pp. 274–75.

ENROLLMENT IN SELECTED SUBJECTS IN PUBLIC HIGH SCHOOLS
RELATED TO TOTAL ENROLLMENT IN GRADES IN WHICH
THE SUBJECTS ARE USUALLY OFFERED, 1960–1961 [1]

Field and subject	Grade	Enrollment Number	Enrollment Percent[2]
ENGLISH:			
Grade 9	9	2,397,708	98.2
Grade 10	10	2,072,940	97.8
Grade 11	11	1,838,189	96.1
Grade 12	12	1,469,897	84.2
College level English	12	9,220	.5
Honors courses	12	2,381	.1
World Literature	12	66,701	3.8
Speech and public speaking	11	454,347	23.8
Creative writing	12	38,097	2.2
Journalism	12	136,071	7.8
SOCIAL STUDIES:			
United States history	11	1,994,068	104.3
World history	10	1,471,531	69.4
Civics (elementary)	9	732,609	30.0
Civics (advanced)	12	780,123	44.7
Problems of democracy	12	480,453	21.8
Economics	12	293,175	16.8
Psychology	12	140,377	8.0
Sociology or social problems	12	289,408	16.6
MATHEMATICS:			
General Mathematics (elementary)	9	1,027,205	42.1
General Mathematics (advanced)	12	349,989	20.0
Advanced high school or college	12	40,031	2.3
Elementary algebra	9	1,607,356	65.8
Intermediate and advanced algebra	11	741,661	38.8
Plane Geometry	10	959,825	45.3
Solid Geometry	12	173,196	10.0
Trigonometry	12	246,225	14.1
Trigonometry-algebra integrated	11	22,995	1.2
SCIENCE:			
General science	9	1,549,271	63.5
First-year biology	10	1,686,318	79.6
First-year chemistry	11	708,143	37.0
First-year physics	12	385,148	22.1
Advanced general and physical	12	276,816	15.9

[1] Digest of Educational Statistics, 1966 Edition (Washington, D.C.: U.S. Department of Health, Education, and Welfare, 1966), p. 34.

[2] Ratio of course enrollment to the total enrollment of the grade where the course is usually offered.

One illustration of the nature of the problem was to be found in the content of compulsory courses. While it was apparent that all students could profit from a study of English, including a study of English literature, it was less apparent that the *traditional* content of courses covering these subjects was appropriate for all. Other great works of literature which had not been selected could equally well be a part of the program. Furthermore, it was apparent that some students did not have the reading ability or the experience background possessed by others and that their reading assignments could appropriately differ even within the same class. It was therefore suggested that material should be selected for the individual, not just on the basis of college entrance requirements.[27]

The emphasis on the general function of the secondary school also caused a review of some course offerings outside of the required areas. General mathematics and general science were introduced to provide a more appropriate survey of certain fields than was being provided in the more restricted courses. The whole movement toward a broad-fields curriculum grew out of a recognition that the secondary school had more general responsibilities than specialized courses could satisfy. A unified course in world history was substituted for the more specialized emphasis in ancient, medieval, and modern European history.[28]

Simultaneously, a tendency has developed to push specialized business and technical training upward toward the thirteenth and fourteenth years. This trend is of course more evident in areas where community colleges and technical schools have been developing most rapidly.[29]

Emphasis on Remedial Work. One promising aspect of the new secondary school program has been emphasis on remedial work. For a long time the assumption was made that reading, writing, and arithmetic skills should be gained in the elementary school. High school teachers were critical of the elementary schools which promoted students who were having difficulty in these areas. A better understanding of the fact that it is possible to help students even of low general ability to develop acceptable skills has made it appear imperative to provide remedial training in the high school itself.[30]

One of the important problems is that remedial work, to be effective, requires diagnostic ability on the part of the teacher. High school teachers have not ordinarily been trained in diagnostic techniques. The emphasis

[27] *Cf.* John R. Searles and G. Robert Carlsen, "English," *Encyclopedia of Educational Research,* 3rd ed. (New York: The Macmillan Company, 1960), pp. 454–66.

[28] Richard E. Gross and William V. Badger, "Social Studies," *ibid.,* p. 1301.

[29] Ralph C. Wenrich, "Vocational Education," *ibid.,* p. 1562.

[30] Arthur E. Traxler, "What Does Research Suggest About Ways to Improve Reading Instruction," *Improving Reading in the Junior High School,* edited by Arno Jewett (Washington, D.C.: U.S. Department of Health, Education, and Welfare, 1957), pp. 5–13.

on subject specialization has tended to hamper their understanding of diagnostic approaches. On the other hand, the elementary teacher's training, while not always adequate in this area, has generally emphasized it more.

Remedial work also requires almost tutorial type instruction. There is little opportunity in the typical high school schedule for such individual attention. No single teacher has a student in his care for long enough either to recognize his problems or to work with him individually. The core approach with its larger block of time and its emphasis on individualization offers some hope in this connection.

Various approaches are being tried to improve students' skill in composition. Smaller English classes and ones requiring more actual composition are being scheduled; readers are being hired to help with the themes, and remedial sections set up for students having unusual difficulty. The older, more formal approach to the study of grammar requiring rules to be memorized and textbook exercises to be done has proven notoriously ineffective. Many students graduate after twelve years of formal instruction in English grammar and still have very little functional skill. On the other hand, even one year of instruction at the high school level based on an individual analysis of difficulty can make a difference.

Remedial help in the field of arithmetic is being provided for individual students. Good mathematics teachers at the high school level are beginning to recognize the importance of grouping within the class. In this way thorough mastery of basic skills may be stressed rather than the mere coverage of the material in some outline or text. There is no particular point in permitting students to proceed to advanced levels without first having overcome the earlier problems.

Even in physical education some schools have recognized the need for individual remedial instruction. Diagnostic and corrective techniques have been developed and marked progress has been made by students in such programs. As in the case of the academic fields, the cooperation of specialists and physicians as well as of the regular teaching staff is required if such programs are to be successful.

Programs of Acceleration and Enrichment. At the same time, there has been progressive recognition of the need for accelerating or enriching the program for those capable of doing more than can be conveniently provided in the regular classroom or curriculum. Such programs have not yet crystallized sufficiently to be clearly recognized as a standard feature of American secondary education. Much experimentation is taking place during the current period.

In some cases provision has been made for a great deal of independent study under the direction of some regular teacher. In others students of unusual ability have been grouped together to pursue the regular sequence of courses at a faster pace and to study some college level material. In still other special sections, the effort has been to provide for "more depth" in the study of the regular subjects by using more advanced or varied text materials.

As a result of Conant's *The American High School Today,* there has been pressure to make the high school cover some of the work now taught in the freshman and sophomore years at college. Courses designated as "advanced placement courses" are being offered in the sciences, mathematics, and foreign languages. The presumption (and much of the practice) is that students will be given credit for completion of college requirements. Similarly there has been pressure to move high school content, particularly in foreign languages, into the elementary school.

While it is generally recognized that many high and elementary school students are capable of mastering advanced subject matter, there is much opposition to this approach. Most education specialists prefer "enrichment" to "acceleration." "Enrichment" refers to the idea that students should be encouraged to pursue particular studies in more depth rather than more hastily. The elementary specialists insist that the elementary program is already sufficiently crowded. The secondary education specialist is concerned lest such areas as social studies will be pushed out in order to provide college level work.

Programmed Instruction and Language Laboratories. Interest in acceleration and enrichment has recently led to a consideration of "automating" learning techniques. Based largely on the studies of Skinner, an educational psychologist of the connectionist school,[31] there have been many kinds of materials developed which would permit students to proceed at their own pace in studying such subjects as plane geometry. Some of the methods require the use of elaborate electronic equipment. Other systems are more similar to the "workbooks" which became prominent in the 1920's and 1930's. Studies of their success or failure when used on a large scale are as yet not conclusive, although some have proved helpful to students capable of using them with relatively little supervision.[32]

The use of electronics to aid instruction takes another form in the language laboratory. The availability of tape recorders and federal funds in recent years has spurred this development. It is assumed that by hearing a language spoken correctly over a tape a student may learn more quickly to pronounce it and to understand native speakers' accents and rhythms. Most of the installations are designed to permit students to work at their

[31] B. F. Skinner, "The Science of Learning and the Art of Teaching," in Wendell L. Smith and J. William Moore, eds., *Programmed Learning: Theory and Research* (Princeton, N.J.: Van Nostrand Company, 1962).

[32] *Cf.* Fund for the Advancement of Education, *Four Case Studies of Programmed Instruction* (New York: Fund for the Advancement of Education, 1964).

own speed, but allow teachers to "listen in" and provide specific help.[33] Critics have questioned the cost of the operation as well as the emphasis on "mechanical gadgets." Proponents have generally been satisfied with the results.

Automated Learning. In addition to programmed learning and the use of language laboratories, a few schools across the country are attempting to develop what may be referred to as automated learning, individually prescribed instruction, or individually managed learning.[34] In theory the approach is little different from earlier efforts referred to as the Winnetka Plan, the Morrison plan, and the Dalton contract. The teacher is expected to work out individual assignments based on some careful diagnosis of the student's needs or interests. Extensive use is then made of programmed texts, films, and even computers. The student proceeds on his own using the teacher as an instructional counselor. The approach will probably get continued attention, but is likely to influence only a few of the better-equipped school programs.

Some educational innovations and possibilities discussed here are elaborated in the "Technology and Teaching" section of Chapter 15.

Teaching by Television. During the past 20 years much effort has been made to discover appropriate uses for television in the public high school programs. It has generally been agreed that "live" events, such as the Presidential inauguration, might be viewed appropriately by social studies classes in the school. Similarly students might be advised to watch particular programs broadcast after school or during free time at school.

The advisability of actually teaching classes by television has been debated more vigorously. Generous grants from private foundations have been supplemented from funds of particular schools systems in an effort to study or promote the possibilities of such use. The usual practice has been to have a television teacher teach for approximately half the period and then a classroom teacher continue the discussion. Studies have not been conclusive. Some have been criticized for failure to provide adequate statistical controls. In general no particular financial savings have been affected. Mastery of information has been approximately the same for classes taught by television and those taught in the regular way.[35] There has been perhaps better lecturing by the television teacher because he has had more time to prepare, but some classroom teachers have found their

[33] Ernest Siegel, "Every Classroom an Electronic Classroom," *Audiovisual Instruction* 13:722–23 (Sept., 1968).

[34] Anna L. Meyer, ed., "New Teaching Strategies," *Audiovisual Instruction* 13:8: 820–59 (Nov., 1968).

[35] Donald W. MacLennan and Christopher J. Ried, *Abstracts of Research in Instructional Television and Film: An Annotated Bibliography* (Stanford, Calif.: Institution for Communication Research, April, 1964), p. 4.

teaching regimented and have complained that the particular techniques used in some experiments reduced them to mere technicians. Some students have been enthusiastic, others have been opposed. Scheduling of classes has been complicated by the fact that all participating schools must follow the timing of the television station.

Flexible Scheduling through Independent Study. One well publicized and funded attempt to modify traditional procedures has been that carried on under the direction of Dr. Frank Brown at the Melbourne, Florida, High School. This school organized the day around shorter "modules of time" which were then combined in various ways to provide for different types of subject matter. The student spent much of his time in independent study and teachers were freed for work with a variety of large and small groups. Proponents argued that the scheme permitted students to proceed at their own pace and provided for more satisfactory use of teacher time. Systematic evaluation of the procedures tried was not seriously undertaken and the variety of different experiments being carried on would complicate assessment. Nevertheless the feasibility of dramatic variations in the scheduling of student and teacher time has been demonstrated and the publicity given the school will probably produce a willingness among other schools to modify their practice.

Team Teaching. There have within the past few years been experiments in using teams of teachers. The general idea has been that by getting together different teachers with different areas of competence (or, in some cases, different amounts of experience) more flexibility and variety could be provided, and students could be taught in small or large groups according to the needs of the subject matter.[36]

Proposals for the size of teams and their organization have varied. Some have suggested that a number of specialists should work together. For example, four or five specialists might work simultaneously with a group of 100 students. This type of team teaching would require various sizes of teaching spaces to be available, so that the teachers could work with small or large segments of the group. The emphasis in this approach is on correlation and integration of the team's work, and occasionally members would use materials researched by other teachers in the team.

Other proposals have put forward the idea of a team headed by a master teacher with much professional experience. The other members might consist of a fully-certified teacher with less experience or perhaps a different specialization; two teaching aides with little or no professional preparation; a clerk to handle the more routine work. Advocates of this idea have stressed its administrative efficiency, its advantage of presenting an integrated instructional program, and the possibility of using it for

[36] L. S. Michael, "Team Teaching," *NASSP Bulletin* 47:36–63 (May, 1963).

in-service training. Its critics are primarily concerned about using untrained personnel to carry out teaching responsibilities.[37] Some of these questions are discussed in more detail in the readings in Chapter 15. It will also be interesting to see whether or not the introduction of more computer-assisted programs will create a necessity and a basis for the development of teaching teams.[38]

The Concept of the Comprehensive High School

Perhaps as a summation of the program modifications during the past 50 years, there developed the concept of the comprehensive high school. Its significance is likely to be missed by the college-oriented layman. The idea includes, in its simplest form, an emphasis on the importance of providing an appropriate curriculum for the whole secondary school population, an emphasis on the development of a variety of curricular offerings, and an acceptance of vocational and general education as fundamental responsibilities of the public high school.

The general trends in public education theory have already been described. In this section, discussion will be limited to one or two aspects which have had particular effects on the development of the comprehensive high school.

The European concept of separate schools for students with separate objectives has been rejected in America in favor of the concept of a single high school in each community providing for a variety of different objectives. The factors which made this decision the logical one included concern for democratization and the need for secondary schools in sparsely populated areas.

In an effort to provide greater flexibility for a wide range of students, some schools eventually established up to ten or more different curricula. But this development proved unsatisfactory in some ways, since students whose objectives altered during their high school years found difficulty in changing curricula and were thus handicapped in their later careers. Also the assignment of a particular curriculum to a particular student was sometimes arbitrary. As it became clear that, in American communities, students neither could nor should make an irrevocable vocational choice at an early age, a form of school organization was sought which would allow a later choice. One answer was to provide the common elements of the curricula in the first two years, and to cater for some specialization

---

[37] J. E. Morland, "Think Twice about Team Teaching," *The Instructor* 73:65 (Sept., 1963).

[38] *See* G. Heathers, "Research on Implementing and Evaluating Cooperative Teaching," *The National Elementary Principal* 44:27–33 (Jan., 1965).

in the junior and senior years. Giving students greater freedom of election, and assigning specific courses rather than a complete set of them, also allowed more real flexibility and tended to reduce any artificial social distinctions which had become attached to particular curricula.

Further influences on the development of the comprehensive high school included the increased interest in vocational schooling. One influence which has been partially overlooked is that, following the generous financial help which vocational education received as a result of the 1917 Smith-Hughes Act, federal-state supervision of the programs led to an improvement in teaching techniques in these areas. For instance, more effective use was made of project methods and better contact was established between school and home. A secondary, but significant result of these developments was that more students stayed on in school who felt that the traditional college-preparatory bias of secondary education was inappropriate for them. They and their parents put further pressure on schools to modify programs.

In the exuberance of a child with a new toy, some schools tried to provide training in quantity for every major trade in the community. For example, some printing departments soon found themselves with expensive presses but without students, since they had already trained more printers than could be used in the whole state within a ten-year period. It also became evident that some vocational training could be offered more economically on the job or in the industry.

Gradually there evolved programs described as "diversified occupations" and "distributive education" which operated under the supervision of the school and as a part of the school curriculum. This type of program made it possible for students to study their occupations at school and to practice their skills in regular jobs under the close supervision of their teachers. In this way the benefits of school supervision and assistance were maintained while the dangers of training too many workers or of giving training inappropriate to local conditions could be largely avoided. The continuance of federal support prevented such programs from being too heavy a financial drain on local school budgets.

General Education versus College Preparation. The shift from viewing the public high school's program as exclusively college preparatory to emphasis on its primary function as the general education of all students of secondary school age has had effects throughout the secondary school curriculum. It is to be found in the additional courses which are offered by the comprehensive high school. It is to be found within the outlines of courses which were previously oriented solely to college preparation. It is to be found in the abandonment of curricula bearing specific labels such as "college preparatory-classical" and "college preparatory-general." It is to be found in acceptance of the extracurricular activities of the school as a valid part of the school program. It is to be found in the teaching techniques being used. It is to be found in the increasing proportion of the secondary age youth attending school.

Summary

The past 40 to 50 years have witnessed considerable modification within the framework established at the beginning of the century. Departmentalization is still a major feature of the program of the high school but the structure of the subject matter being offered is under considerable scrutiny. New arrangements within subject areas and the possibilities for cutting across areas have been explored. The relationships between the elementary school, the high school, and the college have been modified. The four-year high school has in a majority of the school systems given way to a junior and senior high school on one end of the scale and to the development of the community college on the other. Stress on provisions for the needs of the individual student and the tremendous increase in the number of different types of students have brought a variety of responses including an increase in the variety of course offerings, a reduction in the number of required courses, a view of secondary education as general rather than college preparatory in function, an increase in remedial work, and a greater concern for adapting coursework to suit individual progress. The various pressures and the changes which they have wrought have been accompanied by acceptance of the idea that the American public high school is to be a comprehensive rather than a specialized institution.

8

The Informal Phases of
the School Curriculum

ONE OF THE SIGNIFICANT CHANGES IN THE PUBLIC HIGH SCHOOL PROGRAM during the past 50 years has been the development of what is referred to variously as its "extra-class," "extracurricular," "co-curricular," or "activities" program. Although the elaborateness of this program varies from school to school, even the smallest is likely to have some form of it.

Informal Learning in the School Program

While there were school-related activities in American schools 75 to 100 years ago, they became more important during the period between 1920 and 1945. The new emphasis, most forcefully stated in the 1930's, was referred to as "the activity principle." The notion that learning was a process of developing the mind's faculties through exercise in academic pursuits gave way to a stress on the importance of learning by doing. The elementary school responded to this emphasis by modifying its teaching procedures and classroom content. The high school added "extracurricular activities."

First, some of the practical arrangements and considerations which these activities involve will be mentioned.

Activities in the School Day. Activities of an informal nature carried on within the school day fall into five categories (1) club-type activities, (2) publications, (3) dramatics, debating, and musical activities, (4) intramural athletics, and (5) student government.

Club-type activities are typically arranged on a regular schedule during the school day. Many schools have what is called an activities period with a weekly schedule set up for different meetings. Others provide within the class schedule for activities or "interest subjects" without designating a single "activity period." The variety of clubs is likely to be limited by (1) the interests of the students and (2) the availability of staff and financing.

Many schools require all their students to participate in some club activity. Some schools permit the setting of restrictive qualifications for membership in certain clubs, such as election by the membership or approval by the faculty sponsor. Others insist that any such restriction is contrary to the school's aim of permitting each student to benefit from the program to the limit of his own potential. Where the club's purpose is to produce some spectacle for public performance such restriction may become necessary. In such cases tryouts open to the entire student body and carefully judged may help relieve the charge of favoritism.

Where clubs act as an extension of class activities on a less formal basis there may be serious question as to what new purpose is served. When these activities are popular with the students or represent the only available approach to informality in the school program, they can be justified. Sometimes club activities are used to pull students from separate classes for larger group or more specialized activity.

In addition to clubs which are extensions of class activity, others provide special types of instruction. There may be, for example, photography, public speaking, hiking, or camping clubs, stamp or coin collecting clubs, and art clubs.

Part of the emphasis in club-type activities is on student operation. The faculty sponsor is in the role of resource person, assisting in the planning but encouraging as much pupil direction as possible. The advantage for training in leadership is obvious. Even the less able student learns about such things as parliamentary procedure. It is presumed that the absence of grades and marks and the students' participation in planning assures greater pertinence to their needs. There is evidence that this is true. Where clubs are dominated by the sponsors, this benefit is reduced.

Next to the club-type activities in prevalence are those related to school publications. Sometimes this kind of activity has become a part of the class schedule under the heading of journalism. It serves two or three distinct functions. It provides some students with an opportunity for learning the basic creative skills in composition. It provides students with news and information about school activities and a medium for disseminating their news. It serves as a public relations contact between the school and the home.

One problem of any activities program is the possibility that students, either from choice or pressure from the authorities, will spend too much time on it. If the paper is published too often and if standards are set too high, long hours of work after school and interference with other important activities may result for the students involved. While student interest seems to be heightened by increases in the amount of time invested, the program may get out of balance. Sporadic publication and low standards may, on the other hand, cause the program to be ineffectual. Spreading opportunities for participation to all students who are interested is sometimes a problem. It is much easier to arrange an organizational pattern in which each member of the staff has a single responsibility than to rotate responsibilities or have distinct staffs to publish alternate issues.

Part of the justification for the expenses incurred for publications must be found in the use made of them after they are printed.

Dramatic, debating, and musical activities provide opportunities for the development of skill and appreciation. The costs involved usually make it necessary to choose between single productions by a limited number of students or participation by many. In drama the choice may be between a single senior play or some club-type activity involving many. In debating the choice often has to be made between forming a school team or arranging different types of public speaking opportunities for a larger number of students in school. In extra-class musical activities the finished performance may sometimes take precedence over provision for broader participation. The choice may also sometimes have to be made between the relatively limited opportunities provided by a marching band and the musically more sophisticated school orchestra.

The intramural athletic program has received increasing emphasis, particularly since the importance has been recognized of providing athletic activity for all students rather than for a few skilled contestants. In the very small school, most of the interested student body may be taken care of in the varsity program. The larger the school, the less likely this becomes. The first emphasis in the intramurals is likely to be on major team sports.

Among the most glamorous but troublesome phases of the extra-class activities are the interscholastic athletic and other contests. In no other aspect of the life of the school is it so difficult to keep the welfare of the individual uppermost. In no other aspect of the school program is the professional leadership of the school principal as likely to be by-passed. No other member of the teaching staff is as likely as the coach to be subject to dismissal for failing to meet popular demand.

Elaborate efforts have been made by school personnel to avoid over-emphasis on varsity competition. In athletics, the satisfactions, both public and private, which can be gained from developing students' skill make it tempting to shape the rest of the physical education program of the school (and even of the elementary and junior high schools) around the varsity program. It is difficult to know the point at which the emphasis becomes too great. If the student enjoys the process, part of the cost can be justified as recreational activity. If the skills gained carry as a by-product the efficient development of the student's physical endowment, they are perhaps worth the effort.

There is some evidence that so high a degree of specialization is not particularly desirable. Careful medical supervision may be necessary to prevent the possibility of physical damage. In some cases, talented students have been encouraged to continue after they have been injured because they were more skillful than their substitutes. That this may have been done at the insistence of the students, under the emotional tension of the situation, does not relieve school personnel of the moral responsibility for their further injury.[1]

Perhaps the change in the entertainment available to the community as a result of television will serve to permit the high school to limit its sports program to those activities which can be justified for educational value alone. Until such a time, careful control by the principal, superintendent, and school board is essential. Adequate financial support from tax funds, rigid insistence on the enforcement of regulations as to eligibility, selection of coaching personnel for their concern for player welfare, supervision by the principal of coaching methods used, and regulation of the amount of practice time, and the number of games played will help the situation in most schools.

The School's Responsibility for Social Life and Recreation. The social life and recreation of high school students is important in their educational development. On the other hand, it has traditionally been the responsibility of the family and of the other agencies of the society to cater to their needs in these respects. In some schools the principal school social activity during out-of-school hours is a very formal junior-senior banquet or dance, although of course the social and recreational aspects of the athletic program cannot be overlooked. Frequently the student council or class groups also sponsor parties or dances at school.

Some schools have found that social activities sponsored by "fraternities" and "sororities" can have harmful effects. In some communities such organizations have been banned either by school board action or by statute.[2] In others the strategy has been to provide a more acceptable substitute at school. Recent years have seen the development of parent leagues to help in the development and policing of acceptable codes of social behavior for those upper-middle class youngsters who were formerly less well supervised. To ignore the fraternity movement has not been acceptable either to parents or to school officials. Unsupervised activity

[1] There were 333 deaths during the period 1931 to 1956 directly or indirectly attributed to high school football. (*See* American Football Coaches Association Committee on Injuries and Fatalities, *Twenty-Fifth Annual Survey of Football Fatalities,* 1957).

[2] *See* Frank Nania, "School Boards Can Abolish Secret Societies," *American School Board Journal* 139:38–39 (Nov., 1959).

has resulted in unsocial excesses and in a cliquishness which interferes with the normal operation of student elections, activities, or even the simple social contact between students at school.

It has now been recognized that a school program for social education should involve more than dancing and that it is appropriate for the school to teach a variety of recreational skills. These skills may be taught during the school lunch hour, during scheduled time within the physical education program, or at the time of the social itself. Social activities provide numerous opportunities for cultivating skills in mingling with other people and for breaking down class barriers. Students need more opportunities for wholesome heterosexual activity.

The School as a Social Laboratory

The homeroom, the class, the school assembly, the student government, and the subsidiary systems of elections, awards, honors, and commencement activities, give corporate life and vitality to the society that is a school. It is through these aspects of group living that the school succeeds or fails in its attempt to democratize American life. If the battles of Britain are "won on the playing fields of Eton and Harrow," the struggle for the American way of life may well be won in the homerooms and assemblies of the public high school.

The homeroom's influence usually operates through two separate types of activity. The first is the morning assembly of students at which time the record keeping activities are carried out, the role is checked, announcements made, and perhaps some type of ritual conducted. The second is the homeroom meeting in which officers are elected, certain committees perhaps appointed, plans for social and athletic activities made, general school problems discussed, delegates to the student council instructed, reports received, and even formal instruction is carried on. Such meetings may be regularly scheduled, or fused into the briefer daily morning routine.

It is frequently the homeroom teacher who is expected to know the student well, receive marks and reports from other teachers, visit the family, advise the student with regard to his academic program, and secure the assistance of the counseling and psychological services of the school. The homeroom was created in the hope that it would make a center for each student and would help him feel that he is an important part of the school community.

The homeroom is usually a subdivision of the class or year group to which students are assigned and designated as freshman, sophomore, junior or senior. In most schools these classes have certain functions in the corporate life of the school, meet periodically as a group, elect officers, and carry out projects. The senior and junior classes are the ones given the most encouragement in this respect. The senior class will publish the yearbook, produce the senior play, and may even take an extended trip to New York or Washington. The importance of the identification with a class group which results from participating in traditional projects is not easy to estimate. Identification with a broad social group should not be overlooked as a technique for breaking down the less democratic bonds of social class.

The third unit to which a particular student belongs is the student body itself, as organized in the school assembly and—in a representative sense—in the student government. The school assembly is perhaps as old as the high school itself. In the one-room school it provided a time for announcements, corporate worship, and the routines of attendance taking. In most modern schools these activities have been taken over by the homeroom, but there are still some functions served by the practice of meeting large segments of the student body in groups. For one thing, it helps group identification. For another, participating in such things as ritual or group singing is designed to improve general morale. An additional function is perhaps simply to teach the techniques of being part of an audience situation.

School assemblies offer chances for mass instruction, for the display of worthwhile accomplishment on the part of a group or club, for the development of poise on the part of student leaders in the orderly discussion of group business. The discussion of moral issues arising in the life of the school may also have an important place in the school assembly program. Obviously such programs vary in quality from school to school. One particularly controversial matter is the place of religious activity in any school assembly. This is being questioned at the moment both in the courts and among school personnel.

The Student Council, Student Government, Student Courts, and Honor Systems. As important to some high schools as the school assembly and closely related to it is the representative student council. In many schools, some of the responsibility for the control and supervision of student life has been delegated to a representative group. This must of course be a tentative delegation. The principal and school faculty have the legal responsibility for school discipline.

The amount of delegation of responsibility varies from one school to another. An elective council will sometimes plan school assembly programs, discuss such simple problems as beautifying the corridors, monitor the halls or study halls, charter extracurricular activities, and schedule or sponsor school socials. Occasionally, the student government has more extensive authority for passing regulations and maintaining a student court.

In such cases it is usually clear that the principal still maintains veto and review authority. Although it is always possible that such delegation of authority will get out of hand, some schools have found such arrangements to be very satisfactory.[3] Critics have feared that use of the veto would create hard feelings, that student courts would deal too harshly or inconsistently, that too much student time would be required for petty problems, and that members of the court would probably develop a feeling of false superiority. Other school principals have found that such problems were not particularly serious, that the school became more of a laboratory for democracy, and that morale was improved. Where student courts were maintained, the court officials faced with responsibility were anxious to obtain guidance from the sponsor. Parents who raised questions seemed satisfied with the desirability of these procedures when they were explained.[4]

In schools with student courts, the students and staff exercise co-ordinate responsibility. The teacher is still responsible for his own class procedures. The student council takes action (subject to review) which seems necessary to the development of a good situation. They may deal with behavior in the lunchroom or hall, vandalism, cheating, or any other problems which may be handled by persuasion or regulation. With proper advice from the faculty sponsor they can be encouraged to stay out of situations which are more appropriately the responsibility of the principal or school staff. It is important that any student council assume such responsibility voluntarily and not simply be forced to take over duties which the principal finds unpleasant.

American democratic government depends less on rules and regulations than on the thoughtful behavior of the populace. This is something which the sponsor of the student council is likely to point out to overly zealous student councils. The council may spend more time appointing committees to study problems than it does passing regulations. Nevertheless, recognition of the place for regulation is important to the process of understanding democratic government.

Some schools have traditions of student government which are well institutionalized and transmitted from one group to the next. There is sometimes a student code and, imitating the colleges, an honor system. To the extent that such codes are the subject for student discussion and acceptance they are worthwhile. The danger is that they are not student codes designed by students for their own direction but are the work of faculty members imposed on the student group. They then may become symbols of hypocrisy. The principal advantage of having a student code

[3] Frederick T. Shipp, "How Can the Student Council Function More Effectively in the Secondary School?" *NASSP Bulletin* 34:28–33 (March, 1950).

[4] Stuart A. Anderson, "Where Students Maintain Much of Their Own Discipline," *Nation's Schools* 67:71–73 (May, 1961).

is in the opportunity it creates for students to study the ethics of student behavior. The student group most benefited is the one which draws up the code.

There is no doubt that cheating represents a problem in most high schools.[5] The system of testing and marking encourages it. Since cheating is a form of dishonesty, the school cannot safely ignore its existence. For so long as the student thinks of cheating as a part of the game by which he avoids adult control it will remain a problem. Honor systems appeal to students to assume more control over their own morals.

Most of the honor systems in use require students to agree not to cheat, to agree to sign a statement that they have not cheated, and in return to be relieved of the symbol of their subservience, the test monitor. Most students are quite willing to have the teacher relinquish his role as test monitor. The big objection comes to the necessity for reporting others who have cheated. It has been found feasible to get sufficient acceptance of an honor system to reduce the incidence of cheating. Discussions which stress the responsibility of a student for his own behavior and for the maintenance of a moral society represent good training for citizenship. The problem comes when the student generation which developed the code has graduated and the system begins to be a means for getting a few students to monitor the class for the teacher.

Honor Societies, Awards, and Valedictorians. The problem in a democratic school is to decide whether it is appropriate to recognize achievement competitively when the school is supposed to be concerned with the development of the potential of each individual. Since each student has a different potential, competitive standards should be less prominent than individual standards. While the existence of competition serves to stimulate some students to improve, there are others for whom the effect is either discouragement or smugness.[6]

In imitation of national societies at the college level such as Phi Beta Kappa, there are two honor groups sponsored by the National Association of Secondary School Principals: the National Honor Society, and the Junior National Honor Society.[7] Members are elected by the school faculty on the basis of scholastic and other qualities such as leadership in the school activities. Those selected are tapped in an elaborate ceremony and encouraged to serve as a service club for the school. While possibly faculty selection is less open to abuse than student selection, there is still a strong tendency to perpetuate social class stratification.

---

[5] *Cf.* K. H. Sandemeyer, "Who is Kidding Whom?" *High School Journal* 43: 17–22 (Oct., 1959).

[6] *Cf.* H. A. Davidson, M. L. Schriver, H. J. Peters, "Should Johnny Compete or Co-operate?" *The NEA Journal* 49:30–32 (Oct., 1960).

[7] *Cf.* I. F. Butterworth, "Why Not a Chapter of the National Honor Society?" *NASSP Bulletin* 43:43–46 (Sept., 1959).

The Administration of Extra-Class Activities

Because of the variety and importance of the extra-class activities, it becomes important to establish basic policies of administration. The following additional points are some which should be borne in mind when a program is being planned.

1. Preference should be given to types of activity in which many students will be able to participate and from which they can gain knowledge and enjoyment.
2. In some situations, more attention could be paid to fitting in the school program with other activities in the community. Some attempt should be made to analyze the opportunities already easily available to the student. Smaller schools or ones with particular staffing problems might find it better to encourage some of their pupils to join certain outside groups. In other cases, both school and community can benefit from some sharing of knowledge, enthusiasm, and facilities.
3. All school-sponsored activities should contribute toward the social growth and happiness of the individual student and the school as a whole.
4. The time and energy spent by any student should not be so great as to interfere with other types of school work, home activities and responsibilities, or his health.
5. Within reason, the more students can participate in the planning and running of these activities, the more they seem to enjoy them and learn from them.

Two other points have to be discussed: staff and finance.

Staffing the Informal Program. Since high school teaching staff members are usually certified and selected on the basis of their suitability to teach the academic aspects of the program, it is little wonder that the extracurricular program may be restricted by their lack of qualifications. This helps to explain the dominance of class-related clubs which seem of less value as a supplementary phase of the school program. The advisers to publications, public speaking, and dramatics, for example, are likely to be English teachers.

The assignment of teachers to act as advisers on related activities is desirable, providing the teacher is competent in the activity and care is taken not to overload a few members of the staff.[8] The determination of what constitutes a full load is not easy, for some work more efficiently or conscientiously than others. In some cases a teacher may have a hobby

[8] L. H. Fritzemeier, "Fair Way to Measure Extra Work for Teachers," *Educational Executives Overview* 4:25–27 (August, 1963).

very different from his regular class work and may be glad to have the chance to change subjects.

Financing the Informal Program. Perhaps the fairest basis for determining the relationship between load and salary is to set what is considered a "full-time" assignment and then to pay people who have equal training and experience proportionately more for more work.[9] The issue is complicated by problems of supply. When it is possible to get a more sought-after or needed person by paying more, there is a temptation to do so. This is true, for instance, with regard to the shortage of men in the classroom and in activities which require them.

While the payment of the staff for supervising extra-class activities is provided out of regular funds, other expenses are not always provided in the same way. The most expensive phase of the program is varsity athletics, because of the cost of uniforms, equipment, and travel, but there is no phase which is entirely free. The additional expense may be borne directly by students, indirectly through money-making activities, by contributions from people in the community, or by additional support by the school board.

Most students of American secondary education agree that the best basis of support is taxation and the poorest is assessment of the students. If an activity is legitimately a part of the school program, is to be supervised by school personnel, and is to make use of tax-provided facilities, there is little justification for not making it a part of the tax-supported program. One of the problems when outside support has to be relied on is the development of a lopsided program. The most spectacular phases get the most money and the least spectacular, the least. Where such a program as the varsity athletic program must depend on outside support it often also has to accept some outside control.

Many students of secondary education are concerned with the time and effort expended on raising money.[10] There is also the question of whether the methods used are always legitimate ones. If it is raised through conducting magazine sales, there may be problems of accounts management, undue pressure on parents to buy publications they do not need or want, and competition with sales by adults. If it is raised through carnivals or from tickets for other entertainments at school, the problem of exploitation of students is still present. Much of the activity of the so-called carnival is traditionally unworthy of school sponsorship. If money is raised through bake sales, it represents a tax on the parents who contributed the materials for the things being sold as well as an exploitation of the time of the students. While such activities may en-

[9] "Extra Pay for Extra Duties," *NEA Research Bulletin* 41:50–51 (May, 1963).
[10] *Cf.* W. E. Kirkpatrick, "Student Organizations and Charity Drives," *School Activities* 35:84 (Nov., 1963).

courage more parent and community interest in school affairs, the problems involved are too frequently overlooked.

Where the money is raised by the Parent Teacher Association or by a boosters club, the problems of controlling the activity and taxing the parents are again raised. There is also the question of whether the raising of money does not keep the PTA from more important matters dealing with the improvement of understanding between school and home.

Perhaps the operation of a school store to sell necessary school supplies represents one of the more legitimate money-raising efforts. Even here, however, the amount of money that can be raised is likely to be quite limited in relation to the amount needed to support an adequate program of informal activities. If such a school store can be operated, why should not the supplies be sold at cost? The profit made in this way is still a charge on the parents and hence to some extent a barrier to school attendance.

The issue being raised here with regard to the informal activities is little different from that raised 100 years ago with regard to the desirability of free public education. It seems better to provide educational opportunity for all in proportion to their need and to that of the society, and to provide for its support through taxation of all in proportion to their ability to pay. If the extracurricular program is a legitimate part of the program of the school, it should be provided at public expense.

Charity Drives in the School

Closely related to the problem of fund raising in the public schools is the problem of charity drives. There is apparently no fund-raising group which does not bring pressure on school authorities to conduct a part of its campaign in the school. The argument is that by starting to give in the school, students will learn to participate in charitable enterprises and will take part in them after graduation. But there are many counter arguments. The amount of money raised is small, while the expense of the drive is carried by the taxpayer. Little thought is given to whether all of the group can afford to give or to the fact that the money given was earned not by the child but by his parents. Some of the money given could better have been spent on a school lunch. Pressures for charity applied to a captive and sensitive audience are almost vicious. If there is a single area in which the family represents a better unit for education than the school it is in the area of charitable giving. Charity may be encouraged and discussed at school, but in the last analysis it is a matter for the family to provide.

9

Guidance and Counseling Services in the School Program

ALTHOUGH THE MODERN GUIDANCE MOVEMENT DATES BACK AT LEAST TO the period between 1910 and 1920, the significant development of the program has come within the past 30 years.[1] In the modern high school guidance and counseling services are a coordinate phase of the program paralleling the formal and informal curricular activities of the school. That there is a distinction made between guidance and teaching or between counseling and teaching is the result of the nature of the school's evolution. The difficulty of modifying the traditional program made drawing lines of distinction necessary.

The school guidance services may be defined as including all activities of school personnel designed to make the school program appropriate to solving the problems of the individual student. Counseling is the process by which the student is assisted in finding the answers to the problems he recognizes. In most instances counseling involves a direct and private contact between a student and a counselor.

The Need for Guidance Services

Although the secondary school has, doubtless, always provided some of the services which would fit the definition above, the emphasis of the modern school on guidance is in large part the seemingly inevitable result of four distinct forces: (1) an expanded school population, (2) a changing pattern of social organization, (3) a changing concept of the school's role, and (4) a growing awareness of the nature of individual differences.

[1] L. M. Miller, "NVGA Historical Highlight," *Vocational Guidance Quarterly* 11:167–72 (Spring, 1963).

182

The Guidance of an Expanded School Population. For a long time the school population was drawn from a single segment of society and the program was viewed as largely academic in content and purpose. Neither the general public nor school officials expected the school to be much concerned with students' problems. If the subject matter which the school was expected to teach had any utilitarian or pragmatic functions, these were subordinate to what was considered the more fundamental aim of developing mental discipline.

As the social forces which combined to force into the school larger and larger segments of the population began to operate, it became apparent that an education whose chief characteristic was its selectivity must be re-oriented. More and more children were being "selected." The enlarged student body came with a greater variety of vocational aspirations and with a greater variety of opportunities open to them. They, also, had a variety of capabilities.

The first of the guidance responsibilities recognized by the school was that for vocational guidance.[2] For a period it seemed as if everyone was assuming that there was some best vocational choice for each student, and that by giving aptitude tests that choice could be determined. The presumption seemed to be that, after the proper vocation had been selected, then the school's guidance responsibility would be met by seeing that each student followed a course of study appropriate to the vocation chosen. Some of the enthusiasts assumed that such vocational choices could be made quite early—even before beginning secondary education.

Gradually it became obvious that vocational guidance must consist of more than aptitude tests. Making a vocational choice was not so simple that it could be achieved by all students during the period of their secondary education. For some students this was rather obviously a time of vocational exploration. For others there seemed to be no need for exploration until after secondary education was over.

Gradually a transition occurred. The emphasis in the guidance movement shifted from "vocational" to "educational" guidance. Many of the students who were not ready for much vocational guidance were the ones who were going on to college. Decisions about whether to go and which college to choose were viewed as requiring guidance. Some of the testing and counseling techniques developed as a part of the vocational guidance movement could also be used in educational guidance. Once the choice had been made to go on to college, the guidance function consisted of determining what the admissions requirements of the appropriate school were and of seeing that they had been met. Different colleges had different standards and it became evident, for instance, that

[2] *See* Donald G. Patterson, "The Genesis of Modern Guidance," in Gail F. Farwell and Herman J. Peters, eds., *Guidance Reading for Counselors* (Chicago: Rand McNally and Company, 1960), pp. 103–105.

the student who might be unsuccessful at one might be successful at another. Also, colleges offered different fields of specialization and a school staff could help to select one which seemed appropriate to a student's current vocational choices.

Gradually, it became apparent that, with the expanding school population, there were many problems which did not fall under the heading either of vocational counseling or educational counseling. There were students for whom the school did not offer any program which would be of vocational value and who were not interested in attending college. Follow-up studies of former students were needed to see how appropriate the school program had been, not simply in vocational training but in meeting its other objectives. There were counseling problems directly related to the teaching role of the school and others which, while only indirectly related, had important implications for the school program.

Collecting information about students and providing it to teachers and staff members became more and more important, partly because of the new diversity of the student population and partly because new techniques had been developed for getting and using the information. The testing movement could be a powerful aid to the effectiveness of the school program provided the tests were given, interpreted, and made available to the people in a position to use them. The work of social workers and school psychologists was likely to be wasted unless there was some systematic attempt to keep the necessary records and to coordinate the efforts of the various parts of the school staff.

The Changing Nature of Society as a Factor. Not only was the population of the school altering but the nature of society itself was changing. Indeed the increase in the school population came because of the changing nature of society. The shift from a rural to an urban culture brought a shift in the vocational opportunities and, more importantly, in the whole environment in which students were being educated. Because they were no longer going to learn the occupation of their parents at home, they were going to have to receive help in deciding on a vocational choice and in learning vocational skills.

The technological unemployment of the 1930's made even more obvious the complexity of both vocational training and guidance. The increasing selectivity of some colleges made the matter of choosing a college in terms of the ability of the student important. The increased complexity of urban living over that of rural life in the horse and buggy days made the supervision of adolescents by their parents seem more and more difficult. As a result the school was called on to provide more assistance in helping students to understand the nature of the problems they faced in such areas as recreation, heterosexual adjustment, and relationships with adults. Even the matter of preparing young men to accept the necessity of military service and to make wise plans for it became a matter of concern to the school guidance officials.[3]

Inevitably as the school program was expanded to include the whole school-age population, changes in the nature of the society became more and more the concern of the school. Leaders of society realized that the school was a social agency which had influence over a wide section of the population at a formative age and which was directly under the control of the government itself. Whatever guidance was needed seemed almost automatically to be considered a responsibility of the school. When accident prevention became obviously important, the school was asked to teach first aid and safety. When the automobile death rate became alarmingly high, the schools were asked to teach driver education. If drinking caused concern, alcohol education was provided. When the incidence of venereal disease created anxiety, sex education was demanded. The school was recognized as the guidance agency for society as a whole.

The extent to which society's nature has changed is apparent from the accompanying chart of the first jobs of high school graduates in 1965

First Job Classification of High School Graduates of 1965 Not Entering College (Percentages)*

Classification	Male	Female
Professional or Technical	2.4	.6
Farmers or Farm Managers	.7	—
Managers, Officials and Proprietors, except Farm	1.6	.4
Clerical and Kindred Workers	12.0	52.3
Sales Workers	2.4	7.6
Craftsmen, Foremen, and Kindred Workers	11.3	.4
Operatives and Kindred Workers	34.1	15.4
Private Household Workers	—	6.4
Other Service Workers	10.6	15.8
Farm Laborers and Foremen	4.2	.8
Laborers Except Farm and Mine	21.3	.4

* Data from Digest of Educational Statistics, 1966 ed. (Washington, D.C.: U.S. Department of Health, Education, and Welfare, 1966), p. 102.

not entering college. A very short time ago many of the students would have entered farming. The changes which have taken place in farming, manufacturing, running a household, marketing, and even in waging war

[3] Cf. William P. McClure, "The Challenge of Vocational and Technical Education," Phi Delta Kappan 43:212–17 (1963).

within the past 60 years have served to replace a rural horse-drawn civilization with an urban mechanical one. The development of testing and counseling methods has assisted in the modification of a school program designed for the more leisurely living of the eighteenth and nineteenth centuries.

The Changing Concept of the School as a Factor. The process of adapting the school program to a changing society is not a simple one. In the first place it is not always clear what represents a necessary modification. One of the traditional functions of education is to conserve the values of the society in which it exists. In a rapidly changing society it is not clear which are the values to be conserved and which are becoming outmoded. It is also not clear who is to make the decision. Frequently it is simpler to maintain all the old procedures and then to add new ones as supplementary than to replace one phase of a program with another. Sometimes the programs resulting from the attempt both to adopt the new and to conserve the old are cumbersome and even fragmentary.

As it became obvious that adapting the school program to the needs of individuals involved more than helping students with their vocational or educational choices, the concept of guidance was expanded. The school guidance services became the coordinating force which not only helped students select courses but helped teachers adapt the courses to the needs of the students.

Fact finding was an important part of the guidance program. What were the responsibilities of the school in a particular community? To answer this question required information about the true nature of the community, including the other agencies operating there. What were the needs of the particular students attending the school? These were questions which it seemed possible for the guidance services to test objectively. There was, however, other information which must be gathered and which could not be obtained from formal testing. For instance, what problems were being faced by particular students in their personal and social development? What were the obstacles being faced by the student in his adjustment to the program of the school itself? Answering such questions became important for modifying the school program both in its totality and in its effect on individual students.

A second vital part of the guidance program was the interpretation of the facts discovered to those who were responsible for administering the school. There was no particular value in knowing how nearly the school was meeting the community's needs unless that information was going to be translated into some changes in the school itself. Similarly, there was no particular point in knowing the problems of an individual student unless the people who were teaching him could make use of that information.

As the school's program came to be viewed as one designed to meet the needs of the entire body of youth of secondary school age, guidance activities became the key to the school's success. The school which did not have some kind of provision for guidance services was operating blindly.

Awareness of Responsibility for Student Welfare. It is obvious that schools must have always had some concern for the welfare of their students. It is however evident that in the late nineteenth century there was little machinery for determining either the nature of students' problems or for modifying the program to meet their needs.

While the school's responsibility for an expanded population, the changing nature of the society, and the changing concept of the school's role all played a part in increased concern for student welfare, other factors were also influential. One of the most important was the testing movement itself. It became possible during the twentieth century to get an objective appreciation of the nature of individual differences within the student body; being able to measure these differences helped staffs to understand that programs should be modified to make provision for these differences.

Two important factors were the growing influence and sophistication of the fields of psychology and sociology. As more and more became known about the nature of human development, it became more obvious that education was a hopeful process. Behavior was caused, and by modifying the influence of the environment the behavior itself could be modified. Because each individual was different both in his inheritance and in his real environment, it was important to see what variations in instruction were appropriate. Group techniques would have to be sufficiently flexible to provide for individual differences. Guidance became one of the techniques by which the group process was modified to meet individual needs.

Recognizing some of the social forces operating brought awareness of the need to consider the effect the school program was having on the students. It became obvious that, unless this program was sufficiently flexible to provide for children with a negative home environment at the same time as for those whose home background was adequate, the whole social fabric might be in danger.

Perhaps the chief influence in the school's developing of an awareness of its responsibility for student welfare has been the refinement of the public's concept of democracy. Educational philosophers played a large part in this movement. The concept of education as a process of adjusting the individual to the needs of the society was reconciled with the idea of it as a process for developing the individual's potential. Only twentieth century educational thought seems to have recognized that these two concepts must and can be reconciled. As a result the individual and his creative potential have become more important than at any other stage in history. School guidance services became one of the tools by which the program is to be adapted to the demands of democracy.

The Nature of Guidance Services

One approach to cataloguing guidance services is by recognizing the different people in the school to whom these services are rendered. There are four categories served: (1) school officials, (2) teachers, (3) groups of students, and (4) individual students. One of the keys to understanding the nature of the guidance program is to recognize that in each case the emphasis is on service rendered. Guidance activities are service activities, not ends in themselves.

Services to School Officials. School officials have the responsibility for helping to design and operate an educational program. The guidance program can provide them with several kinds of information. It can inform them concerning the nature of the community in which the school is located, the nature of the student body, the nature of the holding power of the school, the cause of student dropout, the reactions of former students, and the effectiveness of the school program in dealing with the specific problems of individual students.

Information about the nature of the community may be gathered in a variety of ways. Statistics about its size, industry, rate of growth, the proportion of homes in which both parents may be working, the religious preference of the children in school, and related matters may be gathered from the community library, the local employment agency, the cumulative records kept at school, or by interviewing students, teachers, and others who may have lived in the area for a long period of time.

The program of a school in a community in which two-thirds of the parents are engaged in farming may be quite different from that found in a community where most of the population works in the local cotton mills. A school located in a rural community where it is known that the majority of the students plan to leave the farm may arrange a program different from the one set up by a similar rural school which anticipates that its students will probably remain. School officials are likely to become interested if they find the dropout rate in their school is markedly higher than that for similar schools in other communities. An analysis of the nature of the problem might suggest changes which could be, and should be, made in the school program.[4]

[4] *Cf.* W. H. Bristow, "Curriculum Problems Regarding Early School Leavers," *Education Digest* 29:13–15 (April, 1964).

The policy of schools with regard to the treatment of particularly controversial issues may vary according to whether or not the religious make-up of the community is homogeneous. The discussion of labor relations may be different in a community school in which children of both labor and management are enrolled from what would be found in a school made up largely of children from farm families.

The extracurricular activities and recreational needs of students may be different in a school in which both parents are working from those found in a community in which only one parent works. In one community, the curriculum may need to reflect the fact that most students expect to continue their education in a college or technical school. Student government may be an important activity in an area in which it is known that there is a high rate of juvenile delinquency.

While much of the information which has been mentioned here might be gathered by the school principal rather than by the director of guidance, the fact remains that it ought to be gathered systematically. In addition to information dealing with the community and its relationship to the school, systematically tabulated information is also needed with regard to students' standing on various achievement tests, vocational interest tests, aptitude tests, and health examinations. Since the staff works within the philosophy that the program should be designed to meet the needs of individual students and of the community as a whole, it is obvious that a survey of the nature of the community and of the student group is a necessary part of operating the school.

Services to Teachers. Much of the information needed by the principal is also needed by teachers. In addition, the teacher will want specific information about the background of the students whom he is teaching both as a group and as individuals. It will be helpful for him to have information about the home from which a student comes, his position in the family, his adjustment to his home, his general academic ability, his past record of achievement, his reading level, his skill level in subjects such as composition, his interests both immediate and long-range, and his adjustment to the school program.

Much of the information which a teacher needs he may gather himself; some of it should be made readily available to him from the school records. In any case, the process of gathering and using such information is a part of the guidance function of the school. The more students a particular teacher has, the more difficult it becomes for him to gather all the information he needs; and the more important it becomes to have guidance personnel to help him.

The cumulative record forms, kept in practically all schools, serve as the basis for recording the information likely to be needed by teachers. In understaffed schools these records are often poorly kept because, while they are of great usefulness, keeping them requires time and diligence. Adequate testing programs are similarly time consuming. The record most carefully kept is likely to be the marks received on subjects.

A second type of service which may be rendered by guidance personnel has to do with interpreting the information gathered. Any teacher having difficulty with particular students may wish help in determining the causes of his problem. The guidance worker may be alert to particular situations which the regular teacher may not have been aware of or may have overlooked. Perhaps the student has demonstrated a lack of proficiency in reading or is emotionally upset. He may need remedial help. It may be discovered that a student is having difficulty in other teachers' classes and concerted effort by several members of the staff may be desirable.

New teachers may find that orientation to the community is important to their effectiveness; the guidance services of the school may facilitate this orientation. The social studies teacher may wish to be referred to the local historians for points of local interest or to be briefed on community problems which may serve as appropriate starting points for teaching units in civics or problems of democracy. The science teacher may need to know of possible field trips or resource people available in the community. Even statistical information about the community may prove helpful.

Services to Students in Groups. The guidance personnel also provide systematic assistance to groups of students. There will occasionally be specific classes or courses which are considered more directly a part of the guidance program than of the academic curriculum. Courses in "occupations" and some of the ones labeled "core" courses may be listed under this heading. The more frequent approach, however, to group guidance is in the activities of the homerooms.[5]

One of the oldest forms of group guidance relies on a survey of occupations in the community. In some cases this approach amounted to little more than memorizing descriptions of jobs and job requirements, but in others it has been a very helpful type of study of the nature of different types of work with special provision for field trips and other use of local resources. When the course in occupations was well taught it was not merely an opportunity for vocational exploration for the student, but also a chance to develop better understanding of other people in the community.

When the "core" courses in the school use student problems as a starting point for units of work, they perform a guidance function. Of course the use of student participation in the planning, even when the

[5] *Cf.* C. E. Vontress, "Quacking in the Homeroom," *The Clearing House* 38: 23–25 (Sept., 1963).

central theme is not the solution of student problems, should help very materially in the improvement of student attitudes toward the school program and even in orienting the instruction in directions which students will find more helpful. The chance for the student to develop a feeling of participation in the direction of his own destiny is important.

Perhaps the principal vehicle for a good guidance program is the homeroom organization. It is the homeroom teacher who is responsible for keeping many of the records which serve as a basis for much of the guidance program. It is the homeroom teacher who is expected to make contact with the parents. Much of the school's social life, with its opportunities for guidance in such areas as heterosexual adjustment, is centered on homeroom activities. Frequently the same group of students and the same teachers will stay together for two or more years. This continuity helps the development of a strong sense of group membership and also gives the teacher more time to get to know the students and their problems.

In some schools a weekly discussion program in the homeroom period serves to help students to understand and work out problems which are not likely to be dealt with in the more formal curriculum. In these discussions a variety of problems may be discussed, including the improvement of study habits, getting along with adults, school regulations and student government, cheating and vandalism, and even current events which seem of significance. While, as in the case of good "core programs," there should be stress on student participation in the planning, these activities require stimulation both from the homeroom teacher and from the school guidance director.

Additional guidance for groups of students may be provided during school assemblies and school-planned recreational events. Where care is taken that speakers and programs deal with problems of interest to students in a manner likely to be acceptable to them, the program will be beneficial.

The Need for Counseling Services

Counseling has been defined as the process by which the individual student is assisted to recognize his problems and find answers to them. It is fairly obvious that the justification for counseling is essentially the same as for other guidance services. Three factors influenced the development of counseling services: (1) a new attitude evolved toward students, (2) a new concept of the nature of learning was developed, and (3) the role of the school changed.

The Development of a New Attitude Toward Students. In Puritan
New England the child had been considered a "veritable limb of satan"
to be curbed in the exercise of his natural impulses. While this concept
had not been universal in the colonial period and had been distinctly
modified during the eighteenth and nineteenth centuries, it was not until
the early twentieth century that serious attention had been paid in the
school to the importance of mental hygiene.[6]

As the concept of mental hygiene was developed, it became obvious
that the program must be adapted to the needs and interests of students.
Students in particular need of help must be referred to more competent
personnel than were likely to be available in the school. A larger portion
of the student group, however, were not so much in need of help from
outside sources as they were of an adaptation of the school's formal program to solve their particular problems. They needed to be understood.

Students were no longer encouraged merely to conform, but were to
be inspired to channel their desire for uniqueness into paths of creativity.
The uniqueness of each personality was recognized as being at least as
important as the need for certain types of social conformity. Anything
which would stifle the development of an individual's ability to make
his own contribution to the common life of the society was to be eliminated from the program of education. Undue emphasis on conformity
was dangerous.

The problem was not one merely of eliminating unnecessary pressure
for conformity, but of providing positively for the student's creative development. It was important to be sure that the student was assisted to
become an independent adult capable of managing his own affairs and
of solving his own problems. Independence of action was to be stimulated.
Any personal problems which the student might find as stumbling blocks
to his healthy development must be identified; he must be encouraged
and helped to find solutions to them.

An important part of independent adulthood is spent working. The
individual should be assisted to discover what employment would give
him pleasure and satisfaction and would enable him to make a contribution to the life of the society.[7] Vocational counseling was one of the first
and most obvious of the needs of the individual who was in the secondary
school program around 1920. Gradually, it became clear that students
sometimes required expert help with problems in the area of general
educational development. Finally the possibility for giving assistance in
the other important areas of adolescent concern became evident. The

[6] Cf. William W. Wattenberg and Fritz Redl, "Mental Hygiene," *Encyclopedia
of Educational Research,* revised ed. (New York: The Macmillan Company, 1950),
pp. 733–35.

[7] Joseph L. Norton, "General Motives and Influences in Vocational Development,"
Pedagogical Seminary 82:263–78 (1953).

important motive in each case was the development of healthy individual personality.

Respect for personality, dependent as it was both on the Judeo-Christian ethic and on the political and social ethics of democracy, received additional support from the developing field of psychology. Psychological theories were obviously influential, for instance, in developing the idea of non-directive counseling. In this technique it is the responsibility of the counselor to encourage the counselee to express his own problem and to work out the solution for himself. Unlike most other counseling techniques, this one emphasizes respect for the independence of the student and particularly his independence of the moral judgment of the counselor.[8]

Recently schools have acted on the assumption that behavior has a cause. The principal way to improve undesirable behavior is to find the cause if possible and to take action to modify it. Thus classroom or school misbehavior may call more frequently for counseling than for disciplinary action. Counseling is the positive approach. Disciplinary action without consideration of the cause may be negative. Even when the cause of the misbehavior may be beyond the control of the school (as in the case of the existence of a poor home environment) the counseling procedure may help the student to adjust to the situation and reduce the seriousness of his misbehavior.

The New Concept of the Nature of Learning. For as long as learning was regarded largely as a matter of mental discipline, the problems, interests, and needs of the individual student were of relatively little importance. The emphasis was on subject matter and the discipline available in the study of it. With the change of emphasis which placed the student at the center of the teaching process, the pattern also began to change.

It was not enough in the new pattern for the school to identify the needs, interests, and problems of the student. It became important for *him* to recognize them and to evaluate them as a basis for his learning activities. It was only as he developed an appreciation of the things which he was learning that he could learn efficiently. Furthermore, if he had important problems which interfered with his giving his full attention to the education he was being offered, it was necessary to help him solve those problems so he could get back to his studies.

It became important for the student to question the techniques by which he was being taught—a very revolutionary concept in the history of education. The previous emphasis had been on the unquestioning acceptance by the student of the teachers' authority. Doubtless this was frequently a convenient wall behind which the incompetent teacher could hide. The modern teacher must recognize that the cooperation of the

---

[8] *Cf.* E. G. Williamson, "Counseling as Preparation for Self-Directed Change," *Teachers College Record* 65:613–22 (April, 1964).

student must come more as a result of an understanding of the purpose of the process and not simply as the result of accepting the authority of the teacher.[9]

The new approach recognized that the important objectives in effective teaching are changes in behavior.[10] Changing behavior requires more basic kinds of understanding on the part of the student than does simple rote memorization of information. This more basic understanding requires a different approach by the student himself. He has to know what the desirable change in behavior is, why it is desirable, and how it may be achieved. This can come most efficiently when teaching is carried on in a climate which is conducive to it.

The Change in the Role of the School. As the school began to accept into its program a new population of secondary age youth, its role was transformed. The transmission of classically organized subject matter began to become relatively unimportant. Leadership in learning how to live effectively became important. Nor did the change in the role come too soon. By the beginning of the twentieth century, evidence of mental maladjustment had already become apparent among large segments of the adult population, and juvenile delinquency was quite prevalent.[11]

Much that had been left to the home when the population of the school was largely upper-middle class must now be taught by the public school. To a certain extent the moral code thought necessary for a complex society was the property of the middle and upper classes. Although in the wide spaces of an agrarian society, some moral deviations seemed relatively insignificant, they became important in the congested area of the city. The school found itself in the role of parent for at least a part of its population. Furthermore, the complicated life of an urban civilization created problems which some parents found themselves unequipped to help their children solve. Indeed, some of these problems have been difficult to identify even when both the school and the home are willing to help and are capable of helping.

A larger pattern of course offerings created the necessity of helping the student to choose the ones most appropriate for him. As long as only one very formal program was available, the student simply chose that one or dropped out of school. The fact that the student was expected to stay in school even when there was no appropriate program for him presented problems. Students who had formerly found limited satisfaction in dropping out of school and going to work found that there were no

[9] *Cf.* D. J. Willower and R. G. Jones, "When Pupil Control Becomes an Institional Theme," *Phi Delta Kappan* 45:107–109 (Nov., 1963).

[10] *Cf.* James M. Sawrey and Charles W. Telford, *Educational Psychology* (Boston: Allyn and Bacon, Inc., 1959), pp. 61–108.

[11] *Cf.* G. P. Liddle, "The Secondary School as an Instrument for Preventing Juvenile Delinquency," *The High School Journal* 47:146–52 (Jan., 1964).

satisfactory jobs available. It became important to help them to accept the school program offered or to modify it to fit their needs.[12]

The fact that some of the students who were expected to remain lacked the ability to do the academic work was a problem both to the teacher and the student. The possibility of providing remedial work for some of these can be determined in the counseling program. In some cases it becomes the responsibility of the school counselor to help the parents of children who are having difficulty living up to parental expectations to set more reasonable standards. The broader the responsibility and program of the school the more necessary becomes the counseling program.

School Personnel Concerned in Counseling and Guidance

Just as the curricular and extracurricular activities involve most of the school personnel, so also the guidance and counseling services represent a responsibility of the whole staff. It may be helpful to indicate briefly the role of each group within the school: (1) the teacher, (2) the school counselor, (3) the principal and his administrative staff, and (4) specialized services from social service workers, psychologists, school nurses, and school doctors. Each group has a particular contribution to make to the total program.

The Teacher as a Counselor. The primary person in the contact between student and school is the teacher. It is the teacher who determines whether the students' need or mastery of subject matter is to be emphasized. It is the teacher who determines whether the atmosphere of the classroom is one of solving problems or of conforming to discipline. It is the teacher who is available to answer the questions of students or to refer him to others for additional help. It is the teacher who is in the best position to spot those who are in trouble or who need help. No effective program of counseling in the modern secondary school can ignore the role of the teacher as a counselor.

If the teacher is concerned with organizing his teaching program around the needs of students, he must first collect information about those students and their needs. He may consult their records, he may ask them to fill out questionnaires or write biographies, he may give them tests, he may visit their homes, or he may get some of the information from the school counselor. In any case, getting ready to teach and getting ready

---

[12] *Cf.* J. Otterness and others, "Dropouts in Your School? Causes, Effects, and Solution," *Minnesota Journal of Education* 43:28 (May, 1963).

196 THE PROGRAM OF THE AMERICAN SECONDARY SCHOOL

to counsel involve essentially the same activities. Is it important whether what is done with this information is called teaching or counseling? On the other hand, if instead of gathering the information of the sort described here, the teacher begins blindly to teach the next twenty pages in the text book, can he be a good teacher?

Some teachers seem to view learning as an exciting process. Their classrooms are exciting places to be. It is here that questions may be asked and possible answers explored. In such an atmosphere no question is considered foolish. In such an atmosphere it is not difficult to move from a discussion of the problems of Hamlet to the problems of John. Indeed the study of Hamlet may help to answer the question which John had recognized as posing a problem. If, on the other hand, the atmosphere is such that the only important questions are those which the teacher asks about the use of the subjunctive mood, the atmosphere for counseling may seem weak.

There has been much stress in the last few years on the importance of adapting teaching techniques to the needs of individual students. This is in many respects a "guidance and counseling technique." Thus teachers using the school records and services available to them, supplemented by their own testing and observation, diagnose learning difficulties, assess which students are achieving at a satisfactory level relative to their own potential, and determine what factors in the school and out-of-school environment are affecting success or failure. Having studied the individual learning processes of their students, they then make use of as wide a variety of resources as may be available including textbooks, library materials, and more specialized programmed materials.

New emphasis on the importance of the student's self-concept has particular pertinence in considering the teacher's counseling role. While self-concept is the result of many factors in the life of the individual, an atmosphere of respect for him as a person is important if the school is to achieve its objectives. Similarly differences in learning style must be observed and teaching adjusted accordingly. The cooperation of teachers and other guidance specialists in the school is essential in this process.

Two teachers in the same school may appear to students to perform entirely different functions. One is always pleasant, will make jokes, and is willing to engage in idle chatter. The other seems stern and concerned about maintaining his social distance. One is known to be a good listener and capable of respecting confidences. The other does not want to be bothered with the problems of adolescents. One seems never to be shocked by the indiscretions of students; the other is prim. Students may be respectful of both teachers. One is made a confidant and counselor; the other is left alone.

Many of the students who seem to need help are so shy and introverted as never to get into disciplinary difficulty. Without the help of the teacher, the specialists in the school may never have an opportunity to be of assistance. It is the teacher who must be on the alert to get the clues as to what are the problems and what their causes may be. It is the teacher who must suggest to the counselor the possibility of rendering assistance. It is the teacher who may make it easy for such a student to go with some problem to the specialist. Otherwise the help may be too late; the child may have been dropped, and the school will have failed because the teacher was not alert.[13]

The School Counselor. Perhaps the second most important member of the staff in the program of guidance and counseling is the counselor. Frequently the counselor may have three distinct roles. He may be the director of guidance, the counselor, and a part-time teacher.[14] It is frequently considered wise for the counselors in a school to have some teaching responsibility. This keeps them in touch with this aspect of the school program and gives them a chance to observe some of their students at work. It helps the counselor establish rapport with other teachers. It may also insure that at least a part of the instructional program of the school starts with a guidance point of view.

The tendency to assign the counselor disciplinary responsibility may be unfortunate. Many of the problems which have become serious enough to get to a disciplinary official are at a point where action must be taken which is not consistent with the permissive atmosphere of a counseling approach.[15] Dealing with disciplinary problems may leave the counselor little time for students who are not discipline problems. Some so-called disciplinarians seem to cultivate a manner more calculated to inspire awe than confidence. On the other hand, it may be that the disciplinarian is the only person available to do the counseling. It may be that when he sees students concerning their misbehavior he can seek its cause and help them to find better approaches to their problems. It is undoubtedly true that students who have many adjustment problems are more likely to be in need of counseling than discipline.[16]

The planning of academic programs in some school settings is appropriately the responsibility of the homeroom teachers under the direction of the counselor or principal. If the number of counselors available is small, their time may better be saved for other types of counseling. If the homeroom program is well organized, the teacher may have a better basis for advising the student than the counselor who has responsibility

---

[13] *Cf.* J. W. Porter, "Heart of the Dropout Problem: Early Identification," *Michigan Educational Journal* 40:362–65 (Jan., 1963).

[14] *Cf.* A. V. Boy and H. L. Isaksen, "Ten Secondary School Counselors Determine Their Role," *NASSP Bulletin* 46:97–100 (Oct., 1962).

[15] J. Scott, "Disciplinarian or Counselor?" *Personnel and Guidance Journal* 41: 464 (Jan., 1963).

[16] *Cf.* R. J. O'Donnell, "Guidance and Discipline," *NASSP Bulletin* 46:51–53 (Nov., 1962).

for from 200 to 600 students. In cases where aptitude testing or other specialized guidance services may be indicated, students might be referred to the counselor for assistance.

The counselor has the responsibility for getting together information which students may find helpful in planning for college attendance, such as college catalogues, information about college costs and the availability of scholarships. He has the responsibility for identifying students who should be encouraged to continue their education who may not already be planning to do so. He has the problem of helping students to see that some colleges may be more appropriate to their level of ability or vocational objectives than others and of encouraging them to make application to the appropriate school.

The counselor may play various roles in the program of vocational counseling. He may help in organizing career days or visits to various types of schools and industries. He may help homeroom teachers plan homeroom programs around the things to consider in the selection of a vocation. He may provide for certain types of interest testing at different stages in the school program. He may schedule conferences with students to discuss the results of tests or to help them explore their vocational decisions. He may help homeroom teachers understand the role of vocational interest testing and the interpretation of such tests.

In the role of personal counselor, the school counselor may serve as the agency through which disturbed students may be referred to other experts for more specialized help. He may have the opportunity to help students identify their problems in their relationship with other students or with school officials. He may be able to lead discussion groups with small groups of students who wish to analyze specific questions or problems in such areas as dating or the observance of social convention. He may on occasion be called on to help students who have gotten into conflict with their parents. If he is fortunate, he will be able to help them in the recognition and solution of their problems in growing as mature members of the school community.

The Principal and His Administrative Staff. In the absence of school counselors, more likely to be the case in the very small school, the principal must serve in the capacity of counselor. In the well-staffed school the principal has the responsibility for seeing that the counselors have the opportunity to carry out their responsibilities. This includes seeing that people are selected who by preparation and temperament are suited to the job. Not every teacher would make a good counselor, and even where people are available with adequate preparation there is no assurance that they are temperamentally suited to working with a particular age or social grouping of students. After counselors have been selected, it is important to see that students and staff alike understand their function. On the other hand it is also important to see that the counselors have an understanding of the nature of the school and its philosophy.

The principal must be in close enough contact with the counseling program to be aware of the needs with regard to such items as space for counseling, time for student conferences, the availability of tests and other materials, organization of the staff and student body for efficient utilization of the services available, and the success of the program. The channels of communication between the counselors, the homeroom teachers, the regular teachers, and the school disciplinarians must be kept open and functioning properly. When possible, secretarial assistance should be available so that the counselor can spend more time on counseling and less on clerical work.

Even in well-staffed schools there is counseling which will be done by the principal or his assistant. Parents will wish to confer with the principal himself, although the counselor may sometimes be brought into the conference. Students may have problems which require the attention of the administrative staff but which have counseling overtones. As has been suggested, most of the serious discipline problems of the school are primarily counseling problems. Because they are discipline problems, they may sometimes be dealt with more efficiently by a "guidance-minded" principal or assistant principal than by reference to the counselor.

Perhaps more important than any specific counseling work of the principal is the atmosphere which he creates for the school. In part this atmosphere starts with the relationship which the principal has with the members of the staff. If, in addition to being generally competent, he is warm, fair, and pleasant in his dealings with the teachers, counselors, and students in the school, a good start has been made in the creation of an atmosphere favorable to the development of a good counseling program. If experimentation with new ways of improving the environment of the school is encouraged, then the atmosphere will be one favorable to better programs.

School Social Service Workers, Psychologists, Nurses, and Physicians. In a sense some of the services called "referral" are not so much referral as auxiliary. They include the school social service worker, psychologist, nurse, and physician. In addition a psychiatrist or psychiatric clinic is also sometimes available in the community.

The school social service worker, sometimes going by other names such as attendance officer, visiting teacher, welfare worker, etc., is likely to be responsible for helping school officials get information about the student's home situation and sometimes for helping to relay to the home important information about the school program. While the actual counseling done by such officials is more likely to be with parents than with students themselves, the information they collect is important to the development of an adequate background for counseling. They can also be of help in evaluating the success of the school's program.[17]

The school psychologist, because he may have more training than the counselor or because his responsibility is differently limited, is in a position to deal with problems which may be beyond the capabilities of the counselor. While the number of school psychologists is extremely limited, the range of problems with which they might give assistance is great. The matter of identifying students in need of remedial assistance in such areas as reading alone would generally require his full time even if teachers were available to do the remedial work. Supervising the standardized testing program, giving individual intelligence tests where they seemed appropriate, developing improved teaching techniques, and identifying special problems and needs of students, all represent areas in which such service is needed in the typical secondary school.[18]

The school nurse and physician have several important responsibilities in the counseling program in addition to their general responsibility for keeping adequate health records, planning instruction in such areas as diet, exercise, and other health habits, coordinating the health services in the community working with children and youth, and maintaining a healthy school environment through the identification of health problems. Advising students on how to go about correcting such deficiences as bad posture, eyesight, physical deformity, and bad teeth represents another necessary service. It is important to have such personnel available for discussing student health problems and concerns. Some students are in particular need of reassurance as to their normality during the physical changes of adolescence. Such community health problems as hookworm and tuberculosis need identification and then require special counseling. The availability of such personnel for referral assistance is desirable even where they are not regularly members of the staff.[19]

[17] E. F. DeRoche, "Responsibilities of the School Social Worker," *The National Elementary Principal* 43:50–52 (April, 1964).

[18] J. Rich and J. L. Bardon, "The Teachers and the School Psychologist," *Elementary School Journal* 64:318–23 (March, 1964).

[19] *Cf.* G. E. Cromwell, "Future of School Nursing," *Journal of School Health* 34:43–46 (Jan., 1964).

10

Revitalizing the School Program: Selected Readings

SINCE 1955 THERE HAS BEEN MUCH FERMENT IN THE PUBLIC PRESS AND IN professional journals with regard to the appropriateness of the existing public school curriculum. Some of this ferment, particularly in the years immediately following the launching of Sputnik I, seemed to be directed to a more rigorous study of mathematics and science. The more recent concern with the problems of the poor has tended to shift the discussion of what was previously called a "life adjustment" curriculum. Still other emphasis was placed on an effort to identify the basic structure of the disciplines.

Taking Stock of Today's Program and Procedures

More and more, the lay public as well as the education profession has recognized the need to consider whether existing programs and procedures are those appropriate to the roles being assigned to the public high school. The traditional college preparatory curriculum, the heavy emphasis on rigor, and the need to be adaptable have all come under scrutiny.

Robert Smith, Professor of Education at San Francisco State College, points up the problems of projecting a curriculum for a "revolutionary society." He catalogues the revolutions which seem to be going on in the expansion of knowledge, in population mobility, in the area of civil rights, and in ideals. He recognizes the possibility of, and problems involved in, counter-revolution.

201

Educating Youth in a Revolutionary Society*

Robert Smith

Since Sputnik, the schools have absorbed more than their share of people's projected tensions. This they have done even as they have sought to respond to revolutions in the major fields of knowledge and in social attitudes and have been forced to adjust to an exploding child population. We, in the United States, have a grave problem of perceiving broadly enough the scope of our revolution and the related sources of conflict and turmoil which surround all of our basic social institutions.

As a nation we have brought this revolution on ourselves. Our people, restless and mobile, energetic and ingenious in technology, have long equated progress with breaking from the ways of the past, particularly in the economic and political spheres. Through progress we seek to verify the perfectibility of man and his works. Our liberal traditions have generated the mass educational system which itself accelerates the growing pace of change.

We came into being as a revolutionary nation with widespread authority problems and with deep convictions that individual freedom, political freedom, and economic freedom plus education plus latitude of action for the individual in all dimensions of life would rapidly enhance and improve life for all people. As we harnessed these ideas and put them to work during the past two hundred years, education has become one of the tremendous motive sources in this society that impels change because the results of education are released and used quickly to build and change society.

THE KNOWLEDGE REVOLUTION

The production and use of knowledge has precipitated imbalances within the society. The industrial revolution undergirding the world in which we find ourselves has rapidly shifted from its earlier chief ingredients of land, power, minerals, capital equipment and labor, to what is now being labeled as a "knowledge revolution" in the area of ideas readily

* *Educational Leadership* 23:279–84 (Jan., 1966). Reprinted with permission of the Association for Supervision and Curriculum Development, and Professor Smith. Copyright © 1966 by ASCD.

harnessed to production. Our institutions, however, have been slow to adapt to this fundamental change in the dynamics of society. For example, education, the basic generator of this change, is still widely viewed as a major drain on the resources of the nation.

The "knowledge industry" accounts for nearly one-third of the entire economy and is growing more than twice as fast as the other sectors. Business concerns in the United States spend some seventeen billion dollars yearly to educate personnel, or one-third as much as is spent for the nation's public and private school systems. More than one-fourth of the nation is engaged in being educated and this proportion is increasing. We have about fifty-one million students and two million teachers. Investment in education, according to the Chase Manhattan Bank, has increased the output of the economy and the income of those educated to a return on investment of about ten percent.

A primary task of this nation is to invent ways to divert major portions of our wealth and skilled personnel into health, education and welfare. The needs, viewed in a conventional framework, may appear insatiable. But this is a false perception. For example, in 1929 this nation invested 3.1 percent of its gross national product on education. With the growing implications of the "knowledge revolution," only 5.8 percent was invested during 1963–64, in spite of the relative surge in youth population, costs of education, and the striking rise in gross national product. Many developing nations, despite their poverty, are making far greater relative efforts in the face of much more severe competition for the limited funds available. Instead of shuddering at the "astronomical rise" in educational costs, we might well assess the disposable wealth *left* to this society after deducting educational investments and make comparisons with the other nations of the world on that basis. Reassurance then should replace panic.

Our emphasis upon science and technology and overuse of highly educated personnel there and in industrial and consumer production reflects another growing imbalance as personnel shortages pile up in social service professions such as nursing, social work, and teaching. Research and development have also lagged in the behavioral sciences for a decade and a half as a direct result of the skewing of the National Science Foundation in the direction of natural sciences. One need not argue for a redress of balance at the expense of favored areas. It is not necessary in a burgeoning economy. The problem is one of advancing selected low priority fields of endeavor in terms of current realities, and of preempting rapidly accruing additional wealth. For example, 1964 produced an increase over the previous year of approximately forty billions of dollars in gross national product.

Knowledge is said to have doubled in the past decade and, in the process, has rendered much previous knowledge questionable or invalid. Ninety percent of the scientists in the world's history are alive and work-

ing today. This in itself is one of the driving motive forces of our accumulating revolution. It shakes our institutions, builds cleavages among us,
and makes us struggle in efforts to maintain the kind of multigroup and
complex multi-institutional society we have become. Unfortunately, while
we have moved with dispatch to harness new knowledge to our production
and distribution systems, we have been slow to adapt our social institutions
to the knowledge revolution.

If we grasp the deeper implications of the "knowledge revolution,"
we can readily attain three objectives of revolutionary import: (a) we
can spend all of the funds we can sensibly absorb for creative extension
of educational services; (b) in so doing, we can also assure ourselves of
future increases in wealth hitherto unknown; and (c) at the same time,
we can achieve new levels of human development for the entire population.

MOBILITY AND LEADERSHIP

Population mobility must be recognized as a revolutionary factor in
this society. Clearly the tempo of the times demands institutions attuned
to high mobility and unstable membership. In some slum-area classes, the
teacher's class list by the end of the school year may show triple the
number of names listed in September, though the size of the class may
remain relatively stable. We know of middle-class schools in which, each
September, at least half the youngsters and a third of the teachers are
new to the school.

The shift of personnel in and out of leadership roles also poses difficulties in achieving continuity of leadership. As we seek desperately for
bases of continuity—or certainty—plans are often upset by personnel
problems. This aspect of change, commonly overlooked, raises grave questions about our capacity for insightful control of revolutionary pressures.
Shifts in leadership are often viewed as needed accessories to change, but
the extremely rapid migration of leaders in and out of key roles in our
institutions provides a random factor hampering the functions of institutions and curtailing capacity to respond intelligently to change.

CIVIL RIGHTS STRUGGLE

The explosiveness of this nation's civil rights revolution results from
rising aspirations thwarted by unresponsive institutions. That crisis cannot
subside without basic revisions of social attitudes and drastic rearrange-
ments affecting our major institutions, especially in education.

The importance of the schools and colleges as agents of change is
highlighted by the fact that they were the first among our major institutions to feel the shock of the emerging civil rights struggle a decade ago.
Increasingly, problems growing out of rapid change in the larger society
are promptly short-circuited into the schools with limited lead-time for

planning and with little augmentation of resources. The "war on poverty" comes to mind as the most recent example. Schools and colleges are becoming lightning rods for discharging tensions arising in the society. They are not designed, nor are they yet prepared for this function.

AN EXPANDING WORLD

Developments in transportation and communication join peoples of the world together along with the contagion of their unsolved problems in human relations. On one hand we are told incessantly that the world is getting smaller. In a limited sense this is true. Supersonic transportation and instant global communication coupled with new potentials for rapid cultural diffusion foster an illusion of a shrinking world.

On the other hand, it is crucial that we perceive the world as *expanding* by leaps and bounds as we look out into it and as we interact with it. In the management of human affairs, the world is expanding; problems become more complex and factors governing them have widening sources of origin, the roots of which tend to become, for the individual, more obscure. We live in larger and larger enclaves whether we refer to community, occupation, government, or world affairs. Reconciliation of diversity and the mustering of consensus for action become increasingly complex processes demanding a resiliency difficult for our generation to muster. There is little in present educational theory and less in practice to suggest that today's youth are being helped to cope with this problem.

We should maintain our respect for specialized competence and for educational programs designed for that purpose. However, many such programs are conceived on too limited a base even for the purposes they are expected to serve both as to content and the context in which they are taught. A more serious problem arises in the almost static designs for general and liberal education which pervade the schools and colleges. We have been warned by the psychiatrist, Lawrence Kubie, that specialized erudition without commensurate emotional and social maturity places the tools for destroying civilization in the hands of the erudite immature. Margaret Mead argued, fifteen years ago, that our task is to prepare the young so that they can cope with problems previously unknown and remake themselves in the process. The concept is only currently drawing limited attention.

REVOLUTION AND IDEALS

We are considering here a developmental revolution building at progressively more rapid pace through time, generated by a complementary set of factors which force drastic changes in major sectors of our society. The cumulative impact on our institutions, on our patterns of association and habits of mind has the dimensions of revolution, but ours is a *con-*

tinuing revolution rather than a one-time staccato affair, hence more of it goes on beneath our level of conscious awareness.

What then do we have as a common ideology or set of social ideals to consolidate our continuing revolution? The democratic creed of the Enlightenment provides the baseline. But those ideals to which most of us subscribe seem to many to represent a priori concepts and notions, often out of step with the revolution as it progresses. A significant minority of our people would jettison the ideals of democracy for various anti-democratic alternatives. Perhaps we have been careless in our efforts to clarify and reinterpret our ideals by underestimating the difficulties in sustaining needed consensus in a multi-group society in transition and under stress. Rejecting the efficacy of indoctrination, we experience difficulty in keeping our ideals—our motive forces of direction, bright and sharp.

PROBLEM OF COUNTER REVOLUTION

There is another facet of revolutions which we cannot enjoy. Revolutions tend by and large to be brief and violent—giving many people release from frustration and pent-up anger. They are exhausting and their conclusion is followed by a period of consolidation under the fighting ideals of the revolution, if the revolutionists are successful.

We must, for example, learn to cope with counter revolution *in process* if we are to control our revolution through democratic values and humane goals. While we may have small cause for discouragement, carelessness and non-commitment could spell disaster for an open society. Currently we find counter revolutionaries maneuvering as Minute Men in the deserts of Southern California, the White Citizens' Councils in the South, the Black Muslims in metropolitan ghettos, and the John Birch cadres developing in the suburbs. We find proposals to restrict the level of educational opportunity extended to students of average ability and below-average financial means.

Broad awareness of the meaning and potential of an open society coupled with determined efforts to extend opportunities and freedom to those left behind in the revolution become major antidotes to anti-democratic movements which challenge our persisting ideals.

HUMAN COSTS OF REVOLUTION

Revolutions are marked by the unevenness of their impact on different sectors of the population involved. In this respect, our revolution is characteristic. Large ethnic and socioeconomic groups have been left behind, as Harrington[2] and Sexton[3] have pointed out. They lag in eco-

[2] Michael Harrington. *The Other America: Poverty in the United States.* Baltimore, Maryland: Penguin Books, 1962.
[3] Patricia C. Sexton. *Education and Income: Inequalities of Opportunities in Our Public Schools.* New York: Viking Press, 1961.

nomic status, formal education, citizenship rights and thus suffer severe cultural impoverishment. As a result, large numbers of youth grow up in "cultural pockets" making access to responsible adulthood difficult.

Despite our wealth and increasing investment in education, we permit a third of our young people to leave school before completing high school. Yet unemployment among youthful workers is double that of the working force. Also, we are facing an explosion in the size of our potential work force at a time when manpower needs are shrinking rapidly for the undereducated.

Problems of youth are not confined to the lower socioeconomic and ethnic groups. College-bound students are facing growing problems of gaining admission to and maintaining themselves in colleges and universities. Evidence is accumulating that increasing numbers of promising students are living in anxiety, chronic fatigue, and fear of failure so acute that their health is impaired.

These are the dreary aspects of our revolution and can be viewed as another consequence of it. Large numbers of people suffer grievous impairment of opportunity and health during such periods. Revolutions, once launched, tend to career out of control. We must learn to manage explosive changes so the fruits of progress are more rapidly and evenly disseminated in improved economic health and educational support for all. We must reexamine more carefully the degree to which our major social institutions actually support the dignity and aspirations of the individuals who comprise them, and whom institutions are designed to serve.

Ours is a society born of dissent and one that, in its building, has looted the natural resources of a continent, poisoned its lakes and streams, and polluted its atmosphere in pursuit of immediate and sometimes narrowly conceived goals. It need not stand aghast at the small minority of youth who express their turbulence through negativism, violence and vandalism. It is axiomatic that youth get out of hand—or appear to their elders to do so—in revolutionary periods.

Education is thus no longer a casual affair. It must be granted top priority as a prime instrument through which we realize the constructive potential of our on-going revolution.

A FOCUS ON NEEDS

The problems of youth and the schools demand massive resources and talent drawn from many fields for the following educational needs:

1. Analysis of existing knowledge and support of research in the area of human development and learning so that teaching and school management shall be guided by the best that we know
2. Extension of educational programs designed to complement the family and neighborhood environment—especially for early child-

hood years—thus capitalizing on new evidence of growth potential in both cognitive and affective development

3. Assessment of the social dynamics and human relations within schools in efforts to maximize their supportive potential for personality and character development as well as for effectiveness in more traditional kinds of school learning

4. Development of cultural service and work experience programs designed to lend continuity to youth's experience in and out of school

5. The design of original, experimental curricula with strategies for *unlearning* and *transitional* learning adapted to build self-confidence and improved self-concepts for those impaired by previous experience

6. Reexamination of special fields of knowledge for related integrative concepts functionally related to human development appropriate to a democratic society

7. Reexamination of possibilities for more extensive and creative use of specialized personnel from a broader range of fields

8. Exploration of our on-going revolution for attitudinal and value implications which should shape major objectives of the schools—especially for character and citizenship education

9. Development of patterns of parent participation and in-service education for school personnel aimed at serious involvement in the process of rethinking the role and function of the schools

10. Establishment of research facilities and consultants to work with teachers and specialists in every school district and county in liaison with higher education and state and national agencies.

Such efforts require financial resources and personnel beyond conventional conceptions of educational needs. As a start, we might seriously consider doubling the outlay for education during the next five to ten years. In addition, we might add a modest increment for research and experimentation, broadly conceived. Supposing we were merely to match the existing level of expenditure for research in science, technology, and the development of hardware for war and defense—presently estimated at 22 billions of dollars?

Through such modest efforts, an affluent society might expect to gain greater control of its revolution in service of human values.

The Emerging Curriculum

Pressure for change in the curriculum has been directed primarily toward the updating of subject matter. Much of the pressure for this has come from college-oriented subject specialists. Reinforcement for such a subject orientation has been supplied by a measure-

ment-oriented group of psychologists and test specialists. It has of course been hard for the "student-centered" group of educational theorists to argue either in favor of the existing programs or against the idea of doing a better job of selecting potential curriculum content. One of their real problems has been to get acceptance of the proposition that real individualization of instruction may serve to de-emphasize any prescribed curriculum.

The first selection by Dr. John I. Goodlad, written in 1963, describes some of the changes occurring at that time (and still continuing) and some of the problems inherent in getting really basic change. Dr. Goodlad, Professor of Education at the University of California, Los Angeles, has been widely noted for his practical and theoretically sound proposals for school improvement.

The Changing Curriculum
of America's Schools*

John I. Goodlad

Today's educators have a formidable task in seeking to select what to teach, especially in cumulative fields such as the natural and behavioral sciences. If this accumulation is plotted on a time line, beginning with the birth of Christ, it is estimated that the first doubling of knowledge occurred in 1750, the second in 1900, the third in 1950, and the fourth in 1960.

Whether or not these are only rough approximations, they have impressed upon educators an inescapable fact, well stated by Professor Schwab of the University of Chicago: It is no longer merely difficult to select and package for instruction the most important bits and pieces of knowledge; it is impossible! The search is on for something more lasting than "the bits and pieces" emerging as residue from the advance of knowledge, something more permanent around which to organize learning.

Some of the guiding questions are old ones. What is worth knowing? What knowledge prepares for the acquisition of new knowledge? What kind of education is most likely to help individuals become self-propelling during a lifetime of learning?

Clearly, a massive reformulation of what is to be taught and learned in the schools of the United States is under way. Talk of the "new"

* *Saturday Review*, Nov. 16, 1963, pp. 63–67+. Copyright Saturday Review, Inc., 1963. Reprinted by permission of publisher and author.

mathematics, the "new" physics, and the "new" biology is now common-place. Various scholarly groups and individuals, handsomely supported by the National Science Foundation—and, to a lesser degree, by private philanthropic foundations—have developed new course outlines and instructional materials for mathematics, physics, chemistry, biology, anthropology, economics, geography, English, and foreign languages. New textbooks are in wide use, both in this country and abroad. Tens of thousands of teachers and students in elementary and secondary schools have participated in the preparation and trial use of these materials. Many of these teachers and thousands more have attended institutes on the new content and how to teach it.

The beginnings of the current curriculum reform movement are commonly identified with the successful launching of the first Russian satellite in the fall of 1957. This spectacular event set off blasts of charges and countercharges regarding the effectiveness of our schools and stimulated curriculum revision, notably in mathematics and the physical sciences. But the roots of change go back further, to the years immediately following World War II. The recruitment of young men for the armed services had revealed shocking inadequacies in the high school science and mathematics programs of high school graduates. The problem was partly the limited quantity of work in these fields, partly the quality of what had been taken. The high school curriculum too often reflected knowledge of another era, not the scientific advances of the twentieth century. Recognizing their responsibility for this unhappy state of affairs, scholars in a few fields began to participate actively in what has now become a major curriculum reform movement.

Sometimes an individual took the initiative, sometimes a learned society (the American Mathematical Society, for example), prompted by a few articulate members. In either case, the subsequent course of events was surprisingly similar from project to project. First, a group of scholars came together to review the need for pre-collegiate curriculum change in their field. Then, in subsequent summers, scholars and teachers invited from the schools planned course content and wrote materials. These materials were tried out in cooperating schools during the regular school year and revised in the light of this experience. Meanwhile, in summer and year-long institutes, teachers were educated in the new content and methodology. Throughout, participants have been agreed, apparently, that new materials are central to basic curriculum change.

The current curriculum reform movement is now too far advanced to warrant the adjective "new." In some fields, notably mathematics, the first wave is about to be followed by a second. The "new" new mathematics is in the offing.

There is grave danger, however, in assuming that curriculum change has swept through all of our 85,000 public elementary and 24,000 public secondary schools during this past decade of reform. Tens of thousands of schools have been scarcely touched, or touched not at all, especially in areas of very sparse or very dense population. Tens of thousands of teachers have had little opportunity to come to grips with what advances in knowledge and change in subject fields mean for them. Tens of thousands hold emergency certificates or teach subjects other than those in which they were prepared. In elementary schools, teachers with any appreciable backgrounds in science and mathematics constitute a species that is almost as rare as the American buffalo.

Suburban schools have fared well by comparison, with extensive participation in curriculum projects, ability to attract qualified teachers, and resources for providing in-service education. The gap between the haves and have-nots persists and, in some ways, is accentuated.

Curriculum planning is a political process, just as it is an ideological process of determining ends and means for education. Proposals must find their way successfully through the political structure into educational institutions or slip into obscurity. Almost without exception, those projects have had their genesis outside of the formal political structure, having been conceived primarily by scholars in colleges and universities who were joined by teachers from elementary and secondary schools.

Projects have been generously supported from funds that are predominantly federal in origin, testifying to the fact that the education of its youth is a primary interest of the nation. But the relationship among local, state and federal governments in the support and conduct of school affairs is a sensitive one that has materially affected the ways by which the various curriculum projects have entered the bloodstream of American education. Conditions of the grants have cautioned recipients against promoting their wares in any way; project directors have been limited to descriptive information, articles and, on request, speeches. But their efforts are in vain unless the benefits find their way to local schools and school systems. It is not surprising, therefore, that products, largely in the form of textbooks, often have been turned over to commercial publishers who have their own effective means of reaching state and local school authorities. These products now come into the schools through the expenditure of state and local funds. This whole fascinating series of events warrants further study.

The curriculum reform movement has been sharply focused on single subjects planned, generally, from the top down. This focus and the "national" character of the projects have attracted first-rate scholars into pre-collegiate curriculum planning. But these characteristics have also attracted scholars from fields not normally included in pre-collegiate schooling, who sense, apparently, a fresh opportunity to include their particular roads to the good life in the curriculum of elementary or secondary schools.

This competition among fields places severe burdens upon instructional time. Just how all of the subjects will share this time remains to be seen. Demands will exceed time, even if the school day, week, and year should be lengthened. Some subjects will have to be combined or left out—there is not room for twenty academic disciplines in the kindergarten. Arguments for the root nature and basic value of a discipline notwithstanding, problems of what subjects shall prevail are resolved largely in the political realm at federal, state, and local levels of educational responsibility, with national concerns largely determining the priorities today. Consequently, the humanities and social sciences will gain increasing favor with any appreciable reduction in world tension.

The strengths and weaknesses of the several projects stem in part from the nature of American education, with its characteristic strengths and weaknesses. For example, there is no single set of aims for America's schools; there are many. Therefore, each curriculum project is free to formulate objectives for its own particular segment of the curriculum. Some have; some have not. Rarely are objectives defined with such precision that one would know exactly what to evaluate in determining the success of a given project. It might be argued that those undertaking the various curriculum activities have no responsibility for the formulation of objectives; that local school districts set their own and gear materials to them. Each project is responsible only for setting forth what to teach in a given subject. But can ends and means be thus separated in any aspect of curriculum planning?

Although objectives are vague or not stated, documents describing the several projects express an almost uniform point of view. The current curriculum reform movement is seeking more in the student than the mere possession of information, however updated that information may be. The student is to sense *intuitively* the *structure* of a field. By "structure" is meant the concepts, principles, and methods that constitute the discipline. "Intuitive" refers to glimpses of abstraction that go beyond immediate practical experience. Sometimes the stated goal is for the student to think like the physicist or the historian.

Goals of this kind have a certain mystical quality. What does a student do when he senses the structure of a field intuitively or thinks like a physicist? How does a teacher decide that the student has acquired these commendable traits? And how are they best developed? Some project directors are deeply preoccupied with such questions. Others have brushed them aside, either because adequate answers appear to be hard to come by or because they believe that their programs already answer such questions reasonably well.

Most of the projects have sought to bring the student into the structure of the subject by identifying a few key concepts (number, quantity, energy, time, space, supply, and demand) which are to be developed persistently and with increasing depth over several years of schooling. The curriculum is thus organized into units, each unit progressing in difficulty and both reviewing and extending one or more concepts introduced earlier in the student's experience. Very often, the subject-matter is similar to that of conventional programs. But the treatment called for is different, For example, the textbook for grade 9 in the program produced by the School Mathematics Study Group concentrates on algebra, as is common in conventional curricula. Emphasis, however, is on the behavior of numbers rather than the solving of algebra equations.

Some of the new programs depart radically from conventional context. Suppes and his associates, in their Experimental Project in the Teaching of Elementary School Mathematics at Stanford University, are developing their instructional materials around the concept of set. A set is simply any collection or family of objects. The putting together of sets of physical objects is a more concrete operation than the addition of numbers. According to Suppes, operations on sets—rather than the more abstract and difficult operations on numbers—permit the child to understand the way a number is related to a set of objects and lays the groundwork for the abstractions constituting mathematical thought. This is quite different from the arithmetic most of us learned in the primary grades!

Those involved in the various curriculum projects may have started out to reform the *content* of their fields, but few stopped there. In many instances, content has been pushed down or expectations for the year increased. There sometimes is provision for gifted high school students to go as much as two years into work normally reserved for college. Throughout, as noted earlier, emphasis is upon unifying concepts, principles, and methods of inquiry, with each successive topic designed to develop a central theme or element. Usually, subject matter is very carefully arranged—"programed" in the jargon of the trade—in a step-by-step sequence. Often, self-instructional programed workbooks accompany the familiar textbook. By means of these workbooks, students are able to work independently and at their own speed part of the time.

Perhaps the most comprehensive instructional package is that produced by the Physical Science Study Committee for a year-long course in high school physics. The first tool of learning is a new textbook, carefully developed by a team of outstanding physicists working in collaboration with high school teachers. Other tools include laboratory experiments and bits of simplified apparatus, a set of films, achievement tests designed to test the application of knowledge and techniques to new problems, a library of paperbound books on special and related topics, and a teacher's guide. Neither laboratory activities nor films are supplementary or for enrichment. Films demonstrate experiments that go beyond the confines of high school laboratories or otherwise provide a perspective not attainable in the classroom. Textbooks, films, laboratory experiments, and class discussions are planned to fit into a consistent, unified whole. With such tools so conveniently available, teachers' talk and chalk are extended as never before.

With grade placement of content determined, and with textbooks, teachers' guides, and supplementary materials published, some project directors see their work as nearing completion. Fearful that the relentless quest for knowledge in their own fields will pass them by, they are anxious to get back to research and teaching, usually maintained only with tag ends of energy during project years. Others, however, have become inescapably caught up in those fascinating learning and pedagogical problems that have alternately intrigued and frustrated psychologists and educationists. Patrick Suppes, for example, of the Stanford Institute for Mathematical Studies in the Social Sciences, as much a psychologist as a mathematician, wants to know what mathematics young children can learn, what they learn with ease and what with difficulty, and why. His materials on sets and numbers for the primary grades are little more than by-products of his central activity.

David Page, now of Educational Services Incorporated in Watertown, Massachusetts, is not enamored with the search for precise grade placement of subject matter. He seeks, instead, what he calls an "intermediate invention" of great power: power to stimulate an almost infinite number of mathematical operations, power to incorporate most of the basic mathematical concepts and principles, power to absorb and challenge children of vastly differing abilities. In one of his intermediate inventions, "maneuvers on lattices," children explore general rules, laws, and proofs for numbers through a simple table of numbers and a system of arrows variously pointing up, down, to left, to right, and diagonally. With the teacher's sweep of an eraser and scratch of the chalk, a new set of stimuli is on the board before the class. The limits of exploration and invention defy grade barriers. There is something here for children of all ages.

Although there are gross similarities in approach among the several dozen curricular projects now under way, probing reveals marked differences. Mathematics, with an array of projects embracing both elementary and secondary education, again provides an excellent illustration. Is mathematical insight enhanced by the verbalization of concepts? The organization of some projects reveals the careful coordination of mathematical operations and their verbal counterparts. Others, however, are casual in their concern for and approach to this question.

Beberman and his associates of the University of Illinois Committee on School Mathematics maintain that the early, often glib and incorrect, verbalization of mathematical concepts inhibits or distorts insight. They believe that precise verbalization is necessary for purposes of communication and proof, but this verbalization should come *only after* the individual has become thoroughly familiar with the generalization and has had adequate opportunity to test and refine it. "Precise communication is a characteristic of a good textbook and a good teacher; correct *action* is a characteristic of a good learner."

Mayor and his associates of the University of Maryland Mathematics Project seek a close and supporting relationship between the verbal and the operational components of mathematics. Both the sequence of mathematical operations and the appropriate vocabulary for them should be planned side by side and pedagogy designed to promote the simultaneous attainment of both.

Page, in the University of Illinois Arithmetic Project, is impatient with "the hindering verbiage (minuend, dividend, partial product, and the rest)" of conventional arithmetic. He seeks what he calls "new frameworks for mathematical ideas" through which children are challenged to explore mathematics—to develop, invent, and extend. Page avoids technical language in his teaching, encouraging children to invent their own, which, he says, often is better. They will come to the use of precise language soon enough, he thinks, when situations demand appropriate communication.

One of the shortcomings of the current curriculum reform movement, running almost uniformly through the projects, is the poverty of data regarding their effectiveness. There are, indeed, gratifying testimonials from teachers and students who have been involved. But are students learning fundamental concepts better than they did in conventional programs? If so, does insight into these concepts provide increased power in dealing with unfamiliar problems? Are all students able to proceed satisfactorily and with satisfaction to themselves in the new mathematics, physics, chemistry, and biology, if allowed adequate time? If so, does this place a solid high school curriculum in these subjects within the reach of all?

Most of the testing to date has compared students in new curricula with students in the old, using test items based on the latter. This is hardly fair to the new ventures. Nonetheless, students in the new curricula have shown up about as well as their counterparts on these conventional achievement tests, except where vocabulary or other specific memory items were called for. In those few instances where students in new curricula have been compared with students in the old using items thought to be more appropriate to the former, students in the old have performed rather poorly.

The scarcity of evaluative data has been defended on the ground that an overwhelming job of curriculum reform had to be accomplished quickly. Time and resources have not yet permitted broad-scale appraisal. The argument has merit. Nonetheless, one must still regret the disproportionate attention to evaluation in projects that sometimes have gobbled up as much as a million dollars a year, not collectively but individually. By and large, the several projects have been conducted apart from the regular teaching and degree-granting structure of universities. Consequently, there have not been the theses and dissertations that might have been stimulated otherwise.

Prospects for the future look somewhat brighter. Several projects have built long-term evaluation into their fiscal and personnel policies. Some have contracted with private testing agencies for the preparation of instruments appropriate to project goals. These provisions, in turn, should force the more precise definition of each project's goals.

The most significant question for the future is whether the current curriculum reform movement, long overdue, has built-in mechanisms to guarantee continuing self-renewal. Are present accomplishments to be enshrined within the covers of textbooks, there to remain (with periodic minor revisions) until some crisis precipitates another massive reform? The answer probably depends on whether or not highly competent, dedicated educators can either reproduce their own kind or attract successors of like competence and reputation into the enterprise. This, in turn, depends on the continuing intellectual challenge of that enterprise.

First-rate curriculum development demands the coordination of a vast array of resources: subject matter specialists, experienced teachers, educationists with a broad understanding of the schools, psychologists, programers, film makers, publishers, and skilled managers to get the most out of this talent. Experience has shown that scholars will participate for a few days during the year and for several weeks during the summer. But pre-collegiate curriculum building is not their primary interest. Nor is textbook writing a rewarded activity in universities. Some psychologists are interested in the learning problems involved but the contribution demanded of them usually is of an applied rather than a basic research nature. Most of the problems are of central concern to educationists but their interests usually cut across subject lines. They know only too well the difficulties of putting together all the separate subjects so that a reasonable and realistic curriculum emerges. Further, they are more than a little skeptical about establishing pre-collegiate curriculum building as an ongoing university enterprise in view of their own long-term frustrating efforts to have such activity recognized as important by the academic community. If the current effort is to continue with vigor, it must either become established within the research and development framework of universities or be taken over by new institutions capable of reaching both the resources needed and the schools.

Whether the controlling agencies be universities or other nonprofit institutions, they must exert influence on the education of teachers. Today's teachers came up through the programs which they are now being asked to replace. The college curricula from which they graduated are in need of wholesale reform. To expect these teachers to depart radically from what they know best is expecting a great deal. Many are making the change—and experiencing a sense of adventure in doing so. But the big change in pre-collegiate schooling will come about in twenty years when today's children in changing schools are teachers—provided the present momentum of reform is maintained.

It is fair to say that the current curriculum reform movement has not yet developed effective means for influencing content and pedagogy in those colleges and universities preparing tomorrow's teachers, school leaders, and teachers of teachers. Until it does, it will not provide for continuing self-renewal.

> *One of the burning issues in twentieth century educational philosophy has been whether the schools had the right or the responsibility as the agents of the society to attempt to modify the society itself. Can the school be both agent and master? Should the school dare to create a new social order? Is the school always doomed to the possibility of a curriculum devised for the previous generation rather than to the present? Harold and June Shane, both professors of education at Indiana University, discuss some aspects of this problem in the following article.*

Future-Planning and the Curriculum[*]

Harold G. Shane and June Grant Shane

During the past decade, and particularly in the last four or five years, the concept of *future*-planning has been explored in such fields as business, government, the military, and certain sciences. *Future*-planning involves a number of promising procedures *for anticipating and shaping or influencing the various possible futures which lie before mankind.*

The concept is of major importance to education, yet it is little known in educational circles. The times now seem right for educators to consider applying these challenging methodologies in the identification of acceptable educational alternatives and for developing school policies and programs.

[*] *Phi Delta Kappan* 49:372–77 (March, 1968). Reprinted by permission of publisher and authors.

Future-planning is proposed as a procedure for creating curricular and instructional strategies that are more than hindsight remedies for today's problems. It employs a sophisticated means for combining values as well as data from education and related disciplines. These, together with the power of controlled imagination, are deliberately employed to *create the particular educational future that our beliefs recommend from among the many less desirable alternative futures in which education, by default, may find itself.*

In this article it is our purpose to explain what *future*-planning is, and to suggest what it could mean for curriculum design, research, and development in the 1970's and 1980's.

What future-*planning is.* *Future*-planning should not be confused with future *planning.* The latter has been commonplace in education for generations as teachers and administrators have endeavored to determine what current circumstances and trends suggested. In other words, much future *planning* has been passive, generally linear, and most frequently based on intuitive guesses or estimates as to the nature of tomorrow.

Future-planning, on the other hand, is active, conceives of the future as a fan-like spread of many "possibles," and assumes that the nature of our tomorrows can be mediated, even to some extent determined, through systematic conjecture based on analysis and projection of data. A few months ago Olaf Helmer of RAND Corporation phrased it this way:

> . . . in the last few years . . . a wholly new attitude toward the future has become apparent among policy planners and others concerned with the future of society. Customary planning horizons are being extended into a more distant future, and *intuitive gambles are being replaced by a systematic analysis of the opportunities the future has to offer.*[1]

Ways[2] contends that the "art of futurism" will be recognized within 10 years, both at home and abroad, as a salient American characteristic Other interest-compelling viewpoints are abundant. Alexander[3] wrote about the procedures and developments in U.S. corporations as they strive to design tomorrow, and Kopkind[4] made a highly informative 1967 status report on the future-planners and "technopols" who are now working in the heartlands of government and industry. Bell,[5] who discusses the concept of the "post-industrial society," also suggests ways in which pro-

---

[1] Olaf Helmer, "The Future of Science," unpublished typescript of an article prepared for October, 1967, publication in *The Science Journal*, pp. 2–4 (italics added).

[2] Max Ways, "The Road to 1977," *Fortune*, January, 1967, p. 94.

[3] Tom Alexander, "The Wild Birds Find a Corporate Roost," *Fortune*, August, 1964, pp. 129–34; 164–68.

[4] Alexander Kopkind, "The Future-Planners," *The New Republic*, February 25, 1967, pp. 19–23.

[5] Daniel Bell, "Notes on the Post-Industrial Society (I)," *The Public Interest*, Winter, 1967, p. 29.

jected and applied theoretical knowledge have become "the matrix of innovation" by which society now lives and grows.

Since applied and informed conjecture is the fuel that feeds the art of studying the implications of probable future developments, from what is the fuel extracted? A concise statement of the background of *future*-planning and its potential contributions to curriculum change is in order.

A *capsule history.* Voltaire (1694–1778) appears to have been one of the first men to have the idea of deliberately peering into the future. Back in the seventeenth century he proposed the term "prevoyance" for the process. But it was Louis XV—a man with an understandable uneasiness about the future—for whom the first predictive study was made. A document, subsequently found in the *armoire de fer* or strongbox of Louis XVI in the aftermath of the French Revolution, revealed that a Foreign Ministry employee, one J. L. Flavier, had made a 1773 report based on a system of "reasoned conjectures" which presented probable foreseeable changes.[6]

H. G. Wells, who was quick to foresee the impact of industry and technology on early twentieth century life, also seemed aware of the power of reasoned prediction. "Every disastrous thing that has happened in the past 20 years," he said, "was clearly foretold by a galaxy of writers and thinkers 20 years ago."[7]

Future-planning began to assume its present form in the later years of World War II. During this period operations research, with its stress on model-building based on the best available information, was first used. New techniques for planning were developed to deal with "multiple possibilities" and "alternate outcomes" in military landings, campaigns, and bombings.

During the postwar years, Olaf Helmer and T. J. Gordon[8] of the RAND Corporation explored some highly interesting techniques for *future*-planning. Olaf Helmer[9] in his *Social Technology*, for example, offers specific suggestions for applying operations research techniques to the social sciences. He feels that the rewards resulting from development of a social technology must not be disregarded if the gap between the physical and social sciences is to be lessened. A number of fugitive materials associated with the application of knowledge to the modulation of future "possibles" are to be found in RAND document files.[10] Henry

[6] *Cf.* Bertrand de Jouvenel, *Futuribles*, a paper presented at a RAND Seminar, November 30, 1964, p. 4.

[7] Cited by Edgar Dale in "What Can Literature Do?" *The Newsletter*, November, 1967, p. 3.

[8] *Cf.* the RAND Archives: *Report on a Long-Range Forecasting Study*, Olaf Helmer and T. J. Gordon, September, 1964.

[9] RAND Archives: *Social Technology*, Olaf Helmer, February, 1965.

[10] An example from RAND's Archive Copies: *Management Science Frontiers: 1970–1980*, E. U. Denardo and M. S. Geisler, June, 1967.

S. Rowen, young (41) new president of the corporation, seems likely to stimulate further a scrutiny of tomorrow. Until 1965 he was a top long-range *future*-planner in the Defense Department.[11]

To conclude our capsule history, the Bell Telephone Laboratories are credited with the origin of the systems approach,[12] and by the mid-Fifties General Electric had created TEMPO for socioeconomic forecasting. Westinghouse—along with the major automotive companies—rapidly followed suit.[13] During the same period, business management consultants such as Booz, Allen, and Hamilton, Inc., began using PERT (Program Evaluation and Review Techniques—a systematic method for planning for many diverse activities) as a management information device. As a means of coping with the future, PERT was ". . . generally credited with a major contribution in making the Polaris missile operational two years ahead of the original schedule."[14]

By 1967, *future*-planning and methodical speculation had become widespread both in the U.S. and overseas. If it were not for certain "internal" or "process" complexities that served as safeguards, it might now be almost of epidemic proportions. England, France, and Germany are among the countries that now have well-developed groups and teams making intellectual forays into the future. In Paris, for example, Bertrand de Jouvenel has become a kind of intellectual dean of futurists. The Ford Foundation has sponsored a group called the *Futuribles*, a small international group of social scientists, for which de Jouvenel is chairman. Their scholarly series of essays reflecting opinions about possible future developments has awakened widespread interest, and de Jouvenel's book, *L'Art de La Conjecture*, has recently been translated into English. Further, at the initiative of Pierre Massé, a 155-page report on changes anticipated by 1985 in 16 dimensions of Franco-European living has been published.[15]

In our own country current interest in future scanning and *future*-planning, as of 1968, has become too widespread even to summarize here. A few examples:

- *The New York Times* has appointed a "Committee on the Future" for editorial planning that *anticipates* news a decade hence.
- In the groves of academe, the American Academy of Arts and Sciences (at Lawrence K. Frank's urging) has established a "Commission on the Year 2000" under the chairmanship of Daniel Bell. It has already (1967)

---

[11] Max Ways, *loc. cit.*

[12] Lawrence Lessing, "Systems Engineering Invades the City," *Fortune*, January, 1968, p. 157.

[13] Brownlee Haydon, "The Year 2000" Typescript dated March, 1967. Read at Wayne State University, March 2 and 23, 1967, p. 5.

[14] Booz, Allen, and Hamilton, Inc., *New Uses and Management Implications of PERT*. New York: Booz, Allen & Hamilton, Inc., 1964, p. 1.

[15] *Cf. Réflexions Pour 1985*. Paris: La Société Industrielle D'Imprimerie, 1964, 155 pp.

devoted a 363-page issue of its 50,000 circulation magazine, *Daedalus*, to a progress report on the commission's deliberations.[16]
• *Resources of the Future*, an organization aided by the Ford Foundation, has completed an excellent group of publications.
• The RAND Corporation has sponsored a series of predictive studies under Helmer and Gordon.
• The U.S. Future Society has been organized and is publishing a "Newsletter for Tomorrow's World."
• A 431-page "framework for speculation on the next 33 years," a book entitled *The Year 2000*, appeared during the winter of 1967-68 and became a popular nonfiction title.

Further "historical" or "present status" data would probably extend our remarks from the verge of tedium to the border of ennui.

What future-*planning can contribute to the curriculum.* Because the shaping of educational policies presumably can be improved by employing systematic conjectural techniques as has been done in science, government, business, and the military, what are some of the values suggested by a careful reading of the current literature of futurism?

At least two direct "outcome values" of future-probing are virtually self-evident. Seven "process values" based on the emerging techniques of *future*-planning also appear. Let us take them in order.

Outcome values. The use of *future*-planning in education is supported by two highly persuasive points: 1) It can help us to avoid just plain stupid mistakes, blunders that could have been by-passed if we had only expended the effort to look ahead intelligently and systematically; and 2) it enables us to foresee dangers and problems in time to consider alternatives, preventing possible unpleasantness, lost time, faulty learning, or human maladjustment.*

Process values. Bear in mind that *future*-planning of the curriculum is inherently a *process* for encouraging change to occur within an educational system. It does not involve a body of dogmatic rules to be followed. It provides a means of changing education and its processes so that individuals may better control and influence forthcoming developments that seem likely to shape their lives. Process values are derived from the interplay of participants with the procedures and ideas that are involved. Some of these values are as follows:

1. Careful consideration is given to the identification of a wide range of possible educational developments. Thus planning is brought into sharp focus as alternative futures are suggested and explored.
2. When a spectrum of possible outcomes in education has been determined, appropriate criteria can be used to assess the means to be employed in obtaining particular ends.
3. Progress is assessed continually through such devices as PERTing, which serve to keep persons working with curriculum models from

---

[16] "Toward the Year 2000: Work in Progress," *Daedalus*, Summer, 1967.
* *Cf.* Haydon, Footnote 13, p. 17ff., for examples from the field of conservation illustrating resources wasted through non-planning.

getting too far out of synchronization. Continuing evaluation also permits in-process changes (i.e., flexibility) in moving toward established ends when mitigating needs become evident.

4. *Future*-planning employs intellectually demanding but rewarding procedures as carefully derived information and referents are fed into the framework for speculation. The input of specialized knowledge or data based on "expertise" constantly validates the sequential decisions that are made in developing a model for curriculum change. The input also serves to reaffirm or to modify educational ends.

5. *Authoritarian* direction becomes subordinate to *authoritative* leadership provided by a) information input, b) the persuasive *merit* of a given idea, and c) the continuing use of research relevant to (or generated by) the processes of *future*-planning.

6. The processes of *future*-planning encourage synergistic* outcomes. In other words, prediction, research, process, and interaction taken together produce an outcome greater than the sum of the input. Also, in *future*-planning, we increase our potential ability to predict outcomes when several lines of thought modify one another and thus increase overall accuracy.**

7. In education as in the social sciences, the techniques of *future*-planning (operations research and expert judgment) offer considerable promise for developing an "interdisciplinary systems approach" to the study of curriculum problems.[17] In effect, we should be able to adapt and reconstruct some of the operational methods from the realm of physical technology to the domain of social and educational technology.[18]

So much for some of the promising elements which seem to support the infusion of *future*-planning in curriculum change. Let us now consider some of the conjectures about the next 50 years—years in which today's children and youth will spend most of their productive adult lifetimes. What "contextual map" can be drawn for society's educational needs? What ideas do we need to explore, test, and apply?

Raw material for future-planning the curriculum. At least in a general way, much of the input needed for effective *future*-planning in education is already available. Books such as Kahn and Wiener's *The Year 2000*,[19] and journals such as *Daedalus* with its issue "Toward the Year 2000,"[20] the *Futuribles**** essays, articles and books listed in Harrison's

---

* Webster defines "synergism" as the simultaneous action of separate agencies which, together, have a greater total effect than the sum of their individual effects.

** Points such as those given here have been carefully assessed by social scientists. Cf. Herman Kahn and Anthony J. Wiener, *The Year 2000*. New York: The Macmillan Co., 1967. Synergistic interrelationships are discussed on pp. 67–71.

[17] Lessing, *op. cit.*, pp. 157, 217.

[18] This point is developed in Olaf Helmer, *Prospects of Technological Progress*, RAND typescript of speech given in Tokyo, dated August, 1967, pp. 9–10.

[19] *Ibid., et passim.* Cf. esp. Chapters I–IV.

[20] *Ibid.* Cf. footnote 15 *supra*.

*** A series of essays by experts in different fields in which opinions about possible future developments are expressed. These are prepared by the *Futuribles* group chaired by Bertrand de Jouvenel.

Bibliography on Automation and Technological Change and the Future, * and literally dozens of other sources have been appearing in increasing numbers since the early 1960's.[21]

These publications have not only made available both the general concept and design of prevoyance or future-peering; they also suggest abundant factors and developments which highly reputable specialists in the physical sciences, social sciences, and other relevant fields feel should be considered and tested as we move into the future. Kahn and Wiener provided especially interesting information when they cited 100 "likely," 25 "less likely," and 10 "radical" innovations that could occur by 2000 A.D.** A quick check of the 100 "likelies" indicates that as many as 40 of the forecasts either directly or indirectly relate to education, hence provide data for conjecture by the educator.

Not only do we have the prospective scientific and technical innovations needed to stimulate and develop educational *future*-planning, we also have much theoretical data, based on trend projection, suggesting that during the next 30 years: 1) five billion people will be living; 2) population increases will begin a relative decline; 3) major increases in food production will occur (e.g., through "ocean farming"); 4) the world GNP will triple and perhaps quadruple; and 5) that automated urban complexes will house most Americans, who by then will be living in a credit-card economy. Also, 6) educational technology will be much more sophisticated; 7) drugs to effect desired therapy related to personality modification will be widely used; and 8) life-spans will be appreciably increased with 9) both our leisure habits and patterns of job-retraining changed as a result.[22]

In other words, if properly developed techniques, policies, and procedures (already offering exciting possibilities) are applied to education, we now have sufficient available socio-scientific "information-input" to begin reasoned conjectures for *future*-planning. But educational planning must also be done methodically. While educational futures could be arrived at in a haphazard manner, it is an inefficient and possibly dangerous way to approach them.

An approach to future-planning the curriculum. What opportunities reside in creative educational conjecture, or "educonjecture," about tomorrow's schools? What techniques can be used in *future*-planning

---

* A listing of materials assembled for two RAND projects by A. Harrison dated March, 1967.

[21] *Cf.* June Grant Shane, "Contemporary Thought, with Implications for Counseling and Guidance: A Bibliography." *Bulletin of the School of Education,* Indiana University, July, 1967, 106 pp.

** Kahn and Wiener, *ibid.,* pp. 51–57. It is significant that two of the 100 "likely" innovations forecast had become realities while this book was being published: major organ transplants and laboratory-created life forms.

[22] *Cf.* Olaf Helmer, *ibid.,* p. 2ff.

instructional programs and how do they differ from procedures ordinarily employed in planning intelligently for the next decade?*

The processes of *future*-planning, as reviewed here, depend on the use of the ORPHIC techniques: *a cluster of procedures based on the systematic use of coordinated expert opinion in education and in related disciplines for purposes of 1) exploring numerous possible educational futures, 2) selecting the best possible futures among them, and 3) developing models for helping achieve desired educational goals.* **

"ORPHIC" is an acronym for ORganized Projected Hypotheses for Innovations in Curriculum. Its dictionary meaning is "oracular." ORPHIC techniques were introduced during 1967–68 to chart educational changes for a large metropolitan school survey conducted under the auspices of the Midwest Administration Center of the University of Chicago.*** Within the limitations imposed by space, we will attempt to review the various steps that may be used in applying ORPHIC techniques, the criteria for selecting experts for educational *future*-planning, and some means of enhancing the value of expertise in such planning.

ORPHIC *procedures in educational* future-*planning.* ORPHIC procedures, in the exploratory stages they have reached thus far, bring together in an "arena for conjecture" two kinds of experts who are important in educational *future*-planning: the specialist with his data and predictions and the generalist who formulates, analyzes, assesses alternatives, and contributes to conceiving and building models.

The action in the arena for conjecture does not have as one of its features gladitorial confrontation, debate, or refutation. It is concerned with creating an intellectually tested consensus with respect to ideas or hypotheses for curriculum changes that are based on the best information available. A persistent effort is made to achieve synergistic outcomes (see footnote 18) through which the product of several minds assumes a more advanced and precise form than such minds would have attained by working alone.

The arena for conjecture may be thought of as an intellectual amphitheater for *future*-planning; one in which the ideas of experts have an opportunity to prove their survival value and to sharpen the thinking of

* *Cf.* Edgar Morphet and C. O. Ryan. *Designing Education for the Future,* 1967, three volumes, published by Citation. These materials are excellent illustrations of intelligent planning for the future but are *not* based on the use of *future*-planning as described here.

** Recognition is due RAND, Inc., for pioneering in *future-planning* through the controlled use of expert judgment. The little-known Delphi technique, which involves the use of a panel of specialists, was used by RAND and appears in the literature as far back as the late 1950's.

*** In an initial venture in educational future planning during January, 1968, Edward T. Hall, Robert Havighurst, and Herbert Thelen were the interdisciplinary participants. A second planning group, one meeting a few weeks later, consisted of Robert H. Anderson, Frank Estvan, and Sidney P. Martland, Jr.

others. The interaction of the experts differs from that of a conventional panel discussion, symposium, or "bull session" in several respects:

1. Each specialist methodically prepares a preliminary résumé of possible futures in his discipline (e.g., anthropology, biochemistry) that relate to futures which fan out ahead for education. This is the *trend census*.

2. In exercising his authoritativeness a consultant is requested to pretest his thinking and suggestions by considering such factors as a) the "half-life of validity" (valid premises and ideas age so quickly now we must allow for their possible demise and anticipate their successors), b) possible "pseudo-experimentation" (since some ideas are dangerous, others costly or difficult to attempt, how would the expert develop a hypothetical experiment, and what possible findings might result?), c) what "scenario" would he plan when conceiving of a curriculum for 1985 as he envisions it evolving day-by-day from its precursor?

3. When ORPHIC techniques are used, heed is methodically given to checking the relationship between hypotheses and evidence.* In other words, a continuing effort is made to insure that a possible proposed educational future has evidence supporting it. Any viable hypothesis pertaining to the curriculum also passes at least the three following tests: a) *technical*—the curriculum innovation is possible; b) *economic*—it is financially feasible; c) *operational*—it is worth doing in terms of the school's philosophy, clientele, view of learning theory, and so forth.

4. The expert places in the arena for conjecture the curricular changes (e.g., 1970–1985) his field of specialization suggests for a) substantive content, b) instructional procedures, or c) para-curricular experiences that might better permit schools to maximize human development.

The foregoing explanation of how ORPHIC planning departs from casual discussions or symposia also serves to explain the essence of the *future*-planning technique itself. It is a pragmatic-empirical chain-series of reasoned predictions looking at the many tomorrows that could ensue in education and following a process designed to permit a particularly acceptable educational future to have a better chance of becoming a reality through creative imagination and hard work. By its nature and processes, *future*-planning can help make our schools important and interesting educational outposts on the borders where people strive for better tomorrows.

Criteria for selecting experts. *Future*-planning inherently serves to encourage qualified persons in both education and related disciplines to work together to improve the curriculum. These experts are selected to

* We have based this on the Helmer-Rescher degree of confirmation concept and formula, and their "personal probability" measure. *Cf.* Olaf Helmer and Nicholas Rescher. "On the Epistemology of the Inexact Sciences," *Management Science* 6:25–52, 1959. Note pp. 34–36, where [de (H, E) = m/n] is presented, E being based on m/n—P (m out of n objects having the property P.)

facilitate reaching a balanced predictive consensus. At least to a considerable degree, the expert sharing in ORPHIC processes should meet all or nearly all of the following criteria:

- Specialized information and skill.
- Ability to apply both his expertise and evidence in the process of prediction; the power to see, in the absence of data, the main alternatives or future developments on which education should hinge.
- A high "reliability quotient"; when previously confronted with hypotheses, he generally has identified the ones which proved to be sound.
- A past record marked by stable and sustained expertise, including that of making pronouncements which subsequently earned acceptance among his peers.
- Breadth within his discipline.
- Intra- and multidisciplinary understandings and insights.
- Imagination with respect to both theory and its applications, and well-developed idea-exchange skills.
- A grasp of educational realities.
- A willingness to support socio-economic equalitarianism created by opportunities made available through the schools.

Enhancing the efficiency and intellectual power of the expert. Once a team of highly qualified persons has been assembled to study possible educational futures what are some of the commonsense things that can be done to facilitate their communications? Here are several useful suggestions.

For one thing, easy and rapid access to a wide range of educational and other types of information is of great importance when specialists meet. Also, the construction of models* can be very helpful in explaining problems, clarifying concepts, and avoiding misinterpretations. An actual 3-D model could be of value, for instance, to a team planning for space use on the campus thus simulated. Likewise, a model of a school's administrative structure could be valuable to a team of consultants about to begin studying data prior to engaging in forecasts regarding a "best" future.

Finally, a carefully nurtured series of opportunities to interact with others also is vital. What is sought here is the synergistic outcome which the combined efforts of experts from related disciplines and education hopefully will produce; an outcome which proves to be greater or more effective than the sum of its individual or isolated parts.

Caveats for educational future-planners. Future-planning of curricula should be undertaken with several cautions in mind as educators use the available "raw materials" extracted from interdisciplinary sources to

---

* As used here, "model" refers to a graphic-visual concept portrayal of relevant elements and their relationships in a situation. There are three-dimensional, pencil and paper, and mathematical models. Each type should provide the best data and perceptions available on a given situation or problem when properly constructed.

channel the fan-shaped multiple futures that lie before the schools into emergent "good" futures consistent with sound societal values. To illustrate, many technical innovations have proved to be mixed blessings. It is important to remember that an automobile, for example, when driven 25 miles, consumes the breathable air that seven million people use during a 30-minute interval. Nuclear technology used commercially also creates a plutonium by-product that could increase the ownership of nuclear weapons. Weather control could throw entire areas out of balance. To cite one more illustration, the use of insecticides and weed killers is becoming one of our greater long-term causes of dangerous chemical pollution of the environment.

In educational conjecture, therefore, prudence must be mingled with foresight so as to avoid inadvertent "pollution" also, be it from education itself or from inept efforts of its well-meaning friends in other disciplines. Obvious caveats in curriculum planning include the danger of subordinating human values to technological ones; random tinkering with human personality; diminishing the importance and significance of individuality; and clothing obsolete goals, content, and procedures with computer-assisted techniques that only serve to help children and youth learn the wrong things more rapidly than they do now.

Another danger could be that of a small, powerful, and autocratic group appointing itself to mastermind the content and procedures of education for 1980 or 1990. A more disastrous "victory" for either physical or social technology would be difficult to imagine than one that led to a system in which a few central *future*-planners—no matter what their field of specialization—superimposed only their values on the schools and on the brain banks of the computers which seem certain to gain in educational importance.

The future belongs to those who plan it. It has been evident for some time now that education is beginning to be recognized for what it is: a force of such social and political importance that it cannot remain laggard, adolescent, or inefficient. In fine, *someone* is going to determine the shape of our emergent educational futures because they are too portentous to be left to chance.

The future belongs not to those who plan to *meet* it, but to those who actively *plan* it. In education we are placed on our mettle not to do battle against persons in other disciplines who are also concerned with creating a better world of teaching and learning. Rather, we are challenged to encourage leadership within our own ranks—a leadership based on the merits of creative ideas and their implications for more adequate educational tomorrows. Thus we undertake to do *future*-planning *along with* rather than *against* those who strive, in their respective specialties, to sharpen the directions, improve the methods, and enhance the power of education's tomorrows.

Providing for Change

It has been recognized in educational circles that it may be easier to get some significant curricular change instituted than it is to get it really understood and accepted by those in a position to make it work. Recent pressures have resulted in much that was identified as innovative. Eugene Howard as Director of Innovation Dissemination for the Kettering Foundation's Institute for the Development of Educational Activity is in a good position to understand the problems involved when innovation becomes an end in itself.

Organizing the High School for Change*

Eugene Howard

There is an old French saying that the more things change the more they stay the same. It seems to me that this saying applies very aptly to much of what is termed "innovation" in our rapidly changing schools.

Scratch the surface of what a high school principal tells you is an innovation and you are likely to find a hard core of conventional practices. I can report to you that there is a lot of superficial, off-the-top-of-the-head, half-baked, under-planned, under-organized, under-financed and under-staffed innovation going on.

Team teaching, for example, too often turns out to be a reorganization of mediocrity—the practice of teachers doing together the kind of teaching which should not be done at all.

Flexible scheduling, when examined closely, often means the substitution of a computer-built rigidity for a hand-built one.

Independent study, in many instances, turns out to be a plan for allowing students to do their homework in the cafeteria; in other cases it becomes a plan for allowing students choices of ways in which they may be coerced.

Seminars have too often become small classes devoted to the sharing,

---

* *The North Central Association Quarterly* 41:293–99 (Spring, 1967). Reprinted by permission of publisher and author.

among students, of prejudice and ignorance. Or worse, yet, a means whereby the teacher can teach conventionally to smaller groups of students.

Architects are designing so-called innovative buildings for us which group conventional classrooms in circles and hexagons instead of in rectangles.

Innovation in curriculum typically means that the teachers have been permitted to adopt the newest form of rigidity conceived by a group of scholars sitting on a campus somewhere.

Educational television as an innovation has been used to impose an electronic lockstep on the student to partially replace the teacher-built lockstep of the past.

I don't want you to get the idea from what I have said about team teaching, independent study, flexible scheduling, newly designed buildings, and seminar instruction, that I am opposed to these innovations. Certainly not. What I am objecting to is the use of these labels as substitutes for meaningful change. What I'm trying to illustrate is that the more things change the more they stay the same.

This is the age of the easy solution to the complex problem. It is the age of instant coffee and tea, instant TV suppers, and instant innovators.

The instant innovator can be defined as an educator who wants to do things differently without really changing anything. His principal method is the technique of label-switching, i.e.—the pinning of an innovative label onto an obsolete practice.

But change in education does not *have* to be superficial. It *can* be basic, meaningful, lasting change. It *can* mean a change in learner and teacher roles, for example. It *can* be change based on information instead of prejudice; and it *can* be change based on a thoughtful analysis of a situation instead of on intuition or expediency.

Systematically planned trial and error must, in our innovative schools, replace capricious trial and error.

Suppose each of you were to go home next week and immediately be able to implement the following changes:

1. Build a new organizational plan for your school which would place every teacher on a teaching team.
2. Add non-certified instruction assistants and clerical assistants to your staff.
3. Redesign your school plant so that the 900 square foot classrooms were replaced by large, open spaces, labeled "learning laboratories," and so that special facilities were provided for independent study and small group instruction.
4. Install a computer-built modular schedule patterned on the Bush-Allen model.

What have you accomplished? You have now made it *possible* for innovation to take place in your school.

What haven't you done?

1. You have made no change yet in what learners do when they learn, or what teachers do when they teach.
2. You have not yet affected the content of the curriculum.
3. You have made it organizationally possible for teachers to break the lockstep and to implement a continuous progress curriculum but it is not very likely that they will do so.
4. You have set the stage, but only set the stage, for the development of a program of independent study in your school.
5. You have made it possible for teachers to use the seminar method of stimulating critical and analytical thinking but you have no assurance that this will happen.

There is an important difference between superficial change and basic change. Organizational innovation will not by itself solve non-organizational problems.

The purpose of this presentation is to explore with you some principles of organization which when applied to a high school, will make basic, meaningful change possible. Let's look at the question, "How do you organize a school so that the improvements which take place are genuine and not superficial?"

I would like to suggest for your consideration four organizational principles which, when translated into an organizational plan for your school, show promise of giving you a plan which will stimulate thoughtful change.

CLIMATE FOR INQUIRY

1. Principle number one has to do with the organizational climate of the school. I would suggest that the climate most appropriate to the innovative school is that which is commonly referred to in the literature as a "climate for inquiry." This organizational climate is characterized by:

   a. a higher degree of openness of communication—among faculty members, between administration and faculty, and between faculty and students—than is found in schools not devoted to inquiry;
   b. a desire on the part of teachers to ask meaningful questions about the results of well-defined instructional procedures;
   c. a willingness on the part of the faculty to devote time and energy to the collection of information pertinent to the questions being asked;
   d. a willingness on the part of the faculty to make new decisions regarding instructional procedures on the basis of the information acquired;
   e. a systematic school-wide plan to evaluate its program and to identify areas in need of improvement, and

f. a high degree of commitment on the part of faculty and students to the basic principles underlying the innovative efforts of the school, but a willingness to subject specific procedures to careful scrutiny.

In the inquiry-centered school, the teacher is actively engaged in performing a number of roles in the change process: innovator, adapter, action-researcher, diffuser. As Fox[1] has said, "The teacher could, in fact, contribute to all of the processes described by Guba in his *Schema of Processes Related to Change in Education.* He is certainly not limited to being a target for somebody else's change efforts." The major purpose of such a school is to produce self-evaluating individuals—teachers and pupils.

But teachers need help if they are to make effective decisions about instruction at the operational level. The organization plan for the school devoted to the inquiry approach must provide for appropriate staff support for day-to-day decision-making by the teacher. A kind of "inquiry specialist" is needed—a person who personifies the philosophy of the school by establishing his own position on educational questions in a rational manner. Teachers have to be *helped* in asking the right kinds of questions about what they *propose* to do, *are* doing, and *have* done. In team planning, for example, teachers need to ask two basic questions—

1. is the proposed path of action consistent with the philosophy of the school, and
2. what are the predicted outcomes of the proposed path of action and how can we determine, on completion of the project, the extent of success or failure of the idea?

TO REPEAT AN OFTEN-UTTERED STATEMENT

A climate for inquiry is a climate which encourages people to inquire. This climate must be built by *people*—people who understand the inquiry approach to problem solving and who help one another raise answerable questions, then *proceed* to find information on which to base a plan of action.

To the extent that a faculty can become proficient in this process, to that extent decision-making regarding instruction can be made at the operational level. To the extent that teachers can learn to operationalize the philosophy of the school—to that extent they can make decisions with confidence that they will not be reversed at a higher level.

The pay-off for the school which implements decentralized, inquiry-based decision-making is two-fold:

[1] Fox, Robert S., "In-Service Education for Innovation and Change," University of Michigan, Center for Utilization of Scientific Knowledge, a paper delivered to the conference on the Role of Demonstration Centers in Educational Change, Urbana, Illinois, March 2, 1966.

1. increased efficiency—that is, decisions can be made more rapidly and more accurately, and
2. a higher level of commitment, on the part of the staff, to the philosophy of the enterprise.

ADMINISTRATIVE AND SUPERVISORY SUPPORT

The second major principle for an organizational plan for an innovative school is the principle of administrative and supervisory support for faculty and student decision-making.

Let's assume that the basic organizational unit of the faculty is the teaching team. There should be available to the team members a wide variety of talent which will support and assist them as they make educational decisions. Most of this specialized talent is already available in the school but organizational debris often separates it from teachers and students who need it. Available to the members of the team should be specialists in the characteristics of the learners (the counseling staff), specialists in learning materials (the staff of the library or IMC), specialists in curriculum (the supervisors at the school and district level), specialists in action research (the school research director), and specialists in organization and communication (hopefully, the school's administrators).

If this talent is to be made available to the teaching team on a regular basis while the team is in the process of making decisions, there must be no hierarchical barriers separating the teachers from the specialists. That is, for example, a team must not be handicapped by having to go through a department chairman in order to get to the research director or to an administrator.

The organizational plan of such a school would be just as flat as you can make it.

One principal suggested to me the other day that the plan should not only be flat but it should be inverted. The principal, supervisors, and specialists, he suggested, should be shown as a kind of foundation, or base, for the school; supporting, not directing, the activities of teachers and learners.

In such a plan, you would broaden the peak of the organizational triangle by implementing a process of shared decision-making at the top. You would then invert the triangle.

Supervision in such a school is seen as the process of improving instruction through assisting the teaching staff in the making of decisions which will (a) be consistent with the school's philosophy, and (b) result in the predicted outcomes.

Administration is seen as the process of improving instruction through the systematic study and improvement of the organization of the school. Organization is seen as consisting primarily of (a) the organizational climate, which we have said should be a climate for inquiry, (b) the communications structure, and (c) the assumed and assigned roles of employees. The principal is the school's specialist in these areas.

EMERGENT VS. DESIGNATED LEADERSHIP

Principle number three has to do with emergent versus designated leadership functions. It is closely related to but not the same as the principle of administrative and supervisory support of faculty decision-making.

This principle recognizes that in an institution dedicated to the fostering of leadership ability among students, such ability must also be recognized among the faculty.

It is unrealistic to divide a staff arbitrarily into "leaders" and "followers." Every study of power structures I have ever heard of has shown that leadership in most organizations, including practically all schools, is widely disbursed, sometimes residing in persons you would hardly expect to be leaders—the principal's secretary, for example.

An organizational plan for an innovative school would provide for, in fact encourage, leadership to emerge from many sources—students, noncertificated employees, teachers, supervisors, and administrators.

The *situation* confronting the decision-making group should determine who should assume a leadership role.

A major responsibility of all designated leaders in a school should be to work with the staff and students in such a way that the most appropriate leadership talent in the school can be made available at the time and place it is needed. In other words, a major responsibility of the designated leader is to foster growth in leadership ability among others.

Leadership on a faculty will emerge when: (1) the climate of the school is perceived by the staff as being one which encourages risk-taking and which does not penalize mistake-making, (2) when it becomes clear that teachers are expected to make decisions and to justify them on professional bases, and (3) when communication in the school is sufficiently open so that students, teachers, administrators, and supervisors are beginning to understand one another's point of view on important educational issues.

FUNCTIONAL FLEXIBILITY

Principle number four has to do with flexibility.

"Flexibility" in schools today is rapidly becoming a dirty word. That's because, in part, it has been confused in practice with sloppiness.

A flexible school is not a school which lacks organizational structure. It is a school which has replaced a rigid, inefficient structure with a more functional one. In the flexible school the structure serves the learners and teachers, not the other way around.

Decisions are made in such a school by people on the basis of their perceptions of the needs of the learners, not by rigid schedules or mouldy procedures handbooks.

In our rigid conventional schools today the learner has almost nothing to say about what he will learn, where he will learn it, who will help him, how he will learn it, when he will learn it, or what materials he will use *for* learning it. The most important decisions in our schools today are made by others on the learner's behalf. Then we wonder why we have trouble motivating students.

Our schools are extremely well designed to serve the needs of the bright conformist.

Likewise, our teachers have little to say about the size of the instructional group, the facilities and materials available to the group, the personnel available to the group, the composition of the group, or the length of time that the group should meet. These decisions are typically made for every teacher in the school for nine months in advance. English 12 will meet in room 127 with Miss Jones, from 10:00 to 10:56, five days a week, for the entire school year. It will because the schedule says it will and the schedule can be changed only with considerable difficulty.

These and other kinds of rigidities plague our schools and make them places where learning goes on under unnecessarily difficult circumstances.

There is no reason why the membership in a teaching team or in a learning team should remain constant for an entire year. Any teaching team in the school should be able to reach out to the entire faculty—and even to the community at large—and attach to itself on a temporary basis a new member who has talents not available among the team members. When a humanities team is planning a unit on Colonial America, for example, they should feel free to include the art teacher for his special understanding of Colonial architecture, or a history teacher from another team who did his master's thesis on Colonial trade with England. These people should join the team not only for planning but for implementation as well, and the organizational structure of the school should permit them to do this.

Four key concepts, then, basic to building an organizational structure conducive to thoughtful innovation, are (1) a climate for inquiry, (2) the principle of administrative and supervisory support, (3) the principle of emergent leadership, and (4) the principle of flexibility.

An organizational plan built on these four principles will be a plan which will go a long way towards encouraging thoughtful innovation to take place.

What, more specifically, might such a plan look like?

It will, as I stated previously, be a flat plan, with no hierarchical steps between the principal and his teachers.

Designated leaders will be organized into a team, perhaps designated as the "inquiry team" or the "program development team"—that part of the organization designed to support instruction by providing specialized talent to the teaching teams when such talent is needed. This inquiry team will be composed of the principal, who is the designated team leader and the specialist in organization and communication; his assistants; the research director, who is the school's specialist in action research; the guidance director, who is the school's specialist in the characteristics of learners; the school's two curriculum coordinators; and the learning materials specialist.

Teaching teams will be formed, in some cases across discipline lines, for the purpose of making a wider variety of teacher talent available to the learner than would otherwise be possible. Each team will be supported by an adequate staff of clerical and instruction assistants and will be provided by the school schedule with adequate unscheduled time so that they can plan together and meet with individual students and with learning teams.

The composition of the teaching team will change from time to time as additional talent is required on a temporary basis.

Students will earn unscheduled time by demonstrating growth in responsibility. A mature senior might have two-thirds of his time unscheduled. It would be his responsibility to schedule this time in a way most appropriate to his own learning needs. A very immature student might have unscheduled time only for lunch, and he might even be required to eat that under supervision.

Each student would have a personal counselor and at least one academic adviser. He would see his counselor only on a self-referral basis. Academic advisers would, however, see their advisees on a regularly scheduled basis. The academic adviser would be chosen by the student and would not necessarily be the same person all year. A student's adviser when he is deeply emersed in an astronomy project might well be a science teacher; when he goes out for football, his adviser might be a member of the coaching staff.

The curriculum would be organized in such a way that individuals and learning teams can go through a course at varying rates. Provision would be made for depth and quest options on the completion of each unit of study. On completion of each unit and on completion of the course, an evaluation of competence would be made. Credit would be given on the basis of work completed and competence demonstrated and on no other basis.

There would be several curricula and several variations of the same curriculum so that content can be as appropriate to the learner as possible in terms of his present interest, future plans, and level of competence.

Computers will probably be used to assist learners and teachers in assessing student progress towards preconceived goals, in diagnosing difficulties, and in suggesting options for future learning activities.

The classroom of the future will be the learning laboratory—a classroom specifically designed for continuous progress. Materials, equipment, and teaching teams will be scheduled into these laboratories but most students will schedule themselves in.

Most large group instruction, as we now know it, will be videotaped and available to the learning team by dial-access. It will not be necessary for a teacher to present a lesson more than once—to a television camera. Some live large groups for motivation purposes and for enrichment will be scheduled in the auditorium. Attendance at such affairs can be entirely optional or a combination of required and optional, as appropriate.

Scheduled seminars will continue as in our flexibly scheduled schools of today. Such seminars will be rather well planned discussion groups, as is now the case, with a teacher present. Students may, however, with their adviser's permission, call their own seminars, announcing the discussion topic in advance and inviting other students to attend if they have an interest in the topic proposed.

Likewise, students should be encouraged to volunteer to teach one another. Any student, with the approval of his adviser, should be able to initiate a course of instruction for other students. Such courses might last anywhere from one week to six months, depending on the objective of the course.

The school should be open at least twelve hours a day and twelve months a year. An organizational plan needs to be devised which would make this possible. Assuming that each student spends about the same amount of time in school as he does now, such a plan would thin out the school and relieve everyone of the claustrophobic, pressure-cooker-like overcrowdedness which now plagues every high school.

When will schools be organized in this way? Some schools may reach this point in 10 to 15 years. The Bush Allen type computer-built modular schedule was a big step in this direction. But Drs. Bush and Allen have not answered the most important questions about organizing the school of the future—they have merely raised them. We have yet, for example, to learn how to teach students in such a way that they will learn to handle unscheduled time responsibly; and we have yet to learn how to organize curricula in such a way as to provide well defined options to students and teachers.

We seem, however, to be progressing rapidly. The recent national study on innovative practices completed by the North Central Association and the Institute for Development of Educational Activities, has shown, among other things, that Paul Mort's much quoted diffusion rate has speeded up significantly in the past few years.

The change process itself is now the subject of a considerable amount of study and experimentation. Some schools, such as University City, Missouri, are experimenting with various kinds of "change agents"— persons specifically hired to bring about planned, appropriate innovation. Some systematic efforts are being made to explore new techniques of action research which will enable teachers to make decisions on the basis of the results of their own practices. I am happy to be associated with a project dedicated to this important objective. Money is now becoming more plentiful to support systematic change.

So there is reason for optimism.

But much needs to be done if we are to learn how to accommodate organizationally the kinds of educational programs now on the drawing boards. The organizational plan of the school of the 1980's must be basically different from the plan now used by most high schools. The plan of the future must encourage an organizational climate which nourishes inquiry; it must provide for new supportive roles for supervisory and administrative staffs and for a moving of decision-making closer to the teacher-pupil interaction level; it must encourage emergent leadership on the part of students and staff; and it must provide for orderly flexibility.

Such an organizational plan could be built in a school within the next ten years. Promising beginnings have been made already.

I am happy to report to you that insofar as organization for change is concerned, our public and private high schools of this country are finally beginning to pull themselves painfully out of the 19th century.

The Middle School

One of the innovations proposed in the 1960's has been the middle school. It has arisen in part out of the need in some urban areas for a different grouping of students to provide for reintegration of segregated schools. Many of the proponents of the 6-3-3 or junior high school pattern of organization do not expect the middle school to become more than one viable alternative to the junior high school. One of the problems of the junior high school has been its designation as a junior high school. In the minds of many, including members of staffs of junior high schools, this has been justification for making it a carbon copy of the high school.

Perhaps the foremost of the specialists in secondary education advocating the middle school as a replacement for the junior high school is William Alexander. In this article he and Emmett Williams describe the argument for a four-year school. William Alexander and Emmett Williams are Professor and Associate Professor of Education at the University of Florida.

Schools for the Middle School Years*

William M. Alexander and Emmett L. Williams

What school organization is best for pupils in that stage of development between childhood and adolescence? Some fifty years ago, the answer was to be a new *junior high* school for grades 7, 8 and 9. This pattern spread relatively rapidly, and a six-year (or six plus kindergarten) elementary followed by a three-year junior and three-year senior high has become the prevailing school organization in the United States.

Yet while these past decades of experience with this pattern have produced many significant and lasting features, there seems today increasing disenchantment with the schools for the middle school years. Some question whether the junior high school is a bridge between elementary and high school or a vestibule to the latter; others are urging change upon the typical graded, self-contained classroom of the elementary school, especially in its upper grades.

THE 6–3–3 PLAN?

Certainly there is not an adequate basis in research for strict adherence to the status quo. Research on school organization does not demonstrate the clear superiority of any one organizational arrangement over all others. Anderson's review (1) of research on organization in relation to staff utilization and deployment led him to conclude that ". . . recent research upon which policies of staff utilization and deployment must be based, at least temporarily, is woefully inadequate." What can be con-

---

* *Educational Leadership* 23:217–23 (Dec., 1965). Reprinted with permission of the Association for Supervision and Curriculum Development, and the authors. Copyright © 1965 by ASCD. [These ideas are developed more fully in a recent publication by these authors and others, *The Emergent Middle School* (Holt, Rinehart and Winston, 1968).]

cluded from a review of the literature is that existing arrangements do not seem to satisfy some criteria for a school organization and a program consistent with psychological and physiological needs of pupils and relevant to modern societal demands.

For example, there is little research evidence to support, and some reason to question, the assumption that a junior high, separate and distinct from both elementary and senior high school, is a necessity because of the unique characteristics of the age group. On the contrary side, Margaret Mead (8) argues that the grades included in junior high "were postulated on age, and not on size, strength, or stage of puberty." As a result she observes that:

> They have resulted inadvertently in classifying together boys and girls when they vary most, within each sex, and between the sexes, and are least suited to a segregated social existence. Also, they have divorced them from the reassurances of association with the children like their own recent past selves and older adolescents like whom they will some day become. When a type of school that was designed to cushion the shock of change in scholastic demands has become the focus of the social pressures which were once exerted in senior high school, problems have been multiplied.

From his viewpoint as a psychiatrist, Berman (2) sees the change from elementary to junior high school as quite poorly timed for children. He declares that "in the midst of deciding who they are, they shouldn't have to waste any energy finding out where they are." His opinion is that "during the highly volatile years of eleven through thirteen or fourteen, youngsters should have a familiar, secure background in which to operate."

Dacus' (3) study of pupils in grades five through ten raises interesting questions. On the criterion measures of social, emotional, and physical maturity, and opposite-sex choices, the *least* differences were found between pupils in grades six and seven, and pupils in grades nine and ten. Yet it is between these grades that our present 6-3-3 plan divides children.

The junior high school is most often defended on the grounds of the *bridge* function. It is supposed to serve as a bridge between the relatively untroubled, relaxed world of childhood and the more rigorous, stressful, disciplined world of high school. Johnson (6) declares: "In a world in which adults expound one set of values and espouse another, in which schooling is prolonged and economic dependence is protracted, and in which social life is largely outside the family, the value of a haven the junior high attempts to be is readily recognized" but notes that not all junior high schools have succeeded in this regard. He criticized the junior high for its tendency to imitate the senior high.

Hull (5) claims that junior high "is a poor investment," and that "it puts the unstable child at a most vulnerable period in his life in a situation more appropriate for older youth." On the other hand, it is commonly observed that today's children grow up faster in many ways. Havighurst (4) states that ". . . the adolescent today is more *precocious* and more *complex*. . . . He has many experiences *earlier* than his parents had these experiences." But does the present "bridge" school serve the intellectual needs of such children? Lounsbury and Marani (7) concluded from "shadow studies" in grade 8 classrooms across the country that the learning environment "was often unstimulating; there was lack of diversity in the program of required subjects; and there was little provision for individual differences among pupils."

PROPOSED: A MODEL MIDDLE SCHOOL

Along with the scholars and researchers cited, the present authors seriously question whether the currently dominant organizational arrangements for educating older children, preadolescents, and early adolescents provide optimum possibilities. New middle school organizations and programs (9) now being developed in various communities across the United States indicate considerable interest in experimentation with patterns differing from those now characteristic of the upper elementary and junior high school years. For consideration by others interested in developing alternative models, we offer the following as one set of possibilities for a model middle school.

Guidelines

A real middle school should be designed to serve the needs of older children, preadolescents, and early adolescents. Pupils would enter the middle school at the approximate age of ten years and would progress to the upper or high school at the approximate age of fourteen. Today's children in this age bracket need freedom of movement, opportunities for independence, a voice in the running of their own affairs, the intellectual stimulation of working with different groups and with different teacher specialists.

They are eager and ready for experiences quite different from those available in the typical elementary school. On the other hand, a congenial school environment for these children should be free of the rigidity of total departmentalization, the pressures of interschool competitions, and the tensions of older adolescent social functions that loom so large in typical junior high schools. The middle school would be planned to serve a truly transitional function from childhood to adolescence. Its organizational arrangements should foster growth from childhood dependence toward a high degree of self-sufficiency.

A middle school organization should make a reality of the long-held ideal of individualized instruction. Every pupil would be assigned a teacher-counselor who coordinates the learner's total program throughout the middle school years in conjunction with other teachers and specialists who know him. An adequate program of diagnostic services would permit teachers to plan individual deviations from standard programs.

Pupils would be scheduled to work in special instructional centers where they may either catch up on needed skills or branch out into further exploration. Programmed instructional materials and other individually paced approaches would be utilized, and self-directed learning emphasized. Non-graded arrangements could permit students to progress at different rates and to different depths.

A *middle school program should give high priority to the intellectual components of the curriculum.* There should be a planned sequence of concepts and skills for the general education areas of the curriculum. This does not imply emphasis on mastery of content of a narrow range of academic subjects, but rather that every effort would be made to create a climate in which learning is exciting and rewarding. What is required is not attainment of uniform standards but that every learner be challenged to perform well at whatever level he is capable of attaining.

In such an environment, intellectual pursuits would be as respected as the social and athletic components of the program, and children would be helped to see that learning can be its own reward uncluttered by any extrinsic system of grades as reward or punishment. Every pupil would be scheduled in a series of planned opportunities for developing both creative and disciplined thinking.

A *middle school program should place primary emphasis on skills of continued learning.* Direct instruction in use of various modes of inquiry and the discovery method helps children to experience joy in learning. In all studies, continued attention would be given to the learning process itself. Teachers would guide pupils in the use of sources, teach them to formulate questions, gather information and materials, and test hypotheses. Pupils would be given increasing opportunities to assume responsibility for portions of their own learning through use of independent study plans.

A *middle school should provide a rich program of exploratory experiences.* The child of middle school age needs many opportunities to explore new interests. Special interest centers, competently supervised and operated on a flexible time basis, should provide individualized instruction in each curriculum area and also in such varied activities as reading, acting, photography, ceramics, typing, personal grooming, and many others. Boy Scout merit badge and Girl Scout proficiency badge work, and other youth programs could be incorporated into the school program under the coordination of the teacher-counselor. A portion of every pupil's schedule would include exploratory experiences.

A *program of health and physical education should be designed especially for boys and girls of the middle school years.* Direct instruction in essential knowledge of personal hygiene would be combined with regular participation in fitness activities, heterosexual group games, and carry-over sports activities. Adequate facilities and specialized supervision should be provided for a total range of physical and health needs including corrective and remedial programs.

An emphasis on values should underline all aspects of a middle school program. A middle school should offer unique advantages for helping children to formulate personal values and standards, and to analyze and question social attitudes and group behaviors. Children of this age are approaching or undergoing physical and psychological changes which they are striving to understand. They are beginning to establish new roles for themselves which sometimes conflict with adult expectations. They are increasingly aware of discrepancies between stated ideals and observed actions. Intellectually honest and emotionally calm exploration of these value areas with competent adult guidance would be a part of each pupil's regularly scheduled program.

The organization of a middle school would facilitate most effective use of the special competencies and interests of the teaching staff. Cooperative arrangements for teaching and guidance, special instructional center personnel, technicians and other aides, and ample supervisory staff would be utilized to enable each person to make his maximum contribution to the total program. Ample instructional planning time and in-service training opportunities would be provided for each teacher. The staff should be employed on a twelve-months contract with provisions for periodic study-leave.

The Curriculum Plan

The curriculum plan of a real middle school would consist of planned programs in three phases: Learning Skills; General Studies; and Personal Development. Every pupil would be scheduled into each of the three phases each year in school. The time requirements and the nature of the work in each phase would vary for individual pupil programs, but the general plan is seen as follows:

1. *Learning Skills Phase:* Continues and expands basic communicational and computational skills development begun at the primary school level, with increasing emphasis on use of library tools and skills of independent study. Skills for emphasis are identified and included along with content goals in each unit of work in all General Studies areas. A remedial program of skills development is conducted in special laboratory centers.

2. *General Studies Phase:* Includes those learning experiences which give the learner a heightened awareness of his cultural heritage and those other common learnings essential to civic and economic literacy. Content would be focused on major concepts and unifying themes drawn from the areas of literature, social studies, mathematics,

science, and fine arts. Some of the instruction in this phase might
be in groups of up to 100 pupils.

3. *Personal Development Phase:* Includes those experiences which fulfill personal and remedial needs, permit exploration of personal interests, and promote physical and social growth; health and physical
education geared to the 10-14 year-old; individually planned experiences in foreign languages, typing, technical training, music, art,
dramatics, journalism; student-managed enterprises; community work
projects; advanced work in science, mathematics, and other areas of
individual special competence and interest.

Organization for Instruction

The organization for instruction would be designed to facilitate an
optimum curriculum and continuous progress for every pupil. Pupils in
the middle school would not be expected to progress at the same rate or
to the same depth. Neither would a student be expected to be at the same
graded level in all of his studies. Planning and evaluation of an individual's
progress through the curriculum should be a cooperative process based
on diagnostic and evaluative data and involving his homeroom teacher,
other teachers who work with him, and other special personnel, with the
pupil himself involved at appropriate levels. Most children would remain
in the middle school for a period of four years; however, some might be
ready to move into the upper or high school after three years, and some
might need to remain in the middle school for a fifth year.

The basic instructional unit of a middle school should be the individual. The significant organizational arrangements can be described by
analyzing the various groups and centers through which an individual
student would be scheduled.

1. *Homeroom Unit:* Each pupil would be a member of a homeroom
group of about 25 pupils who are in the same year in school but are
heterogeneously grouped on other criteria. A homeroom teacher-
counselor, competent to give basic instruction in the General Studies
area, and skilled in planning individual programs, would be assigned
to each Homeroom Unit. The Teacher-counselor would work out an
individual program with each pupil, mandated by diagnostic and
performance data and on the judgments of other teachers who also
work with the pupil. The amount of time spent with the Homeroom
Unit would vary with individuals, and typically decrease as a pupil
moves from the first through later years in the school.

2. *Wing Unit:* A Wing Unit would combine four homeroom units and
their teachers for cooperative planning and instruction in the
General Studies area. The pupils in the Wing Unit would be in the
same year in school but otherwise heterogeneously grouped. Four
homeroom teachers, each representing a special competence in one
of the General Studies areas of language arts, social studies, science,
or mathematics would meet regularly to cooperatively plan the instruction for the 100 pupils in the Wing Unit. The teachers in the
Wing Unit would function as a curriculum planning committee and

as a teaching team. The team may arrange for some of the instruction to be in large groups containing all of the 100 students, and some of the work to be in small groups for interactive discussions, or instruction in basic skills.

3. *Vertical Unit:* The Vertical Unit, consisting of approximately 400 pupils and 16 teachers, would provide an environment that is at once stimulating and secure, stable and flexible. The Vertical Unit (a "school within a school") gives the pupil a wider community in which to live, explore, and develop new social understandings. At the same time, this unit is small enough to promote a sense of identity and belongingness. All four year levels of the school would be represented in the Vertical Unit, and provisions for vertical acceleration through any area of the curriculum would promote greater individualization and program flexibility. Younger students would have opportunities to work and plan with and learn from more mature ones, and the older student would have special opportunity to provide leadership within the Vertical Unit.

4. *Special Learning Centers:* The use of Special Learning Centers to serve the exploratory interests and the special and remedial needs of the middle school pupils would be a distinctive feature of the organization. Pupils would be scheduled for work in these centers on an individual basis for both short-term and long-term instruction in the Personal Development and Learning Skills portions of the curriculum. The centers should be adequately equipped and manned by special personnel competent to direct group study and individual projects. Special Learning Centers would include: library, reading laboratory, home arts, typing and writing laboratory, foreign language laboratory, arts and hobby center, music room, and physical education-recreation center. Centers would be operated on a flexible schedule and would be open to pupils after school and on Saturday.

The key to the implementation of a successful middle school program is a staff of adults of uncommon talents and abilities. The teachers must be as knowledgeable as possible in their chosen academic fields and must have training in the guidance and counseling of children of middle school age. A program of selection, recruitment, and training would be necessary to develop a staff with these special qualifications.

Obviously such a school would be expensive—perhaps costing up to half as much more per pupil than average schools for children of the middle school years. But the loss of human potential in current educational organizations and programs for this age group may be far more costly.

If these ideas merit investigation, increased costs for their careful testing could surely be justified.

REFERENCES

[1] Robert H. Anderson. "Organizational Character of Education: Staff Utilization and Deployment." *Review of Educational Research* 34:455–69; October, 1964.

[2] Sidney Berman. "As a Psychiatrist Sees Pressures On Middle Class Teenagers." *NEA Journal* 54:17–24; February, 1965.

[3] Wilfred P. Dacus. "A Study of the Grade Organizational Structure of the Junior High School as Measured by Social Maturity, Emotional Maturity, Physical Maturity, and Opposite-Sex Choices." *Dissertation Abstracts* 24 (1963): 1461–62. University of Houston, 1963.

[4] Robert J. Havighurst. "Lost Innocence—Modern Junior High Youth." *Bulletin of the National Association of Secondary-School Principals* 49:1–4; April, 1965.

[5] J. H. Hull. "The Junior High School Is a Poor Investment." *Nation's Schools* 65:78–81; April, 1960.

[6] Mauritz Johnson, Jr. "Schools in the Middle—Junior High: Education's Problem Child." *Saturday Review* 45:40–42, 56; July 21, 1962.

[7] John Lounsbury and Jean Marani. *The Junior High School We Saw: One Day in the Eighth Grade.* Washington, D.C.: Association for Supervision and Curriculum Development, 1964.

[8] Margaret Mead. "Early Adolescence in the United States." *Bulletin of the National Association of Secondary-School Principals* 49:5–10; April, 1965.

[9] Judith Murphy. *Middle Schools.* New York: Educational Facilities Laboratories, 1965.

Family Life Education

If the school is to modify its program to deal more directly with the problems of modern living, one area of curriculum innovation is family-life education. There has been considerable discussion of this possibility for at least a whole generation. Some circles have been concerned lest such an emphasis would be an infringement on the responsibility and rights of parents. Some powerful church groups are also opposed on religious grounds to such teaching.

Several forces seem to be operating in the society at the present time to reduce opposition to school programs in family-life fields. Sex has become a more open and accepted topic for polite conversation. The possibility of disastrous population explosion has been recognized by large numbers of respected and well-informed people. The position of the Catholic Church on family planning seems to be changing. Concern for the welfare of the poor has emphasized the role of the large family in creating conditions of poverty.

The two articles in this section give different aspects of the problem. The first deals with one of the basic needs and the second with the nature of a curriculum.

John Dykstra, Associate Professor of Social Science at Jersey City State College in New Jersey, viewing the demographic problems facing the world, stresses what seem to him the urgent dimensions of the problem and an apparent unwillingness of curriculum specialists to deal with it.

Imperative: Education
for Reproductive Responsibility*

John W. Dykstra

In November, 1960, a statement of conviction concerning population growth was presented to the Secretary-General of the United Nations. It said in part:

> In spite of technological advances the earth cannot provide much longer enough food and minerals for a population which is increasing more than geometrically. Unless a favorable balance of population and resources is achieved with a minimum of delay, there is in prospect a Dark Age of human misery, famine, under-education, and unrest which could generate growing panic, exploding into wars fought to appropriate the dwindling means of survival; . . .
> . . . we urge that the United Nations, dedicated to the service of mankind, take the lead in establishing and implementing a policy designed to limit population growth the world over—in order that human beings everywhere may grow on a qualitative rather than on a merely quantitative level, and in order that they may be assured of the opportunity to develop their highest capacities, and to enjoy individual freedom, the advantages of education and public health, privacy, abundance, security, and the beauty and wonder of the world.[1]

The views indicated are not those of an unstable, ill-informed fringe of alarmists. This statement was signed by 216 of the world's most eminent men and women, including 17 Nobel Prize winners, and such other renowned figures as Jonas E. Salk, Arnold Toynbee, Sir Charles Darwin, Lewis Mumford, and Aldous Huxley.

Three years later the prestigious National Academy of Sciences issued a report in which it urged our federal government to participate actively in fostering international birth control studies as part of a major attack upon uncontrolled population growth. The committee gravely warned, "It

---

* *Phi Delta Kappan* 49:9:503–506 (May, 1968). Reprinted by permission of publisher and author.
[1] *The New York Times*, Sept. 20, 1961, carried a full-page advertisement reproducing the statement.

is an international problem from which no one can escape. Other than the search for lasting peace, no other problem is more urgent."[2]

Demographers and scholars from related areas are in almost total agreement that continuation of existing rates of population increase will have disastrous consequences for mankind. They differ only in their calculations as to whether, if present trends continue, man will first exhaust the supply of food, water, oxygen, or space.

In sharp contrast to the air of urgent concern manifested in statements by scientists has been the continuing neglect of the subject in American education. One looks in vain for evidence that American educators are significantly involved in communicating the nature and seriousness of the situation, or in stimulating thought concerning the kinds of social policies called for to deal with this demographic menace.

The secondary social studies classrooms would seem the most logical settings for such activity; social studies time, however, is still heavily committed to the memorization of a vast array of facts about the past, with occasional forays to discover lessons for the present. The tendency for the social studies to avoid coming to grips with the admittedly controversial but vital issues of the present has never been better illustrated.

Textbooks in use are probably as accurate an indicator as any available with respect to topics treated in social studies courses at the secondary level. A sampling of texts in such courses as social problems, world geography, sociology, economics, and world history provides convincing evidence that little is being done to convey an awareness of the challenges that a surging population poses to the world.

In one 660-page tome dealing with problems confronting the United States there is a single index reference to population, and there is a three page discussion of the contribution that population growth makes to prosperity.[3] The most recently published sociology text in our random list avoids any treatment of population.[4] Those world history students who have the sort of conscientious teacher who will reach the end of the book will encounter, on page 743 of a 745-page text, a capsule presentation of the population explosion.[5]

A text used in the less conventional "preparation for family life" courses proved to be just as wary of the subject. Neither "population" nor "birth control" nor any related topic was listed in the index. A chapter entitled "The Children in Your Future" avoided any intimation that it

[2] *The New York Times,* April 18, 1963, p. 1.

[3] Robert Rienow, *American Problems Today* (Second Edition). Boston: D. C. Heath, 1958. (A third edition has been on the market since 1965, but is probably not yet as widely used as the second.)

[4] Jack H. Curtis, John A. Coleman, and Ralph Lane, *Sociology.* Milwaukee: Bruce, 1967.

[5] T. Walter Wallbank, *Man's Story.* Chicago: Scott, Foresman, 1964.

is either possible or desirable to limit the number of children. A subtopic, "The Enjoyment of Children," is handled without suggesting that either the number or spacing of children is in any way related to enjoyment.[6]

Most typically, texts contain a handful of scattered references to population growth. In my sampling only two of the books designed for use in the infrequently offered secondary sociology course devoted so much as a chapter to the "population explosion." One can hardly expect students to take the threat of an overcrowded world very seriously so long as more space is allotted in their text to the federal reserve system, American social classes, or the monsoons.

To the extent that the existence of a population problem is acknowledged, it is rather consistently portrayed as the exclusive concern of the underdeveloped nations. Students are usually assured that all is well in the United States, since productivity continues to outrun population growth. A constantly increasing number of Americans is in fact often alleged to be a very desirable condition, creating growing demand for goods and services and thereby assuring the continuance of prosperity.[7]

Those texts that do most in the way of conveying something of the magnitude of population problems confronting nations such as India and Pakistan nevertheless manifest an aversion to discussing the possibilities of curtailing population increases. Suggestions as to remedial action invariably involve the production of more and more. If the high school student had no other access to information on this subject he would necessarily conclude that surging population growth is one of the inevitabilities of human existence.

To gather further evidence concerning the attention given the subject of population in our high schools, I administered a questionnaire to a group of newly arrived college freshmen. In a sample of 119, only eight students reported that population was given considerable attention in any course in high schools they had attended. The abysmal lack of factual knowledge concerning the subject was reflected in answers to subsequent questions; again only eight, for example, were able to give estimates of world population within a half billion of the generally accepted figure. With few exceptions, such knowledge as was possessed was reportedly derived from magazine and newspaper articles and from television treatment of the subject.[8]

[6] Mollie Stevens Smart and Russell Cook Smart, *Living in Families*. Boston: Houghton-Mifflin, 1965.

[7] See Paul Driscoll Lindholm, *Our American Economy*. New York: Harcourt, Brace, 1959. Students are assured, "The fact that more population means more demand for housing, for food and clothing, for household appliances and furniture, and for many other goods and services is itself an encouragement to production, and therefore to prosperity," p. 400.

[8] A more detailed presentation of the findings of this study is presented in my article, "The Population Explosion; A Neglected Topic," *The Social Studies*, October, 1965, pp. 190–93.

The failure of our schools to give adequate attention to the nature and significance of present population increases is reflected in the tremendous contrast between the alarm manifested by much of the scientific world and the tepid concern of the man in the street. A Gallup Poll conducted in June, 1963, found three out of four Americans unconcerned about the "population explosion," with one out of three not even aware of its existence. Another poll taken two years later found that crime, racial discrimination, and poverty were all ranked ahead of population growth as serious problems for the United States. Factual knowledge about population was meager.[9] Considering that one can experience 12 or even 16 years of formal education without encountering more than a passing reference to the "population explosion," the minimization of its significance is hardly surprising.

When those manifesting indifference are questioned further, some simply insist that God will take care of us; others show a comparable faith that science will rise to every challenge, whatever our numbers. Geophysicist Harrison Brown, in *Challenges to Man's Future*, has shown in a dramatic way the fatuity of thinking which is oriented toward using science to increase productivity and unconcerned about curbing population increase. Brown holds that all conceivable present forms of food will be over-consumed in the present century. He postulates that our ingenious scientists will helpfully enable us to eat rock. But, he calculates, by 2700 A.D. the earth will be consumed by our burgeoning population. Now all migrate to other planets; but by 3200 A.D. all these planets are also devoured. Our swarming billions next turn their attention to the sun; the last of it is consumed by 3700 A.D.[10] Planned parenthood might not have been such a bad idea.

In addition to the central population problem of making survival possible in the face of a constant accretion of humans, there are an array of other problems in which population growth looms as a crucial factor. The combating of air and water pollution, the eradication of illiteracy, the reduction of traffic congestion, the satisfying utilization of leisure, the preservation of beauty, the defense of privacy, and the fight against poverty—all are causes that would be substantially furthered by the curbing of population increase. Not only does there appear to be neglect in our schools of the central issue of man's survival, but the extent to which population growth contributes to these other problems is frequently minimized or ignored. In a widely used world geography text, for example, a section is allotted to the poverty of Latin America without a single

[9] Population Reference Bureau, Inc., "The American Public Looks at the Population Crisis," news release of Feb. 16, 1966.

[10] Harrison Brown's illustration is presented by Lloyd V. Berkner in his article "Man versus Technology," *Population Bulletin*, November, 1966.

reference to the rate of population increase, a rate which exceeds that of the Orient.[11]

Typical is the consistency with which conservation education circumvents the population factor. In a conventional treatment by a weekly for juveniles, the young readers were warned, "Inch by inch, mile by mile, the cities are creeping into country areas. Unless careful plans are made and followed all our wild lands are in danger of becoming cities."[12] What the young folk were not told anywhere in this issue—nor are they in most such discussions—is that unless these "careful plans" contain effective programs for reducing the American birthrate all the planners in the world will be to little avail.

Even in those rare instances in which there is acknowledgment of the fact that population increase is a basic source of pressure upon resources, the attitude assumed seems to be that the increase is an inevitable element around which adaptive programs must be built. In the "Conservation of Natural Resources" chapter in one of our social problems texts there is a brave sentence that warns, "Because of the rapid shrinkage of our resources and the expansion of our population, good citizenship demands that we practice more conservation."[13] One looks in vain in the remainder of the chapter for any intimation that good citizenship might also call for fertility control so as to reduce this pressure of population upon resources.[14]

Social science texts repeatedly reassure their trusting readers that vastly more humans can be supported within the confines of the United States. It would seem highly pertinent also to give consideration to the quality of life that will be possible once our population has increased twofold, and shortly thereafter, at present rates of increase, threefold.[15] For it is in the realm of the resources that enrich life with beauty and aesthetic satisfactions that the challenges posed by an expanding population are most difficult to meet. In the short run, at least, more Americans can be provided more houses to live in, more clothes to wear, and more food to eat. But more Americans cannot be provided more Yosemite Valleys, more Grand Canyons, more Niagaras, or more areas of unsullied wilderness.

[11] Clyde F. Kohn and Dorothy Weitz Drummond, *The World Today*. New York: McGraw-Hill, 1963.
[12] "Conservation—A Constant Battle," *My Weekly Reader*, March 16–20, 1964, p. 113.
[13] Lawrence V. Roth, Stillman M. Hobbs, and Alan C. Drake, *Living in Today's World* (Second Edition). New York: Laidlaw Brothers, p. 107.
[14] One of the best treatments of the interrelationship between population increase and conservation is found in Samuel P. McCutchen, George L. Fersh, and Nadine I. Clark: *Goals of Democracy—A Problems Approach*. New York: Macmillan, 1962.
[15] Population Reference Bureau, Inc., "U.S. Population: 200 Million Plus," news release of Nov. 6, 1967, p. 1.

Already, the combination of increased numbers, expanded leisure, and greater mobility has tarnished the beauty and lessened the possibilities of enjoyment in our once magnificent national parks. In the most popular ones campsites are packed tent-peg to tent-peg throughout the summer. Bumper-to-bumper traffic crawls along park roads. The recently completed jet-port next to the Grand Canyon insures that this once-remote refuge will reverberate with the roar of jets.

The future of forms of recreation requiring space appears exceedingly bleak in the metropolitan areas in which most of our population lives. Golf courses continue to capitulate to the blandishments of real estate interests. Waiting times at the surviving courses effectively limit usage. Many an urban college campus is a microcosm of the national scene, as tennis courts are transformed into parking areas and other more "practical" uses.

Fishing in our more populated Eastern states has come to assume ludicrous proportions. Each weekend throngs of anglers jostle each other on the banks of the less heavily polluted streams, entangling their lines amidst the detergent foam in the frantic effort to hook some docile hatchery-bred trout planted there a few days earlier. Fishing pressure has already spread this "put and take" travesty of fishing to many Western states still viewed, in the popular image, as the "wide open spaces."

While the need for population stabilization is patently more acute for the densely settled have-not nations, it is equally obvious that no nation can indefinitely add to its population. First it is the quality of life that is threatened; later comes the challenge to maintain life at all. The question is not whether an equilibrium between births and deaths is to be established, but when and how. Will a halt to population growth be achieved while there is still open space and forests and opportunities for privacy; or will we delay until such amenities are merely distant memories? Will the stabilization result from a voluntary limitation on births, or will it result from an increase in deaths as a consequence of malnutrition and resultant disease?

Firmly ensconced in the mores of our society is the belief that parents have the right to bring into the world as many children as they wish. If this right gets continued recognition, population stability will only be attained through a massive educational effort. It is not simply knowledge of the techniques of birth control that is needed, but also of the facts that make population stabilization an urgent necessity for the future of man.

In those nations that fail to educate their peoples effectively concerning national population needs, an increasing amount of coercive governmental intervention in the determination of family size can be anticipated. Compulsory sterilization or imprisonment are the likely fate of those who jeopardize the future of their society through an irresponsible incidence of reproduction. A bill providing for the sterilization of those males with three or more children was introduced last year in the Indian parliament. Some Indian states now provide sums of money to those who volunteer to be sterilized, as well as to those social workers who recruit such volunteers.[16] If present research efforts are successful, the vaccination of a population against pregnancy during much of their fertile life will be another measure available to governments.

Novelist Anthony Burgess, in *The Wanting Seed,* envisions a future in which governments, seeking desperately to halt runaway populations, utilize increasingly repressive measures. In the first stage propaganda, free contraceptives, the fostering of homosexuality, and the encouragement of infanticide are utilized. These efforts failing to stem the tide, parenthood becomes a crime, and pregnant women are executed. In the last stage roving masses of men seek to exterminate each other, and we observe once again the Malthusian conception of warfare as a negative check upon population.

Pro-natal influences abound in most cultures which resist any revolutionary message regarding the necessity of curtailing births. Since for the great bulk of the period that man has been on the earth the great need has been to insure the launching of enough children to maintain the group, favorable attitudes toward fertility have been nurtured. Means of sexual gratification that have not involved the possibility of conceptions occurring have been generally condemned.

Although the United States lacks the cult of virility so prominent in Latin America, there are still strong tendencies toward stereotyping the large family as a happy one, while the childless couple is presumed to be joyless, and if so by choice, "selfish." A periodic offering in Sunday magazine supplements is a glowing account of life in a family of 20. "Mothers of the Year" typically have children in excess of the national norm.[17]

The foregoing suggests that the curtailment of population growth is not likely to be attained through oblique references to the responsibility of the individual. The intellectual case for birth control will have to be developed fully and forcefully if it is to make headway against the emotional attachments to the birthways of the past.

Undoubtedly one of the greatest deterrents to the classroom treatment of population issues has been the religious involvement in the subject. The traditional Roman Catholic opposition to the use of contraceptives is well-known; lesser resistance has existed in some fundamentalist Protestant and Orthodox Jewish circles. Under the circumstances, the

[16] *The New York Times,* Dec. 18, 1967, p. 12.
[17] This subject is treated more fully in my article "Pro-Natal Influences in American Culture," *Sociology and Social Research,* November-December, 1959, pp. 79–85.

prudent teacher could hardly be expected to become involved in discussions which might logically seem to lead to the conclusion that the universal practice of birth control is one of the greatest needs of a nation.

Whatever the final papal declaration on the subject, however, the past five years have seen major changes in the climate in which the discussion of population growth is conducted. Catholic publications have become increasingly receptive to articles that point out the evils of uninhibited population increase. Many of the more progressive priests and laymen have unequivocally advocated a change in church teaching concerning birth control. Given such ferment within the church, classroom discussion of population issues is today much less likely to polarize into pro- and anti-Catholic positions.

The evidence does not necessarily indicate that mankind is utterly lost, overwhelmed by the inexorable effects of his fertility. It does suggest, however, that without delay vast energies must be directed toward effective education on this subject. Effective education is that which induces couples to have no more than the two children which most must settle for if population growth is to be halted. Man must extricate himself from a situation in which he must run faster and faster merely to stand still.

If the United States, with its tremendous educational resources, cannot educate its populace to reproductive responsibility, the most pessimistic predictions of demographic disaster ahead would seem certain of realization. If such a task is beyond our capacity, surely the populous underdeveloped lands, struggling now to create a literate citizenry, can hardly hope to convey with the needed haste an awareness of the harsh demographic realities to their population, and the consequent need to curtail births. The metamorphosis from manhood to anthood will then be completed.

The term family life education has seemed to some simply a euphemism for what was previously called sex education. There is probably no single area of curriculum concern for which more attention has been given to the preparation of curriculum materials. The following article by Michael A. Carrera, Assistant Professor of Health Education, Kingsborough Community College, Brooklyn, New York, gives in outline form the topics which are frequently included in curriculum guides. Curriculum specialists have generally agreed that it would be desirable to have family life education begin even before the child enters the first grade; to have such content treated in the regular courses in social studies, science, and health rather than in special and separate sections in the high school; and to have as much of the work as possible done in coeducational rather than in separate sex settings.

Family Life Education: A Curriculum Proposal for High Schools*

Michael A. Carrera

The trend in contemporary society toward youthful marriage has been the focus of numerous sociological studies. The apparent instability of these marriages shown clearly by divorce rates which are far above the norm have been illustrated by significant empirical evidence.[1,2,3]

This trend is receiving considerable encouragement from the adolescent milieu which is saturated with the vocabulary and symbols of romance, love, and marriage. Fairy tales, dolls, television, movies, and songs perpetuate the fantasies of love, how it feels to fall in love, what one does when in love, and how young people can maximize their opportunities to experience this state.

In view of the foregoing statements a clear challenge faces the secondary school educator, for family life specialists agree that marriage and family education on the junior and senior high school level can play a significant role in (1) reducing the number of youthful marriages and (2) providing an education which not only imparts facts but will develop meaningful attitudes and values towards a sound marital experience in contemporary life.[4]

It is in response to this challenge that the effective educator must provide the necessary intellectual climate to assist young people in acquiring accurate and comprehensive knowledge in this area. Acknowledging, however, that there exist many deterrents which prevent the achievement of this goal, there are specific programs which will afford the students the

---

* *The Clearing House* 42:394–97 (March, 1968). Reprinted by permission of publisher and author.

[1] Thomas P. Monahan, "Does Age of Marriage Matter in Divorce?" *Social Forces*, October 1, 1953, p. 86.

[2] Harvey T. Locke, *Predicting Adjustment In Marriage*. New York: Henry Holt, 1951.

[3] Robert C. Cook, *Population Bulletin 17*, Population Reference Bureau, Washington, D.C., June, 1961.

[4] Lee G. Burchinal, "Research on Young Marriage: Implications For Family Life Education." *The Family Life Coordinator*, No. 9 (1960), pp. 6–24.

opportunity to become confident and successful in their heterosexual inter-action, while providing them with a sound and meaning dialogue in marriage and family life.

The following is an outline, including specific teacher references, which covers topical considerations in preparation of a secondary school marriage and family curriculum. The instructional approach should be an eclectic one, with the emphasis on *active reciprocal communication* in the classroom. Maximum effectiveness of the educational process is one in which both student and teacher are involved in a constant dialogue concerning the issues at hand.

The extent and depth of the coverage of the listed topics should relate to the maturity level and real needs of the individual students.

I. *The Nature of Man-Woman*
   Biological
   Emotional
   Physical
   Sexual—Including a frank discussion of the male and female reproductive process.
   1. Johnson, Warren R., *Human Sex and Sex Education Perspectives and Problems.* Philadelphia: Lea and Febiger, 1963.
   2. Mead, Margaret, *Male and Female.* New York: Mentor Books, New American Library, 1955.
   3. Montagu, Ashley, *The National Superiority of Women.* New York: Macmillan Co., 1953.
   4. Reik, Theodor, "Men and Women Speak Different Languages," *Psychoanalysis*, Spring-Summer Publication, 1954, pp. 3-15.
   5. Watts, Alan, *Nature, Man and Woman.* New York: Mentor Books, 1960.

II. *Dating and Courtship in Transition*
   Definitions
   Purposes
   Ancient Dating Customs
   Modern Dating Concepts
      Random Dating
      Going Steady
      Pinning
      Petting
   (Venereal disease should be discussed in this general area.)
   1. Bernard, Harold W., *Adolescent Development in American Culture.* Yonkers, N.Y.: World Book, 1957.
   2. Bernard, Jessie, Helen Buchanan, and William Smith, Jr., *Dating, Mating and Marriage.* New York: Arco Publishing Co., 1958.
   3. Burgess, Ernest W., *Courtship, Engagement and Marriage.* Philadelphia, Pa.: J. B. Lippincott, 1954.
   4. Cavan, Ruth S., *Marriage and Family in The Modern World.* Thomas Cromwell Co., 1960, Chapters 3, 6, 7, 8, 9, 11.
   5. Fielding, William J., *Strange Customs of Courtship and Marriage.* New York: Hart Publishing Co., 1942.

    6. Merrill, Francis, *Courtship and Marriage*. New York: Holt-Dryden, 1959.

III. *Love*
Definitions
Love vs. Infatuation
Historical Concepts of Love
Love and Maturity: Characteristics

1. Duvall, Evelyn, *Love and the Facts of Life*. New York: Association Press, 1963.
2. Fromm, Erich, *The Art of Loving*. New York: Harper Colophon Books, 1965.
3. Hall, Edward, *The Silent Language*. Garden City, N.Y.: Doubleday, 1959.
4. Hunt, Morton, *The Natural History of Love*. New York: Knopf Co., 1959.
5. Sussman, Marvin B., *Sourcebook In Marriage and The Family*. Boston: Houghton Mifflin Co., 1963, pp. 86, 93.
6. Udry, J. Richard, *The Social Context of Marriage*. Philadelphia and New York: J. B. Lippincott Co., 1966.
7. West, Jessamyn, *Love is Not What You Think*. New York: Harcourt, Brace & World, 1959.
8. Winter, Gibson, *Love and Conflict*. New York: Dolphin Books, 1961.

IV. *Readiness For Marriage*
Mate Selection
Religious Factors
Endogeny-Exogeny
Interfaith Relationships
Interracial Relationships
Premarital Sexual Experiences including a discussion of mature, responsible sexual behavior
Transition of courtship to marriage emphasizing the engagement period
Historical concepts of Marriage
    Monogamy
    Polygamy
    Polyandry

1. Bossard, James and Eleanor Boll, *One Marriage and Two Faiths*. New York: Ronald Press, 1957.
2. Crawley, Malfetti, Stewart, and Vas Dias, *Reproduction, Sex and Preparation for Marriage*. Englewood Cliffs, N.J.: Prentice Hall, 1964.
3. Duvall, Evelyn, *Why Wait Till Marriage*. New York: Association Press, 1965.
4. Gordon, Albert, *Intermarriage*. Boston: Beacon Press, 1964.
5. Kirkendall, Lester, *Premarital Intercourse and Interpersonal Relationships*. N.Y.: Matrix House Ltd., 1966.
6. Lee, Alfred & Elizabeth, *Marriage and The Family*. New York: Barnes and Noble Inc., 1967. Chapters 1, 2, 3.
7. Morgan, William and Mildred, *Thinking Together About Marriage and Family*. New York: Association Press, 1955, Chapters 8-14.

8. Stein, Joseph, *Maturity In Sex and Marriage.* New York: Coward, McCann, 1963.
9. Sussman, Marvin B., *Sourcebook In Marriage and The Family.* Boston: Houghton Mifflin Co., 1963, pp. 101, 115, 120, 125.
10. Winch, Robert F., "Mate Selection: A Study of Complementary Needs," *American Sociological Review,* Vol. 20, 1955, pp. 552-555.

V. *Marriage*
   Youthful Marriages
   Realistic Expectations in Marriage
   Fantasies and Fears
   Meaning of Compatability
   Recognition of Marriage Roles
   Family Ties
   1. Bowman, Henry, *Marriage For Moderns.* New York: McGraw-Hill Co., 1965.
   2. Clemens, Alphonse, *Design For Successful Marriage.* Englewood Cliffs, N.J.: Prentice Hall, 1965.
   3. Duvall, Evelyn, *In-Laws, Pros and Cons.* New York: Association Press, 1954.
   4. Mudd, Emily and Aron Krech, *Man and Wife.* New York: W. W. Norton, 1957.
   5. Polatin, Phillip and Ellen Philtine, *Marriage In the Modern World.* Philadelphia: J. B. Lippincott, 1956.
   6. Rainer, Jerome and Julia, *Sexual Adventure In Marriage.* New York: Julian Messner, 1965.
   7. Stein, Joseph. *Maturity in Sex and Marriage.* New York: Coward, McCann, 1963.
   8. Sussman, Marvin B., *Sourcebook In Marriage and The Family.* Boston: Houghton Mifflin Company, 1963, pp. 3-14.

VI. *Preparation For a Family*
   Management in Family Living
   Family Planning
   Methods of Child Spacing
   Parenthood
   Marriage Problems and Crises
   1. Anshen, Ruth, *The Family: Its Function and Destiny.* New York: Harper and Brothers, 1950.
   2. Bossard, James and Eleanor Boll, *Why Marriages Go Wrong.* New York: Ronald Press, 1958.
   3. Cohen, Jerome and Arthur Hanson, *Personal Finance.* Homewood, Ill.: Richard Irwin, 1964.
   4. Leslie, Gerald, *The Family In Social Context.* New York: Oxford Press, 1967.
   5. Stroup, Atlee, *Marriage and Family: A Developmental Approach.* New York: Appleton-Century-Crofts, 1966.
   6. Winch, Robert, *The Modern Family.* New York: Holt, Rinehart, and Winston, 1963.
   7. Womble, Dale, *Foundations For Marriage and Family Relations.* New York: Macmillan Co., 1966.

Section III

The Operation of the
Public High School

THE ACTUAL OPERATION OF THE AMERICAN PUBLIC HIGH SCHOOL IS A
complex process. In order to understand the school, it is important to
consider the teaching method, discipline and morale, provision for group
instruction, and the mechanical operations concerned with records, reports,
marks and graduation.

Discussion of teaching method will include consideration of five
important concepts which have served to revolutionize the role of the
teacher: (1) individualization of instruction, (2) unit teaching, (3) teaching as supervision of learning, (4) concern for the effect of teaching techniques on the student, and (5) concern for academic freedom. The
discussion of discipline and morale points to an important relationship
between the nature of student control and the school's mission in the
development of civic and ethical understandings.

The problem of grouping students for instruction and the closely
related problems of scheduling bring into focus the question of providing
for individual students in the social setting of the school. Consideration of
problems in keeping records, making reports, assigning marks, and preparing for graduation makes apparent the crucial significance of personality
in even the mechanical operation of the secondary school.

The availability of a new technology is producing excitement among
some of the students of the American public high school. Consideration is
being given to many different possibilities from programmed learning and
computer-assisted instruction through team teaching and improved counseling techniques.

11

The Revolution in Teaching Method

THE SHIFTING EMPHASIS OF THE AMERICAN SECONDARY SCHOOL, FROM EDU-
cation of the few to education of the masses, would by itself have
required a wholesale revision in teaching methods. This revision was given
a very powerful assist by the modification of old theories of learning. Let
us examine some concepts which have had an important impact.

Individualization of Instruction

Democratic educational theory, as it developed during the nineteenth
century, continued to put stress on developing the potential of the individual. Gradually, as the testing movement began to develop in the twentieth century, it became obvious that there were tremendous differences
between individuals of approximately the same age level. Furthermore, it
became important to determine the nature of the differences and to recognize them in the process of teaching.[1]

Emphasis on Diagnosis. One important dimension, then, of the idea
of individualizing instruction is the idea of diagnosing the nature of the
learning problems being faced. Good diagnosis requires the collection of
information about students and the maintenance of adequate records.
Departmentalization of the high school makes this important and at the
same time difficult. One phase in the collection of information is, of
course, the use of standardized tests. Standardized testing began to make
considerable headway in the twenties and has become increasingly refined
within the past 40 years. The emphasis has been on intelligence testing
with a subsidiary interest in achievement testing both in general and spe-

[1] See Roy O. Billett, *Provisions for Individual Differences, Marking, and Promotion*
(Washington, D.C.: U.S. Office of Education Bulletin 1932, No. 17, Government
Printing Office, 1933).

cific areas, diagnostic testing particularly in reading and arithmetic, and testing for vocational interests.[2]

Most public schools have at some time during the student's school career given an intelligence test and recorded the score. Too frequently this has not been followed up with other testing to check its reliability. Some poorly prepared teachers seize on a low score as a sufficient reason for making no further effort to teach a particular student. Many teachers, however, recognize the limitations of intelligence tests and try to supplement them with other tests, comparisons with earlier tests, analysis of the student's actual school performance, and—where possible—more individual testing. One particular use of the intelligence test has been to identify students who are not achieving up to their reasonable capacity.[3]

Standardized achievement tests also prove helpful in planning the program of a class. The high school English teacher, for example, can get some appreciation of the status of particular students in his class. The achievement test may or may not serve also as a diagnostic test in terms of indicating the specific types of problems which individual students may be having. If a student shows up poorly on the English section of a general achievement test, the secondary school teacher may follow up with more specific testing to determine areas which are worthy of attention.[4]

Various types of interest testing, while of more direct use in the guidance program, are also helpful in the diagnostic teaching process since they may indicate ways of improving motivation.[5]

Related to the testing program of the school is the system of cumulative records. These contain information about the family of the student, his previous school experience, the tests which he has taken, his social development, his health, his disciplinary problems, and his vocational interests and objectives. Sometimes a reference to these records will provide clues to understanding a student which will save a teacher much additional testing.[6]

A third technique available to teachers is the use of his own tests. Important in this connection is the pre-test. Thus the teacher who has tentatively identified his objectives for the term's work tests to see whether these will be appropriate.[7]

    [2] Chester W. Harris, "Intelligence," Encyclopedia of Education Research, 3rd ed. (New York: The Macmillan Company, 1960).
    [3] Cf. W. Mays, "Philosophic Critique of Intelligence Tests," Educational Theory 16:318–32 (Oct., 1966).
    [4] P. L. Dressel, "The Role of Evaluation in Teaching and Learning," National Council for the Social Studies Yearbook 35:10–20 (1965).
    [5] R. C. Craig and M. C. Holsbach, "Utilizing Existing Interests to Develop Others in General Science Classes," School Science and Mathematics 64:120–28 (Feb., 1964).
    [6] Gordon Ellis, "A New Approach to Student Records," Personnel and Guidance Journal 42:166 (Oct., 1963).
    [7] W. J. Laidlaw, "Teacher-Made Tests: Models to Serve Specific Needs," The Clearing House 39:336–39 (Feb., 1965).

The teacher may use a formal type of test requiring direct answers or he may engage in informal activity such as analysing errors made by students in their daily speech or on some written assignment. Much emphasis on the test as a basis for formal grades and reports to parents gets in the way of teaching, but there can hardly be too much emphasis on diagnosis of the nature of the learning that is taking place. Although in the departmentalized program this emphasis on diagnosis seems much more complicated than in the elementary school, the aim of the secondary school to provide for the needs of all of its students makes it seem imperative. There is, however, no particular point in diagnosis unless there is to be some follow-up and adaptation of the teaching process.

Grouping Within the Class. Some aspects of the problem of grouping students will be discussed at length in Chapter 12. Discussion is concerned here specifically with the use of small groups *within the class.* To the extent that it has been assumed that it was possible to grade instruction at the high school level into sequential and carefully defined courses which were to be mastered before students proceeded, it was considered less necessary to break the class group into smaller segments. With the recognition of the importance of individual differences, the picture has changed.

Good teachers divide their larger groups into smaller groups for several distinct purposes. In the first place such grouping makes it possible to deal with different levels of ability. It becomes possible to provide for three or four distinct levels of *group* instruction.[8]

More important, perhaps, is the fact that within a group of six or ten students it becomes more nearly possible to recognize the individuality of each student. Although the teacher obviously cannot spend the whole class period working directly with each small group, the time he does spend may be designed to have a greater impact on the *individual.*[9]

A third factor in evaluating the importance of small groups is the usually improved morale. Students are able to be more active participants in smaller groups than in larger ones. A chance for participation is important in the motivation of students who have become discouraged. In larger groups they are in competition with students who may have had more ability or poise. When placed in groups of smaller size and more nearly at their own interest or ability level, they have more opportunity for communicating with and learning from each other, for leadership and participation.

Individualized Assignments. Individual assignments were much used during the early thirties, but less use is made of this technique today in modern secondary schools than seems theoretically desirable. Nevertheless, most teachers make use of it with at least a few of their students.

---

[8] R. S. Jones, "Instructional Problems and Issues; Ability Grouping and Related Issues," *Review of Educational Research* 36:419–20 (Oct., 1966).
[9] H. A. Jeep and J. W. Hollis "Group Dynamics in Action, *The Clearing House* 41:203–209 (Dec., 1966).

Much of the work of the high school is concerned with the development of concepts rather than simply of skills. Even here, it is evident that where there are large apparent differences in ability or in achievement, individualized assignments should be tried. Students may be better motivated by being allowed to undertake projects which seem of particular interest to them. Some teachers have developed a number of alternate assignments dealing with the same areas of concept and skill development, and students are encouraged to choose the one which interests them most. Others make extensive use of individual conferences to plan with students their assignments for projects which may proceed independently for several days or even weeks. Exceptionally capable students who have already mastered basic material available in the text may move to greater depth in the same material or even to new material. Less capable students may be given more elementary material and may make more progress if they feel that they are not being asked to tackle work beyond their capabilities.

While the use of programmed materials is still in an experimental stage, the principal arguments in its favor revolve around the possibility for allowing students to proceed at their own rates. One role of the teachers in such a situation is to provide for special situations not anticipated in the programs and to suggest which programs may be appropriate.[10]

The concept of the class moving in a single unit with everyone doing or trying to do the same thing at the same time is less easily justified than that of each student proceeding at a rate appropriate to his own needs and interest.

Modified Use of the Textbook. Until recently the basic instructional procedure was perhaps best described as "digestion" of the textbook. The teacher started at the front and together with the class moved to the end of the book, being careful to "consume" its contents on the way. This method is contrary to the idea that instruction must be provided for each individual at his own level of difficulty. Using this method is made more difficult because many modern textbooks are still not well suited to the grades to which they are generally assigned.

Even when all of the students in the class can read and comprehend the material in the text, there is still considerable question as to the appropriateness of everything in the text for every class group which may be using it. For instance a grammar text may include material dealing with certain mistakes common to students in one section of the country but not to students somewhere else. Within any particular class the same kind of difficulty based on student differences will arise. Teachers who use diagnostic techniques in their teaching will make more judicious use of the text materials which are furnished.

---

[10] *Cf.* L. M. Stolmow, "Problems, Procedures, Pitfalls and Promise of Programming Practices," *NASSP Bulletin* 48:256–70 (April, 1964).

Some teachers use texts as reference books either assigned to particular students for specific purposes, or to be used independently by the student to find background material for special assignments. More use is made by such teachers of material from periodical literature, parallel reading, and other sources. While the outline of the text may sometimes be a guide to the activities of a particular class, the scope of its work may sometimes be much broader or on rather different lines. Frequently, state courses of study, locally designed materials, or even materials planned cooperatively by teachers and students serve as the basis for organizing class activities. The need for individualization within this framework may determine how much use of the text seems appropriate.

The teacher is in a better position to diagnose the needs of his class than is the author of the textbook who must of necessity write for the whole population of students who may use his material. Current emphasis in improvement of teacher education programs is both on developing skill in meeting the individual student's needs and on providing a high level of competence in basic subject matter.[11]

Unit Teaching

A development in methodology which has taken place within the last 50 years is the concept of unit teaching. This seems to combine at least three different characteristics. They result for recognition of the importance of (1) wholeness in the development of understanding, (2) the learner's participation in the structuring of the learning situation, and (3) intrinsic motivation. It might be noted that the emphasis on unit teaching is essentially an emphasis on the management of groups of students, although of course provision is made for individualizing instruction. Thus, diagnostic teaching and unit teaching are complementary activities designed to get at both the problems of individual differences and those of group instruction.[12]

One aspect of the unit approach involves organizing a period of time, consisting of from several days to several weeks, as a unit. The central theme may consist of a particular body of subject matter such as the Westward Movement, or Back Country America,[13] a project such as the making of a telescope, or an experience such as a study of the

---

[11] Cf. W. B. Spalding, "Evaluation of Proposals for Change in Teacher Education," *National Commission on Teacher Education and Professional Standards Official Report*, 1963:37–49.

[12] Jack Blackburn, "The Learning Activity Approach in Unit Teaching," *The High School Journal* 47:201–209 (Feb., 1964).

[13] See The Commission on the English Curriculum, National Council of Teachers of English, *The English Language Arts in the Secondary School* (New York: Appleton-Century-Crofts, Inc., 1956), pp. 70–112.

recreational needs of the community. The central theme provides for one basis of continuity from one day to the next.[14]

Unit teaching will also frequently involve getting at least part of the class to participate in making decisions as to how the work will be carried out. The amount of student participation must depend on a number of other factors to be discussed later. The third factor in effective unit teaching is identification by both students and teachers of objectives sought and evaluation of how well those objectives are achieved. Unit teaching is goal directed.[15]

The unit approach is less helpful in skill subjects such as typing or elementary French or in subjects such as geometry which have a clear sequential logic in the organization of the material. It is in social studies, science, and literature, where the concepts being developed are of more apparent importance than the mastery of information, that such an approach is most helpful. A convincing case can be built for saying that even the skill subjects such as typing and language should be taught as part of an experience curriculum. Many skillful teachers are doing this.

Wholeness and the Development of Understanding. An important development of twentieth century educational theory has been recognition of the value of teaching subject matter in its total context or *gestalt*.[16] Part of the problem in older and more atomistic approaches was that each part of the operation was taught without reference to its connections with or effects on the rest. If in the study of history each important bit of information was learned separately, its significance as a part of the whole picture was likely to be lost. The history student was expected to transfer his knowledge that Wilson was reelected President in 1916 to his understanding of American participation in the First World War. While some of this transfer did occur it has been indicated that the most effective learning is that which occurs in as nearly a complete situation as can be constructed.[17]

In unit teaching every effort is made to see that students have a chance to learn important concepts in the situations in which they actually occur.[18] Thus related concepts take on richer meaning. If the purpose in studying American participation in the First World War is to help students understand, say, how wars get started, how countries get involved in them, how much wars cost, and how peace may be maintained,

[14] J. B. Chase, Jr. and J. L. Howard, "Changing Concepts of Unit Teaching," *The High School Journal* 47:180–87 (Feb., 1964).

[15] W. E. McPhee, "The Teaching Unit: What Makes It Tick," *The Clearing House* 38:70–73 (Oct., 1963).

[16] *Cf.* T. L. Hawk, "School Practices and Certain Principles of Learning," *The Elementary School Journal* 64:36–41 (Oct., 1963).

[17] The atomistic approach has been adapted by the developers of programmed materials for the teaching of skills and for the study of certain types of logically organized content material.

[18] *Cf.* H. B. Shane and R. B. McQuigg, "Unit Teaching and the Integration of Knowledge," *The High School Journal* 47:188–93 (Feb., 1964).

then it is important to set up the learning process in a way that such general questions may be studied. In a more atomistic approach questions were dictated and answers were memorized. In the unit approach students are urged to raise questions for themselves and, by reconstructing the events of the period, to find clues to the answers. The same information may serve as a clue to the answer of several questions or may serve merely to help complete the picture itself. By striving to build a whole picture, students learn to answer new questions using the same information and understanding.

Participation of the Learner in Planning. The idea of including the learner in the planning is something misunderstood both by those who are sympathetic to the idea of unit teaching and by those who are critical. It is important to recognize that including the learner will not mean that the teacher will lose control over the process. The teacher has a continuing responsibility for the planning, but he still may include the student as a participant. The teacher does the pre-planning. He sets the stage as to the nature of the plans to be made by the students and decides when they will take part. He makes suggestions as to practical approaches. He encourages particular courses of action; he may actively discourage others. The teacher sees that the time taken for the planning does not use up too much of the total time available. The teacher may veto too large a project or one which does not seem worthwhile. He may redirect a committee which has bogged down in relatively unimportant activity.

Why then should the student be encouraged to participate in the process? In the first place, it is important for the student to understand why he is taking part. Activity which has no meaning becomes a drudgery. Perhaps more important, such activity may be wasted and misdirected. The importance of purposefulness in study has been demonstrated. The student is able to become in a sense his own teacher or his own critic. The teacher who has helped the students plan the process has shifted part of the teaching responsibility to those taught. Because they helped to plan, they are able to do a better job of self-evaluation.

The Intrinsic Nature of Motivation. Partly as a result of pupil participation in planning, the unit approach stimulates intrinsic motivation. Motivation based on such external forces as grades or threats or competition is likely to be wasteful. It also encourages such shortcuts as cheating or cramming. The competition may lose its effectiveness on the one hand or may lead to unpleasantness on the other. Motivation based on a genuine interest in the completion of a project tends to result in reinforcing the objectives of the instruction.[19] Intrinsic motivation

<hr/>

[19] *Cf.* J. Crescimbeni, "Values in Motivation, Extrinsic or Intrinsic," *Education* 84:160–62 (November, 1963); and David G. Ryans, "Motivation in Learning," *The Psychology of Learning*, 51st Yearbook, Part II, National Society for the Study of Education (Chicago: University of Chicago Press, 1952), pp. 289–331.

also has the advantage of being more pleasant. Most students are curious about the world in which they live, and they participate more enthusiastically in activity which seems designed to satisfy part of that curiosity.

The tendency in unit teaching is to relate the activities of the classroom to the problems and concerns of students. Equally important is to select activities for which teachers will have a sustained interest.

Stress in unit teaching is on learning as a process of solving problems or at least of testing solutions.[20] Marks and tests become peripheral to the important outcomes of learning.

Teaching as Supervision of Learning

The principal teaching techniques of the nineteenth century school were the lecture and the recitation. Modern teaching emphasizes more subtle and more efficient procedures. The concept of teaching as the promulgation of the truth in the form of closely reasoned lectures has given way to the concept of teaching as the supervision of learning.[21]

Limitation of the Lecture Technique. As the importance of providing for the needs of the whole population of school age began to be accepted, it became apparent that the lecture had serious weaknesses.[22] The range of abilities in any classroom made a single approach to the lesson material impractical.

In addition, a lecture is essentially a passive process. A few students might be so stimulated by what they heard as to be taught effectively, but listening is a poor substitute for more active engagement. The problem of remaining passive became acute for students who had to spend six hours a day listening to lectures. For students who had difficulty comprehending material in the lecture, the best alternative was sometimes to go to sleep.

The necessity of providing four or five good lectures a day five days a week made great demands on the teacher's time. One solution was to write the lectures out and save them from one year to the next. The difficulty with this process was that the lecture soon became dated and stale. Furthermore good lecturing required a degree of showmanship and a great output of energy on the part of even the skillful. Some teachers who were capable of doing a fine job of teaching did not have these particular talents.

[20] J. V. Marani, "Problem Centered Learning," *Education* 84:231–34 (Dec., 1963).

[21] *Cf.* L. Pulliam, "The Lecture: Are We Reviving Discredited Teaching Methods?" *Phi Delta Kappan* 44:382–85 (May, 1963).

[22] G. Max Wingo, "Methods of Teaching," *The Encyclopedia of Research*, 3rd ed. (New York: The Macmillan Company, 1960).

The lecture technique also required a sophisticated reaction from the students. It was necessary for the student to identify the important ideas, take good notes, recognize vocabulary, and apply what was being said to other situations. Some instructors worked to help their students develop the necessary skills, but were likely to find themselves bogged down in *techniques* when they were more concerned with *content*.

The crucial problem in overdependence on the lecture was how to check that the instruction was getting across. Unless students were given a great deal of encouragement to ask questions during the lecture, there was no way to know until later what they understood. The fact that each class was different made it uncertain whether a lecture that had been relatively successful in the preceding class would be successful in this one. In either case, the one-way nature of the lecture made it wasteful of time. If the class already knew the material being given in the lecture, there was no way of indicating that fact.

Most high school students, and indeed a large portion of college age students, find extensive formal lecturing boring. This by itself is enough to bring it into disrepute as an efficient instructional technique for general use. There are many situations in which the teacher may appropriately talk informally for varying lengths of time about various aspects of the work of the class. Such talking, however, is not to be confused with the more formal lecture because it takes into account the need for student participation.

Limitation of the Recitation Approach. Although most high school classrooms have begun to abandon dependence on the lecture technique, there is still great dependence on the almost equally ineffective recitation technique. In its most typical form the entire class will be asked to read the next 20 pages in the text and be prepared to recite on them. Sometimes the material will actually be read aloud in class, each student reading a paragraph, and sometimes it will be read silently during the class or as a homework assignment. The teacher then will ask questions orally or perhaps give a brief written quiz. The most obvious objection to this technique is its failure to provide for differing needs within the class.

The second objection to this approach is that it is uninteresting. Material that may be inherently fascinating is so routinized that even the most imaginative are likely to miss the possibilities inherent in it. Learning is deprived of its vitality. Motivational problems grow where they should not have been found. Students become rebellious or listless, and school becomes unpleasant for both teachers and students.

A third objection is that it represents inefficient use of class time. Even if differences in individual ability were recognized, it would still not be an effective approach. Learning *about* something is substituted for learning something. Students who might be led through other techniques to do, or feel, or think, are encouraged merely to memorize or to recall the descriptions of the action, feeling, or thought of others. As in the case of the lecture, the emphasis is on learning as a passive process. It is of course possible for a student to get effective stimulation from the process of reading and then reciting, but this stimulation is not so likely in the mechanical process of recitation as in some of the more recently developed techniques. There is still too much left to the chance of transfer.

Where this technique involves the reading aloud of material by the students to the rest of the class, other objections may be raised. In the first place the effectiveness of the instruction may be reduced by the distracting influence of poor reading. The poor reader is not likely to improve his reading skill in the process either. In the second place the process is slow and may also be boring to the group as a whole.

Too much emphasis on recitation without attention to the development of study techniques can be disastrous. The student who regularly misses questions may be unable, unless he is given additional help, to develop a better technique for studying. Constant embarrassment over his failure does not make it easier for him to enjoy participating in the learning process.

Limitation on the Use of Homework. Reliance on homework has been one avenue of escape from the inefficiency of the lecture and recitation as teaching procedures. Since most of the class time was taken up in recitation, actual study and learning became relegated to the home or the study hall. In some schools teachers seemed in competition with each other for the reputation as the hardest taskmaster. Some teachers around the turn of the century argued that each hour of class time should demand two hours of preparation. Some high school students were working as much as 60 hours a week.

Fortunately, many of the schools which make use of homework have recognized that a work load of more than two hours of out-of-school preparation per day is undesirable.[23] Aside from deciding how large a portion of a student's time can be devoted to school work, there are other important considerations. If a single assignment is made to an entire class, the problem arises as to the varying abilities within the class to profit from the assignment or even to complete it within a reasonable period of time. There is also the problem of what the opportunity may be for out-of-school study. Some students have time on their hands. Others may have time-consuming chores to be done. Nor do all the students have an adequate place to study, reference books to use, or even sufficient lighting. Emotional conditions in the home are also important. Large

---

[23] *Cf.* G. D. Maybre, "Homework in the Junior High School," *NASSP Bulletin* 47:16–17 (Oct., 1963).

families who live in one or two rooms with sick older people and crying babies may complicate the student's problems.

There is strong feeling in some quarters that the 30 hours a week at the disposal of the school probably represents a reasonable limit for most of the important assignments of the teacher. Some students may profitably have additional assignments, but these should require little specific supervision from the teacher or parents, and interfere little with important family projects, recreation, and sleep.[24]

Emphasis on Supervision of Learning. Throughout the criticism given above of the lecture, recitation, and homework there has been implicit an emphasis on teaching as a process of supervising learning. Learning has been viewed as a process in which the activity of the learner is the important factor. Teaching is viewed as a process of helping the student to study rather than of forcing him to recite. Even the motivation of study is viewed as arising from the student's own recognition of his need.

Through the dual process of diagnosing learning difficulties and directing the development of units of instruction, a teacher may help the student to recognize his needs, capitalize his interests, and look for the solution to his problems. His development as a mature person capable of self-direction is the primary goal. Motivation is a primary concern because the student must use his time willingly if he is to use it efficiently.

The supervisor of learning helps the student to formulate the objectives of his study. To spend time on the formulation of objectives increases the likelihood of more effective study.[25] If the student does not understand where he is going, he will have difficulty assisting himself in the process of getting there. Furthermore he will resent having to wander blindly at the whim of someone else.

The supervisor of learning helps the student to determine how to approach his objectives. The teacher may suggest that the approaches which are tried could be improved by more use of reference materials. He points out other activities which might be undertaken in the meeting of the original objectives or he helps in formulation of new objectives. When he recognizes that there is basic information or skill which must be learned before the group can go on profitably to another activity, he takes the time to develop that information or skill. Where possible, he keeps his class informed as to what is being done and most important of all, why.

The supervisor of learning helps the student evaluate both progress toward objectives and the objectives themselves. Testing processes are

[24] G. Langdon and I. W. Stout, "What Parents Think of Homework," *NEA Journal* 52:9–11 (Dec., 1963).

[25] A. W. Combs, "Fostering Self Direction," *Education Digest* 31:5–7 (May, 1966).

such as to encourage the student to analyze which study techniques and activities have been effective and which need improvement. The supervisor of learning is concerned that the student sees new skills and new information which he needs to master, and also that he recognizes progress toward his objectives.

The Development of Self-Discipline. The newly developing theories of teaching give great importance to the development of self-discipline. The nature of the situation may require external control, but the primary emphasis is not on external control but on self-control. As noted above, the role of the teacher is one of encouraging the student to assume responsibility for his instruction. Unnecessary control and discipline implies a lack of respect for the personality of the individual and hence is undemocratic. The purpose of teacher-imposed discipline must be the protection of the individual from himself or from others. When, however, its effect is to prevent the student from developing the ability to take care of himself, it has gone too far.

The importance of self-sufficiency on the part of high school age students becomes more obvious when it is remembered that within one year many of them will be on their own as active citizens. Those who drop out of school or fail to continue into college are those who are least likely to have been successful in getting a measure of independence in the high school.

The term "self-discipline" refers not just to the matter of avoiding infringement of rules. It refers more positively to ability to recognize worthwhile objectives, to select activities which will help in the attainment of those objectives, to work industriously at those activities, and then to evaluate the results in order to redefine the objectives. Such discipline is acquired through practice that has been criticized. The teacher who shies away from providing an opportunity for practice has to prove that the techniques he used were better in the attainment of objectives that were more important.

The Importance of Variety. Much that has been said about newer approaches to teaching in the secondary school may be summarized by the phrase "appropriate variety." Each learning situation and each student in a group is different. Each skill, concept or attitude to be taught is somewhat different from others. Each teacher is himself different in each situation and from other teachers. There are thus many dimensions to be considered in planning for instruction.

A textbook dealing with understanding the nature of the American high school cannot describe in detail all of the appropriate variations in teaching method. The need for variety in all of the situations described is obvious. The best teaching provides for flexibility both in terms of the needs of different students in the class, in terms of changing circumstances, in terms of modified objectives, and in terms of the mood and success of the teacher himself.

The Effect of Teaching Techniques on the Student

A fourth dimension of the revolution in teaching methodology during the twentieth century is perhaps best described as concern for the techniques' effect on the student. This concern has been reflected in the discussion above of the importance of individualizing instruction, the emphasis on unit teaching, and the emphasis on teaching as the supervision of learning. Most attention has been given to three problems: (1) indoctrination, (2) mental health, and (3) how to encourage creativity.

The Problem of Indoctrination. Respect for student personality sometimes conflicts with what seem to be effective teaching techniques. Simply stated, the problem of indoctrination is the problem of deciding whether each individual is to be left free to decide for himself the important issues which he faces as an individual and as a member of a social group or whether he is going to be required to accept the point of view held by his teachers.

If he is going to be required to accept the solution of others, the teaching process is one of telling him what that solution is and then of telling him that it is not possible for him to make a different decision for himself. This indoctrination is sometimes accomplished simply by constant repetition of the solution, started before he has had any opportunity to arrive at any other solution. This may, for example, involve the use of a ritual—as in the case of certain church dogmas or in the pledge of allegiance to the flag—or the arraying of respected authority on the side of the solution being advocated. The intent in such cases is to set up such emotional walls that an individual will feel uncomfortable questioning the point of view expressed.[26]

Respect for the right of each individual to make his own decisions free of interference seems basically democratic. Of course inevitably so complex a society as ours does have important rules which it is dangerous for a student to disobey. A student is required for instance to recognize the importance of respecting other people. He is required to accept constituted authority and to obey the law. There are certain standards of decency which he must accept whether he likes them or not. What is

---

[26] *Cf.* E. D. Pannes, "The Relationship Between Self-Acceptance and Dogmatism in Junior-Senior High School Students," *Journal of Educational Sociology* 36:419–26.

the distinction between teaching an individual the basic regulations of social living and indoctrination?

It is perhaps accurate to recognize that there is a difference between realizing that regulations exist and accepting them as desirable. Social education could stop with pointing out what the rules are and then leaving the individual free to accept or reject them. Whether the society would agree that as a social institution the school should go no further is not so clear. The student should certainly be helped to see the advantage in having such rules and the disadvantage of not having them. On the other hand it is important to let him see that while he questions them at his own peril he may have to question them if he wishes really to understand them. The next step is to point out that understanding the need for rules and regulations is crucial for the fullest participation in the life of the society.[27]

There is also the necessity of encouraging some caution in questioning the rules which seem to have developed as a result of the long experience of the race. There is sometimes a fine line between helping the student to learn vicariously from racial experience and using accumulated authority to stifle the development of independent maturity. When emotional techniques are used to get acceptance of ideas which are capable of rational defense, both the individual and the society suffer.

The Problem of Mental Health. As it becomes more and more important for everyone to have a secondary education, mental health becomes more and more a school problem. Some of the students who must come to school are likely to have mental health problems resulting from factors not under the school's control. It becomes the school's duty to offer whatever assistance it is capable of rendering and at the least to avoid complicating these problems.

For a few students at least, the competitive atmosphere of the school, coupled with pressure from parents for good grades, may itself create serious mental health problems.[28] Teachers have to make allowances for the fact that what is a reasonable assignment for some students may be a strain for others; they also have to avoid giving the impression that only the most capable students are worthwhile.

Since high school students are going through the changes and stresses of adolescence, the school has to try to provide them with an adequate understanding of the nature of adolescence. Thus the school may appropriately spend time on discussion of such matters as sexual maturation, the changing relationship of the student to the adults who

[27] *Cf.* W. H. Boyer, "Have Our Schools Kept Us Free?" *School Review* 71:222–28 (Summer, 1963).

[28] *Cf.* Frances M. Briggs, "Grades: Tool or Tyrant? A Commentary on High School Grades," *The High School Journal* 47:280–84 (April, 1964).

work with him at home and at school, the problems of choosing and preparing for a vocation, the problems of courtship and marriage, and his relationship with his peers. These are all matters which give healthy adolescents concern, and if they are ignored they tend to become serious problems both for some of those who are healthy and for those who are less so.[29]

The Problem of Creativity. Because the school is a large and complex institution, it is likely to place more stress on conformity than on creativity. In a society which depends on the ability of each individual to make some contribution to the total life of the group, creativity is vital.[30] It is not simply a matter of recognizing the creative genius who may prove to be a great inventor, artist, or statesman. It is also important to encourage the average citizen to become as creative as possible in his approach to life. For the teacher, the problem is that little is known about the nature of creativity.[31] Whether it may be caught or taught has been the subject of speculation by philosophers for centuries. There is, however, some evidence that success encourages success. The student who has been encouraged to exercise his own initiative and has found it pleasant is more likely to continue to develop his ability to assume initiative.[32] The student who is criticized when he first ventures out from his traditional role may be afraid to try again.

The so-called extracurricular activities may prove to be more helpful than the regular classroom activities in developing creativity. In the first place, there is more room for student initiative in leadership roles: In the second place, there is less attempt to control the content of the program. Unfortunately, however, many of the students in the school are not able to get into a position to develop their own initiative because of the competition with more capable or self-assured youngsters.[33]

The teacher can find many opportunities in the regular classroom for student initiative when he is alert to the need and secure enough in his role to be willing to take the chance. The planning of units of instruction, the carrying out of individual assignments, the presentation of material to the class, the discussion of current problems, all provide opportunities for creativity. Conversely, strict teacher domination, in-

---

[29] Robert J. Havighurst, *Developmental Tasks of Education,* 2nd ed. (New York: Longmans, Green and Company, Inc., 1952).

[30] *Cf.* N. E. Wallen, "Creativity, Fantasy and Fact," *The Elementary School Journal* 65:438–43 (May, 1964).

[31] *Cf.* R. J. Hallman, "Can Creativity be Taught?" *Educational Theory* 14: 15–23 (Jan., 1964).

[32] *Cf.* J. K. McFee, "Developing the Creative Potential," *Classroom Teachers Association Journal* 60:25–26 (Jan., 1964).

[33] *Cf.* T. H. Smith, "The Case of the Overactive Student," *Pennsylvania School Journal* 112:232 (Jan., 1964).

sistence on adherence to a single pattern of study, insistence on high but external standards of performance, and dependence on grades and marking systems for motivation are likely to stifle the sparks of creativity.[34]

Concern for Academic Freedom

The Treatment of Controversial Issues. Tolerance of differences of opinion occasionally creates a problem for the teacher who is alert to the importance of encouraging full consideration of important economic, political, and social problems. During the nineteenth century there was a tendency to say that controversial issues could be avoided in the public school and that academic freedom was an issue only in the setting of the University.[35] More recently there has been emphasis on the necessity of gaining the widest possible understanding of controversial issues. In addition it has been considered important to give students an opportunity to develop their capacity for thinking through important problems even as children.[36]

Economics, the relative merits of the different political parties, the theory of evolution, sex education, and even religious controversy may be discussed openly and freely in many American public high schools. That this is permitted is a measure of the respect of the general public for the fairness and integrity of the public school teacher. It may also reflect a growing recognition on the parents' part that children of high school age are capable of handling such discussion. It is worthwhile to consider for a moment what the important ground rules are.

The teacher should insist that any discussion of controversial issues be conducted on a high plane. Issues and not personalities should be the matters for consideration. There must be an attempt to understand the points of view which may be different from those probably most familiar to the student. Students should be encouraged to look for acceptable evidence to support their argument, and the distinction between evidence and propaganda must be considered. The teacher should attempt either to remain neutral or at least to make clear to his students the nature of his bias.[37]

The teacher may legitimately indicate that, where it is not possible to deal with an issue in an atmosphere of tolerance, discussion must wait

---

[34] *Cf.* E. Margolin, "Do We Really Prize Creativity?" *The Elementary School Journal* 64:117–21 (Dec., 1963).

[35] *See* Howard K. Beale, A *History of Freedom of Teaching in American Schools* (New York: Scribner and Sons, 1941).

[36] *Cf.* A. W. Dulles, "Diplomacy, Strategy and Intelligence," *NASSP Bulletin* 48:281–88 (April, 1964).

[37] C. W. Fawcett, "Teaching About Controversial Issues," *Classroom Teachers Association Journal* 60:25–26 (March, 1964).

until this is possible. In such instances freedom of discussion is not denied but delayed until the conditions for it can be established. To avoid discussion of all controversial issues would be to deprive the student of the practice necessary for the highest level of participation in the public life. It seems better that such practice should be acquired in the public school under the leadership of impartial teachers in preparation for discussion in more partisan circles.

The Importance of Mutual Respect of Teacher and Student. Much has been said of the importance of respect for the personality of the student. Any discussion of academic freedom must recognize the importance of an atmosphere of *mutual* respect of student and teacher. Indeed without such respect the teaching methods which seem based on the concept of teacher guidance are doomed to failure. For instance, when a teacher finds it necessary to tell a student that he has not done an assignment as well as was expected, it should be clear that the teacher is displeased with the performance and not with the student.

The kinder discipline of modern schools has done much to help students learn to respect their teachers rather than to fear them. Discipline is not, however, the important reason that the pupil must respect the teacher. In the efficient operation of the teaching process, the energies of the pupil should be spent on the consideration of the issues at hand, on the learning of the important attitudes, skills, and concepts which it is the business of the school to teach. The student may also derive his view of authority from his relationships with his teachers.[38] For a few students, the teacher is the only person with whom they have ever come in contact who seems to regard them as worthy of respect. They may lack the ability to respond consistently to such respect. Nevertheless, it is important for him to make the effort.

The Response to Pressure Groups. Pressure groups seem to be characteristic of American political life. Indeed they represent the avenue by which the average citizen makes his wishes known. Unfortunately, it is difficult to be sure whether a particular pressure group expresses the wishes of the majority, and, if it does, whether the rights of the minority have been taken into consideration. The teacher may feel pressure which is basically contrary to the responsibility of the public schools.[39]

While some pressure groups manage to get legislation passed which would restrict teachers' freedom, or which—more frequently—may specify some of the curriculum content, such legislation is usually repealed later in the interest of academic freedom and professional responsibility. The danger in such legislation is most frequently in the zealousness with

[38] *Cf.* F. M. Newman, "The Consent of the Governed and Citizenship Education in Modern America," *School Review* 71:404–24 (Winter, 1963).

[39] *Cf.* C. H. Wilson, "Local Pressures in Education," *The National Elementary Principal* 43:32–36 (Jan., 1964).

which it is advocated rather than in its intent to override the professional decisions of school officials.[40]

One largely American institution, the school board, is responsible for absorbing public criticism of the school. Aggrieved citizens or groups of citizens may easily get a hearing with this group, which carries the legal responsibility for policy decisions. It is the responsibility of the school board to determine both what is the will of the majority of the citizens in the community and what is in the opinion of the professional school personnel in the interest of all of the children. After the pressure group has had its hearing, the school board assumes responsibility for the final decisions.[41]

The unfortunate influence of some minority pressure groups may be reduced if members of the teaching profession are vigilant. While the principal or staff of a small school may, occasionally, be swamped by the pressures of the local situation, groups of the profession may be able to gain more careful consideration of the issues at stake. Both the regional accrediting associations and the local, state, and national units of the National Education Association may serve in this capacity.[42]

[40] Cf. D. J. Willower, "Lay and Professional Decisions in Education," Peabody Journal of Education 41:226-28 (Jan., 1964).

[41] Cf. D. C. Chaput, "Who Determines Policy," The Clearing House 37:521-22 (May, 1963).

[42] Cf. R. B. Kennan, "Protecting the Teachers Against Unjust Treatment," New York State Education 51:30 (March, 1964).

12

Discipline, Morale, and the Values
of Adolescents

MODERN EDUCATIONAL THEORY RECOGNIZES THAT EMPHASIS ON SCHOOL DIS-
cipline as a contest between teachers and students for control is inconsistent with the idea that the school is a proving ground for democracy.
While there must be an atmosphere of orderliness, self-discipline is better
than teacher-imposed discipline. "Morale" is a better word to describe the
desirable quality of student behavior than "discipline."

The Need for a Democratic Outlook

The danger in using the word "discipline" is that the older approach, in
which discipline was the imposition of force from without, will over-
shadow emphasis on self-discipline. The teacher in the democratic school
is as responsible for the quality of the classroom situation as before. His
objective is the development of student maturity through the sharing of
responsibility.

Self-Discipline. An important consideration in developing a philosophy of student control is recognition that self-discipline is basic to democratic social life. Social control which is based primarily on obedience to
rules and regulations becomes a police action. On the road, for example,
if every driver chose his own path, straight or crooked, left or right, most
cars would crash. If there is a motorist who for some reason does not know
which side of the road he is to proceed on or who takes no heed of regulations, it is important that he be required to conform. This is both for
his safety and for that of his fellow citizens. Similarly in the classroom
there must be regulations with regard to talking and, for the protection

of all concerned, such regulations should be enforced. In both cases the enforcement of the regulation must be subordinate to the basic intent of the regulation either to provide safer travel or to promote learning.

If the motorist or the student understands the nature of the regulation and the purposes which it is meant to serve, he has a better basis for recognizing the justice in its enforcement and the times when it may be relaxed. Although some motorists are inclined to question the validity of the speed limit on some section of the highway, most motorists recognize that the death toll on the highway makes it necessary to establish limits and most of them are embarrassed to be caught violating the law. Similarly, while some students may prefer to talk during the time set aside for reading the assignment, most of them recognize the necessity for observing silence.

Without a large measure of self-discipline both traffic regulation and student control would become impossible. There are not enough policemen to enforce obedience to all the traffic regulations if a large segment of the population does not accept them as valid. Furthermore, a single teacher in a classroom of 30 students is helpless unless part of the group accept the idea that control is necessary. There is, even in the least democratic school, a large measure of self-discipline.

To insist, however, that all the discipline in the modern school is self-discipline would be foolish. Part of the motivation to obey traffic regulations is fear of the policeman. Similarly, part of the motivation in obeying the teacher is distaste for the consequences of disobedience, but where fear is the only deterrent to misbehaving, students are likely to get pleasure in getting by with misbehavior.

Practice in self-discipline is important to the society at large. A reasonable amount of time devoted to understanding the nature of democratic social control in the classroom is helpful both in the immediate improvement of the morale of the class and as civic education.

Respect for Others is Contagious. Not only is self-discipline basic to democratic social life, but there is a contagiousness to democratic values. It is easier to respect those who are respectful of us. Indeed the teaching of democratic values is difficult in an autocratic setting. If there is any single characteristic of the democratic teacher, it is the quality of respecting and conveying his respect for his students. Respect for students is conveyed in the manner in which the teacher addresses them, the considerateness which he expresses in making assignments, and the care with which he corrects their mistakes. Conversely the teacher who is inconsiderate conveys his lack of concern for democracy.

Respect for others need not involve loss of dignity. In the autocratic society there is an assumption that authority is to be exercised as a right.[1]

---

[1] *Cf.* A. R. Dykes, "Democracy, Teachers, and Educational Decision-Making," *School and Society* 92:155–56 (April, 1964).

Discipline in such a society is based either on fear or on a kind of distance that defies consideration for the inferior by the superior. On the other hand, the democratic philosophy requires recognition that each individual is important and must be respected. Good discipline comes as a result of affection or at least of respect for the one in authority based on his ability to merit respect.

Respect for the young by the old, of the group for the individual, of the underdog by the stronger, has become entrenched in the thinking of the American people. The autocratic approach goes contrary to the training not only of the school but also of the home, the church, and even the gang. Hence the teacher who might wish to use the authoritarian techniques more characteristic of the European school will find himself going contrary to the basic attitudes of the society itself.

Some educators have suggested the importance of establishing a high level of expectation, so that students understand that they are thought capable of behaving well.[2] Whether respect for the student begets respect for the teacher as a result of the example that is set, as a result of the notion that this represents fair play, or as a result of the student's desire to maintain his apparently established status, there seems to be little doubt that the teacher who is respectful of his students finds them more likely to be respectful of him.

Freedom within Limits. One of the important conditions of a desirable relationship in the classroom is recognition that—while there are limits imposed by the nature of the situation—there is freedom within those limits.

The limits are created by the nature of the school itself and by the necessity for efficiency in the learning process. Among the necessary limits is, for instance, recognition that other classes in the building have to work too and that unnecessary noise may interfere with what they want to do. Within a particular classroom also students must learn to respect the rights of others.

Similarly the nature of a particular learning activity seems to set certain limits. If it is important for the class to be listening to the teacher or to a student, then each person in the group must restrict himself so that it is possible for the others to hear. On the other hand there may be other times, when the groups are singing, for instance, that good discipline may call for noise rather than silence.

The limit to liberty is to be found at the point at which the rights of other individuals will be abridged.[3] In the school setting the immediate focus is on the right of the individual and those with whom he is to

---

[2] *Cf.* J. E. Winkler, "Reflections on Discipline," *The Clearing House* 39:113–14 (Oct., 1964).

[3] *Cf.* J. L. Lennon, "Authority, Freedom, and the Teenager," *Catholic Schools Journal* 65:34–36 (April, 1965).

learn. Whenever the school by its insistence on quietness or conformity interferes with the opportunity of the student to explore, to create, to consider, or to communicate, it may be defeating its own purpose. While quietness may be necessary to some types of learning, to insist on quietness all the time may be abridging freedom both unnecessarily and unwisely.

Too much control by external authority actually robs the student of the chance to learn to discipline himself. It may be well to permit a little more freedom than seems consistent with some of the other objectives of the school in order to permit students the opportunity to learn the importance of self-control.

The Teaching of Self-Discipline. The teaching of self-discipline, like the teaching of any other subject in the school program, may be carefully planned. It may follow the same procedures of diagnosis, organization, and evaluation. It has been pointed out that there are two kinds of student misbehavior. One is the result of not knowing the proper way to behave. The other is the result of unmet basic drives or unreasonable expectations. We must of course recognize that while we may describe these as two distinct types of misbehavior in practice they do not separate themselves so easily. Most human behavior is the result of many causes and misbehavior in the classroom is no exception.[4]

The teacher who is faced with misbehavior, or perhaps simply with deciding what is desirable behavior, must analyze the situation. What are the limits which seem desirable? To what extent can the inclinations of the student group be permitted free expression? At what point must they be limited? If there has been misbehavior, what was its cause? Was the lesson material interesting? Was the classroom routine well enough established to make it clear to the student what was expected? Were there other factors which made the group hard to manage, such as plans for a holiday or a ball game? Is this a time of day when students are likely to be exhausted or excitable?

In the case of individual students there are usually a variety of considerations. Students habitually in trouble have particular problems of their own. They may be in need of attention, of self-assurance, of affection. The pressure to conform is so strong that the student who is a consistent nonconformist is likely to be one who is driven by powerful forces. It is important for the teacher and the school to look for the nature of these forces. Other serious problems are to be found among students who are too quiet and who conform too readily. Where the difficulty is with a single student and not with a whole group, then the teacher is perhaps safe in looking first not at himself but at the student's background to determine the causes.

Conversely, the teacher who has difficulty with a whole class may need to look at his relationship to the class to find the cause of the diffi-

---

[4] *Cf.* James L. Hymes, Jr., "Good Discipline," *Grade Teachers* 81:21 (Feb., 1964).

culty. Whether it is lack of respect for the group, ineffectiveness in the management of routine, failure to insist on the importance of reasonable behavior, dull material or poor methods of presentation, or some combination of these, he may need to plan carefully as to how he can regain sufficient control of the situation. If the need is for more student assumption of responsibility for behavior, this may require carefully planned analysis on their part as well as on the part of the teacher.

Because students come from a variety of homes and social backgrounds, what may seem to teachers and school authorities to be abnormal behavior may seem perfectly normal to the students who are misbehaving. The expectations of the teacher must not be unreasonable. The school is not interested in simple conformity. The important concern is for behavior which demonstrates understanding and respect for others.

The Need for a Respectful and Friendly Atmosphere

The atmosphere of a school is important to the effort to improve and to maintain morale. There are apparently three distinct relationships which contribute to the development of a wholesome atmosphere: those within the staff, those between the members of the staff and the students, and those between the members of the student body. These relationships have a profound effect on each other.[5]

Good Relationships within the Staff. Students pattern much of their behavior on their interpretation of how adults behave. When they see teachers being respectful of each other, they see that respectful treatment is possible. For some of them this is a revelation because the adults with whom they come in contact outside of the school may be neither respectful nor considerate. When they see adults plan together, conceding to each others' wishes, coming to good compromise, they may be learning that this is a way to avoid conflict. They can sense an atmosphere of mutual trust, of team work, of pleasant working relationships.

The relationship of the principal to the school staff is likely to be reflected in the relationship of the staff to the student.[6] Where the principal is stern and exacting, there is a tendency for the teachers to be stern and exacting in their demands on their students. For whatever reason, the pattern seems to remain consistent throughout the school. In such a situation the students themselves tend to react in the same way to each other. Where there is a relaxed relationship between the principal or members of the supervisory staff and the classroom teachers, there is a tendency

[5] *Cf.* L. H. Fritzemeier, "Pupil Programs, Discipline, and the Counselor," *NASSP Bulletin* 47:40–47 (Sept., 1963).

[6] *Cf.* D. Duncanson, "Democracy and School Administration," *The Teachers College Journal* 35:165–67 (March, 1964).

for the teachers to have a relaxed relationship with their students, and for the students to feel relaxed in their dealings with one another.

In most schools it is the teachers' meeting which presents the best opportunity for the development of a wholesome working relationship within the staff. Unfortunately, the teachers' meeting is usually held in the afternoon when everyone is tired and relationships are most likely to be strained. Often the administrative staff is unaware of the importance of these relationships to the total morale of the school. Frequently, speed in making decisions is mistaken for efficiency. Since the fastest approach to decision-making is to have the principal or some other official make the decision, many decisions which would have profited from debate are made prematurely and discussion is by-passed. On the other hand, there is sometimes a tendency in faculty meetings to have the group make decisions which are of little consequence and which could in the interest of efficiency have been delegated to the principal or to a committee working with the principal.[7]

A second matter of concern has to do with the way in which suggestions or directions may be passed on. Some principals disseminate regulations and announcements in a manner that maintains the pleasantness of the working relationship. Others are cold and lack understanding of the importance of good personal relationships in this matter. Because this contact between teacher and administrator is likely to occur in the presence of students, it is particularly important that it be illustrative of democratic relationships.

The Relationships Between the Members of the Staff and Students. In some schools the relationship between staff and students seems coolly formal; in others, it may seem to some to verge on the too familiar. In either case it is a part of the atmosphere of the school. It is well understood among teachers in the American high school that the adult need not, and indeed probably cannot, be accepted as a part of the adolescent gang. It is recognized, for instance, that it is dangerous to the morale of the school for the teacher to date a student or for the young teacher to take part in the out-of-school amusement of high school age students. It is assumed by other teachers and by the community at large that the disciplinary role of the teacher is likely to be compromised by such activity.

On the other hand, a friendly relationship between teachers and students is more appropriate in the democratic school than the more stiffly formal relationship customary in Europe.[8] Social distance is certainly not considered the principal tool of democratic discipline. It is because

---

[7] A. Blumberg and E. Amidon, "Teacher Reactions to School Faculty Meetings," *Journal of Educational Research* 56:466–70 (May, 1963).

[8] *Cf.* Zane E. Eargle, "Social Selectivity of Secondary Schools as National Policy in Four Countries," *The High School Journal* 47:161–62, (Jan., 1964).

the teacher is expected to maintain some status as a symbol of adult responsibility that he cannot relax entirely the traditional barrier between the adult and the adolescent.

In the classroom itself the teacher is expected to maintain sufficient formality to have control of the teaching situation. At the same time he should be careful to respect the students' feelings. It is seldom appropriate to ridicule students or to be sarcastic in references to them. Rebukes are best delivered privately in such a manner as to avoid unnecessary embarrassment. Wherever possible, points of view which may clash sharply with those stated by a student should be presented tactfully in such a way that the idea is permitted to stand on its own merit rather than on the authority of the teacher.

It is important for the teacher to know his students and to demonstrate his understanding of their problems and sensitivities. One of the problems for the large school is the difficulty of being certain that each student feels he is known and appreciated. Sometimes the schedule of the school is such as to keep a student body under tension. The practice of changing classes every 45 or 50 minutes contributes to this tension. The practice of having a longer break in the middle of the morning is gaining favor and tends to permit some relaxation of strict formality. Scheduling students for longer periods of time with the same teacher tends to increase the opportunity for making the school a place in which the student feels that he is known and liked.[9]

The Atmosphere in the Student Body. Much of the morale of a school is built on the relationships of students with students. Although this relationship is affected by such things as the homogeneity of the community, the fact of heterogeneity within family social groupings is no excuse for failing to use student relationships as a positive part of the school educational program.

One of the most obvious approaches to building student morale is through careful use of the opportunities within the curriculum itself. The social studies teacher and the English teacher have both opportunities and responsibilities for helping students to understand the backgrounds of others within the school. Teachers can help shy students gain necessary skills and poise in the regular classroom activities. Occasional discussions of the nature of democracy and of the warmness or coldness of the school may help to alert students.

The homeroom activities provide informal contact between members of the student body, and the skillful homeroom teacher can work to improve social adjustments within the group. Opportunity can be provided for learning social skills like dancing and for discussion of such things as

[9] *Cf.* J. R. Seeley, "Mental Health and the Secondary School," *The Teachers College Journal* 35:84-85 (Dec., 1963).

dating practice. Class parties, if not expensive, may provide some opportunities for practicing social skills and for learning to appreciate different members of the group.[10]

The athletic program of the school may serve to improve the morale of the members of the teams and of the spectators. Care must be taken, however, because emphasis on competition may hamper the development of the social skills which these sports were intended to improve. If the rivalry with a neighboring school is allowed to get out of hand, the student body may be welded together at the expense of creating mistrust of outsiders.[11]

Other aspects of the extracurricular activities programs have similar contributions to make to the morale of the student body. Some students who are not athletically inclined find satisfaction through the musical activities of the school or through being a part of the newspaper staff. Because students are in smaller, less formal groups, they have an opportunity to build friendships more easily than in the regular program of the school. The contribution of an effective program of student government to the morale of a school is hard to overestimate. Emphasis on morale is quite legitimately a function of the student council. Furthermore, an opportunity for constructive responsibility for various phases of the school program may consume the energies of students who otherwise might remain negative toward the school and school personnel.[12]

Positive Discipline as Continuous
Orientation to Responsibility

Since the entire student body of the school changes completely within three or four years, it is necessary to be constantly reteaching lessons that have already been taught. Fortunately or unfortunately, there is a tendency for certain attitudes to become traditional with a student body.

The Development of Ethical Maturity. There was discussion in the previous section of the importance of student morale and the effect of interpersonal relationships on that morale. Even more important is the contribution which the school as a social laboratory can make to the development of ethical maturity on the part of students within the student body.[13] Good discipline and ethical maturity may be distinguished by

[10] K. Weikel, "Where the Homeroom Fits In," *School Activities* 34:273–75 (May, 1963).

[11] W. R. Reed, "Intercollegiate and Interschool Athletics, Assessing the Accomplishments and Problems," *NASSP Bulletin* 48:271–80 (April, 1964).

[12] J. R. Zimmerman. "Please Don't Say No to the Extracurricular Program," *School Activities* 35:152 (Jan., 1964).

[13] F. B. Dixon, "The Student Council Organizes to Promote Citizenship," *School Activities* 34:259–61 (April, 1964).

pointing out that "discipline" refers more shallowly to the surface behavior and control, while "ethical maturity" describes the understanding of important principles of social behavior. Some of those who would have the schools assume more responsibility for religious instruction argue the need for more instruction in ethics. Some theorists indicate that there are other avenues open to the school which, while not in conflict with the instruction usually offered by the church or home, are not so dependent on religious indoctrination.[14]

The emphasis of democracy itself on the principle of respect for the individual provides an important ethical base from which to study honesty, selflessness, kindness, loyalty, friendliness, courtesy, and related character traits. The school situation provides the opportunity for both precept and example, for discussion and practice. While it is clear that in the teaching of democracy what is done speaks much louder than what is said, it is important that understanding ethical principles should not be left to chance any more than understanding concepts in geometry or science is left to chance. Formal attention to the teaching of ethical principles is a desirable feature of the school instruction program.[15]

Cheating is a common practice in many public secondary schools.[16] The school system which bases most of its motivational effort on grades has created a situation in which cheating is perhaps inevitable. A truly objective grading system evaluates achievement on an impersonal scale. Such a system seems unfair in that it rewards ability rather than effort. While ethical behavior is not the automatic result of instruction in ethics or even the development of ethical understanding, the school which ignores the existence of cheating, or which fails to provide an opportunity for understanding the ethical problems involved, need not expect to have made much of a contribution to student morality.

Time spent in discussion of ethical relationships between members of opposite sexes in their dating practices is likely to pay off in more wholesome practice.[17] Vandalism of public property has been markedly decreased in some schools as a result of getting the students to think about the problems involved. The courtesy of students toward each other, and toward school visitors has been notably improved by planned attention to it by teacher or student council members. Improved behavior, however, is not always indicative of improvement of understanding. Behavior may be improved simply by coercion. The concern of the school

[14] Cf. D. A. Erickson, "Religious Consequences of Public and Sectarian Schooling," School Review 72:22–33 (Spring, 1964).

[15] R. L. Hunt, "How Schools Can Teach Religious Values Legally," Nation's Schools 73:48–49 (Feb., 1964).

[16] L. J. Becker, "Changing Moral Values of Students." Journal of Home Economics 55:646–48 (Oct., 1963).

[17] Cf. E. M. Duvall, "Exploring Students Attitudes About Dating," Journal of Home Economics 56:86–88 (Feb., 1964).

staff should be primarily for the development of understanding. Planned study is the safe approach to the development of understanding.

The Role of Self-Evaluation. The most important step in planned study is self-evaluation. The school staff or student council which is concerned about attitudes in the school can start with a diagnosis of the various kinds of relationship which already exist. A survey of class behavior, cheating, vandalism, safety, or courtesy will generally suggest where the main problems arise. The involvement of as many students as possible in the process of analysis may serve to increase both the effectiveness of the original diagnosis and also the enthusiasm for later discussion and follow-up.[18]

If the study is carried out by the student council or committees, serious acceptance of the program by the staff seems to increase its value to the students involved. Also, there is no particular reason why the school cannot harness the intense drive for peer group acceptance, although there is some danger in generating too much enthusiasm among the students in case some of them become excluded from the group for nonconformity.

The impact which some schools are able to make in a reasonably short time on the behavior and even on the thinking of their students serves as a challenge to the rest of the secondary schools to give serious attention to the possibilities. The chance to analyze mistakes, to verbalize the problems, to plan for improvement, and then to re-evaluate, represents all of the elements for a good learning situation with the opportunity to develop new insights. Where the Marine Corps may achieve its results through indoctrination, the public school has the opportunity to provide even more effective learning through demonstration.

Perhaps the important aspect of self-evaluation is that it gives assurance that the instruction which is given is appropriate. This is true both in the grosser recognition of the problems in need of attention and in the more minute recognition of the nature of the problems. Just as effective instruction in English grammar deals with the questions which the students actually face rather than with those faced by children in some other area, the techniques of group living are more likely to be learned when the ethical problems discussed are the ones the students come across daily rather than those which might be described in a text book. The fact that at present there are few text materials available for formal instruction in the ethics of democratic living is probably fortunate.

The Opportunity to Make Mistakes. The development of ethical maturity may result from a situation in which there is an opportunity to make mistakes. Some of the critics of student government in the public high school dwell at length on the immaturity of the students and suggest

[18] F. R. Petrillo, "How the Student Council Can Enrich the Guidance Program," *School Activities* 35:77–80 (Nov., 1963).

that any participation by them in the control of the school should be purely advisory. Certainly it is easy to see that the staff has some responsibility to protect each individual in the school from the immaturity of his associates. Yet, without the chance to make some mistakes, there is no opportunity to learn the finer points which the mistakes help to emphasize.

While much can be learned vicariously in the area of ethical understanding, it seems wise to use the realism provided by delegating responsibility for behavior to the students themselves. This does not mean, however, total abrogation of responsibility by the school staff. It might involve development of coordinate responsibility. Indeed, unless the members of the staff are to operate largely as policemen, there must be responsibility on the part of students themselves. To formalize that responsibility, and to encourage its thoughtful use, is a practical exercise in democracy.

The student who is caught cheating and encouraged to recognize his mistake has been helped; the student caught cheating who is merely ridiculed may simply learn that it is unwise to get caught. The nature of the treatment may determine to a large extent the learning which takes place.

Recognition, whether by a student or by a large part of the student body, of the nature of mistakes which are being made within the social life of the school provides for understanding of social relationships outside it. The success of student codes or honor systems is not in the code or system itself, but in the orientation which it provides for the students who develop it and for those who accept it as valid.[19]

Maintaining Interest. When objectives become obscured or attention diverted, discipline becomes a problem. There is a contagion in the class of the enthusiastic teacher even when the material may seem to the casual observer to be potentially dull. Whether the teacher is concerned with transmitting information, skills, or concepts, students seem eager to learn. Inevitably when interest has dropped, the opportunity to learn has in some way been reduced.

It is not always possible to maintain an interesting pace in teaching. Some types of learning require tedious drill or laborious work of some other sort. In these cases there are still ways to give the process more vitality. The teacher who anticipates the difficulty and helps his class to be prepared for it is less likely to have trouble. For instance, a teacher planning a field trip can help his class to visualize some of the problems which may be faced and to work out procedures for dealing with them. Wherever possible, the class itself is asked to participate in making the rules. Possible delays in transportation are anticipated, behavior on buses

[19] *Cf.* "Lubbock High's Honor System," *School Activities* 35:101–102 (Dec., 1963).

is identified in positive terms, the need to leave a good impression on strangers is stressed, and the eating arrangements are discussed in advance.[20]

Where unforeseen difficulty arises, the effort to be positive in the approach is maintained. Minor breaches in discipline are ignored if a positive contribution does not seem likely to result from taking action. Care is taken to praise positive behavior rather than to stress negative aspects.[21]

To catalogue the possible breaches of discipline is to make them attractive. The teacher, the principal, or the student council group who wishes to improve school morale can best start by identifying the aspects of the program which seem good. It is the winning team which is likely to have the most spectators, not because the game is likely to be better but rather because people want to be identified with success. A class group which has been given a good reputation is likely to get satisfaction from its maintenance.

Occasionally, because of some unfortunate sequence of events, a class group builds a reputation for being hard to discipline. In such instances it seems almost as if the group was trying to live up to the reputation. In any case, once they miss the satisfaction of being identified as a good group, they lose incentive. The same sort of thing seems to happen with individual students who recognize that they have been identified as "problems." It gets to the point that their chief claim to personality is through identification with their reputation. It is terrifying to think of the contribution which the school may make in thwarting the development of wholesome personality traits in such individuals.[22]

Punishment as a Negative Approach

Despite the stress in the three previous sections on the importance of a positive emphasis with regard to school discipline and morale, there is a negative aspect which seemingly cannot be completely avoided. One of the hopeful signs in American life, as well as in American education, has been the steady advance from an emphasis on cruelty and punishment to one on kindness.[23] Conditions in early American schools as well as those

[20] Cf. D. C. Koch, "Class Trip," *The NEA Journal* 53:17–20, April, 1964.

[21] Cf. D. L. Barnes, "Analysis of Remedial Activities Used by Elementary Teachers in Coping with Classroom Behavior Problems," *Journal of Educational Research* 56: 544–47 (July, 1963).

[22] Cf. D. J. Willower and R. G. Jones, "When Pupil Control Becomes an Institutional Theme," *Phi Delta Kappan* 45:107–109 (Nov., 1963).

[23] L. D. Harris, "Positive Approach to Student Behavior," *NASSP Bulletin* 40: 117–18 (1956).

in Europe during the seventeenth century were evidently deplorable. It is obvious that these conditions reflected similar attitudes and conditions in society itself. In an age in which debtors were thrown into prison, it is not surprising that children who were thought incapable of learning were caned.

Punishment as a Symbol. In some cases it seems as if punishment is inevitable. There has perhaps been a challenge to the authority of the teacher or the school. The only alternative to chaos may be strong action directed toward the threat. There is, perhaps, a well-defined school regulation which has been deliberately flouted. To ignore the breach of the rule will lead to further infringements, and similar rules will be in jeopardy. It is the opinion of some of the most idealistic that some type of punishment is necessary in such cases. Nor is it likely to be argued by the sternest disciplinarian that the punishment of the offender in such a situation served any particularly positive purpose. It simply gives notice that the regulations of the school are going to be enforced. It is designed as a deterrent, not as a positive educational force.[24]

Punitive enforcement seems most necessary where the rule is not accepted as useful by the student to whom it is applied. Thus if school officials believe that it is dangerous for students to cross the street to get refreshments, they may pass regulations forbidding them to go across. The student who fails to recognize the threat to his safety may be willing to cross the street anyway. The school then has to announce that punitive action will be taken against students who violate the regulation. Similarly the parents of small children find it necessary to reinforce their own safety regulations with punitive action.

Even in the most democratic school there are many situations either in which students do not recognize the necessity for a regulation or in which the temptation to violate it is so strong as to require the establishment of what must be recognized as negative incentives. For instance, if the school day is sometimes long, tedious, and tense, student attention will begin to wane before it is over. The teacher may have to resort to the threat of punishment to maintain a reasonable teaching situation. Some students come to school tense and would be inclined to become aggressive; the threat of punishment may be necessary for the protection of other students, although it obviously should be avoided if a better substitute can be found. The goals of part of the school curriculum are sometimes obscure or remote and it becomes necessary to require students to meet some assignments under threat of punishment. Generally the regulations dealing with class attendance must be vigorously enforced. While it may be that the class should be sufficiently interesting to attract the students who are supposed to be there, the nature of the

[24] J. R. Wilson and J. M. Spinning, "Opinions Differ: Corporal Punishment?" *The NEA Journal* 52:18–20 (Sept., 1963).

situation may make that difficult. The inexperienced teacher may need the threat of punishment as a crutch until he can learn to provide better incentives.[25]

In each case punishment stands as a symbol of the school's authority over the individual. While it is still perhaps a necessary symbol, it is also a relic of the days when society was organized on a more highly authoritarian basis. It is better to avoid the use of symbols of authority wherever possible. By the same token it would be better not to need traffic regulations and policemen to enforce them. Nevertheless, when it is recognized that there are people who will violate the law and that their action is likely to result in the injury of innocent people, the necessity for the law and for its enforcement is recognized.

For so long as it can be shown that laws are necessary, the legislatures will be negligent when they fail to pass them and officials will be negligent when they fail to enforce them. Similarly teachers and school administrators must inevitably in the exercise of their duties make and enforce regulations which provide for the protection and education of their students. Just as the citizens must obey reasonable or duly promulgated legislation, the student must in the interest of the common good accept the regulation of school authorities and the punishment which is necessary to its adequate enforcement.

The Punishment Should Seem Logical and Fair. There are various conditions which would seem to make punishment more acceptable in a democratic school. Such action as is taken must be both logical and fair. In the typical, well-regulated school, it is logical to expect that some punitive notice will be taken of a clear violation of regulations. This may consist merely of a reprimand or it may be a good deal more severe, depending on the nature of the violation. The severity of the punishment is expected to be gauged to the seriousness of the offense. It is assumed by some that two different offenders would receive approximately the same punishment for the same offense.

One of the problems is that, while the need for equal punishments is recognized, differences among the students makes each offense different.[26] Since the school must be concerned with the effect of the punishment on the student being punished, it must exercise caution even in insistence on equal treatment. This is, of course, an indication of the inconsistency between punishment as an authoritarian symbol and teaching as a democratic process.

It is generally accepted that cruel or unusual types of punishment should be avoided because they will appear to the student as either unfair

[25] *Cf.* H. Vincent, "Are Your Teachers Handcuffed on Discipline?" *School Management* 8:107–108 (April, 1964).

[26] J. Marcus, M. Richardson, and J. Gray, "Discipline Problems," *The NEA Journal* 56:60–63 (Dec., 1967).

or illogical. It is considered logical to require the student to repair damage done to property. It is generally understood in American high schools that corporal punishment is undignified and inappropriate. It might be noted that use of corporal punishment in elementary schools will vary somewhat with the customary punishment used in the home. Where corporal punishment represents the normal punishment at home, it is not likely to be considered cruel or unusual at school.[27]

Criticism of corporal punishment is usually based on the assumption that it represents an unwarranted attack on the student and is a denial of his personal integrity. There is the possibility of permanent injury. This also may be possible in subtle ways in any type of punishment although it is less likely with some than with others.[28]

Loss of privilege is usually considered a logical and fair punishment. The problem in the typical high school is that there are really few privileges to lose. To require students to stay in after school seems to make of school attendance a drudgery, penalizes the teacher, and for some students loses its effectiveness rather quickly.

Occasionally, teachers will wish to banish students from their classrooms. This practice has many disadvantages. In the typical school there is nowhere for him to go from class. Movement in the halls is usually closely regulated to prevent unexcused absence from class, and other teachers object to having students who are likely to be discipline problems wandering where they may disturb classes.

It is a tribute to the American school, the teachers, and the students that with so few punitive measures available, schools are so orderly. The teacher in general may make special assignments of work to be done, have special conferences, rebuke, ask a student to stay after school, or send him from the room, or to some other official. The principal may take the various types of action taken by the teacher, confer with the parents, or send the student home for varying periods of time. Punishment is only a minor aspect of the educational program of most American school children.

The Role of Firmness, Consistency, and Acceptance. In addition to the requirement that punishment should be logical and fair, it is also desirable that it should be firm and consistent. With the limited range of penalties available to the teacher, it becomes important that they be used sparingly. The effect of any penalty tends to be dulled with use. The experienced teacher is likely to move carefully and then to see that the punishment is applied firmly enough to be effective the first time.

---

[27] For consideration of the legal status of corporal punishment see Robert R. Hamilton, *Legal Right and Liabilities of Teachers* (Laramie, Wyoming: School Law Publication, 1960).

[28] *Cf.* P. Nash, "Corporal Punishment in An Age of Violence," *Educational Theory* 13:295–308 (Oct., 1963).

He attempts to be consistent in his insistence on whatever standards it is that he wishes to maintain. If any uncertainty exists as to whether the rule will be enforced, it may become a game for students to determine how far they may go.

More basic than any other factor in the success of punishment is its acceptance by students as just. If there is to be any educative effect, the student must recognize that the punishment was deserved and understand that it is important that the action which required punishment not be repeated. The severity of the punishment is related to these two points: recognition of the fact of punishment and reinforcement of the desire not to repeat the offense. Too severe a punishment may result in resentment rather than acceptance.

Frequently, the acceptance of punitive action is as important a symbol as the fact of punishment itself. When the student willingly accepts punishment in order to get the record straightened out, the situation may be healthier mentally than one in which nothing much happens but the student is left with the feeling that the teacher or the principal "is down on him."

Toward More Positive Action. One educator has suggested that punishment should be reserved for the normal, healthy student and that punishment of the chronic offender should be avoided because he is obviously not healthy enough to be able to take it.[29] Punishment is thus viewed as a teaching technique which can be safely used only with those who do not already feel rejected by the society and the school. Only when they feel secure can the school risk the possibility of making them feel rejected. This view of punishment leaves unsolved the question as to what can be done about the just enforcement of important regulations made for the safety and welfare of students too immature to understand the need for them. It also neglects the fact that the students themselves may feel a certain security if they know the school will exercise a paternalistic control over the possible excesses of the student body.[30]

Both the long- and the short-range effects of any punitive action must be taken into consideration. If the short-range effect is to provide a situation in which more positive types of action may be initiated, and the long-range is to encourage the development of self-discipline, then the punishment is apparently acceptable. On the other hand, if the short-range effect may be to provide for orderliness, but the longer-range effect is to make still more stringent punishment necessary, the punishment is unacceptable. Some teachers have orderly classrooms, but their classes

[29] James L. Hymes, Jr., *Behavior and Misbehavior: A Teacher's Guide to Action* (Englewood Cliffs, N.J.: Prentice-Hall, Inc., 1955).

[30] *Cf.* J. Yoder, "Creative Discipline," *School and Community* 50:28–29 (Oct., 1963).

seem dependent on them for the maintenance orderliness. Other teachers develop a kind of group responsibility for orderliness which is relatively independent of their presence. The same observation can be made of whole schools.

It is generally safer to judge the effect of punitive action on the particular student being punished than to attempt to justify harsh action on the grounds of the welfare of other students. Doubtless there are times when the safety of the rest of the student body is jeopardized by the continued attendance of particular students. A student may be banished from school but he can hardly be banished from society. School officials have some responsibility for trying to see whether another agency that can help him more will assume responsibility for the social development of the unsocial student whom the school dismisses. While dismissal from school may seem just, its completeness is disturbing.

For the emotionally sick children who must come to classes, the school becomes a hospital rather than a disciplinary barracks. It must first help them to regain a measure of health before it is ready to treat them as healthy young people ready to be disciplined to social living. It is unfortunate that the school must operate in these cases in a dual capacity. It is tragic that the psychological services which are needed to help it to perform if it is to function as a hospital are usually lacking. Nevertheless, the school is sometimes the only hope for children who will otherwise be permanently problems of the society.[31]

The Values of Adolescents

Much is being said in current periodical literature about the value system of American teenagers and about the use of the school to teach moral and spiritual values. Previous chapters have indicated that American society is socially stratified and that each social level tends to have a system of its own. It has also been indicated that there seems to be a developing tradition for using the school to teach those values which would improve the quality of democratic living.

The Social Behavior of High School Students. Recent studies of adolescent social behavior have furnished some evidence of the extent of variation from commonly accepted norms. Cheating, vandalism, car stealing and speeding are problems both among high school students and recent school leavers. Drinking and drug addiction are recognized as

[31] D. J. Lyons and V. Powers, "Follow-up Study of Elementary School Children Exempted from Los Angeles City Schools During 1960–1961," *The Exceptional Child* 30:155–62 (Dec., 1963).

problems in some communities. Sexual immorality seems to have increased among middle-class students perhaps partly as a result of the parents' difficulty in supervising dating and recreation in the age of the automobile. In some of the metropolitan areas serious gang violence is a problem among youth of school age in slum areas.[32]

Overt behavior problems of the sort described indicate important areas of concern for the value system of our youth. There are also personal values which may be of as much or more significance. The view which the young person has of his role in life, the basis of his choice of a vocation, his sense of responsibility for his family, his community, other individuals in his society, and his civic responsibilities may not be so easily observed.[33]

The Role of the School in Teaching Values. Pressure has been applied by agencies outside the school which has resulted in teaching about the effects of alcohol and narcotics, courses in driver education, in sex or family-life education, and the values of democracy as opposed to totalitarianism. In most cases professional school people have recognized as valid the public's concern for these aspects of safety and morality. They have frequently resisted, on other grounds, the legal prescription as to how values were to be taught in the school curriculum.[34]

The appropriateness of indoctrination as a teaching technique has been questioned in a previous chapter. The importance of using the school as society's agent for the improvement of the life of the community has also been emphasized.

The Role of Identification in the Learning of Values. Too little is known about the teaching of moral values. It seems to be the consensus among educational theorists that the student's identification with a particular role is important. The role identified may be the father's, or it may occasionally be that of some person such as the teacher or minister. Acceptance of that role may be largely unconscious, but it may presumably be influenced by an understanding of the consequences of the action. Thus there may be a place both for precept and for example.[35]

The school is operating against a serious handicap with those students for whom the role presented by the family and the peer group differs sharply from that of the school itself. To the extent that it can help students see the long-range consequences of the roles which the school and other forces may present, it may be able to have an effect.

[32] *Cf.* M. F. Baer, "Juvenile Court Statistics," *Personnel and Guidance Journal* 42:744–45 (April, 1964).

[33] F. G. Jennings, "Adolescents, Aspirations, and the Older Generation," *Teachers College Record* 65:335–41 (Jan., 1964).

[34] J. H. Bunzel, "Pressure Groups in Politics and Education," *The National Elementary Principal* 43:12–16 (April, 1964).

[35] *Cf.* A. B. Heilbrun, Jr., "Parental Model Attributes, Nurturiant Reinforcement, and Consistency of Behavior in Adolescents," *Child Development* 35:151–67 (March, 1964).

The school must strive for understanding, and for the kind of acceptance which comes from understanding, if it is to act consistently with democratic principles: respect for the individual personality and his right to make his own choice must be maintained.[36]

[36] Cf. G. I. Brown, "Meaning of Democracy and the Methods Course," *Educational Forum* 28:323–26 (March, 1964).

13

Providing for Group Instruction

ALTHOUGH INDIVIDUALIZING INSTRUCTION IS AN IMPORTANT AIM, IT IS OBVIously necessary to carry on much of the instruction in groups. In the first place it is impossible to provide one teacher for each student in school. If it were possible it would not be efficient use of teacher time, nor would it provide a good learning situation. The social setting of the classroom provides many lessons which no tutor could teach alone.

The Individual and the Group

Democratic educational theory has two dimensions. On the one hand, the individual is recognized as the basic unit of society. Such institutions as the family or the state have no existence except as they are made up of individuals. Nor can they be said to be good or bad except as they affect the lives, meet the needs, of the individuals who make them up. On the other hand, the individual is dependent on the society in which he lives for his development. He is a social animal. His adjustment to the rest of his society is a paramount condition for his satisfactory development.

Just as democracy has two dimensions, learning seems to have two dimensions. One is personal and private. It occurs within the organism. Such learning seems limited by the potential of the individual and his own nervous system. The other is public. The individual is influenced by the group in his decisions as to what to value, what to learn, how to use, and the significance of what he is learning.

The group furnishes the climate for learning. Much of the motivation must come out of the basic interactions of individuals within the group. The opportunity for testing the significance of insights occurs when ideas are exchanged within the group.

298

There is no real question whether or not the school must deal with students in groups. The essential question is what will be the basis for deciding how to group. How can a maximum of opportunities for individual and social learning be provided?

Homogeneity in Grouping. While students differ from one another there are similarities between them. Each situation provides a homogeneous basis for grouping. In the one-room school, the only homogeneity that could be provided was geographic. The children lived in the same community. When the one-room school gave way to the two-room school it became possible to provide for homogeneity on the basis of age or scholastic attainment. Age and scholastic attainment did not always go together and so there had to be some compromise if both were important. As students progressed beyond the level of general education, a third factor in providing homogeneity was introduced—the nature of the subject matter itself. When current school practice is examined it is found that the present emphasis on grouping in the elementary school is primarily on age, adjusted somewhat for ability and achievement. In the secondary school there is more emphasis on subject matter, although age is still a factor. At the college level the emphasis is still more largely on subject matter, although there is still selectivity both on the basis of previous achievement and between colleges on the basis of ability.

There is considerable discussion in current popular literature of the possibility of paying more attention to ability grouping, both at the elementary and secondary school levels. Proponents of ability grouping stress the possibility of covering more material with the better students and of concentrating on basic skills with the slower students. The opponents point out some serious disadvantages. Brighter and slower students can learn something from each other which they might miss in separate groups. The tendency for ability grouping to emphasize social stratification was mentioned in Chapter 3. Proponents of racial integration have pointed out the present tendency of grouping practices in some schools to resegregate classes which have been integrated. The tendency of children from socially prominent families to do better on tests used to determine ability may in part be the result of inherited ability or it may be the result of their having better educational opportunity outside of the school. In either case the effect on school social stratification has been found in some communities to be strong.

There are some other pertinent problems. Where separate measures of ability are used—such as ability in arithmetic and reading—different groupings become apparently appropriate for each measure. If different groupings are compared, as much as half of the total group may be grouped differently on the two measures. Where a third aspect of the program is considered, a third type of grouping might be proposed. It becomes apparent that, while groups may be set up for some particular aspect of the program, they become inappropriate for other aspects.[1]

The solution generally accepted by education theorists has been to provide some slight homogeneity on the basis of age, maturity, and subject preference, and then to keep class size small. The teacher who recognizes several levels of ability within a relatively small class can arrange his teaching techniques so as to take this into account. To recall the example of the one-room school, it is not necessary that everyone in the class be doing the same thing at the same time. No matter what basis is used for arriving at homogeneity, a more refined technique will distinguish still other differences between students.

Promotion Policy. Closely related to the question of homogeneity in grouping is the matter of promotion policy. A lot is sometimes said about what is called "social promotion." Almost every instructional problem at the high school level has been said by someone to "result from whole-sale promotion in the lower levels." Thus the English teacher who realizes that some of his students cannot read at better than the fifth grade level wonders why these students were ever promoted out of the sixth.

It is unreasonable to expect the whole population of a particular age group to reach the same level of proficiency in a skill like reading. All learn at different rates because all start with different inheritances and have grown up in different environments. With special attention it may be possible to establish a minimum level which each student in a particular group should attain. This attention may require the help of much special personnel if the level set is close to the grade level in which students are currently placed. For some students the meeting of this new standard may not be worth the effort required both from him and from his teachers.

Within some limits, students will learn faster studying new material with a congenial age group than if they are kept back. Frequently retention seems to result in repetition of the same experience. Furthermore, while reading is important, it is not the only subject which the school is interested in teaching. Some students who do poorly in reading are doing satisfactorily, and a few are doing well, in arithmetic. Students who are much retarded are likely to drop out of school at an earlier age than the students of the same general ability level who are with approximately their own age group.[2]

The social benefits of school attendance seem more easily achieved in the regular chronological age groups than in groups with wide age differences. From the standpoint of classroom management at the elementary

---

[1] J. Franseth, "Research in Grouping: A Review," *School Life* 45:5–6 (June, 1963).

[2] *Cf.* G. L. Chamberlin and E. D. Catterall, "Acceleration for the Average Potential Dropout?" *Phi Delta Kappan* 45:98–100 (1964).

school level the over-age student creates a problem both in class and on the playground. There are, however, cases in which there are some valid reasons for saying that a student would be better off repeating.

At the first grade level there are frequently less mature students who may profit more from staying with the same teacher than from being promoted. For this and other reasons, some systems have organized what are referred to as ungraded primary groups in which promotion from one level of material to another can proceed without regard for the customary promotion dates.[3] In some schools there is a rule that children should not be retained more than one year in the first eight except under special circumstances. Retardation for more than two years is considered even more questionable.

The social problems of retardation may not be apparent at the time the student is retarded but become more serious during the high school years when social development seems more crucial. The fact that any class or age group contains several different maturity groups provides for some flexibility, but a strain is placed where students are seriously retarded.[4]

In modern school practices, individual differences seem to be better catered for by the use of flexible teaching procedures, more remedial instruction where it seems desirable, and more variety and depth of treatment for those at the upper end of the achievement scale.[5] The tendency of a few teachers to put the blame on the promotion policy of the elementary school for something which is partly due to their own inability to provide for flexibility seems unfair and misleading.

Multiple Tracks. One suggested solution to the problem of providing for differences in student ability has been referred to as a multiple track approach or "streaming." Tried out on a limited scale in the elementary and junior high schools in the 1920's and 1930's, it was then found not to be particularly appropriate. More recently it has been suggested again for junior and senior high schools.

In essence it advocates that students be grouped according to ability in such a way that some of them might cover a three-year course of study in two years and still others might require four. There could still be a shifting from one track to the other for students who were misclassified. This could occur at convenient time intervals within the program, or students could change grouping at the end of the term year interval.[6]

[3] *Cf.* J. W. Halliwell, "Comparison of Pupil Achievement in Graded and Non-Graded Primary Classrooms," *Journal of Experimental Education* 32:59–64 (Fall, 1963).

[4] *Cf.* C. Vaden, "Should Johnny Be Retained?" *Texas Outlook* 48:37 (April, 1964).

[5] *Cf.* R. G. Shadick, "Individualization in the Instructional Program," *Association for Student Teaching Yearbook* 42:39–56 (1963).

[6] A. S. Jewitt and Others, *Teaching Rapid and Slow Learners in High Schools* (Washington, D.C.: U.A.O.E. Bulletin 1954 No. 5, Government Printing Office, 1954).

Educational theorists have generally opposed such schemes in recent years on several grounds. In the first place they have argued that it placed the emphasis on covering a specific body of content or course of study rather than on providing an appropriate use of two, three, or four years for each type of student. In the second place it is felt that it is better to modify work within the classroom than to rely on mechanical (and cumbersome) administrative devices. In the third place, the track system was felt to duplicate the other problems of ability grouping.

Flexible Grouping. Grouping within the classroom was discussed in the previous chapter as one method of individualizing instruction. It is important to refer to it again here because it seems to be the answer to the problem of providing within the school for the needs of the whole age group of students.

In the first place grouping within a class is essentially a flexible arrangement. It can be provided for within a class period and may last for as long as it seems appropriate to the activities at hand. Furthermore, it can be changed from one type of activity to the next. Time may be taken to work on particular skills with one group while another is permitted to go on with other activities. Enrichment may be provided for some students while others are working on remedial activities.

In the second place, social class distinction that becomes a problem with less flexible types of grouping may be avoided. During each day students will join several different groups. The emphasis is not on social distinction but on problems in learning. Some of the groupings may be used consciously to provide for better integration of different social groups represented within the class.

The emphasis of the high school on marks and on the teaching of fixed bodies of content has had its effect. The question has been raised, for instance, as to how students were going to be marked if there were several different groups in one class.[7] The problem of marking systems will be discussed at more length later. The question which might be raised here is whether the more important function of the school is to assign marks or to teach students what they are capable of learning. If the assignment of marks is secondary to the matter of teaching, then a satisfactory arrangement can be worked out. For instance, if the idea of mastering one set of competences before moving on to the next is the goal, then the mark can be based on the amount or quality of work actually completed. If the mark is to be a motivational device, then it may reflect evaluation of the student's effort.

Groupings and Standards. Discussion of homogeneous grouping, promotion policy, and grouping within the class suggests the question of the relationship between such matters and the standards of the school. Traditionally, both teachers and parents have considered promotion from

[7] *Cf.* P. DePue, "Rubber Yardstick and the Pursuits of Excellence," *The Clearing House* 38:248–50 (Dec., 1963).

one grade level to the next as indicative of having completed certain fixed standards of work. A school which required the achievement of a higher level of skill was said to have higher standards than one which did not require so high a level. Any promotion policy which permitted all students of secondary school age to enter the secondary school would, in this traditional view, represent a serious watering-down of the standards.[8]

If traditional teaching techniques (which required each child in a particular class to move at the same pace) were used, this would indeed seem to be the case. If the pace of the whole class is to be that of the slowest student, then the presence of all, or nearly all, the students of a particular age group will insure a tortoise-slow pace. If, on the other hand, the school uses techniques for individualizing instruction the effect would be very different.

It becomes important to consider whether the traditional approach to consideration of standards is at fault. Should the term "standard" be descriptive of how well the school is doing what it is trying to do, or should it describe how difficult it is for a particular student to get a diploma? Is a school to be considered good because it provides for the needs of a large number of the students for whom it is responsible, or is it to be said to be good because it concentrates on the portion of an age group that may be planning to attend college?[9] It would seem apparent that the modern high school is committed to providing for the education of all of the students who can profit from attending.

It is, of course, obvious that to have committed itself to making some provision for all students still does not require it to neglect developing the capacity of any particular student. How many students are promoted or even graduated is not relevant in discussing the standards of the school because the school standards should be defined on other bases. This issue will be discussed at greater length in the chapter on records and reports.

Grouping and the Learning Process

There seem to be at least three different considerations which arise from the necessity for providing for teaching of students in groups. The first is is provision for individuality, the second is variation in teaching materials and techniques, and the third is recognition of the social aspects of the learning process. While each of these considerations is almost automatically apparent from the previous discussion of homogeneity in grouping, there are other dimensions which are not so readily seen.

---

[8] Cf. John I. Goodlad, "Classroom Organization," Encyclopedia of Educational Research, 3rd ed. (New York: The Macmillan Company, 1960).

[9] W. H. Bristow, "Curriculum Problems Regarding Early School Leavers," Education Digest 29:13–15 (April, 1964).

Respect for Individuality in Grouping. While the emphasis in a discussion of grouping is likely to fall on the nature of the teaching group or situation created, it is important to remember that the function of the school is to provide for the needs of the individual. It is difficult for the high school teacher to realize the differences which exist between the various students in his classroom because of the number with whom he comes into contact. Respecting the individuality of 150 different students during the day is not easy. The fact that contact with any portion of that large group is for so short a period as 50 minutes complicates the problem still further. Nevertheless, neither the size of the group nor the shortness of contact changes the fact that effective teaching must be based on recognition of individual needs. The nature of the learning process is not changed by the complexity of the group even though the nature of the teaching process may be materially altered.

There should be respect for individuality inherent in the grouping process. When a class is sectioned in such a way as to call attention to important differences in ability to learn, or to social distinctions, there is a serious risk of offending the students who are classified as inferior. That the classification is accurate does not make it excusable unless it is necessary. If the classification is not accurate, the difficulty is compounded almost to the point of slander.

Respect for individuality may be seriously neglected if in any one room more students with serious problems are collected than the teacher is capable of helping. Some schools, which practice what is called ability grouping, assign teachers with the slowest groups fewer students. Otherwise these teachers may have so many problems that no one student in the group gets as much help as he might be able to obtain if the group were dispersed among the various sections of the school. Those with serious problems may actually irritate one another and develop problems that did not exist before.[10]

Respect for individuality may suffer if in the process of grouping more provision is made for similarities between members of the group than for the important differences which exist between them. When all of the students in the seventh grade who are reading at the fourth grade level are grouped together, the fact may be ignored that some of them need help on word-attack skills, while some have poor eyesight, and others weak experience backgrounds. To improve their reading may well require different teaching techniques.[11]

---

[10] *Cf.* R. Tillman, J. H. Hull, "Is Ability Grouping Taking Schools in the Wrong Direction," *Nation's Schools* 73:70–71 (April, 1964).

[11] *Cf.* V. W. Mitchell, "Analysis of the Grade Expectancy and Actual Reading Achievement of Sixth Grade Pupils with Special Attention to Six of the Possible Factors in Reading Underachievement," *Teachers College Journal* 35:52–53 (Nov., 1963).

Some teachers, when told that their groups are homogeneous, forget that they are still dealing with students who are in every respect different from each other. They feel justified in using the same techniques of mass instruction which have been so often and effectively criticized.

What has been indicated in the preceding paragraph bears directly on the crucial fact that any system of grouping is obviously and seriously artificial. This applies both to the differences which did not serve as the basis of the grouping process and to the more minute characteristics of the traits which were actually used. Thus if scores on an intelligence test were used as a basis, then the group may well differ in age, achievement on other tests of ability, social status, health, physical size, reading, previous grades, etc. There may also be differences in some aspects of intelligence itself.[12]

The attempt to use more than one basis for arriving at homogeneity of groups must amount to a compromise. Doubtless this is essentially desirable. It is necessary to group on some basis of homogeneity. The important matter is to be sure that the basis which is used is one which will facilitate instruction in all of the phases of the school program. Extreme emphasis on any single measure, whether it be chronological age, sex, reading skill, or mental age, is likely to do a disservice by complicating the problems outside of the area being emphasized.

Since, for example, the students who may profitably be studying the same social studies concepts are of varying levels of reading ability, have different skills in composition, and different experience backgrounds, it is necessary to recognize the importance of providing different materials and using different techniques. The problem of using varying techniques and materials has been discussed in Chapter 11. The important consideration here is that whatever system of grouping is used there is a continuing need for recognition of the value of variety not only from one unit of instruction to another, but immediately and directly in the treatment of each unit. That this complicates the work of the teacher does not change the fact that the nature of the student body with which he is trying to work requires it.

Social Aspects of the Learning Process. The individuality of students has been strongly emphasized. This point has been coupled with recognition of the social function and nature of the American public high school. It is important to keep these two facets in focus at the same time. If a teacher concentrates entirely on the importance of individuality, he makes of the teaching process a tutorial one in which each student is dealt with separately. Doubtless in learning basic skills this emphasis on individual help sometimes becomes an efficient and even necessary process.

[12] *Cf.* J. S. Braun, "Relation Between Concept Formation Ability and Reading Achievement at Three Development Levels," *Child Development* 34: 675–82 (Sept., 1963).

There are, however, at least two other important considerations to be kept in mind.

Some of the skills which should be taught are social in nature. One can read about civics, but an understanding of civic relationship may come from living with other people in a setting in which the adjustments necessary to that living are felt. One learns to write a composition not simply to be able to record his thoughts but rather for the sake of passing his ideas along to someone else. It is not possible to justify any of the skills which are taught in the school apart from the fact that they have social as well as personal implications. Many of them lose their significance completely when taught apart from their social setting.

The student whose entire education is carried on in a tutorial arrangement is likely to develop some skills to a fine point. Nevertheless, his education is incomplete unless some provision is made for his development of social skills and understanding.[13] The student who is educated in a private school in which he comes in contact with only a very limited sampling of the social strata of the total population can be socially handicapped. Recognizing this danger, some of the better-endowed private schools have made an attempt to include in their student bodies representatives of various social groups. Unfortunately, the fact is that they must of necessity represent too small a proportion of the group to be representative. The traditions and setting of such schools are likely to be such as to encourage their assimilation into the school rather than to make the atmosphere of the school more democratic. Also, some students sent early to boarding schools miss the opportunity to develop wholesome attitudes to family life, since they leave a home that is conducive to the right kind of development before attitudes toward family relationships are fully established.

Scheduling and Grouping

Perhaps the most significant single factor in the grouping practices of the modern school has to do not with homogeneous or heterogeneous grouping but rather with the schedule of the day and week. It takes a very large school to have much opportunity for ability grouping because of the other complications in the operation of the schedule.[14]

Weakness of the Typical Schedule. While the typical elementary school teacher is expected to deal with approximately 30 students during

---

[13] *Cf.* S. N. Fen, "Social Relations as the Content of Intellectual Learning," *Social Studies* 55:138–43 (April, 1964).

[14] D. W. Allen, "Elements of Scheduling a Flexible Curriculum," *Journal of Secondary Education* 38:84–91 (Nov., 1963).

the course of the school day, the typical secondary school teacher must deal with as many as 150. The difference lies primarily in traditional differences in the philosophy of the two systems. While these traditional differences may no longer represent current educational philosophy, nevertheless the emphasis continues to be on specialization in the high school and on personalization in the elementary school.

Not all elementary school teachers take full advantage of the greater flexibility of activity provided by the self-contained class, and some elementary schools are abandoning it. Nevertheless, the opportunity for flexibility is there and at least some teachers make the most of it.[15] Some high school teachers, too, achieve a surprising amount of flexibility within the limits imposed by the daily schedule. The obstacles are serious. In the first place the problem of getting to know 150 students is itself a major hurdle. It is relatively easy to know the extroverts in the class well enough to teach them effectively after the first day, but there are inevitably a few students who remain faces in assigned seats throughout the entire year.

The second important limitation is the shortness of the time available in any single day. Each lesson must take only 45 or 50 minutes. The fact that the development of some lessons requires more time and that some lessons might profitably take not so long is overlooked. Also overlooked is that impetus is likely to be lost in shifting classes, in reintroducing material first introduced on the preceding day, and in establishing new motivation each day. The life of the student is forced into the rigid mould of 50-minute periods. He is expected to shift from the rigors of mathematics to the different concepts of social studies in five minutes. The more engrossed he has become in one area, the more difficult the shift. He is at the same time shifting from a teacher who by personality and training expects one type of behavior into the classroom of another teacher with another set of expectations.

The teaching techniques that are appropriate for the short class period are likely to be very formal and to ignore approaches which are built on student motivation and activity. The mechanics of the situation make laboratory work, committee process, planned discussion, and indeed the logical development of ideas difficult. It is easy to lecture, to make formal assignments, to give frequent tests, and in short to treat students not as separate personalities but as members of a class unknown to the teacher and frequently even to each other.

The third limitation is the emphasis which such an approach puts on subject specialization. The teacher in such a situation feels the responsibility to teach within the given period only that single body of material assigned to him. Furthermore he will feel most comfortable if he is teaching it as a logically organized body of subject matter with a

15 T. D. Butterfield, "Self-Contained Classroom: The Stage for Pedagogical Practice in the Elementary School," *New York State Education* 51:12 (Feb., 1964).

central basis for organization and with the central core receiving the primary emphasis. To the subject specialist at the college level this approach is the natural, or at least the familiar one. College scholarship emphasizes the same kind of specialization. The college-prepared high school teacher may feel more comfortable in such a teaching situation, but the justification for the school curriculum must be made in terms of the needs of the students to whom it is being taught. Emphasis on the logic of subject matter represents a serious threat to efficient instruction.[16]

Limitation of the formal instruction in any given year to the central areas of four or possibly five subjects—such as Latin III, U.S. History, English (American Literature and Grammar), Algebra II, and possibly Chemistry I—seems to some observers, at least, to be a very limited approach to meeting the developmental needs of even that portion of the high school population who may be planning to go to college.

Some of the changes which are suggested in this section must come not as a result of changes in the mechanics of the daily schedule, but rather as the result of basic changes in teaching methodology. Some of them cannot be effected until the schedule has been altered to provide conditions more hospitable to the philosophy of such changes. The interrelatedness between educational philosophy, physical facilities, schedule, and teaching methodology is more basic than is sometimes recognized.

Modifications in the Length of the Period. Some reduction in tension has been achieved by lengthening the periods in the schedule day and reducing their number. Thus within a single day the teacher might come in contact with only five or six distinct groups of students rather than the six, seven or eight groups with which he formerly worked either on a teaching or study hall basis. In some cases this reduction was accomplished by eliminating the existing study halls and adding the time saved to the other periods in the day. The study hall had become obviously out of place in an education which placed the emphasis on variety in the learning process and on teacher direction of study. The study hall had also become a disagreeable chore because the supervising teacher was cast in the role of monitor rather than director of activity.

A second technique for lengthening the class period has been to reduce the number of periods within any single day but to keep the same number of class hours of instruction. Thus six class periods would be rotated through a five-period class day and one would be omitted each day. This approach has the advantage of reducing the number of different teachers students meet in any one day and of giving a longer class period on the days on which the classes meet. An additional advantage is that it prevents any one subject from coming at the poorest time in the day every day. Class activities can be chosen in such a way as to take

[16] *Cf.* M. Scherwitzky, "Obituary for the Early Childhood Major," *New York State Education* 51:11 (Dec., 1963).

advantage of the relative alertness of the student group with high interest material saved for the times when student attention is more difficult to maintain.

A third method has been to group subject fields in such a way that a particular teacher teaches the same students two or more subjects and has at his disposal two or more consecutive periods. In some cases the subject matter is actually reorganized to constitute a new and larger body of material (or group of experiences) with a new designation or name. Even if there is no attempt to correlate or integrate the material involved, there is still an advantage in reducing the number of students whom the teacher is expected to know, and in giving him more flexibility in the use of the time he has with them.[17]

One Subject at a Time. A more radical approach to flexibility, but one which preserves the concept of subject specialization, is commonly referred to as the one-subject plan.[18] In this system a student studies one subject at a time for some fixed period of time, usually at least six weeks, and then moves to another. This system has been used extensively by Hiram College in Ohio, by the Kiskamentas preparatory school in Pennsylvania, by the Eureka High School in Mississippi, and more briefly by the Mangum High School in Durham County, North Carolina.

A teacher has only one class of students during the day, although he may have four, five, or six during the year, depending on the length of the period assigned. The whole day is at his disposal and he is free to take field trips or other projects which would otherwise have interfered with the rest of the school program. Because students are not moving about every period, the teacher assumes much of the responsibility for pupil management customarily taken by the elementary school teacher but in the high school likely to be relegated to the principal or counselor's office. The formal class procedures of the short class period give way to more individual study, committee work, and small group activity.

The student by concentrating on a single subject is encouraged, or perhaps forced, to give it his attention—there is nothing else in the school day which is likely to take precedence over it. Thus the advantage of the summer music camp, or of the intensive approach to language instruction, is brought into the regular high school instructional program. If a student desires to complete a two-course sequence in language or mathematics during his senior year, it may be managed simply by arranging two courses sequentially without having to wait for an additional year.

The school system which wishes to provide a specialist to teach in several different high schools might then have him teach for the first six or eight weeks at one school and then for the second at the next

---

[17] *Cf.* W. B. Jennings, "Core and Activities at Como Park," *Minnesota Journal of Education* 44:12 (Feb., 1964).

[18] *See* Samuel M. Holton, "Flexibility in Secondary Schools Through the One-Subject Plan," *The High School Journal* 32:113–22 (May, 1949).

without having to go during the same day from one campus to the other. The transportation of specialized equipment is considerably simplified when this method is adopted. It would also make feasible the transporting of students from one school to another for a particular course.

The basic advantage, however, is that each teacher has enough contact with each student in the class to know him personally and to plan an appropriate program of activities suitable to his stage of development.

Specialized Curricula and Grouping. One of the most important influences on grouping procedures is the result of two related aspects of the curriculum: elective courses and specialized curricula. To the degree that students may choose the courses which they are going to take they tend to group themselves. Particularly in the small school the decision to take physics, for instance, not only places the student in the class with others who want and are considered able to profit from a study of physics, but it is also likely to put him in classes with the same students in other aspects of his program. The scheduling of classes in the small school becomes so inflexible that there may be only one such choice available and making that one choice, of necessity, determines the rest of the student's sectioning for that year.

When the selection of courses becomes formalized into specialized curricula leading perhaps to secretarial employment or attendance at a college concentrating on science, in some schools a choice is made but once for the whole four-year program. While this is not necessarily bad, it may have some disturbing results. Course or curriculum selection tends (even more than attempts at homogeneous grouping by abilities) to classify students according to the social status of their parents. Some moderately large schools take pains to see that grouping in courses not requiring specialized content avoids following the same pattern of class stratification as the specialized courses. This is easier to do in large schools than in the smaller schools. Fortunately, perhaps, the smaller school is more likely to provide homogeneity within the social life of the school as a whole.

Some schools develop special sections of English and social studies for the college preparatory student, the commercial student, the technical student, and the general student. Unless the actual content is to be modified significantly, the social stratification which results cannot be justified.

Providing for Special Education at the Secondary Level

One of the important problems facing American education deals with making special provision for three classes of students: the handicapped, the slow-learners, and the gifted. Since all students are different from each other, the fact that these three groups are more markedly different has less significance than is commonly assigned to it by the layman or sometimes by the apologist for special treatment. We must then ask the question as to what the responsibility of the public school should be in dealing with these children. The answer is, of course, in one dimension quite simple. We must make the same effort that we would make to provide for every other individual difference which we recognize to be important to the individual's development. We must develop his potential as an individual and as a contributing member of the society. In the case of the distinct deviant, both self-gratification and social contribution may present potentially grave problems.

Provision for the Physically Handicapped. The range of possibly serious physical handicaps is tremendous.[19] Those who are able to attend the public school include principally the crippled, the epileptic, the hard of hearing, those with speech handicaps, and those who are blind or nearly blind. For the physically crippled, the teacher's chief concern is to help them recognize that they can be active and useful members of the group. This provision will probably involve providing such activities as they are capable of participating in and, if it is possible, affording worthwhile substitutes for such activities as they may not be able to participate in. For the hard of hearing the answer may be simple: providing a hearing device, special training in lip reading, or special placement in the classroom may solve the problem. On the other hand it may sometimes be necessary to provide special instruction. Similarly special instruction may be provided for those needing speech therapy. The emphasis is on providing the necessary special instruction within the regular school setting wherever possible. The point in this case is that the child should recognize that, in all essentials but that of hearing, he is a normal part of the social group.[20]

The same general approach is taken with the blind as with the deaf. Where provision can be made for instruction in the regular classroom this is considered desirable. Specially printed materials are sometimes available, as are funds for employing readers. Where special instruction is required outside of the regular classroom, it is frequently provided in the regular school system. Only in extreme cases or in complicated situations is it considered desirable to place such students in institutional boarding centers.[21]

The opportunities for helping the regular student body recognize the importance of accepting the disabled as regular members of the social group should not be overlooked. The best approach is to emphasize the

[19] *Cf.* F. W. Doyle, "Educating the Handicapped," *California Education* 1:31–32 (Sept., 1963).

[20] *Cf.* S. R. Silverman, "Educating Deaf Children," *School Life* 46:24–28 (Jan., 1964).

[21] *Cf.* Maurice H. Fomacre, "Visually Handicapped," *Encyclopedia of Educational Research*, 3rd ed. (New York: The Macmillan Company, 1960), pp. 998–1000.

similarities rather than the differences. Emphasis on acceptance becomes most difficult when deviation is considered sufficient ground for segregating students into special situations or institutions.

Providing for the Slow-Learner. The same principles which have been suggested for dealing with the physically handicapped would seem applicable in dealing with the slow learner. In the first place, being markedly slower than the average for the group still does not mean being different in kind, but only in degree. The same laws of learning seem to be appropriate. It is important for the slow learner to participate with others of the same general age in as many activities as possible. Special remedial help should of course be provided by the regular teacher or, if this is not enough, by specialists; but remaining a member of the social group in which his social education can progress is also important.

The epileptic is faced with many problems of a very different nature. It becomes particularly important to help the rest of the student body adjust to the possibility of his having seizures at school. Protecting the student from physical danger is important, but his emotional problems must not be overlooked either. The restrictions typically placed on the social life of the epileptic are quite extensive and must not be magnified unduly if complications are to be avoided. Some of the drugs used to control seizures seem to leave the patient somewhat less effective mentally during and after the period of the seizures and the seizures themselves may be exhausting. All of these factors require understanding and patience on the part of school personnel.[22]

In the second place, the learning activities of the slow learner, like those of learners at any other level, should be selected for their appropriateness to his stage of development. Simply repeating experiences which have not proved profitable before, or which are obviously intended for less socially mature students, is poor pedagogy. Thus the eleven-year-old who is at the second grade level in reading should not be required to use reading materials geared to the interest level of seven-year-olds. He may find such materials both insulting and uninteresting.

At the high school level it is necessary to recognize the presence of slow learners and to provide, within the general framework of the curriculum, opportunities for them to receive help. Thus in the English class they may need to work on developing skills which other students have mastered in the fifth or sixth grade. In the social studies and science classes it may be desirable to recognize that the regular text materials must be supplemented with others more appropriate to fifth or sixth grade reading levels. The mathematics classes must make some provision for the continued development of elementary arithmetic skills.

It is possible to provide for the slow learner as well as for the average and the quick. It requires, however, a willingness on the part of the staff

[22] C. Kram, "Invisible Illness," *Illinois Education* 52:70 (Oct., 1963).

and, importantly, a willingness on the part of the public to pay for such a program.

Providing for the Gifted. At the other end of the scale of abilities is the "gifted" student. The aristocratic traditions of the high school make it somewhat simpler to get special assistance for this group. It might be noted that the lower and lower-middle classes have as many children in this category as are to be found in the upper and upper-middle classes, even when it is recognized that environmental factors of the upper-class groups have given them an advantage on the test scores used in measuring intelligence. Simply to provide the traditional college preparatory curriculum is a poor approach to providing for the gifted.[23]

As for the handicapped and slow learners, it is recognized that it is desirable to give special assistance to the gifted within the regular social setting wherever possible. Social education is at least as important for them as for any other group, and segregation into an elite class is not considered desirable in a society which wishes to avoid social stratification in adult life. For similar reasons the attempt to provide for gifted students by acceleration into other age groups has not proved particularly desirable. Acceleration, beyond one or occasionally two grade levels, tends to place students outside of the social group in which they could operate most effectively. They are frequently unable to compete in the physical, and sometimes the social, activities with the older students with whom they are thrown. More effective experiments have been made to permit students to accelerate their studies while remaining in their own age group.[24]

While the gifted are capable of a good deal of self-direction, they still need, and are entitled to, help from the regular teacher. They may profitably be encouraged to go more deeply into the areas being studied in social studies, science, and English literature—delving into more advanced material than that in the regular text, making wider use of library resources, undertaking more and more ambitious projects, helping —where it is profitable for them to do so—with the instruction of other members of the class. In skilled areas such as arithmetic, mathematics, reading, and composition, they should be encouraged to develop skills beyond those for the grade levels in which they are placed. Specialized help from skilled teachers is also appropriate for this group whenever it can be provided.

One of the handicaps to the provision for both the retarded and the gifted is the tendency to regard the body of content material used in high school courses as static. As the teacher of the one-room school knew well, it is not necessary for every student in the class to be working at the

[23] R. L. Hamm, "Integrated Program for the Gifted," *Minnesota Journal of Education* 44:8 (Dec., 1963).

[24] G. A. Swenson, "Acceleration Versus Enrichment," *NASSP Bulletin* 47:9–10 (Oct., 1963).

same level or dealing with the same material. It is, of course, convenient in handling large groups of students for them to be working on similar types of material, and even to be working on the same problems at particular times. Nevertheless, there is no reason for failing to recognize that some students must work at a more elementary level or that some must be encouraged to work on entirely different material at a more advanced level.

14

Records, Reports, Marks, and Diplomas

MUCH OF THE MECHANICAL OPERATION OF THE AMERICAN PUBLIC HIGH school is dependent on the use of records, reports, marks, and diplomas. The departmentalization of the curriculum has been partly responsible for the elaborateness of the system. Emphasis on efficiency of administration has also contributed.

Records

Records must not become ends in themselves. This is one of the problems to be faced in developing any record system. Thus the principal who recognizes that some particular type of record might be useful must further ascertain whether the cost of making and keeping it in terms of student and staff time will be justified. Some schools, for instance, have embarked on elaborate testing programs from which valuable information might have been gleaned. However, the tests were often filed without any adequate interpretation of the results. The school was perhaps able to say to some critics that it had an elaborate testing program, but the instructional program was not materially affected.

If on the other hand too conservative an attitude is taken toward the collection and recording of pertinent information, the possibility of systematically studying problems may be hampered. Modification of a school program requires that there be available some basis for determining the success of changes. In the absence of records it is difficult to know the starting point from which achievement can be measured. Furthermore, a study of school records may suggest problems which might otherwise have been overlooked.[1]

[1] A. R. Lichtenberger, "Educational Records are Useful in Making Decisions," *School Life* 47:20–22 (Nov., 1964).

It is helpful, for instance, to have a record of the size of the enrollment for any particular class group for each of the preceding years back
to the one in which the group entered the first grade. This record, when
corrected, gives an indication of the holding power of the school program
which may not be readily apparent to someone who is looking merely at
the enrollment for a particular year. Attendance records may have seemed
a chore at the time they were first recorded, but the information has
uses which may not have been originally recognized.

Those who wish to understand a particular student better may find
a wide variety of material from his cumulative record helpful. They may,
for instance, be interested in his overall academic record with the insights
it may provide as to if and when he had difficulty in mastering basic
skills. They may be interested in his attendance record and the clues it
offers to such things as parental attitudes toward school attendance,
childhood illness, important changes resulting from a loss of interest in
the school program, and truancy. The test record will also furnish clues
as to general ability, the appropriateness of the school program, the need
for remedial attention, and the interests and problems of the student.
Most cumulative records also provide a health record, and information
about the family situation.

There seems to be a tendency to collect some records of slight value
to the instructional program and to neglect others which would seem
particularly desirable. Because in most areas school funds are allotted on
the basis of attendance and enrollment, elaborate reports on these items
are made by each teacher, principal, and superintendent of schools. In
some cases these reports require many hours of time otherwise available
for instructional purposes. Elaborate cross checks are provided to determine the accuracy and sometimes the honesty of those making the
reports. Similarly, some school systems have elaborate accounting systems
established for keeping up with such property as textbooks. The cost of
accounting is probably greater than any loss which would result from the
absence of such a system.

What Records Are Kept in the Public High School? The typical high
school keeps several kinds of records. They may be classified as follows:
(1) records necessary to the financial operation, (2) records necessary to
the mechanical operation, (3) records helpful in the teaching and counseling, (4) records used in the recommendation of students to colleges or
employers, and (5) records helpful in maintaining public relations.

The records kept as a part of the financial operation of the school
are of two types: those used as a basis for getting tax appropriations, and
those used to assure the honesty of students and teachers who handle
money from various sources. The records used for getting tax funds, besides student attendance data, include such other items as teacher
qualifications and attendance, payrolls, and reports on related operations

such as the school cafeteria. While such records must be efficiently kept, the amount of staff time devoted to the process is seldom appreciated.[2]

Most of the schools also handle large sums of money from sources other than tax sources. It is not uncommon for the sums involved in a school of less than a thousand students to run in excess of $100,000. Protection of the public and the school staff requires systems for accounting and the auditing of the accounts. It is considered wise to require all student activities with funds at their disposal to make use of the school accounting system. Student fees, book rentals, club dues, athletic funds, cafeteria funds, library funds, and money collected for such things as field trips all become a part of the total picture.

The records which are kept as a part of the mechanical operation of the school have to do primarily with where students and teachers are supposed to be at particular times of the day. It is at this level that simplifying school organization would make a difference in the problem of record keeping. It is necessary to keep a schedule for each student, unless students are kept together in blocks, in which case it is sufficient to know which block a student is in and the schedule for the block. It is also necessary to have a schedule of each teacher's activities. The use of particular school facilities such as the gymnasium, the auditorium, the library, motion picture projectors, instructional films, and other important items must also be scheduled. In most cases procedures for pupil accounting are set up to see that each student is where he is supposed to be at any particular time. This system, like some other types of accounting, may require a great amount of staff time which might be spent in other ways.

Records which are more basic to the school program are those which help with counseling and teaching. The most important record in this category is the cumulative one. This record is supposed to be started when the student enters school and to continue until he graduates. It is the one which serves as his permanent record in the school. Commonly the information which is recorded on this permanent record is first recorded in other forms in the teacher's grade book, on standardized test forms, on report cards, on health record cards, or on check sheets, and then is transcribed by some teacher or clerk on to the form which is kept in the record files.

It is also customary to keep records of a more temporary nature. In this category may be the test scores on subject matter recorded in the teacher's roll book, the records of disciplinary action which may be kept in the principal's office, samples of student work, autobiographies, anecdotal comments, correspondence with parents, and summaries of conferences held with students or others about the student's work. With

2 N. P. Moyle, "Registers: A Protest," New York State Education 50:15 (June, 1963).

much of this material, the decision which has to be made is essentially whether or not to preserve for the use of other teachers or school personnel what would otherwise be available only to the collector. The filing system of the school office or of individual counselors should be arranged so that it can be conveniently consulted by other members of the staff.

Some of the information which is later used for making recommendations to employers or college personnel was first collected for other purposes in the cumulative record form. It is particularly important where such use is anticipated to get as complete a record of the total life of the student in school as it is convenient to preserve. Records of participation in extracurricular activities are important in this connection. Frequently the principal or assistant principal may have no other basis for filling in requested reference forms than that which is available in such records. The student may have graduated during a previous principal's administration or may have been one of several hundred with whom the principal himself had contact in any particular year. Even a picture of the student may be helpful.

Some of the records may be helpful in interpreting the school program to the public at large. Descriptions of the later success of students, figures on enrollment in particular curricula, figures on the holding power of the school, records of the standing of students on national examinations, special honors to faculty members or students, and information as to teacher load all tend to help improve the quality of the public support for the school. If an experimental program is undertaken, it becomes particularly important to have available figures which may be indicative of its success.

Which Records are Confidential? It is difficult to decide which records should be kept and also to whom they should be made available. Should all teachers have access to all of the records of a particular student? Should parents or students have access to the school records? How long should records of disciplinary action be kept in the file? These and similar questions are likely to have an important influence on the nature of the records kept. Basic to the keeping of any record is the question as to whom it is addressed. How will it be interpreted?

Generally the assumption must be made that the professional staff of a school, including the principal, the counselors, and the teachers, are sensitive to the importance of keeping confidential matters confidential. Furthermore, it is important to have as complete a picture of a student as possible if the program is to be adapated to provide for his developmental needs and interests. When records are to be kept confidentially and used in the interest of the individual student, it becomes feasible to get and keep some information which would otherwise not be available or of which it might be unwise to make a record.

For this reason it is important that most records be protected from careless disclosure. Those who need the records must have them where they can make full use of them and yet at the same time students must not be given an opportunity to pry. Too strict guardianship of the records defeats the purpose for which they are kept, and yet the confidential nature of material must be respected. Sometimes portions of the record which do not have to be protected may be duplicated for more easy access. New copying machines make much possible now that would formerly have been laborious. Sometimes central record facilities can be designed for more easy access by authorized personnel.

The amount of information which can be safely passed along to parents will depend on their level of training and attitudes, and on the nature of the information itself. In general, as much information should be given as will be helpful, while care must be taken to avoid possible misunderstanding. Student standing on standardized intelligence tests is a case in point. The significance of such test results is difficult for some teachers to recognize, and it is to be generally expected that parents will have similar difficulty. If such information is ever disseminated, care should be taken that its significance is explained at the same time.[3]

Records of student misbehavior, disciplinary action taken, teachers' opinions, and certain types of information on the health or family status of a student are important parts of the school record but are by their nature confidential. It is generally considered wise to keep at least the disciplinary record separate from the general permanent record and to provide for its systematic destruction after it has served its usefulness. There is no particularly good reason for keeping it after a student has graduated from a school, for its possible misuse is obvious. Even the courts recognize the importance of protecting the immature from the stigmas attached to youthful misbehavior.

Reports to Colleges and Employers. It has become customary for schools to recommend students to colleges and employers. This of course is a service both to the college or employer and to the student. The general practice is to make such reports only on the request of the student himself on the grounds that at least part of the recommendation process involves the confidential relationship between the student and the school. By its nature the report must be an honest one, and yet the possibility is that it will be damaging to the student's chance to do something he wishes to do.

The problem is complicated further by the desire of the college or employer to have the school keep some type of record which it has no other good reason for keeping. For example, some colleges request that the school furnish the rank of a student in his graduating class. To fail

---

[3] School board policy, and—in the case of one state (New York)—rulings at the state level, sometimes require that parents be informed of their children's scores.

to furnish this information may put the student in a bad light, but to try to furnish it may involve lengthy and unreliable calculation. Similarly the colleges may want the academic program of the student reported under traditional titles which no longer accurately describe the courses themselves.

Despite these problems, it is important from the standpoint of articulating the educational program to give the college as much basis as possible for understanding the academic and personal qualities of students. It is also in the interest of the student to see that he gets into the school in which he is likely to be most successful in furthering his educational development.

Employers are also likely to want help in determining which students may be desirable employees. Again, the general rule is that such information should be given only after a request from the student himself. Some of the vocational programs prepare students directly for employment and the school may receive calls for students who are available. The school may furnish a list of such students or may give a more detailed recommendation for some of them. The placement function of the school may sometimes seem in conflict with its responsibility for providing evaluative recommendations. Honesty is the best policy. It is desirable for the employer to know how strongly the school is willing to recommend a student. This protects the status of future recommendations and helps make certain that students are able to be successful in the jobs which they get.

The desirability of moving away from the notion that the diploma is a passport either to college or to vocational employment makes it essential for the school to furnish such information as it ethically can to colleges and employers. In this case recommendation is based on the particular job for which a student is applying and is not just a general statement of his excellence to do anything. Criticism of the school for the quality of its program will become less pronounced when the public understands the school's responsibility to provide as broad an educational opportunity as possible for as large a segment of the population as can appropriately take it.

Marking Systems

Naturally related to the problems of records is a discussion of school marking systems. The marking system is nothing more than the code by which some aspect of the student's work is made a matter of record. Marking is not, however, a simple matter. It is not always even clear either from the record or in the mind of the teacher as to exactly what it was the record was supposed to represent. The problem is complicated and even within a single school there is not likely to be agreement as to what a particular symbol in the marking system, such as an "A," means.

What is to Be Recorded? One of the basic problems in determining what a particular symbol should mean is how to decide whether the main concern is mastery of appropriate subject matter or relative achievement. It is generally conceded that there are no well-standardized bodies of subject matter which can be used as a scale for measuring accomplishment in high school courses. No two students have learned the same body of content. Once it is conceded that instruction should be based on the background, needs, and interests of students, it has been conceded that no two students should be expected to have learned the same thing. Not only does each student start from a different point, but each one finds different significance in what he is studying.[4]

On the other hand, if marks are supposed to represent the progress which a particular student has made from his own starting point, many complications are introduced into the system. It becomes necessary to know where each student was when he started, and there is no very adequate scale by which to measure his progress. It is not appropriate to compare the work of two students because each is different in some degree and in every respect from the other. It is equally difficult to determine any good basis for comparing the present status of a particular student with his own status at sometime in the past.[5]

While these difficulties are not easily resolved, it seems likely that marking systems of some type will be used for some time to come. It is desirable to recognize that they are likely to be invalid and that at best they are estimates rather than precise measurements. Because of the tendency to regard marks as rewards for work done, grades are sometimes lowered for unexcused absence, raised for extra work, lowered for lack of neatness, raised for originality, lowered for bad conduct, and raised for effort or good conduct. Studies have tended to show that men gave boys better grades and women gave girls better grades, that foreign students were likely to get lower grades than native-born students, and that there was likely to be a halo effect on the grades of students who were considered good students. Thus it may be difficult to say whether a particular grade represents achievement, effort, attendance, conduct, sex, place of birth, or previous reputation.[6]

It may be that if the grade is to be the basis for moving a student up to the next level of instruction it should mean something different

[4] C. D. Jarrett, "Marking and Reporting Practices in the American Secondary School," *Peabody Journal of Education* 41:36–48 (July, 1963).

[5] G. W. Walker, "Make Those Marks More Reliable and Valid," *School and Community* 50:12–13 (Jan., 1964).

[6] C. J. Finley "How Well Can Teachers Judge Pupil Achievement?" *California Journal of Educational Research* 17:126–32 (May, 1966).

from what it should mean if it is to report to parents the student's effort and attitude. For it to be used as a punishment for unexcused absence or misbehavior seems to the student unfair and dishonest and makes the grade become too important a part of the motivational pattern. Where the grade is used to represent many different things it loses its value as a description of any of them.

How Is It To Be Recorded? One of the old devices for marking involved the use of the percentage grading system. In this system the assumption was made that there was a known standard of work which could be called the 100 per cent level (or the base), and then the rest of the work of a class could be judged in relation to that level. It was even considered possible to designate some particular level, say 70 per cent, as the passing level. Each test or examination was then scored on a success-percentage basis.

Gradually, it became evident that there was no single standard which could be used as a base for determining percentage scores. Because students might appropriately learn different things in the same class, there was no way even of approximating such a basis. Furthermore, such a system presumed an accuracy of measurement which was unrealistic. Even in such apparently simple areas as mathematics, it was never clear whether points should be subtracted for simple errors in arithmetic when the method used was right, or whether the problems given were of equal difficulty and should be assigned equal weight in the total grade. It was apparent that differences of one grade point in many subjects were arbitrary and that differences of as much as ten or even 20 points were likely if two readers read the same papers.

With the gradual abandonment of the percentage system, the present system which depends on the use of numbers or letter symbols arranged on a scale came into use. In some cases, by assigning plus and minus symbols, the number of gradations may reach 13. Some students have pointed out that, while 13 symbols is certainly better than the 35 or more commonly used under the percentage grading system, it still represents a degree of accuracy that the techniques in use would not justify.

While there seems to be fairly general use of letter symbols as the basic marking system, the significance of the symbol is not uniformly clear. In some cases there is an attempt to define the meaning of the symbol by the use of such terms as excellent, very good, good, fair, satisfactory, and unsatisfactory. This attempt, of course, refines the meaning only slightly. In some cases the definitions used revert to the already discredited percentage system, and the letter grade is defined as the equivalent of some range of the percentage system. For instance the "A" may be defined as being between 90 and 100. Some report cards actually define the symbols both in terms of the words and the percentage designations.[7]

Scores on standardized tests are usually reported in terms of some standard score. One of the most important of these is the percentile rank. This differs entirely from the old percentage score in that the percentile rank enables direct comparison of the performance of the student with other students in the same population. Thus a student who ranks at the seventieth percentile ranked as well or better than 70 per cent of the students with whom he was compared. Other scores may indicate the grade placement of students on particular content or sometimes their mental age.

What About the Normal Curve? Recognition that the marking system could better be used for comparing the work of one student with another's than with any particular arbitrary standard led some people to suggest the employing what is referred to as "the normal curve." It had been observed that most human traits which were measured on a continuous scale seemed to be distributed in large unselected populations according to a mathematical formula. By making certain assumptions, it was possible to assign marks to each score which was obtained on a particular test. Since the normal curve was symmetrical it was convenient to define the grading system as "symmetrical." Where the grading system A, B, C, D, F was used, the same number of A's would be assigned as F's and the same number of B's as D's. In some systems the actual percentage of student scores to be expected in each group was arbitrarily specified.

There are several weaknesses in this system. In the first place, one of the assumptions on which the system is based calls for the existence of a large group. The typical class group of 30 students is considered too small. In the second place, the assumption is made that the population is unselected with regard to the particular trait being measured. This assumption is probably false in any group at the high school level. Students who would appear at the bottom of the scale have been retarded or dropped from school. The assumption that there is merit in balancing the A's with the F's is also probably invalid. Failure is likely to be defined as indicating the need for a student to repeat the course. It does not seem justified to decide that a student needs to repeat a course simply on the basis that he falls within a certain percentage of a group. Repetition should be based instead on evidence that a student might profit from repeating.

A more defensible approach retains the idea of defining the upper portion of the grade system in terms of expected percentages of successful students, but sets up some criteria for defining the significance of lower

[7] *See* Ann Z. Smith and John E. Dobbins, "Marks and Marking Systems," *Encyclopedia of Educational Research*, 3rd ed. (New York: The Macmillan Company, 1960), pp. 783–88.

portions of the scale. In such a system it might be stated that, over a long period of time, a certain percentage of students enrolled in a particular required course would be expected to receive an "A". It would be recognized that for any particular class such a definition would not be valid, but the teacher assigning the mark would judge the work of particular students not only against the small group to which they were assigned, but also against a larger group which he has had previously or which he expects to have. His judgment is to be based on an imaginary standard which he has set for the achievement of the group, but it is to be checked periodically against the actual proportion of students which he may have had over a longer period of time.

The assumption is still being made that the teacher is competent to rank the students in order and that what is needed is a basis for determining the mark to be assigned to each level. This assumption is a questionable one, but if there is to be a marking system it must be made. The criteria to be set for determining whether a particular student will fail or pass might be based on some other assessment than the simple rank of the student in the group. One of the important considerations is whether the student will benefit from repeating the course, or from suffering whatever other penalty is associated with failure, as much as he would benefit from not failing. (Most of the studies of trial promotion have indicated that students were as likely to benefit from not being retained in a course after receiving a failing mark as they were from being retained.)

In schools which define an "appropriate" distribution of grades, some elective courses might expect to have a much larger proportion of A's and B's than some others. Physics and Chemistry may be elected almost entirely by students in the upper percentiles. It seems important that within a particular school particular grades have approximately the same significance from one teacher to the next within the same course and probably also from one course to another.[8]

Reports to Parents

One of the complications in the marking system arises from the tendency to send home to parents the mark which might more appropriately have been reserved for the school files. The parent should be more concerned with how well the student is measuring up in terms of his own abilities than with a comparison of his work with that of other students. It is the school which must teach students in groups and therefore may justifiably

[8] Cf. James B. Conant, The American High School Today (New York: McGraw-Hill Book Company, 1959).

compare them with one another. Recognition of the need for better means of communicating with parents has led to several approaches at both the elementary and secondary school levels.[9]

Why Report to Parents? It is not easy to determine how much contact the school and the parents should have with one another. Since the school is in a sense a secondary educational agency and the home has the primary responsibility, there must be some effort on the part of the school to cooperate with the home. This cooperation is complicated, however, by the fact that, as adolescents, high school students are beginning to wish to assume responsibility for their own lives. They tend to regard any attempt of the parent to contact the school or of the school to contact the parent as unnecessary interference in the relationship of the student with each. This desire for independence of action is a necessary part of the process of maturing.[10]

Additional problems arise from parental misunderstandings of the nature of reports and of appropriate action to be taken. Some parents are known to have unreasonably high standards for their children and consequently put unreasonable pressure on these children to succeed. It is sometimes found that there is rivalry among a particular group of parents concerning grades and social skills. Such a competition, while not always injurious to the children involved, is at least irrelevant to the work of the school.[11]

A third problem has to do with the time and effort necessary to making the report. In some schools it seems that the reporting process has become more important than teaching itself. Tremendous amounts of teacher time are spent in the construction of tests, in recording marks, in exchanging marks with the teachers responsible for making out the report, and finally in copying them on the various forms. Frequent reporting calls for frequent testing, and these tests may be designed, not for their appropriateness as teaching devices, but only as devices to assist in the ranking. Student attention is diverted from the learning process to the process of receiving a mark. Many of the important outcomes of instruction which cannot be easily tested become subordinated to less important outcomes which can be more objectively measured.[12]

Perhaps the major problem in reporting to parents is to be found just at the point where the report is most likely to misrepresent vital parts of

[9] C. D. Jarrett, "Marking and Reporting Practices in the American Secondary School," *Peabody Journal of Education* 41:36–48 (July, 1963).

[10] E. F. DeRoche, "My Parents, My Teacher, and Me," *The NEA Journal* 52: 16–17 (Dec., 1963).

[11] S. P. Williamson, "Good, Average or Poor," *Kentucky School Journal* 42:42–43 (Jan., 1964).

[12] T. L. Hawk and L. M. DeRidder, "Comparison of the Performance of Pre-Graded Students with Grade Motivated Students," *Journal of Educational Research* 56:548–50 (July, 1963).

the school program. The mastery of factual information is much less important than the development of concepts and modifications in behavior which cannot be accurately measured or recorded. An emphasis on test scores not only diverts the teacher's attention from his primary responsibility, but may also mean that the school fails to give the parent any real basis for understanding what is supposed to be happening to the child. The school is failing to tell the parent what he needs to know to be a partner with the school in the education of his child.[13]

Still another problem in the reporting process is that it is likely to be a one-way process. The school reports to the parent, but there is very little encouragement to the parent to report to the school. There is no good opportunity for an exchange of information between the parent and the school. Thus the teacher is deprived of a chance to discover how what the school may be teaching is carried into the home.

What Kind of a Report? When it has been agreed that the report should reveal more than the quantity of factual information mastered, as measured on objective tests, it has to be decided what additional information should be given. The simplest addition is an extra grade on effort or attitude. In this way the school attempts to indicate whether the student is doing as well as should be expected or whether his attitude toward his work seems to be wholesome.

In some cases a check list of important character traits or school objectives is provided, and students are rated on these as well as on strictly academic work. This system seems to have the advantage of indicating to parents that the program of the school has broader concerns than those reported academically. The disadvantage is that sometimes teachers have not had any particular occasion to observe some of the traits listed, or they may be at a loss as to how to use the check list in rating them. Some schools try to have all of the teachers working with a particular student give a composite rating of the traits listed. This is easier in the smaller school than in the larger ones.[14]

In some cases teachers are asked to write descriptive comments on the report card or to write letters to the parents at the time the reports are sent. This personalized approach has the advantage of facilitating the discussion of particular strengths and weaknesses which would not be easily reported on a standard form. It also may stimulate the development of a correspondence between the home and the school which will help in the creation of mutual understanding. The principal problem is in the volume of letters which would have to be written if the teacher tried to contact all of the 150 or more homes of children in his classes. In addition,

[13] G. H. Farwell and others, "Pressures Behind the Grade," *The Clearing House* 38:462–66 (April, 1964).

[14] N. M. Chansky, "Elementary School Teachers Rate Report Cards," *Journal of Educational Research* 56:523–28 (July, 1963).

teachers who have had little contact with particular children may have difficulty in making meaningful assessments of the kind necessary.

Some schools have made elaborate efforts to substitute parent conferences for the less satisfactory report card system.[15] In this way the teacher is able to interpret the meaning of the report to the parent and to adapt its nature to the apparent ability of the parent to understand. Furthermore the parent himself is able to discuss the problems of the child from his own point of view. The report becomes appropriately a two-way conference. The trouble with this approach is that it is so time-consuming if all the parents are to talk with all their children's teachers. On the other hand if they are not to talk with all of them, then the opportunity for an exchange of ideas will be materially reduced. A second problem is to be found in the reticence of some of the parents, particularly of those from the lower social and economic groups. They may even hesitate to come to school.

Any system of reporting which fails to meet with the approval of the parents involved is likely to fail to achieve its purpose. It is therefore important that representative parents be included in the process of approving major modifications of the reporting system. It is also important that teachers and other members of the professional staff have an understanding of what the changes are designed to accomplish. Progress from a simple statement of the comparative achievement of students toward the regular parent conference has been most satisfactory in those schools which were willing to move patiently from one level to the next with the full concurrence of those who were concerned.

How Often Should a Report Be Made? As has been indicated, the frequency of reporting is sometimes so great as to interfere with the teaching process itself. Furthermore, the nature and completeness of the report-filling is affected by how often it must be made. It is much easier to do a complete job if sufficient time is available to do it at a leisurely pace. Some schools, which depend on letters and parent conferences, try to stagger the reports for different students in such a way that only a few of them are due on any one day. Regular periods are provided in the school schedule for such conferences, and parents are encouraged to make appointments at times when there will be ample opportunity to give full consideration to any problem which may be noted.

Certain types of reports and conferences may need to be emergency reports. Particular situations may require special attention. This might be true for instance when a student has been sick, is in a particular difficulty, or for some other reason seems to need coordinated help from the school and his home. When students have made unusual progress or have done particularly well in some extracurricular activity, it may be well to send

[15] W. H. Graves, "Parent Conferences Pay Off," *Texas Outlook* 47:16–17 (June, 1963).

a particular report to the homes noting this accomplishment. There is too great a tendency for all of the reports which the school sends at irregular times to be of a negative character.[16]

Some secondary schools find monthly and six-weeks report periods of the usual type much too frequent and have gone to a system of reporting less often. In some cases the full report is a semester report and reports over shorter intervals deal with special aspects of the program which it seems important to emphasize. Thus the citizenship and attitude reports might be made every six weeks and the formal academic reports might be made only at the end of the semester. Such a system helps to relieve the pressure on the learning of mere factual information and to stress other outcomes which the school may feel to be more important.

Where schools change the frequency of the reporting period, care is usually taken to encourage parents to come for conferences with teachers at more frequent intervals if such conferences seem desirable. In some cases teachers will, on request, send additional estimates concerning the student at more frequent intervals. The intention in decreasing the frequency of the report is to increase its accuracy, not to decrease the amount of contact with the parent.

What About Home Visitation? It is obvious that where a teacher has as many as 150 different pupils it is virtually impossible for him to visit each one's home. He may, however, be able to visit those in his homeroom or perhaps those whom he feels in need of understanding better.

The same problems mentioned earlier concerning the reluctance of adolescents to have home and school get together will enter the picture in the decision as to when it is wise to have home visits. Both parents and children from some of the poorer social and economic levels may be embarrassed to have teachers visit the home. The children feel awkward because they recognize their home conditions are of a lower standard than those of the teacher himself. Where the objection on the part of either the child or his parent is strong, it is doubtful if much is to be accomplished by a home visit.

On the other hand it is important for the teacher and other school personnel to have a chance to know the child in his home setting. The program of the school can then be seen in better perspective. It is also important for parents to realize that school officials are interested in the welfare of the children.[17]

School systems which have found home visits most profitable have generally suggested the advisability of making the first visit early enough in the school year for it to be obvious that is was essentially a call for

---

[16] V. C. Wooden and M. E. Gardner, "Are Failure Notices Effective?" *The Clearing House* 38:399–400 (March, 1964).

[17] William G. Kornegay, "Another Look at Home Visiting," *The High School Journal* 40:166–68 (Jan., 1957).

the purpose of getting acquainted and not designed to report on misbehavior or to discuss unpleasant problems.

Some teachers and school officials will be more successful in making
home visits than others. The personality and general tone of the relationship of the teacher with the community will have a great deal of effect in
determining the way in which he is likely to be received. Care in timing
the visit is important. Some teachers prefer to send a notice to a parent
to ask if it is convenient to call or to make an appointment on the telephone. Where there is provision for regular parent conferences at the
school, the necessity for home visits is reduced, although there is still
some advantage in being able to observe the nature of the home setting
itself.

Diplomas

One of the most formal and sought-after records which the school provides
is the high school diploma. The matter of graduation requirements has
been discussed in detail in Chapters 6 and 7. The more specific problem
here is the adequacy of the diploma as a record.

The increased responsibility of the secondary school for all of the
students of secondary age has made it seem unwise to restrict the diploma
to those students who are planning to continue in college. On the other
hand, there is a tendency on the part of some critics of the secondary
school to assume that when the diploma becomes available to any student
in attendance at the school, the standards have been lowered. Their criticism may be easily countered by reminding them that the school is not
concerned with maintaining any uniform standard, but rather with meeting the needs of individual students. It is doubtful if the anticipation of
the diploma ever induced many students to work more effectively.[18]

As was pointed out above, prospective colleges or employers can ask
for a detailed recommendation from school officials, and it is better if
they do not try to rely on diplomas or marks alone. The chief advantage
in specifying a particular quantity of work to be completed before the
diploma is awarded is to make it appear essential for students to stay in
school. Sometimes, it seems desirable for some students to complete their
contact with the public school earlier than the usual four years. At other
times, the educational program of the school is sufficiently rich in opportunity to justify encouraging students to remain in school for more than
the prescribed time. When the diploma is to be awarded would seem

---

[18] L. V. Stahlicker, "High School Graduation for Slow-Learners," *Peabody Journal
of Education* 42:166–72 (Nov., 1964).

much less important than whether the school had been able to provide the education which the student seemed to need.

Schools wishing to maintain some of the selectivity of the old style diploma have awarded different kinds of diplomas to different students, based on the courses which they have pursued. Thus there might be a college preparatory diploma, a commercial diploma, and a general diploma. The distinction being made in this way seems somewhat foreign to the purpose of the comprehensive high school. Indeed, differences are not as great as the titles indicate.[19]

It has been suggested in some circles that it might be well to have on the back of the diploma or on a separate card the transcript of the record of a student.[20] While this approach would be more accurate than designations of diploma types, it would still seem an incomplete record of the student's high school program. It would have no place for a record as to what he had gained from his participation in the out-of-class activities of the school. Furthermore, the transcript is now available from the school when the student has any real need to ask for it. Most school records are protected from fire or other destruction. Indeed few colleges will now accept transcripts which are presented by the student himself. The official transcript must be sent by the principal along with his recommendation form.

[19] Cf. J. R. Eales, "Programs Completed by 1963 Graduates from California Public High Schools," California Education 1:31 (Nov., 1963).
[20] Cf. E. E. Lohman, "High School Diploma Is Not Enough," Ohio Schools 41:20–21 (Nov., 1963).

15

Restructuring Teaching:
Selected Readings

EXPANSION OF THE ROLE OF THE PUBLIC HIGH SCHOOL, COUPLED WITH RECOGnition of the existence of a technological revolution, has led to the question of how to make teaching more efficient. Paradoxically, the need to individualize instruction has become greater at a time when mass production seems ever more vital. Several alternatives to traditional teaching procedures are being considered. Discussion has wandered from systems analysis to programmed learning, computer-assisted instruction, team teaching, independent study and various combinations, logical and illogical.

The New Technology

Some of the writing on educational innovations has sounded more like Buck Rogers than serious proposals for real schools. Recent experience with the fact that the science fiction of one generation turns out to be prophetic of the everyday experience of the next cautions against discounting altogether even the wildest-sounding proposals.

Attempts to exploit modern technology in the improvement of teaching in the twentieth century have included the use of motion pictures and various recording devices. More recent additions have included emphasis on programmed and computer-assisted instruction. Programmed materials do not necessarily have to be used with a machine, but most teaching machines use some sort of programmed sequence of organized teaching materials. Similarly, it is quite feasible to find various uses for the computer, but perhaps the most fascinating involves its use as a teaching device. Together these innovations offer possibilities for freeing the teacher of certain routines of instruction and giving him more time to devote to the rest of his responsibilities. There does not yet seem to be any likelihood of being able to dispense with the teacher altogether.

Some see the computer as a sensible and efficient machine to use in programmed learning, a machine that is capable of being used for intensive individual instruction. Others see it as a potential threat, something that will dehumanize the educational process. Others see it as a means of useful, rapid, and efficient record keeping and storage. In the following selection, Gerald Gleason, Director of Research, School of Education, University of Wisconsin, Milwaukee, relates the potential and the problems of computer-assisted instruction.

Computer Assisted Instruction:
Prospects and Problems*

Gerald T. Gleason

Computer assisted instruction (CAI) for several years only a vague, ill-defined and non-demonstrable dream in the minds of computer specialists, engineers, and technologists, has emerged during the past year as a specific, demonstrable and potentially powerful instructional tool.

Educators, at all levels from pre-school through university and including industrial and vocational trainers, have indicated growing interest in the possibilities of computer controlled presentation of instructional materials.

We appear to be approaching significant breakthroughs in CAI hardware and software. Consequently, we face the necessity of intelligent decision-making regarding possible applications and implications. The purpose of this article is to describe the "state of the art" in CAI and to suggest some crucial issues and problems which must be widely and openly discussed by many individuals and groups within and related to the educational endeavor.

WHAT IS IT?

In this developmental stage, CAI defies precise definition. In its simplest form, a computer-connected typewriter can provide drill materials

* *Educational Technology* VII:1–8 (November 15, 1967). Reprinted by permission of the publisher and author.

to students in subject areas such as arithmetic and spelling. The materials can be carefully and logically sequenced and can be presented to the student on the basis of his past performance in a manner that insures continuous feedback. Appropriate branching sequences are designed to accommodate a variety of individual differences.

In its most sophisticated form, material in virtually any subject area can be presented to the student using a variety of presentation modes (e.g., printed, audio, visual, graphic). A variety of response modes are available (e.g., written, typed, response selection, audio, light pen). Feedback techniques which permit student control of the learning strategy and sequencing of materials, and make possible an almost unlimited analysis of student performance and program effectiveness can be incorporated. A wide variety of hardware and software is currently in use in a number of institutions throughout the country.

CAI is based upon some of the same theoretical foundations as programed instruction. In fact, many persons, now active in the field, cite their own personal experiences with programed instruction (PI) as the basis of their current interest in CAI. In its early stages of development, PI included the following essential characteristics:

1. Precise statements of instructional objectives in behavioral terms.
2. Presenting material in a carefully and logically sequenced order leading to criterion performance.
3. Providing for continuous and active student involvement—overt, if possible.
4. Providing continuous feedback on student performance.
5. Providing continuous reinforcement—usually in the form of success.
6. Permitting the student to proceed at his chosen rate of speed.

The implementation of this approach occurred in significant works in the late 1950's and early 1960's. To most careful observers, PI, even in its most primitive forms, has demonstrated the capability of helping students "learn" a variety of skills, concepts, principles, generalizations, and attitudes. Admittedly, PI is a long way from universal acceptance but the overwhelming generalization from the research evidence is that PI can be an effective and efficient instructional technique.

PI TO CAI

Interestingly, however, it was the shortcomings of "conventional" PI which stimulated interest in CAI. Most of the early teaching machines were quickly discarded in favor of the programed textbook for economic as well as logistical reasons. Most machines simply were not capable of implementing the principles of PI due to the inherent restrictions of the machines themselves (i.e., the long delay between response selection and confirmation).

Unfortunately, from this writer's perspective, the programed textbook imposed even further restrictions from a theoretical point of view by virtually precluding the use of audio and visual presentation and response modes. The programed textbook publishers, admittedly in a profit-conscious, high-risk field, seemed to forget the old adage "A picture is worth a thousand words." Few programed textbooks have even a scattering of pictures, maps, charts, or graphs. Most rely solely on the printed word.

With these restrictions even the best programed textbook materials could not really implement all of the "basic" principles of PI. For example, linear programing assumes that the devised sequence of frames is *the* appropriate sequence for all students. While some programers have attempted to incorporate branching sequences in linear programs, these have been largely ineffective due to the limitations of the presentation device, either "hard" or "soft."

As early as 1960 some writers began to look to the computer as an aid in overcoming the inherent shortcomings of the simple teaching machine or the programed textbook. Computer based programed instruction added these capabilities:

1. Sequencing of frames as a function of student performance. For example, on the basis of his response on a specific criterion frame, and/or his history of performance on related criterion frames, a student can be, a) given additional remedial or practice material, b) continued in the linear sequence, c) branched ahead to more challenging material.
2. The student is given truly "immediate" response confirmation or correction. The most sophisticated CAI systems provide feedback in less than a second and some strive for a millisecond time lapse. This has significant implications from a theoretical as well as a practical point of view.
3. The most highly developed CAI systems utilize a wide variety of presentation modes, including audio, slides, motion pictures and graphics.
4. These systems also provide for a wide variety of student response modes ranging from simple selection ("Strike the 'A' key") to typing and light pen selection or sketching. Voice-recognition techniques which will enable the computer to respond to spoken commands of the student will almost certainly be available within the next several years.
5. CAI can provide a much broader range of reinforcement techniques than is available in PI and will also enable the programer to utilize the demonstrated power of several reinforcement schedules in sustaining attention and performance level.
6. A computer-assisted machine enables the student to proceed at a pace that is appropriate to his interest and ability. However, there may be some restrictions based on the capacity of the particular computer in use and the number of student terminals.

Thus, CAI would seem to provide the opportunity to expand the demonstrated effectiveness of PI by overcoming some of the restrictions imposed by the simple machine or the programed textbook.

The growing body of research evidence on CAI strongly indicates that the technique can be effective and efficient in assisting students to learn specified skills and concepts. In addition, most students express generally positive reactions to the technique. Much more research is needed, however, before widespread implementation can be justified. Hopefully this research will not fall into the trap of comparing CAI with "conventional" instruction but will assess the effectiveness of CAI in helping students attain specified behavioral objectives.

WHAT IS GOING ON TODAY?

As with most significant developments, concurrent activity is under way at a number of installations in the United States. The author has recently visited many of these sites. Several of the more dramatic developments are:

1. In the Computer-Assisted Instruction Laboratory at the Brentwood School in East Palo Alto, California, Suppes, Atkinson and others are developing reading and mathematics materials at the primary school level. Children from a broad socioeconomic range have been involved in the developmental activities. In an excellent example of cooperation between university scholars and public school educators, this project, even with its preliminary and partial data, has demonstrated that young children can readily adapt to a highly mechanized instructional approach. Significantly these investigators have found that the multi-media capability of the system requires a comprehensive and time-consuming curricular analysis of the content field.

2. The Plato IV system at the University of Illinois has evolved from the earlier "Socrates" and "Plato I-III" systems. In the Computer Based Education Research Laboratory developmental work is under way in a variety of content fields. Potentially the most significant research is aimed at developing a plasma display device which will be more economically feasible than the cathode-ray tubes used on most available systems. The University of Illinois plans to have several hundred student terminals available for research and instruction during the coming year.

3. In a recently announced project, elementary school students in 15 New York City schools will be using an RCA Spectra 70/45 system for drill and remedial work in arithmetic and spelling. Supported by a grant from USOE, this project plans to assess the reactions of disadvantaged children to CAI as well as to provide a large scale field test for one of the major systems under development.

4. The Philadelphia public schools will be testing the new Philco CAI system this fall.

5. In the Oak Leaf School in Pittsburgh, the Research and Development Center at the University of Pittsburgh is experimenting with individually prescribed instruction (IPI) which relies upon the computer for continuous analysis of student performance and progress through a series of carefully sequenced lessons. While this use is not actually CAI, the project is demonstrating some of the contributions of computers to individualizing instruction.

6. Science Research Associates (SRA) have established a CAI Laboratory in Chicago to demonstrate the IBM 1500 system. The Laboratory is used as a testing site for materials being prepared by SRA for the 1500 system under a working agreement with IBM. Major attention is being given to courses designed for use at the high school or early college levels in mathematics, science and social science. These programs will use a newly developed programing language called APL (A Programing Language) which has the capability of allowing the student to use the computer to solve a variety of problems incorporated into the materials. Thus, problem solving skills can be developed and utilized in conjunction with other lower-order learning tasks. The working arrangement between SRA and IBM is especially significant since it recognizes the critical relationship between hardware and software. IBM plans to lease 1500 systems to some 40 institutions of higher education for research and development purposes, with installation beginning this Fall.

These developments are representative of many other similar activities currently under way throughout the country. In addition, some experimental work is in progress in Europe and a recent report of a conference in the Soviet Union indicated plans for extensive research in CAI.

SYSTEMS AVAILABLE

In contrast to the teaching machine movement, the extremely high costs of developing CAI systems have restricted the activity to a relatively small group of large corporations with the necessary capital support for research and developmental work. IBM, RCA, Philco and Westinghouse all have systems in various stages of development. A few smaller companies also report some activities.

Fortunately, all of these companies appear to be resisting the "get rich quick" attitude which characterizes so many new developments. Most companies emphasize the tentative and research nature of their systems and are not currently offering them to prospective buyers. We can anticipate, however, increasing pressure on these companies to mass-produce a viable and reliable system for the vast educational market. We can only hope that these pressures will not cause premature closure on any system which does not realize the full potentiality of CAI.

PROBLEMS AND ISSUES

In the face of these rather encouraging developmental activities, a number of problems require continuing attention.

1. The seemingly impossible cost of CAI causes many educators to despair of any widespread implementation. At this stage, such despair may be justified. For example, the lease charges for an IBM 1500 system with 16 student terminals are in excess of $7,000 per month. This does not include personnel costs to operate the system

or the costs of developing software for the system. Even assuming 100% utilization of each student station, the per pupil per hour cost would probably exceed $7–$8 over a period of time, which is far greater than "conventional" instruction costs.

Education, however, is rapidly being forced to do a more precise cost-benefit analysis of its operation. What are the real costs of having a trained professional teacher using his time performing menial and time-consuming tasks which the computer can do far more efficiently and possibly more effectively? What are the real costs resulting from our lack of precise knowledge of a student's level of performance and instructional needs? Perhaps the costs of CAI should be weighed against the true costs of an inefficient and ineffective system for some students and some teachers.

Another aspect is worthy of note with regard to costs. The decision to undertake long-range and very expensive developmental work in CAI has been made by some of our largest and most successful business enterprises. It is highly probable that these decisions have been made only after a systematic analysis of the potential marketability of such systems. Each of these companies has said, in effect, "We believe that CAI is an economically feasible product." It remains to be seen whether these companies can convince the public of their judgment.

2. Another problem might be called the hardware-software interface. The multi-media capability of CAI presents a challenge to producers of programs that has probably never been faced before. What is the optimal "mix" of a software package? How much audio and what kinds, at what speeds? Are still pictures as effective as motion pictures? What types of overt responses facilitate what kinds of learning for which students? The capability of CAI to provide answers to these questions presents a tremendous challenge to researchers and practitioners. The old cliche, "It's not the machine that counts but the program that is in the machine," may have to be modified to something like, "It is the machine that really challenges the programer to make full use of its capabilities."

3. The costs of software production virtually preclude local school activity without substantial investments for production facilities. Professional teachers can learn to write CAI programs but they will need extended support facilities to produce really effective packages of materials. In all probability, the major hardware producers will be required to make substantial investments for related software production. The best that educators can do is to insist on the rigorous research and field testing standards that were so woefully lacking in the teaching machine era.

4. The perennial dilemma of curricular decision-making may raise the issue of centralized control of education at the state or even federal level. Concerned educators and laymen must prevent this, not by outlawing computers, but by vigilant surveillance and insistence on involvement in the decision-making process. We now have such involvement; we can only lose it by refusing to carry out our responsibilities as professionals and citizens.

5. Some persons see an increasing "dehumanization" of the educational process, and may suggest steps to cease all developmental work on CAI. The vision of a student isolated in a learning carrel, being manipulated by the flashing lights of a computer, may be reminiscent

of the Skinner box or Orwell's 1984. This may be a very real problem which defies solution in advance. Perhaps one day we will look back at the 1960's and say, "We should have destroyed all computers." But we cannot see that far into the future. The best we can do is to jealously guard and retain those values which are important to us. However, we cannot, and must not do this by refusing to consider, examine, try and evaluate new devices and methods which may help us achieve more effective and efficient educational programs.

SUMMARY

Computer-assisted instruction, based upon the same theoretical foundations as programed instruction, appears to be on the verge of a major breakthrough in hardware, software and implementation. A number of CAI systems are currently in operation throughout the United States. Preliminary evidence suggests a capability of providing effective and efficient instruction in a variety of content fields. Major problems appear to be in cost, program development, curriculum decision-making and potential dehumanization of the educational process.

One of the most exciting technical developments in secondary and higher education is the development of the information retrieval system. The potential for use of such an aid is perhaps exceeded only by that of the motion picture projector (and in time the potential of the projector will be incorporated). Ted Johnson, Library Project Director at the Oak Park and River Forest High School, Illinois, describes in this article the system being put into effect at the school.

An Information Retrieval System
of the Future*

Ted Johnson

In discussing the topic, "An Information Retrieval System of the Future," I must confess my concern about the perspective from which we examine the subject.

Retrieval systems are a part of today's new-wave spectrum. They can be exciting, even to the point of intoxication. Some observers are so enamored of such systems they would have us believe we are about to eliminate all the drudgery elements of teaching.

Pursuing this perspective far enough, it is easy to imagine the classroom of the future as being equipped with an overstuffed tilt-back twirl-around chair and a computer control panel for the teacher with each student safely stored in a womb-like study carrel. In such an educational system perhaps the prime qualifications of a good teacher would be a physique appropriate to such a chair and the capacity to push the right button at the critical moment of the attention span.

Of course, there are also those who, with only moderately controlled disgust, view retrieval systems as one more example of over-rated gadgetry which appeals to the racoon impulse of many teachers and administrators. At the same time, there are a few individuals who cry out in desperation that our technology is reducing teaching from an exalted art form to the level of a technician's job.

Hopefully, there is a perspective which involves less distortion. Without going all the way back to Gutenberg, we can contend that the audio-visual "revolution" is by now a mature one. In fact, we probably improve our accuracy when we call the changes evolutionary.

In a very spotty fashion I have tried to illustrate the perspective with the records of my own school.

In gathering materials for the preparation of a publication which will mark the centennial of the Oak Park and River Forest High School, I uncovered some 1903 photographs and a 1909 course of study book. Describing equipment used in the history department, this book reports the "Stereopticon run by electricity, (is) always ready." One of the photos prepared for a 1903 visual display supports this fact. Further, the course of study notes that "lantern projection" was used in Elementary Science and that the lantern used in Zoology was "supplied with a microscopic attachment, (and) also a vertical attachment for the study of live material." Other photos substantiate some of these facts. I wonder if the reactions to electric current were noticeably different from those mentioned earlier.

Skipping two generations, in 1965 the Knapp Foundation selected three secondary schools across the nation as demonstration centers for its School Library Project. As a part of its participation in this grant, the Oak Park and River Forest High School created a new system of resource centers in its library program. Math-science and foreign language resource centers were created while a long-established American history resource center was improved.

Such centers add much flexibility to a library program. A variety of audio-visual equipment and instructional materials can be made available

* The North Central Association Quarterly 41:309–315 (Spring, 1967). This paper was presented at the annual meeting of the North Central Association, April 5, 1967. Reprinted by permission of publisher and author.

to students on an individual basis. Librarians who are also subject matter specialists can be utilized in centers specifically adapted to the respective disciplines of these librarians. Faculty members can be given an opportunity to participate more directly in the program of the library and to more effectively employ the services of the library with their students in small groups or through individualized instruction. The library can become more than one large, quiet study area for reading and reference.

The retrieval system which we are now developing is still in its gestation period. In another five months it will be retrieving on site. I would like to recommend a perspective which includes the stereopticon of 1903, the resource centers of 1965, and the retrieval system of tomorrow. It has been a long time since electricity and audio-visual equipment began providing additional opportunities for the improvement of instruction. The work of 1965 owes much to the accomplishments of 1903. At the same time, the work of 1965 has made significant changes. Of even greater importance, the work of 1965 has suggested new avenues to be explored for the future. An information retrieval system is central to the pursuit of these suggestions.

A COOPERATIVE PROJECT . . . TO IMPROVE LEARNING

As you will recall, Title III of the Elementary and Secondary Education Act of 1965 was enacted to encourage innovations and to demonstrate exemplary programs of innovations in educational practice. On the basis of a study conducted by its faculty in the winter and spring of 1966, the Oak Park and River Forest High School made application for financial assistance under this act. A total of $1,500,000 was requested to assist in the development of a library-located instructional resource center which would be capable of electronically storing vast amounts of information and making that information instantly retrievable for individual or group instruction.

The project bears the title "A Cooperative Project Among Teachers, Schools, and Industry for Continued Development of Means to Improve Learning." While it does at first glance seem to be concerned primarily with machinery, its intention and justification are the development of additional methods and devices with which to assist the essentially human tasks of teaching and learning.

The Oak Park proposal grew out of two facts of concern to all schools. In the first instance, we are confronted by an information explosion, a problem being compounded so rapidly that at least one observer estimates we are approaching the time when our publications will weigh more than the planet on which they are being published. There is more significant information available to our school libraries than can be effectively utilized in instruction through existing procedures. The physical problems alone are prohibitive. New methods of storage and use must be perfected.

In the second instance, the possibilities of truly individualized instruction are finally being realized on a large scale. The many proposals for flexible scheduling, the new independent study programs, and the revolution in school libraries are but a few examples of the expanding activities on behalf of student programs designed one at a time.

RANDOM ACCESS RETRIEVAL SYSTEM

In response to the two concerns of the information explosion and individualized instruction, the Oak Park and River Forest High School faculty concluded that a *random access* retrieval system would be an innovation which would have a significant impact on both problems at the same time. In support of this conclusion, the United States Office of Education awarded a sum of $1,486,200 in an operational grant intended to cover the period of November 1, 1966, through October 31, 1969.

This grant will finance a major part of the research and development necessary for the creation of such a retrieval system. Local and private funds in excess of $1,000,000 are now at work with the federal funds, and private industry is financing related research programs. A minimum of three years will be required to reach the intended goal, though in the most basic sense it is not realistic to speak of the project actually drawing to a close.

STAGE ONE: ELECTRONIC EQUIPMENT

The first stage (1967) of the project is scheduled to be in operation by September. At that time a random access audio retrieval system will begin operation. This part of the projected system is now being engineered by the Ampex Corporation on the basis of a design created by their research staff last spring.

This audio random access retrieval system will consist of a master storage bank, a program control center, and twenty-five student carrels or stations. From his carrel the student will select the item in the storage bank he desires or to which he has been assigned, and within thirty seconds he will be able to begin listening to that program. To this point the system may sound simply mechanical and not at all unusual. Any language lab is an audio retrieval system.

Similar retrieval systems are now in use in schools and colleges in many parts of the nation. Millions of dollars of public and private funds are currently being spent to extend such retrieval systems. However, these systems all lack *random access*. On the basis of a rather exhaustive study, it is clear that no school or college is now able to provide random access to the material subject to retrieval.

Retrieval systems now in operation are all handicapped by a basic lack of flexibility. This deficiency can be seen in the fact that retrieval systems available today must employ scheduled programming or have any one program taken out of circulation by a request from just one student. If assistance in math is offered at 10 A.M., but the student is in class until 11, he misses the scheduled program. Or if one student requests a thirty-minute German lesson at 1 P.M., no other student will be able to start that lesson until 1:30.

The retrieval system I am describing will eliminate such problems through the remarkable innovation of random access. Because this system will enjoy this facility, each student will be able to select the program he needs at any time. Regardless of how many students are selecting programs, regardless of which program each student chooses, and regardless of how many programs are available in the storage bank, each student addressing the system will be able to start his individual lesson in less than one minute.

The random access will be made possible by a combination of recording devices. The storage bank will contain several multiple-track master tapes on which individual fifteen-minute lessons or programs will have been recorded. Each student carrel will be equipped with a high-speed recording device which will be able to copy any one fifteen-minute program in the storage bank, make the copy available to the student, and free the master tape for another student within thirty seconds. The master tapes, the carrel control panels, and the high-speed recording devices will be directed by a custom-tailored general-purpose computer.

The first stage system will include a storage bank capacity of 224 fifteen-minute programs and 25 student carrels, but the random access capacity makes possible an expansion to a literally unlimited number of programs and carrels in the future. That is to say, random access will make available the flexibility in use and storage capacity required to cope with the fundamental problems identified above.

BEYOND STAGE ONE

The second and third stages of the project are necessarily less well defined. No random access audio retrieval system currently exists, but the devices to make it possible do. Thus, Ampex is pioneering with the Oak Park and River Forest High School through its creative engineering of the necessary existing components. The devices and techniques for the second and third stages of the project do not now all exist.

The project is a research and development one; it does have an aura of blue sky dreaming about it. So much so, in fact, that last spring a few of America's giant corporations listened to the proposal with condescension and veiled snickers.

Ampex and some other leading corporations responded differently. With enthusiasm, confidence, and dollars, they have committed themselves to the necessary research. Dealing with the Ampex engineering and design staff has proven to be a particularly exciting experience. The command of ESEA Title III is to accomplish innovation. Random access to audio material will meet this command. Progress in the direction of random access to video programs will also be a significant response to this command.

In the second stage (1968) an expansion of the capacity of the storage bank and the addition of 150 more carrels are planned. These steps are certain. The introduction of a video storage and random access capacity and the addition of a video screen to the student's carrel to take full advantage of the resources of the library are also planned for this stage.

Video random access of still material is now possible on a device called a video file. This device can store and provide random access to 500,000 single still pictures of objects or printed pages. No motion is currently possible in true random access, however, because our technology has not advanced to the point of high-speed reproduction of motion pictures or video tape materials. A video random access capacity truly useful for education must include motion and color. Such a capacity is a part of the goal for the third stage of the project.

The third stage (1969) will involve continued development of the audio and video facilities. It will also include the addition of audio and video retrieval in each of 200 classrooms and other group-instruction stations in the high school.

This facility will enable the individual teacher to employ the audio and video materials of the library within his classroom as a part of his basic instruction. By simply selecting the correct number, the English teacher will be able to present our Mr. Radford reading "The Congo," Lawrence Olivier performing Hamlet, or T. S. Eliot reading his own poetry; the history teacher will be able to present F.D.R.'s first inaugural address, or a collection of slides on pre-Columbian architecture; the homeroom teacher will be able to show guidance material such as college counseling programs. These are but a few examples of the types of valuable material which can be made more readily available, or in some instances made available for the first time, for classroom use through a developed random access retrieval system.

The classroom retrieval unit will free the teacher from any number of mechanical problems which currently drain teacher energy. The teacher will not need to handle the machinery, but more importantly, the class will not have to leave the classroom to join other classes in a central viewing area. Regardless of how many class groups are watching a particular program, each teacher will be in command of the presentation as it is made to his own class. Familiar tools and supporting materials will be at hand. Eventually the teacher will be able to select any one part, or several parts of a film, television, or slide show to serve the requirements of his class.

In this third stage, preparation will be made to transmit or broadcast the resources of the retrieval system to the other schools and colleges, public and private, in at least the villages of Oak Park and River Forest. Representatives of the Oak Park Elementary Schools, the River Forest Public Schools, Fenwick High School, a Catholic school for boys in Oak Park, Trinity High School, a Catholic school for girls in River Forest, and the several Lutheran and Catholic elementary schools in the two villages participated in our retrieval-system study and will continue to work with us in the development of the system. Concordia Teachers College and Rosary College, both in River Forest, have indicated a desire to be associated with the project when a proper role can be defined.

A large-scale inter-library program may well be the logical extension of the retrieval center. Whether our broadcasting will be done by closed circuit, micro-wave, or U.H.F. channel is at this point unknown. Whatever method is selected, it will be possible for all these schools to draw upon the resources of the Oak Park and River Forest High School library without in any way limiting the high school program because of the flexibility and unlimited capacity which random access makes possible.

INSTRUCTIONAL MATERIALS

Of course, the key to the significance of this slightly spectacular hardware will be the instructional materials, the software, available in the storage bank. As defined by the faculty, this library-located retrieval system will be utilized to supplement and enrich classroom instruction. This retrieval system will not be a programmed instruction center.

The goals defined by the classroom teacher will be served by the electronic facilities of this resource center. Consider, as an example, the mathematics teacher who is demonstrating the solution of a quadratic equation by completing the square. Two of his students are absent; four students have considerable difficulty and do not grasp the concept as rapidly as others; five students readily understand the procedure. The five advanced students can be referred to a lesson in the retrieval system demonstrating another method of solving a quadratic equation. The four students who are having difficulty can be directed to a review lesson in the storage bank. This tape can include several sample problems and can be used in conjunction with work sheets. The two students who are absent can be sent later to the retrieval center for a make-up lesson before they ask the teacher for after-school time.

Each teacher will be able to utilize these same services in his own subject area. The history teacher will be able to make available to his students a wide selection of specialized topic presentations either for individual or class assignments. Recordings of the actual sounds of history, including the voices of leading personalities both past and present, and interpretive commentary by prominent historians can be readily available to the individual student.

For the English teacher, the retrieval system can be used to provide additional emphasis, explanation, and reinforcement on selected points of grammar. With a near maximum of convenience, his students can listen to recorded readings of poetry, prose, or drama. The speech teacher will be able to take advantage of this same function. Because the students will be able to record responses on a separate tape track while listening to a program track, speech skill exercises will also be possible. Through the same function, much of the work of the foreign language laboratory can be handled by the retrieval system.

While the first stage of the retrieval system will include random access to audio presentations only, visual materials can be co-ordinated with the taped lessons. Thus, the art department will gain a means by which to widen student access to pertinent subject matter through joint tape and photographic slide programs. So too, foreign language instruction based on tape-slide tours of foreign countries can be expanded. Work sheets, slides, and loop films are only some of the visuals which can be used in conjunction with the audio programs.

The retrieval system will also make it possible to supplement classroom instruction by improving the use of class time. Mr. Geisert, a biology teacher, has already tested one sample of this benefit. In his biology classes, Mr. Geisert requires of each student a research project. Most of the projects require data and statistical procedures in order to arrive at any conclusion. Through the use of an audio and visual lesson already tested in the math-science resource center, Mr. Geisert has been able to remove his instruction on elemental statistical procedures from the classroom and gain time for an additional topic in the laboratory.

Members of the faculty will also gain opportunities to share and utilize each other's special talents. The English and history teachers will be better able to draw the work of the art and music teachers into their respective courses of study. The humanities classes will have the necessary range of talent on tap. Material on the Chicago school of architecture prepared by the architectural drawing teacher will be readily available to history students.

PROJECT GOALS

These examples are but a few of the software possibilities, but they do illustrate certain key features of the retrieval system and its rationale. Improvements in the methods of teaching and learning are the ends sought. Enrichment and supplement materials will be employed. Dramatically increased flexibility of access to instructional materials will be achieved. Opportunities for individualized instruction and independent study will be expanded. A number of mechanical problems which currently plague teachers will be eliminated. The materials of the library and the activities of the classroom will be combined much more thoroughly for both teachers and students than has been true or possible in the past.

Initially, virtually all the software will of necessity be prepared by the high school staff. During the present semester several teachers are teaching reduced class loads so they can prepare instructional materials for the system. In our next summer session approximately twenty teachers will be working on these materials. When it is appropriate to do so, we are adapting existing materials to the uses of the retrieval system, but the bulk of the software is originating with members of the faculty. Once the most desirable methods and the effectiveness of the center have been demonstrated, we anticipate that commercial firms will enter this particular market. To this end we have established preliminary contact with some of the likely firms. All that is required to bring them into this production field is evidence of a market.

Even after mass producers enter the field, we will still be in the production business, of course. The unique needs of any one school can not be precisely met in all cases by general presentations. At the same time, schools similar to ours would probably be able to effectively employ some of our own materials. In fact, some schools have already requested access to the instructional materials we prepare. Such should be a result of this nationally subsidized project, and on a limited-quantity basis we will be equipped to supply such requests at cost to the consumer. The production of copies, I assume, will be limited to audio and video taped programs. I do not envision our entering into the reproduction of motion pictures or records.

Finally, this retrieval system project is part of a larger process which is having a significant impact on the relationship between industry and the common school. I have already referred to the different attitudes of major electronics firms to our initial proposals. It has not been easy for industry to recognize that funds have been made available for research under the direct command of elementary and secondary school people. Manufacturers have had some difficulty in shifting gears from supplying products to creating products for these schools. At least one of our largest electronics and communications producers is still deliberately committed to a policy of pioneering nothing but manufacturing everything for schools.

Let us hope that the necessary communication can be achieved and that the required expertise will be brought to bear on the problem by both industry and the schools. We are all too familiar with the great rush into the federally created market by both parties. The idle sophisticated equipment and the hurriedly, but ill-adapted machinery thrust into schools are mute testimony to the chaos and waste which result when funds, sales-manship, and eagerness precede a careful study of function and purpose. It would seem that a corner has been turned away from this unfortunate scene, however. Major segments of American business are showing or developing an understanding of school problems equal to their financial and technological power. If the worldly wisdom of school men operates at the same level, the future should be orderly and productive.

The retrieval system project which I have tried to describe here will supplement all aspects of the school program. The project is being con-structed on the foundation of a continually evolving school program, comprehensive library services, and substantial community support. In a program of studies of more than 300 course offerings, selected innovations and experiments are tested. Over 1,000 students a day voluntarily use the main library for reading and reference work, while an additional 350 use the math-science, foreign language, and American history resource centers by individual choice. In a November 1965 referendum the community approved a $9,000,000 building program which includes the physical facili-ties required for the retrieval system.

WANTED: EFFECTIVE UTILIZATION

Inherent in this project to develop a random access retrieval system are many exciting possibilities. Yet it must be remembered that the elec-tronic devices on which the project rests will only be tools in the hands of teachers and students. These tools will not make trivial material signifi-cant. They will not make poor teaching good. They will not convert the contrary, dull, or listless student into a co-operative, perceptive, or inspired paragon of academic virtue. They will not make these resources for learn-ing any different tomorrow than they were yesterday or 3,000 years ago. But these tools can serve the cause in which every good teacher struggles. They can serve the most effective utilization possible of the knowledge and understanding acquired in the past on behalf of a more civilized future.

A second rather fascinating area for speculation about possible solutions to learning problems deals with research into the chemical processes in the brain. Possibilities for further development range from the somewhat fantastic idea of a learning pill and memory drugs to the more apparently plausible and important understanding of brain injury and disease. David Krech, Professor of Psychology,

University of California at Berkeley, discusses some experiments and trends in this area.

The Chemistry of Learning*

David Krech

American educators now talk a great deal about the innovative hardware of education, about computer-assisted instruction, 8 mm cartridge-loading projectors, microtransparencies, and other devices. In the not too distant future they may well be talking about enzyme-assisted instruction, protein memory consolidators, antibiotic memory repellers, and the chemistry of the brain. Although the psychologists' learning theories derived from the study of maze-running rats or target-pecking pigeons have failed to provide insights into the education of children, it is unlikely that what is now being discovered by the psychologist, chemist, and neuro-physiologist about rat-brain chemistry can deviate widely from what we will eventually discover about the chemistry of the human brain.

Most adults who are not senile can repeat a series of seven numbers— 8, 4, 8, 8, 3, 9, 9—immediately after the series is read. If, however, they are asked to repeat these numbers thirty minutes later, most will fail. In the first instance, we are dealing with the immediate memory span; in the second, with long-term memory. These basic behavioral observations lie behind what is called the two-stage memory storage process theory.

According to a common variant of these notions, immediately after every learning trial—indeed, after every experience—a short-lived electro-chemical process is established in the brain. This process, so goes the assumption, is the physiological mechanism which carries the short-term memory. Within a few seconds or minutes, however, this process decays and disappears; but before doing so, if all systems are go, the short-term electrochemical process triggers a second series of events in the brain. This second process is chemical in nature and involves, primarily, the production of new proteins and the induction of higher enzymatic activity levels in the brain cells. This progress is more enduring and serves as the physiological substrate of our long-term memory.

* *Saturday Review*, Jan. 20, 1968, pp. 48–50+. Copyright Saturday Review, Inc., 1967. Reprinted by permission of publisher and author. The article is adapted from a speech to Seminars on Innovation sponsored by the U.S. Office of Education and the Charles F. Kettering Foundation in Honolulu, July, 1967.

It would follow that one approach to testing our theory would be to provide a subject with some experience or other, then interrupt the short-term electrochemical process immediately—before it has had an opportunity to establish the long-term process. If this were done, our subject should never develop a long-term memory for that experience.

At the Albert Einstein Medical School in New York, Dr. Murray Jarvik has devised a "step-down" procedure based on the fact that when a rat is placed on a small platform a few inches above the floor, the rat will step down onto the floor within a few seconds. The rat will do this consistently, day after day. Suppose that on one day the floor is electrified, and stepping onto it produces a painful shock. When the rat is afterward put back on the platform—even twenty-four hours later—it will not budge from the platform but will remain there until the experimenter gets tired and calls the experiment quits. The rat has thus demonstrated that he has a long-term memory for that painful experience.

If we now take another rat, but this time *interfere* with his short-term memory process *immediately after* he has stepped onto the electrified floor, the rat should show no evidence of having experienced a shock when tested the next day, since we have not given his short-term electrochemical memory process an opportunity to initiate the long-term protein-enzymatic process. To interrupt the short-term process, Jarvik passes a mild electric current across the brain of the animal. The current is not strong enough to cause irreparable harm to the brain cells, but it does result in a very high level of activation of the neurons in the brain, thus disrupting the short-term electrochemical memory process. If this treatment follows closely enough after the animal's first experience with the foot shock, and we test the rat a day later, the rat acts as if there were no memory for yesterday's event; the rat jauntily and promptly steps down from the platform with no apparent expectation of shock.

When a long time-interval is interposed between the first foot shock and the electric-current (through the brain) treatment, the rat *does* remember the foot shock, and it remains on the platform when tested the next day. This, again, is what we should have expected from our theory. The short-term electrochemical process has now had time to set up the long-term chemical memory process before it was disrupted.

Some well known effects of accidental human head injury seem to parallel these findings. Injuries which produce a temporary loss of consciousness (but no permanent damage to brain tissue) can cause the patient to experience a "gap" in his memory for the events just preceding the accident. This retrograde amnesia can be understood on the assumption that the events immediately prior to the accident were still being carried by the short-term memory processes at the time of the injury, and their disruption by the injury was sufficient to prevent the induction of the long-term processes. The patient asks "Where am I?" not only because he does not recognize the hospital, but also because he cannot remember how he became injured.

Work conducted by Dr. Bernard Agranoff at the University of Michigan Medical School supports the hypothesis that the synthesis of new brain proteins is crucial for the establishment of the long-term memory process. He argues that if we could prevent the formation of new proteins in the brain, then—although the short-term electrochemical memory process is not interfered with—the long-term memory process could never become established.

Much of Agranoff's work has been done with goldfish. The fish is placed in one end of a small rectangular tank, which is divided into two halves by a barrier which extends from the bottom to just below the surface of the water. When a light is turned on, the fish must swim across the barrier into the other side of the tank within twenty seconds— otherwise he receives an electric shock. This training is continued for several trials until the animal learns to swim quickly to the other side when the light is turned on. Most goldfish learn this shock-avoidance task quite easily and remember it for many days. Immediately before— and in some experiments, immediately after—training, Agranoff injects the antibiotic puromycin into the goldfish's brain. (Puromycin is a protein inhibitor and prevents the formation of new proteins in the brain's neurons.) After injection, Agranoff finds that the goldfish are not impaired in their acquisition of the shock-avoidance task, but, when tested a day or so later, they show almost no retention for the task.

These results mean that the short-term memory process (which helps the animal remember from one trial to the next and thus permits him to learn in the first place) is not dependent upon the formation of new proteins, but that the long-term process (which helps the animal re-member from one day to the next and thus permits him to retain what he had learned) is dependent upon the production of new proteins. Again, as in the instance of Jarvik's rats, if the puromycin injection comes more than an hour after learning, it has no effect on later memory—the long-term memory process presumably has already been established and the inhibition of protein synthesis can now no longer affect memory. In this antibiotic, therefore, we have our first chemical memory erasure—or, more accurately, a chemical long-term memory preventative. (Almost identical findings have been reported by other workers in other laboratories working with such animals as mice and rats, which are far removed from the goldfish.)

Thus far I have been talking about disrupting or preventing the formation of memory. Now we will accentuate the positive. Dr. James L. McGaugh of the University of California at Riverside has argued that injections of central nervous system stimulants such as strychnine, picrotoxin, or metrazol should enhance, fortify, or extend the activity of the short-term electrochemical memory processes and thus increase probability that they will be successful in initiating long-term memory processes. From this it follows that the injection of CNS stimulants immediately before or after training should improve learning performance. That is precisely what McGaugh found—together with several additional results which have important implications for our concerns today.

In one of McGaugh's most revealing experiments, eight groups of mice from two different hereditary backgrounds were given the problem of learning a simple maze. Immediately after completing their learning trials, four groups from each strain were injected with a different dosage of metrazol—from none to five, 10, and 20 milligrams per kilogram of body weight. First, it was apparent that there are hereditary differences in learning ability—a relatively bright strain and a relatively dull one. Secondly, by properly dosing the animals with metrazol, the learning performance increased appreciably. Under the optimal dosage, the metrazol animals showed about a 40 per cent improvement in learning ability over their untreated brothers. The improvement under metrazol was so great, in fact, that the dull animals, when treated with 10 milligrams, did slightly better than their untreated but hereditary superior colleagues.

In metrazol we not only have a chemical facilitator of learning, but one which acts as the "Great Equalizer" among hereditarily different groups. As the dosage was increased for the dull mice from none to five to 10 milligrams their performance improved. Beyond the 10-milligram point for the dull mice, however, and beyond the five-milligram point for the bright mice, increased strength of the metrazol solution resulted in a deterioration in learning. We can draw two morals from this last finding. First, the optimal dosage of chemical learning facilitators will vary greatly with the individual taking the drug. (There is, in other words, an interaction between heredity and drugs); second, there is a limit to the intellectual power of even a hopped-up Southern Californian Super Mouse!

We already have available a fairly extensive class of drugs which can facilitate learning and memory in animals. A closer examination of McGaugh's results and the work of others, however, also suggests that these drugs do not work in a monolithic manner on something called "learning" or "memory." In some instances, the drugs seem to act on "attentiveness"; in some, on the ability to vary one's attacks on a problem; in some, on persistence; in some, on immediate memory; in some, on long-term memory. Different drugs work differentially for different strains, different intellectual tasks, and different learning components.

Do all of these results mean that we will soon be able to substitute a pharmacopoeia of drugs for our various school-enrichment and innovative educational programs, and that most educators will soon be technologically unemployed—or will have to retool and turn in their schoolmaster's gown for a pharmacist's jacket? The answer is no—as our Berkeley experiments on the influence of education and training on brain anatomy and chemistry suggest. This research is the work of four—Dr. E. L. Bennett, biochemist; Dr. Marian Diamond, anatomist; Dr. M. R. Rosenzweig, psychologist; and myself—together, of course, with the help of graduate students, technicians, and, above all, government money.

Our work, started some fifteen years ago, was guided by the same general theory which has guided more recent work, but our research strategy and tactics were quite different. Instead of interfering physiologically or chemically with the animal to determine the effects of such intervention upon memory storage (as did Jarvik, Agranoff, and McGaugh), we had taken the obverse question and, working with only normal animals, sought to determine the *effects* of memory storage on the chemistry and anatomy of the brain.

Our argument was this: If the establishment of long-term memory processes involves increased activity of brain enzymes, then animals which have been required to do a great deal of learning and remembering should end up with brains enzymatically different from those of animals which have not been so challenged by environment. This should be especially true for the enzymes involved in trans-synaptic neural activity. Further, since such neural activity would make demands on brain-cell action and metabolism, one might also expect to find various morphological differences between the brains of rats brought up in psychologically stimulating and psychologically pallid environments.

I described briefly one of our standard experiments. At weaning age, one rat from each of a dozen pairs of male twins is chosen by lot to be placed in an educationally active and innovative environment, while its twin brother is placed in as unstimulating an environment as we can contrive. All twelve educationally enriched rats live together in one large, wire-mesh cage in a well lighted, noisy, and busy laboratory. The cage is equipped with ladders, running wheels, and other "creative" rat toys. For thirty minutes each day, the rates are taken out of their cages and allowed to explore new territory. As the rats grow older they are given various learning tasks to master, for which they are rewarded with bits of sugar. This stimulating educational and training program is continued for eighty days.

While these animals are enjoying their rich intellectual environment, each impoverished animal lives out his life in solitary confinement, in a small cage situated in a dimly lit and quiet room. He is rarely handled by his keeper and never invited to explore new environments, to solve problems, or join in games with other rats. Both groups of rats, however, have unlimited access to the same standard food throughout the experiment. At the age of 105 days, the rats are sacrificed, their brains dissected out and analyzed morphologically and chemically.

This standard experiment, repeated dozens of times, indicates that as the fortunate rat lives out his life in the educationally enriched condition, the bulk of his cortex expands and grows deeper and heavier than that of his culturally deprived brother. Part of this increase in cortical mass is accounted for by an increase in the number of glia cells (specialized brain cells which play vital functions in the nutrition of the neurons and, perhaps, also in laying down permanent memory traces); part of it by an increase in the size of the neuronal cell bodies and their nuclei; and part by an increase in the diameters of the blood vessels supplying the cortex. Our postulated chemical changes also occur. The enriched brain shows more acetylocholinesterase (the enzyme involved in the trans-synaptic conduction of neural impulses) and cholinesterase (the enzyme found primarily in the glia cells).

Finally, in another series of experiments we have demonstrated that these structural and chemical changes are the signs of a "good" brain. That is, we have shown that either through early rat-type Head Start programs or through selective breeding programs, we can increase the weight and density of the rat's cortex and its acetylocholinesterase and cholinesterase activity levels. And when we do—by either method—we have created superior problem-solving animals.

What does all of this mean? It means that the effects of the psychological and educational environment are not restricted to something called the "mental" realm. Permitting the young rat to grow up in an educationally and experientially inadequate and unstimulating environment creates an animal with a relatively deteriorated brain—a brain with a thin and light cortex, lowered blood supply, diminished enzymatic activities, smaller neuronal cell bodies, and fewer glia cells. A lack of adequate educational fare for the young animal—no matter how large the food supply or how good the family—and a lack of adequate psychological enrichment results in palpable, measurable, deteriorative changes in the brain's chemistry and anatomy.

Returning to McGaugh's results, we find that whether, and to what extent, this or that drug will improve the animal's learning ability will depend, of course, on what the drug does to the rat's brain chemistry. And what it does to the rat's brain chemistry will depend upon the status of the chemistry in the brain to begin with. And what the status of the brain's chemistry is to begin with reflects the rat's early psychological and educational environment. Whether, and to what extent, this or that drug will improve the animal's attention, or memory, or learning ability, therefore, will depend upon the animal's past experiences. I am not talking about interaction between "mental" factors on the one hand and "chemical" compounds on the other. I am talking, rather, about interactions between chemical factors introduced into the brain by the biochemist's injection or pills, and chemical factors induced in the brain by the educator's stimulating or impoverishing environment. The biochemist's work can be only half effective without the educator's help.

What kind of educational environment can best develop the brain chemically and morphologically? What kind of stimulation makes for an enriched environment? What educational experiences can potentiate the effects of the biochemist's drugs? We don't know. The biochemist doesn't know. It is at this point that I see a whole new area of collaboration in basic research between the educator, the psychologist, and the neuro-biochemist—essentially, a research program which combines the Agranoff and McGaugh techniques with our Berkeley approach. Given the start that has already been made in the animal laboratory, an intensive program of research—with animals and with children—which seeks to spell out the interrelations between chemical and educational influences on brain and memory can pay off handsomely. This need not wait for the future. We know enough now to get started.

Both the biochemist and the teacher of the future will combine their skills and insights for the educational and intellectual development of the child. Tommy needs a bit more of an immediate memory stimulator; Jack could do with a chemical attention-span stretcher; Rachel needs an anticholinesterase to slow down her mental processes; Joan, some puro-mycin—she remembers too many details, and gets lost.

To be sure, all our data thus far come from the brains of goldfish and rodents. But is anyone so certain that the chemistry of the brain of a rat (which, after all, is a fairly complex mammal) is so different from that of the brain of a human being that he dare neglect this challenge—or even gamble—when the stakes are so high?

Emphasis on Individualization

J. Lloyd Trump, an official of the National Association of Secondary School Principals, has been quite influential in suggesting the importance of change in the secondary schools of the country. The "Trump Plan" (detailed in 1959 in a widely-circulated NASSP pamphlet titled Images of the Future) *was a proposal for reorganizing the use of teacher and student time through the employment of teacher aides and through more attention to the possibilities for independent study on the part of the students themselves. The key concern was greater flexibility.*

The following article is something of a distillation of his thought

on the key ingredients in the instructional program of a good second-
ary school. He argues for a change in the teachers' mode of presenta-
tion, more emphasis on student discussion, and modification of the
process of evaluation of student achievement. It is hard to disagree
with the outline which he presents, even though many other
competent observers of the secondary scene are inclined to disagree
on some of the specifics of his other proposals for the secondary
school.

Secondary Education Tomorrow:
Four Imperatives for Improvement*

J. Lloyd Trump

When we think about secondary education tomorrow, if we *are* genuinely
interested in improving the quality of teaching and learning, it seems to
me there are a number of changes that are imperative. Here I suggest
four changes in what teachers and pupils do regardless of whether a
school is relatively conventional or if such innovations as team teaching,
television, resource centers, varied size pupils groups, flexible schedules,
or nongraded programs are in operation. Most of the proposals may be
put into practice immediately in any school. So I hope what I say will be
useful to you even in the *near* future, which is later this week or next week.

The first of the four imperatives is to change the nature of teacher
presentations. I refer to what teachers say while conducting class. Teachers
at the present time, in conventional classrooms with 25-35 students, spend
almost half of the time talking *to* the students. Whether this talking is
done by one physically-present teacher in a regular classroom with 25-35
students, or by one of a team of teachers, or by means of television, film,
or recording, there are actually only *three* activities that are appropriate.

The first of these three is to motivate. A teacher needs to present
topics with such commitment and intrigue that the pupils will want to
learn more. Although motivation is one of the most frequently researched
and discussed topics, it is full of mistaken ideas. For example, back in the
20's motivation was encouraged by letting students do what they wanted to
do. This proposal which goes under the topic of "Progressive Education"

* *NASSP Bulletin* 50:87–95 (April, 1966). Reprinted by permission of the National Association of Secondary School Principals. Copyright 1967 by the NASSP.

was discounted and is not being followed. The substitute is also a blind alley. It is called "teacher-pupil planning." The teacher uses a variety of ruses to get the students to do what the teacher already has determined he wants them to do. Present research goes beyond these concepts to consider the effects of praise, a smile, a pat on the back, or extrinsic rewards—another series of ruses to make the pupil feel good about what he is supposed to do anyway.

The trouble with much of the research about motivation is that it is done with isolated segments of the whole teaching-learning process rather than to recognize the totality of it. Motivation is actually a very complex matter. It involves a number of things. For instance, is requires removing the causes of frustration or boredom. Many students in conventional classes of 25-35 are frustrated because what the teacher and other students say is over their heads. They do not understand and they hesitate to ask questions. Or for other students, they are bored because the teacher is telling them things they already know. We need to remove the causes of these factors. Also, we need to provide better guidance for students through the learning process by means of immediate reinforcement, telling them whether or not they have learned, or through programs of continuous progress that make it unnecessary for a student to sit there until the rest of the students catch up.

Motivation is effected also by whether or not appropriate materials are available immediately for the student to get his hands on, and whether he has adequate time to do it when he becomes interested in the subject. Probably even more important in motivation is the provision of exciting and intriguing teaching. This need, of course, is one of the important arguments for team teaching. But even in regular classrooms, the teachers need to spend time in selecting that part of the subject which will intrigue the students most. Or he uses a superior film or recording to help him provide motivation. In other words, when the teacher talks to students, he always asks himself the questions, "Will what I say actually motivate the students? Will my enthusiasm rub off on them? Will it result in a real desire to learn more about the topic? Is there somebody or something that can do it better than I?"

The second appropriate activity when a teacher talks is to provide information *not readily available* to students elsewhere. Conversely, this means to refrain from telling too much, thus taking the edge off the topic or making it less necessary for pupils to study. Teachers talk so much that some students get enough out of the teacher's presentation that they feel they can get by without doing homework.

The teacher's goal is *not* to cover the subject, but rather to get the students to do so. I could give you many illustrations of this. Not too long ago I was observing a lesson. This one happened to be by television in a relatively large group, but television could have been used in a conventional classroom. Moreover, what the television teacher was talking about is analogous to what teachers often do in conventional classrooms. In this particular lesson the teacher was talking about the New Deal in the 30's. I assume his purpose was to get the students to read about the New Deal in their textbooks. For 27 minutes he talked to them about the NRA, the CCC, the NYA, various procedures used to control production and distribution of goods, and to provide employment and programs for youth. He talked about the president at the time, Franklin D. Roosevelt, who of course is ancient history to most of these students now. The only thing you saw during the 27 minutes, incidentally, was the teacher's face, except for a brief presentation of an art drawing of the NRA eagle.

If the teacher's purpose is to get the students to read about the New Deal, think how much better it would have been for the teacher to have talked about the Great Society, today; to have shown some pictures, films, or recordings of President Johnson, the Economic Opportunity Program, the Job Corps Camps, etc., and talked to students about why these things are being started. Near the end of the lesson the teacher could point out that we have done many of these things before. We have some recordings. Or you can read in your textbooks about the NRA, the CCC, and the NYA. My point is that the teacher should provide information not readily available—the Great Society is not included in their textbooks.

Teachers have to avoid either telling too much or telling too little. Both are wrong. On the other side of telling too little we must remember that students do not have to discover everything—even though we are on sort of a discovery binge these days. There are some things that students should be told in order to avoid a lot of wasted time and frustration. The teacher can put ideas on tape so the students can listen to the tapes if they wish. They can assemble a lot of other material. But the teacher needs to tell them *how* to get at it.

The third thing a teacher does while talking is to assign. They make an assignment so carefully that students of diverse talents and interest in the subject know precisely what they have to learn—what knowledge, what skills, what attitudes are considered *essential* for anyone to know and what are *desirable* or *enriching* for more talented or more interested pupils. Teachers need to do this assigning in such a way that all students find something to do, so they are stimulated in most instances to go beyond the minimum either in depth or creativity. Research is clear on this point. Students who fail, or make poorer grades than they are capable of making, or who drop out, complain that they do not understand the assignments; they do not know what the teacher expected them to do. The teachers, on the other hand, quickly respond that the students did not listen. As the old cliché goes, "If the learner has not learned, then the teacher has not taught." This is appropriate with respect to assignments. Teachers need to develop *guidesheets* that describe precisely what the students are supposed to know, and the *worksheets* that direct them into a variety of activities to learn what to read, what to listen to, and what to view. You can do these things in a regular class or you can do it in the setting of team teaching.

I would like to emphasize that these teacher presentations to motivate, to provide information not readily available elsewhere, and to assign should occupy no more than 40 per cent, and preferably less, of the class time per week. The pupils need class time for other activities.

The second of the four imperatives is to change the character of independent study. I mean by independent study what students do after the teacher has finished talking. There is as much independence from teacher supervision as possible as students develop responsibility for their own learning. The quality of teacher presentations, particularly the assignments, directly affects the quality of pupil study and learning.

In addition to the assignments, we need to provide spaces in every classroom where students can work with a variety of materials, covering wide ranges of difficulty as they think, read, view, listen, write, discuss, make, experiment, and discover. The library and other work rooms can supplement the classrooms. But the classroom itself must provide places for independent study. Independent study is done individually, although at times it occurs in small groups. Some of it is required, some is selected, some is routine, some is imaginative. But I remind you that the goal always is to reduce teacher supervision, in order to develop more pupil responsibility.

Some schools, of course, provide a greater variety of separate resource centers, libraries, laboratories, workshops, remedial areas, and conference rooms for independent study activities to complement large group instruction and small group discussion areas. Regardless of the setting, teachers can improve what they do with respect to the character of independent study.

Let me give you an illustration from one of the schools involved in the NASSP Internship Project for Secondary-School Administrators. One of our interns last year, in trying to find an area in his school where he could work most effectively, found that one of the problems was with what the English teachers called their "terminal" students. These are students who had failed English a number of times. They had not dropped out of school—unfortunately in some respects for the English teachers. They were still there, causing discipline problems. Their attendance was poor; they were learning very little. The intern went to his university, talked with his professors, and then came back with a solution to their problem. He asked the teachers if they were willing for a while to stop teaching so much and give the students more time to learn. Since they were more than willing to try anything reasonable, they left the chairs in this conventional classroom (with one teacher and about 30 students) but along one wall collected a wide variety of reading materials. They bought some paperbacks and in addition, asked these students and others in the school to bring materials from home—magazines, newspapers, catalogues, a breakfast food box (everyone has something). They had a wide variety of materials in varying levels of reading difficulty.

On another wall they had two tape recorders. The students could listen to tapes with earphones; some, teachers had prepared and others were bought commercially. On a third wall, they placed a filmstrip projector. The closets around the school provided some old filmstrips, the kind with pictures and reading materials on them. They had quite a collection of these. On the fourth wall, the window wall, in cardboard boxes arranged alphabetically so the students could find them easily, were various exercises—on capitalization, sentence structure, spelling, and many others. Any student could go and pick out an exercise—on a single sheet usually—do it, and then go back and get the answer sheet and find out immediately how well he had done. This is a kind of immediate reinforcement, or programed learning approach. When the students came into the room, they could go to any one of the four areas, and if they got tired after 10 minutes or so, they could go to another.

I was a visitor for two hours in the classroom. At the beginning of the second period, the teacher got a telephone call and was 10 minutes late. No one missed her. The students were now working. Discipline problems were fewer and attendance was better; reading scores improved and so did writing. The teachers in this conventional classroom gave the students time to do the necessary independent study and provided them with materials to do it.

I could give you many other illustrations. For instance if you want students to read more, then you have the English teachers hold fewer class periods per week so that the students have time to read, either in the classroom or in the library. You can quadruple the amount of pupil reading that way.

An important aspect of independent study is that all pupils are able to spend at least 40 per cent, and preferably more, of their class time in a variety of activities. The time requirement is true whether the work is done in a conventional classroom or in a school with a variety of specially equipped learning resources centers.

The third imperative is to provide for student discussion. Students need to learn how orally to express ideas effectively, to listen to the ideas of others, and to identify areas of disagreement and consensus—and to respect each other in the process. These skills have to be taught and they have to be practiced. I am sorry to say, as you know very well, that these skills are not practiced in today's classrooms. What is called classroom discussion is little more than an oral quiz conducted by the teacher.

The point is that students need training in the skills of oral communication. They need small groups to do it properly. A teacher with a conventional class of 30 or 35 students can divide the class into three subgroups. Certainly there must not be more than 15 in any one group and 12 is probably better. Then the students have to be trained for various roles—to be discussion leader, discussion recorder, observer, and for the various kinds of member roles.

The teacher has to learn new roles, too. Teachers do not conduct oral quizzes or lectures during these discussion sessions. Once again the purpose of this discussion is not to cover the subject, not to rehash teacher presentations, and not to report on all that occurs in independent study. The emphasis is on good discussions and improved interpersonal relations. Unless the pupils are taught *how* to discuss and unless the teacher helps them by making observations about what was right or what was wrong with the discussion itself, students will not improve their discussion techniques.

Students need about 20 per cent, or perhaps a little less, of the class time per week in every subject field for these discussion activities. We emphasize *every subject field,* because students need to learn how to talk about health and how to talk about mathematics, as well as in the more common fields of social science and English language arts.

The fourth imperative is to change the process of evaluation. I want to suggest very dogmatically three present practices that need to be abandoned immediately. The first practice to eliminate are the oral quizzes, which erroneously are called classroom discussion. This oral quiz, or recitation, is an ineffective way for teachers to discover what students know and for students to show what they know or do not know. Moreover, these oral quizzes or recitations waste a significant amount of pupil time. While one student answers, the rest of the class is passive. Their time could be spent better in independent study. The teacher's time could be spent in preparing better presentations or improving evaluation.

The second practice to be abandoned is the use of multi-purpose letter grades. That is, the A, B, C, D, or F, or whatever equivalent you use that combine such unrelated matters as achievement, attitude, personality, obedience, attendance, or whatever else the teacher wants to include. It is a terrible thing, for instance, to allow attendance to influence this multi-purpose grade. However, as long as only one grade is given, the teacher tries to combine all of them into a single grade which, of course, provides inaccurate information to pupils, parents, colleges, and employers.

The third practice to abandon is emphasis on the comparison of individual pupils in groups. Included are such activities as grading on a curve and preparing class ranks. These comparisons give some pupils and their parents a false sense of security. That is, they think they know more than they do because the competition in that particular group is not very challenging. Such comparisons also give other students constant frustration, as they are compared to other people and always come out at the bottom of the totem pole.

A first step in replacing these three practices is to identify and to describe the goals that teachers seek for pupils. One of these goals is to grow in knowledge or skills. Then teachers need to prepare written tests or exercises. Programed materials can be used to reveal to students and to the teachers how each individual pupil is growing in the knowledge or the skills that he is supposed to have. Standardized tests provide base line data.

If the teacher needs to check on growth in discussion skills, this is easy to do. The teacher sitting in as the observer and critic keeps a tally of how often the students participate in the discussion and the quality of what they say. For example, if one of the students is Margaret, the teacher discovers by keeping tally, that during this six weeks' grading period Margaret has talked 17 times. Incidentally, that is better for her because during the preceding six weeks she talked only 12 times. So there is growth. In addition, the teacher makes, after each statement, a tally indicating the quality of what Margaret said on that particular occasion. If it was a good statement, a plus is put after the tally. If what Margaret said was wrong, or it was a smart-alecky reply or it took the students away from the discussion, a minus is recorded. If what Margaret says really did not matter one way or the other, the teacher records a zero.

These data, reported to parents, are of tremendous interest to them and also to Margaret. But we do not compare Margaret with the other students. It is her own personal growth in discussion that concerns us. Also, in evaluating Margaret's discussion, we need to know about her relations with other pupils. We use sociometric techniques to see what is happening to interpersonal relations among students.

We can evaluate the quality of independent study by using scales of one kind or another. Dr. Max Griffin of Boston College, former principal of the Wayland, Massachusetts High School, developed a series of such scales. A teacher looks at the product and evaluates on a five-point scale a student's use of material resources. Or he evaluates the use of human resources—who did the student talk to? Were they the right people? He judges the self-discipline of the student—did he stay at the job until it was finished? How creative was it? How imaginative?

The point is that matters such as independent study, oral discussion skills, habits of inquiry, interpersonal relations are reported to parents and to students, to colleges and employers, along with achievements in knowledge and in skills.

Evaluation also occurs in all of the educational settings. Program instruction devices and written tests are used in regular classes or they can be used in large groups or during independent study. Attention profiles and the quality of independent study show the quality of teacher presentations. Regardless of the setting, we must change our procedures of evaluation, because *how* we evaluate speaks much louder than what we say in influencing that which teachers and pupils do.

So, here are the four imperatives that I think need to be changed immediately:

1. Change the nature of teacher presentations
2. Change the character of independent study
3. Provide for student discussion
4. Change the process of evaluation.

Unless we accept these four imperatives—regardless of whether we continue with one teacher and 30 students per class, whether we go into team teaching, or whether we use modern technological devices such as television, programed instruction, computer-assisted learning, or any of the rest—the quality of learning in the secondary school of tomorrow will not be materially better than it is today. That is why I think these suggestions are so important.

If you want more detailed guidance regarding any or all of these four imperatives, write me at the NASSP. We will send without charge some longer papers on each one. Principals and supervisors need to work with teachers in the classrooms, in the places where teachers teach and pupils learn. I believe you need to start next week and continue with patience and understanding, until the quality of teaching and learning in your school is improved. It can be done.

Team Teaching

Efforts to provide greater flexibility in the scheduling and instruction of high school students have led to the development of what is referred to as team teaching. The term has been used to describe everything from simple departmentalization of instruction, through multiple assignment of teachers to a single classroom, to really flexible use of teacher and student time. The central consideration is, of course, that there be some type of coordination of two or more adults' activity in instructing a group of students.

The following article reports favorably on the activities of one team of teachers at the proudly innovative school at Melbourne, Florida. Kenneth Jenkins is Assistant Principal at the Miami Springs Senior High School and was administrative intern with Dr. B. Frank Brown at the Melbourne High School.

Teaming and Teaching*

Kenneth D. Jenkins

Better than six years have passed since the presentation of Lloyd Trump's *And No Bells Ring,* followed by *Focus on Change—Guide to Better Schools.* Since these educational milestones, much of our world has changed. Great leaders have fallen; protest movements have lost their aura of respectability; hallucogenic drugs and mod fashions are in. But much of our world, unfortunately, has instead remained static. Men are no closer to peaceful understanding; minorities still suffer indignities; and men still toil to achieve even submarginal self-sufficiency.

As Dr. Trump so accurately predicted in 1961, many facets of education have changed. Education is becoming a major force in the American culture; innovation, in general, has become more acceptable; programs of independent study are materializing at an increasing rate. One such prediction which has achieved wide use is the concept of team teaching. The teaching team has become so accepted, it is a virtual educational cliché.

Classically, team teaching has come to be regarded as a means by which a group of teachers coordinate their particular abilities for the purpose of improved instruction, the rationale being that one teacher cannot be an authority on all knowledge for all students. This premise was given succinct expression by Lloyd Trump's statement: "Educational opportunities should not be limited by the accidents of the schedule or the one teacher a student has assigned to him."

Perhaps the ultimate team is one composed of a master teacher, several other subordinate teachers, and qualified instructional aides. Seldom, however, does a teaching team reach this plateau. Most ordinarily, a team is comprised of two or three individual teachers whose particular specialities complement each other. Such was the case when I was involved in a teaching team for a course in American Studies. While my speciality

* *The Clearing House* 42:80–82 (Oct., 1967). Reprinted by permission of publisher and author.

is literature, a second member of the team was a specialist in history, and a third in philosophy and humanities. Each took the responsibility for developing and presenting that aspect of the course curriculum which was most within his province.

Still another common practice in the name of team teaching is to rotate teachers or students so that one teacher teaches his speciality to one group, then moves on to another. This might more appropriately be called "turn teaching," since it fulfills little of the other functions of a team such as varying class size or team evaluation. This year at Melbourne High School another variation is being utilized, one which may prove to be quite effective.

For all the favorable arguments presented on behalf of team teaching, there is something to be said for the continuity and rapport which is engendered by one effective teacher in a classroom. The advocates of team teaching, myself included, would argue that such an arrangement contains a built-in preventative of flexibility. It became the task of a group of English teachers at Melbourne High School to reconcile these two organizational methods. Facilities were not available for a conventional team approach. The inclinations of the teachers forbade an attempt at turn teaching, although the fact that they were dealing with world literature offered an easy "out" for this type of organization. Further, the teachers were disinclined to rotate students according to ethnic specialities or genre. At this point, a plan began to evolve that would slip between the horns of the dilemma.

Most English teachers have one area of world literature in which he feels most comfortable. If his academic background in world literature is typical, however, he obtained most of his information in one or two survey courses in European literature. Thus it was that all of the teachers concerned here had a highly general background, with emphasis in an area of special interest. Their plan of organization attempts to gain the flexibility of team teaching, while maintaining the continuity of the classroom.

Initially, their plan calls for each teacher to develop materials, bibliographies, and aids in his particular specialty. Thus, each teacher researched, developed, and duplicated information in areas of French and Spanish literature, Russian literature, classical literature, Hebrew literature, Oriental literature, Scandinavian and German literature, and the development of language—areas which form the core of the higher ability English classes. These materials were then made available to all other teachers in the team. So, to a great extent, the strengths of each team member are made accessible to all other members, certainly a major asset in implementing a team approach.

An example might serve to illustrate such an operation. At the beginning of the school year, each teacher researched, gathered, organized, and duplicated highly relevant source materials to supplement or substitute for the text. Upon completion of the first unit, teacher A, who developed materials in Hebrew literature, moved into classical literature. She then used, to whatever extent she desired, the materials developed by teacher B. Accordingly, teacher B, who developed the classical materials, planned to move into French and Spanish literature; she would use materials developed by teacher C. On it goes, each set of materials being further defined and modified as each subsequent teacher applies the materials to her classes and unique situations.

It was further agreed that each teacher would act as prime resource person in his speciality for students wanting to go on a limited independent study in that given area. Thus, a student, regardless of who his regular teacher happens to be, would work with that teacher who is a specialist in the area of concern. If the student wants to do further investigation into Chekhov, Corneille, or Sappho, he will work with a special teacher for the duration of his investigation. This move not only makes each teacher available to each student, but it also makes the use of limited independent study more meaningful.

To bring another dimension of flexibility to this team, classes have combined to meet as one group when the occasion demands it. Recently, a guest speaker here to talk on Japanese literature spoke on various aspects of Oriental literature to three classes each period. When we received the film series on *Oedipus Rex*, those classes dealing with classical literature met as one group to view the films. They then returned to their smaller classroom units, where they subdivided even further to criticize various aspects of the films. Thus, in our team, we have provisions for large or small groups, seminar or discussion groups, and independent study. Teachers develop materials according to their strengths and make them available to others in that team. Almost all of the necessary components of team teaching are present; even team evaluation.

The team is currently working on a means by which each team member will evaluate at least one major theme for each student each marking period. Roughly, the idea is to circulate the themes during the marking period in order that all of the work will not accumulate at the end. The rationale is based on a desire to test one's judgment and bias against others so as to find a firmer base upon which to evaluate subjectively. Many problems still need to be worked out, but the desire is there. Something will evolve, at least for team consideration.

Much has been said about team teaching and its undoubted success. However, the implementation of the team concept is not always feasible in all situations. There are times when team teaching has fewer answers or offers little relief for the needs that exist. The alternative proposed herein gives a means by which flexibility can be achieved without an overwhelming transition.

Francis Bacon has said that "He who will not try new remedies must expect new evils, for time is the greatest innovator." The team is already feeling the first fruits of its success. Hopefully, others may see this as an answer, at least until such time that they are willing to take the "big plunge" into a full team situation.

There have been many criticisms of team teaching. Perhaps the most cogent is that it may increase rather than decrease the likelihood that particular students will be neglected. Another results from some of the problems involved in getting several teachers or a teacher with several aids who work well together. In the following article, William Goldstein, a Junior High School Principal in Plainview, New York, catalogs these and some other possible problems.

Problems in Team Teaching*

William Goldstein

All stories, if continued far enough, end in death, and he is no true story-teller who would keep that from you.

Ernest Hemingway

Similarly, all new approaches to teaching, if not analyzed enough, end in atrophy. Logic and research tell us that the teaming of teachers to achieve certain desirable instructional ends has become a highly accepted, fashionable mode of teaching—to date perhaps the most compelling and attractive instructional approach to inquiry, transmittal of subject matter, use of teacher talent, and flexible grouping of students known. On the other hand, it is not difficult to see how one may be blinded by the dazzle of exotica triggered by such currently romanticized notions as large group instruction, seminars, pre- and post-testing, regrouping, sophisticated team planning, instructional analysis, and the like.

No responsible schoolman would quarrel with the need to develop new teaching-learning situations to deal with new knowledge and a "new breed" of students who continue to become increasingly demanding as well as hungry for broader and more lasting mastery of that in our en-

* *The Clearing House* 42:83–86 (Oct., 1967). Reprinted by permission of publisher and author.

vironment which needs to be controlled and mastered. However, vacuous acceptance of ideas which are, in the words of Riesman, "other-directed" is tantamount to the establishment of superficiality at best and, at worst, predestined to certain failure. The dream and the real experience, the symbol and its substance, appearance and reality must be viewed as distinguishable and frequently separable commodities.

THE PROBLEM OF CHOICE

In its brief but singularly successful history, team teaching, for better or for worse, has meant almost anything its constituents wanted it to mean. For instance, some secondary schools organize teams of teachers on what is commonly called a "horizontal" basis, *i.e.*, where four teachers in the academic disciplines (English, social studies, mathematics, and science) are responsible for the basic instructional program of approximately 120 students. Other secondary schools, organize teaching teams on a "vertical" basis, *i.e.*, where three teachers within a single academic discipline (let us say, mathematics) are responsible for the instructional program of all students at a grade level (*e.g.*, grade 7).

Possible variations on these two major themes are legion, and all may have considerable relevance to sound educational objectives. Whichever direction toward the teaming of teachers a school chooses to take, it must first overcome the two most conspicuous problems—those of *choice of commitment* based on theoretically determined and desired outcomes and of the *organizational schema* to fit this choice.

One is reminded of little Alice and her charming egg-acquaintance, Humpty Dumpty, in Lewis Carroll's brilliant work, *Through the Looking-Glass*:

'When I use a word,' Humpty Dumpty said, in a rather scornful tone, 'it means just what I choose it to mean—neither more nor less.'
'The question is,' said Alice, 'whether you can make words mean so many different things.'
'The question is,' said Humpty Dumpty, 'which is to be the master—that's all.'

OPERATIONAL PROBLEMS

Humpty Dumpty, though, like all characters populating lands of fantasy, could luxuriate in dismissing problems once he tired of them; such is not the case here. Once decisions on direction have been made, they must be dealt with. Team teaching raises a number of continuous and rather deep problems which need, quite expectedly, continuous and, sometimes, rather deep analysis. Examination of some of these may prove fruitful.

The Time Volcano. C. Northcote Parkinson in his humorous "law" states that "Work expands so as to fill the time available for its completion." Team teaching formulates its own paradoxical judicial maxim: As work or the perception of needed work expands, the time available for its completion contracts. Foremost among problems central to successful programs of team teaching seems to be the problem of a lack of time to plan programs and, indeed, sometimes even to execute instructional plans. Commitment to the teaming of teachers requires new looks into the organization of the school; these "new looks" may need to include the possibility of a complete reconstruction of the teaching load to allow for better planning and, most importantly, *analysis* and *evaluation* of the teaching-learning process. Failure to come to grips with the new realities created by a new process amounts not only to playing ostrich, but perhaps also to cheating at it.

Space Exploration. Space, like time, is a fascinating scientific contemporary phenomenon receiving much attention. New use of building space is corollary to team teaching. Nothing provides greater frustration to students and faculty alike than short-circuitry in the use of building space. Varying class sizes, frequent regroupings of students, and sophisticated uses of audio-visual devices derive much of their existence from the idea of team teaching; attendant to these notions, logic directs that new and older school buildings alike must adapt their organization of building space to the instructional demands of the team rather than allow plastic instruction to take place in an unbending container.

Staff Relationships. Placing personalities into mandatory juxtaposition creates all kinds of new relationships and problems. To belabor the enigmas of human behavior is a fruitless adventure at this time; however, to ignore these enigmas altogether is similarly fruitless.

When teachers sit down to plan together (one of the essential ingredients of team teaching) and, indeed, when they stand up to teach together or separately, new roles and perceptions of roles are born. Changes in both the image a teacher has of himself as well as changes in the image he broadcasts to others must and do occur. The resulting new teacher posture gives rise to new masks which the teacher wears in his new roles.

As dialogue between teachers increases and sharpens in focus and quality, academic productivity of a new and vibrant order may result; this is no problem except insofar as harnessing the new energies is concerned. On the other hand, experience yields other results also.

Negative, sometimes destructive behavior comes about when teachers, ill-suited to cooperative efforts, are thrust into continuous professional contact with one another. Disagreements, if frequent enough, rupture the team process and children are the big losers. For if adults cannot deal with one another productively, certainly no tangible good can come of team teaching, since the name becomes hollow and the process a mockery.

When personalities clash, whether via disagreement, insecurities, perpetual defensiveness, or other aspects of human abrasion, team teaching is doomed on that particular team. Failure on the parts of responsible individuals to react and reconstruct the team immediately could calcify the breach and make irretrievable the process of team teaching for the individuals involved.

On the other hand, recognizing that human frailty is one of the most serious threats to the success of team teaching, supervisors can contain, control, or even eliminate problems to a large extent with careful screening, selection, and assignment of teaching personnel. This takes perception, insight, patience, and virtuosity with human behavior—and even then there is no guarantee, so complicated are the human factors.

Paradox of Over-Productivity. As in the inversion of Parkinson's Law stated earlier, team teaching reaches new heights of productivity. Frequently, it finds itself so paradoxically successful, that it outruns itself both intellectually and logistically.

Intellectually, successful teams discover new relationships of, let us say, one academic discipline to another, but may not have access to the wherewithal or the mechanics to cement the relationship. New teaching techniques frequently point the way to new class sizes and new teacher-pupil ratios; yet, if the available logistical support is threadbare, the new idea predictably atrophies.

The point is that if a school commits itself to a system, in this case team teaching, it must also commit itself to supporting systems since imagination, when unbuttressed, is quickly frustrated and ultimately dissolves into mediocrity. It is hardly fair or even real to expect productivity and a new energy if a teaching team stands chained like Prometheus to a rock of convention. One cannot view new horizons and countless directions from a limited environment.

The New Technology. Experience with team teaching proves mightily that no discussion of it is complete without pointing up relationships to the uses of educational "hardware." Several key questions need to be asked and, in the asking, the problems reify themselves:

1. To what extent do teaching teams need technicians or, at the very least, technical assistance in organizing and using educational machinery?
2. What equipment is used with what frequency in varying sized groups?
3. What is the relationship between types of educational hardware and the concept of "independent study?"
4. Is "programmed learning" obsolescent or does it have a role in the teaming process?

5. As the team plans for use of audio-visual materials, should it not also plan *against* overuse of these materials?
6. What role should teacher aides or paraprofessional personnel play in the use of machine in teaching?
7. What degree of technical competence or accomplishment may a school reasonably expect from its professional teaching personnel? Should one expect a minimal level of competence in this respect from all or should the team train individuals for this kind of specialized role?

In an exploding technological environment, in an era where students and faculty alike are bombarded by data from all kinds of mass media of communication, a whole new area of involvement opens to teachers—an area, however, which carries with it new problems requiring new answers in new surroundings.

Finance. Team teaching costs money; it does not save it. However stark this may sound, it is unavoidably accurate. If teaming is to succeed, it must be given more-than-adequate funding. Once the momentum of "over-production" begins, support must be available or the program withers—ironically as a result of its own success.

Cost analysis here is out of place. Suffice it to say that staffing (professional and paraprofessional) coupled with the needs of time, space, and technology make rather self-evident the need for sound and reasonably generous fiscal moorings.

New Responsibilities for Professional Personnel. From the ashes of traditional approaches to instruction, new responsibilities accrue to professional personnel. Teachers, for example, now must deal in new data for the regrouping of students on different bases from what once was. Guidance counselors, formerly almost the only ones concerned with initial grouping data, now work actively in new roles as members of teaching teams. The possibilities for worth, contribution, and status are almost limitless, but need focus as the idea of team teaching develops and matures. Trite as it may sound, the challenge and the problems of coping with the unknown provide teaching teams with a fuel which generates not only abundant energy, but also phenomenal candle-power for intellectual illumination.

POSSIBLE DIRECTIONS FOR TEAM TEACHING

Team teaching is not without its problems, but nothing else worthwhile is either. If those responsible for quality instruction in the schools attack each problem responsibly, progress is assured. Once teams of teachers are established in a school and gain experience in the new venture, there are three major options open: (1) team teaching can fail because its problems are not confronted and solved, (2) team teaching can remain at a *status quo*, superficial level, or (3) team teaching begins, through a vigorous attack on an amelioration of its problems, to provide a continuous vehicle for teacher growth, student learning, teacher involvement in key academic decision-making, teacher status, sound research, and modern evaluation. Team teaching is a continuous "action" device, one whose problems may even provide the sources of its major strengths. To ignore this would not be unlike Gilbert & Sullivan's Duke of Plaza-Toro, who, with such caution, "led his regiment from behind. He found it less exciting."

One curriculum development making headway prior to the excitement over Sputnik was the core curriculum. While it was more popular at the junior high school level, there was some evidence that it was becoming accepted in the more rigidly traditional high school program. As defined by some of its advocates, core curriculum was an attempt to go beyond the mere correlation and fusing of subject matter areas to a greater focus on the specific problems of individual students. The following article by one of the most able specialists in the area of the junior high school curriculum raises serious questions about the appropriateness of team teaching to meeting the objectives of the core curriculum. Gordon Vars in 1966 was Associate Professor of Education at Cornell University.

Can Team Teaching Save the Core Curriculum?*

Gordon F. Vars

"Both the principles and the early patterns of core are now advancing under the banner of team teaching."—Harold Spears[1]

"Team teaching and the core curriculum are as far apart as the poles in their underlying philosophical and psychological assumptions."— Nelson Bossing[2]

* *Phi Delta Kappan* 47:258–62 (Jan., 1966). Reprinted by permission of publisher and author.

[1] Paraphrased from: Harold Spears, "A Second Look at *The Emerging High School Curriculum*," *Phi Delta Kappan*, November, 1963, p. 102.

[2] Paraphrased from: "S-R Bonds," *Phi Delta Kappan*, February, 1964, p. 268.

"Team teaching in reality can become an extension, a further refinement, and an improvement of the core."—Vernon Anderson[3]

How is it possible for eminent educators, all experts in curriculum, to come to such contradictory conclusions? Clarification of this issue is vital to anyone interested in team teaching, core, or curriculum in general.

CORE CURRICULUM

Spears states:

> Among the common features of both core and team teaching are: 1) a large group of pupils assigned to a team of teachers, 2) a curriculum block assigned as the area to be covered, 3) a block of time longer than the usual period provided for the work, 4) the provision within the program of class groups varying in size from exceedingly large to exceedingly small, 5) freedom for the teachers to plan among themselves the flexible scheduling within the program that meets the instructional objectives of the moment, and 6) the correlation of curriculum content naturally related.[4]

Here and in his earlier writing Spears applies the term "core" to any program "involving a longer period than the popular forty-to-sixty-minute period and dependence for material upon an area which under a subject curriculum would comprise two or more subject fields."[5] More appropriate for this concept is the generic term "block-time," proposed by Grace Wright in her definitive 1958 study of block-time and core programs.[6]

Both Bossing and Anderson restrict the term core to a *particular type* of block-time class that goes beyond correlation to focus directly on the needs, interests, and problems of students.[7] In such a program subject matter is brought in as needed to deal with problems, clearly distinguishing core from programs in which primary commitment is to preselect subject matter. As Anderson describes it:

> The core curriculum is a way of organizing some of the important common learnings in the high school curriculum, using a problem-solving approach as its procedure, having social and personal problems

[3] Vernon Anderson, "The Evolving Core Curriculum," in *The High School Curriculum*, Harl R. Douglass (ed.), Third Edition. New York: Ronald Press, 1964, p. 266.

[4] Spears, *op. cit.* See also Spears introduction to: David W. Beggs, III, ed., *Team Teaching: Bold New Venture*. Indianapolis: Unified College Press, 1964, pp. 8–9.

[5] Harold Spears, *The Emerging High School Curriculum and Its Direction*. New York: American Book Company, 1940, p. 63.

[6] U.S. Office of Education, *Block-Time Classes and the Core Program in the Junior High School*, by Grace S. Wright, Bulletin 1958, No. 6. Washington: Government Printing Office, 1958, pp. ix, 9–19. See also: William Van Til, Gordon F. Vars, and John H. Lounsbury, *Modern Education for the Junior High School Years*. Indianapolis: Bobbs-Merrill, 1961, pp. 92–104.

[7] Roland C. Faunce and Nelson L. Bossing, *Developing the Core Curriculum*, Second Edition. Englewood Cliffs, New Jersey: Prentice-Hall, 1958, p. 58.

significant to youth and society as its content, and focusing upon the development of behaviors needed in a democratic society as its purpose.[8]

It is the latter, more precise definition of core that is applied in this analysis. Since both Bossing and Anderson have similar definitions of core, the clue to their disagreement must lie in their conceptions of team teaching. In listing the characteristics of core, neither Anderson nor Bossing makes explicit reference to teaching teams or to "exceedingly large groups," although both stress cooperative planning among core teachers.[9]

TEAM TEACHING

In team teaching, two or more teachers are given joint responsibility for all or a significant part of the instruction of the same group of students. Team teaching is a key element of the plan proposed by J. Lloyd Trump and the Commission on the Experimental Study of the Utilization of the Staff in the Secondary School.[10] Besides team teaching, Trump advocates flexible scheduling, the use of nonprofessional personnel as teacher aides, and increased utilization of modern instructional media. Instruction is to be provided through independent study, small-group discussion, and presentations in groups larger than the usual class.

As indicated by its title, the commission is primarily concerned with redeployment of staff rather than curriculum reform. Implications for core must be inferred from the commission's publications, from other writings on team teaching theory, and from reports of team teaching experiments. Core is seldom mentioned in Trump's publications, but clearly consonant with the core idea are his goal of helping students learn to think and solve problems on their own, his emphasis upon the guidance role of the teacher, and such features as flexible use of large blocks of time, cooperative planning among teachers, and varying the size and composition of class groups.

INTERDISCIPLINARY TEAMS

Correlation of subject matter is facilitated by an interdisciplinary team, which Trump illustrates as follows:

> A teacher of United States history, a teacher of United States literature, teachers who know the music and arts of the country, and special-

[8] Anderson, op. cit., p. 248.

[9] Faunce and Bossing, op. cit., pp. 59–60, and Anderson, op. cit., pp. 248–252.

[10] See for example: J. Lloyd Trump, Images of the Future: A New Approach to the Secondary School. Washington: National Association of Secondary School Principals, 1959; and J. Lloyd Trump, New Directions to Quality Education: The Secondary School Tomorrow. Washington: National Association of Secondary School Principals, 1960.

ists who can improve students' writing and speaking could team together to teach various phases of the culture of this country. . . . This approach would provide a natural synthesis of subject matter and the most competent teaching in the various subject areas.[11]

Brownell and Taylor also hypothesize "improved correlation of subject matter because of cooperative planning in team meetings,"[12] and cite as an example a three-period "core" arrangement composed of three seventh-grade teachers, specialists in English, social studies, and mathematics, respectively.

In 1940 Spears described four programs involving interdisciplinary teams, giving particular attention to the Evansville (Indiana) Plan, initiated while he was director of secondary education in that city. In this program three teachers were given responsibility for 100 ninth-graders in a three-period block of time. The "General Living Core," as it was called at the Benjamin Bosse High School, included experiences drawn from English, social studies, everyday business training, practical mathematics, art, music, and science. The "main threads of instructional experience" were school life, community life, home life, and vocational life; various ways of grouping and regrouping students were suggested for carrying out the program.[13]

Since 1958, special issues of the *Bulletin of the National Association of Secondary School Principals* have been devoted to reports of experiences with the Staff Utilization Commission's recommendations. The May, 1963, issue revealed the extent to which the interdisciplinary team idea had caught on. Fully half of the team teaching programs described in this issue included at least one team that teaches two or more subjects. Of the thirteen schools having junior high teams, nine had the "block-team" arrangement.

All these programs fall within the definition of block-time; they provide for flexible use of an extended period of time and correlation of subject matter. Many include small-group work and independent study. The interdisciplinary team may eliminate a persistent problem in block-time programs, the tendency of some teachers to stress one of the subjects absorbed into the block more than the others. Judicious use of small-group work may enable team teachers to establish rapport with a few of their students sufficient for them to exercise the guidance function typically assigned to block-time teachers. Also, the variety of teacher personalities on a team increases the likelihood that any one student will

[11] J. Lloyd Trump and Dorsey Baynham, *Focus on Change, Guide to Better Schools.* Chicago: Rand McNally, 1961, p. 106.

[12] John A. Brownell and Harris A. Taylor, "Theoretical Perspectives for Team Teaching," *Phi Delta Kappan*, January, 1962, p. 151.

[13] Spears, *op. cit.*, 1940, pp. 289–320.

find an adult to whom he can relate easily. Little wonder, then, that team teaching may appear to be compatible with the core idea, at least in its older, more general sense of block-time, as used by Harold Spears.

Anderson sees further possibilities, saying:

> Team teachers have good opportunities to use teacher-pupil planning, problem solving, personal and social problems, related subject matter from different fields, and skills in relation to ongoing situations. They have the opportunity to use the experience-centered approach. Moreover, they have the propitious opportunity to use their subject specialities and talents, a lack in the core program.[14]

He makes it clear, however, that these are opportunities, not inevitable results of team teaching. It is the likelihood of this happening that is doubted by Bossing on both philosophical and psychological grounds. To examine this question we must go beyond the Trump proposals, preoccupied as they are with organizational matters, to examine team teaching theory. For this we rely on *Team Teaching*, edited by Judson Shaplin and Henry F. Olds, Jr., one of the most penetrating analyses of team teaching extant.[15]

It is important to note first that comments on the integration of learning experiences from several curriculum areas appear but rarely in this book. The word core is not listed at all in the index, is mentioned only two or three times in all 430 pages, and is used to refer to an arrangement more accurately labeled block-time. While pointing out that team teaching arrangements have forced teachers to take a new, critical look at the curriculum, Shaplin states quite frankly that "the staff utilization studies, including team teaching, have most frequently been primarily concerned with administrative reorganization and adaptation of the existing curriculum to the new organization."[16] A consistent curriculum theory of any kind is notably lacking in most of the major publications on team teaching, least of all the relationship of team teaching to the problem-centered core.[17]

DRAWBACKS IN TEAM TEACHING

Moreover, certain features of team teaching appear to militate against effective core teaching. Take the matter of time. Those who expect team

[14] Anderson, *op. cit.*, p. 266.
[15] Judson T. Shaplin and Harry F. Olds, Jr. (eds.), *Team Teaching*. New York: Harper and Row, 1964.
[16] *Ibid.*, p. 42.
[17] See, for example: David W. Beggs, III, *Decatur-Lakeview High School: A Practical Application of the Trump Plan*. Englewood Cliffs, New Jersey: Prentice-Hall, 1964; David W. Beggs, III, ed., *Team Teaching, op. cit.*; Medill Bair and Richard G. Woodward, *Team Teaching in Action*. Boston: Houghton Mifflin, 1964.

teaching to give the teacher more time for planning and for counseling with students are doomed to disappointment. The many complicated administrative decisions that are delegated to the team are tremendously time-consuming. Speaking from his experience with elementary team teaching in Lexington, Joseph C. Grannis says: "It seems likely that team teaching will demand as much time as the self-contained classroom, if not more, for a long time to come."[18]

Even large-group instruction, which is supposed to give teachers some released time, may fail to deliver. "Not only do these lessons require a great deal of time to prepare," Grannis says, "but it is also generally necessary for teachers who are not directly responsible for the lesson to be present anyway, or at least to be involved in the planning, in order to insure the articulation of these lessons with others that precede and follow them."[19] Core teachers have for years complained that a major obstacle to success of their program was lack of adequate time for staff planning and for counseling with students. They may well be jumping from the frying pan into the fire if they embrace team teaching.

Teacher-student planning within a broadly defined problem area is another key feature of core that may be difficult to carry out in a team. Clearly, cooperative planning is impossible with a large group of 100 or more students. It also is difficult to see how small groups could carry out their own plans and still keep their schedules close enough together to profit from large-group instruction. In other words, classes or small groups would be so tied to the schedule of large-group instruction that their freedom to evolve their own plans would be severely restricted.

Otherwise, after the initial overview of a problem area (which might well be carried out with combined groups), each core class would inevitably go its own way. This would not rule out the possibility of combining groups whenever a film, visiting speaker, or field trip happened to be appropriate to more than one group, a practice possible in any kind of program. Joint action to carry out a unit-culminating activity, such as a school assembly or service project, also would be difficult if each group selected its own learning experiences through teacher-student planning. Loren Tompkins reports that whole-group culminating activities have been abandoned by the core team at Northern Hills Junior High School in North Topeka, Kansas, because it proved almost impossible for each teacher to finish a unit on the same day. "It is easy to fill in until the team is ready to begin a new unit," he writes, "but it is most difficult to maintain pupil interest in postponed culminating activities."[20]

18 Shaplin and Olds, *op. cit.*, p. 163.
19 *Ibid.*, pp. 163–64.
20 Loren Tompkins, "Background of the Northern Hills Core Program." Unpublished manuscript, 1964, p. 7.

Another difficulty in harmonizing team teaching and core lies in the area of guidance. Trump makes much of the opportunities for personal teacher-student conferences in a team teaching program, but we have already pointed out that teachers in a team may actually have little time for these. Assignment of a guidance specialist to a team, helpful as that may be, is hardly an adequate substitute for the teacher-counseling provided by a core teacher who has developed a close personal relationship with his students.

The small-group discussions inherent in most team teaching proposals are expected to provide excellent opportunities for developing teacher-student rapport. However, the fact that these are so often called "discussion groups" rather than counseling groups, work groups, or even study groups, leads one to wonder how far they go beyond the mere rehashing of information presented in large-group sessions.[21] Apparently little has been done thus far to exploit the guidance potential of small-group sessions. In fact, some teams deliberately rotate their small-group leadership, sacrificing sustained contact between a teacher and a few students in the hope that all team members will become somewhat acquainted with all the students.

Robert A. Anderson has this to say about the oft-reported problem of getting to know the students in a team teaching situation:

> In the beginning, elementary teachers in a team will tend to be alarmed by the fact that it takes much longer to become acquainted with the pupils than it did in the self-contained classroom. They need reassurance on this point, since the evidence from pilot teams very clearly shows that the problem is a temporary and soluble one. In fact, the data suggest that by approximately midyear the team members are in possession of much more information about each child than their counterparts in self-contained classrooms, even though the latter have only one-third to one-sixth as many pupils.[22]

A core teacher who takes his guidance responsibilities seriously would hardly be willing to wait half a year to get to know his students well. Moreover, although information about one's students is important, even more important are the emotional overtones of the teacher-pupil relationship. The continued presence of other adults in a team teaching situation may affect the quality of these relationships. Dan Lortie raises this question in discussing the high rapport possible under the "autonomy-equality" (self-contained) teaching situation:

> What we do not yet know is whether such states of high rapport can arise where more than one adult is teaching in a single classroom. Under autonomy-equality the teacher unselfconsciously relates directly

[21] See, for example: David W. Beggs, III, *Decatur-Lakeview High School, op. cit.,* pp. 99–113.
[22] Shaplin and Olds, *op. cit.,* p. 214.

to the class and need not concern himself with the possibly different reactions emanating from other adults. Can adults work together in a way which permits them the same free-wheeling emotional freedom and which results in an equally intense relationship?[23]

The most serious conflict between core and team teaching stems from the emphasis upon subject matter specialization in most team teaching proposals. Shaplin states this quite frankly:

> One of the major goals of many team teaching projects has been to increase the amount of subject specialization among teachers at all levels of the school system. At the secondary school level this means further division of a broad subject area. An English teacher, for example, may become a specialist in language, in some phase of literature, or in developmental reading.[24]

In the same book, we are told by Glen Heathers that "the self-contained classroom is being destroyed by insistent pressures toward greater teacher specialization and toward greater diversity in the instructional arrangements made available to the individual student."[25] This, despite his candid admission that "*specialization offers no guarantee whatsoever that teaching of a subject will improve with respect to such goals as critical thinking, inquiry, self-instruction, or command of theory.*"[26] While no instructional arrangement can guarantee results, one cannot but wonder what motivates the drive toward specialization if there is not at least the expectation of better achievement of these vital objectives.

In addition to subject matter specialization, the hierarchical team advocated by Trump involves further specialization in terms of roles, such as team leader, general teacher, teacher aide, clerk, and the like. Even when no formal team structure is provided, some specialization of functions must take place simply to enable the team to operate. Whether specialization is planned for or "just happens," the question remains: Can a team of staff members fully exploit the interrelatedness of learnings inherent in a core problem area, or must plans be filtered through the mind of a single person, someone who knows intimately the interests, capacities, and previous experiences of a relatively small group of children?

Problems encountered whenever two teachers try merely to correlate their courses should be sufficient warning of the well-nigh insuperable difficulties facing a team who would teach core. Robert Ohm tells us that "specialization of tasks, functions, and jobs tends to pull the organization apart and to split the central unity of the teaching process."[27]

[23] *Ibid.*, p. 278.
[24] *Ibid.*, p. 82.
[25] *Ibid.*, p. 372.
[26] *Ibid.*, p. 352 (Italics mine).
[27] Robert E. Ohm, "Toward a Rationale for Team Teaching," *Administrator's Notebook*, March, 1961, p. 2. (Publication of the Midwest Administration Center, University of Chicago.)

Specialization, the inevitable concomitant of team teaching, is thus destructive of the very unity of teaching process which core is designed to promote.

CONCLUSION

Team teaching is a pattern of staff organization that seems at first glance to be eminently suited to core, when the latter is defined in the older sense of block-time. Incompatibilities begin to appear, however, when core is defined more precisely as a curriculum organization with primary focus upon the personal-social problems of the learner. The staff time absorbed in just keeping a complex team in operation, the limitations on teacher-student planning imposed by the team schedule, the difficulties of establishing close teacher-student rapport, and above all the staff specialization that seems inevitable in a team, all militate against successful core teaching. Far from being the "salvation" of core, team teaching may prove to be "the Devil in disguise."

Counseling and Self-Direction

Almost any consideration of the restructuring of the relationship of teachers and students in the high school raises questions with regard to counseling services and pupil self-direction. The more varied the school population, the greater the need for counseling. In the setting in which relatively little is being done to modify the real curriculum content, counseling becomes the effort to make the existing program more palatable to those students for whom it has seemed inappropriate. Similarly effective use of the school situation as a practice field for the learning of democratic techniques becomes complicated as the proportion of the student population from lower class backgrounds increases.

The first article catalogs some of the problems which have arisen in the conditions of change which seem to prevail at the present time. Counseling for the future, like teaching for the future, seems to pose a special dilemma. The solution suggested here is that counseling services should concentrate on teaching an approach rather than the more unstable world of facts. The important approach taught in the counseling situation is to be self-direction. Adolph

Unruh is Dean of the School of Education, University of Missouri, Saint Louis; O. T. Richardson is Dean of Instructional Services at Ball State University.

Counseling in an Age of Change*

Adolph Unruh and O. T. Richardson

Change is a constant variable in life. Inanimate and animate things are constantly changing and in various ways. It is also obvious that institutions change. Change may be from good to bad or from poor to better, but change is a constant factor. Even the requirements for membership in certain institutions change from year to year. And it is fascinating to watch great cities undergoing the processes of razing, face lifting, rebuilding, and redevelopment.

If one understands change, then it is possible to do something about the direction it takes to effect some control over it. Change may be deliberately sought in social institutions in which people are encouraged to adopt new patterns of behavior. In educational institutions change is deliberately sought as youth are guided away from certain subjects, or toward an approved type of learning. Some students are assisted in changing their study habits so that learning may be more effective. In business, in economics, and in society changes are sought and are expected. The counselor who does not understand the phenomenon of change, or who assumes that his experience is sufficient to meet all the problems his students will bring him, is surely obsolescent.[1]

CHARACTERISTICS OF CHANGE

If one can describe change by indicating its various characteristics, then it is possible to observe it more closely and to have some management of it.

(1) One characteristic is rate. When one remembers that 90 per cent of all the scientists who have ever lived are still alive, it is possible to see that change has come upon us very rapidly. Twenty years ago a

* *The Clearing House* 41:148–52 (Nov., 1966). Reprinted by permission of publisher and authors.
[1] Wrenn, C. Gilbert, "The Culturally Encapsulated Counselor," in Mosher, Ralph L., Carle, Richard F. and Kehas, Chris D., *Guidance: An Examination*. Newton: Harcourt, Brace & World, Inc., 1965, pp. 214–224.

Congressional report stated that ten mathematicians were all that were needed for all industry in the United States. Today, however, more than 200,000 are needed simply to operate the various computers. It is said that 50 per cent of the children in the elementary grades today will be employed in occupations that do not now exist. It is possible, then to see that rate may be accelerated or decelerated depending upon the circumstances and the factors involved. Intense acceleration might result in a revolution, whereas change that takes generations for its completion would be more descriptive of evolution.

(2) A second characteristic of change which can be observed is volume. Innovations may begin in one school department and spread quickly to another. Significant changes at school can affect what happens at home. When schools begin to strengthen their curricula and assignments, the increased homework makes it difficult for the family at home to help and a change in family relationships results. When the school and the home change it is obvious that relationships with the church probably undergo some changes also.

(3) Another characteristic is that change has direction. The easiest way to illustrate this concept is to note that the population is fleeing the center of the great cities and arriving in vast numbers in the suburbs.[2] The continuing development of machines, tools and gadgets makes life much easier in the home and on the farm, and so there is a change from drudgery and long days of hard manual labor to a life of mechanized labor and leisure. This much description may point out that there is a movement in an observable direction.

Perhaps a brief look at some of the results of change may be useful. The scientific way of thinking often clashes with the modes of thought one finds in rather stable and staid communities. Innovations in business and industry, in organizational structure and in the community itself, may be forced on people. If these people are not prepared for rapid change they may find themselves engaged in controversies and beset with fears and frustrations, so much so that they may lose sight of the real issues.

In such situations, one may find youth quite disturbed about its role in society, and its present status.[3] Often several youths separate from the main body into their own groups and become fiercely loyal to their gangs. They are searching for identity and they look for security among themselves, paying much attention to what the peer groups have to say. These may, in turn, be controlling factors in school achievement, the motivation to drop out and obtain employment, and other teenage behavior.

[2] Davis, Kingsley, "Urbanization—Changing Patterns of Living" in Simpson, H. S., *The Changing American Population*. A Report of Arden House Conference. N.Y.: Institute of Life Insurance. 488 Madison Avenue. Chapter 3.

[3] Coleman, James S., *et al.*, "Emergency of an Adolescent Subculture in Industrial Society," in *Social Climates in High Schools*. Washington, D.C.: U.S. Department of Health, Education, and Welfare. 1961. Bulletin OE 33016. pp. 1–34.

SOME CONDITIONS WHICH INFLUENCE COUNSELING

When one tries to look ahead to the days when change is common for everyone, including counselors and students, it becomes obvious that prediction is hazardous. Today, even families are less competent to counsel youth than they once were, because conditions relating to employment and the vocations are no longer stable. Children thus become more independent from parental influence, control and advice. They look to the outside for counsel with regard to educational opportunities and advantages. The same is true with regard to vocational opportunities.

Attention should be given to the fact that an increasing percentage of high school graduates goes on to college. Before many years elapse, the educational ladder will extend from age three and Project Headstart, through college. How much does the counselor know about his students' socio-economic background and the changing nature of the social, economic, and cultural world into which they will graduate? The great metropolis, constantly increasing in size, continues to absorb the major portion of the population, but at the same time it becomes more impersonal and objective. Soon much of the work, and many jobs will be automated and programmed. Uneducated and unguided youth will find little sympathy in the business community. They will find it necessary to return to some source for additional counseling, perhaps several times, and some will need retraining more than once.

More and more women will prepare for a variety of careers including positions in business and industry and proprietorships. Many will take time out to rear a family and then will return to institutions of higher learning or resume their interrupted careers. The percentage of women in the labor force of this country has already grown to one-third of the total number employed. While there may be some uncertainty in some quarters of the future of women in the manpower market, their continued influx is a certainty and presents the counselor with a challenge. For example, what kinds of jobs or positions would he predict will be available for them in 1975 which are not available now? If it is true that half of the fifth graders will be employed in occupations that do not now exist, then how would he suggest that a young lady prepare for this new world?

Changes in business and industry and the innovations of electronics have uprooted many formerly stable occupations. Some jobs appear briefly and within a few years are gone as a result of these newer developments. The realization that today a machine can perform work on the same level as a person with a twelfth grade education places a premium upon, not only more education and counseling, but a better quality of both.

These changes and uncertainties of the future have had an impact on youth. Counselors are finding more pupils with problems of emotional imbalance and feelings of insecurity. Symbols of security such as ancestral lands or homes are vanishing. The idea of condominium or joint owner-ship of apartments is new, presenting new modes of living and hence new problems of social behavior. Added to this condition is the great mobility of the American people and a diminution of the feeling of being an integral part of a community. Indeed, some families will have no homes in the usual sense of the word, but rather six or ten residences scattered about the country in the same way their work is. This kind of life will affect the kind of education a student obtains, and he must develop new resources for personal growth, stability and security. Modern youth is freer from parental restraint than he has been in the past. They have much more money to spend and they have been responsible for developing a large and lucrative market for the things that teen-agers buy. All of this leads to a growing feeling on the part of youth of not being wanted, or being ignored, and a sense of ineffectiveness of what they do.

In attempting to help persons solve their problems under conditions such as these, counselors will require a much greater understanding of the nature, the functions, and the implications of change in society for the individual and the kinds of choices he is compelled to make. The counselor must be aware of the montage of a variety of extremes in society, of opposing pressures, of competing and compensatory forces and agencies. As much as anyone in the school system, he may need a com-puter to keep information on educational changes and social and economic trends in order to match the counselee's needs.

In general, one may anticipate that the conditions described above will continue to exist. Furthermore the rate of change in many areas will accelerate. One may also assume that the volume of problems will rise as increasing numbers of people are involved. Finally, as the third character-istic of change suggests, the trend away from present social and cultural traditions and habits will continue.

Thus, the situation for the school counselor becomes a serious one. Unless he is a constant and critical student of the socio-economic scene and endowed with vision, he may be counseling his students for an assault on the Maginot Line. But counseling is by nature aimed at the future. The problem is to untangle the mixed cues that come from countless im-pressions, and to analyze the seeming instability and insecurity which the future presents.

FACTS ARE NOT ENOUGH

The modern high school counselor needs to know more about which behavior patterns are waning in their use and effectiveness in society. He needs to know that knowledge is increasing at an accelerated rate and he needs to know in which areas his knowledge of the situation is becoming less valid. He cannot place implicit faith in the facts and information he currently possesses. Nor can he predict accurately, day after day, what knowledge, information or skills will be needed to gain a profitable entrance into the market place. Neither can he know what kinds of experiences are available in other institutions which may be expected to maximize the student's potential.

He knows about the extreme mobility of the American people, but he cannot know where his student will find a new home, what friends he shall have, or what his future may be. He may know that research is an initiator of change and a producer of new opportunities, but he cannot predict what they will be or what use will be made of them. He knows there will be racial problems, problems of employment, questions about social behavior, and inter-cultural relations, but he cannot predict their intensity, frequency, nor the degree of his counselee's personal involvement in them. He does know, however, that his student must learn to approach each new challenge or innovation with equanimity, with intelligence, and with a problem-solving attitude. Information is, by nature, temporary and changing, and problems once solved have a way of coming unglued.

COUNSELING IN AN AGE OF CHANGE

If counselors will accept the assumptions that decisions once made are quite likely to need revision and that life consists of continuous decision making, they may adopt an approach that will yield results of greater permanency,[4] paradoxical as that may seem. Let the counselor be reminded that, as an illustration of this point, within a two year-period 73 per cent of the juniors in the Project Talent in 1960 changed their decisions regarding careers.

In the difficult task of counseling youth, one tool would be of considerable help to the counselor. He should strive to develop the ability to use the conceptual tools of the modern educator. One such example is a typology of change. This example consists of four panels, although the counselor may create panels to develop his own conceptions and understanding.

If the counselor will accept that it is possible to build into students' mental structures the image of the change process and a perception of themselves as change agents, then he may assume that students can begin to conceptualize their problems in a way that develops a measure of strength, security, and purpose. The age of the teens is a critical one for building personality, and for building a concept of the world that clearly reflects an expectation that change and innovation are a part of it. Such

---

[4] "News and Trends," NEA *Journal*, 55:3, Washington, D.C.: National Education Association, December, 1965.

a mental structure is required for the building and the development of an identity in the world.

Every problem that confronts the student has in it the element of novelty. It requires ways of thinking and behaving that are foreign to the

PANEL 1	PANEL 2	PANEL 3	PANEL 4
Characteristics of Change	Agents of Change	Focus of Change	Implications for Counseling
(1) Rate (2) Directions (3) Volume	a. Technology b. Cultural Interaction c. Research d. Interest Groups	A. Institutions B. Occupations C. Attitudes D. Values	I. Temporary nature of knowledge and conditions II. New diagnostic tools III. New programs of orientation and feed back into the curriculum IV. More inquiry and creativity

person and must be learned somehow. It requires divergent thinking, inventiveness, and practice in synthesis. The student must learn new ways of analyzing his data and information and of teasing out of them new meanings and interpretations. The counselor should be able to teach these lessons to his counselee and to assist teachers in building these qualities into the curriculum.

Counseling would require, then, that in every counseling situation emphasis be given to the decision making process itself. It should provide the student with opportunities to learn how to collect data and to discover sources of additional information on the basis of one's own efforts. He should be taught to utilize the institutional and community resources available to him for improving his understanding, and for sharpening his information. In this way he will learn to use the method of inquiry. He will increase his powers of observation and will learn to be resourceful.

Every counseling situation should provide the counselee with opportunities to organize his information and data in different ways.[5] He should learn to make projections, and guesses, contrasts and comparisons so as to extract every possible interpretation and meaning from his study of the information. He can learn to suspect the existence of unknown factors as he makes his guesses or generalizations. In other words, as he improves his powers of critical thinking, his powers of analysis and evaluation, he is developing a capacity for self-reliance and a valid approach to changes he will encounter. He becomes an information processor rather than an

[5] Kneller, George F., The Art and Science of Creativity, Chicago: Holt, Rinehart and Winston, Inc., 1965, p. 7.

information gatherer and storer. He does not approach the future with memorized answers but rather with procedures for processing alternatives.

In this manner, the student learns self-direction, if not self-discipline, because of the necessity of learning how to be objective; how to be thorough in the search for evidence; and how to be impartial in evaluation. There will be much greater premium on independent, self-directed, self-programed, self-paced learning in the next few years. A student cannot consort with tutors indefinitely. Each change or innovation he faces, each decision he must make, provides him with an opportunity for another stimulating intellectual exercise which he approaches confidently. These problems are no longer sources of frustration to be solved by asocial behavior and hostility.

For the counselor, change is reality. His challenge is to teach each counselee the methods, the approaches, the attitudes with which to participate in the process of change in a constructive and satisfying way.

In the following article, Matthew W. Gaffney suggests some ways in which the adolescent can be encouraged to develop the right perspective for self-direction and self-discipline. He maintains that by allowing opportunities for self-direction the incidence of school misbehavior is decreased. What is probably more important, the school is used more wisely as a learning laboratory. Matthew Gaffney is district principal of the Cold Spring Harbor (New York) schools.

Student Behavior:
Vital Part of the Instructional Program
in the Secondary School*

Matthew W. Gaffney

The discipline and control of students in the secondary school deserves considerable attention. The American high school is a complicated social institution. Anyone even remotely connected with such an institution,

* *The Clearing House* 42:222–23 (Dec., 1967). Reprinted by permission of publisher and author.

bringing together as it does a large number of growing adolescents for the purposes of education, shortly realizes that such a task cannot be accomplished without clear and concise patterns of teacher and pupil movements within the buildings and within the allotted time span. The issue soon becomes clear that the operation of the school will either result in a controlled environment in which the activities of the school can proceed successfully, or it will be a disorganized disaster.

Impending disaster is such an ever-present fear, that the administrators in charge often create rules and conditions for student movements and control which operate for the purposes of the administration and teachers without taking into consideration the ulterior purposes of the school—the building of a self-directed student; a truly maturing adolescent.

The basic philosophical position from which a policy regarding student discipline and control originates is quite simple. The only purpose of the secondary school is the education of students. The students come to high school just growing out of childhood and it is expected that they will leave six years later quite mature, capable of self-direction and, ultimately, self-instruction. It is important that the basic climate be established and maintained that the school is a workshop. It is a place to get a job done. It is expected that the rules will be reasonable and will be directed toward the ultimate welfare of the students. The school takes the position that the students wish for the success of the school and that they will live within its reasonable rules.

The nonconforming student, violating the basic rules of the school, must be brought to realize that he is acting in such a way as to injure his own educational opportunity. In addition, he must see that his acts may prevent the school from reaching its purposes for the other students. Discipline, therefore, will take the posture of correction, not punishment. The disciplined student must be brought to realize that the aim of the the corrective experience is to create an experience whereby he will learn to be self-directed and to conform to reasonable rules. The school is the last chance for society to help the undisciplined. No opportunity to help should be overlooked.

SELF-DIRECTION THROUGH FREE PERIODS

The nature of the secondary school with the self-directed assignment of one, two, or more free periods in the course of each instructional day, offers to the school administration the opportunity to establish a setting in which the student may learn the important lesson of self-direction. The older practice of an assigned study hall with a study monitor taking roll and enforcing silence in a confined and sometimes sterile atmosphere falls short of providing this opportunity for self-direction. In its place, the following practice has been instituted.

The central office is provided with the names of students who are not assigned to a specific class instruction for each period of the day. Students who are free in a particular period may elect each day the area to which they wish to report. For students who desire to go to a library area, a language practice room, an independent laboratory, or to the office of a particular teacher who is free at the same time, this choice is open. On arriving at this location, they sign a sheet noting the area and the particular period. This sheet, shortly after the opening of the period, is sent to a recording clerk in the central office.

Students wishing to go to a room where absolute silence is guaranteed and large enough table space is available so that their books and papers may be laid out, can choose the study area noted as the "Independent Study." Here a teacher is in charge and is responsible for guaranteeing the contract of silence; silence from teachers and custodians as well as fellow students. Students in this area also sign a sheet which is forwarded to the recording clerk in the central office.

Students wishing to converse with fellow students or to work with groups of four to six where no restrictions are placed on conversation in a normal tone of voice, can go to the "Cooperative Study Area." Here the rules are those of ordinary decorum. Students are expected to select a table of four but may move around freely from table to table as the occasion arises. Talking is permitted at normal voice levels. Students also sign the entry slip which is forwarded to the recording clerk.

Students who have chosen either an independent study area or the library, but do not conform to the rules of quiet studious application are immediately asked (i.e., sent) to the Cooperative Study Area where their impulsive desire to talk with neighbors may be exercised without restraint.

These three areas of choice are open during any free period during the day and may vary from day to day as the desires of the student dictate.

The task of the recording clerk in the central office is to match the students lists arriving from each of the study areas against the list of students who are unassigned according to the particular period. In the event that a student failed to sign into a particular area, he is presumed to be loose within the building or to have taken French leave. The name of the student is then reported to the assistant principal in charge of discipline and the student, when found, is brought before him. His case is reviewed as to whether there has been some error in reporting.

If the student is found to have been unable to assign himself to a particular area and wanders loose, he is now recognized as a student in personal difficulty and unable to operate within a free-choice situation. He is then assigned to a "Directed Study Area."

A Directed Study Area operates each period of the day in the charge of a teacher who is to make sure that the student arrives promptly, that he stays in the room in a condition of absolute silence. No excuses are permitted for leaving the study area except for a dire emergency. The minimum time of assignment to this area is one full school week. At the end of one school week the student may petition for release from this area in a letter of petition addressed to the assistant principal and forwarded to the principal with the approved endorsement of the teacher-in-charge of the Directed Study Area.

Each student who has been assigned to the Directed Study Area is asked to discuss this with his parents. The office of the school sends to the parents an explanation of the assignment of the student to the Directed Study Area. This letter explains its purposes and invites the parents to discuss with their son or daughter the importance of developing self-control and good study habits.

Warning notices of unsatisfactory scholastic success are prepared monthly and at each of the marking periods a list is prepared of the students receiving such notices. This list is placed in the hands of each of the teachers in charge of the cooperative study areas. The students who are on this list and are in regular attendance and seem to appear more than a few times in this study area, are asked to discuss with the teacher-in-charge as to whether they are making the proper choices of their free time.

In addition, the records clerk, who has on file the names of the students who have elected the cooperative study area, makes a tabulation of the number of times the failing or warned student has studied there. A form letter is sent to the parents of the student informing the parents of the continued choice of the student in the Cooperative Study Area and requests the assistance of the parents in reminding the students that this choice may be one of the reasons for their lack of success in their scholastic endeavors. The individual guidance counselor of each of these failing students is given a copy of the letters sent to the parents and is kept informed of the frequency of the non-succeeding student's presence in the Cooperative Study Area.

MINOR VIOLATIONS OF SCHOOL RULES

School tardiness and tardiness in arriving at assigned classes repeated for more than a relatively few occasions is viewed as evidence of a personality defect. Persistent school tardiness is reviewed by the assistant principal with the offending student. The cause of the tardiness is reviewed and examined on an individualized basis. Where it appears that the home is contributing to the tardiness of the student, a letter to the parents is formulated requesting their assistance. Where the problem of school tardiness appears to be the individual student's personality pattern, a full dress review of the situation is made using the guidance counselors and, if necessary, the services of the parents. The student evidencing a regular pattern of tardiness to school, unexplainable through any outside force, is required to report regularly every day to the assistant principal for discipline. If a penalty seems in order, it is worked out on an individualized basis depending upon the circumstances.

Tardiness to class is charged to the attention of the individual classroom teacher. The tardy student is noted by the classroom teacher and an individual discussion with the student is required. Frequent tardiness to class on the part of the student is reported to the assistant principal for discipline who calls the offending student in for a discussion of the cause of the tardiness. Punishment or penalty are here also worked out on an individual basis.

MAJOR VIOLATIONS OF SCHOOL RULES

There are certain actions of students which give evidence of serious social sickness on the part of the student. In addition, certain of these actions profoundly affect fellow students and, if continued unchecked, could well destroy the fabric within which the institution is able to continue. Among these acts are truancy, leaving school in the middle of the session without formal dismissal, insolence to a faculty member, deliberate acts of insubordination to the administration or the faculty, fighting ending in physical violence, the use of tobacco or alcohol, and deliberate destruction of school property.

The discovery of a student engaging in any of these major violations requires immediate action. The offending student is referred to the assistant principal in charge of discipline. It is extremely important that at this point the student not be reprimanded as being a bad person or as one with whom the school must disassociate itself, or one from whom the school authorities will extract penalties and punishment as restitution to the school. Rather, the initial conference with the pupil should search for the cause of the action, inviting the pupil to enter into intellectual search for the reason for his or her actions. In serious cases, the parents are contacted and invited to come to the school and discuss the matter with the school authorities.

The discipline action takes the form of placing the student on probation. A student under probation is required to carry with him throughout the school day and for as long as the probation needs to be continued, a complete schedule of his or her locations in the building at all times. Each subject matter teacher and each study hall teacher is required to initial for each period for each day under the heading of satisfactory or unsatisfactory conduct. In the event that the student has lost time in school, there is a requirement that the time be made up at the close of school in the afternoon by working silently in one of the school libraries for a minimum period of one hour each day. In the event of destruction of school property, the parents and pupil are requested to make restitution for the amount of damages the school has suffered.

Each student placed on probation has sent to his home a letter to the parents explaining what probation is, the reasons for placing the student on probation, and a determination of the minimum length of time which the student should be on probation. At the conclusion of the probationary period, the student may come into the office of the high school assistant principal and request release from probationary status. His sheets are reviewed and he must next request and receive an interview with the principal of the school. At this time the entire case is reviewed: the causes of the action, the penalties and punishments extracted, and whether the student understands completely the reasons for probation. This is the opportunity for the principal to make sure that the student understands that conduct of this sort cannot be condoned, for the welfare of the pupil and the school system is at stake. The principal alone can remove the student from probation. A follow-up letter is sent to the parents at the time of the removal of the student from probation.

Actual suspension from school for any period of time is used only in the most serious of circumstances and when it is absolutely necessary to protect the school from the presence of a seriously disturbed individual. The services of the school psychologist and other experts are brought in for a full case conference leading to a discussion of and preparation for permanent expulsion.

DOES THE SYSTEM WORK?

The evaluation of a program of discipline is quite easy. How many repeaters are found on probation? How about the percentage of students in the "directed study halls." An "opinion poll" of teachers, parents, and most important of all, students, can easily be prepared and evaluated. If the repeaters are few and far between, if the percentage in the directed study areas is under 2 per cent, and if it is the opinion of the students that the system is fair but firm, then the system works!

Section IV

The Staffing and Housing
of the Secondary School

BEFORE THE PROGRAM OF THE AMERICAN PUBLIC HIGH SCHOOL HAD BECOME
so complicated, staffing and housing were themselves simple. As the school
developed into a more complex enterprise, teaching became more professional and specialized staff personnel became more and more important.
At the same time that the staff was becoming more specialized, it became
evident that a more elaborate physical plant was needed to house the
program.

Increased professional status for teachers involved the clarification
of the teacher's relationship with other members of the staff, with the
students, and with the community. It became important for the teacher
himself to recognize the nature of his role and to formalize his recognition
in a code of ethics.

The secondary school staff is now divided into three different categories and within each category there is still more delineation of responsibility. There are administrative personnel, the professional teaching staff,
and the staff operating the auxiliary services of the school. How they
function as a team is determined by the degree to which they understand
their relationship to the other members of the staff.

Consideration of the secondary school plant includes recognition of
the principles involved in locating a school in a community, of the
function and peculiar problems in the use and construction of the different parts of the plant, and of the role of the professional staff member
in the proper utilization of the facilities provided.

Significant changes appearing on the horizon make it important to
consider, among other things, the need for flexible types of construction

393

and for a more functional approach to school design. Possibilities which may have a profound influence on the shape and organization of schools in the future include: information retrieval systems for expanding school library and other resources; the development of educational parks.

Recent political developments have suggested the possibility of fundamental shifts in the political relationship between the secondary school and the parent community. Teacher militancy, unionism, and student power must all be considered as potentially significant features in the operation of the American public high school of the future.

16

The Teacher's Relationship
to his Profession

IMPLICIT IN ALL THAT HAS BEEN SAID ABOUT THE AMERICAN PUBLIC HIGH
school is recognition that school operation is primarily the responsibility
of professional teachers. As a professional the teacher has to be aware of
his relationship to the students he teaches, to the other members of the
staff, to the community in which he works, and to the profession itself.

Being Part of a School Staff

One of the distinguishing qualities of a professional group is to be found
in the relationship which the members have to each other.[1] The primary
functions of teachers are service functions. Both the schools and the profession of teaching exist for the service which teachers render to students.
A teaching staff is bound together by responsibility for service. Within
the school they also work with others who share their service function
but who do not share their professional preparation.

Working with Other Teachers. In school, each student comes into
contact with several teachers during the course of the day. In the course
of his high school career he is likely to come into contact with as many
as 20 or more. Both the effectiveness of his school day and the total effect
of his high school education is dependent to some degree on the planning
and cooperation of these teachers. Planning takes place in the formal
faculty meetings, in the discussions of any group of teachers instructing
a particular grade level, in the meetings of departmental groups, and in
the informal contact of the teacher's lunchroom or lounge. The plans

[1] V. M. Rowley and S. H. Flint, "Re-shaping the Professional Image," *Educational
Forum* 28:481–84 (May, 1964).

may have to do with the length of the school day, with the sequence of course materials, with arrangements for special trips or excursions, with the schedule for tests and examinations, with the problems of particular students, with school policy in regard to pupil traffic, or with any of the other decisions which affect the welfare or morale of students individually or of the school as a whole.

In the professional contact of teacher with teacher the service being rendered to the student is expected to be the primary consideration. For instance, scheduling should be made with regard for the educational service being rendered, not simply the convenience of the teacher. There should be a high level of respect of teacher for teacher. Each should be able to feel that his opinion is respected by the others with whom he works. It is natural that older teachers are going to regard younger teachers as immature. It is also natural that younger teachers are likely to regard older teachers as conservative. It is important, however, that each be able to demonstrate respect for the other's professional competence.

In the close confines of the school faculty some of the same tensions develop as in any other situation in which people live and work together for a long period of time. The sharing of equipment, for instance, may be a source of friction. The allocation of limited funds for supplies may be another. Decisions as to which teachers will be on duty at a particular time may be a source of concern. Teachers are human beings.

One of the most crucial relationships in the school is that of the teaching staff with the new teacher.[2] The new teacher is likely to be immature and insecure. His college or university training has included a brief period of student teaching but otherwise he is likely to be faced with the full responsibility for his job with little orientation as to what to do. He will probably feel that to ask for much help is to display his incompetence. He may also recognize important differences between the ways in which things are being done at the school and the ways in which he has been encouraged to teach in his own preparation. The assignment by the principal of an older teacher to help the younger one in his initial orientation to the staff and to the profession of teaching is frequently made. Many school systems provide in other ways for the orientation of new staff members.

Many principals recognize that the extra strain of organizing new courses and of making adjustments to teaching make it advisable to see that new teachers are not permitted to carry too large a load. It is important that new teachers be given a chance to make adequate preparation for their teaching.[3]

[2] J. Moroney, "Helping the Beginning Teacher," *The Clearing House* 38:360–64 (Feb., 1964).

[3] A. Frazier, "New Teachers and A New Kind of Supervision?" *Educational Leadership* 21:97–100 (Nov., 1963).

The NEA Code of Ethics is one statement which makes specific reference to several aspects of the teacher's commitment to the profession. In this "code" the teacher is urged to "recognize that a profession must accept responsibility for the conduct of its members and that our [his] own conduct may be regarded as representative." He is to participate responsibly in the development and implementation of educational policies. He is to cooperate in the selective recruitment of prospective teachers. He is to work for equitable treatment of all members of the profession. He is to "keep the trust under which confidential treatment is exchanged." He is to deal honestly in such matters as use of time granted for professional meetings, public criticism of education, in the representation of his own professional qualifications and in the recommendation of his colleagues for advancement.[4]

Working With Administrative Personnel. Young teachers and outsiders sometimes assume that the relationship of the teacher to the principal and superintendent is analogous to that of the factory worker to the foreman or plant superintendent. This is a poor assumption. Teaching provides a great amount of autonomy for even the newest teacher. While the principal has supervisory responsibilities, the teacher is free to adapt his own teaching techniques within broad policy limits. Usually help in instrumental procedures is offered only at the request of teachers or in situations where discipline or instruction has broken down spectacularly.

Because the principal is himself an experienced teacher, he and his assistants are resource persons to the inexperienced teacher in the solution of problems which he may have either in teaching methodology or in the routine of classroom management. It is important, however, that the new teacher move in the direction of self-sufficiency in these areas. It is not considered fair to the responsibilities of the principal to send to him problems which the teacher could solve for himself. Furthermore, it is unfortunate to indicate to a class group that the teacher cannot work out a solution to less severe problems which may have arisen. Successful management of a crisis will build confidence in the teacher as a leader.

It is important for the young teacher to recognize the necessity for loyalty to the administration of the school.[5] Loyalty is a trait which has become important in American social philosophy, and disloyalty is not likely to be acceptable even when the grounds for disloyal conduct or criticism may have seemed adequate. The important consideration is that, while a particular official may not be personally deserving, the welfare of the institution suffers from disloyalty. Because individuals and institutions are closely associated in the public mind, it is important that public

[4] National Education Association, "Code of Ethics of the Education Profession," *The NEA Handbook 1963–1964* (Washington, D.C.: NEA, 1963), p. 68.
[5] *Cf.* W. J. Congreve, "Role of the Principal in School Improvement," *NASSP Bulletin* 48:3–9 (March, 1964).

respect for the administration of the school be maintained. Young teachers are expected to be particularly careful of their conversation if they are discussing school affairs. A recommended practice is to avoid shop talk when others who are not members of the school staff are present. It is suggested that comment to outsiders about school personnel whether of the teaching staff or the administration should be positive and constructive.

The cheerful acceptance of special duty assignments can make the whole atmosphere of the school more pleasant. Where the decision made has been the result of democratic discussion each person involved should be most alert to accept the outcome cheerfully and work to make the process involved successful. After there has been time for a thorough trial, there may be opportunity for renewed discussion. Participation in the democratic process carries unusual responsibility for cooperation in the execution.

Sometimes the young teacher fails to realize the impact of a decision which he may make unilaterally on the whole program of the school. Thus a teacher who becomes irritated with a student and tells him to leave the room may not realize that within the school as it is organized there is no other room to which he may go. The more experienced teacher will recognize this fact and will take other action more apppropriate to the situation in which he operates.

Among the important relationships which the teacher has with administrative personnel is that relating to contracts and employment. There are generally accepted principles under which the teacher maintains a contractual relationship with his employer. These are based on the principle of mutual respect and good faith. They provide convenient ground rules for the inexperienced teacher in his decision as to his initial employment.

In the first place it is understood that the teacher conducts professional business through professional channels. Thus the teacher should make application to the professional person in the school system who is responsible for nominating teachers. In this way undue pressure from laymen in the community is avoided. The teacher should wish to be employed on the basis of his competence and not on the basis of his knowing members of the school board or prominent citizens in the community. Application should be made only to school systems in which the prospective teacher is willing to work, and confidential information about the nature of vacancies should be kept confidential. The professional teacher will avoid seeking a position known to be filled by another teacher. Nor will he accept a vacancy created through unprofessional activity, or pending controversy over professional policy or the application of unjust personnel practices and procedures.[6]

6 National Education Association, "Code of Ethics of the Education Profession," *The NEA Handbook 1963–1964* (Washington, D.C.: NEA, 1963), p. 69.

"The professional teacher will adhere to the conditions of a contract until the contract has been terminated legally or by mutual consent, give prompt notice of a change in availability of service, status of application or in change of position. Care will also be exercised in avoiding conflicts of interest by accepting gifts or gratuities of significance that might influence his judgment in the exercise of his professional duties. Similarly teachers should not engage in outside employment that will impair the effectiveness of their professional service."[7] It should be noted that these statements of ethics are not regulations of an employing board but rather the formulation by representatives of the profession itself of the reasonable standards expected.

Working with Supervisory Personnel. The supervisory personnel in a school have two important responsibilities: (1) coordinating the work of different teachers and (2) assisting individual teachers in the improvement of instruction. In carrying out these duties the supervisor is usually free of other administrative responsibilities for the work of the teachers whom he is supervising. He is usually not responsible for the employment of teachers or for their retention. He is frequently not responsible for decisions as to their work load. He is likely to be responsible for getting groups of teachers together to plan their work, to prepare courses of study, to discuss better or different teaching approaches, and to request equipment and material for instructional purposes. He is likely to encourage teachers to ask for help in locating instructional supplies and equipment, in evaluating some particular teaching techniques which they may be using, and in general improving their effectiveness as teachers.[8]

The supervisor is usually a well-trained and experienced teacher who has the confidence of the administrative staff as one who is capable of rendering assistance. He is a helping teacher. It is therefore important for the young teacher to recognize the help that may be available from him. It is appropriate to ask the supervisor to visit the classroom and to discuss any teaching problems. Requests for help will be recognized as confidential when this seems necessary. When the supervisor visits on his own initiative, it should be recognized that he has general responsibility for coordinating the work of the whole teaching staff and must therefore have a basis for knowing the nature of the program itself, including both its strengths and needs.[9]

In the absence of a supervisory staff, the principal must carry his full load of supervising instruction as well as of administering the school. In most instances this is likely to mean that work is not as well coordi-

---

[7] *Ibid.*

[8] F. P. Morley and others, "Roles of Supervisors and Administrators," *The ASCD Yearbook 1964* (Washington, D.C.: The Association for Supervision and Curriculum Development, 1964), pp. 125–58.

[9] J. A. Richard, "The Art of Creative Supervision," *Educational Leadership* 21: 80–83 (Nov., 1963).

nated as it might or should be. It becomes the responsibility of the teacher to make the supervisory aspect of the job as easy as possible. Permission and encouragement to visit the classroom should be freely and enthusiastically given. Attendance at meetings called to discuss problems should be prompt and participation whole-hearted. Requests for instructional materials should be carefully prepared and made well in advance of the need. In the absence of a supervisor, planning for departmental instructional meetings should be cleared with the principal, but the initiative may have to come from the teachers concerned.[10]

The general attitude of the young teacher toward the supervisory personnel should involve acceptance both of the need for supervision and of the desire of the supervisor to be helpful. This need not involve a loss of self-respect on the part of the teacher. Paradoxically, the more competent the teacher, the more profitable the supervisor's assistance becomes. The supervisor becomes a sounding board for discussion of new projects and for the projection of new plans. The supervisor is able to help in the location of resources which may not be available to the teacher alone. The plans of the individual teacher can be more easily dovetailed with the plans and aspirations of other professional workers in the school and community. It is the secure teacher who can most easily and profitably have assistance. It is the insecure teacher who has the most difficulty accepting the assistance by which security could be achieved.

Working with the Non-Teaching Staff. The complexity of the organizational structure of the school has made necessary the addition of non-teaching personnel to the staff. Non-teaching personnel include not only the janitors, but the engineers, the nurses, and others whose training may be extensive but whose responsibility is for some aspect of the school program other than regular instruction.

The nature of the job performed by these people usually determines the lines of authority which they may follow. They are likely to have less autonomy within their sphere than the teacher has in his. They are more directly responsible to the principal. Requests of them for special service should be within clearly established authority or through the principal's office. It is not customary, for instance, for the janitor to be permitted to run errands for the teachers. Such tasks would be likely to interfere with his ability to complete the duties assigned him for the day. Whether or not it is appropriate for the teacher to make suggestions about the way in which the room is cleaned can be determined on the basis of the administrative practice in the school.

Care must be taken to respect the position and personality of the non-teaching staff. This respect is important not only because it is consistent with democratic doctrine but also because of the example being set the students. Teachers are expected to use proper titles of respect,

---

[10] *Cf.* Calvin Greider, "Let High School Department Heads Be Responsible for Supervision of Instruction," *Nation's Schools* 71:84 (April, 1963).

show consideration both in the form in which requests are worded and in the demands made, and to be concerned for the personal welfare of the people themselves. It is important to indicate in various ways the importance of the job being done to the mission of the school itself. Stimulating staff pride in the institution is an important aspect in developing the pride of the community in its schools.

The relationship of the teachers to school personnel with other kinds of technical or professional training is also important. While teachers may be appropriately jealous of what seems to be an encroachment on their independence to do the regular professional job of teaching, they must also recognize the need to cooperate with such other personnel as the school nurse or the secretarial staff. It may in some cases be necessary to get clarification from the school principal as to what is the dividing line between the responsibility of the teacher and of the nurse or clerk. At other times it is necessary only to work out a reasonable basis for cooperation, founded on mutual respect and an understanding of each others' problems.

It is important for the teaching staff of the school to make appropriate use of the services available through the non-teaching personnel. If, for instance, some students need assistance from the school nurse, it is likely to be the teacher who is in a position to make the necessary referral. If specialized teaching equipment is needed, the teacher may appropriately request it through the principal who may be able to get the engineer to supervise its construction. The case workers may have to get their start from a reference by a teacher or the counseling office.

Being a Part of the Community

Not only the teacher's cooperation with other members of the staff is important; his relationship to the community at large is also of consequence. In a sense the relationship of the teacher to the community is one of employee to employer. It is not, however, the relationship of the "hired hand" to the employer, but rather that of the professional person to the client. The teacher is not only the employee of the community but he is also a part of the community. This matter creates an interesting situation because it is never quite clear as to when the teacher is simply acting in his rightful position as a citizen and when he is still the representative of education and culture as the teacher of the school. Nor is it particularly worthwhile for the teacher himself to try to make the distinction. His effectiveness as a teacher and as a citizen are in a sense enhanced by the fact that the two roles are somewhat inseparable.

The Community's Expectations. In the early days of American education before teachers had much specialized professional status or training, it became customary for the school board or school committee to define carefully the relationship of the teacher to the community. The teacher might be expected to stay in one boarding house, keep specified hours, agree not to dance or smoke, attend church regularly, and sing in the church choir or teach a Sunday school class. Whether such regulations were liked by the teacher is not clear; they certainly left the teacher's position in the community clearly defined.[11]

In modern times, partly because the standards of the profession are better understood, partly because teachers themselves are better prepared and more highly professional, and partly because the improvement of travel and communications has made the general population less suspicious of outsiders, these requirements have been relaxed. The teacher in the smaller community is still expected to set a higher standard of public morality than would be characteristic of the general population, but the application of the standard is not formalized in the contract nor made the concern of the school board. Only gross violation of the moral code is likely to bring dismissal from a teaching position.

Wherever the teacher is called on to teach the Sunday school class or lead the scout troop, he should be free to indicate that he has other important commitments or that such service is too much like his daily routine for him to feel it wise to undertake it. His personal habits are his own concern except where they come into direct conflict with the moral standard of the community. In this case he is more likely to weaken the status of the school as an institution than to jeopardize his own job. The chief restriction on his social life is as it relates to his students. It is, for instance, considered unwise for him to date members of the student body of the school not so much because of community censure as because of its possible effect on his handling of school discipline and teaching relationships.

While the extent of his participation in community activities is the decision of the teacher himself, it is evident that participation in the civic life of the community does generally improve the relationship of the community to the school. The school becomes less simply a physical entity sitting out on the hill. In time of crisis over the issuance of school bonds or discussion of the appropriateness of some portion of the school curriculum, the feeling that the teachers are well known and trusted members of the community is an important influence for the good of the school.[12]

Although it is sometimes considered unwise for school teachers to take an active part in election campaigns in which school board members may be nominated, they have a responsibility to vote and to insist on exercising their rights as citizens. Their responsibilities as citizens to work for the welfare of the communities in which they reside are intensified

---

[11] Adolph E. Meyer, *An Educational History of the American People* (New York: McGraw-Hill Book Company, 1957).

[12] M. J. Peterson, "The Community and the Man," *Agricultural Education Magazine* 35:251 (June, 1963).

by the fact that they should be in a position to judge the issues being raised and to set an example of high-minded citizenship.[13]

One problem for teachers relates to the treatment of controversial issues in the classroom. The distinction between study and partisan indoctrination is important both to democracy and to public relations. Certainly no partisan point of view need be sponsored as "official." It is, of course, possible that the interest of the individual student may require a degree of partisanship. For some, the importance of consulting a physician in the case of illness is controversial. Nevertheless, most teachers of hygiene feel that they are acting ethically when they support the partisan point of view that it is desirable to consult a doctor.[14]

Teachers who are adequately paid for their services have a duty to devote most of their productive energies to their teaching jobs. They should not have to carry other work in order to support their families. The decision should, however, be left to the teacher since he is the one in a position to see the adequacy of his salary to meet his obligations. It would, perhaps, be unfortunate to have teachers leaving the profession who by carrying part-time jobs on the side would be able to stay on; there may be no replacements for them if they leave. The existence of such a situation should be called to the attention of the professional associations and public pressure applied by those groups in order to secure better salaries.[15]

Although in some communities it is considered important that the public employees live and trade in the communities in which they work, the unavailability of suitable housing and the trend toward considering the teacher as a state rather than a local employee has resulted in the gradual modification of this practice. The fact that modern transportation makes it convenient to get into the school for special functions has played a part. The trend toward suburban living and commuting has reduced the pressure.

Getting to Understand the Community. The teacher needs to understand the nature of the community in which the school is located and from which students come to school. One of the best ways to gain this understanding is by becoming a part of the community and its activity. Thus the teacher becomes alert to the problems most likely to concern the inhabitants in the operation of the school. Controversial issues may be identified and the nature of public concerns recognized.

Local traditions and the peculiarities of local speech may become the basis for some of the planning of courses in social studies and English.

[13] T. E. Robinson, "What's So Unreasonable About A Teacher's Wanting to Participate in Politics," *The NEA Journal* 53:39–40 (May, 1964).

[14] "Social Issues and the Schools; A Symposium," *CTA Journal* 60:7–30 (March, 1964).

[15] *Cf.* H. Davis and others, "Economic, Legal and Social Status of Teachers: Income From Additional Employment," *Review of Educational Research* 33:400 (Oct., 1963).

Even the mathematics and science teachers may make their instruction more appropriate when they understand the daily lives of their students and the students' families. In isolated communities there may be quite distinct problems which only the teacher who is becoming part of the community can really appreciate or cope with. While the nature of learning may have some universal characteristics, its application to local life and conditions is dependent on a thorough knowledge of the locality itself.

The best approach to becoming a part of the community is by doing what comes most naturally. Taking part in local affairs or church activities, joining civic clubs, accepting invitations to speak to local clubs, playing on a community athletic team, joining some kind of sports club, and simply being neighborly will all help the young teacher become accepted as a part of the group. As in any social situation, it is well for the newcomer to avoid getting involved in any highly controversial issues. Nor does it help to take sides with any faction in the community. In many cases the basis for the factionalism does not concern the newcomer.

Systematic study of the community's problems is important. It is wise to know whether the community is primarily industrial, agricultural, or suburban. The nature of the industry or agriculture involved is a part of the picture. Whether the community is relatively prosperous or poor is important. The causes of prosperity or poverty may be analyzed. The political structure of the community also has bearing. Is it controlled by a limited number of people or is there a large measure of democracy? Who are the influential citizens and what is their point of view on important issues? Who are the people who represent the conscience of the community and how do they exercise influence? How reliable is the local newspaper as a reflector of community opinion?

The desire of the teacher to become a part of the community's social life must not be allowed to make him insensitive to such problems as social class in the area. While the teacher may take part appropriately in the middle class activity in the community, he must be careful not to give offense to other groups. It is recognized in the Code of Ethics "that the public schools belong to the people of the community" and teachers are urged to acknowledge the right and responsibility of the public to participate in the formulation of educational policy.[16] Perhaps uniquely among American professions and among the teachers of the world, the American teaching profession recognizes this basic requirement of lay participation in the formulation of policy for the public school system. Equally important is the matter of keeping the public informed of the nature of the program provided. In spite of his special professional training and understanding of the nature of the educational process, the professional teacher in a democratic society shares the decision-making

[16] National Education Association, "Code of Ethics of the Education Profession," *The NEA Handbook 1963–1964* (Washington, D.C.: NEA, 1963), p. 68.

responsibility with his employer. The presumption is that this does not require him to act contrary to his understanding of the student's own welfare.

Living in a community is not synonomous with understanding it. There are many people who have lived all of their lives in a particular community and never developed any understanding of the conditions around them. There are others who with more systematic study have come to know their surroundings quickly.

Responsibility to the Student. It is service to the children (and to the adults who are students) which is the first responsibility of teachers as members of the profession. The teacher's responsibility is to deal justly and considerately with each student.[17] The more diverse the school population has become and the greater the emphasis on the use of the school as a social escalator, the more importance has been attached to the matter of equal treatment for all of the children. It is not enough for a teacher to disseminate information to his prospective students. It is important that he disseminate that information and use those techniques which are appropriate to the needs of the students themselves.

Those stating the Code of Ethics for the Education Profession emphasized the importance of measuring the success of each student in terms of his progress toward his own maximum potential. They stressed the importance of stimulating a spirit of inquiry, the acquisition of knowledge and information, and the thoughtful formulation of worthy goals. They recognized the importance of cooperative relationships with other community institutions, especially the home.[18]

In addition to these matters of a general nature dealing with the relationship of the teacher to the student, there are also items concerning special situations. One deals with the teacher's responsibility to withhold confidential information about students "unless we deem its release serves professional purposes, benefits the student, or is required by law."[19] Another states that the teacher should not accept remuneration for tutoring except in accordance with officially approved policy. The withholding of confidential information seems an almost automatic result of the nature of the teaching relationship. It is important for the teacher to have information which may be very personal to the student himself. Respect for the personality of the student and recognition of his need for privacy leave no other alternative than respect of confidence.

Remuneration for tutoring raises the question of double payment for services rendered. Since the teacher is paid to do the best job he can do in the instruction of each individual in the group, the requirement of additional pay for the same service is obviously unwarranted. Also, there is the possibility that pressure might be felt by a student to accept tutor-

[17] *Ibid.*, p. 67.
[18] *Ibid.*
[19] *Ibid.*

ing. The teacher is in the position of determining the educational fate of the student through the system of grading and promotion. He cannot therefore afford to have the question of monetary reward for additional assistance brought into the picture.

Responsibility of the Teacher to the Parent. The relationship of the teacher to the parent is one derived from the relationships of the teacher to the student and to the community. Because the child is immature and is under the guardianship of his parents, the teacher has a responsibility to parents which is somewhat different from his responsibility to other adults in the society. Because the school and the home have important shared responsibilities, the teacher must be especially concerned to respect the relationship of child and parent and school and parent.

The code of ethics specifies that the teacher is to cooperate with the home.[20] Since the parent in this country is the primary agent of the society for the education of the children, the teacher must respect this responsibility. There is sometimes a problem when there seems to be a conflict between the interest of the child and the wishes of the parent. It is obvious that the teacher must move most cautiously when this conflict seems to exist, recognizing at all times both the importance of respect for parental responsibility and for his own duty to the student.

As far as confidential information is concerned, parents should be furnished such information as will serve the best interests of their children, and teachers must respect also the confidential nature of the information received from parents. There is a distinct problem in this area with regard to information about high school age students which they may not wish divulged to their parents. The basic concerns are, of course, for the welfare of the student and the way in which information was obtained.

An additional injunction relates to the necessity of informing appropriate individuals and agencies of the student's educational needs and of helping to provide understanding of his educational experiences.[21] The concern here is not merely to keep parents and other appropriate agencies informed as to the progress of the children but also to interpret the purposes of the school as they relate to student development.

The Satisfactions of Teaching as a Career

Discussion of the secondary school teacher's role as a professional person seems incomplete without mention of the sources of satisfaction in teaching as a career. It seems obvious that, while teacher salaries will continue to rise and that while there are some positions in the teaching profession which are adequately compensated, teachers' remuneration at the second-

[20] *Ibid.*
[21] *Ibid.*

ary school level is not a positive factor in the choice of teaching as a career. The satisfactions of teaching are not to be found in the salary of the teacher.

The Status Role of the High School Teacher. Doubtless the position of the teacher in the community varies considerably from one place to another. In some communities the teacher ranks as a part of the upper class, in others as upper-middle. In a few others the rank may be more nearly that of the lower-middle class.[22] In each case, however, there are aspects of the teacher's role in the community which have little bearing on its class structure. It is recognized that the teacher's mission is to provide service. Other job relationships may put the community on guard against the person holding the job, but the teacher usually is regarded as one to be trusted.

For instance, the community is frequently suspicious of the politician because it fears his motive may not be service but a love of power. Similarly, the motive of the salesman may be questioned. The minister may be hampered by people's fearing that he is trying to interfere with the beliefs or behavior of the individual. The physician may be considered too aloof. The lawyer, while sometimes respected, is not always trusted. The teacher, however, is likely to be held in affection. The teacher is able to achieve a quality of classlessness not available to the same degree to many other public figures.

It is interesting to compare the conditions under which the service of the teacher is rendered. The doctor must work with the sick, the lawyer with those who are in trouble, the undertaker with those who are bereaved. The teacher, most of the time, is working with the young and their parents under the normal and usual conditions of life. His service to them is concerned with their hopes, fears, and aspirations. They are likely to make some progress under his tutelage whether he is particularly effective or not. If his students turn out well, he may claim a measure of credit. If they do not, then he can point to other influences which were probably more responsible than he was for their failure.

The class status of the teacher is much less important than his directly personal relationship to the community and the position he holds in the lives of the children and adults who make up that community. The question for the prospective teacher may be whether the opportunity for service and acceptance in the lives of the vast bulk of the population is sufficiently important to justify the penalty in terms of low monetary rewards.

Other Rewards in Teaching. In the previous section attention has been given to the relationship between social status and the opportunity for service. The two matters seem clearly related even though the nature of the relationship is a complicated one. One satisfaction in teaching is to

[22] *Cf.* S. Tenenbaum, "The Teacher, the Middle Class, The Lower Class," *Phi Delta Kappan* 45:82–86 (Nov., 1963).

be found in the opportunity for service. Closely related to that satisfaction is the quality of the relationship between those engaged in social service.

The congeniality of teachers engaged in a common project of service is a source of mutual satisfaction. In addition the similarity of background, experience, and ideals is likely to be productive of a high level of con-geniality. There is an atmosphere of mutual trust as well as of companionship. The typical school staff is large enough and sufficiently representative of different age groups to provide even for the factor of similarity of age, interest, and activity.

While the low salary of the teacher makes it often necessary to engage in other types of remunerative activity during long vacation periods, the breaks in the school schedule tend to prevent monotony. There is opportunity for the continued pursuit of intellectual and cultural interests both in association with others of similar interests and through use of summer periods. Only in the teaching profession is there so great a premium on the pursuit of knowledge for its own satisfaction.

For teachers who remain in the same community or at least within the same vicinity for long periods of time, there is satisfaction from the association with former students and their families. In part, the vicarious satisfactions of recognizing the progress of students toward success is a rich reward for the teacher. The teacher who teaches only 35 students a year for 40 years has had an influence of some kind on approximately 1,500 peoples' lives. This may represent a large part of a small community's population. The influence of the teacher who has taught over 100 different students a year within a teaching career is destined to have affected in some way the very fabric of the society. Knowledge of the nature of such influence is perhaps the richest of the rewards of teaching.

The intellectual satisfaction of the teaching process itself has not been touched on at much length. Some teachers find both the content which they are teaching and the workings of the human mind fascinating media for their own creative endeavor. For the artistic teacher the satisfactions of a job creatively done are more important than either the financial remuneration or even the opportunity for service to others. Teaching is fun because it is challenging, because it is full of complexity, and because there are so many possible avenues for expressing the personality of the teacher through the liberation of his students' individuality. English, music, arithmetic, and science achieve their significance as they are studied by teachers and students and come to influence the behavior of those teachers and students.

Maintaining One's Integrity. Much has been said about the importance in the teacher's role of the element of service to others. A little has been indicated in the previous section of the rewards which teaching offers the teacher himself. Perhaps the most important facet of participation in the professional life of the school and community is at the same time the most intangible. It has to do with the maintenance of one's integrity or individuality as a person.

In spite of the fact that the public school teacher is of necessity a part of a very large and complicated piece of machinery, he is primarily a person and an individual. It would be contrary to the core of the democratic principle to insist that his importance in the school setting derived mainly from his position. His influence arises not from single acts which he performs, but rather from their total effect. The same laws of psychology which recognize that the student is not simply the sum of his individual acts must hold for the teacher. The integration of the personality traits of the teacher is important for the same reasons that the integration of those of the student is important.

The teacher must be encouraged to recognize that, in spite of the necessity for group control, he has the opportunity and duty to use his creative talents to stimulate and enrich the lives of his students. Probably no other social institution, with the possible exception of the home, places so much stress on the importance of the interaction of person with person. It is desirable that the teacher maintain himself as a vigorous, well-integrated personality. His own physical, mental, and emotional health is important to his effectiveness in his dealings with others.

The teacher is entitled to develop his own point of view on important moral, political, aesthetic, and ethical problems. He is entitled to think for himself and to follow the logic of his thought. He is entitled to live his own life, to choose his own friends, and to plan for his own future.

Teachers are a source of new thought in the life of the community. The teacher may be the employee of the society, but he is not the hireling. His service must be the thoughtful service which goes beyond the capacity of his employer to give instruction. His responsibility is to instruct his employer.

When the teacher has ceased to be a free man, thinking his own thoughts and carrying out his responsibilities according to his own understanding of them, the school has ceased to perform its function in the democratic society. The integrity of the teacher is of much greater importance than the nature of the curriculum, the quality of the physical plant, the pattern of administration and supervision, or even the teaching methodology. It is the quality of the respect for the teacher's integrity which will determine the success or failure of all these other aspects of the school operation.

The Professional Preparation of Teachers

One important dimension of the teacher's professional status is the nature of specialized preparation required. During the early 1960's there was much discussion of teacher education. Several laymen including Koerner and Conant have written extensively and critically about what seemed to them to be involved.[23] A series of annual conferences has been held by the Commission on Teacher Education and Professional Services of the National Education Association. Money has been received from the Ford Foundation and other groups for special projects designed to modify existing procedures. Some criticism has been justified. Some of it seems designed to reduce rather than to increase the professional status of teaching.[24]

The Selection of Teachers. One element in the improvement of teaching at the secondary level is the initial selection of candidates. One of the problems is that high school teachers are in short supply, particularly in certain specialties such as mathematics and science. It is argued by those desiring to be more selective that greater selectivity will lead to higher salaries which will in turn lead to a better supply.[25]

There seem to be three levels at which selection might be made. One is at the time of admission to teacher education programs. The second is at the time of certification. A third might be at the end of some probationary period on the job. Some teacher education institutions exercise a high level of selectivity at the time of admission to the college itself. Usually, selectivity at later stages is on the basis of general ability, emotional and personal qualities, adequacy of background in terms of general culture and in the specified fields which the teacher wishes to teach, and technical competence.[26]

Any program of selectivity faces two important questions: How adequate are the measures being used? How adequate is concern for the welfare of the candidate being selected? Any positive selection should be on the basis of as many factors as seem appropriate to the situation for which there is evidence. This evidence might appropriately be gathered through testing, evaluation of academic records, and the recommendations of those in a position to judge. Unfortunately most of this evidence is likely to be inconclusive or even erroneous. By gathering as much information as possible, some of the problems of judgment may be reduced.

The question of the welfare of the candidate himself must be balanced against the welfare of the students he will teach. The teacher preparation institution is the agency in the best position to recommend

[23] J. B. Conant, "Teacher Education and the Preparation of Secondary School Teachers," *NASSP Bulletin* 48:192–208 (April, 1964); J. D. Koerner, "Findings and Prejudices in Teacher Education," *School and Society* 92:127–34 (March 21, 1964).

[24] *Cf.* "Three Slants on Curriculum," *Michigan Education Journal* 41:11 (Jan., 1964).

[25] H. H. Punke, "The Pay and Competence of Teachers," *The High School Journal* 47:13–21 (Oct., 1963).

[26] R. V. Buckland, "Admission to Student Teaching," *Kentucky School Journal* 42:20 (Feb., 1964).

students for a license (certificate) to teach. It therefore must be in the position of protecting the public from incompetence. The philosophy of general education in a democracy which says that each individual is to be taught those things which he needs to know is inappropriately applied to the professional preparation of teachers, doctors or lawyers. The impact of professional certification makes it more necessary for the professional school to be selective. Only those should be certified who are likely to be successful practitioners.[27]

Elements of the Program of Teacher Preparation. There are three reasonably distinct elements generally considered in discussion of appropriate education for teachers: the general, the special, and the professional. The proportion of time to be allotted to each type has been much discussed in recent years. Nevertheless there seems to be agreement that there is the necessity for all three.

The definition of what constitutes an adequate general education for teachers is necessarily vague. Most frequently it is defined as consisting of a variety of college level courses from the areas of English, the humanities, the sciences and mathematics, and history or the social sciences. Usually the courses required for college freshmen and sophomores and a certain proportion of electives are specified as contributing to "general education." Teacher preparation institutions may use some test or battery of tests to determine whether candidates possess a "sufficient background" of general culture. If so, general culture has been defined by the content of the tests used.

The amount and nature of course content in the field which a student expects to teach is likely to be specified either in requirements for certification or by the institution responsible for teacher preparation. In most states which certify teachers on the basis of a four-year bachelor's degree program, the requirements for most high school teaching fields are similar to those necessary for a college major in the same field. Exceptions to this rule deal with possibilities for certification to teach in more than one field or with areas in which there is an insufficient supply of teachers. In some states the special preparation in such areas as science and social studies may include work from more disciplines than college majors would. States which certify students only on the basis of a minimum of five years of preparation will require a larger amount of course work in the field of teaching specialization.

Much of the lay criticism of teacher education programs has dealt with the nature of course content and amount of work required in the professional field of education. Conant, for instance, seems to suggest that the amount of time given to professional course work might be reduced.

[27] "How Good Are Our Teachers?" *Education Digest* 29:1–4 (Nov., 1963).

Koerner and others criticize what they believe to be the nature of that content. Typically, professional content includes study of the school's role in American society, the nature of child and adolescent development, the principles of educational psychology (including learning theory), the specific problems of the secondary or elementary school, and the theory, organization, methods, and materials appropriate to the teaching of the particular subject to be taught. In addition there is provision for actual teaching under the supervision of the preparing institution.

Most professionals in the field of teacher education are convinced that any serious reduction in the time allotted to study of the problem of teaching will result in a less competent teacher. They have pointed out that foundation-sponsored programs attempting to do this have failed to provide for satisfactory evaluation on this point. Most of the critics have not themselves been through professional preparation programs nor are they professionally trained students of public education.

Time Allotments for Teacher Education. Throughout the nation at least four years of undergraduate preparation is the basic requirement for certification of new secondary school teachers. Some states now require five years of preparation or a masters degree for permanent certification. Most of the others provide additional salaries and recognition for those with more than the minimum. A few school systems have a significant proportion of their teaching staff with the Doctors degree.[28]

Much thought has gone into the problem of how to organize teacher preparation courses. The stronger teacher preparation institutions have carefully planned sequences of professional course work to form a program rather than permitting courses to remain discrete items. Similarly, it has been suggested that, if a fifth year is to be added to the preparation program, it should be a part of a planned five-year program and not simply an appendage to a four-year liberal arts degree. This would be in opposition to the programs supported by the Ford Foundation, most of which are designed to entice liberal arts graduates to become teachers.[29]

Much of the reorganization of teacher education programs is based on new approaches to student teaching. Where older programs tended to be based on teaching a single class or perhaps two or three for part of a semester, the newer ones tend to require that the student teacher be in the school for the whole day for several weeks at a time. Stress is placed on having responsibility for all of the usual duties of a regular classroom teacher. Some of the programs which are based on five years of preparation provide for as much as a full semester of student teaching. It has been

[28] J. C. Stone, "Teacher Certification, Supply and Demand," *Review of Educational Research* 33:343–54 (Oct., 1963).

[29] F. E. Heinemann, "The History of the Fifth Year Program," *Minnesota Journal of Education* 44:12–13 (Jan., 1964).

suggested that, in addition to student teaching for half a semester in the fourth year, students might then proceed to an internship for at least part of the fifth year.

Most of the more adequately staffed school systems provide for close supervision of first year teachers in order to be sure that teachers are well prepared for assuming professional responsibility. Teacher preparing institutions are also concerned both to provide better supervision of internships in the fifth year and to maintain supervisory contact in the first year of teaching. It is generally agreed that some experience similar to an internship should be provided for most young teachers as a basis for further graduate work.

Whether graduate work should be primarily in the field of education or in the field of subject specialization would depend on both the particular strengths or weaknesses of the teacher, on his previous undergraduate program, and on his teaching interests. Certainly teachers planning to work in special fields, such as counseling or work with the handicapped, will need specialized preparation beyond that usually available at the undergraduate level. Similarly there are many areas of study in the field of education which the graduate teacher has had little opportunity to explore but which would improve his competence as a teacher. There are also many subject areas which students need to explore in order to keep raising their level of competence above that of the undergraduate major.

As in other professional fields, there is a need for teachers to keep up. In-service education may appropriately be provided in workshops in large school systems, in summer programs in graduate schools of education, and under the supervision of state departments of education. Some states are making extensive use of television for this type of program.[30]

Responsibility for Certification. One of the matters at issue between educational theorists and their critics is the question of who should have responsibility for issuing teaching certificates. A related problem deals with the desirability of reciprocity from one state to another. Conant has recommended that the teacher preparation institutions have the responsibility.[31] Others, however, cite the need for more control over the standards of different institutions.[32]

In each of the states the final licensing authority is in the hands of state departments of education. For many years these made specific regulations dealing with the courses and hours required in general educa-

[30] *Cf.* D. G. Tarbet, "Use of Television in In-Service Education," *The High School Journal* 47:112–17 (Dec., 1963).

[31] J. B. Conant, "Teacher Education and the Preparation of Secondary School Teachers," *NASSP Bulletin* 48:192–208 (April, 1964).

[32] W. E. Armstrong (Interviewed), "Accreditation: Quality Control on Teacher Education," *Ohio Schools* 42:12–13 (March, 1964).

tion, special subject matter, and professional education for certificates in each teaching field. Since not all states had the same regulations, some teachers could not move easily from one teaching job to another. Usually, however, teachers certified in one state could meet requirements in other states while teaching on a temporary certificate.[33]

More recently, a commission representing the teaching profession and known as the National Council for the Accreditation of Teacher Education (NCATE) has been accrediting college and university programs of teacher education; some states now recognize graduates of these programs as having met certification requirements. In addition, some states are providing in other ways for reciprocity on certificates, while some are setting up programs for approval of those institutions which may not have been accepted by the NCATE.[34]

Those concerned with raising the status of teachers have insisted that professional control of entrance into the profession is essential.[35] Critics, generally opposing professionalization of teaching, have complained that there is already too much professional control. Some of the critics have been opposed to the "progressive" philosophy of many of the leaders of the profession.[36] Others are perhaps afraid of the possibility of increased costs when teachers supply is limited to those adequately prepared.

Proposals for Merit Rating. Related to the problem of selectivity in teacher education, and to certification, is the question of providing for extra payment for better teachers. Most teacher salary scales provide for higher salaries for those with more training and experience. Generally there is little or no provision for "merit" pay.[37]

Most teachers and school administrators are opposed to trying to provide for merit increments for several reasons. They feel that the techniques for measuring teacher effectiveness are too unreliable. They argue that the personnel who would be required for merit rating could be more profitably employed in supervision, and they believe that a rating system would strain unnecessarily the relationship between teachers and administrators. They also argue that most salary scales are so near subsistence levels that increases could more fairly be spread over the entire teaching staff. The surest approach to improving teaching, they believe, is to

[33] Earl W. Anderson and Elfreda M. Rusher, "Staff-Certification," *Encyclopedia of Educational Research*, 3rd ed. (New York: The Macmillan Company, 1960), pp. 1354–56.

[34] C. C. Travelstead, "NCATE Yesterday, Today, and Tomorrow," *Phi Delta Kappan* 45:38–42 (Oct., 1963).

[35] W. C. Lovinger, "Accreditation of Teacher Education: Why, How, and By Whom," *Journal of Secondary Education* 38:289–95 (May, 1963).

[36] See R. B. Brown, "Issues in the NCATE Controversy," *American Teachers Magazine* 48:9–10 (Dec., 1963).

[37] J. C. Moffitt, "Differences in Teaching: Can They Be Recognized and Compensated?" *The National Elementary Principal* 43:54–56 (Nov., 1963).

raise the supply of teachers by raising salaries and then selecting those best prepared for the jobs.[38]

Those educators who favor merit rating argue that more reliable procedures can be developed. Some school systems with higher than average salary scales have found less objection to merit pay increments. Others have made merit increments available on plans developed by teacher representatives who volunteered to be rated.[39]

---

[38] V. M. Rowley and S. H. Flint, "Re-Shaping the Professional Image," *Educational Forum* 28:481–84 (May, 1964).

[39] I. Gerber, "In Defense of a Merit System," *High Points* 46:62–63 (March, 1964).

17

Personnel Engaged in Secondary Education

ORIGINALLY THERE WAS BUT ONE TEACHER WHO SERVED AS TEACHER, principal, janitor, superintendent, clerk, and librarian. He reported to the trustees or board of education. Budget making was no particular problem because there was not much to budget. The principal item of expense was the salary of the teacher. Gradually, the problems involved in school operation become more and more complex and the variety of personnel needed to operate it has increased.

The Administrative Personnel

One group which exercises a strong influence on the quality of American secondary education is classed as administrative. It is this group which stands between the public as represented by the school board and professional teachers who do the actual teaching. It is perhaps the most highly professionalized of the groups concerned with the operational aspect of the program. Generally the administrators have had more professional training and more experience. While basic policy decisions are supposed to be made by the lay personnel of the school board, the detailed program is dependent on the administrators and on their leadership of the professional staff. Whether or not the school is to be democratic or aristocratic, progressive or conservative will be determined by the school administrators.

The Superintendent of Schools. While the superintendent of schools is not likely to be housed in the high school building, he is probably as crucially a part of the administration of the secondary school as the principal himself. It is the superintendent who nominates the principal to the lay board. It is the superintendent who recommends the budget for the operation of the school. It is the superintendent who determines the way in which the members of the high school staff will be selected. Although he may delegate some of this function to the principal, he is likely to make the final decision on which teachers will be selected. It is the superintendent who must first be convinced there is a need for major revision of the school curriculum. It is the superintendent who will recognize the need for setting up new secondary schools or for expanding the physical plant to provide more adequately for existing schools.[1]

The problem of how to relate the school program to the needs of the community devolves largely on the superintendent himself. The superintendent may use the school board as a sounding forum for discussion of the nature of the present program and the desirability of modifying it, but the initiative must usually come from him. Any setting up of other lay groups to examine the program is also likely to be recommended by the superintendent himself. The definition of what is lay responsibility will often be suggested by the professional superintendent. The need for a broader tax base and the budgeting of available funds requires the attention of the staff of the superintendent.

The overall supervision of the curriculum and staff in-service training, as well as the articulation of the various school levels within the system, are all responsibilities of the superintendent. The maintenance of such central facilities as a professional library and the distribution of basic instructional supplies is the responsibility of the superintendent and his central staff. The development of full use of the resources of the community for the better education of its children is also largely the responsibility of the superintendent.

Conducting basic research as to the needs of the community and students is likely to require the careful attention of the superintendent and members of his staff. It is this function which seems most likely to be neglected in the modern public school system. Nevertheless, it is basic both to the modification of the school system and to doing a better job within the existing framework. The research effort may start with the comparatively simple study of such things as the holding power of the school, but it will also need to be concerned with more complicated studies of the needs of the students, with the effectiveness of particular systems of grouping and teaching, and with the true nature of the curriculum itself.

The Principal of the School. While the superintendent has responsibility for the program, the administrative official directly responsible for the day-to-day operation of the high school and for the development of the curriculum is the principal. The complexity of the departmentalized program places more responsibility on the high school principal than is

[1] P. J. Misner, "The Superintendent's Job Can Be Well Defined," *Nation's Schools* 71:81 (May, 1963).

carried by the elementary school principal or even the college president.[2] It is the principal and his assistants who keep the whole clockwork-like schedule running. Operating within whatever policies may have been laid down by the superintendent of schools and board of education, they have direct supervision over the teachers and students in the school. It is they who are responsible for the safety of the school in the case of fire or other catastrophe. They are responsible for general morale and discipline of the student body and of the faculty. They determine the nature and frequency of the interruptions which are made in the work of the teachers and students for the handling of administrative routine. Similarly they have considerable responsibility in most school systems both for the initial employment of teachers and for recommending their continued employment or dismissal.

The responsibilities of the principal include not simply supervision of administrative routines, but also responsibilty for the general quality of the curriculum of the school. Operating within the policies established by the board of education and superintendent of schools, the principal and his assistants are responsible for specific decisions as to which teachers will teach which classes and for the make-up of the classes which they teach. While the teacher must have control over his own techniques, the principal is still generally considered responsible for much supervision of instruction. He and his assistants suggest ways of improving teacher effectiveness, provide better teaching materials, and encourage or require participation in in-service education programs, faculty meetings, or workshops. He determines the nature of the departmental organization of the staff.

The principal is responsible for the planning and staffing of the extracurricular activities program. He and his assistants have general financial control and responsibility for funds which may be collected or spent in connection with this program. He determines which activities are appropriately a part of the program and which students and staff members are eligible to participate. Although the policies for the operation of the program should be developed cooperatively with the other members of the staff and, where it seems desirable, approved by the superintendent and board of education, the recommendation of such policy is likely to rest initially with the principal.

The general atmosphere and point of view of the school staff towards its responsibilities to students is very much influenced by the attitude and point of view of the principal. If the school is to be a laboratory of democracy, then the principal must see that his exercise of authority and responsibility is an example of democratic administration.[3]

[2] *Cf.* J. M. Richards and J. K. Hemphill, "A Progress Report: A Study of the Secondary School Principalship," *NASSP Bulletin* 48:211–30 (April, 1964).

[3] R. L. Lien, "Democratic Administrative Behavior," *NASSP Bulletin* 48:31–38 (March, 1964).

The Assistant Principalship. As the size and complexity of the school increases, it becomes desirable to have one or more assistant principals. It is usual for these officials to take over some particular phase of the work of the principal. In such cases they exercise the responsibility subject to the direction of the principal. The first responsibility which is likely to be assigned is that of disciplinarian. While this is not the most important of the responsibilities of the principal, it has in some schools become one of the most time-consuming. It is certainly one in which it seems important that the official responsible be permitted to keep his schedule free of other work which cannot be dropped in the case of some emergency. Such a person may of course help with other administrative routines such as the working out of the details of the schedule for the following year, the planning of various school activities and assembly programs, and perhaps the supervision of portions of the extracurricular activities program. He is also likely to be responsible for contacts with parents, welfare officials, health authorities, and social service workers.

Another function which may be assigned to an assistant is the direction of guidance activities. While this and the responsibility for disciplinary activity in the school must be closely coordinated, there is danger of neglecting the guidance function for the more immediately time-consuming activities of interviewing troublemakers and checking pupil attendance. Bad discipline does suggest the need for guidance activity, but the guidance function is more basic to the program of the school. The planning of a well-coordinated program of counseling, testing, and individual instruction should not become subordinate to the maintenance of discipline. In most cases the director of guidance activities will also have responsibility for counseling. Even in schools which still maintain the titles "dean of boys" and "dean of girls" for disciplinaries, it is being recognized that there is still a need for counselors and directors of guidance activities.

A third function which may be assigned is that of coordinator of instruction or curriculum coordinator. It is the responsibility of this official to do what he can to improve the quality of the instructional program. He has general responsibility for the distribution of necessary materials including audio-visual aids, textbooks, and reference materials. He gets groups of teachers together to coordinate their planning. He plans workshops and helps with the instructional aspects of the faculty meetings. He is able to spend his full time on the instructional aspects of the school programs without having to be concerned with the other administrative or disciplinary problems.

Where there is a six-year type of school organization and in some exceedingly large four-year schools, there has been a tendency to assign assistant principals responsibility for one or more years. Thus there might be an assistant principal in charge of the junior high school and another in charge of the senior high school. Each of these would then be encouraged to organize his staff and program somewhat independently of the other, but coordinating where necessary through the principal's office. The advantage of such an arrangement is that it makes possible some of the values of a small school—in particular, more attention can be paid to individual students. Some of the newer secondary schools have purposely provided physically for smaller units which would house perhaps 500 students and would be supervised by separate assistant principals.

Another type of arrangement has been to assign an assistant principal as a general administrative assistant and understudy to the principal. In this case, a principal who is about ready to retire may shift the responsibility of the school over to his successor somewhat more gradually than might otherwise be the case. The newcomer can learn the staff, students, and routines of the school, and the transition is easier.

The Clerical Staff. Much of the administrative routine of the secondary school is dependent on the efficiency of its clerical staff. Keeping the many reports and records both concerning finance and the students themselves is time-consuming. Since these records are the basis for much of the operation of the school they must be kept accurately. There are elaborate statistical reports, transcripts of the records of students, grades to be recorded, schedules of students and staff members to be maintained, records of participation in extracurricular activities, records of conferences with students and parents, and reports to the superintendent of schools, to the state superintendent of schools, to accrediting associations, and to the U.S. Office of Education.

In addition to the records and reports mentioned above, there is the correspondence with parents, colleges, former students, governmental agencies requesting information about students or former students, citizens of the community, employers requesting recommendations, and others doing business with the school. Some of these may be handled by a clerk or stenographer, some may be dictated by the principal or one of his assistants, and some may be taken care of by an office manager. While these activities may seem peripheral to instruction, they have a bearing on the public attitude toward the school.

Unless the principal or one of his assistants is to be confined to the office during the entire school day, it is important to have someone who acts as a receptionist to answer the telephone and manage the traffic around the office. Since the receptionist may have a great amount of contact with students coming to the office for information and assistance, it is important that she be a pleasant person who can encourage a wholesome attitude toward the principal and school administration. The tactful handling of visitors who may not understand why the principal or members of the staff are not immediately available for conference may prove very important in the public relations aspect of the school program.

Some schools have recognized that the clerical staff can make a contribution to the efficiency of the teaching as well as administrative staffs. Many of the routines of reporting can be handled in the central office. The preparation of mimeographed materials to be distributed to students can reduce the time spent in copying material from the chalk board or other sources. Occasionally, certain types of objective tests may be scored by school clerks, and some schools have experimented with the possibility of hiring teaching assistants who can help by reading English themes and doing some clerical chores. The use of teaching aides in the classroom is being widely discussed and provided as a possibility for improving teaching effectiveness.

As various labor-saving devices have come into general use in the business world, they have also proved helpful to school personnel. Public address systems, duplicating machines, calculators, and electric typewriters have been accepted for a long time. More recently copying machines of various types are being used more and more, and other business machines are being employed in some schools for the registration and scheduling of students. The public schools probably have more need for efficient utilization of limited personnel than any business operation. Care must be taken, however, to avoid the de-personalization of the program. For instance, a misused public address system is a serious threat to the instructional program of the school. Similarly, the automation of the scheduling process may make adjustments to the needs of individual students more difficult. It may be questioned as to whether the need for such devices is not an admission that a particular school has already become too large to render the kind of personal attention which seems basic to democratic secondary education.

The Professional Non-Teaching Staff

The heart of the educational process is still to be found in the daily relationship of teacher and student. In the modern school, however, the teaching staff and the administrative personnel directly concerned with the teaching program no longer work alone. Some of the duties which once devolved on the teachers and some new responsibilities are now handled by other professional staff on a full- or part-time basis. Often their work can make or mar the success and atmosphere of the school program.

The School Librarian. One of the professionally prepared members of the staff is the high school librarian. The librarian serves the instructional program both through his direct contact with students and as an expert resource person assisting the teachers to find teaching materials. In addition he has an administrative responsibility in the ordering, cataloguing, displaying, and repairing of books. Thus he must be prepared as a teacher in the understanding of the interests and needs of high school students and teachers and as a librarian in the technical skills of librarianship. He should have a knowledge of the general field of books for children and adolescent youth, a knowledge of the problems in providing materials appropriate to the development of skills in reading and use of reference materials, a knowledge of the materials available in fiction and non-fiction areas which support the instructional programs in the various subject fields, and an understanding of the use of the library resources in unit teaching.[4]

It is important that the librarian have an appreciation of the educational philosophy of the secondary school. The development of attitudes, skills, concepts, and factual information is of more importance in the school library than the collection and preservation of books. Many of the attitudes of the public or reference librarians may have to be modified in the school library in the same way that the attitudes of the specialist in music, art, English, language, or history have to be modified in the high school classroom.[5] The traditional characterization of the library as a dreary and quiet place where children are seen but not heard, and where regulations keep one from enjoying the books must give way to the more functional idea that the library is a place for pleasant work and relaxation. The librarian is the key to the change.

The Counselor. The counseling and guidance services of the modern public high school have been described earlier. The counselor, like the other professionally trained members of the teaching staff, has a specialized role which supports the basic teaching responsibility of the secondary school. He must have preparation in the specialized techniques of counseling while at the same time understanding the program and philosophy of the school. Just as the school librarian and the history teacher are not merely librarians and historians, the school counselor is not merely a counselor.

The counselor will typically devote a minor portion of his time to classroom teaching. His teaching duties serve to keep him in touch with students as students and also with the problems of other members of the teaching staff. Developing an understanding of the counseling program by teachers who may be new to teaching or to the school is an important part of his responsibility. He must encourage an atmosphere sympathetic to the students' needs.

The basic responsibility of the counselor is the personalization of the program. He should have wide latitude, within the policy of the school, in helping students to develop worthwhile programs based on an understanding of their needs and interests. He should have the confidence of

[4] A. B. McGuire, "School Librarian: A New Image," *Educational Leadership* 21:227-30 (Jan., 1964).
[5] M. G. Mitchell, "What's Going On in the School Library," *Phi Delta Kappan* 45:44-47 (Oct., 1963).

students in his interest in their welfare and his willingness to help them solve their own problems. While his relationship to them may and should be on a professional plane, it is also important that there be no effort to be critical or moralistic. Understanding and not domination should be the basic aspect of the relationship.

The certification requirements for school counselors frequently specify that he must have had previous teaching experience. Generally the specialized and professional nature of counseling requires preparation beyond that minimum required in most states for teaching. (It might be noted also that professional levels of teaching also require more than the minimum required for simple certification.) This preparation includes more specialized study of the problem of high school youth, the use of tests and other techniques for assessing pupils status, the reference materials available for giving assistance in vocational choice, and an understanding of the relationship of the counselor to the other aspects of the school program.[6]

The Auxiliary Services to the School

In addition to the personnel concerned in the professional administration of the school, and those even more directly concerned with its teaching function, there have developed a number of other important activities which may be referred to as auxiliary services. Some of these are essential to the school's operation. Others, while not accepted as essential, are clearly important to the fullest development of high school youth.

Engineering Services. As school plants and facilities have become more and more elaborate, it has been necessary to provide technical engineering services to keep all the equipment in working order. The heating systems alone may require elaborate control by a specialist. Public address systems, plumbing, and lighting are likely to present additional problems. The supervision of the custodial help, the care of the buildings and grounds, and the routine maintenance of office equipment in the school office and commercial departments of the school are all time-consuming. While the school principal has general responsibility in these areas, it is becoming common practice to employ school engineers to handle large plants or school systems.

Because these people work closely with pupils and teachers and because they are looking after investments running into hundreds of thousands and sometimes millions of dollars, it is important that they be

---

[6] The American Personnel and Guidance Association, "The Counselor: Professional Preparation and Role; A Statement of Policy," *Personnel and Guidance Journal* 42:536–41 (Jan., 1964).

well trained in their duties and in the public relations techniques necessary in public positions. Where these officials are under the direct supervision of the superintendent or business manager of schools, it is also important for them to have a clearly defined working relationship with the principal of the building in which they are working.

The School Janitor or Custodian. The modern custodian has to have much more technical training that was necessary in former times, when the principal job was sweeping out the school. The care of modern floors has become more complicated than merely mopping or sweeping them. In many schools the routine operation of the heating system falls to the lot of the custodian and, when this is done efficiently, it requires more than simply shoveling coal or taking out the ashes. Even the replacement of light fixtures requires more knowledge now.

The care and sanitation of the toilets and plumbing fixtures of the school is complicated and yet important. The school must set a good example for its student body. Modern detergents make it quite feasible to have clean schools, but their use requires personnel able and willing to do the job.

Most school principals recognize the importance of having custodial staff of good integrity and character. Like everyone else in the school, these people come in daily contact with students and their example is sometimes likely to be followed. In some schools the custodian seems even to perform some of the functions of the counselor. While this counseling may not be the best school practice, the people who are the custodians should be of a sufficiently high moral character that their counsel will be positive.

The Dietitian and Cafeteria Workers. The increase in the size of the school cafeterias and the increased complexity of the records which must be kept by the schools participating in the federal lunch programs has made the job of the dietitian important in the operation of the school. The administrative responsibility for feeding perhaps a thousand students cheaply and efficiently and for giving them a well-balanced meal requires distinct ability. The variety of skills in meal planning, record keeping, cooking, and management of help requires both training and experience. When it is recognized that the cafeteria can also serve as a means of improving dietary habits, the selection of personnel becomes more obviously important.

The number of students being fed daily in school cafeterias and the infrequency of cases of food poisoning or epidemics traceable to them is a tribute both to the dietitian and to the vigilance of public health officers. The standards they may teach students to expect in other public eating establishments should have a beneficial effect on practice in the community at large.

As in the selection of other personnel to work with school children and teachers, it is important that the people chosen represent high personal and moral standards. It is important that they have adequate professional preparation to do the job and a sufficient educational background to understand some of the services to the program of the school which may be rendered by cafeterias and cafeteria workers. They should be led to feel that they are appreciated as part of the teaching team of the school. Their contribution to the morale of the school should be recognized.

The use of students as part-time workers in school cafeterias seems of dubious value. In general, the time which they have for such work could be spent to better advantage in the educational or recreational phases of the school program. If they are in need of free lunches or part-time employment, these may be provided in other ways. If students must be employed in the lunch room, great care must be taken to protect the rest of their educational program. Their identification as students who must work for their lunches is in some cases bad for their morale.

The School Nurse. It is customary in most areas to have either a school nurse or the part-time services of a public health nurse. These people have several distinct functions. They help to identify students in need of private or public medical attention. They help to call the attention of school personnel to important public health problems within the school. They help school officials in spotting communicable diseases among the student population. They help carry out the teaching function of the school in the area of health and sanitation. They help in giving first aid to students hurt or taken ill at school.[7]

Where the nurse is not a regular member of the school staff but comes in from the public health department, there is a problem in working out her role within the school. In some cases she is likely to regard herself as a kind of supervisor who is to give directions to the teachers on how to perform their particular functions in regard to the health of students. On the other hand, there is also the possibility that the regular teachers may feel that they have been relieved of their particular responsibilities for the health of their students by the presence of the school nurse. While it is generally more satisfactory in the larger school to have a full-time nurse directly responsible to school officials, the part-time nurse's responsibilities can be sufficiently well defined to avoid the development of bad working relationships with the teaching staff.

It is important in either case that the school nurse have a thorough knowledge of the educational philosophy of the school and of her relationship to the teachers, counselors, and administration. The fact that within the school the pattern of relationships is likely to be distinctly more democratic than within the hospital should be clear and the reasons for the difference should be equally clear.

[7] G. E. Cromwell, "The Future of School Nursing," *Journal of School Health* 34:43–46 (Jan., 1964).

The School Physician and the Dentist. Some schools have part- or full-time school doctors and dentists. Not only can these people perform an important function in the recognition and recommendation for treat-ment of students with special health problems, but they can also help to provide for other very important medical services of an instructional nature. For instance, the moderately large secondary school has a number of students who need corrective physical education. Such programs benefit from the supervision of a physician and may be neglected in the absence of one. Participation in both the sports program and the required physical education program also should be based on careful and regular physical examination. The need for dental work, glasses, hearing aids, corrective orthopedic assistance, and routine medical care may be hampering materially the effectiveness of certain students. Public health problems such as hookworm can also be recognized at school.

It is important for medical personnel who work closely with the school to have some type of orientation to the school program similar to that needed by the school nurse. In some cases there is the problem of showing medical personnel that school health programs are not competi-tive with private practice but more probably serve to advertise the im-portance of the service rendered to the community by the medical profession. The democratic relationship within the school staff is also sometimes different from the relationship of the doctor with the nurse or the patient. Some of the health services which the community sees fit to carry out through the public schools are not purely educational in their purpose. There is probably none of them, however, which does not have important implications for the effective learning of the students in school. The sick student can not be an efficient student. Furthermore, attitudes toward health must be frequently taught at school if they are to be learned by all of the children of all of the people.

The School Psychologist. The dependence of the educational pro-gram on sound psychological insights and the need for individualizing the school's impact on the student in attendance has made it seem im-portant to have in the school or closely available such specialists as psy-chologists, psychometricians, and even psychiatrists. It is the function of these specialists to keep tab on the psychological implications of the things which the school is doing in the lives of the students and teachers who are participating in the program. Where these services are not directly present in the school itself, it is important that they be available on a consulting or referral basis and that there be no great amount of red tape to their use.[8]

The work of these specialists is obviously related to that of the school counselor but is more highly specialized. In most cases it is wise that they

[8] A. W. Hepburn, "The School Psychologist," *Education* 84:137–40 (Nov., 1963).

have had some teaching experience as a part of their training program. They must realize that they are a service agency in the school and that they must work democratically with the other members of the school staff as members of the professional team.

They will be concerned with giving tests, the analysis of the relationships within the school program, the discovery of the problem areas in the instruction of students, the improvement of working relationships between teachers and disturbed students, the development of modified programs for students who may be under too much tension or who may need reassurance, the interpretation of test results to teachers, the development of better understandings within the teaching staff of the nature of teaching, and in general with an improvement of the teaching aspect of the school program.

The School Social Worker. Schools have for a number of years had staff members who performed the duties of attendance officer, case worker, visiting teacher, or some other social service functions. Sometimes these people have worked under the supervision of the superintendent of schools and at other times they have been under the supervision of the welfare department. Most of their responsibility has been in working with the elementary schools because the students from many of the homes needing such assistance have tended to drop out at an early age. With a shifting toward a more pervasive responsibility of the school for all of the youth of secondary school age, there is more need for these officials as a part of the secondary school program.[9]

It was noted in the third chapter that the program of the school is too directly a middle-class program. One of the functions of the case worker or social service worker is to understand its problems for and responsibilities to students in the lower levels of society. Without such assistance the best intentions may fail to provide an effectively democratic program of public education. Few public school teachers are trained to get the necessary facts and to see that the right help is provided.

In order for this service to be focused directly on the work of the school, it is desirable that at least some social service workers be a regular part of the school program. They need to be participating members of the faculty in regular attendance at faculty meetings. Every aspect of the program has to be viewed in terms of its effect on improving the school's holding power and instructional capability. The curriculum, the teaching methods, and the organizational operation of the school are all in need of scrutiny from the point of view of their effect on the submerged element of the school population. The function of the school in reconstructing society cannot be met in any other way.

[9] E. F. DeRoche, "Responsibilities of the School Social Worker," *The National Elementary Principal* 43:50–52 (April, 1964).

18

The Secondary School Plant

PARTLY BECAUSE OF THE INCREASE IN THE NUMBER OF PERSONNEL CON-
cerned in the operation of the high school but more directly because of
the increased functions of the school, the nature of the secondary school
plant has changed drastically since the days of the one-room school.
Because it is readily visible, this phase of the American high school is
most impressive both to the local visitor and to the foreigner. The revolution in school housing has achieved its greatest momentum in the period
since the Second World War. About that time the revolution in the
school's role in American life coincided with a revolution in the nature
of building materials and in the field of architecture itself. In all three
revolutions the emphasis was on functionalism as opposed to classicism.

The Style and Location of the Plant

The most obvious aspects of the school's physical plant are its architectural style and the location and size of its site. During the early part of
the twentieth century it was apparently important that the new secondary
school be built along classical Greek or Gothic lines on the principal hill
or thoroughfare of the community. This reflected the new-found concern
of the community for public secondary education. The imposing site and
nature of the building were to reflect dignity on the internal operation of
the school and on the community itself. Gradually the emphasis on mere
architectural beauty gave way to recognition of the need for economy.[1]
The money which was being spent had to provide for a maximum amount
of educational value for a maximum number of children. During the same

[1] *Cf.* C. D. Gibson, "Are School Buildings Costing Too Much?" *California
Education*, 1:7–12 (Sept., 1963).

period the architects felt the challenge not only in school housing, but in industrial, public, and residential building, to develop a style which was at once handsome and functional. New construction techniques using steel and concrete made the shift possible; and the development of engineering skill in the areas of heating, lighting, ventilation, and acoustics also made a contribution.[2]

In some communities the argument over functionalism tended to cloud the issue of whether money appropriated for school buildings was to be spent for educational purposes or in the creation of architectural monuments.[3] That the period of indecision was brief is a tribute to the ability of the modern architect to create beauty out of simplicity, or perhaps it is a tribute to the sense of the American people. The question is no longer one of whether there will be Greek columns or adequate shop facilities, but of what kind of facilities are adequate for an expanding program.

Building Around the Program of the School. After the revolution in school building the ruling idea was to make the building appropriate to the program which it was to house.[4] The core of the building was to be its classroom, but because each subject required a different kind of classroom, not even all of the classrooms were to be alike. Since the school's program involved other kinds of activities besides attending classes, there were libraries, science and language laboratories, shops, auditoriums, gymnasia, cafeterias, offices, conference rooms, and specialized areas for music, art, the storage of special equipment, and even for the relaxation of the staff and of the student. It was no longer sufficient to tell the town architect to construct a building with sixteen classrooms and the related facilities. It became important to have an architect or consultant familiar with the problems of school housing to consult at length with the professional staff as to what was going to be done with the building after it was complete. Because each school community and school population was unique, each program was to be somewhat different from every other one. It was no longer desirable to build the same kind of school in every community.[5]

In some cases it became obvious that, although the community could not afford to build a new school, the existing building was not appropriate to the kind of program which should be offered. It became desirable to remodel and redevelop the facilities which were available. Again the

---

[2] J. Silinsh, "Modern Steels Add New Dimensions to School Design and Construction," *American School Board Journal*, 148:21–25 (Jan., 1964).

[3] J. M. Barrow and M. R. Sumption, "How to Measure Building Cost by Educational Opportunities," *Nation's Schools* 73:60–61 (Jan., 1964).

[4] *Cf.* D. A. Willey and N. W. Hanson, "Is There Vision in Your Educational Specifications?" *American School Board Journal* 146:33–36 (June, 1963).

[5] *Cf.* W. Fox, "You Need a School Building Consultant," *American School Board Journal* 148:52 (Jan., 1964).

school staff worked in coordination with the architect in the planning. Perhaps the efficient teaching of commercial subjects required a new classroom or a larger one. Perhaps the school had decided to abandon the use of study halls. The use of audio-visual aids required facilities for storing equipment and films. The science laboratories had to be designed for multiple use by several kinds of science classes. Language laboratories required a different kind of space. Unit teaching required more space than was required by the traditional lecture techniques. Vocational shops had changed in character, and there was perhaps more emphasis on industrial arts and less on vocational skills which could better be learned in a co-operative diversified occupations program.

New concepts as to the possibilities for correctional physical education led to the need for rooms for physical examinations and for correctional training. Instruction in swimming seemed important, so swimming pools were sometimes added. Student parking facilities became important. Counseling, guidance, and testing required special conference facilities, additional space for records, and always more storage than was available. The extra-class activities of the school required special facilities—perhaps a small theater, space for the newspaper staff and the student council, space for the various athletic teams and activities.

Building to Change the Program. More radical than the idea of building the plant around the program has been a movement which seemed designed to reshape the program. Spearheaded by national firms of consultants to school architects, and sponsored by such groups as the National Association of Secondary School Principals, this movement may have a significant influence on the typical American high school.[6]

Among the modifications which have been suggested have been the campus school, the school-within-a-school, and more recently a wholesale revision of the use of school space. The campus school represented a move toward a college-type complex: separate phases of the program were located in separate and specially designed buildings. The school-within-a-school approach was based on a modification of team teaching. It provided for joint use of a variety of teaching facilities by a small group of teachers and a fraction of the total population of the school.[7]

The idea of more use of such facilities as the language laboratory and more individual responsibility on the part of the student has led to the construction of school buildings in which the individual study cubicle rather than the classroom is the central feature. Such a facility would have the effect of forcing a revision of the curriculum or at least the schedule of the school. While classrooms are still provided, only a fraction of the

    [6] W. J. Stone, "Schools of the Future, Now," *NASSP Bulletin* 46:241–49 (May, 1962).
    [7] Francis G. Cornell, "Plant and Equipment," *Encyclopedia of Educational Research*, 3rd ed. (New York: The Macmillan Company, 1960), pp. 1008–1028.

population of the school would be expected to be using them at a particular time.[8]

The Location of the Site and the Arrangement of the Buildings. With renewed emphasis on relating the building to the program of the school, it became obvious that the selection of a site and the location of the activities on the site were important. In the first place much more space seemed desirable than had been typically allotted. It was important for the school to be free of interference from the noises of city living and traffic. It was important for students to be safe both from hazards at school and from traffic while going to and from school. It was important to have ample space to provide for such things as student and staff parking, for outdoor physical education and recreation, for the study of plant life, and for freedom from congestion and noise within the building itself.[9]

The typical school needed a minimum of ten acres if it had only 300 students and it might need as much as 30 acres if it had as many as 1,000 students.[10] Within the building different types of activities could be zoned to avoid the competition of noise and odors. The cafeteria would be on one wing or in a separate building. The shops, and music education facilities would need to be separated from the libraries and other classrooms as well as from each other. Classrooms requiring joint use of such facilities as laboratories or the libraries might be built adjacent. Multiple use of classrooms was planned for, as well as the development of specialized rooms for special purposes.

With the improvement in transportation much less attention is now paid to the problem of a central location than to the matter of adequate size and freedom from congestion. The trend over the past three or four decades toward suburban living and toward decentralization of shopping areas indicate that some of the same forces have been at work in the other phases of community life. It has been pointed out that where towns are large enough to justify planning facilities for more than 1,000 students it is time to begin to think in terms of two or more high schools at opposite ends of town with not less than 500 nor much more than 1,000 students in each.[11]

It is felt important that play space, including the playing fields and gymnasiums which house a part of the school program, should, where

[8] Harold B. Gores, "Schoolhouses That Work," *NASSP Bulletin* 49:69–76 (March, 1965).

[9] *See* George W. Holmes III, "Decade of Secondary School Plant Planning," *The High School Journal* 44:130–34 (Jan., 1961).

[10] R. W. De Remer and B. G. Lauda, "Need for Large School Sites," *American School Board Journal* 148:71–74 (April, 1964).

[11] *Cf.* Walter H. Gaumnitz and Ellsworth Tompkins, *Holding Power and Size of High Schools* (Washington, D.C.: U.S. Office of Education Circular Number 322, Government Printing Office, 1950).

possible, be at the site of the school. Having the facilities near the main school helps to make the athletic program a part of the general program and minimizes the tendency for varsity games to be simply amusement spectacles. Furthermore, the safety hazards incident to crossing traffic in going from the school to playing fields may be kept under some control. The use by the community of school facilities when this does not interfere with the school's own needs is encouraged both because these facilities are in reality community property and because public relations are generally improved.

The Educational Park. De facto segregation of minority groups in large metropolitan areas has brought about the development of what have been referred to as educational parks. The theory has been that, by building large new school complexes, children from several attendance areas could be transported in sufficient numbers to provide for adequate representation of minority and majority groups in the school population. This has been made possible in part by the availability of land purchased for urban renewal near the central city core. It frequently served an additional purpose of permitting outmoded facilities to be abandoned.

Some professional school men have been concerned at the size of the student bodies thus created. One technique for dealing with this problem has been to set up several schools on the same park or campus, each self-contained with approximately 1,000 students. Expensive facilities such as auditoriums could then be shared.

Attempts to see that classrooms are more representative of the larger community have been the result of the twentieth century view that the school is an agent for the socialization of the population. Obviously the mere provision for physical integration of minority groups does not solve the problems of group living. On the other hand, instruction in group living must become more meaningful in such an environment.

The Parts of the School Plant

It seems well at this point to stop to catalogue the different features of the school plant in order to indicate the part that each may play in the educational program. In some cases it seems sufficient simply to mention that a particular facility is provided. In others it seems helpful to indicate the ways in which the adequate provision of such a facility seems to assist the operation of the instructional function of the school itself.

The Classrooms. As has already been indicated, the classrooms form the core of the school plant, and it seems desirable to provide different types of rooms for different types of subject matter and methods of teaching. Discussion of the classroom seems to come under about three headings: comfort, attractiveness, and instructional utility. These are not exclusive categories because there is a clear relationship between each of the three. Both comfort and attractiveness improve instructional utility.

One of the most important aspects of classroom comfort is the matter of lighting. While it is essential that there be enough light for the type of work to be done, the amount of light contrast between different areas in the field of vision is equally important. Since most of the material which children read is on a white surface, it is considered desirable for the other things which they see to be light. The walls, the ceiling, the floor, the table surface, and the chalk boards should be light. Related to this is also the idea that the amount of usable light is dependent on the amount of reflectance of these surfaces. The green chalk boards, which have come into wide use recently, not only are aesthetically more appealing but they help to increase the light in the room and to decrease the amount of contrast in the field of vision.

Because of the importance of diffused light, the use of indirect or semi-direct lighting has been closely studied. No child should be required to face a bare light source. If fluorescent lights are used, it is important that bulbs that have become dim with age or have begun to flicker be easily replaced.

The ventilation and heating of a room are also important to comfort. Teachers should be sensitive to the fact that students may be differently dressed and require less heat than that at which the teacher would be most comfortable. Generally, classrooms may be better a little cool than too warm. Some schools ask that teachers leave the regulation of classroom temperature to the janitor, particularly when older style heating plants are used and it is easy to warm rooms near the boiler but difficult to get heat to those further away. Ventilation should be such that no student is sitting in a draft; frequently window deflectors are necessary in classrooms where window ventilation is used. It is sometimes necessary to ventilate rooms during periods in which classes are changing.

The attractiveness of a classroom is dependent on a number of factors. It is important in the first place that it be clean and reasonably tidy. In general, students will be more cooperative in keeping a classroom clean than in cleaning one up. Only a little encouragement is necessary, and the lesson in tidiness is perhaps a part of social education. Displays of work in progress may increase attractiveness. It seems to help if the classroom carries the flavor of the intrigue of the subject to be studied. On the other hand it is unfortunate to use all of the available display space for aesthetic purposes if there is an opportunity to use the space for instructional purposes. The two aspects should be combined.

Some teachers complain that their classroom settings do not permit the use of newer teaching techniques. In most cases such complaints are only partially true. It is perhaps easier to do projects, use committee work, and carry on other space-consuming procedures in a large room than in a small or narrow one, but much more can be done in the standard high school classroom than appears at first sight. There is no more wasteful style of seating arrangement than the traditional five or six rows. Nor is there one which seems more monotonous to the student or visitor. The amphitheater arrangement is one simple variation. Zoning of the classroom for different types of activity is feasible even in the standard room. A space for teacher/student work conferences can be provided in a front corner, another for use of reference materials in a back corner. If students are grouped in interest or ability groups, it is possible to move chairs about from period to period to provide for this grouping. If chalk board space is needed, different groups may face or be near different sections of the board. If the group activity consists largely of listening, then part of the classroom will be arranged so that students face the teacher. If there are to be motion pictures or slides, it must be possible to dim the room.

The mathematics classroom may have need for a great amount of chalk board space and ample opportunity for the teacher to move about to help students with individual work or to confer with small groups of students. There may be a need for display models of various mathematical concepts or charts ruled for plotting graphs. The storage of plane tables and surveying instruments may present a problem or perhaps the storage of exercises and work books may have to be provided for.[12]

The social studies classroom on the other hand might need much more extensive space for committee or group work. More space would be needed for reference material and it is likely that much more space could be used in bulletin boards than in chalk boards. The need for teacher domination of the class would probably be less than in some other classrooms. It would be most helpful to have adequate space for the storage and display of maps and charts as well as of student projects. There should probably be space within the room for housing library books both of a fiction and a non-fiction nature dealing with topics being studied in the class. There should also be files of current newspapers and other periodicals which would prove helpful to committee groups or for individual projects under the supervision of the teacher.[13]

The English classroom, since it is likely to be the center for the study of grammar, literature, speaking, writing, and listening skills, might have a variety of special features. It might be helpful to have the same kind of space for the display of books as in the social studies room. It should be possible to arrange the seating in the room for debates, panels, or informal play readings. A browsing corner might be desirable, and facilities for

[12] Cf. Paul W. Briggs, "New High Schools Staff Planning and Teamwork," *American School and University* 35:37–40 (1963).
[13] Cf. T. Bell, "Why not a Social Studies Laboratory," *Social Studies* 54:181–83 (Oct., 1963).

students to do committee work or work in pairs on special projects would be helpful. A glassed conference room which might be supervised by the regular teacher while the rest of the class was engaged in some other activity might be helpful. Space for the use of a tape recorder or record player would also be important.[14]

The science classroom, which is to be used by students studying general science and by others studying biology, might appropriately contain space both for laboratory experiments and for general class discussion and work. The older concept of the separate laboratory is giving way to the idea of moving from one activity to another with more flexibility. Tables must be provided for teacher demonstrations and for student work. Space is also needed for growing plants, for observing water life, for storing equipment and materials, for committee as well as individual work, and for use of reference materials. Since some of the materials used and stored are likely to be hazardous, it is important that part of the storage be locked.[15]

Other academic classrooms have particular needs. Special provisions should be made for language teaching, geography, art, music and other activities requiring different kinds of space and equipment.

The Impact of Team Teaching and Flexible Scheduling on Classrooms. The development of the idea that more than one teacher will be working with varying sizes of student groups will obviously have an impact on classroom construction. In some schools operating in what is called the "school-within-a-school," various size rooms are clustered together. In such a situation students frequently have carrels or study stations and much of their time is spent in these stations pursuing individual study projects. More space is allocated than in the typical school to teacher conference space.

In planning for team teaching and for flexible scheduling, many variables need to be taken into consideration. Among these are the need for specialized space and equipment for certain fields of study, the need for multiple use of space, the nature of the relationships between members of the team, the size of groups which will be likely to work together at any given time, and the possibility of changing the schedule on short notice. There is of course the real danger that the physical plant may crystallize the program around a particular approach before that approach has been carefully tested.

With the development of school architecture as a special field, a fund of experience in solving the particular problems of school construction is being created. There is a trend away from stock plans and the standard

[14] *Cf.* Nicholous L. Engelhardt, Jr. "Laboratories for Learning," *American Schools and Universities*, 26:135–40 (1954).

[15] *Cf.* "Where Science Facilities are Heading," *Nation's Schools* 72:44 (Dec., 1964).

classroom toward building for particular programs. The development of movable partitions has made it possible to experiment with different types of classroom design.

The Shops and Specialized Classrooms. The kind of shops or specialized classrooms which will be needed will depend entirely on the program. The trend in smaller schools is toward general shops with divisions for special work in woodworking, metal working, electrical and electronic work, and drafting. As schools become larger and offer more specialized vocational training, other facilities may be added. Usually, how often the space will be utilized is considered before the decision is made to provide specialized types of shop equipment. On the other hand, it is frequently possible within the concept of the general shop to provide a wide variety of opportunity.[16]

The home economics program is also likely to require specialized facilities. Opportunities are needed for learning to use standard cooking and sewing equipment and household appliances. In most situations, the provision of elaborate housekeeping suites is not practical; but, where multiple use is possible, dining room space may be used for instruction and serving meals, living room space for instruction and informal class activity, and even bedrooms may be made to double as health clinic facilities. In this way areas for demonstrating furnishings and the care of the home may be provided.[17]

Commercial courses require space for teaching typing, shorthand, and the use of office machines. It becomes important for the schools to stay up-to-date in such programs, and this may require constant remodeling to accommodate new and different types of equipment. The demand for typing by students other than the commercial students is constantly increasing and requires ever-increasing amounts of space. It is possible that eventually most students may want to know how to type. This function may eventually be taken over by the elementary school.[18] Whether this shift to typing will eventually require additional space in the typical classroom for student typewriters remains to be seen.

Teaching drama seems to call for the development of small theaters in which instruction may be more easily given and supervised without the problems involved in the use of an auditorium. Similarly instruction by television seems to offer some special problems requiring different style rooms from those of regular classrooms. The old style study halls have proved so unsatisfactory that many new schools have no special provision for them. Either study halls are conducted in regular classrooms, are

[16] J. B. Morgan, "Waupaco's Senior High School Comprehensive General Shop Design," *Industrial Arts and Vocational Education* 53:48–50 (March, 1964).

[17] L. M. Ehman and G. Marks, "Home Economics Facilities: Tools for Learning," *American Vocational Journal* 39:26–28 (Jan., 1964).

[18] *Cf.* C. D. McConnell, "Typing in the Sixth Grade," *The National Elementary Principal* 43:67–68 (Sept., 1963).

provided for in the longer class period, or students are assigned to the library space. The latter arrangement is not particularly popular with the librarians and seems to interfere with some other uses of the library itself. Where study halls are provided, it is frequently suggested that there should be space in the study hall for reference materials and perhaps also for periodicals which may be helpful.[19]

The School Library and Instructional Materials Center. There has been much discussion as to whether the high school library is to be primarily a place for storing and cataloguing books which are then distributed to classrooms or whether it is to be the center in which the books are to be used. There is much to be said for the idea of making books available in the classrooms in which they are going to be used. On the other hand this availability may sometimes require expensive duplication. Some schools have provided reference books such as encyclopedias in practically every high school classroom and then provided for the transfer of books being used at any particular time from the central library to the classroom library.[20]

Some authorities, basing their figures on usual use of library facilities where time is provided for students to go to the library voluntarily or for classroom groups to be taken while working on particular projects, have suggested the need for table seating for a minimum of 50 students and at least ten per cent of the high school population. Most of the books should be shelved for easy access.[21]

The school library is the logical place for student committees to meet in a glassed-off area under the supervision of the librarian. Space may also be provided here for instruction of class-size groups in the use of the library, and for using specialized audio-visual equipment including overhead and opaque projectors, film strips, and motion pictures. The cataloguing and supervising of such equipment and aids is most logically related to the functions of the school librarian. It is of course well, whenever possible, to take audio-visual materials directly to the classroom rather than to rely primarily on central facilities, but some of the facilities are not easily portable. There must also be provision for previewing films by teachers and students alike.[22]

It is important that the library be attractive, that the number of regulations governing student conduct be kept as small as possible, that students should have the opportunity to confer with one another and with

[19] M. P. Heller, "Outmoded Study Halls Give Way to Learning Centers," *The Clearing House* 38:231–33 (Dec., 1963).

[20] C. Dane, "The School Library as an Instructional Materials Center," *Peabody Journal of Education* 41:81–85 (Sept., 1963).

[21] *Cf.* W. S. Corliss, "On Planning Library Rooms," *American School Board Journal* 147:27–28 (July, 1963).

[22] *Cf.* R. B. Hudson, "New and Future Trends in the Use of Audio-Visual Materials," *The ALA Bulletin* 58:39–42 (Jan., 1964).

the librarian, and that conditions conducive to pleasant but effective use of materials be maintained. Acoustical treatment of ceilings and walls, bright but glare-free lighting, as well as furniture and walls light enough to provide a good reading background, are all features which can make working in the library easier and more agreeable.

Work space for the librarian and his staff is important, and should be arranged so that the librarian can supervise the library while engaged in other types of work. The library should be planned to facilitate the assistance of students wishing help in reference work as well as the comparative seclusion of those who may wish to settle back to read or browse. Some schools have arranged to have the library near to student lounge facilities. Such arrangement tends to strengthen the idea that the library is a part of the recreational life of the school. Provision should also be made for students wishing to listen to recordings either for their own enjoyment or as a part of a music appreciation program.

The Auditorium, Gymnasium, and Lunchroom. One of the problems which disturb school planners is that some facilities are used infrequently in proportion to their size and cost. The auditorium, gymnasium, and lunchroom fall into this category; there has been a great deal of emphasis in recent years on the possibility of constructing facilities for multiple use which would combine the features of all three types of room. In some of the smaller schools this combination has met with success, but scheduling conflicts and problems of conversion had made it unpopular. A newer trend has been toward reducing the size of the auditorium to the point that it would normally seat not much more than the total enrollment of the school. In some schools of more than 1,000 or 1,200 students, the student body has been divided to meet in two or more assemblies. Where extensive community usage has made it important to seat larger audiences, the stress has been on recognition that the auditorium was a community auditorium; assistance has been asked in paying for the cost of building, maintenance, and heating. It is not considered worthwhile to build an exceedingly large auditorium for the once-a-year commencement activities, but rather to use gymnasium or stadium facilities for this purpose if there is no community auditorium available. It is felt that auditoriums seating more than 1,500 lose most of the feeling of audience participation important to student assemblies.

While there is a strong temptation to construct gymnasiums with the varsity athletic program as the primary consideration, it is physical education and not athletics which must be considered first. The use of folding seating has made possible the more efficient use of floor space, and the development of durable floor finishes has made it unnecessary to restrict the use of the playing court to the practice of the varsity team. The gymnasium of the modern high school must be used for a variety of recreational purposes for which street shoes as well as basketball shoes are appropriate. Provisions must be made for ample shower and dressing facilities and for a well-rounded physical education program. Proper ventilation both of the gymnasium itself and of the locker and shower space is important.

The lunchroom of the modern secondary school must be large enough to feed the whole school population within a reasonably short period of time, usually not more than two regular class periods. It is considered better not to try to seat more than 300 students in one room at the same time, and so it may be necessary to have more than one lunchroom served by a central kitchen. It is also helpful to have conference type small dining rooms in which teachers, students, or others conducting school business may eat. These rooms may be used at other times of the day for conference purposes or for small class or committee work.

The Administrative and Counseling Suites. The administrative offices must be located so as to facilitate school administration and contact both with the school itself and with the public which may want to consult with staff members. Typically, the principal's office is so arranged that a receptionist may assist in meeting students and the public, in handling routine requests for information, and in managing the office itself. Other offices also need to be located near to the secretarial staff.

It is being recognized that more and more space needs to be available for keeping office supplies and for the permanent storage of valuable student records. The fact that most of the counseling and guidance services require extensive use of student records makes it desirable to have counseling offices convenient to the record facilities. The disadvantage in this arrangement is the tendency to lose sight of the counseling function in the routine administrative operation of the school. The counseling facilities generally include in addition to private conference facilities, space for the display of vocational and occupational materials, reading and waiting room space, and facilities for testing (including adequate storage for tests and materials). If there are health clinic facilities, they may be associated with the guidance facilities or they may be located near the physical education facilities. It may also be helpful to have the student lounge facilities near the guidance facilities because of the relationship between these two aspects of the program. While this location facilitates supervision of the student lounge by the counselors, it may bring the student lounge closer to the administrative suite, which is not considered so desirable.

Conference Facilities and Lounges. Because the modern philosophy of the secondary school places so much stress on the use of conference and small group work, there is seldom enough conference space available. While it is not considered economical to provide offices for all the teachers, it is desirable to provide space for them to keep records and materials and to hold conferences with students or parents. Small offices or conference booths might be shared by several teachers or classrooms. There should also be space where teachers may work in committee, planning their work, previewing films, agreeing on various types of curriculum material, or discussing the problems of their students.

Teacher lounges which provide facilities for making coffee and for some relaxation during the day are also important both for the mental health of the teachers and for the creation of esprit-de-corps. This space may be convenient to the cafeteria for use during the lunch hour, but should not be too remote from the teachers who may need to make use of it during other times of the day. It should be large enough to accommodate the teachers who are likely to be free during any class period or special work groups who may wish to use it after school.

Rooms for use by students in connection with various phases of the extracurricular program are important and should include adequate file and storage space. Among the more important items are a dark room for processing film and space for the newspaper staff and student council. Of course, the same principles of multiple use must be observed in this matter as in other phases of the use of the school facilities. The fact that the space required is not very large makes provision more feasible.

Student lounges are becoming an important part of the school plant. Lunch-time recreational facilities are needed in bad weather, and some schools also provide more freedom of movement during the school day, including a milk break in the morning. Space for students' getting to school early or needing to remain after school tends to reduce problems of student control during these periods. Furthermore, as the school assumes some responsibility for the recreational education of students, the possibilities in providing opportunities for dancing, use of television, listening to records, or simply browsing in books becomes evident.

The Teacher's Role in Plant Planning

Since the school plant is one of the most important tools provided for the development of an appropriate educational program, the prospective teacher needs to know how to use it and have a part in planning it. Where the plant is not adequate, it is probably the responsibility of the staff working with the principal and superintendent to see that the needs become known and the plant is remodeled or replaced. It is the prerogative of any craftsman to insist on adequate tools with which to work. It is of course the mark of the artist to be able to use the tools available.

The Teacher and the Architect. It is becoming more imperative to involve the entire professional staff (as well as students and interested parents) in the planning of new facilities for an existing school. The first step in the process is usually drawing up a description of the school program, including features already well-established and those which appear desirable but which may not yet have been developed.[23] From this description it is then possible for the educational consultants to the architect to draw up what are commonly referred to as the educational specifications.

If the educational consultants see aspects of the program which may not have been carefully considered by the professional staff, they may then discuss them with the staff before the specifications are turned over to the architect. Space requirements are indicated; the relationships which must be provided for are noted; the arrangement of the space itself is suggested. Sketches may supplement written descriptions of the nature of the facilities desired and the use to which they are to be put. After all of the educational specifications are in, the architect then begins to prepare material for consideration by the professional staff and their consultants. Representatives of the teaching staff may visit other schools of similar construction and get ideas for the improvement of their own programs and of the physical facilities.

Care should be taken throughout the process that at each stage the professional staff understands the decisions being made and approves of them. Otherwise, there may be serious wastage in the use of the complete building. It is important that the staff understand what is expected of a new plant in order to know how to use it. The best way to assure staff understanding is to have staff participation in the planning. Where facilities represent the development of a new school, it is still important to select the principal and staff of the school as early as possible in the planning stage so that the building may be designed to fit a program rather than vice-versa.

The architect may wish to consult both with the educational consultants and with the teachers themselves for more specific details of the nature of the program and of the facilities which may not have been indicated in the educational specifications. The expression of the educational philosophy of the school in the plant itself has ramifications which do not appear at first glance even to the architect. Every effort must be made to see that everyone concerned can help to interpret the philosophy and to visualize its application in the new plant.

[23] Frances G. Cornell, "Plant and Equipment," *Encyclopedia of Educational Research*, 3rd ed. (New York: The Macmillan Company, 1960), pp. 1008–1028.

19

Toward a New Political Orientation:
Selected Readings

IN THE FIRST HALF OF THE TWENTIETH CENTURY, THE AMERICAN SECONDARY school and its leadership have been closely allied with the conservative political power structure of the country. Schools were supposed to be kept out of politics. School elections were supposed to be non-partisan and were generally held at different times from those for the rest of the governmental structure of the country. Teachers were themselves either considered members of the conservative middle class elements of the community or were upwardly mobile from the lower middle class and were warned not to "rock the boat." Students, while not always quiescent, were not particularly aware of the potential power available in student strikes and protests. For various reasons the situation is changing. The school leadership, the teachers, and the students are all reconsidering the role of the school in politics.

The Impact of Teacher Militancy

For a long time a very insignificant portion of the teachers of American secondary schools were willing to consider even the possibility of strikes and collective negotiations. Within the last few years there has been a significant shift in attitude on this point. The National Education Association now approves of collective bargaining, the use of sanctions (including withholding services in extreme situations such as the absence of a suitable contract), and the word "strike" is occasionally being used. The principal teachers' union, the American Federation of Teachers, is becoming stronger and is in

442

active competition with NEA affiliates as the bargaining agent for local groups of teachers.

The first article by Donald W. Robinson, Associate Editor of the Phi Delta Kappan, reports an interview with Albert Shanker, President of the United Federation of Teachers, the teachers' union representing New York City teachers. At the time of the interview Mr. Shanker had just finished serving a 15-day sentence for leading an illegal strike. In the fall of 1968, Mr. Shanker again led the teachers in a strike because a group of teachers were fired from a ghetto school by the newly-organized school district board. While not discussed in this interview, the implications of this second strike relate to the effect of decentralization of big city schools on the power of teachers' unions and associations in the big city school systems.

A Talk with Albert Shanker*

Donald W. Robinson

Albert Shanker, relaxed, soft-spoken father of four, looks more like the philosophy professor he started out to be than the militant union leader he is. He reflects a quiet dedication to the cause he adopted 15 years ago when financial pressures led him to interrupt his doctoral studies in philosophy (including a teaching assistantship with Charles Frankel) and accept a long-term substitute job in the New York City schools.

Shanker is proud that one of the little-noticed provisions of his hard-won strike settlement last September specifies that the board will cease giving substitute licenses. "Furthermore," he says, "there is a penalty clause attached. If the board should continue to give substitute examinations after a certain date it would be required to place all substitutes on the appropriate salary schedule and pay other benefits and penalties to the tune of somewhere between $30 million and $50 million."

Almost immediately upon assuming his teaching duties Shanker became interested in teacher organization. He admits that his mother's involvement with the Garment Workers' Union had created a family environment favorable to unions. Not surprisingly, this atmosphere continues. Recently Shanker's five-year-old son, asked to identify George

* *Phi Delta Kappan* 49:255-6 (Jan., 1968). Reprinted by permission of publisher and author.

Washington, promptly replied, "He was the first president of the United Federation of Teachers."

The immediate condition that fed and has continued to feed Shanker's union zeal was the way New York teachers were treated. At the outset he objected to their being ordered to sacrifice part of their lunch periods for "snow duty." The objection was met with a curt, "You're lucky you have a job at all." Shanker admits that he dared to be bold because he had no intention of staying.

At this time (1952) New York City teachers were represented by 106 competing organizations. Shanker saw the need for teacher unity and he believed in the union concept. The achievement of that unity within the union has been a 15-year accomplishment to which he has been a major contributor. This has meant unending negotiation among teachers themselves. All 106 groups are now within the fold, and all competing interests must be reconciled.

That the union has achieved unity Shanker does not doubt. He says, "If there ever needs to be a stoppage in the future we can do it without pickets, without written resignations, without a strike vote. Two years from now if the contract is rejected by a majority of teachers, 50,000 teachers will just stay home, without being told by the leadership or by anybody else. We have our weapon for future use; it is individual teacher commitment."

Actually, the teacher resignations were never submitted during the September stoppage. Shanker had every intention of submitting them, but was dissuaded when a deputy superintendent threatened to turn men's names over to draft boards.

Shanker sees no evidence at all that a damaging public image of the teacher as a law-evader has been created, or that student idealism has suffered. Any student reaction, he believes, is very temporary. At the same time, the imperturbable president of the UFT does expect (as of October 25) that he will have to serve at least 10 days in jail.

If Shanker is pleased with the contract provision eliminating the substitute teacher, he is even more pleased with the proviso that insures an additional $10 million for experimental programs. Five million of this will finance additional intensive effort in elementary schools serving disadvantaged areas, including the controversial More Effective Schools (MES).

Shanker explained the origin of the MES schools, concerning which conflicting evaluations have been submitted. When Bernard Donovan was acting superintendent, he says, Donovan proposed that $2 million be set aside to provide $1,000 premiums for each of 2,000 teachers serving in "intolerable" schools. The union dubbed this hike "combat pay" and successfully opposed it. The acting superintendent then proposed the "Effective Schools" plan, with smaller classes. When the board objected to the implication that other schools were ineffective, the name was changed to *More* Effective Schools. When the cost was estimated at $1,200 per pupil, Donovan opposed the plan on the ground that the city could not afford it.

A little later, Superintendent Calvin Gross, under pressure from the union and the community, sanctioned the first 10 MES schools. A year later 11 more were added. Shanker asserts that teachers and pupils share the union's enthusiasm for the plan, and he predicts the continuation and expansion of the program or another like it.

Asked for his reactions to talk of an NEA-AFT merger, the UFT president expressed his disbelief that this could happen in the next few years. "It is impossible," he said, "for the NEA to make the necessary structural changes. The NEA is too rigid. Their elections are closed affairs. Our elections are wide open. When Carl Megel was elected UFT president, a shift of 15 votes in the convention would have beaten him. Charles Cogen won by 16 votes. The delegates control the AFT convention, but this cannot be said of the NEA."

The conversation turned back to the benefits gained by the New York strike. "The salary gains are fantastic, with 25 percent of our teachers receiving take-home increases of $2,300 over a two-year period, and no one gaining less than $1,500. In addition we won valuable fringe benefits. Extra-duty activities—moonlighting, if you wish—will be paid for at the median salary for classroom teachers, which during this contract period will be $10.25 per hour. This agreement will benefit 20,000 of New York's 55,000 teachers. For the first time we have established the principle that a teacher's time is just as valuable after school as it is during the school day. This rate will apply to after-school recreation programs, to summer school work, and to other programs.

"We also had an expansion of our welfare fund this year. I think most teachers fail to realize that New York City teachers have a completely paid health plan covering major medical expenses. They have a dental plan for the entire family. They can walk into any of 3,000 drugstores and have any prescription filled for 75 cents. They can get a free pair of eyeglasses for each member of the family every two years. This year we got a $50 per teacher addition to the welfare fund. We expect to use most of that $50 for college scholarships for children of teachers within the school system. And this will be another first. I do not think that such benefits—these welfare benefits and these scholarship benefits—will very long remain a secret, and I think teachers in other districts will be demanding the same thing.

"It is also a clear gain that teachers in our special service elementary schools and in our ghetto schools will have a daily preparation period, and every two out of three years each junior high and senior high school teacher will have 10 unassigned periods a week, which is double the number they previously had. We accomplished this by eliminating the amount of time the principal can assign teachers to routine chores within the school.

"Finally, I would say that the stoppage showed a virtually new relationship between the city administration and the Board of Education. The Board of Education really is dead; it did not function throughout the whole stoppage situation. Only the president of the board functioned. In the final analysis the mayor had to tell him what to do and call the whole board together to override this one man, who had created a rather rigid position. He really refused to negotiate or to bargain. He's an attorney for the shipping industry of New York City. I guess he thought he could use some of the hard management techniques and win.

"At one point most of the city administration sat with him for something like 30 hours and put it to him very bluntly. They said either you find a way of running the school system without 50,000 teachers or you find a way of replacing these 50,000 teachers or you go down there and negotiate with them.

"All those hours the administration had to pound away, and finally when he still wouldn't move the whole Board of Education had to be called in and told that the school system was going to be wrecked unless they bought this package we had proposed.

"I would say that probably at the present time there is no real function for the Board of Education within the City of New York. The city administration is calling the shots on all important matters, not only budgetary but in such areas as community involvement. I can't think of any major decisions that will be made in the near future by the board and not by the city administration."

This interviewer sees no reason to doubt Albert Shanker's assertion of concern for the proper education of pupils. His dedication in the welfare of teachers is not inconsistent with a simultaneous concern for the improvement of instruction, especially for pupils in disadvantaged areas. Shanker himself says that the last six days of the stoppage were devoted to tying down non-money matters after all the teacher benefit clauses had been finally agreed upon. And anyone who has seen Albert Shanker with Bernard Donovan knows that this tough union leader has earned the unqualified respect of his equally tough superintendent.

The second article by Lloyd S. Michael, Superintendent-Principal of Evanston Township High School in Evanston, Illinois, describes some of the potential concerns of experienced school principals and administrators for the effect of collective negotiations on the nature of the relationships within the school.

The Principal and Trends
in Professional Negotiations*

Lloyd S. Michael

MYRON LIEBERMAN WROTE IN LAST OCTOBER'S *American School Board Journal* that as of June 1, 1967, approximately 34 percent of the nation's teachers were teaching in states which specifically required some type of negotiations. He predicted that by 1972 about 80 percent of the nation's teachers either will be teaching in states with some type of negotiations statute or will actually be engaged in negotiations which will require significant changes in school management. He advised that vigorous action is needed now to enable school administration to confront the problems inherent in collective negotiations.

There is a rising teacher demand for collective action about many educational matters, including staffing, curriculum, and instruction. Don Davies, speaking at the annual convention of AASA here two years ago, identified one of the chief demands of teachers: "We want to have a more important part in managing our own affairs, in making decisions about what shall be taught, how, when, by whom, and under what conditions." A study of the professional agreements reveals the extent to which many teacher groups in the intervening two years have been successful in gaining their objectives.

Professional negotiations in an increasing number of school districts include considerably more than demands for increased salaries and better working conditions. Teachers seek the right and responsibility to participate and share in the development of educational policy and procedures that can influence significantly the program of the school system. A recently adopted negotiation agreement in a New York school district clearly illustrates a new role for the teacher in school management. The contract states: "The . . . Teacher Association shall discuss, participate

* *NASSP Bulletin* 52:105–110 (May, 1968). Reprinted by permission of the publisher and author.

in, and/or negotiate on the following matters of mutual concern: recruitment of teachers, teacher turnover, in-service training, teaching assignments, teaching conditions, class size, curriculum, district planning, budget preparation, school calendar, salaries, communications, protection of teachers, leaves of absence, general absence provisions, sabbatical leave and other fringe benefits, dues deductions, grievance procedures, and other matters which affect the quality of the education program and the morale of the teaching staff." This board of education, and the trend is in this direction, agreed that their teachers were qualified to make significant contributions to educational matters of the district and should share in the development of policy and program.

DETERRENT TO INNOVATION

Teacher demands, with or without negotiation agreements, are tending to support a traditional and less useful model of the school. Strong pressures in many school districts are being exercised to narrow and regiment the task of teachers, their compensation, class size, work load, and working conditions. The effect of these demands and pressures may seriously deter the diffusion of promising practices in the allocation and utilization of all types of school personnel, as well as of many other innovations in curriculum and instruction.

The school principal should have serious concerns about the dissatisfaction, aggressiveness, and militancy that are increasingly prevalent on his faculty. How does he meet this problem when, at the same time, he must work with his staff cooperatively to cope with a complexity of problems including the knowledge explosion, population growth, technological innovations, urbanization, and changing social relationships? Our Association urges principals to become instructional leaders and to act as managers of change.

How effective is the typical secondary school principal? Many able educators who serve as principals are thwarted in nearly every aspect of instructional leadership. In the first place, the everyday "line" problems and emergencies which the building principal must shoulder as his responsibility prevent him from functioning as an effective leader of his faculty. He is fortunate if he has the time and the authority to help select and retain a good staff. Further, increasing specialization and diversification of the teaching task preclude any one educator from becoming a master teacher or supervisor of all subjects at all levels for all categories of learners. The need is for adequate assistance and support at the building level and from the central office staff. Most principals can and do keep up with innovations and experiments but find serious obstacles in inadequate budgets, bureaucratic restrictions, inferior facilities, as well as teacher and school-system inertia. In all fairness, some principals block change because of scheduling difficulties, apathy, lack of involvement, and their own inertia.

PRECARIOUS POSITION

The greatest problem facing the secondary school principal today is his attempt to fulfill his role as an instructional leader and as a manager of change in his precarious and frequently untenable position caused by the schism developing among teachers, boards of education, and chief school administrators.

Principals have met the challenge to their role in essentially two ways: We will have business as usual or we will set up a business of our own. In the "business as usual" approach, principals are rapidly losing ground in their attempt to have a voice in and make a contribution to their school's program. Teachers, in their attempt to bypass the superintendent, are either ignoring principals or are including them in negotiation agreements which severely limit administrative prerogatives previously within the province of the building administrator.

In the second instance, principals band together to protect their own rights by emulating strong union or teachers' association organizations. School principals become militant and build up their own organizations to have a more effective voice. Albert Shanker, president of New York City's teachers union, said: "If they don't have strong organizations of their own, they will get killed every year in negotiations." This "solution" rigidifies all battle lines and widens the breach among the four major groups concerned: teachers, board members, superintendents, and principals. Obviously, a collective position by principals on such matters as teaching load, schedules, professional meetings, curriculum decisions, methods of supervision, and other issues on which change is now being won or sought by teaching staffs defines disagreements more sharply and splits the educational enterprise into four separate and perhaps self-serving groups. In this situation, students and their parents are often caught in a no-man's-land and either become pawns in the conflict or are subjected to a series of work stoppages and other activities detrimental to the best interests of all concerned.

COLLABORATIVE LEADERSHIP

One alternative to negotiations or collective bargaining as presently constituted is collaborative leadership, which Dunn and Stafford[1] define

---

[1] Kenneth John Dunn and Rita Lynne Stafford. "Collaborative Leadership for School Systems." *Suggested Rationale and Action Patterns.* New York: Education Council for School Research and Development, January, 1968.

as "the process of intergroup interaction and involvement whereby representatives of the educational hierarchy cooperatively accept the responsibility for policy and program decisions, thereby producing an integrated power-equalization structure." In this "power-equalization" model, problems, issues, policies, decisions, and joint tasks are designed and implemented by principals, teachers, board members, and superintendents. This suggested model of collaborative leadership, as an alternative plan to negotiations, should be tested in a number of school systems.

Recently 45 suburban school systems organized a Center for the Study of Educational Personnel Policies. The focus of the Center's activities is twofold: (1) the development of innovative practices in personnel policies, particularly in those areas of staff employment, changing roles of educators, and teacher compensation; and (2) the provision of consultative services on policy formulation which would develop new and improved answers to personnel problems. The Center seeks to provide a means through which all members of the educational enterprise may participate in the process of collaborative discussion, analysis, and solution of the various personnel problems that school systems face.

A profound change is taking place in the guardianship of public education. Doherty and Oberer[2] emphasize that teachers are beginning to assert a much greater influence on how our schools are run and that this movement will continue. They predict: "If teacher leaders and school officials learn to use the development wisely, it may prove to be the most therapeutic educational development of the century. If they do not, it may freeze into our system more firmly than ever before those personnel practices that can only lead to mediocrity." The stakes are high; principals must be involved.

The quantity and quality of personnel, both professional and non-professional, are vital to the successful operation of good schools. It is essential that we continue to search for the highest possible dividend on our investment in people. The building principal has the strategic and vital leadership role in the wise and effective utilization of personnel.

Student Power as a Force in Determining
Educational Policy

Not only are the administrators and teachers reassessing their relationship to the rest of the power structure of the society and to each other, but in at least a few schools the question is being raised as to

---

[2] Robert E. Doherty and Walter E. Oberer. *Teachers, School Boards, and Collective Bargaining.* Ithaca, N.Y.: Cayuga Press, 1967, p. 125.

what the role of the students themselves will or should be. It was perhaps inevitable with the black power movement and the student power crisis at Berkeley and then at Columbia that public school students would become involved in some demonstration of the possible uses of power. Student strikes were not new in the Spring and Fall of 1968, but there seemed to some observers to be a more national significance to them. Johns H. Harrington is editor of school publications, Division of Instructional Planning and Services, Los Angeles City Schools.

L.A.'s Student Blowout*

Johns H. Harrington

A new kind of monster raised its head in Los Angeles last spring when the city school district faced its first student walkouts in a 113-year history. Whatever happens to the 13 grand jury indictments for conspiracy that are still pending as this is written, the repercussions of the events during the week of March 5 are likely to produce shock waves that will affect schools and minority groups in urban areas throughout the country. Certainly there are lessons to be learned from the "student blowout" that should be helpful to public school teachers and administrators elsewhere.

Five Mexican-American high schools on the east side were involved, but the primarily Negro Jefferson High School also closed its doors for three days. In two predominantly Negro junior high schools as well, pupils left classes for a time. Some set fires in trash cans and broke windows. As a side effect, 800 white students and non-students clashed with police in Venice some 18 miles across the city on the west side.

In addition to its large Negro population, Los Angeles is unique in that it has 800,000 citizens of Mexican descent—the greatest concentration outside Mexico itself. The city is also the most popular "port of entry" in the southwestern United States for immigrants from Mexico.

The extent of participation in the blowouts is difficult, if not impossible, to measure accurately. Estimates vary with the point of view and knowledge of the observer. School spokesmen report that some 2,500 students joined in the walkouts, and another 1,000 stayed away from classes because of apparent fear of violence. In the main, however, demonstrations

* *Phi Delta Kappan* 50:74-79 (Oct. 1968). Reprinted by permission of the publisher and author.

were nonviolent. Demands of demonstrators, agitators, and the few teachers who joined with them ranged from sweeping educational changes to abolishment of corporal punishment and permission to wear miniskirts.

Although the district staff said that newspapers exaggerated the extent and nature of the disorders, an indication of events during the week-long demonstrations can be gleaned from such reports as the following:

> "Police and school authorities today are probing possible underground agitation as the cause of disorders Tuesday and Wednesday at four Los Angeles high schools. . . .
>
> "One school official attributed the walkouts and rock-throwing, bottle-throwing demonstrations to editorials in an 'underground magazine' which urged students to 'rise up' and protest any conditions they did not like. Two policemen dispersing students at Roosevelt High were hit by flying bottles yesterday. One was hospitalized for treatment of an eye cut. . . . At Lincoln High about 400 young persons refused to attend classes. They were urged, a school official said, to attend a rally at a nearby park by a bearded youth who wore the uniform of the 'Brown Berets,' a militant Mexican-American group. . . ." (Los Angeles Herald-Examiner, March 7)
>
> "Police Chief Tom Reddin warned today that 'professional agitators' are in for trouble for inciting school walkouts like the one at Belmont High School yesterday, where fires were set, police cars stoned, and six persons arrested." (Los Angeles Herald-Examiner, March 8)
>
> "Two hundred young persons broke up a meeting of the City Board of Education and sent most board members fleeing out a rear door Thursday as a climax to a day of boycotts, arson, and the stoning of police cars at schools attended by minority groups.
>
> "Mrs. Georgiana Hardy, board president, pounded her gavel and adjourned the meeting as a bearded member of the Brown Berets strode down the aisle and took over the guest speaker's microphone.
>
> " 'If you walk out today, we will walk out tomorrow,' shouted the youth." (Los Angeles Times, March 8)

In a statement to the press issued March 8, Jack Crowther, city schools superintendent, declared:

> "Every effort is being made to maintain an orderly and normal educational process in the Los Angeles city schools. Representatives of the Board of Education and Secondary Division staff are meeting today with student representatives of protest groups to discuss grievances which have been raised regarding some of the high schools.
>
> "It is important to note that, despite the many disturbances at these schools in the last few days, the overwhelming majority of students have remained in class and continued their studies. . . ."

On the following Monday, Crowther addressed a letter to teachers in the schools concerned and asked that they read a message to students. It included:

> "Let me emphasize that all of us agree with the desperate need to improve the educational program, buildings, and equipment in your

schools. These are the very things which we are fighting for—and indeed on the very day that classes were being disrupted, I and members of the Board of Education were in Sacramento making a desperate plea to the State Legislature for more money to improve our schools.

"I think we can all agree that your viewpoint has been heard— and has been made known dramatically during the last four days of last week. Today your representatives will present their views to the Board of Education.

"Therefore, I am asking each one of you from this moment on to remain in school and continue your class work. Nothing further can be gained by leaving your classes, and the only result of such action will be further harm to your education. *Time lost from classes is gone forever and cannot be regained.* We know that your parents are anxious and eager for school to continue without further interruption."

Shortly after the first walkouts, the Board of Education took the following actions:

1. Agreed to hold a special meeting at Lincoln High School to discuss educational problems in the East Los Angeles area.
2. Granted amnesty to the students who boycotted classes since March 7.
3. Appointed a Negro principal, vice principal, and head counselor at Jefferson High School. (These assignments were already in process, however, when the demonstrations at Jefferson took place.)

But the board refused to order removal of police from the high school campuses or to ask for release of students who had been arrested during the demonstrations.

The demands and recommendations with which the board and staff were deluged both for and against the walkouts came from a wide variety of sources, including the Educational Issues Committee, a community group in East Los Angeles; the California Association of Educators of Mexican Descent; the East Los Angeles Coordinating Council; the Broadway-Central Coordinating Council; the Citizens' Compensatory Education Advisory Committee; the Los Angeles Teachers Association and the American Federation of Teachers; faculty and student groups, both official and unofficial; the community press; and "underground" newspapers.

The demands themselves covered almost the entire spectrum of the educational program, including:

• Free press • Free speech • Bilingual school personnel • Bilingual instruction • School buildings • Cafeteria service • Community relations • Corporal punishment • Counseling ratio • Electives • Fences around campuses • Reading • Reallocation of R.O.T.C. funds • Suspension policies • "Community parents" as teacher aides • Dress and grooming • Homogeneous grouping • Mexican-American contributions to U.S. society • Administrators of Mexican-American descent • Teachers of Mexican-American descent • Nonacademic assemblies • I.Q. tests • Library facilities • Academic courses • Prejudice of school personnel • Open restrooms • Eligibility for student body office • Swimming pools • Dismissal or transfer of teachers because of political or philosophical views

Ironically, some of the demands were direct quotations from statements by Crowther or Stuart Stengel, associate superintendent, Division of Secondary Education, regarding improvements in the educational program that they were seeking. Objectives that have been emphasized by Stengel as "imperative" include:

1. Development of practical testing instruments which will measure the disadvantaged pupil's true potential
2. More counseling services to provide continuous encouragement of pupils to fulfill their potential
3. Full elective programs available in all schools or within a reasonable geographic area, despite comparatively low enrollments in such electives
4. An expanded program for educable mentally retarded pupils
5. Improvement of vocational education programs which will train noncollege-bound pupils for gainful employment and the increased development of placement services
6. Improvement of textual and supplementary additional materials which are at both the pupil's ability level and the pupil's interest level
7. An expanded program of English as a second language
8. Provision for experimental classes taught in Spanish in various subject fields
9. Provision of sound human relations training for teachers and administrators
10. Provision for continuous follow-up studies to determine what's happening to the high school graduate

"It is my belief that the staffs of East Los Angeles secondary schools are doing an outstanding job, within the limitations of what is financially feasible," Stengel said. "I think that our program constantly improves, although not as rapidly, of course, as school personnel and community would like it to ideally."

Since the student blowout, the Board of Education and staff have been working on responses to the 36 major demands that were presented. As a barrage of scathing criticism from militant groups continued, Crowther told the board:

"It needs to be emphasized that, in the main, many of the items [demands] are essentially the same as projects which staff has, from time to time, presented to the board for its consideration. The list of demands has created two erroneous implications: 1) that little, if anything, has been attempted by the board and the district in trying to carry out educational improvements demanded by the students and community; and 2) that improvements have been carried out in other schools throughout the district, particularly in more affluent areas, at the expense of East Los Angeles schools.

"One other impression also needs to be clarified: that funds are available to carry out the list of demands. The fact is that no such funds are available without cutting elsewhere. The facts are that a major share of funds is already being allocated to minority area schools (an average of $53 more annually per student than in so-called advantaged areas). . . ."

When the Board of Education granted amnesty to students and appointed Negro administrators at Jefferson High School, the actions were criticized by demonstrators as not going far enough and also by some teacher and other groups for yielding to pressure.

A statement signed by 101 teachers from Roosevelt High School read in part:

"Let it be clearly understood that no teacher whose name appears on this petition wishes to leave Roosevelt. On the contrary, this petition is intended to reflect our loyalty to our school and our deep concern for our students.

"Under the present circumstances, however, we feel that, by submitting to the intimidation of a small militant faction, the Board of Education has acted in error.

"The board's lack of firm action, its display of divided authority, and its nonsupport of local administrators and teachers in their efforts to uphold the provisions of the Education Code and the Administrative Guide of the State of California have made teaching virtually impossible.

"Because of the board's vacillation, teacher morale is depressed, student attitude is confused, and administrative authority is undermined."

Despite the crisis and conflicts of views, however, within a week after the boycott school programs were resumed as Superintendent Crowther and his staff continued to seek additional funds to strengthen the educational program and made both immediate and long-range plans to heal the wounds.

Observers within and without the school system attributed the walk-outs to a wide range of causes. Obviously, some were related to recent incidents, such as dissatisfaction with local policies, cancellation of a local high school play, and unrest on college campuses. Others, however, concerned problems that have been growing in intensity for years. Although all agreed that additional help is needed for pupils in East Los Angeles—as in many other urban areas throughout the nation where students should have better educational opportunities and there has been an influx of new residents—some have claimed that the blowout was spontaneous while others have contended that the "rabble-rousers always present" somehow had managed to gain enough momentum to enlist widespread student and community support. Another version was that political opportunists saw a power vacuum and seized the opportunity to cut a niche for themselves. In referring to the blowout in the *Los Angeles Times* for March 17, 1968, Dial Torgerson wrote, "It was, some say, the beginning of a revolution—the Mexican-American revolution of 1968."

Whatever the cause, or combination of causes, there were many advance indications that storm clouds were reaching threatening proportions. In its February 11 issue—nearly a month before the crisis—the *East Los Angeles Gazette* carried a banner on page one which read, "Walkout by Students Threatened at Garfield, Five Other Schools." The story began as follows:

> "The threat of a student walkout, dramatizing overcrowded conditions and alleged disregard of cultural heritage in Eastside high schools, which may be staged May 3 (or sooner), is presently hanging over the heads of school administrators.
> "The original area of concentration was considered to be Garfield, Roosevelt, Lincoln, and Wilson high schools, but it was learned this week that planners are now trying to encompass both Huntington Park and Bell high schools in the proposed mass absence. . . ."

Julian Nava, Mexican-American member of the Board of Education and a history professor at San Fernando Valley State College, was quoted in the February 25 issue of the *East Los Angeles Gazette* as saying, "It is 'a healthy sign that [East Los Angeles] students are finally speaking up' in regard to educational demands and threats of a walkout if the student's voice goes unheeded." The story added:

> "The Board of Education member made it clear he did not favor any form of student violence but, rather, regarded the complaints of local students as a major step for the Mexican-American people."

In contrast with Nava's position, "underground newspapers" published many inflammatory articles for months prior to the walkout. For example, in the December 25, 1967, issue of *La Raza*, one of the militant community publications that have recently been established, a columnist said:

> "I almost vomited in the Belvedere auditorium recently. The place was jammed with people when some guy . . . leader of some Daddy Club spouted nonsense. He gave a talk about the group and then fell apart saying that his group are good guys. WE ARE NOT AGITATORS, he said over and over.
> "All he had to say was something like this: 'I'm a good Mexican. I keep my mouth shut. I don't make waves. I keep my blind followers doing the same. Please don't criticize this school or any other or I won't get a chance to speak at things like this. I'm in with all the Gringos here and they all like me so don't ruin anything. I like this even though the strings on my back itch and the top of my head aches from getting patted so much by my blue-eyed friends. Please join us but only if you don't bring up anything important like changing the schools so they do

a better job. Just come to the meetings, keep your mouth shut, and come to our dances. Oh Goodie!' . . ."

This item appeared in *East Side* on December 8, 1967:

"The boys' vice principal would make an excellent night watchman and the registrar could always tag along and help with the flashlight or keys or something.
"The principal should remain at home. I mean, really, he doesn't do anything. He could always telephone or write a letter once every two or three weeks and I'm sure he could accomplish as little as he has by being present. Why be only ninety percent ignorant of the school's problems when you could be completely ignorant. . . ."

The *Free Student*, another underground newspaper, carried an attack labeled "Student Gov't a Farce," which read in part:

"There are basically two ways of ending the administrative control of student government. Different schools may find one or the other more effective. . . . By acting and not talking, we can end the farce of student government."

These excerpts are mild compared with other items in the underground press, many of which ridiculed individual members of school staffs. In spending a few hours scanning a sampling of the papers, a reader gets the impression that the writers consider nothing right with the educational program—including personnel, facilities, and governing policies.

Since the educational blowout, many steps have been taken to help meet the needs it dramatized. Most of the measures, however, were already on the drawing boards before the shrill voice of dissent shattered the educational calm. Among innovations have been:

1. Appointment of James Taylor, a Negro, to the newly created post of assistant deputy superintendent of instruction (with the rank of an assistant superintendent).
2. Assignment of John Leon, a Mexican-American, as head of a new instructional planning center in East Los Angeles.
3. Authorization by the Board of Education of two highly "innovative" educational "complexes," to be located in East Los Angeles and the Watts area. (Plans for the complexes were initiated long before the blowout.)

"This project is an approach to provide a real breakthrough in the education of minority-group young people by doing an all-out job of providing a variety of services and programs in a concentrated area and by using the newest ideas to put them into effect," Crowther commented. "A flexible, specific program for each school in the complexes will be developed. Our plan is to have ideas come from the school community —by involving parents, other community members, teachers, and administrators."

4. Appointment of Edward Moreno as supervisor of bilingual education in the Instructional Planning Branch and issuance of a study report on what has been done, is being done, and is planned in the Elementary Curriculum Bilingual-Bicultural Program.
5. Conduct of the largest summer school in the history of the Los Angeles city schools, involving 149,000 pupils at 259 locations.

Both elementary and secondary schools offered special classes of various types. One program included five educational enrichment centers for elementary school pupils of varying socioeconomic backgrounds.

6. Teaching of conversational Spanish to 210 teachers in summer workshops.
7. Establishment of the Eastside Bilingual Study Center for approximately 1,800 adults at Salesian High School.
8. Employment of 88 bilingual clerks.
9. Provision of workshops for school personnel to develop greater understanding of the Mexican-American culture and community.
10. Establishment of a classified personnel office for the school system on the east side.

Although instructional materials had already been designed especially to help minority group students, more have been developed and others are on the way. An instructional guide on Mexico was published in 1959, and *Angelenos—Then and Now, Californians—Then and Now,* and *Americans—Then and Now* were issued in 1966. The latter series consists of pupil materials for elementary schools which describe the contributions and achievements of members of minority groups. Spanish editions of various pupil materials have been printed or are now being translated. A leaflet called "Blending of Two Cultures" focused on service for Mexican-American pupils.

Reference lists for teachers and pupils include "A Selected List of Books on American Ethnic Groups for Secondary School Libraries," "Recommended Books on American Cultural Minority Groups for Elementary School Libraries," and "Bibliography of Books in Spanish Compiled from Recommended Titles for Secondary Libraries."

Although it is too early to say whether L.A.'s student blowout has been properly patched up or what organizers may think of next, it must be evident to most observers that a heavy thrust is being made by the Los Angeles city schools to provide the kind of education that all pupils need. Many would agree with John Leon, director of the new instructional planning center in Los Angeles, when he recently said:

It seems to me that in American education we have three major phases. In the first, the schools blame the homes for the failures of children. In the second, the parents and other citizens blame the schools. Now we must enter the third phase, in which schools and homes share the blame for educational problems and work together toward their solution.

Unlike a Grade B movie, however, the story does not necessarily have a happy ending. In fact, for the time being, at least, there seems to be no ending at all. An article in the *Los Angeles Times* for August 4 reported that the Educational Issues Coordinating Committee of East Los Angeles had "rejected" the Board of Education's handling of the 36 "student" demands for educational reforms. The coordinating committee also has requested status independent of the board and asks that the committee and the district staff choose an independent group of educators to investigate East Los Angeles problems.

"We are not going to be put off," the *Times* quoted the Rev. Vahac Mardirosian, chairman of the committee, as saying. "We are not going to go away."

The student blowout and its aftermath in Los Angeles have dramatically illustrated the need for better communications between schools and community, more financial help, and greater emphasis on minority group culture. Perhaps the most important lesson, however, is the urgency of decentralization in urban areas to encourage local participation and to assure provision of an educational program that meets local needs. In the future, community influences undoubtedly will have a greater impact on curricular offerings and other aspects of individual school programs.

Bibliography

History of Education

BAILYN, BERNARD, *Education in the Forming of American Society* (Chapel Hill, N.C.: University of North Carolina Press, 1960).

BAYLES, ERNEST E. and B. L. HOOD, *Growth of American Educational Thought* (New York: Harper and Row, 1966).

BOYD, WILLIAM, *The History of Western Education*, 8th revised ed. (New York: Barnes and Noble, Inc., 1967).

BRUBACHER, JOHN S., *A History of the Problems of Education*, 2nd ed. (New York: McGraw-Hill Book Company, 1966).

BUTTS, R. FREEMAN, *A Cultural History of Western Education* (New York: McGraw-Hill Book Company, 1955).

CREMIN, LAWRENCE A., *Transformation of the School* (New York: Alfred A. Knopf, Inc., 1961).

FRENCH, WILLIAM M., *America's Educational Tradition: An Interpretive History* (Boston: D. C. Heath & Company, 1964).

GOOD, H. G., *History of American Education*, 2nd ed. (New York: The Macmillan Company, 1962).

———, *History of Western Education*, 2nd ed. (New York: The Macmillan Company, 1962).

GROSS, RICHARD E., *Heritage of American Education* (Boston: Allyn and Bacon, Inc., 1962).

MEYER, A. E., *An Educational History of the American People*, 2nd ed. (New York: McGraw-Hill Book Company, 1967).

———, *An Educational History of the Western World* (New York: McGraw-Hill Book Company, 1965).

MULHERN, JAMES, *History of Education*, 2nd ed. (New York: The Ronald Press Company, 1959).

MYERS, E. D., *Education in Perspective of History* (New York: Harper and Brothers, 1960).

NAKOSTEEN, M. K., *The History and Philosophy of Education* (New York: The Ronald Press Company, 1965).

POUNDS, R. L., *The Development of Education in Western Culture* (New York: Appleton-Century-Crofts, 1968).
THUT, I. N., *The Story of Education* (New York: McGraw-Hill Book Company, 1957).
WILDS, ELMER H., and K. V. LOTTICH, *Foundations of Modern Education*, 3rd ed. (New York: Holt, Rinehart, & Winston, Inc., 1961).

The Aims of Education

BLOOM, BENJAMIN S. and D. R. KRATHWOHL, *The Taxonomy of Educational Objectives*; Book I *Cognitive Domain* (New York: David McKay Co., Inc., 1956), Book II *Affective Domain* (New York: David McKay Co., Inc., 1964).
BRUNER, JEROME S., *The Process of Education* (Cambridge: Harvard University Press, 1960).
Educational Policies Commission, *The Central Purpose of American Education* (Washington, D.C.: NEA, 1961).
FLAUM, LAURENCE S., *Credo for American Public Education* (Minneapolis: Burgess Publishing Co., 1962).
FRENCH, WILL, *Behavioral Goals of General Education in High School* (New York: The Russell Sage Foundation, 1957).
KELLEY, EARL C., *In Defense of Youth* (New York: Prentice-Hall, Inc., 1962).
LINDVALL, C. M., *Defining Educational Objectives* (Pittsburgh: University of Pittsburgh Press, 1964).

The Sociology of Education

BELL, ROBERT R., and HOLGER R. STUB, *Sociology of Education, a Source Book*, revised ed. (Homewood, Ill.: Dorsey Press Inc., 1968).
BROOKOVER, WILBUR B., and DAVID GOTTLIEB, *Sociology of Education*, 2nd ed. (New York: American Book Company, 1964).
COOK, LLOYD A., and ELAINE F. COOK, *A Sociological Approach to Education*, 3rd ed (New York: McGraw-Hill Book Company, 1960).
CORWIN, DONALD G., *Sociology of Education* (New York: Appleton-Century-Crofts, 1965).
GWYNN, J. MINOR, and JOHN B. CHASE, JR., *Curriculum Principles and Social Trends*, 4th ed. (New York: The Macmillan Company, 1969).
HALSEY, A. H., and others, *Education, Economy, and Society* (Glencoe, Ill.: The Free Press, 1961).
HAVIGHURST, ROBERT J., and BERNICE L. NEUGARTEN, *Society and Education*, 3rd ed. (Boston: Allyn and Bacon, Inc., 1962).
HODGKINSON, HAROLD L., *Education in Social and Cultural Perspective* (New York: Prentice-Hall, Inc., 1962).
PAGE, CHARLES H., *Sociology and Contemporary Education* (New York: Random House, Inc., 1964).

President's Commission on Law Enforcement and the Administration of Justice, *Juvenile Delinquency and Youth Crime* (Washington, D.C.: U.S. Government Printing Office, 1967).

RATHS, J. D., and J. D. GRAMBS, eds., *Society and Education, Readings* (New York: Prentice-Hall Inc., 1965).

THAYER, V. T., and MARTIN LEVIT, *The Role of the School in American Society* (New York: Dodd, Mead, & Company, 1966).

WALLER, W. W., *The Sociology of Teaching* (New York: John Wiley and Sons, Inc., 1965).

WESTBY-GIBSON, DOROTHY F., *Social Perspectives on Education: The Society, The School* (New York: John Wiley and Sons, Inc., 1965).

American Education Today

BEREDAY, GEORGE Z. F., and LUIGI VOLPICELLI, *Public Education in America: A New Interpretation of Purpose and Practice* (New York: Harper and Brothers, 1958).

CRAIG, ROBERT C., and ADRIAN M. DUPUIS, *American Education: Its Origins and Issues* (Milwaukee: The Bruce Publishing Company, 1963).

CREMIN, LAWRENCE A., *The Transformation of the School* (New York: Random House, Inc., 1964).

DEYOUNG, CHRIS A., and R. WYNN, *American Education*, 6th ed. (New York: McGraw-Hill Book Company, 1968).

GRIEDER, CALVIN, and S. A. ROMINE, *American Education*, 3rd ed. (New York: The Ronald Press Company, 1965).

GROSS, R. E., *American Education* (New York: Holt, Rinehart & Winston, Inc., 1964).

HALL, CLIFTON L., and others, *Readings in American Education* (Chicago: Scott, Foresman and Company, 1963).

HARTFORD, ELLIS F., *Education in these United States* (New York: The Macmillan Company, 1964).

HILLWAY, TYRUS, *Education in American Society* (Boston: Houghton Mifflin Company, 1961).

HUGHES, JAMES M., *Education in America*, 2nd ed. (New York: Harper and Brothers, 1965).

KEPPEL, FRANCIS, *The Necessary Revolution in American Education* (New York: Harper and Row, 1966).

KIMBALL, SOLON T., and JAMES McCLELLAN, *Education and the New America* (New York: Random House, Inc., 1962).

KING, EDWARD A., *The Shaping of the American High School 1880–1920* (Milwaukee: The University of Wisconsin Press, 1969).

MOORE, HARRY, *Modern Education in America* (Boston: Allyn and Bacon, Inc., 1962).

POUNDS, RALPH L., and ROBERT L. GARRETSON, *Principles of Modern Education* (New York: The Macmillan Company, 1962).

RUDY, WILLIS, *Schools in an Age of Mass Culture* (New York: Prentice-Hall, Inc., 1965).

WOODRING, PAUL, and JOHN J. SCANLON, *American Education Today* (New York: McGraw-Hill Book Company, 1963).

464

BIBLIOGRAPHY

Traditional Aspects of the Secondary School Curriculum

ANDERSON, VERNON E., *Principles and Procedures of Curriculum Improvement*, 2nd ed. (New York: The Ronald Press Company, 1965).

BRUBACHER, JOHN D., *A History of the Problems of Education*, 2nd ed. (New York: McGraw-Hill Book Company, 1966).

CAY, DONALD F., *Curriculum: Design for Learning* (Indianapolis: The Bobbs-Merrill Co., Inc., 1965).

DOLL, RONALD C., *Curriculum Improvement: Decision Making and Process* (Boston: Allyn and Bacon, Inc., 1964).

DOUGLASS, HARL R., *The High School Curriculum*, 3rd ed. (New York: The Ronald Press Company, 1964).

FORD, G. W., and L. PUGNO, eds., *The Structure of Knowledge and the Curriculum* (Chicago: Rand McNally & Company, 1965).

GOODLAD, JOHN I., *School, Curriculum, and the Individual* (Waltham, Mass.: The Blaisdell Publishing Company, 1966).

GWYNN, J. MINOR, and JOHN B. CHASE, JR., *Curriculum Principles and Social Trends*, 4th ed. (New York: The Macmillan Company, 1969).

HAAS, G., and K. WILES, *Readings in Curriculum* (Boston: Allyn and Bacon, Inc., 1965).

JOHNSON, H. T., *Foundations of Curriculum* (Columbus: Charles E. Merrill Publishing Co., 1968).

KRUG, EDWARD A., *The Secondary School Curriculum* (New York: Harper and Row, 1960).

LEESE, JOSEPH, and others, *The Teacher in Curriculum Making* (New York: Harper and Row, 1961).

OLIVER, A. I., *Curriculum Improvement* (New York: Dodd, Mead & Company, 1965).

SAYLOR, JOHN G., and WILLIAM M. ALEXANDER, *Curriculum Planning for Modern Schools*, revised ed. (New York: Holt, Rinehart & Winston, Inc., 1966).

TRUMP, J. LLOYD, and DORSEY BAYNHAM, *Focus on Change* (Chicago: Rand McNally & Company, 1961).

WILES, KIMBALL, *The Changing Curriculum of the American High School* (Englewood Cliffs, N.J.: Prentice-Hall, Inc., 1963).

Modification of the Secondary Curriculum

ALBERTY, HAROLD B. and ELSIE J., *Reorganizing the High School Curriculum*, 3rd ed. (New York: The Macmillan Company, 1962).

ALEXANDER, W. M., and others, *The Emergent Middle School* (New York: Holt, Rinehart & Winston, Inc., 1968).

Association for Supervision and Curriculum Development, *Balance in the Curriculum Yearbook 1961* (Washington, D.C.: NEA, 1961).

———, *Changing Curriculum Content* (Washington, D.C.: NEA, 1964).

———, *Curriculum Materials* (Washington, D.C.: NEA, 1964).

——, *New Dimensions in Learning* (Washington, D.C.: NEA, 1962).

——, *Using Current Curriculum Developments* (Washington, D.C.: NEA, 1963).

——, *What Are the Sources of the Curriculum?* (Washington, D.C.: NEA, 1962).

BERMAN, L. M., *New Priorities in the Curriculum* (Columbus: Charles E. Merrill Publishing Co., 1968).

BUSH, R. N. and D. WALLEN, *A New Design for High School Education* (New York: McGraw-Hill Book Company, 1964).

FAUNCE, ROLAND C. and NELSON L. BOSSING, *Developing The Core Curriculum*, 2nd ed. (Englewood Cliffs, N.J.: Prentice-Hall, Inc., 1958).

LURRY, LUCILLE L. and ELSIE J. ALBERTY, *Developing a High School Core Program* (New York: The Macmillan Company, 1957).

National Education Association, American Educational Research Association, *Curriculum Planning and Development* (Washington, D.C.: NEA, 1960).

——, Center for the Study of Instruction, *Deciding What to Teach* (Washington, D.C.: NEA, 1963).

——, *Project on the Instructional Program of the Public Schools, Schools for the Sixties* (New York: McGraw-Hill Book Company, 1963).

The Activities Program of the School

American Association for Health, Physical Education, and Recreation, *Athletics in Education* (Washington, D.C.: NEA, 1963).

BAILAND, VIRGINIA and HARRY C. McKOWN, *So You Were Elected*, 2nd ed. (New York: McGraw-Hill Book Company, 1960).

FREDERICK, ROBERT W., *Third Curriculum*. (New York: Appleton-Century-Crofts, 1959).

——, *Student Activities in American Education* (New York: Center for Applied Research, 1965).

GEARTTS, SISTER MARY M., *Critical Analysis of the Objectives of Extra-Curricular Activity Programs in Catholic High Schools* (Washington: Catholic University of America Press, 1960).

KILZER, LONS R. and others, *Allied Activities in the Secondary School* (New York: Harper and Brothers, 1956).

MILLER, F. A. and others, *Planning Student Activities* (Englewood Cliffs, N.J.: Prentice-Hall, Inc., 1957).

MUELLER, PAT and ELMER D. MITCHELL, *Intramural Sports*, 3rd ed. (New York: The Ronald Press Company, 1960).

National Association of Secondary School Principals, *The Effective Student Council* (Washington, D.C.: NEA, 1964).

——, *Evaluation of Student Activities* (Washington, D.C.: NEA, 1966).

——, *The Student Council Adviser* (Washington, D.C.: NEA, 1963).

——, *The Student Council in the Secondary School* (Washington, D.C.: NEA, 1962).

ROBBINS, J., and S. WILLIAMS, *Student Activities in The Innovative School* (Minneapolis: Burgess Publishing Co., 1969).

STROUP, HERBERT H. *Toward a Philosophy of Organized Student Activities* (Minneapolis: University of Minnesota Press, 1964).

Guidance Services in the Secondary School

ADAMS, JAMES F., ed., *Counseling and Guidance: A Summary View* (New York: The Macmillan Company, 1965).

American Educational Research Association, *Guidance, Counseling, and Personnel Services* (Washington, D.C.: NEA, 1966).

ARBUCKLE, DUGALD S., *Pupil Personnel Services in American Schools* (Boston: Allyn and Bacon, Inc., 1966).

BLANCHARD, HOWARD L., and LAWRENCE S. FLAUM, *Guidance, A Longitudinal Approach* (Minneapolis: Burgess Publishing Company, 1968).

BOY, ANGELO O., and G. J. PINE, *Client-Centered Counseling in the Secondary School* (Boston: Houghton Mifflin Company, 1964).

CALDWELL, EDSEN, and CLARENCE MAKLER, *Group Counseling in the Secondary Schools* (Chicago: Science Research Associates, 1962).

COTTINGHAM, H. F., and W. E. HOPKE, *Guidance in Junior High Schools* (New York: Taplinger Publishing Co., Inc., 1961).

CROW, LESTER D., and ALICE, *Readings in Guidance* (New York: David McKay Co., Inc., 1962).

DOWNING, L. M., *Guidance and Counseling Services* (New York: McGraw-Hill Book Company, 1968).

FARWELL, GAIL F., and HERMAN PETERS, eds., *Guidance Readings for Counselors* (Chicago: Rand McNally and Co., 1960).

GLANZ, EDWARD C., *Foundations and Principles of Guidance* (Boston: Allyn and Bacon, Inc., 1964).

GLENNEN, ROBERT E., *Guidance, an Orientation* (Boulder, Colo.: Pruett Press, Inc., 1966).

HILL, GEORGE E., *The Management and Improvement of Guidance* (New York: Appleton-Century-Crofts, 1965).

HOLLIS, JOSEPH W., and LUCILLE, *Organizing for Effective Guidance* (Chicago: Science Research Associates, 1965).

HUMPHREYS, J. ANTHONY, and others, *Guidance Services*, revised ed. (Chicago: Science Research Associates, 1960).

JOHNSON, WALTER F., and others, *Pupil Personnel and Guidance Services*, (New York: McGraw-Hill Book Company, 1961).

JONES, ARTHUR J., *Principles of Guidance and Pupil Personnel Work*, 5th ed. (New York: McGraw-Hill Book Company, 1963).

KOWITZ, G. J., and N. G., *Operation Guidance Services for the Modern School* (New York: Holt, Rinehart & Winston, Inc., 1968).

LEE, J. M., and N. G. PALLONE, *Guidance and Counseling in Schools* (New York: McGraw-Hill Book Company, 1966).

LONGHARY, JOHN W., *Counseling in Secondary Schools* (New York: Harper and Brothers, 1961).

MATTHEWSON, ROBERT H., *Guidance Policy and Practice*, 3rd ed. (New York: Harper and Brothers, 1962).

MILLER, CARROLL H., *Guidance Services: An Introduction* (New York: Harper and Brothers, 1965).

MILLER, FRANK W., *Guidance Principles and Services* (Columbus: Charles E. Merrill Publishing Co., 1961).

MORTENSEN, DONALD G. and A. M. SCHUMULLER, *Guidance in Today's Schools*, 2nd ed. (New York: John Wiley and Sons, 1966).

MOSER, LESLIE E. and RUTH D., *Counseling and Guidance: An Exploration* (New York: Prentice-Hall, Inc., 1963).

National Association of Secondary School Principals, *Aspects of Guidance and Counseling* (Washington, D.C.: NEA, 1963).

——, *Guidance Practices in the Secondary School* (Washington, D.C.: NEA, 1962).

——, *Guidance Procedures in the Secondary School* (Washington, D.C.: NEA, 1961).

——, *Phases of Guidance in the Secondary School* (Washington, D.C.: NEA, 1961).

OHLSEN, MERLE M., *Guidance Services in the Modern School* (New York: Harcourt, Brace and World, Inc., 1964).

PATTERSON, CECIL H., *Counseling and Guidance in Schools* (New York: Harper and Brothers, 1962).

SALTZMAN, G. A. and H. J. PETERS, *Pupil Personnel Services* (Itasca, Ill.: E. Peacock Publ., 1967).

SHERTZER, BRUCE and HERMAN J. PETERS, *Guidance* (New York: The Macmillan Company, 1965).

TRAXLER, ARTHUR E., *Technique of Guidance*, 3rd ed. (New York: Harper and Row, 1966).

Teaching Methods in the Secondary School

ALCORN, MARVIN DOUGLAS, and others, *Better Teaching in Secondary Schools*, revised ed. (New York: Holt, Rinehart & Winston, 1964).

BILLETT, ROY O., *Teaching in Junior and Senior High Schools*, 2nd ed. (Totowa, N.J.: Littlefield, Adams and Co., 1967).

BLOUNT, NATHAN D. and H. J. KLAUSMEIER, *Teaching in Secondary School*, 3rd ed. (New York: Harper and Row, 1968).

BOSSING, NELSON L., *Teaching in Secondary Schools*, 4th ed. (Boston: Houghton Mifflin Company, 1967).

CALLAHAN, STERLING G., *Successful Teaching in Secondary Schools* (Chicago: Scott, Foresman and Co., 1966).

CLARK, LEONARD H., ed., *Strategies and Tactics in Secondary School Teaching* (New York: The Macmillan Company, 1968).

CLARK, LEONARD H., and L. S. STARR, *Secondary School Teaching Methods*, 2nd ed. (New York: The Macmillan Company, 1967).

CYPHERT, FREDERICK R., and others, *Teaching in The American Secondary School* (New York: McGraw-Hill Book Company, 1964).

FAUNCE, ROLAND C., and CARROLL L. MUNSHAW, *Teaching and Learning in Secondary Schools* (Belmont, California: The Wadsworth Publishing Company, 1964).

HOOVER, KENNETH H., *Learning and Teaching in the Secondary School*, 2nd ed. (Boston: Allyn and Bacon, Inc., 1968).

INLOW, GAIL M., *Maturity in High School Teaching* (New York: Prentice-Hall, Inc., 1963).

LEE, FLORENCE H., ed., *Principles and Practices of Teaching in Secondary Schools* (New York: David McKay Co., Inc., 1965).

LEE, J. M., *Principles and Methods of Secondary Education* (New York: McGraw-Hill Book Company, 1963).

McKean, Robert C., *Principles and Methods in Secondary Education* (Columbus: Charles E. Merrill Publishing Co., 1962).

National Association of Secondary School Principals, *Instructional Procedures in the Secondary Schools* (Washington, D.C.: NEA, 1962).

Risk, T. M., *Principles and Practices of Teaching in Secondary Schools*, 4th ed. (New York: American Book Co., 1968).

Samford, Clarence D., and others, *Principles and Practices in Secondary Education* (Dubuque, Iowa: William C. Brown Company, 1963).

Steeves, Frank L., *Fundamentals of Teaching in Secondary Schools* (New York: Odyssey Press, Inc., 1962).

Walton, John, *Toward Better Teaching in the Secondary Schools* (Boston: Allyn and Bacon, Inc., 1966).

Classroom Management and School Discipline

Association for Supervision and Curriculum Development, *Discipline for Today's Children and Youth*, revised ed. (Washington, D.C.: NEA, 1956).

Bany, Mary A., and Lois V. Johnson, *Classroom Group Behavior* (New York: The Macmillan Company, 1964).

Brown, Edwin J., and A. T. Phelps, *Managing the Classroom*, 2nd ed. (New York: The Ronald Press Company, 1961).

Gnagey, William J., *Controlling Classroom Misbehavior* (Washington, D.C.: NEA, 1965).

———, *The Psychology of Discipline in the Classroom* (New York: The Macmillan Co., 1968).

Hymes, James L., Jr., *Behavior and Misbehavior: A Teachers Guide to Action* (Englewood Cliffs, N.J.: Prentice-Hall, Inc., 1955).

Larson, Knute G., and Melvin R. Karpas, *Effective Secondary School Discipline* (New York: Prentice-Hall, Inc., 1963).

National Education Association; *High School Discipline in American Society* (Washington, D.C.: NEA, 1956).

Parody, Ovid, *The High School Principal and Staff Deal with Discipline*, revised ed. (New York: Teachers College, Columbia University, 1965).

Phillips, C. Lakin, Daniel M. Wiener, and Norris G. Haring, *Discipline Achievement and Mental Health* (Englewood Cliffs, N.J.: Prentice-Hall, Inc., 1960).

Zapf, Rosalend M., *Democratic Processes in the Secondary Classroom* (New York: Prentice-Hall, Inc., 1959).

Grouping, Scheduling, and Provision for Special Classes

Anderson, Vernon E., and W. T. Gruhn, *Principles and Practices of Secondary Education*, 2nd ed. (New York: The Ronald Press Company, 1962).

Austin, David B., and others, *American High School Administration*, 3rd ed. (New York: Holt, Rinehart & Winston, Inc., 1961).

Barker, Roger G., and Paul V. Gump, *Big School, Small School: High*

School Size and Student Behavior (Stanford: Stanford University Press, 1964).

BAUGHMAN, M. DALE, ed., *Block of Time Scheduling Practices in Junior High Schools* (Danville, Ill.: Interstate Printers and Publishers, Inc., 1960).

BEGGS, DAVID W., *The Decatur-Lakewood High School: A Practical Application of the Trump Plan* (New York: Prentice-Hall, Inc., 1964).

BROWN, BARTLEY F., *The Nongraded High School* (New York: Prentice-Hall, Inc., 1963).

BROWN, FRANK B., *Appropriate Placement School* (New York: Prentice-Hall, Inc., 1965).

COPLEY, FRANK O., *The American High School and the Talented Student* (Ann Arbor, Mich.: The University of Michigan Press, 1961).

DeHAAN, ROBERT F., and ROBERT J. HAVIGHURST, *Educating Gifted Children*, revised ed. (Chicago: University of Chicago Press, 1961).

DOUGLASS, HARL R., *Modern Administration of Secondary Schools*, 2nd ed. (Waltham, Mass.: Blaisdell Publishing Company, 1963).

ELICKER, PAUL E., *Administration of Junior and Senior High Schools* (New York: Prentice-Hall, Inc., 1964).

FLIEGLER, LOUIS A., ed., *Curriculum Planning for the Gifted* (New York: Prentice-Hall, 1961).

FRENCH, JOSEPH L., II, *Educating the Gifted*, 3rd ed. (New York: Holt, Rinehart & Winston, Inc., 1964).

GOLDBERG, MIRIAM L., and A. H. PASSOW, *The Effects of Ability Grouping* (New York: Teachers College Press, 1966).

HANSEN, CARL F., *The Four-Track Curriculum in Today's High Schools* (New York: Prentice-Hall, Inc., 1964).

JOHNSON, GEORGE O., *Education for the Slow Learners* (New York: Prentice-Hall, Inc., 1963).

KEPHART, NEWELL C., *Slow Learner in the Classroom* (Columbus: Charles E. Merrill Publishing Co., 1960).

KOUGH, JACK, *Practical Programs for the Gifted* (Chicago: Science Research Associates, 1960).

———, *Look at Acceleration and Enrichment* (Washington, D.C.: NEA, 1963).

National Association of Secondary School Principals, *Student Differences and Secondary School Offerings* (Washington, D.C.: NEA, 1963).

National Council for the Social Studies, *How to Work With the Academically Talented in the Social Studies* (Washington, D.C.: NEA, 1960).

OVARD, GLEN F., *Administration of the Changing Secondary School* (New York: The Macmillan Company, 1966).

———, *Change and High School Administration* (New York: The Macmillan Company, 1968).

SUMPTION, MERLE R. and EVELYN M. LUECKING, *Education of the Gifted* (New York: The Ronald Press Company, 1960).

TANSLEY, A. E. and R. GUILFORD, *The Education of Slow Learning Children* (New York: The Humanities Press, Inc., 1960).

TRUMP, J. LLOYD and DORSEY BAYNHAM, *Focus on Change* (Chicago: Rand McNally and Company, 1961).

WARD, VIRGIL S., *Educating the Gifted* (Columbus, Ohio: Charles E. Merrill Publishing Co., 1961).

WILLIAMS, STANLEY W., *Educational Administration in Secondary Schools* (New York: Holt, Rinehart & Winston, Inc., 1964).

School Marking, Records and Reports

ADAMS, GEORGIA S. and T. L. TORGESON, *Measurement and Evaluation in Education, Psychology and Guidance* (New York: Holt, Rinehart & Winston, Inc., 1964).

AHMAN, J. STANLEY and MARVIN D. GLOCK, *Evaluating Pupil Growth*, 2nd ed. (Boston: Allyn and Bacon, Inc., 1959).

ANDERSON, ALBERT F. and BERNICE P. BRIGGS, *Focus on Rebellion*, 2nd ed. (San Francisco: Chandler Publishing Company, 1962).

BARON, DENIS and H. W. BERNARD, *Evaluation Techniques for Classroom Teachers* (New York: McGraw-Hill Book Company, 1958).

Classroom Teachers Association, *Evaluating and Reporting Pupil Progress* (Washington, D.C.: NEA, 1955).

DAVIS, FREDERICK B., *Educational Measurements and Their Interpretation* (Belmont, California: Wadsworth Publishing Company, 1964).

HORROCKS, J. E., and T. I. SCHOONOVER, *Measurement for Teaching* (Columbus: Charles E. Merrill Publishing Co., 1968).

National Association of Secondary School Principals, *Rank In Class* (Washington, D.C.: NEA, 1962).

STRANG, RUTH, *Reporting to Parents* (New York: Teachers College, Columbia University, 1959).

THOMAS, ROBERT M., *Judging Student Progress*, 2nd ed. (New York: David McKay Co., Inc., 1960).

The Education and Professional Status
of High School Teachers

American Association of Colleges for Teacher Education, *Foundations for Excellence*, Fifteenth Yearbook (Washington, D.C.: NEA, 1962).

———, *Liberal Arts Colleges and Teacher Education* (Washington, D.C.: NEA, 1963).

———, *Roles and Relationships in Teacher Education* (Washington, D.C.: NEA, 1963).

BEGGS, WALTER K., *The Education of Teachers* (New York: The Center for Applied Research, 1965).

BEREDAY, GEORGE L. F., and JOSEPH A. LOUWERYS, eds., *The Education and Training of Teachers* (New York: Harcourt, Brace and World, Inc., 1963).

BOYLAN, JAMES R., *School Teaching as a Career* (New York: Henry Z. Walck, Inc., 1962).

COMBS, ARTHUR W., *The Professional Education of Teachers* (Boston: Allyn and Bacon, Inc., 1965).

CONANT, JAMES B., *The Education of American Teachers* (New York: McGraw-Hill Book Company, 1963).

GARBER, LEE O., and CHARLES M. MICKEN, *The Commonwealth, the Law and the Teacher* (Danville, Illinois: Interstate Printers and Publishers, Inc., 1963).

GARBER, LEE O., and NEWTON EDWARDS, *The Law Governing Teacher Personnel* (Danville, Illinois: Interstate Printers and Publishers, Inc., 1962).

GAUERKE, WARREN C., *Legal and Ethical Responsibilities of School Personnel* (New York: Prentice-Hall, Inc., 1959).

HEALD, J. E., and S. A. MOORE, *The Teacher and Administrative Relationships in School Systems* (New York: The Macmillan Company, 1968).

HODINFELD, G. R., and T. M. STINNETT, *The Education of Teachers: Consensus and Conflict* (New York: Prentice-Hall, Inc., 1964).

KERSHAW, JOSEPH A., and ROLAND H. MCKEAN, *Teacher Shortage and Salary Schedules* (New York: McGraw-Hill Book Company, 1962).

KINNEY, LUCIUS B., *Certification in Education* (New York: Prentice-Hall, Inc., 1964).

KLEINMANN, JACK H., *Fringe Benefits in Public Education* (New York: Teachers College, Columbia University, 1962).

KOERNER, JAMES D., *The Miseducation of American Teachers* (Boston: The Houghton Mifflin Company, 1963).

LIEBERMANN, MYRON, *Education as a Profession* (New York: Prentice-Hall, Inc., 1956).

——, and M. MOSKOW, *Collective Negotiations for Teachers* (New York: Rand McNally & Co., 1967).

MASSEY, HAROLD W., and EDWIN E. VINEYARD, *The Profession of Teaching* (New York: The Odyssey Press, 1961).

MCGLOTHLIN, WILLIAM J., *Patterns of Professional Education* (New York: G. P. Putnam's Sons, 1960).

MCGRATH, EARL J., and CHARLES H. RUSSELL, *Are School Teachers Illiberally Educated?* (New York: Teachers College, Columbia University, 1961).

MCKENNA, BERNARD H., *Staffing the Schools* (New York: Teachers College, Columbia University, 1965).

National Education Association, *The Teaching Career Fact Book* (Washington, D.C.: NEA, 1964).

——, Ethics Committee, *Opinions of the Committee on Professional Ethics,* revised ed. (Washington, D.C.: NEA, 1964).

——, Research Division, *The Economic Status of Teachers in 1963–1964* (Washington, D.C.: NEA, 1964).

——, Research Division, *Teacher Supply and Demand in Public Schools* (Washington, D.C.: NEA, 1964).

REDEFER, FREDERICK, and DOROTHY REEVES, *Careers in Education* (New York: Harper and Brothers, 1960).

ROGERS, VIRGIL M., ed., *Do We Want Merit Salary Schedules?* (Syracuse: Syracuse University Press, 1960).

RYANS, DAVID G., *Characteristics of Teachers* (Washington, D.C.: American Council on Education, 1960).

SMITH, ELMER R., ed., *Teacher Education* (New York: Harper and Brothers, 1962).

STILES, LINDLEY J., and others, *Teacher Education in the United States* (New York: The Ronald Press Company, 1960).

STINNETT, T. M., *Professional Negotiations in Public Education* (New York: The Macmillan Company, 1966).

Teacher Education and Professional Standards Commission, *Manual on Certification Requirements for School Personnel in the United States,* 3rd ed. (Washington, D.C.: NEA, 1964).

WALLER, WILLARD, *The Sociology of Teachers* (New York: John Wiley & Sons, Inc., 1965).

The Role of School Personnel

ANDERSON, CARL L., *School Health Practice,* 3rd ed. (Saint Louis, Mo.: C. V. Mosby Company, 1964).

BYRD, OLIVER E., *School Health Administration* (Philadelphia: W. B. Saunders Company, 1964).

CROMWELL, GERTRUDE E., *The Nurse in the School Health Program* (Philadelphia: W. B. Saunders Company, 1963).

DOUGLASS, HARL, and others, *Democratic Supervision in Secondary Schools,* 2nd ed. (Boston: Houghton Mifflin Company, 1961).

FAWCETT, CLAUDE W., *School Personnel Administration* (New York: The Macmillan Company, 1964).

FRANSETH, JANE, *Supervision as Leadership* (New York: Harper and Brothers, 1961).

GEORGE, NOVIL L., and RUTH D. HECKLER, *School Food Centers* (New York: The Ronald Press Company, 1960).

GRAY, SUSAN W., *Psychologist in the Schools* (New York: Holt, Rinehart & Winston, Inc., 1963).

GWYNN, J. MINOR, *The Theory and Practice of Supervision* (New York: Dodd, Mead & Company, 1961).

HAAG, J. H., *The School Health Program,* revised ed. (New York: Holt, Rinehart & Winston, Inc., 1965).

HARRIS, BEN M., *Supervising Behavior in Education* (New York: Prentice-Hall, Inc., 1963).

JACOBSON, PAUL B., and others, *The Effective School Principal,* 2nd ed. (New York: Prentice-Hall, Inc., 1963).

JOHNSON, ARLIEN, *School Social Work, Its Contribution to Professional Education* (Washington, D.C.: National Association of Social Workers, 1962).

JONES, J. J., and others, *Secondary School Administration* (New York: McGraw-Hill Book Co., 1969).

KEPPEL, FRANCIS, *Personnel Policies for Public Education* (Pittsburgh: University of Pittsburgh Press, 1962).

McCLEARY, LLOYD E., and S. P. HENELEY, *Secondary School Administration: Theoretical Bases of Professional Practice* (New York: Dodd, Mead & Company, 1965).

National Association of Secondary School Principals, *Phases of Supervision in the Secondary School* (Washington, D.C.: NEA, 1961).

NEIMER, ALMA, *The School Health Program,* 2nd ed. (Philadelphia: W. B. Saunders Company, 1965).

Professional Rights and Responsibilities Commission, *Developing Personnel Policies,* revised ed. (Washington, D.C.: NEA, 1963).

VALETT, ROBERT E., *The Practice of School Psychology, Professional Problems* (New York: John Wiley & Sons, Inc., 1963).

WILSON, ROBERT E., *The Modern School Superintendent* (New York: Harper and Brothers, 1960).

ZWOLL, JAMES A., *School Personnel Administration* (New York: Appleton-Century-Crofts, Inc., 1964).

Planning and Utilization of the School Plant

American Association of School Administrators, *Planning America's School Buildings* (Washington, D.C.: NEA, 1960).

BAKER, JOSEPH J., and JON S. PETERS, *School Maintenance and Operation* (Danville, Ill.: Interstate Printers and Publishers, Inc., 1963).

BRAINARD, ALANSON D., *Handbook for School Custodian*, 5th ed. (Lincoln, Nebraska: University of Nebraska Press, 1961).

BURSCH, CHARLES WESLEY, and J. L. RIRD, *High Schools: Today and Tomorrow* (New York: Reinhold Publishing Corporation, 1957).

Building Research Institute, *School Building Research* (Washington, D.C.: Building Research Institute, 1963).

McCLURKIN, WILLIAM D., *School Building Planning* (New York: The Macmillan Company, 1964).

MacCONNELL, JAMES D., *Planning for School Buildings* (Englewood Cliffs, N.J.: Prentice-Hall, Inc., 1957).

National Education Association, Research Division, *Studies of Utilization of Staff, Buildings, and Audio Visual Aids in the Public Schools* (Washington, D.C.: NEA, 1959).

OTTO, KARL, *School Buildings* (New York: W. S. Heirman, 1961).

Index

A

AFT (*see* American Federation of Teachers)
Academic freedom, 276–278
Academies, 6–8, 127, 158
Acceleration, of program, 164–165
Achievement tests, 261, 262
Activities program, 171–181
Adolescent unwed mothers, article about, 107–118
Adolescents, values of, 295–297
Affective objectives of education, 26–27, 122
Agranoff, Bernard, 350, 352, 354
Administration, of extracurricular activities, 178–181
Administrative offices, 439
Administrative personnel, 416–421
relationship with teachers, 397–399
Aims, of public secondary education, 20–28, 44
Alexander, Tom, 218
Alexander, William M., article by, 238–245
America, social-economic goals of, 21–22
American Academy of Arts and Sciences, 220

American Federation of Teachers, 442, 445
American Mathematical Society, 210
Anderson, Robert A., 377
Anderson, Robert H., 238
Anderson, Vernon, 372, 373
Architect, 440–441
Articulation, importance of, 150–152
Assemblies, school, 176
guidance and, 191
Assignments, individual, 263–264
Assistant principal, 419–420
Athletics, intramural, 173
Atmosphere, school, 283–286
Audio-visual materials, 331–332
Auditorium, 438
Automation, education and, 65–73
Automated learning, 166
Auxiliary services, 423–427
Awards, 178

B

Balistrieri, J., 78
Beberman, Max, 214
Behavioral Goals of General Education in High Schools, 24–25

474